W9-ATF-874

A DICTIONARY OF SYMBOLS

A DICTIONARY OF SYMBOLS

Second Edition

by

J. E. CIRLOT

Translated from the Spanish by

JACK SAGE

Foreword by Herbert Read

PHILOSOPHICAL LIBRARY
New York

Translated from the Spanish
DICCIONARIO DE SIMBOLOS TRADICIONALES

English Translation
© *Routledge & Kegan Paul Ltd., London, 1962*
Published by Philosophical Library, Inc.
200 West 57th Street, New York, N.Y. 10019

Second Edition 1971

ISBN 0 8022-2083-5

Printed in the United States of America

CONTENTS

PLATES

FOREWORD

IN THE INTRODUCTION to this volume Señor Cirlot shows his
wide and learned conception of the subject-matter of this dictionary,
and the only task left to me is to present the author himself, who
has been familiar to me for some years as the leading protagonist
of a very vital group of painters and poets in Barcelona. Juan
Eduardo Cirlot was born in Barcelona in 1916, and after matriculat-
ing from the College of the Jesuits there, studied music. From 1943
onwards he was active as a poet, and published four volumes of
verse between 1946 and 1953. Meanwhile the group of painters and
poets already mentioned had been formed (*Dau al Set*), and Cirlot
became its leading theoretician. For historical or political reasons,
Spain had been slow to develop a contemporary movement in the
arts comparable to those in other European countries; its greatest
artists, Picasso and Miró, had identified themselves with the School
of Paris. But now a vigorous and independent 'School of Barcelona'
was to emerge, with Antonio Tapies and Modesto Cuixart as its
outstanding representatives. In a series of books and brochures
Cirlot not only presented the individual artists of this group, but
also instructed the Spanish public in the history and theoretical
foundations of the modern movement as a whole.

In the course of this critical activity Señor Cirlot inevitably
became aware of the 'symbolist ethos' of modern art. A symbolic
element is present in all art, in so far as art is subject to psychological
interpretation. But in so far as art has evolved in our time away
from the representation of an objective reality towards the expression
of subjective states of feeling, to that extent it has become a wholly
symbolic art, and it was perhaps the necessity for a clarification of
this function in art which led Señor Cirlot to his profound study of
symbolism in all its aspects.

The result is a volume which can either be used as a work of
reference, or simply read for pleasure and instruction. There are
many entries in this dictionary—those on Architecture, Colour,
Cross, Graphics, Mandala, Numbers, Serpent, Water, Zodiac, to
give a few examples—which can be read as independent essays.

But in general the greatest use of the volume will be for the elucidation of those many symbols which we encounter in the arts and in the history of ideas. Man, it has been said, is a symbolizing animal; it is evident that at no stage in the development of civilization has man been able to dispense with symbols. Science and technology have not freed man from his dependence on symbols: indeed, it might be argued that they have increased his need for them. In any case, symbology itself is now a science, and this volume is a necessary instrument in its study.

HERBERT READ

INTRODUCTION

ACTUALITY OF THE SYMBOL

Delimitation of the Symbolic On entering the realms of symbolism, whether by way of systematized artistic forms or the living, dynamic forms of dreams and visions, we have constantly kept in mind the essential need to mark out the field of symbolic action, in order to prevent confusion between phenomena which might appear to be identical when they are merely similar or externally related. The temptation to over-substantiate an argument is one which is difficult to resist. It is necessary to be on one's guard against this danger, even if full compliance with the ideals of scholarship is not always feasible; for we believe with Marius Schneider that there is no such thing as 'ideas *or* beliefs', only 'ideas *and* beliefs', that is to say that in the one there is always at least something of the other—quite apart from the fact that, as far as symbolism is concerned, other phenomena of a spiritual kind play an important part.

When a critic such as Caro Baroja (10) declares himself against any symbolic interpretation of myth, he doubtless has his reasons for so doing, although one reason may be that nothing approaching a complete evaluation of symbolism has yet appeared. He says: 'When they seek to convince us that Mars is the symbol of War, and Hercules of Strength, we can roundly refute them. All this may once have been true for rhetoricians, for idealist philosophers or for a group of more or less pedantic *graeculi*. But, for those who really believed in ancient deities and heroes, Mars had an objective reality, even if this reality was quite different from that which we are groping for today. Symbolism occurs when natural religions are degenerating.' In point of fact, the mere equation of Mars with War and of Hercules with Labour has never been characteristic of the symbolist ethos, which always eschews the categorical and restrictive. This comes about through allegory, a mechanical and restricting derivative of the symbol, whereas the symbol proper is a dynamic and polysymbolic reality, imbued with emotive and conceptual values: in other words, with true life.

However, the above quotation is extremely helpful in enabling us to mark out the limits of the symbolic. If there is or if there may be a symbolic function in everything, a 'communicating tension', nevertheless this fleeting possession of the being or the object by the symbolic does not wholly transform it into a symbol. The error of symbolist artists and writers has always been precisely this: that they sought to turn the entire sphere of reality into a vehicle for impalpable 'correspondences', into an obsessive conjunction of analogies, without being aware that the symbolic is opposed to the existential and instrumental and without realizing that the laws of symbolism hold good only within its own particular sphere. This distinction is one which we would also apply to the Pythagorean thesis that 'everything is disposed according to numbers', as well as to microbiological theory. Neither the assertion of the Greek philosopher on the one hand, nor the vital pullulation subjected invisibly to the science of Weights and Measures on the other, is false; but all life and all reality cannot be forced to conform with either one theory or the other, simply because of its certitude, for it is certain only within the limits of theory. In the same way, the symbolic is true and active on one plane of reality, but it is almost unthinkable to apply it systematically and consistently on the plane of existence. The consequent scepticism concerning this plane of reality—the magnetic life-source of symbols and their concomitants—explains the widespread reluctance to admit symbolical values; but such an attitude is lacking in any scientific justification.

Carl Gustav Jung, to whom present-day symbology owes so much, points out in defence of this branch of human thought that: 'For the modern mind, analogies—even when they are analogies with the most unexpected symbolic meanings—are nothing but self-evident absurdities. This worthy judgement does not, however, in any way alter the fact that such affinities of thought do exist and that they have been playing an important rôle for centuries. Psychology has a duty to recognize these facts; it should leave it to the profane to denigrate them as absurdities or as obscurantism' (32). Elsewhere Jung observes that all the energy and interest devoted today by western Man to science and technology were, by ancient Man, once dedicated to mythology (31). And not only his energy and interest but also his speculative and theorizing propensities, creating the immeasurable wealth of Hindu, Chinese and Islamic philosophy, the Cabbala itself and the painstaking investigations of alchemy and similar studies. The view that both ancient and oriental man possessed a technique of speculative thought which assured them of some success in prophecy is affirmed by, for example, the archaeologist and historian, Contenau, who maintains that the schools of soothsayers and magicians of Mesopotamia could not have continued to flourish without a definite proportion of correct prognostications; and again by Gaston Bachelard (1), posing the question: 'How could a legend be kept alive and perpetuated if each generation had not "intimate reasons" for believing in it?' The symbolist meaning of a phenomenon helps to explain these 'intimate reasons', since it links the instrumental with the spiritual, the human with the cosmic, the casual with the causal, disorder with order, and since it justifies a word like *universe* which, without these wider implications, would be meaningless, a dismembered and chaotic pluralism; and finally, because it always points to the transcendental.

To revert to the question of the limits of the symbolic and to fix more precisely the aims of this work, let us consider how, on the façade of a monastery, for example, we may note: (*a*) the beauty of the whole; (*b*) the constructional technique; (*c*) its period-styling, bearing in mind the geographical and historical implications; (*d*) the implicit or explicit cultural and religious values, etc.; and also (*x*) the symbolic meaning of the forms. In this instance, the appreciation of the symbolical implications of an ogival arch beneath a rose window could constitute an item of knowledge different in kind from the other items we have enumerated. To facilitate analyses of this kind without, let us repeat, confusing the symbolic essence of an object—the transitory symbolic function which heightens it at any given moment—with its total significance as a real object in the world—that is our main aim. The fact that a Romanesque cloister corresponds exactly to the concept of *temenos* (sacred precinct) and to the images of the soul, the fountain and the central fount—like *sutratma* (silver thread), linking a phenomenon by way of its centre to its origin—does not invalidate or even modify the architectural and utilitarian reality of this cloister; it enriches its significance by identifying it with an 'inner form'.

SYMBOLISM AND HISTORICITY

One of the most deplorable errors of symbolist theory, in its 'spontaneous' as well as in its occult and even its dogmatic interpretations, lies in opposing the symbolical to the historical. Arguing from the premise that there are symbols—and, indeed, there are many—which exist only within their own symbolic structure, the false conclusion is then drawn that all or almost all transcendental events which appear to be both historical and symbolic at once —in other words, to be significant once and for all time—may be seen simply as symbolic matter transformed into legend and thence into history.

The most authoritative students of religion, orientalists and even esoteric scholars have recently raised their voices in protest against this error. Mircea Eliade asserts that 'the two points of view are only superficially irreconcilable . . ., for it must not be thought that a symbolic connotation annuls the material and specific validity of an object or action. Symbolism *adds* a new value to an object or an act, without thereby violating its immediate or "historical" validity. Once it is brought to bear, it turns the object or action into an "open" event: symbolic thought opens the door on to immediate reality for us, but without weakening or invalidating it; seen in this light the universe is no longer sealed off, nothing is isolated inside its own existence: everything is linked by a system of correspondences and assimilations. Man in early society became aware of himself in a world wide open and rich in meaning. It remains to be seen whether these "openings" are just another means of escape or whether, on the other hand, they offer the only possible way of accepting the true reality of the world' (18).

In this quotation we can see clearly formulated the distinction between the historical and the symbolic. We can also see the ever-present possibility of a bridge linking both forms of reality in a cosmic synthesis. The hint of scepticism in the concluding words of this Rumanian scholar should be ascribed to his predominantly scientific training at a time when science, with its emphasis upon the analytical approach, has achieved admirable results in every sphere of reality without showing itself capable of grasping the overall organic pattern, that is: as 'multiplicity in unity'. This scientific disaffection has been well defined by Martin Buber: *Imago mundi nova, imago nulla*. In other words, the world today lacks its own image, because this image can be formulated only by means of a universal synthesis of knowledge—a synthesis which, since the Renaissance and the *de omni re scibili* of Pico della Mirandola, has daily become more difficult.

In connexion with this question of the relationship between the historical and the symbolic, René Guénon has observed: 'There is indeed over-eager acceptance of the belief that to allow a symbolic meaning must imply the rejection of the literal or historical meaning; such a view shows an ignorance of the law of correspondences. This law is the foundation of all symbolism and by virtue of it every thing proceeding essentially from a metaphysical principle, which is the source of its reality, translates and expresses this principle in its own way and according to its own level of existence, so that all things are related and joined together in total, universal harmony which is, in its many guises, a reflection, as it were, of its own fundamental unity . . . One result of this is the range of meaning contained in every symbol: any one thing may, indeed, be regarded as an illustration not only of metaphysical principles but also of higher levels of reality' (25).

The above considerations make it clear that the symbolic in no way excludes the historical, since both forms may be seen—from the ideological point of view—as functional aspects of a third: the metaphysical principle, the platonic 'idea'; or all three may be seen as reciprocal expressions of one meaning on different levels. Going to the kernel of the problem, religion—which naturally absorbs so much of his attention—Jung agrees with Eliade and Guénon in his belief that 'the psychic fact "God" is a collective archetype, a psychic existent, which must not in itself be confused with the concept of a metaphysical God'. The existence of the archetype (that is, of the symbol) 'neither postulates a God, nor does it deny that he exists' (31); yet although this is, strictly speaking, unquestionable, it must surely be agreed—if only in theory—that the universality of an archetype affirms rather than denies the reality of the principle in question. Consequently the symbolic, being independent of the historical, not only does not exclude it but, on the contrary, tends to root it firmly in reality, because of the parallelism between the collective or individual world and the cosmic. And because of the great depth of the hidden roots of all systems of meanings, a further consequence is our tendency to espouse the theory that all symbolist traditions, both western and oriental, spring from one common source. Whether this one source once appeared in time and space as a primeval focal point, or whether it stems from the 'collective unconscious', is quite another matter.

We should like to emphasize that when we refer, in the various passages quoted and paraphrased, to 'tradition' or 'traditional doctrine', we are referring only to the continuity—conscious or un-conscious—and the coherence of a system, as much in the dimension of space as in that of time. Some writers favour the doctrine of a spontaneous growth of historically unrelated ideas, while others believe only in the spread of ideas through culture. Loeffler, for example, comments upon the importance of proving that the creation of the storm-myth belongs neither to race nor tribe, since it occurred simultaneously in Asia, Europe, Oceania and America (38); this is akin to the contention of Rank that: 'The myth is the collective dream of the people', a concept substantiated by Rudolf Steiner. Bayley, following Max Müller, believes in the common origin of the human race, which he contends is proved by the universal themes of folklore, legend and superstition. Orientalism, the study of com-parative religion, mythology, cultural anthropology, the history of civilization and art, esoterism, psychoanalysis, and symbological research have all combined to provide us with ample material to substantiate 'psychological truth', and this 'essential oneness';

further evidence has been forthcoming from the psychic and also from physiological bases common to us all on account of the importance of the human body—its shape as well as its postures—in relation to the simplest elements of symbolist dialectic.

ORIGIN AND CONTINUITY OF THE SYMBOL

The Development of Symbolism   Diel rightly asserts that the symbol is a vehicle at once universal and particular. Universal, since it transcends history; particular, because it relates to a definite period of history. Without going into questions of 'origin', we shall show that most writers agree in tracing the beginnings of symbolist thought to prehistoric times—to the latter part of the Palaeolithic Age. Our present knowledge of primitive thought and the deductions which can justifiably be drawn concerning the art and the belongings of early man substantiate this hypothesis, but substantiation has been forthcoming particularly from research upon epigraphic engravings. The constellations, animals and plants, stones and the countryside were the tutors of primitive man. It was St. Paul who formulated the basic notion of the immediate consequence of this contact with the visible, when he said: '*Per visibilia ad invisibilia*' (Romans i, 20). The process whereby the beings of this world are ordered according to their properties, so that the words of action and of spiritual and moral facts may be explored by analogy, is one which can also be seen, with the dawning of history, in the transition of the pictograph into the ideograph, as well as in the origins of art.

We could adduce an immense weight of testimony offered by human faith and wisdom proving that the invisible or spiritual order is analogous to the material order. We shall come back to this later when we define 'analogy'. Let us recall the saying of Plato, taken up later by the pseudo-Dionysius the Areopagite: 'What is perceptible to the senses is the reflection of what is intelligible to the mind'; and echoed in the *Tabula Smaragdina*: 'What is below is like what is above; what is above is like what is below', and also in the remark of Goethe: 'What is within is also without.' However it may be, symbolism is organized in its vast explanatory and creative function as a system of highly complex relations, one in which the dominant factor is always a polarity, linking the physical and metaphysical worlds. What palaeolithic Man evolved out of this process is impossible to know except through indirect deductions. Our knowledge about the latter part of the Neolithic Age is considerably wider. Schneider and Berthelot both consider that this was the period (that is: possibly the fourth millenary before history) when man underwent that great transformation which endowed him with the gifts of creation and organization, qualities which distinguish him from the merely natural world. Berthelot, who has studied this process in the Near East, has given the name of 'astrobiology' to the religious and intellectual cultures of that epoch. The evolution of Man up to this point in history must have passed through the following stages: animism; totemism; and megalithic, lunar and solar cultures. The subsequent stages must have been: cosmic ritualism; polytheism; monotheism; and, finally, moral philosophy. Berthelot considers astrology, astronomy, arithmetic and alchemy of Chaldean origin, a contention which points conclusively to a single focal point in time and space.

He defines the value and significance of astrobiology in the following terms: 'Between on the one hand the world-vision—in many other respects variable and complex—of primitive races, and the vision of modern science and Western Europe on the other, an intermediary view has long held sway in Asia and the Mediterranean. It is what may be termed "astrobiology" or the interplay of astronomic law (the mathematical order) and vegetable and animal life (the biological order). All things form at one and the same time an organic whole and a precise order. The domestication of animals and the care of plants (agriculture) had become a reality long before history began, both in Chaldaea and in Egypt—that is, before 3,000 B.C. Agriculture ensures the regular production of precisely determined species of vegetable, and also ensures an appreciation of their annual "rhythm" of growth, flowering, fructifying, sowing and harvesting, a rhythm which is in direct and constant relation to the calendar, in other words, the position of the heavenly bodies. Time and natural phenomena were measured by reference to the moon before they came to be measured by the sun . . . . Astrobiology hovers between a biology of the heavenly bodies and an astronomy of human beings; beginning with the former, it tends towards the latter' (7). During the neolithic era the geometric idea of space was formulated; so also were the significance of the number seven (derived from this concept of space), the relation between heaven and earth, the cardinal points, and the relations between the various elements of the septenary (the planetary gods, the days of the week) and between those of the quaternary (the seasons, the colours, the cardinal points, the elements). Berthelot believes in the slow spread of these ideas, rather than in their spontaneous and independent appearance. He points to their probable dissemination through either the northern or southern areas of the Pacific, mentioning in passing that America may well have been, in spirit, a colony of Asia before that of Europe (7); and another stream may have been flowing in the opposite direction: from the Near East into Central Europe.

The argument about whether European megalithic culture came before or after the great oriental civilizations is far from settled. Here questions of symbolism arise. The importance of the Franco-Cantabrian zone in the Palaeolithic Age is well known; it is also known that the art forms of this district spread across Europe in the direction of Siberia and southwards across North Africa to the southernmost part of the continent. There was, no doubt, a period of transition between this early flowering and the great megalithic monuments. However that may be, Schneider specifically says in connexion with the symbolic forms studied by him (50): 'In the sixth chapter I shall try to summarize this esoteric doctrine, the systemization of which seems to have been originally the work of megalithic cultures.' And his attitude towards the zone of origin leaves little room for doubt for he states that 'the megalithic must have spread from Europe to India via Danubian culture, a new stage of development beginning with the Age of Metals'. He points out that there are marked similarities between the ideas of regions as far apart as America, New Guinea, Indonesia, Western Europe, Central Asia and the Far East, that is to say, of areas in all parts of the world.

Let us consider now the similarity between the discoveries attributed by Schneider to megalithic European culture and those ascribed by Berthelot to the Far East. In Schneider's opinion the final stage of neolithic development differed from the earlier stage 'in the preference it showed for static and geometric forms, in its organizing and creative genius (evolving fabulous animals, musical instruments, mathematical proportions, number-ideas, astronomy and a tonal system with truly musical sounds). The carrying over of totemistic mystical elements into a more advanced, pastoral civilization explains some of the fundamental characteristics of the new mystique. . . . The entire cosmos comes to be conceived after the human pattern. As the essence of all phenomena is, in the last resort, a vibrant rhythm, the intimate nature of phenomena is directly perceptible by polyrhythmic human consciousness. For this reason, imitating is knowing. The echo is the paradigmatic form of imitation. Language, geometric symbols and number-ideas are a cruder form of imitation.' Schneider then observes that according to Speiser and Heine-Geldern, 'the outstanding cultural elements of megalithic culture are: cyclopean buildings, commemorative stones, stones as the dwelling-places of souls, cultural stone-circles, *palafittes*, head-hunting, the sacrifice of oxen, eye-shaped ornaments, death-ships, family-trees, signal-drums, the sacrificial stake, and labyrinths' (50).

It is precisely these elements that have most successfully preserved their symbolic form down the ages. And did not these express, even in megalithic times, the very essence of human life, bursting from the unconscious in the shape of a constructive and configurating longing? Or was it, rather, the ever-present, primary forms of life, sacrifice and intellection of the world which found everlasting expression in these cultural creations, making an ineradicable impression on the mind of Man? One may unhesitatingly answer in the affirmative to both questions, for they refer to the different but parallel phenomena of culture and psychology.

SYMBOLISM IN THE WEST

It was Egypt who gave shape, in her religion and hieroglyphics, to Man's awareness of the material and spiritual, natural and cultural duality of the world. Either independently or together, the various civilizations of Mesopotamia developed their own particular systems; yet these systems were but outward variations of the one true, innermost, universal pattern. There are differences of opinion about dating the first appearance—or at any rate the final crystallization—of some of the most important and complex symbols. Some writers argue strongly in favour of remote origins. Krappe (35) holds that the scientific study of the planets and their identification with the gods of the Babylonian pantheon date only from the 7th century B.C.; but others trace these beginnings as far back as the age of Hammurabi (2000 B.C.) or earlier. Father Heras, for example, says: 'The early Indians, as has been revealed by inscriptions, were the discoverers of the movements of the sun across the sky—the basis of the zodiacal system. Their Zodiac had only eight constellations and each constellation was supposed to be a "form of God". All these "forms of God" in the end became deities, each one presiding over one particular constellation; this is what happened in Rome, for example. The eight Indian signs of the Zodiac are: Edu (ram), Yal (harp), Nand (crab), Amma (mother), Tuk (balance), Kani (arrow), Kuda (pitcher), Min (fish).' The dodecatemorian system of the Zodiac first appears in the form in which we know it as late as the 6th century B.C. Egyptian and Chaldean science was partly assimilated by the Syrians, Phoenicians and Greeks, reaching the latter largely through secret societies. Herodotus points out, in writing of the Pythagoreans, that they were obliged to wear linen clothes 'in accordance with the Orphic ceremonies, which are the same as the Egyptian . . .'.

The mythologies of the Mediterranean peoples were characterized by a vivid, dramatic vitality which came to be expressed both in their art and in their myths, legends and dramatic poetry. These myths enshrined the moral principles, the natural laws, the great contrasts and the transformations which determine the course of cosmic and human life. Frazer points out that 'under the names of Osiris, Tammuz, Adonis and Attis, the peoples of Egypt and Western Asia represented the yearly decay and revival of life, especially of vegetable life' (21). The tasks of Hercules, the legend of Jason, the 'histories' of the heroic age of Greece which provided the inspiration for the classical tragedies, have such great archetypal power that they constitute timeless lessons for mankind. But beneath this mythological and literary symbolism and allegory, a subterranean stream of oriental influence was beginning to flow in from the East.

Principally during the Lower Roman Empire, when the cohesion of the classical world was beginning to dissolve, Hebraic, Chaldean and Egyptian elements began to ferment. Dualist Manichaeism and Gnosticism began to threaten the position of early Christianity. Among the Gnostics, the emblem and the graphic symbol were used for the propagation of initiatory truths. Many of the innumerable images were not of their own creation but were compiled from various sources, mainly Semitic. Symbolism veers towards the Unitarian doctrine of reality and comes to be a specialized branch of speculation. Diodorus Siculus, Pliny, Tacitus, Plutarch, Apuleius all reveal some familiarity with oriental symbolism. Aristotelian thought also contained a strong element of symbolism. In Syria, Mesopotamia, Transcaucasia and Egypt, oriental Christianity had absorbed a vast symbological inheritance. Similarly, those Roman colonies in the West that survived the Nordic invasions retained many attributes of ancient times, including traditional symbols. But, according to the Rev. Fr. Festugière, in *La Révélation d'Hermès Trismégiste*, one of the currents which were most able to contribute to the formation of the symbolist and alchemic 'corpus' was that of the literature of the 'Mirabilia'. This was apparently founded by Bolus the Democritean during the 3rd–2nd centuries B.C. and was continued for centuries in a virtually unbroken tradition by Pseudo-Manetho, Nigidius Figulus, Demetrius, Apollodorus, etc., culminating in the *Book of the Things of Nature*, a Syrian work of the 7th century A.D.

The concept of the analogy between the visible and the invisible world is, then, held jointly by the pagan religions of the Lower Empire, by neoplatonic and Christian doctrines, except that each one of these three systems uses this concept for its own ends. According to Eliade, Theophilus of Antioch would point out, to those who denied the resurrection of the dead, the signs which God places in reach of Man in the realm of natural phenomena: the cycle of the seasons, of the days and nights. He would even go further and say: 'May there not perhaps be resurrection for the seeds and the fruits?' (18). In his *Letter* number LV, St. Augustine shows that teaching carried out with the help of symbols feeds and stirs

Title-page of book of emblems by Joachim Camerario
(Nuremberg, 1590) with symbolic tree, circle,
precinct and grotesques.

the fires of love, enabling Man to excel himself; he also alludes to the value of all things in nature—organic and inorganic—as bearers of spiritual messages by virtue of their distinctive forms and characteristics. All the mediaeval lapidaries, herbals and bestiaries owe their origin to this concept. Most of the classical Fathers of the Church have something to say about symbolism and since they enjoyed such a high reputation in Roman times, one can see why this was the period when the symbol came to be so deeply experienced, loved and understood, as Davy emphasizes (14). Pinedo mentions the immense cultural value, particularly during the Middle Ages, of the *Clavis Melitoniae*—an orthodox version of ancient symbolism. According to Cardinal Pitra—quoted by Pinedo—an awareness of this 'Key' is to be found in most mediaeval authors. This is not the place to give a summary of their ideas or works, but we should like to mention in passing the important works of: Alan of Lille, *De Planctu Naturae;* Herrad of Landsberg, *Hortus Deliciarum;* Hildegard of Bingen, *Scivias Domini, Liber Divinorum Operum Simplicis Hominis;* Bernard Silvestris, *De Re Mundi Universitate;* Hugh of St. Victor, *Didascalion, Commentarium in Hierarchiam Coelestem,* etc. The *Key* of St. Melito, bishop of Sardis, dates from the 2nd century A.D. Some other sources of Christian symbolism are: Rabanus Maurus, *Allegoriae in Sacram Scripturam;* Odo, bishop of Tusculum; Isidore of Seville, *Etymologiarum;* Johannes Scotus Erigena, John of Salisbury, William of St. Thierry, etc. St. Thomas Aquinas himself speaks of the pagan philosophers as sources of external and demonstrable proofs of Christian truths. Concerning the intimate nature of mediaeval symbolism, Jung observes that, in those days 'analogy was not so much a logical figure as a secret identity', that is to say, a continuation of primitive, animistic thought (32).

The Renaissance also showed great interest in symbolism, although in a manner more individualistic and cultured, more profane, literary and aesthetic. Dante had fashioned his *Commedia* upon a basis of oriental symbols. In the 15th century particular use was made of two Greek writers of the 2nd and 3rd centuries A.D. They are Horapollo, with his *Hieroglyphica*; and the anonymous compiler of the *Physiologus*. Horapollo, inspired by the Egyptian hieroglyphic system, the key to which had been lost by his time, tried to reconstruct its meaning upon the basis of its configuration and elemental symbolism. In 1467, an Italian writer, Francesco Colonna, wrote a work, *Hypnerotomachia Poliphili* (published in Venice in 1499), which enjoyed widespread success and in which the symbol had now acquired the particular, mobile significance which has come to characterize it in modern times. In 1505, Colonna's editor published Horapollo's work, which in turn in-

fluenced two other important writers at the same time: Andrea
Alciati, author of *Emblemata* (1531), which was to arouse a dis-
proportionate taste for profane symbolism throughout Europe
(Henry Green in his *Andrea Alciati and his Books of Emblems*,
London, 1872, names more than three thousand titles of books
dealing with emblems); and Giampietro Valeriano, author of the
compendious *Hieroglyphica* (1556). In 15th-century painting there is
abundant evidence of this interest in symbolism: Botticelli, Mantegna,
Pinturicchio, Giovanni Bellini, Leonardo, for example; later,
during the 16th, 17th and 18th centuries, this interest tended towards
the allegorical. One may say that, from the latter part of the Middle
Ages onwards, the West lost that sense of unity which characterized
the symbol and symbolist tradition. Yet proof of its continued
existence is offered by the occasional revelation of diverse aspects
in the work of poets, artists and writers, from Giovanni da Udine
to Antonio Gaudi, from Bosch to Max Ernst. In German Roman-
ticism, the interest in the deeper layers of psychic life—in dreams
and their meaning, in the unconscious—is the fount which has
given rise to the present-day interest in symbology, which, although
still partially repressed, again dwells in the deep wells of the spirit,
as it did before being circumscribed by a system with a rigid cosmic
pattern. Thus, Schubert, in his *Symbolik des Traumes* (1837), says:
'The prototypes of the images and forms utilized by the oneirocritic,
poetic and prophetic idioms, can be found around us in Nature,
revealing herself as a world of materialized dream, as a prophetic
language whose hieroglyphics are beings and forms.' Most of the
literature of the first half of the 19th century, especially the Nordic,
presupposes a feeling for the symbolic, for the significant. Thus,
Ludwig Tieck, in *Runenburg*, says of his protagonist: 'Insensitive
from that moment to the beauty of flowers, in which he believes
he can see "the gaping wound of Nature" throbbing' (the theme of
Philoctetes as well as of Amfortas in *Parsifal*), 'he finds himself
drawn towards the mineral world.'

Innumerable *genera* still conserve symbols in semeiotic form,
ossified and sometimes degraded from the universal plane to the
particular. We have already referred to literary emblems. In a
similar class are the distinctive marks used by mediaeval and
Renaissance paper-manufacturers. In this connexion, Bayley says
that, from their first appearance in 1282 up to the second half of the
18th century, they had an esoteric meaning; and that in them,
as in fossils, we can see the crystallization of the ideals of numerous
mystic sects of mediaeval Europe (4). The popular art of all European
peoples is another inexhaustable mine of symbols. One only has to
glance through a work like that of Helmuth Th. Bossert in order to
find amongst the images such well-known subjects as the cosmic

tree, the snake, the phoenix, the ship of death, the bird on the rooftop, the two-headed eagle, the planetary division into two groups of three and of four, grotesques, rhomboids, lines and zigzags, etc. Furthermore, legends and folktales, when their editors have been faithful, as in the case of Perrault and the Grimm brothers, have retained their mythical and archetypal structure (38). In the same way, in lyrical poetry, alongside works created within the canons of explicit symbolism—best illustrated in the works of René Ghil—there are frequent flowerings of symbolic motifs springing spontaneously out of the creative spirit.

THE SYMBOLIC MEANING OF DREAMS

What a myth represents for a people, for any one culture, or for any given moment of history, is represented for the individual by the symbolic images of dreams, by visions and by fantasy or lyricism. This distinction does not imply dichotomy: many dreams have been known to express premonitions. But when the symbol—or the premonition—goes beyond the particular and the subjective, we find ourselves in the realm of augury and prophecy; symbolic laws can explain both phenomena, but the latter may be a revelation of the supernatural.

Given our contemporary psychoanalytic concept of the 'unconscious', we must accept the placing within it of all those dynamic forms which give rise to symbols; for, according to Jung's way of thinking, the unconscious is 'the matrix of the human mind and its inventions' (33). The unconscious was 'discovered' theoretically by Carus, Schopenhauer and Hartmann, and experimentally by Charcot, Bernheim, Janet, Freud and other psychologists. But this newly acquired knowledge merely showed to be internal what had formerly been thought to be external to Man. For example, Greek seers believed that dreams came from 'without', that is, from the domain of the gods. Now, esoteric tradition, in accordance with the Hindu doctrine of the three planes of consciousness, had always been aware that the vertical division of thought could also be seen on three levels: the subconscious (instinctive and affective thought); consciousness (ideological and reflexive thought); and superconsciousness (intuitive thought and the higher truths). Hence, by way of simplification, we shall adopt the Jungian term 'unconscious' instead of 'subconscious', since one rightly asks oneself when dealing with many authors: 'How can they be so certain that the unconscious is "lower" and not "higher" than the conscious?' (31).

The interest in dreams and their symbolic content goes back to Antiquity, when, although the theory was never consciously formulated, it was implied that the phenomenon could be considered as a kind of personal mythology, even though the manner of its expression was the objective, collective myth. The famous dreams of the Bible; the book of Artemidorus Daldianus; the interpretative dictionaries of Chaldean, Egyptian and Arabic origin bear witness to the attention paid to dreams as harbingers of hidden truths about the submerged life of the psyche and, more rarely, about external and objective facts. The mechanism of oneiromancy, like that of other divinatory or prophetic techniques, is a universal phenomenon; for such techniques are based upon the higher activity of the unconscious in response to certain stimuli, and upon the automatic acquisition of unconscious stores of knowledge remaining unperceived until 'read' in accordance with the principles of numbers, orientation, form and space. We must again underline the way in which Jung approaches this universal phenomenon. He says that the fact of 'an opinion being held for so long and so widely necessarily demonstrates that in some way it must be true, that is, *psychologically true*'. He explains psychological truth as a fact, not as a judgement or an opinion, and he considers that careful demonstration and corroboration are evidence enough for this (31).

Since an extensive bibliography of dreams is already available, it is here intended only to recall that they afford Man another means of making contact with his deepest aspirations, with the geometric or moral laws of the universe, and also with the muted stirrings of the submerged unconscious. Teillard points out that in dreams all layers of the psyche are revealed, including the deepest. And just as the embryo passes through the evolutionary animal stages, so we carry with us archaic 'memories' which can be brought to light (56). On the other hand, Carus believed that the soul was in communion with the cosmic, and that, oneirocritically speaking, the soul was susceptible to truths different from those which rule the waking life; in this way he associated dreams with those rituals which enabled Man to enter into the great secrets of Nature. It is usually accepted that modern ways of thinking differ from primitive thought-processes only with regard to consciousness, and that the unconscious has hardly changed since the Upper Palaeolithic Stage.

Oneirocritic symbols, then, are not strictly different from mythical, religious, lyrical or primitive symbols. Except that, with the primary archetypes, one finds intermixed a kind of subworld consisting of the remains of existential images drawn from reality, which may be lacking in symbolic meaning, which may be expressions of the physiological—merely memories—or which may also possess a symbolism related to the material and primary forms from which they originate. In this dictionary we have kept to traditional symbols only, but it is evident that other more 'recent' symbols must derive from the older—as the motor-car from the carriage—or else must be related through the symbolism of form, although this must always be a question of *similar* symbols, not of the *same* symbol nor of the same order of meaning.

There is another problem which we cannot ignore: not all human beings are on the same level. Even if we do not accept the idea of radical differences, or the concept of spiritual growth—a concept which always has a touch of the oriental and esoteric about it— it is undeniable that differences of intensity (emotion, inner life, richness of thought and feeling) and of quality (intellectual and authentically moral education) bring about essentially different levels of thought, whether it be logical or magical thought, rational speculation or oneirocritic elaboration. Havelock Ellis has pointed out that extraordinary dreams are confined to people of genius, and according to Jung even primitive races make a similar distinction; the Elgonyi tribe in the Elgon jungle explained to him that they recognized two types of dream: the ordinary dream of the unimportant man, and the 'great vision', generally the exclusive privilege of outstanding men (34). Hence interpretative theories of symbolic material must vary according to whether they are drawn from the analysis of the dreams of more or less pathological individuals, from the dreams of normal people, from those of outstanding men, or from collective myths. The materialistic tone pervading the symbolic classifications of many psychoanalysts is accounted for by the nature of their sources of information. On the other hand, the symbology of philosophers, founders of religions and poets is wholly idealist and cosmic in direction, embracing all objects, seeking after the infinite and pointing to the mysteries of the mystical 'centre'. This is verified by Jung, who shows that accounts of fantasy or of dreams always contain not only what is most peremptory for the narrator but also what for the moment is most painful (i.e. most important) for him (31). It is this 'importance' which fixes the plane upon which any system of interpretation must exist. Freud's definition ('Every dream is a repressed desire') points to the same conclusion, for our desires are the index of our aspirations and our potentialities.

THE SYMBOLISM OF ALCHEMY

In his *On Psychic Energy*, Jung has asserted that: 'The spiritual appears in the psyche as an instinct, indeed as a real passion. . . It is not derived from any other instinct, but is a principle *sui generis*, that is, a specific and necessary form of instinctual power.' Apart from the fact that this asseveration would seem to put an end to the assumption that science is necessarily materialistic, its importance lies in that it takes up the essential platonic doctrine of the soul, which we here equate with the Jungian principle of spirituality, even though at times it may be necessary to treat the two principles separately. Plato in *Timaeus*, Plotinus in the *Enneads*, elaborate the idea that the soul is a stranger on earth, that it has descended from the spaceless and timeless universe, or that it has 'fallen' on account of sin into matter, that it initiates a process of life-giving growth corresponding to the period of involution.

At any given moment, the inverse of this downward and inward movement can be produced: the soul recalls that its origin is beyond space and time, beyond living creatures and the world of objects, even beyond images; it then tends towards the annihilation of the corporeal and begins to ascend towards its Origin. Iamblichus explains this as follows: 'A principle of the soul is that it is superior to all Nature, and that through it we can rise above the order and the systems of the world. When the soul is thus separated from all subordinate natures, it exchanges this life for another and abandons this order of things to bind itself inseparably with another.' The idea of rotation is the keystone of most transcendent symbols: of the mediaeval *Rota*; of the Wheel of Buddhist transformations; of the zodiacal cycle; of the myth of the Gemini; and of the *opus* of the alchemists. The idea of the world as a labyrinth or of life as a pilgrimage leads to the idea of the 'centre' as a symbol of the absolute goal of Man—Paradise regained, heavenly Jerusalem. Pictorially, this central point is sometimes identified with the geometric centre of the symbolic circle; sometimes it is placed above it; and at other times, as in the oriental *Shri Yantra*, it is not portrayed at all, so that the contemplator has to imagine it.

But constantly we find a given theme reappearing under the guise of a new symbol: the lost object, the impossible or very difficult enterprise; or else it comes to be equated with a variety of qualities: knowledge, love, obtaining a desired object, etc. Alchemy was developed in two fairly well-defined stages: the mediaeval and the Renaissance, the latter terminating by the 18th century, when it split once again into its two original components: mysticism and chemistry. Alchemy is a symbolic technique which, together with the desire for positive discoveries in the field of the natural sciences, sought to materialize spiritual truths. Instead of confronting the mythical dragon in their search for 'treasure', like Cadmus, Jason and Siegfried, the alchemists sought to *produce* it by means of hard work and virtue. Their work was not aimed at a simple revelation of esoteric truths, nor was it materialistic: both purposes coalesced, however, to achieve something which for them had the significance of the absolute. Each operation, each detail, every subject, every instrument was a source of intellectual and spiritual life: they were authentic symbols. After being forgotten for a period, alchemy was reassessed as 'the origin of modern chemistry', and recently Bachelard, Silberer, Jung and others have come to see the true completeness of its meaning, at once poetic, religious and scientific.

Bachelard points out that alchemy 'possesses a quality of psychological precision' (33) and that, far from being a description of objective phenomena, it is an attempt to project human love into the 'heart' of things (1). Jung insists that the experiments of the alchemists had the sole purpose—like the ancient techniques of divination, though the former was more ambitious and persistent—of stimulating the deepest layers of the psyche and of facilitating psychic projections in material things, or in other words, of experiencing material phenomena as symbols which point to a complete theory of the universe and the destiny of the soul. For this reason, he says that 'the investigator had certain psychic experiences which appeared to him as the particular behaviour of the chemical process'. Elsewhere he defines this as 'chemical research which, through projection, incorporated unconscious psychic material', a remark which he rounds off by affirming that 'the real nature of matter was unknown to the alchemist. He knew it only by allusion. Searching for a solution, he projected the unconscious into the obscurity of matter in order to illuminate it. To explain the mystery of matter, he projected another mystery into what was to be explained' (32). The *summa* of this mystery, the deepest of secret aspirations, was the *coincidentia oppositorum*, of which 'the alchemists are as it were the empiricists, whereas Nicholas of Cusa is its philosopher' (33). But the alchemist did not merely pretend to carry out his experiments; he was, indeed, profoundly and pathetically engrossed in his search for gold. It was this interest, together with his sense of dedication that—as in the search for the Holy Grail—was the guarantee of final success, by dint of the virtuous practice which his unceasing labour demanded. To discover the secret of making gold was the mark of divine favour. Jung interprets the process psychologically as the gradual elimination of the impure factors of the spirit in the progress towards the immutable values of eternity. But this interpretation had been fully grasped by the alchemists themselves: Michael Maier, in *Symbola Aureae Mensae* (1617), says that 'chemistry encourages the investigator to meditate upon celestial blessings'. Dorn, in *Physica* (1661), alludes to the relationship which must exist between the worker and his research when he asserts: 'You will never make Oneness out of Otherness until you yourself have become Oneness.' Oneness was achieved by annihilating the desire for what is different or transitory and by fixing the mind upon what is 'higher' and eternal. Famous indeed is the maxim of the alchemists: *Aurum nostrum non est aurum vulgi.* This assertion—that their gold was not ordinary gold—seems to indicate that their symbolism excluded the material reality of the symbol, in favour of the spiritual. But, of course, it is hazardous to talk as if the varied work of so many researchers with such differing backgrounds was all of a piece. The demand for actual gold could be interpreted as being the same as the longing of the doubting St. Thomas. The chosen few were well content with the dream of the 'subterranean Sun' shining at the bottom of the alchemist's oven like the light of salvation within the depths of the soul, no matter whether this salvation is considered to be the product of religious faith or of that hypothetical 'process of individuation' into which Jung seems to have poured his finest thoughts and sentiments about Man. Of course, beneath this concept there lie hidden none other than the three supreme longings which seem to lead to felicity: first, the alchemic Rebis, or the androgynous being, signifying the conjunction of opposites and the cessation of the torment caused by the separation of the sexes, beginning with the time when the 'spherical man' of Plato was split into two halves; second, the establishing of the 'volatile' principle, that is, the annihilation of all change or transition, once the essence has been obtained; and, finally, the concentrating into one central point, as a symbol of the mystical centre of the universe—that is, of the irradiant origin (32) and of immortality.

DEFINITIONS OF THE SYMBOL

Definitions and analyses of the nature of symbols and of symbolism are all too frequent. But we should like to study some of the more thoughtful suggestions, keeping, as always in this work, within the limits of comparative analysis. For the Hindu philosopher Ananda K. Coomaraswamy, symbolism is 'the art of thinking in images', an art now lost to civilized Man, notably in the last three hundred years, perhaps in consequence of the 'catastrophic theories of Descartes', to quote Schneider. Coomaraswamy, then, shares the views of Fromm and of Bayley, explicit in the titles of their respective works: *The Forgotten Language* and *The Lost Language of Symbolism.* However, this loss—as anthropology and psychoanalysis have shown —is limited to consciousness and not to the 'unconscious', which, to compensate, is perhaps now overloaded with symbolic material.

Diel considers the symbol to be 'a precise and crystallized means of expression', corresponding in essence to the inner life (intensive and qualitative) in opposition to the external world (extensive and quantitative) (15). In this, he agrees with Goethe, who asserted: 'In the symbol, the particular represents the general, *not* as a dream, *not* as a shadow, but as a living and momentary revelation of the inscrutable.' We suggest that the distinction made by Diel between the inner and the outer worlds is a general truth, applicable not only to the Cartesian method: the world of *res cogitans* is one which recognizes extension. How is it possible, then, for it to ignore the quantitative if the qualitative arises from 'groups' of quantity?

Marc Saunier, in his literary and pseudomystical style, points to an important characteristic of symbols when he states that they are 'the synthesizing expression of a marvellous science, now forgotten by men', but that 'they show us all that has been and will be, in one immutable form' (49). He thereby assigns to symbols—or recognizes, rather—their didactic function as timeless objects *per se*, at least in their intimate structure, for the other factors are cultural or personal variants.

The connexion between created and Creator is also apparent in the symbol. Jules Le Bêle recalls that 'every created object is, as it were, a reflection of divine·perfection, a *natural and perceptible sign* of a supernatural truth', thus echoing the Pauline proposition *Per visibilia ad invisibilia*, as well as the assertion of Sallust that 'The world is a symbolic object.' Landrit insists that 'symbolism is the science of the relations which unite the created world with God, the material world with the supernatural; the science of the harmonies existing between the diverse parts of the universe (correspondences and analogies)', operating within the process of involution, that is, of the materiality of all things.

Here we must interpose a distinction and a clarification. Erich Fromm (23), steering his course along the normal channels of symbolic knowledge, lays down three kinds of symbol which are different in degree: (*a*) the *conventional*, (*b*) the *accidental*, (*c*) the *universal*. The first kind comprises simple acceptance of a constant affinity stripped of any optical or natural basis: for example, many signs used in industry, in mathematics and in other fields. The second type springs from strictly transitory conditions and is due to associations made through casual contact. The third kind is that which we are now studying and is defined, according to Fromm, as the existence of the *intrinsic relation* between the symbol and what it represents. It is obvious that this relation does not always have the same vitality. For this reason, as we have already pointed out, it is difficult to classify symbols with exactitude.

This language of images and emotions is based, then, upon a precise and crystallized means of expression, revealing transcendent truths, external to Man (cosmic order) as well as within him (thought, the moral order of things, psychic evolution, the destiny of the soul); furthermore, it possesses a quality which, according to Schneider, increases its dynamism and gives it a truly dramatic character. This quality, the essence of the symbol, is its ability to express simultaneously the various aspects (thesis and antithesis) of the idea it represents (51). Let us give a provisional explanation of this: the unconscious, or 'place' where symbols live, does not recognize the inherent distinctions of contraposition; or again, the 'symbolic function' appears at the precise moment when a state of tension is set up between opposites which the consciousness cannot resolve by itself.

For psychologists, the symbol exists almost wholly in the mind, and is then projected outwards upon Nature, either accepting language as its being and its form or converting being and form into dramatic characters, but it is not seen in this way by orientalists and esoteric thinkers, who base symbolism upon the incontrovertible equation macrocosm=microcosm. For this reason René Guénon points out that: 'The true basis of symbolism is, as we have said, the correspondence linking together all orders of reality, binding them one to the other, and consequently extending from the natural order as a whole to the supernatural order. By virtue of this correspondence, the whole of Nature is but a symbol, that is, its true significance becomes apparent only when it is seen as a pointer which can make us aware of supernatural or "metaphysical" truths—metaphysical in the proper and true sense of the word, which is nothing less than the *essential function of symbolism.* . . . The symbol must always be inferior to the thing symbolized, which destroys all naturalist concepts of symbolism' (29). This latter idea is repeatedly stressed by Guénon, declaring that 'what is superior can never symbolize what is inferior, although the converse is true' (25) (provided, we must add, that one is dealing with a specific symbol of inversion). On the other hand, what is superior can remind us of what is inferior.

The observations of Mircea Eliade are very interesting in this respect. He assigns to the symbol the mission of going beyond the limitations of this 'fragment' which is Man (or any one of his concerns) and of integrating this 'fragment' into entities of wider scope: society, culture, the universe. Even if, within these limitations, 'an object transmuted into a symbol—as a result of its being possessed by the symbolic function—tends to unite with the All . . . this union is not the same as a confusion, for the symbol does not restrict movement or circulation from one level to another, and integrates all these levels and planes (of reality), but without fusing them—that is, without destroying them', integrating them, in short, within a system. On the other hand, Eliade believes that if the All can appear contained within a significant fragment, it is because each fragment restates the All: 'A tree, by virtue of the power it manifests, may become a blessed haven, without ceasing to be a tree; and if it becomes a cosmic tree it is because *what it manifests* restates, point by point, what the totality manifests' (17). Here we have the explanation of the 'intrinsic relation' mentioned by Erich Fromm. Though transmuted to another plane of reality, it consists of the essential relationship between one process and another, between one object and another, an intimate relationship which has been defined as rhythm.

THE 'COMMON RHYTHM' OF SCHNEIDER

The analogy between two planes of reality is founded upon the existence in both of a 'common rhythm'. By rhythm we mean here not 'perceptible order in time', but the coherent, determinate and dynamic factor which a character or figure possesses and which is transmitted to the object over which it presides or from which it emanates. This rhythm is fundamentally a movement resulting from a certain vitality or from a given 'number'. It shows itself as a characteristic expression or formal crystallization. Thus, between the live snake, with its sinuous movement, and the snake appearing in inanimate relief, there may be an analogy which is not only formal (in the design, disposition, or in the specific shape of the animal) but also rhythmic—that is, of tone, of modality, of accent, and of expression.

Martin Buber, in his study of natural, primitive poetry, points out that Man—whether it be megalithic Man, our contemporary Primitive, or 'romantic' Man seeking natural spontaneity in his relations with the cosmos—'does not think about the moon as such, which he sees every night; for what he retains is not the image of a wandering, luminous disc, nor that of an associated demonic being, but that of the immediate emotive image, the lunar fluid flowing through bodies' (quoted by Gaston Bachelard, 2). This is exactly the view of Schneider also, pointing to the aptitude for symbolic and rhythmic thought of Primitive Man, who could identify the movement of a wave with that of the backs of a moving flock of sheep (51). Davy recalls that Boethius had alluded earlier to a 'common rhythm' when he asserted that only those things which have the same matter in common—meaning, in this context, the same 'vital aspect'—can mutually transform and interchange themselves (14). Rhythm may be understood as a grouping of distances, of quantitative values, but also as a formal pattern determined by rhythmic numbers, that is, as spatial, formal and positional similitude.

But there is a deeper meaning to the concept of rhythm, which is precisely that expounded by Schneider upon the basis of Primitive

Man's identification of one 'living, dynamic cell' with two or more different aspects of reality. For this reason, he points out that: 'The definition of the common rhythm varies considerably according to the culture in question. Primitive beings found related rhythms particularly in the timbre of the voice, the rhythm of walking, motion, colour and material. More advanced cultures preserve these criteria, but they give more importance to form and material (the visual) than to the criteria of the voice and the rhythm of walking. Instead of conceiving these related rhythms dynamically and artistically as primitive people did, higher cultures think of them as abstract values and order them according to a reasoned classification of a static and geometric kind. . . . Whereas Primitive Man saw that forms and phenomena are essentially fluid, more advanced civilizations have given pride of place to the static aspect of forms and the purely geometric outlines of shape' (50).

Rhythms and modes, then, allow relationships to be established between different planes of reality. While natural science establishes relationships only between 'horizontal' groups of beings after the classification of Linnaeus, mystic or symbolic science erects 'vertical bridges' between those objects which are within the same cosmic rhythm, that is, objects whose position 'corresponds' to that of another 'analogous' object on another plane of reality: for example, an animal, a plant or a colour. According to Schneider, this idea of correspondences comes from belief in the indissoluble unity of the universe. Thus, in megalithic and astrobiological cultures, the most disparate phenomena are brought together, by virtue of their having a 'common rhythm'; 'hence one finds that such elements as the following are correlated: musical or cultural instruments and implements of work; animals, gods, and heavenly bodies; the seasons, the points of the compass, and material symbols; rites, colours and offices; parts of the human body and phases in human life' (51). Symbolism is what might be called a magnetic force, drawing together phenomena which have the same rhythm and even allowing them to interchange. Schneider deduces some important ontological conclusions from this: 'The apparent multiplicity of outward forms spreading out over concentric planes is deceptive, for, in the last resort, all the phenomena of the universe can be reduced to a few basic rhythmic forms, grouped and ordered by the passage of time' (51). He also draws gnostical conclusions: 'The symbol is the ideological manifestation of the mystic rhythm of creation and the degree of truth attributed to the symbol is an expression of the respect Man is able to accord to this mystical rhythm' (50). The rhythmic link between the world outside Man and the physiology of Man is demonstrated by Schneider's affirming that Primitive Man and his animal-totem—though different beings

—are joined in a common rhythm, whose basic element is the *cry-symbol* (51). Jung has amplified the psychological implications of this concept, demonstrating the deep and constant relationship between rhythm and emotion (31).

At this point we must comment upon the conclusion implicit in Schneider's thesis that, in spite of the multiplicity of forms which phenomena seem to take on, there is a lack of clearly independent forms in the universe. Indeed, morphology in its systematic analysis of forms has found that only a few are fundamental: this is particularly true of biology, in which the ovoid is a basic form from which the sphere, its segment and many intermediate forms are derived. In fact, symbological analyses often seem to offset a certain narrowing of scope by an added richness in depth, for the few basic situations that do exist appear under varying, though secondary, guises. Similarly, the only 'original' numbers are the first decade of the Greek system or the numbers up to twelve in the oriental system. The rest come under the rule of 'multiplicity', which is merely a reordering of the basic series. Besides, the place of symbolism is within the archetypal pattern of each being, each form, each rhythm. Within this archetypal pattern, thanks to the principle of concentration, all like beings can be presented as one being. And in addition, by virtue of this oneness, the predominant rhythm transmutes all that might appear to be separate; so that, to give an example, not only do all dragons stand for The Dragon, but any symbolic daub resembling a dragon is also The Dragon. And we shall see that this is a consequence of the principle of 'sufficient identity'.

JUNG'S ARCHETYPE

In the equation macrocosm=microcosm there is the implied possibility of explaining the former by the latter, or vice versa. The 'common rhythm' of Schneider belongs rather to the tendency to explain Man by reference to the world, while Jung's 'archetype' tends to explain the world by reference to Man. This is logical, since the archetype does not stem from forms or from figures or objective beings, but from images within the human spirit, within the turbulent depths of the unconscious. The archetype is, in the first place, an epiphany, that is, the revelation of the latent by way of the recondite: vision, dream, fantasy, myth. These spiritual manifestations are not, for Jung, substitutes for living things—are not lifeless effigies; they are the fruits of the inner life perpetually flowing out from the unconscious, in a way which can be compared with the gradual unfolding of creation. Just as creation determines the burgeoning of beings and objects, so psychic energy flowers into an image, an entity marking the true borders between the informal and the conceptual, between darkness and light.

Jung uses the word 'archetype' to designate those universal symbols which possess the greatest constancy and efficiency, the greatest potentiality for psychic evolution, and which point away from the inferior towards the superior. In *On Psychic Energy*, he specifically says: 'The psychological mechanism that transforms energy is the symbol.' But, in addition, he appears to give a different meaning to the archetype, linking it strictly with the structure of the psyche, when he distinguishes it from the symbol in so far as its ontic significance goes. To clarify this, let us quote some of Jung's own observations: 'The archetypes are the numinous, structural elements of the psyche and possess a certain autonomy and specific energy which enables them to attract, out of the conscious mind, those contents which are best suited to themselves. The symbols act as transformers, their function being to convert libido from a "lower" into a "higher" form. . . . It was manifestly not a question of inherited ideas, but of an inborn disposition to produce parallel images, or rather of identical psychic structures common to all men, which I later called the archetypes of the collective unconscious. They correspond to the concept of the "pattern of behaviour" in biology' (31). 'The archetypes do not represent anything external, non-psychic, although they do of course owe the concreteness of their imagery to impressions received from without. Rather, independently of, and sometimes in direct contrast to, the outward forms they may take, they represent the life and essence of a non-individual psyche' (33). That is to say, there is an intermediate realm between the oneness of the individual soul and its solitude, and the variety of the universe: between the *res cogitans* and the *res extensa* of Descartes, and that realm is the image of the world in the soul and of the soul in the world, in other words, the 'place' of symbolism 'working' in areas prepared by the archetypes—eternally present, the 'problem being whether the consciousness perceives them or not' (32).

In his *Essais de psychologie analytique*, Jung again defines the nature of the archetypes as the ready-made systems of both images and emotions (that is, of rhythms). They are inherited with the brain-structure—indeed, they are its psychic aspect. They are, on the one hand, the most powerful of instinctive prejudices, and on the other, the most efficient aids imaginable towards instinctive adaptations. Jung points out that the idea of such 'image-guides' of ancestral origin had already appeared in Freud, who called them 'primitive fantasies'. Jolan de Jacobi, in her work on Jung's psychology (30), says that Jung took the expression from St. Augustine, who used it in a sense which is very similar to the platonic 'idea', that is, the primordial reality from which the realities of existence arise as echoes and fragments. Archetypes are like all-embracing parables:

their meaning is only partially accessible; their deepest significance remains a secret which existed long before Man himself and which reaches out far beyond Man. Jolan de Jacobi identifies symbols for practical purposes with the archetypes, mentioning as examples of the latter: the 'night sea-crossing', the 'whale-dragon', figures such as the prince, the child, the magician or the unknown damsel. We cannot further debate Jung's concepts without going more deeply into his psychological and anthropological theory, which would be beyond the scope of this work. To return to the relationship between, or identity of, the symbol and the archetype, we might say that the latter is the mythical and merely human aspect of the former, whereas a strict system of symbols could exist even without human consciousness, since it is founded upon a cosmic order determined by those 'vertical' relationships which we mentioned when commenting upon the 'common rhythm' of Schneider. In short, it is a synthesis which transmutes systems of vibrations, echoing one basic' and original 'model', into a spiritual idiom expressed usually in the numerical series.

ANALYSIS OF THE SYMBOL

The basic ideas and suppositions which allow us to conceive of 'symbolism', together with the creation and vitality of each symbol, are the following:

(*a*) Nothing is meaningless or neutral: everything is significant. (*b*) Nothing is independent, everything is in some way related to something else. (*c*) The quantitative becomes the qualitative in certain essentials which, in fact, precisely constitute the meaning of the quantity. (*d*) Everything is serial. (*e*) Series are related one to another as to position, and the components of each series are related as to meaning. This serial characteristic is a basic phenomenon which is as true of the physical world (in its range of colours, of sounds, of textures, of landscapes, etc.) as of the spiritual world (in its virtues, vices, humours, feelings, etc.). Factors which account for serial arrangement are: limitation; the integration of discontinuity and continuity; proper order; graduation; numbering; the inner dynamism of the component elements; polarity; symmetrical or asymmetrical equilibrium; and the concept as a whole.

If we take any 'symbol'—for example, the sword, or the colour red—and analyse its structure, we shall see that it can be split up into both its real and its symbolic components. First, we find the object in itself, in isolation; in the second place we find the object linked to its utilitarian function, to its concrete or factual reality in the three-dimensional world—directly, in the case of the sword; or indirectly, giving colour, for example to a cloak, in the case of the colour red; in the third place, we find what enables the object to be considered as a symbol: that structure which we have termed 'symbolic function', or the dynamic tendency of the object to link up with its corresponding equivalents in all analogous series, nevertheless principally tending to show the particular metaphysical meaning. In this symbolic function we can still distinguish between the symbolic meaning and the general meaning, the latter being

Engraving in the *Historiarum liber* of Herodotus (Paris, 1510) with the important symbols of the primordial waters, ship, woman, bees and phoenix.

frequently ambivalent and charged with allusions whose variety, however, is never chaotic, for it is marshalled along the co-ordinate line of a 'common rhythm'.

Thus, the sword, iron, fire, the colour red, the god Mars, the rocky mountain, are all interrelated because they are oriented along one 'symbolic line'. They all imply the longing for 'spiritual determination and physical annihilation', which is the profoundest meaning of their symbolic functions; but in addition they are joined together —they beckon to each other, one might say—by virtue of the inner affinity that binds all these phenomena, which are, in truth, concomitants of one essential cosmic modality.

In consequence, apart from this network of relations linking up every kind of object (physical, metaphysical, mental, real and unreal in so far as they have 'psychological reality'), the symbolic order is established by a general correlation between the material and the spiritual (the visible and the invisible) and by the unfolding of their meanings. These components, which account for the 'mode of being' of the object, may be complementary or disparate; in the case of the latter an ambivalent symbol is produced. Schneider mentions the flute as an example (50). The flute in form is phallic and masculine, whereas its sound is feminine. It is an instrument which stands in curious, inverse relation to the drum, with its deep masculine tones and its rounded, feminine shapes. One indispensable aspect of the relationship between abstract forms (geometric or biomorphic, intellectual or artistic) and objects is the mutual influence they have upon each other. Let us analyse another symbol: water, for example. Its predominant characteristics are: (i) it fertilizes; (ii) it purifies; (iii) it dissolves. These three qualities have so much in common that their relationship can be expressed in a variety of ways, although one constant factor always emerges: the suspension of form—that is, the lack of any fixed form (fluidity) —is bound up with the functions of fertilization or regeneration of the material, living world on the one hand, and with the purification or regeneration of the spiritual world on the other. It is this bond which helps to explain the vast symbolism of water, appearing in the midst of solid areas of the cosmos, with the power of destroying the corrupt and of initiating a new cycle of life—the latter meaning is one that extends to the zodiacal signs of Aquarius and Pisces, and confirms the words of the Psalm: 'I am poured out like water, and all my bones are out of joint' (Psalm xxii, 14).

These basic concepts, then, are the justification and the fundament of the symbolic order of things. Jung, however, working within the framework of his symbolic logic, does not accord them the same priority. Speaking of the libido, or vital energy, he says that we have the following possibilities of symbolization: (i) *Analogous comparison* (that is, a comparison between two objects or forces on the same co-ordinate of a 'common rhythm'), as, for example, fire and the sun. (ii) *The objective, causative comparison* (which is based upon the properties of the symbolic object itself), as, for example, the sun as life-giver. (iii) *The subjective, causative comparison* (which functions like the second group, except that it immediately identifies the inner force with some symbol or some object possessing a relevant symbolic function), as, for example, the phallus or snake. (iv) *The functional comparison*, based not upon symbolic objects themselves but upon their activity, informing the image with dynamism and drama; for example, the libido fecundates like the bull, is dangerous like the boar, etc. The relevance to myth of this last group is self-evident (31).

SYMBOLIC ANALOGY

According to the *Tabula Smaragdina*, the threefold principle of the analogy between the outer and the inner world is: (i) the common source of both worlds; (ii) the influence of the psychic upon the physical; (iii) the influence of the physical world upon the spiritual. But the analogy lies not only in the relation between the inner and the outer world, but also in the relation between the various phenomena of the physical world. Material or formal resemblance is only one of the many possible analogies, for analogy can also exist in connexion with function. At times, the act of choosing reveals a basic analogy between the inner motives and the ultimate goal. Let us quote some examples of analogy by way of clarification. From religious literature we learn that the Order of St. Bruno preferred precipitous and remote places for their communities; the Benedictines would choose mountain-heights; the Cistercians, pleasant valleys; and the Jesuits of St. Ignatius, the cities. For those conversant with the character of these foundations it is almost unnecessary to point out that their very choice of situation implies a landscape-symbolism, or that, looked at in another way, the places selected are eloquent proof of the guiding spirit behind each of these communities.

The Pigmies of Equatorial Africa believe that, in the rainbow, God expresses His desire to communicate with them. This is why, as soon as the rainbow appears, they take up their bows and shoot at it. . . . (17). The incomparable beauty of this striking image tells us more about analogy than any analysis can. Other aspects of the same kind of thing may be seen in certain superstitions, such as the belief of many races that by undoing the bolts, locks and latches of the home during the birth of an infant, they can facilitate its coming into the world (21). One more analogy: the process of creation—which oriental theogonies explain as both progressive multiplication and as division, since all things derive from unity—has its analogous counterpart in the related myths of the carving up of the body of Osiris in Egypt, of Prajapati in India and of Dionysos in Greece (40).

As examples of formal analogy or resemblance, we quote four symbolic ways of referring to the Centre: the Hindu Wheel of Transformations in the centre of which is a space which is either quite unadorned or else filled with just the symbol or image of a deity; or the Chinese *Pi*, a disc of jade with a hole in the centre; or the idea that the Pole star, piercing the sky, points the way along which the merely temporal world must move in order to rid itself of the restrictions of time and space; or, finally, in the West, the Round Table with the Holy Grail standing at its centre point. We can see in all these very different objects an almost obsessive repetition of the image of a duality: the centre contrasted with the circumference, as a twofold image of the ineffable origin of the world of phenomena. But there is one legend which opens up great possibilities in analogy, for it contains both formal analogy (resemblance) and functional analogy. It is the myth of the cursed hunter, who leaves the Mass just when the Consecrated Form is being raised aloft, to go hunting. One can see delineated here a spiral movement which 'repeats' the creation of the physical world. The soul abandons the centre (the circular form of the Host) and leaves for the outer part of the wheel, where movement is swifter (symbolized by the endless chase after an unattainable quarry).

Analogy, as a unifying and ordering process, appears continuously in art, myth and poetry. Its presence always betrays a mystic force at work, the need to reunite what has been dispersed. Let us quote two cases—one of art criticism, the other literary but bearing upon the first—which have analogy as their sole foundation. Cohn-Wiener says 'Reliefs enable us to appreciate that there (in Babylon) clothes do not emphasize the shape of the body, as in Egypt: they hide it, in the way that murals conceal the rough marks of a building.' Théophile Gautier characterized Burgos cathedral as: 'Vast as a stone pyramid and delicate as a woman's curl', and Verlaine called the Middle Ages (which had created this cathedral): 'Vast and delicate'.

We have to persist in our study of analogy, for it is perhaps the corner-stone of the whole symbolic edifice. If we take two parallel actions, as expressed in the phrases: 'The sun overcomes the darkness', and 'The hero slays the monster', there is a correspondence between the two phrases (and the two actions). We have to conceive of each one as a three-part series: subject, verb, predicate. There is an analogy in function: both subjects, both verbs, both predicates are interrelated. In addition, as we have chosen two actions with a 'common rhythm', the parts of the series could be replaced or interchanged without causing any break or confusion in the system: we could equally well say 'The sun slays the monster' or 'The hero overcomes the darkness'. To take another example, in the parallel expressions: 'The sun shines with golden brilliance' and 'Gold

shines with golden brilliance', the common predicate allows not
only the interchange but also the identical equation of subject.
From the intermediate phrase: 'The sun shines like gold' or 'Gold
shines like the sun', comes the irrefutable conclusion: 'The sun—
in so far as its brilliance is golden—is gold.' This equation occurs
not because of the intrinsic value of its components but because of
the significance of their position, for the relationship is concerned
only with the dynamic or, in other words, symbolic, position of
objects. This identical equation, then, is what we have called 'the
principle of sufficient identity' and what we consider to be the core of
symbolism. Clearly, this identity is 'sufficient' (that is, sufficient for
symbolic purposes) from the very moment it is created in the very
heart of the dynamic potential of the symbol. When their functions
coincide and reveal their allegiance to one essence, both objects,
although different on the existential plane, become one on the
symbolic plane and therefore interchangeable; they are now—
to use the scholastic terms—the *coniunctio* (integrating conjunction)
of what was formerly *distinctio*. This is why symbolic technique is a
matter of progressively ordering such identities within genuine
common rhythms. Also, for the above reasons, the symbolic image
is not an 'example' (an external and hypothetical relation between
two objects or two correspondences) but an internal analogy (a
necessary and constant relationship).

SYMBOL AND ALLEGORY—SYMBOL AND ARTISTIC EXPRESSION

As a general rule, writers on the subject distinguish in essence
between the symbol and the allegory. Bachelard (3) defines the latter
as 'a lifeless image, a concept which has become over-rationalized'.
For Jung (30), allegory is a limited kind of symbol reduced to the
rôle of a pointer, designating only one of the many potential series
of dynamic meanings. Again, the difference between allegory and
symbol may be understood by reference to the hypothesis of Wirth,
for whom the essential function of the symbol is to explore the
unknown and—paradoxically—to communicate with the incom-
municable, the partial discovery of these unfathomable truths
being achieved through symbols (59). Diel illustrates the difference
between allegory and symbol with a vivid example: 'Zeus hurls a
thunderbolt, which on the meteorological plane is a straightforward
allegory. This allegory is transmuted into a symbol when the act
acquires a psychological meaning, Zeus becoming the symbol of the
spirit and the thunderbolt symbolizing the sudden appearance of an
illuminating thought (intuition) which is supposed to come from the
god himself' (15). This cipher is a semeiotic expression, a conventional abbreviation for a known constant. Allegory is seen therefore

as the mechanism of the symbol, in which the chief characteristic of the latter is devitalized and turned into a mere cipher which, because it is dressed up in traditional, symbolic garb, may even appear to be alive.

Allegories have often been created quite consciously with theatrical or literary ends in mind. Cesare Ripa's *Iconologia* is a vast thesaurus of personifications and allegories. Mythological dictionaries provide many examples in which realistic portrayal deprives them of symbolic value. Thus, according to Cochin, Cruelty is depicted as a fearful hag smothering a child in its cradle and laughing in the firelight; and Dusk as a youth with a star on his forehead and the black wings of a bat, fleeing beneath a veil representing night. Even more mechanical are the allegories representing science, the arts or industry. Cosmography is usually shown as an old woman; she wears a blue cape studded with stars while her dress is earth-coloured. In one hand she holds an astrolabe, in the other a compass. At her feet are the globes of the earth and the heavens. These examples prove that the elements of allegory are symbols which are in no way distinguishable from true symbols. Their function alone is modified and inverted, for, instead of indicating metaphysical and spiritual principles—instead of possessing an emotional content—they are artificial creations designating physical realities and nothing else.

But in certain circumstances the components of allegory can revert to their symbolic state, that is, if the unconscious seizes upon them as such, overlooking their semeiotic and representational ends. Hence we may speak of an intermediate zone of images consciously created, even if calling upon ancestral memories, perhaps through the medium of dreams or visions. We find an example of this in the playing-cards of the Tarot, the compositions of which seem to be carried out according to a criterion analogous to that of many allegories or mythical figures. The only difference is that their mysteriousness places them beyond the reach of reason and enables them to act as stimuli to the unconscious. The same thing frequently happens in art: symbols have come to be placed within conscious, traditional and dogmatic systems, but their inner life still pulses beneath this rationalized order, even becoming audible from time to time. In ornamentation, strict rhythm rather than symbolic rhythm is at work. The inner force of the rhythm is conveyed to the observer who is moved by it according to his nature, but it is rare for even the suspicion of a psychological or cosmic significance to rise to the surface of his consciousness, although he may perceive its dynamic essence. We have read with interest René Alleau's recent work, *De la Nature des symboles*, and find the distinctions he draws between symbol and *synthema* interesting from a formalistic standpoint but of less help than hindrance towards the proper understanding of the spiritual and psychological meaning of symbols.

The same thing occurs with artistic expression, which may be related to symbolization but must not be confused with it. Artistic expression is a continuous, flowing, causal and direct relation between the inspiration and the final representation, which is both the means and the end of the expressive process. Symbolization is discontinuous, static, indirect, transcending the object in which it is enshrined. In music and in painting, one can easily distinguish between the expressive and the symbolic factors. But since we cannot here go into such particulars, we shall confine ourselves to determining the parts played by these factors in some general artistic tendencies. Thus expressionism, confronted with the material world of objects, tends to destroy them and to submerge them in a swirling stream of psychic forces, overwhelming the expressive figures and, with its power, obliging them to become part of a system of free rhythms. Symbolism, on the other hand, while isolating each form and each figure, attracts, as if with magnetic lines of force, all that has 'common rhythm', that is, all that has natural affinity. It thus reveals that the profound meaning behind all series of symbolic objects is the very cause of their appearance in the world of phenomena. Concerning the relationship of the art-form with the author, let us refer again to the concept of endopathy, anticipated by Dante in his *Canzoniere*: 'He who would paint a figure, if he cannot become that figure, cannot portray it.' This is a further affirmation of 'common rhythm', like the earlier observation of Plotinus that the eye could not see the sun unless it became to some degree a sun itself and vice versa. In symbolist doctrine, there is never any question of mere relation between cause and effect but rather of 'mutual causality'. In symbolism, everything has some meaning, everything has a purpose which at times is obvious, and at others less so, and everything leaves some trace or 'signature' which is open to investigation and interpretation.

Perhaps a deeper conception than the scientific ones is that of Sufic mysticism. Henry Corbin, in *Creative Imagination in the Sufism of Ibn 'Arabi* (London, 1969), referring to the idea of the *ta'wil* professed in Sufism, states that it is essentially a method of symbolic understanding of the world, based on the transmutation of everything visible into symbols. He adds that this is practicable through the 'intuition of an essence or person in an Image which partakes neither of universal logic nor of sense perception, and which is the only means of signifying what is to be signified'. Sufism admits an intermediate kingdom (an 'interworld', as it is called) between phenomenic reality and logical or ideal reality. This interworld is the pure truth of all things, but elevated to a magicomystic, angelic position. In other words, according to this doctrine, the Oneness, before reaching material realities, multiplies itself into other realities, which must perforce be objects of amazed contemplation. (These other realities are material realities which have been transformed and appear in the function of their dominant quality, their spiritual 'office'.) Asín Palacios, in his *Escatología musulmana en la Divina Commedia*, proved the connexion between Dantean idealism and the Islamic study of the contemplative life.

APPRECIATION AND INTERPRETATION

The Problem of Interpretation   In the 19th century, mythology and symbolism were much discussed, particularly in connexion with the problem of interpretation. Max Müller derived the majority of myths from solar phenomena, in particular Dawn representing victory over Darkness, while Schwartz and his school gave pride of place to the storm (35). Soon another interpretative approach came into being, in which all celestial and meteorological images came to be considered as secondary to mental and spiritual symbols. So, for example, Karl O. Müller, in his *Kleine deutsche Schriften*, remarked that, essentially, the myth of Orion had nothing astral about it, and that only subsequently did it come to be placed in the heavens. This process of projecting the worldly into the celestial sphere, in particular into the astral, is known as catasterism. The arrival of the psychological thesis, however, did not invalidate the arguments for celestial provenance—such as those put forward by Dupuis in his *L'Origine de tous les cultes*—and this is yet a further proof that the symbol is plurisignal, a term first used by Philip Wheelwright. Basically, all these problems of 'origin' are of very secondary importance. From the point of view of symbolist tradition, there is no question of priority, only of simultaneity: all phenomena are parallel and related. Interpretations only indicate the starting-point of the interpreter, not the causal or prior condition within the system itself.

These inevitable qualifications inherent in symbolic interpretation are underlined by Gaston Bachelard in his prologue to Diel (15), when he says, not without irony: 'Are you a rationalist historian? You will find in myth an account of famous dynasties. Are you a linguist? Words tell all, and all legends are formed around sayings. One more corrupted word—one more god! Olympus is a grammar controlling the functions of the gods. Are you a sociologist? Then in myth you will find the means by which, in primitive society, the leader is turned into a god.' The only all-embracing interpretation which would seem to fit the original meaning of myths and symbols is the one that takes this meaning right back to the metaphysical source, to the dialectic of creation. Louis Renou praises Zimmer's 'intuitive appreciation of the metaphysical approach to the myth', which is to say, his fidelity to his subject, an approach embracing both the philosophical and the religious aspects (60). But argument about all the possible interpretations dates not from our times, nor from recent times, but from Antiquity. Seznec recalls that the ancients evolved theories about the origins of the gods, based upon interpretations which can be summed up as expressions of three essential attitudes: (a) myths are more or less modified accounts of historical facts, of people raised to the rank of gods, as happened in historical time with Alexander the Great; (b) myths express the conflicts inherent in the natural world, for which reason gods had to be supernatural, cosmic symbols; (c) myths are the fabulous expression of philosophical or moral ideas. We would rather say that myths, and a great number of other archetypal symbols, are all three things at once. Or better still, that they are concrete, historical realities, that they are at once cosmic and natural; moral and psychological realities are merely restatements on three planes (history, the physical world, the psychic world) of the same basic ideas. Euhemerism, a system which gives preference to historical interpretation, does not, however, in any way affect the nature of symbol or myth, because, as we have already said, the simultaneous occurrence of an abstract and general manifestation with its materialization in a moment of space-time not only implies no contradiction, but actually is a proof of their true existence on both planes.

In the world of symbols, totemistic interpretation does no more than demonstrate relationships, without elucidating meanings: it forges connecting-links between beings endowed with 'common rhythm', but it does not indicate the meaning of these beings. To say that Athena was the nocturnal owl, the Magna Mater a lioness or Artemis a she-bear, is to say nothing about the meaning of the gods nor about their respective animal-symbols. The analysis of meaning is the only thing which can lead to the reconstruction of the inner structure of each symbol. Similarly, realism, which sees in a fable merely a different version of the original event or an amalgam of varied elements, offers only a secondary explanation of the problem of 'origins' without attempting to go deeply into the *raison d'être* of the entity. To say that the image of the bat gave birth to the idea of the hippogryph, the chimaera and the dragon, is to give the minimal idea of the expressive and symbolic value of such fabulous animals; only an analysis of their context, their behaviour and their purpose can bring us close to the myth of the symbol with its considerable capacity for dynamic transfiguration. Krappe is speaking in terms of realism when he says that the well-known tradition of associating the tree with the serpent can be traced 'quite simply to the fact (easily verifiable in all countries where snakes live) that these reptiles generally make their holes at the foot of a tree' (35). Even if we grant the accuracy of this explanation, what could it tell us about the intensity of this myth, with its powerful symbolism expressing Biblical temptation? Clearly, symbolism is something *quite different*. It is the magnetism which reality—whether it be simple (the object) or complex (the relationship)—is seen to exert by virtue of its spiritual potential within the cosmic system. The snake and the tree are related analogously in their outlines, in the resemblance of the reptile to the roots of a tree, and in the relationship between the tree and the erect snake on the one hand, and the columns of Boaz and Jachin on the other: a binary image of the essential paradox of life—the paradox of Good and Evil. While the tree raises its branches to the sun as if in an ecstasy of adoration, the snake is poised ready to strike. This is the essence of the symbol and not the fact that snakes nest at the foot of a tree. What is more, applying the traditional law that facts never explain anything but are the mere consequence of principle, we can say that if the snake makes its nest beneath trees, this is precisely because of this inner relationship.

PSYCHOLOGICAL INTERPRETATION

Given that every symbol 'echoes' throughout every plane of reality and that the spiritual ambience of a person is essentially one of these planes because of the relationship traditionally established between the macrocosm and the microcosm, a relationship which philosophy has verified by presenting Man as the 'messenger of being' (Heidegger): given this, then it follows that every symbol can be interpreted psychologically. So, for example, the secret room of Bluebeard, which he forbids his wife to enter, is his mind. The dead wives which she encounters in defying his orders are the wives whom he has once loved, that is, who are now dead to his love. Jung emphasizes the twofold value of psychological interpretation; it has thrown new light upon dreams, daydreams, fantasies and works of art, while on the other hand it provides confirmation of the collective character of myths and legends (31). He also points out that there are two aspects of the interpretation of the unconscious: what the symbol represents in itself (objective interpretation), and what it signifies as a projection or as an individualized 'case' (subjective interpretation). For our part, objective interpretation is nothing more nor less than understanding. Subjective interpretation is true interpretation: it takes the widest and profoundest meaning of a symbol in any one given moment and applies it to certain given examples.

Psychological interpretation points the middle way between the objective truth of the symbol and the particular circumstances influencing the individual who experiences the symbol. The prejudices of the interpreter must, in varying degrees, also be taken into account, for it will often be difficult to wean him from his particular likes and dislikes. It is here that symbols acquire secondary, accidental and transitory meanings, quite apart from their universal quality. The sword, without ever losing its objective meaning (which we explained earlier) comes to acquire various secondary meanings —which may even, because of its vital potential, appear momentarily as the primary sense—according to whether the symbol occurs in the mind of a soldier, a priest, a collector of swords or a poet. And this is to mention only one limiting factor, in itself extensive enough, embracing, as it does, character-study. The symbol, then, like water, finds its own level, which is the level of the interpreting mind. The difficulties of interpretation are therefore enormous, whereas the difficulties in the way of appreciating the symbol are almost elementary. Much scepticism about symbolism—especially among psychologists—arises because of the confusion of two quite different aspects of the function of symbolism: (i) the manifestation of the true meaning of the symbolic object, and (ii) the manifestation of a distorted meaning superimposed by an individual mind prejudiced by circumstantial or psychological factors. The difficulties of psychological interpretation concern not so much the series of 'multivalencies' of the symbol (common rhythm), as the variety of outlook of the interpreting mind, influenced either unconsciously by the power of the symbol or consciously by his own *Weltanschauung*.

One example of this kind of prejudiced interpretation can be seen in the Freudians, who claimed to unveil the universal sexuality of all objects and forms because they demonstrably belonged to one or the other of two broadly opposed groups: the masculine and the feminine. But the Chinese, with their Yang-Yin symbol, and the Hindus, and the Hebrews had long ago established the essential polarity of the world of phenomena according to generic principles, including the sexual division. Nevertheless, no matter how an object might be classified, it would never lose its potential significance; for its grouping constitutes only one of its symbolic representations and not, of course, the most important. The Talmud, furthermore, had discovered the interesting method of interpreting sexual dreams not always as immediately meaningful but often as indirectly significant or portentous (Fromm, 23). To dream of sexual relations with, for example, one's mother signified the attainment of the highest degree of wisdom. That Roman divines were also aware of this is proved by the interpretation given to a similar dream of Julius Caesar, to whom it was prophesied that he would inherit the world. But on the other hand one cannot deny those psychological interpretations which point to sexual ends. When a man, in the Talmud, 'sprinkles an olive tree with olive oil', he betrays symbolically an incestuous desire. The distortion of symbols inherent in any method of psychological interpretation derived from abnormal minds and applied to abnormal conditions may be seen in the patterns of meaning evolved by Volmat in his *L'Art psychopathologique*. For him, the symbol 'grows around a dynamic system, that is, around a structure within the dimensions of time and personality'. Such distortion of the true meaning of symbols arises from an over-restriction of their function, from over-identification with the psychological mechanism which construes it and with the *alter ego*, although it makes up for this restriction by its added intensity. Everything is made as subjective as possible: the tree is no longer the cosmic tree, but a projection of the self; and similarly with mountains. Water and fire present only their negative and destructive connotations, not the positive ones of purification and regeneration. By associations, only the tragic and mournful connotations are investigated: such is the construction put upon flowers and animals, for example. In the same way, this kind of interpretation overruns the object, altering it wherever necessary to fit abnormal symbols. Houses lose their doors and windows (symbols of openings, outlets, hopes of salvation); trees lose their leaves and never bear fruit. Catastrophes, which in traditional symbolism have the ambivalent meaning of both destruction and of fecundation and regeneration, are here limited to negative and destructive functions. One can understand that symbology built upon interpretation at this level can lay no claim to objectivity: it is no longer metaphysical but psychological.

On the other hand, to limit symbolic interpretation to the analysis of meaning, or to enumerating the qualities of the thing and its spiritual counterparts, is not enough. Not because the method is inherently deficient, but because in practice no one can see clearly and wholly what the object in question is.

A confrontation with symbolist tradition therefore becomes necessary, a tradition with secular associations and interpretations of undoubted value and universality; it is, then, essential to apply the comparative method whenever possible.

LEVELS OF MEANING

Corresponding to the multiplicity of symbolic objects linked by a 'common rhythm' is the multivalency of their meanings, each one distributed analogously on a separate level of reality. This power of the symbol to evince a meaning not only on one level but at all levels is borne out by all those who have written about symbology, notwithstanding their scientific outlook. Mircea Eliade stresses this essential characteristic of the symbol, emphasizing the simultaneity of its different meanings (17)—although, strictly, instead of 'different meanings' one ought to speak of the different values and particular aspects assumed by the basic meaning. Schneider gives a vivid example of this kind of progressive ordering of meaning, with its separate patterns on each plane of reality. He notes that if we take three fundamental planes: (i) vegetable and meteorological life; (ii) natural human life; and (iii) spiritual growth; then the concepts of death and rebirth—respectively symbolized by the moon in its waning and waxing phases—signify on these three levels: (i) drought and rain; (ii) illness and cure; and (iii) fossilization and flux (51).

Schneider goes on to suggest that the symbol is the inner link between all that is analogous or associated, rather than the dynamic potential of each separate object. He suggests that 'every symbol is a rhythmic whole embracing the essential, common rhythms of a series of phenomena, which are scattered over different planes by virtue of their secondary rhythms. They spread out from a spiritual centre and their clarity and intensity decrease as they approach the periphery. The reality of the symbol is founded upon the idea that the ultimate reality of an object lies in its spiritual rhythm—which it incarnates—and not in its material aspect' (50), or its functional aspect. Diel shares this view, applying it to myths, such as that of Demeter and her daughter Persephone, where he points out that the Eleusinian Mysteries imply three levels of meaning: the agrarian, the psychological and the metaphysical, the mystery lying in the integration of these three levels of reality; and these three levels correspond to the levels of all forms of sense-perception and knowledge. Hence, interpretation becomes the selection of one level as predominant, leaving aside the question of interaction, symbolic degradation and over-restriction within the particular. It is quite legitimate to see Medusa as a cloud, Chrysaor the golden sword as lightning, the galloping hoof beats of Pegasus as the thunder. But by limiting the upwards-tending dynamism of the symbol within these meteorological concepts, the unbounded potential significance of the symbol becomes confined within the limits of allegory.

From the Freudian school onwards, the level of a great many symbolic interpretations has been that of sexual activity. The swan, for example, has come to be seen simply as a symbol of herma-phroditism; yet on the mystical plane it has always alluded to the androgynous god of many primitive and astrobiological religions, as well as to the *rebis* of the alchemists and to the bisexual Man of Plato. Confining the symbol in this way within the narrow limits of allegory, restricting it to a lower plane in the pattern of the universe, is known in symbology as the 'degradation of the symbol'. And this degraded meaning may not only affect the interpretation it receives, but also the symbol itself. At times, degradation is brought about by trivial vulgarization: thus, arising from the myth of Mercury and Perseus flying through space with the aid of their winged sandals, we have the more modest journeyings of those who wear the seven-league boots (38); out of the myth of the 'Islands of the Blessed', which is connected with the mystical 'centre', there has arisen the urge for 'ocean paradises' which even Gauguin sought to turn into reality; out of the mythical battles between Osiris and Set, and Ormuzd and Ahriman, come the struggles between the 'good' and the 'bad' in literature (17). Lévy-Bruhl, in *L'Expérience mystique et les symboles chez les primitifs*, adduces some similar examples of fairy-story deformation of the symbol. Other forms of degradation are: over-particularized interpretation, leading to lengthy and arbitrary descriptions of 'the language of flowers' and so on. Over-intellectualized, allegorical interpretations are another aspect of the same thing—for example, asserting that 'the union of Leda and the swan signifies the pairing of Power and Injustice'; similarly, 'identifications' through so-called analogy. This dangerous tendency is what led to the decadence of symbolist movements during the Renaissance. In all the examples of deformation we have given, one finds the same basic falsification: the creative drive of the symbol—its tendency to revert to its Origin—is restricted, and it is made to bear labels which are over-concrete, too materialized or inferior. Its metaphysical function is arrested, and consequently a single plane of reality comes to be mistaken for the sum of all possible levels of symbolic meaning. If this use of symbols is recognized as deformation, then—as we suggested earlier when commenting upon Caro Baroja—a general distrust of ready-made symbolic meanings and the attempt to use them to explain myth, would seem to be justified. The influence of the symbol must be allowed to pervade all levels of reality; only then can it be seen in all its spiritual grandeur and fecundity.

THE SYMBOLIZING AGENT AND THE SYMBOLIC OBJECT

In accordance with our usual practice of using the comparative rather than the deductive method and avoiding over-classification, we have not drawn rigid dividing-lines between the separate meanings of each particular symbol on its various levels of reality. We have not done so because our sources have been very varied and we have preferred to reproduce their content with a minimum of editorial comment. Another reason for not stating clear-cut conclusions is that in our opinion it is not always possible to accept the particular views of some writers, however estimable they may be as compilers or even as interpreters of symbols. For example, Loeffler says that in oriental and Nordic mythology, each symbol, myth or legend contains 'four superimposed moral lessons: (i) an historical lesson, that is, an epic narration dealing with real facts and people and serving as a kind of "material backing" for the symbolic teaching involved; (ii) a psychological lesson, depicting the struggle between spirit and matter on the human plane; (iii) a lesson bearing upon life on our planet; and (iv) a lesson upon the constitution of matter and cosmic order' (38). This schematic division is surely misleading, for we must remember that, for any given level of meaning, it is not the meaning itself which changes but the way it is adapted or applied. Finally, we have not favoured this kind of classification—despite its serial 'multivalency'—for the reason that symbols, traditionally at least, seem to have an inborn tendency to settle upon one particular plane. Thus, some symbols are primarily concerned with psychology, others with the cosmological or natural orders. There are those too, we must point out, which exist in order to reconcile different levels of reality, particularly the psychic with the spatial. The best example of this is that of the mandala, and all those symbols of conjunction or those uniting the three worlds. Thus, for example, steps are symbolic of the connexion between the conscious and the unconscious, just as they are a connexion between the upper, the terrestrial and the nether worlds. The idea of order is an essential one in symbolism and is expressed through the ordering of space, geometric forms, and numbers, and by the disposition of living beings as symbols in positions determined by the law of correspondences. Another essential idea of symbolist doctrine is that of the cycle, either as a series of possibles—expressed particularly through the septenary and all its associated or derived symbolic forms—or as a process which closes up some of the possibilities once the cycle is completed. Zodiacal symbolism is a perfect illustration of this cosmic structure. The relation of destiny with the cyclic process is implied in the figures of the legendary Tarot pack; the wealth of symbolic knowledge which is contained in each and every one of its cards is not to be despised, even if their symbolic significance is open to debate. For the illustrations of the Tarot afford clear examples of the signs, the dangers and the paths leading towards the infinite which Man may discover in the course of his existence.

The great themes of death and resurrection, related respectively with the cycle of involution (progressive materialization) and evolution (spiritualization or the return to the point of origin), gave rise to many myths and legends. The struggle to come to grips with truth and the spiritual centre appears in the form of battles and trials of strength, while those instincts which shackle Man and hold him down appear as monsters. According to Diel, 'the symbols most typical of the spirit and of intuition are the sun and the sunlit sky; those of the imagination and the darker side of the unconscious, are the moon and night. The sea symbolizes the mysterious immensity from which everything comes and to which everything returns' (15). All natural and cultural objects may be invested with a symbolic function which emphasizes their essential qualities in such a way that they lend themselves to spiritual interpretation. So, for example, rocks, mountains and all topographical features; trees and vegetables, flowers and fruit, animals, works of architecture and the utilities, the members of the body and the four elements. But it should be remembered that this catalogue of objects becomes much shorter when the objects become possessed of certain symbolic potentials, when they are strung together, as it were, along one line of meaning. For example, within the symbolism of levels and of the relation between heaven and earth, the mountain, the tree, the temple and steps can often be equated. On occasions, such a relationship appears to be created by or at least to bear the imprint of one principal symbol. It is for this reason that Mircea Eliade can say that 'the intuitive awareness of the moon as the source of rhythm as well as the source of energy, life and regeneration (of material things) has built up a veritable network between all the different cosmic planes, creating symmetries, analogies and communion between phenomena of infinite variety. . . . We have, for example, the series: Moon, rain, fertility, woman, snake, death, periodic regeneration; but at times only a part of the series is apparent: Snake, woman, fecundity; snake, rain, fecundity; or woman, snake, eroticism, etc. A complete mythology has been built up around these smaller, secondary groups' (17), especially around the principal symbol.

The symbolic object appears as a quality or a higher form, and also as an essence justifying and explaining the existence of the symbolizing agent. The most straightforward of symbological analyses based upon simple enumeration of the qualitative meanings of the object, sometimes, while the 'mode of existence' is being investigated, will reveal a sudden opening which illuminates its meaning through an association of ideas. This association should never be thought of as a mere external idea in the mind of the investigator, outside the symbol itself, but rather as a revelation of the inner link—the 'common rhythm'—joining two realities to the mutual benefit of both. For this reason, when one reads in Picinelli's work: 'Sapphire:—Arouses pity. In colour similar to the sky: it shares its colour. It gladdens the heart. A symbol of heavenly reward. Contemplative', then one must agree that, within the limits of his implicit analysis, the writer is right as far as he goes, although the terms implying anticipation ('arouses pity') and moral effect ('it gladdens the heart'), are not strictly explanations of the symbol but of a reaction arising from its contemplation.

SYMBOLIC SYNTAX

Symbols, in whatever form they may appear, are not usually isolated; they appear in clusters, giving rise to symbolic compositions which may be evolved in time (as in the case of story-telling), in space (works of art, emblems, graphic designs), or in both space and time (dreams, drama). It is necessary to recall that, in symbolism, each detail invariably has some particular meaning (4), and that the way a symbol is oriented also calls for attention: for example, fire pointing downwards represents erotic life; while, pointing towards the sky, it expresses purification. Schneider mentions also the importance of the location of the object: a basket changes its meaning when placed on the head, for 'any given object changes in significance according to the "common rhythm" it is made to respond to' (50). Combinations of symbols evidence a cumulative meaning. Thus, a crowned snake signifies the crowning of instinctive or telluric forces. Emblems are very often based upon a conjunction of various simple symbols in any given sphere. At times they are concordant symbols, at times discordant. An example of the former is the frequent mediaeval emblem of the heart enclosed within a circle from which tongues of flame radiate. The three constituent parts of this emblem refer to the Trinity: the heart represents Love and the mystic centre, the circle represents eternity and the flames, irradiation and purification. On other occasions the symbol is formally simple yet structurally it is made up from two or more sources: thus, the tree is given the form of a cross, or the cross the form of a leafless tree—a symbol which also occurs in mediaeval emblematic designs. An example cited by Bachelard falls within this class of confederate symbol: appearing in a dream of Jean-Paul are 'white swans with wings outspread like arms' (2). This kind of symbolic syntax is found most frequently in allegories and attributes. If the globe, the symbol of the world, has an eagle above it (8), it expresses the consecration of power. Medusa's head—with its negative, destructive character—placed in the centre of a symbolic space, signifies destructiveness (15). Very important, too, is the vertical positioning of the symbol. Higher elevation along a given vertical axis always indicates spiritual superiority—by analogy of physical with metaphysical 'height'. For this reason, the *uraeus* of Egyptian sovereigns expressed the spiritualization of the inner force (symbolized by the snake) when it was positioned on the forehead, on a spot the importance of which is well known to Tantrist Yoga.

Symbolic syntax, in respect of the relationship between its individual elements, may function in four different ways: (a) *the successive manner*, one symbol being placed alongside another; their meanings, however, do not combine and are not even interrelated; (b) *the progressive manner*, in which the meanings of the symbols do not interact but represent different stages in the symbolic process; (c) *the composite manner*, in which the proximity of the symbols brings about change and creates complex meanings: a synthesis, that is, and not merely a mixture of their meanings; (d) *the dramatic manner*, in which there is an interaction between the groups and all the potentialities of the preceding groups are synthesized. We have followed the practice of Enel—who would appear to have settled the problems which preoccupied Horapollo and Athanasius Kircher—and taken several examples from the Egyptian system of hieroglyphics, which well illustrates the last group. Further ideas upon the 'de-ciphering' of complex symbols can be drawn from what we have suggested when dealing with spatial and pictorial symbolism. Moreover, we note that the meaning of any symbol can be enriched by the application of the law of correspondences and its corollaries. In other words, objects possessing 'common rhythm' barter some of their properties. But we must also recall that the Scylla and Charybdis of symbolism are (firstly) devitalization through allegorical over-simplification, and (secondly) ambiguity arising from exaggeration of either its meaning or its ultimate implications; for in truth, its deepest meaning is unequivocal since, in the infinite, the apparent diversity of meaning merges into Oneness.

If we take all the possible applications of an analytical method founded upon the symbolism of space or of lineal direction, or of determinate or indeterminate, regular or irregular forms, or of the gamut of texture and colour, we can see that they are indeed very numerous; one in particular is the comprehension of those works of art which portray the immediate projection of inner forces and fantasies not in the figurative world but in the material. It could here be objected that abstract—geometric, biomorphic or textural —painting, or surrealist visions, do not call for conscious discrimination, since the aim of the creator—as Richard Wagner said of his music—is to forget all about the psychological mechanism and let the unconscious speak to the unconscious. This is as true as it is to note that the implications of symbology are sometimes disturbing and even sinister. For this reason, and others already mentioned, we have not given analytical descriptions of paintings, dreams or literature. This is not the place to discuss the implications of symbolist theory; anyone who wishes is free to make use of the mystic bonds to which we allude or to ignore them as he sees fit. We only wish to add that we regard our work less as a reference-book than a book to be read at leisure. And that only by seeing all the symbols compiled as a whole can the reader learn anything about any one of them; for symbolic meanings are often surprising, such as that implied in the relationship between the *retiarius* and *mirmillo* gladiators and the zodiacal signs of *Pisces* (aquatic forces of dissolution, its attributes being the net and the trident) and *Cancer* (the solar force, its attributes being fire, the shell of the crab and the sword)—a relationship which explains and justifies the gladiators' unceasing struggle in the gilded amphitheatres of Rome. Then again, dynamism plays an important rôle. The sun, for example, may rule over or be ruled by the moon. In the latter case, we are faced with the law of becoming; in the former, with the law of being, as defined by Evola. One last observation: We have on occasion added to the symbolic meaning those allegorical meanings which we have thought might prove of some interest.

Abandonment The symbolism of abandonment has a similar range of reference to that of the 'lost object', and they are both parallel to the symbolism of death and resurrection (31). To feel abandoned is, essentially, to feel forsaken by the 'god within us', that is, to lose sight of the eternal light in the human spirit. This imparts to the individual's existence a sense of estrangement—to which the labyrinth theme is also related.

Ablution To quote Oswald Wirth: 'In alchemy, the subject, having undergone *nigredo* (blackness) followed by death and putrefaction, is subjected to ablution, an operation which makes use of the slow dripping of condensation from the vapours that rise from the carcass when a moderate flame applied externally is alternately raised and lowered in intensity. These continual drops serve to bring about the progressive washing of the material, which changes from black to grey and then gradually to white. The whiteness is an indication of the success of the first part of the *Magnum Opus*. The adept worker achieves this only by purifying his soul of all that commonly agitates it' (59). Washing, then, symbolizes the purification not so much of objective and external evil as of subjective and inner evils, which we might call 'private'. It is hardly necessary to add that the latter kind of purification is much more difficult and painful than the former, since what it sets out to destroy is something which is bonded to existence itself with all its vital urges. The principle involved in this alchemic process is that implied in the maxim 'Deny thyself . . .', and an indispensable precept for true moral progress.

Abnormality In primitive cultures, maimed beings, as well as madmen, were believed to possess supernatural powers—the shamans, for example. In primitive magico-religious thinking, the outstanding ability of physically abnormal individuals is not regarded, as it is in modern psychology, as having been developed in compensation for the abnormality, but rather the other way round: the maiming, the abnormality, the tragic destiny were the price the individual had to pay for some inborn extraordinary gift—often the gift of prophecy. This belief was universal (9). In some mythologies, maimed beings are connected with the moon and its phases; there are mythic lunar beings, with only one hand or one foot, who have the magic power to cure disease, bring rain, and so on (17). This conception of abnormality is not restricted to animate beings, but applies equally to objects. According to Cola Alberich, abnormal objects have always been considered as particularly useful in warding off malignant influences. Such objects are: stones with embedded fossils; amulets shaped like a six-fingered or a four-fingered hand; double almonds in one shell; unusually shaped grains of corn, etc. (12). There is an interesting parallel to be drawn between the spontaneous interest evinced by Primitive Man in strange or abnormal objects, and the more deliberate, 'poetic' treatment bestowed by surrealists upon such objects as elements in the symbolic process. The belief in the magic powers of abnormal objects is connected with the symbolism of the jester (that is, the inverted king, the sacrificial victim) and with the symbolism of the moon.

Abracadabra Many words and phrases relating to rituals, talismans and pentacles have a symbolic meaning, either in themselves or in the way they are used, which is expressed either phonetically or, more frequently, graphically. This word was in frequent use during the Middle Ages as a magic formula. It is derived from the Hebrew phrase *abreq ad hâbra*, meaning 'hurl your thunderbolt even unto death'. It was usually inscribed inside an inverted triangle, or was set out so that it formed a triangle (39) thus:

```
A B R A C A D A B R A
 A B R A C A D A B R
  A B R A C A D A B
   A B R A C A D A
    A B R A C A D
     A B R A C A
      A B R A C
       A B R A
        A B R
         A B
          A
```

This magic word has also been related to the Abracax (Abraxas, Abrasax) of the Gnostics. It is in reality one of the names of the sun-god, Mithras (4).

Abyss The abyss in any form has a fascinating dual significance. On the one hand, it is a symbol of depth in general; on the other, a symbol of inferiority. The attraction of the abyss lies in the fact that these two aspects are inextricably linked together. Most ancient or primitive peoples have at one time or another identified certain breaks in the earth's surface or marine depths with the abyss. Among the Celts and other peoples, the abyss was inside mountains; in Ireland, Japan and the South Sea islands, it was at the bottom of seas and lakes; among Mediterranean peoples it was just beyond the horizon; for the Australian aborigines, the Milky Way is the abyss *par excellence*. The abyss is usually identified with the 'land of the dead', the underworld, and is hence, though not always, associated with the Great Mother and earth-god cults (35). The association between the nether world and the bottom of seas or lakes explains many aspects of legends in which palaces or beings emerge from an abyss of water. After King Arthur's death, his sword, thrown into the lake by his command, is caught as it falls and, before being drawn down to the bottom, flourished by a hand which emerges from the waters.

Acacia This shrub, which bears white or pink blooms, was considered sacred by the Egyptians, partly, no doubt, because of its dual coloration and also because of the great mystic importance of the white-red principle (8). In Hermetic doctrine, according to Gérard de Nerval in his *Voyage en Orient* (9), it symbolizes the testament of Hiram which teaches that 'one must know how to die in order to live again in eternity'. It occurs with this particular symbolic meaning (that is, the soul and immortality) in Christian art, especially the Romanesque (20).

Acanthus The acanthus leaf, a very common ornamental motif in architecture, was, during the Middle Ages, invested with a definite symbolism derived from its two essential characteristics: its growth, and its thorns. The latter is a symbol of solicitude about lowly things. According to Bishop Melito of Sardis, they signify the awareness and the pain of sin. We may mention here that in the *Diary* of Weininger, there is no difference between guilt and punishment. A more generalized symbolism, alluding perhaps to natural life itself, with its tendency towards regression or at least towards stunting, appears in the Gospels in the parable of the sower (Luke viii, 7), where we read that some of the seed (of spiritual principles and of salvation) fell amongst thorns and was choked. And in the Old Testament (Genesis iii, 18) the Lord tells man that the earth will yield to him thorns and thistles (46).

Acrobat Because of his acrobatics, which often involve reversing the normal position of the human body by standing on his hands, the acrobat is a living symbol of inversion or reversal, that is to say, of that need which always arises in time of crisis (personal, social or collective historical crises) to upset and reverse the established order: idealism turns into materialism; meekness into aggressiveness; serenity into tragedy; order into disorder, or vice versa. Acrobats are related to other aspects of the circus and, in particular, to the mystery of the Hanged Man in the Tarot pack, which has a similar significance.

Activity In the mystic sense, there is no activity other than spiritual movement towards evolution and salvation; any other form of activity is merely agitation and not true activity. On this point, the West is in full accord with the East, for, according to the doctrine of Yoga, the highest state (*sattva*), characterized by outward calm, is that of greatest activity (the active subjugation of the lower impulses and their subsequent sublimation). Thus, it is not surprising that Cesare Ripa, in his *Iconologia*, through a process of assimilation with the exalted images of the Archangel St. Michael and of St. George, represents 'Virtuous Action' as a warrior armed in a gilt cuirass, holding a book in one hand and in the other a lance poised ready to be thrust into the head of a huge serpent which he has just vanquished. The head of Vice, crushed under his left foot, completes the allegory. Hence, every struggle or victory on the material plane has its counterpart in the realm of the spirit. Thus, according to Islamic tradition, the 'Holy War' (the struggle against the infidel, depicted with weapons held at the ready) is simply an image of the 'Great Holy War' (the struggle of the faithful against the Powers of Evil).

Adam Primordial Man. The name is derived from the Hebrew *adama* (= earth). G. G. Scholem, in *On the Kabbalah and its Symbolism* (London, 1965), states that, initially, Adam is conceived as 'a vast representation of the power of the universe', which is concentrated in him. Hence the equation macrocosm = microcosm. In both the Bible and the platonic doctrine of the androgyne, Eve appears as an excision of the first being, which integrated sexual duality. Do the tree and the serpent reproduce the same duality on another symbolic plane? Or do they express a different duality to that contained in the first human couple, which is the symbol of the internal and external excision of the living being? Eve, in the rôle of persuader, appears as a mediator between the serpent (the source of evil, which William Blake likened to energy) and man, who would have been free and indifferent, and who would have 'fallen' only under pressure.

Aerolite A symbol of spiritual life which has descended upon earth. A symbol of revelation; of the 'other world' made accessible; and of the heavenly fire in its creative aspect, i.e. as seed. Tradition has it that, just as there are 'upper waters', there is also 'upper fire'. The stars symbolize the unattainable aspect of this fire; aerolites and meteorites are its messengers, and hence they are sometimes associated with angels and other heavenly hierarchies (37). It must be remembered that the iron first used by man was meteoric (which may account for the common root of the word *sidereal* and other words beginning with the prefix *sidero-*). The belief in a symbiotic relationship between the heavenly and the terrestrial worlds lies at the root of the idea of the 'cosmic marriage', a concept with which primitive astrobiological thought sought to explain the analogy, as well as the tangential relationship, between the antithetical worlds of heaven and earth.

Ages, The For the purposes of the morphology of symbols, an age is exactly the same as a phase. The lunar 'model' of the four phases (of waxing, fullness, waning and disappearance) has sometimes been reduced to two or three phases, and sometimes increased to five. The phases in the span of human life have undergone similar fluctuations, but in general they are four, with death either omitted or combined with the final phase of old age. The division into four parts—quite apart from the importance of its relationship with the four phases of the moon—coincides with the solar process and the annual cycle of the seasons as well as with the spatial arrangement of the four points of the compass on the conceptual plane. The cosmic ages have been applied to the era of human existence, and also to the life of a race or an empire. In Hindu tradition, the *Manvantara*, also called *Mahâ-Yuga* (or the Great Cycle), comprises four *yuga* or secondary periods, which were said to be the same as the four ages in Greco-Roman antiquity. In India, these same ages are called after four throws in the game of dice: *krita, tretâ, dvâpara* and *kali*. In classical times, the ages are associated with the symbolism of metals, giving the 'golden age', 'silver age', 'bronze age' and 'iron age'. The same symbolic pattern—which in itself is an interpretation—is found in the famous dream of Nebuchadnezzar (Daniel ii) as well as in the figure of the 'Old Man of Crete' in Dante's *Commedia* (*Inferno*, XIV, ll. 94-120) (60, 27). Progress from the purest metal to the most malleable—from gold to iron—implies involution. For this reason René Guénon comments that the successive ages, as they 'moved away from the Beginning', have brought about a gradual materialization (28). And for this reason, too, William Blake observed that 'Progress is the punishment of God'. So that progress in life—in an individual's existence—is tantamount to gradual surrender of the golden values of childhood, up to the point in which the process of growing old is terminated by death. The myths concerning the 'Golden Age' find their origin, according to Jung, in an analogy with childhood—that period when nature heaps gifts upon the child without any effort on his part, for he gets all he wants. But in addition, and in a deeper sense, the Golden Age stands for life in unconsciousness, for unawareness of death and of all the problems of existence, for the 'Centre' which precedes time, or which, within the limitations of existence, seems to bear the closest resemblance to paradise. Ignorance of the world of existence creates a kind of golden haze, but with the growing understanding of concepts of duty, the father-principle and rational thinking, the world can again be apprehended (31). The aims of surrealism are nothing short of reintegrating, as far as is practicable, this state of emotional irrationality characteristic of primigenial peoples.

Agriculture Its allegorical representation is the figure of a goddess, like Ceres in appearance (with whom it may be identified), but with a plough and a plant bearing its first blossom. Sometimes, the allegorical figure carries a cornucopia full of fruits and flowers, or has both hands leaning on a spade or a hoe. The Zodiac is also included, to indicate the importance of the yearly cycle and the sequence of the seasons and the work that each season implies (8).

Air Of the four Elements, air and fire are regarded as active and male; water and earth as passive and female. In some elemental cosmogonies, fire is given pride of place and considered the origin of all things, but the more general belief is that air is the primary element. Compression or concentration of air creates heat or fire, from which all forms of life are then derived. Air is essentially related to three sets of ideas: the creative breath of life, and, hence, speech; the stormy wind, connected in many mythologies with the idea of creation; and, finally, space as a medium for movement and for the emergence of life-processes. Light, flight, lightness, as well as scent and smell, are all related to the general symbolism of air (3). Gaston Bachelard says that for one of its eminent worshippers, Nietzsche, air was a kind of higher, subtler matter, the very stuff of human freedom. And he adds that the distinguishing characteristic of aerial nature is that it is based on the dynamics of dematerialization. Thoughts, feelings and memories concerning heat and cold, dryness and humidity and, in general, all aspects of climate and atmosphere, are also closely related to the concept of air. According to Nietzsche, air should be cold and aggressive like the air of mountain tops. Bachelard relates scent to memory, and by way of example points to Shelley's characteristic lingering over reminiscences of smell.

Alchemy The real beginnings of alchemy date back to the first centuries A.D., when it was practised mainly by Greeks and Arabs. Elements from various traditions, including Christian mysticism, were later incorporated. It was essentially a symbolic process involving the endeavour to make gold, regarded as the symbol of illumination and salvation. The four stages of the process were signified by different colours, as follows: black (guilt, origin, latent forces) for 'prime matter' (a symbol of the soul in its original condition); white (minor work, first transmutation, quicksilver); red (sulphur, passion); and, finally, gold. Piobb analyses the symbolic meaning of the various operations. The first, known as *calcination*, stood for the 'death of the profane', i.e. the extinction of all interest in life and in the manifest world; the second, *putrefaction*, was a consequence of the first, consisting of the separation of the destroyed remains; *solution*, the third, denoted the purification of matter;

Athanor, the alchemists' oven (after an old engraving).

distillation, the fourth, was the 'rain' of purified matter, i.e. of the elements of salvation isolated by the preceding operations; fifthly, *conjunction* symbolized the joining of opposites (the *coincidentia oppositorum*, identified by Jung with the close union, in Man, of the male principle of consciousness with the female principle of the unconscious); *sublimation*, the sixth stage, symbolized the suffering resulting from the mystic detachment from the world and the dedication to spiritual striving. In emblematic designs, this stage is depicted by a wingless creature borne away by a winged being, or sometimes it is represented by the Prometheus myth. The final stage is *philosophic congelation*, i.e. the binding together inseparably of the fixed and the volatile principles (the male/invariable with the female/'saved' variable). Alchemical evolution is epitomized, then, in the formula *Solve et Coagula* (that is to say: 'analyse all the elements in yourself, dissolve all that is inferior in you, even though you may break in doing so; then, with the strength acquired from the preceding operation, congeal') (48). In addition to this specific symbolism, alchemy may be seen as the pattern of all other work. It shows that virtues are exercised in every kind of activity, even the humblest, and that the soul is strengthened, and the individual develops. Evola (*Tradizione Ermetica*) writes: 'Our Work is the conversion and change of one being into another being, one thing into another thing, weakness into strength, bodily into spiritual nature. . . .' On the subject of the hermaphrodite, Eugenio d'Ors (*Introducción a la vida angélica*) writes: 'That which failed to "become two in one flesh" (love) will succeed in "becoming two in one spirit" (individuation).'

Alcohol Alcohol, or life-water (*aqua vitae*) is fire-water, i.e. a symbol of the *coincidentia oppositorum*, the conjunction of opposites, where two principles, one of them active, the other passive, come together in a fluid and shifting, creative/destructive relationship. Particularly when burning, alcohol symbolizes one of the great mysteries of Nature; Bachelard aptly says that, when alcohol burns, 'it seems as if the "female" water, losing all shame, frenziedly gives herself to her master, fire' (1, 2).

Almond Tree Traditionally, a symbol of sweetness and delicacy. As it is one of the first trees to blossom, late frosts can destroy its flowers. The precise observation of Nature, constantly practised by primitive man, is the source of this symbolic analogy, as of so many others which might at first seem merely artificial allegories.

Alpha and Omega The first and last letters of the Greek alphabet, standing, therefore, for the beginning and end of all things. They are very frequently used in this sense in Romanesque art. Because of its shape, alpha is related to the pair of compasses, an attribute of god the creator; while omega is similar to a torch, i.e. to the fire of apocalyptic destruction. Animal figures have also been associated with this symbolism. In the frontispiece of a 12th-century manuscript of Paulus Orosius (Bibl. Laon, 137) alpha and omega appear respectively as a bird and a fish, i.e. the upper and the lower abyss.

Amphisbaena A fabulous animal, keeper of the 'Great Secret', according to a 16th-century Italian manuscript which belonged to Count Pierre V. Piobb. It is a symbol which occurs with some frequency in heraldic images, marks and signs. It was known to the Greeks, and it owes its name to the belief that, having a head at both ends, it could move forward or backward with equal ease. Sometimes it is depicted with the claws of a bird and the pointed wings of a bat (48). According to Diel (15), it was probably intended to express the horror and anguish associated with ambivalent situations. Like all fabulous animals, it instances the ability of the human mind to reorder aspects of the real world, according to supra-logical laws, blending them into patterns expressive of man's motivating psychic forces.

Anchor In the emblems, signs and graphic representations of the early Christians, the anchor always signified salvation and hope. It was often shown upside down, with a star, cross or crescent to denote its mystic nature. The Epistle to the Hebrews says: 'Which hope we have as the anchor of our soul' (4).

Anchor of Salvation, an
early Christian symbol.

Angel A symbol of invisible forces, of the powers ascending and descending between the Source-of-Life and the world of phenomena (50). Here, as in other cases (such as the Cross), the symbolic fact does not modify the real fact. In alchemy, the angel symbolizes sublimation, i.e. the ascension of a volatile (spiritual) principle, as in the figures of the *Viatorium spagyricum*. The parallelism between angelic orders and astral worlds has been traced with singular precision by Rudolf Steiner in *Les Hiérarchies spirituelles*, following the treatise on the celestial hierarchies by the Pseudo-Dionysius. From the earliest days of culture, angels figure in artistic iconography, and by the 4th millennium B.C. little or no distinction is made between angels and winged deities. Gothic art, in many remarkable images, expresses the protective and sublime aspects of the angel-figure, while the Romanesque tends rather to stress its other-worldly nature.

Animals Of the utmost importance in symbolism, both in connexion with their distinguishing features, their movement, shapes and colours, and because of their relationship with man. The origins of animal symbolism are closely linked with totemism and animal worship. The symbolism of any given animal varies according to its position in the symbolic pattern, and to the attitude and context in which it is depicted. Thus the frequent symbol of the 'tamed animal' can signify the reversal of those symbolic meanings associated with the same animal when wild. In the struggle between a knight and a wild or fabulous animal—one of the most frequent themes in symbolism—the knight's victory can consist either in the death or in the taming of the animal. In Chrétien de Troyes' mediaeval romance, Yvain, the hero is assisted by a lion. In the legend of St. George, the conquered dragon serves its conqueror. In the West, some of the earliest references to animal symbolism are found in Aristotle and in Pliny, but the most important source is the treatise *Physiologus*, written in Alexandria in the 2nd century A.D. Another important contribution was made one or two centuries later by Horapollo, with his two treatises on *Hieroglyphica*, based on Egyptian symbolism. From these sources flows a stream of mediaeval animal symbolism which produced such notable bestiaries as that of Philip of Thaun (A.D. 1121), Peter of Picardy and William of Normandy (13th century); or the *De Animalibus*, attributed to Albertus Magnus; *Libre de les besties* of Raymond Lull; and Fournival's *Bestiaire d'Amour* (14th century). The primitives' view of animals, as analysed by Schneider (50), is mirrored in all these works, namely that while man is an equivocal, 'masked' or complex being, the animal is univocal, for its positive or negative qualities remain ever constant, thus making it possible to classify each animal, once and for all, as belonging to a specific *mode* of cosmic phenomena. More generally, the different stages of animal evolution, as manifested by the varying degrees of biological complexity, ranging from the insect and the reptile to the mammal, reflect the hierarchy of the instincts. In Assyrian and Persian bas-reliefs, the victory of a higher over a lower animal always stands for the victory of the higher life over the lower instincts. A similar case is in the characteristic struggle of the eagle with the snake as found in pre-Columbian America. The victory of the lion over the bull usually signifies the victory of Day over Night and, by analogy, Light triumphing over Darkness and Good over Evil. The symbolic classification of animals is often related to that of the four Elements. Animals such as the duck, the frog and the fish, however much they may differ one from the other, are all connected with the idea of water and hence with the concept of the 'primal waters'; consequently, they can stand as symbols of the origin of things and of the powers of rebirth (37, 9). On the other hand, some animals, such as dragons and snakes, are sometimes assigned to water, sometimes to earth and sometimes even to fire (17). However, the most generally accepted classification—which is also the most fundamentally correct—associates aquatic and amphibious animals with water; reptiles with earth; birds with air; and mammals (because they are warm-blooded) with fire. For the purposes of symbolic art, animals are subdivided into two categories: *natural* (often in antithetical pairs: toad/frog, owl/eagle, etc.) and *fabulous*. Within the cosmic order, the latter occupy an intermediate position between the world of fully differentiated beings and the world of formless matter (50). They may have been suggested by the discovery of skeletons of antediluvian animals, and also by certain beings which, though natural, are ambiguous in appearance (carnivorous plants, sea urchins, flying fish, bats), and thus stand for flux and transformism, and also for purposeful evolution towards new forms. In any event, fabulous animals are powerful instruments of psychological projection. The most important fabulous animals are: chimaera, sphinx, lamia, minotaur, siren, triton, hydra, unicorn, griffin, harpy, winged horse, hippogryph, dragon, etc. In some of these the transmutation is a simple one, and clearly positive in character—such as Pegasus' wings (the spiritualization of a lower force)—but more often the symbol is a consequence of a more complex and ambiguous process of the imagination. The result is a range of highly ambivalent symbols, whose significance is heightened by the ingrained belief in the great powers exercised by such beings as well as in the magic importance of abnormality and deformity. In addition, there are animals which, while hardly or not at all fabulous in appearance, are credited with non-existential or supernatural qualities as the result of a symbolic projection (for example, the pelican, phoenix, salamander). There is a fragment by Callimachus on the Age of Saturn, in which animals have the power of speech (this being a symbol of the Golden Age which preceded the emergence of the intellect—Man—when the blind forces of Nature, not yet subject to the *logos*, were endowed with all sorts of extraordinary and exalted qualities). Hebrew and Islamic traditions also include references to 'speaking animals' (35). Another interesting classification is that of 'lunar animals', embracing all those animals whose life-span includes some kind of cyclic alternation, with periodic appearances and disappearances (18). The symbolism of such animals includes, in addition to the animal's specific symbolic significance, a whole range of lunar meanings. Schneider also mentions a very curious primitive belief: namely, that the voice of those animals which can be said to serve as symbols of heaven is high-pitched if the animal is large (the elephant, for example), but low-pitched if the animal is small (as the bee); while the converse is true of earth-symbol animals. Some animals, in particular the eagle and the lion, seem to embody certain qualities, such as beauty and the fighting spirit, to such an extent that they have come to be universally accepted as the allegorical representations of these qualities. The emblematic animals of Roman *signa* were: eagle, wolf, bull, horse and wild boar. In symbolism, whenever animals (or any other symbolic elements) are brought together in a system, the order of arrangement is always highly significant, implying either hierarchical precedence or relative position in space. In alchemy, the descending order of precedence is symbolized by different animals, thus: the phoenix (the culmination of the alchemical *opus*), the unicorn, the lion (the necessary qualities), the dragon (prime matter) (32). Symbolic groups of animals are usually based on analogical and numerical patterns: the tetramorphs of Western tradition, as found in the Bible, are a fundamental example; another example would be the Chinese series of the four benevolent animals: the unicorn, ·phoenix, turtle and dragon. The following animals occur particularly in Romanesque art: the peacock, ox, eagle, hare, lion, cock, crane, locust and partridge (50). Their symbolic meaning is mainly derived from the Scriptures or from patristic tradition, though some meanings, arising from analogy, such as that between cruelty and the leopard, are immediately obvious (20). The importance in Christianity of the symbols of the dove, the lamb and the fish is well known. The significance of the attitudes in which symbolic animals are depicted is usually self-evident: the counterbalancing of two identical—or two different—animals, so common in heraldry, stands for balance (i.e. justice and order, as symbolized for instance by the two snakes of the caduceus); the animals are usually shown supporting a shield or surmounting the crest of a helmet. Jung supports this interpretation with his observation that the counterbalancing of the lion and the unicorn in Britain's coat of arms stands for the inner stress of balanced opposites finding their equilibrium in the centre (32). In alchemy, the counterbalancing of the male and the female of the same species (lion/lioness, dog/bitch) signifies the essential contrast between sulphur and mercury, the fixed and the volatile elements. This is also the case when a winged animal is opposed to a wingless one. The ancient interest in animals as vehicles of cosmic meanings, over and above the mere fact of their physical existence, persisted from the earliest beginnings of the Neolithic Age up to as late as 1767, with the publication of such works as *Jubile van den Heyligen Macarius*. This treatise describes processions in which each symbolic chariot has a characteristic animal (the peacock, phoenix, pelican, unicorn, lion, eagle, stag, ostrich, dragon, crocodile, wild boar, goat, swan, winged horse, rhinoceros, tiger and elephant). These same animals, together with many others (such as the duck, donkey, ox, owl, horse, camel, ram, pig, deer, stork, cat, griffin, ibis, leopard, wolf, fly, bear, bird, dove, panther, fish, snake and fox) are those mainly used also as watermarks in papermaking. The use of watermarks, undoubtedly mystical and symbolic in origin, spread throughout the Western world from the end of the 13th century onwards. All the above particular symbolic uses rest on a general symbolism of animals, in which they are related to three main ideas: the animal as a mount (i.e. as a means of transport); as an object of sacrifice; and as an inferior form of life (4). The appearance of animals in dreams or visions, as in Fuseli's famous painting, expresses an energy still undifferentiated and not yet rationalized, nor yet mastered by the will (in the sense of that which controls the instincts) (31). According to Jung, the animal stands for the non-human psyche, for the world of subhuman instincts, and for the unconscious areas of the psyche. The more primitive the animal, the deeper the stratum of which it is an expression. As in all symbolism, the greater the number of objects depicted, the baser and the more primitive is the meaning (56). Identifying oneself with animals represents integration of the unconscious and sometimes—like immersion in the primal waters—rejuvenation through bathing in the sources of life itself (32). It is obvious that, for pre-Christian man (as well as in amoral cults), the animal signifies exaltation rather than opposition. This is clearly seen in the Roman *signa*, showing eagles and wolves symbolically placed on cubes (the earth) and spheres (heaven, the universe) in order to express the triumphant power of the force of an instinct. With regard to mythic animals, a more extensive treatment of this subject is to be found in the *Manual de zoología fantástica* of Borges y Guerrero (Mexico and Buenos Aires, 1957), in which such creatures are characterized as basically symbolic and, in most cases, expressive of 'cosmic terror'.

Anjana A type of witch in Hispanic folklore, the name perhaps being derived from Jana or Diana. These witches take on the form of old women to test out the charity of human beings. In their true form they are beautiful young women, fair haired and blue-eyed, clothed in tunics made of flowers and silver stars. They carry a gold staff and wear green stockings. They watch over animals and have underground palaces full of jewels and other treasure. The touch of their staff turns everything into riches (10). Symbolism of this kind reveals ancestral memories of druidesses; at a deeper level it also signifies the soul renewed by fusion with the 'mana personality'. The staff, a sigmoid symbol, is the emblem of those relationships linking apparently unrelated things. The green stockings allude to the primitive forces of virgin nature. The treasures and riches signify the spiritual powers harboured by the unconscious.

Antiquity The age of an object confers upon it an additional significance which eventually becomes more important than the original significance of the object itself. The significance of antiquity is derived from the following considerations: (i) Whatever is old is authentic, unadulterated, true, a link with the other world; old things do not deceive, therefore they stand for truth itself; (ii) Whatever is old is primitive, closer to that 'primigenial era' which boasted the 'Golden Age' of humanity; (iii) By analogy, whatever is old is related to the primitive stages in the individual's life, i.e. to the carefree life of the child, the 'paradise lost' of childhood.

Ants An attribute of Ceres, ants were utilized in soothsaying (8). There is an Indian myth in which they symbolize the pettiness of all things living—the fragile character and impotence of existence; but they also represent the life which is superior to human life (60). On account of their multiplicity, their symbolic significance is unfavourable.

Anvil A symbol of the earth and of matter. It corresponds to the passive and feminine principle, as opposed to the hammer, which denotes fecundation.

Apocalyptic Beast A symbol of matter in the process of involution: a snake or a dragon, for example, in so far as they are enemies of the spirit and a perversion of higher qualities (9). It has sometimes been equated with the feminine principle, in so far as this is a source of temptation and corruption, and particularly of stagnation in the process of evolution. Myths such as those of Calypso or the sirens are related to this theme.

Apollo In mythology and alchemy, his spiritual and symbolic significance is identical with that of the sun (15). The spreading golden hairs which crown the god's head have the same meaning as the bow and arrow (sunrays) (8). The Greek name for Apollo is, of course, Apollon, which means 'from the depths of the lion' and expresses the meaningful relationship of the sun with the fifth sign of the Zodiac, Leo (48).

Apple Being almost spherical in shape, the apple signifies totality. It is symbolic of earthly desires, or of indulgence in such desires. The warning not to eat the forbidden apple came, therefore, from the mouth of the supreme being, as a warning against the exaltation of materialistic desire (15). The intellect, the thirst for knowledge—as Nietzsche realized—is only an intermediate zone between earthly desire and pure spirituality.

Aquarius The eleventh archetypal sign of the Zodiac. Its allegorical representation is a figure of a man pouring water from an amphora. In the Egyptian Zodiac of Denderah, Aquarius carries two amphorae. This version merely affects the numerical symbolism;

it affords clearer proof of the dual force of the symbol (its active and passive aspects, evolution and involution), a duality which is of the essence in the important symbol of the Gemini. All Eastern and Western traditions relate this archetype to the symbolic flood which stands not only for the end of a formal universe but also for the completion of any cycle by the destruction of the power which held its components together. When this power ceases to function, the

   Zodiacal Sign of Aquarius

components return to the Akasha—the universal solvent—which is symbolized by Pisces. In these two signs of the Zodiac, then, the cosmic *pralaya*, or Brahma's night, runs its course. Its function, according to Hindu tradition, is to reabsorb into Oneness all those elements which originally seceded from it to lead separate individual existences. Thus, each end carries the seed of a new beginning (Ouroboros). The Egyptians identified Aquarius with their god Hapi, the personification of the Nile, whose floods were the source of the agricultural, economic and spiritual life of the country. Consequently, Aquarius symbolizes the dissolution and decomposition of the forms existing within any process, cycle or period; the loosening of bonds; the imminence of liberation through the destruction of the world of phenomena (40, 52).

Arabesque A type of ornamentation which appears to imply, apart from the cultural context of its proper name (Arabia, Islamic art), the idea of repetition, of turning back on oneself, of intertwining. To a certain extent, this idea relates it to Celto-Germanic ornamentalism and Irish and Viking art, but with profound differences. On the other hand, the arabesque has been associated by literati with the grotesque, because of its labyrinthine, sinuous form. There is more freedom in the Nordic plaits than in the oriental arabesques, which sometimes assume a circular shape, forming a kind of mandala.

Architecture The symbolism of architecture is, of course, complex and wide-ranging. It is founded upon 'correspondences' between various patterns of spatial organization, consequent upon the relationships, on the abstract plane, between architectural structures and the organized pattern of space. While the basic pattern of architectural relationships provides the primary symbolism, secondary symbolic meanings are derived from the appropriate selection of individual forms, colours and materials, and by the relative importance given to the various elements forming the architectural whole (function, height, etc.). The most profound and fundamental architectural symbol is the 'mountain-temple' (the Babylonian *ziggurat*, Egyptian pyramid, American *teocalli* or stepped pyramid, Buddhist *stupa*). It is based on a complex geometrical symbolism including both the pyramid and the ladder or staircase, as well as the mountain itself. Some of this symbolism can also be found in Western religious building, particularly Gothic cathedrals. Such temples often include essential elements from the *mandala* symbolism (that is, the squaring of the circle, through a geometrical diagram combining the square and the circle, usually linked through the octagon as an intermediate step) and from the symbolism of numbers (the significant figure standing for the number of essential factors: for example, 7 is very common in stepped pyramids; and, in the Temple of Heaven in Peking, 3—the number of floors—is the basic number, multiplied by itself because of the 3 platforms and the 3 roofs) (6). The figure 8, as we have seen, is of great importance as the link between 4 (or the square) and the circle. The Tower of the Winds, in Athens, was octagonal in plan. The eight pillars of the Temple of Heaven in Peking are another instance (6). As the cave inside the mountain is an essential element in mountain symbolism, it follows that the 'mountain-temple' would not be complete without some form of cave. In this sense, Indian rock-cut temples are a literal expression of the mountain-cave symbol: the temple actually *is* the cave cut into the side of the mountain. The cave stands for the spiritual Centre, the heart or the hearth (cf. the cave in Ithaca, or the Cave of the Nymphs in Porphyry). This symbolism implies a displacement of the symbolic centre, that is, the mountain peak of the world 'outside' is transferred to the 'inside' (of the mountain, and so of the world and of Man). The primary belief in the fundamental significance of an external form (such as the menhir, omphalos or pillar) is replaced by an interest in the space at the centre of things', identified as the ancient symbol of the 'world egg'. One of the specific symbols of this is the dome, symbolizing also the vault of heaven (which is why domes in ancient Persia were always painted blue or black). In this connexion, it is important to note that, in the geometrical symbolism of the cosmos, all circular forms relate to the sky or heaven, all squares to the earth, and all triangles (with the apex at the top) to fire and to the urge towards ascension inherent in human nature. Hence, the triangle also symbolizes the communication between earth (the material world) and heaven (the spiritual world). The square corresponds to the cross formed by the four Cardinal Points (6). And, of course, the pyramid is square in plan and triangular in section. This general symbolism, however, can be profoundly modified in certain directions by the addition of powerful secondary meanings or associations.

Thus, whereas Christianity comes to stress the importance of the human individual rather than the cosmos, temple-symbolism emphasizes the transcendence of the human figure rather than the contrast between heaven and earth—though the primary meaning can by no means be ignored. Already in Greek, Etruscan and Roman temple-building, this symbolic contrast, as well as the symbolism of gradual ascent (as in Babylonian *ziggurats*) had become subservient to the concept of a temple mirroring on earth the division of the heavens into an ordered pattern, and resting on supports (pillars, columns) which—since they originate from primitive lake-dwelling structures—relate the earth's surface to the 'primordial waters' of the ocean. The typical Romanesque church combines the symbolisms of the dome, and of the circle and the square, with two new elements of the greatest importance: the subdivision of the main body of the building into nave and two aisles (symbolic of the Trinity) and the cross-shaped plan, derived from the image of a man lying prostrate with his arms outstretched whereby the centre becomes not man's navel (a merely symmetrical division) but his heart (at the inter-section of nave and transept), while the main apse represents the head. As indicated above, each architectural element contributes to the general symbolism. Thus, in Gothic architecture, the symbol of the Trinity occurs repeatedly in triple doors, trefoiled, scalloped and pointed arches. The ogive in itself is nothing but a triangle with curved sides, with all the specific implications of triangle-symbolism outlined above (14, 46). The flammigerous arch, as the name indicates, is a symbol of fire, and it would be possible to see in the formal evolution of 15th-century Gothic a return to the apocalyptic meanings which were so important in Romanesque iconography (46). Jambs, pillars and side columns can be interpreted as 'guardians' of the doorway. Porches are the external counterpart of the altar-piece which, in its turn, is—as it were—the 'programme' set up in the heart of the temple. Cloisters also possess cosmic and spiritual implications. On the cosmic plane, and regarded as a spatial expression of a period of time, they stand for the cycle of the year, and by analogy, for the life-span of Man. The correlation is as follows: North-East side of the cloister—October December; North-West—January/March; South-West—April June; South-East —July September. The four divisions of the year (or of the human life-span of which it is an analogical image) are further correlated to the four phases of a ritual cycle of healing (or salvation): the first phase—death, danger and suffering; second phase—purifying fire; third—cure; fourth—convalescence (51). According to Pinedo, the South side, whence the warm winds blow, pertains to the Holy Spirit, inspiring the soul with the fire of charity and divine love; the North side, exposed to the cold winds, pertains to the devil and his insinuations that freeze the soul (46). As regards one of the most characteristic features of Gothic cathedrals—the twin frontal towers—Schneider points out that they are related to the two peaks of the Mountain of Mars (with its related symbols of the Gemini, Janus and the number 2), while the dome over the intersection of the nave and transepts stands for the Mountain of Jupiter (or unity). Paradise is above the platform and Hell (represented by the gargoyles) beneath. The four supports, pillars or piers which sub-divide the façade and determine the location of the three doorways are the four rivers of Paradise. The three doors stand for faith, hope and charity. The central rosette is the Lake of Life, where heaven and earth meet (sometimes it also stands for heaven, towards which the apex of the triangular ogive points) (50). Attempts have also been made to define the probable allegorical significance of other parts of the architectural fabric of the cathedral. Thus, according to Lampérez, the church walls stand for humanity redeemed; the counterforts and flying buttresses for uplifting, moral strength; the roof for charity and shelter; the pillars, for the dogmas of the faith; the ribbing of the vaults, for the paths of salvation; the spires, for God's finger pointing to the ultimate goal of mankind. It will be seen that the special symbolic meanings here are obviously related to the appearance and functions of the various architectural elements. Two further facts should also be mentioned: the 'degraded' interpretation suggested by psychoanalysts whereby every building is seen as a human body (doors and windows—openings; pillars—forces) or spirit (cellars—subconscious; attics—mind, imagination)—an interpretation arrived at on an experimental basis; and the possibility of elaborating increasingly complex systems by combining a number of symbolic principles. Kubler, in his *Baroque Architecture*, analyses the case of Fr. Giovanni Ricci who, following the example of his mannerist forerunners Giacomo Soldati and Vincenzo Scamozzi, endeavoured to develop a new 'harmonic'—or ideal—architectural order, by integrating the existing systems (Tuscan, Doric, Ionic, etc.) into a scheme whereby each different mode was related to a specific temperament or to a certain degree of holiness (Plate III).

Aries The Ram, a symbol of the creative impulse and of the spirit at the moment of its inception (4). The first sign of the Zodiac. In Hindu symbolism it stands for Parabrahman, that is, for the undifferentiated whole. Because the Zodiac is the symbol of the cycle of existence, Aries, its first sign, stands for the original cause or the thunderbolt which emerges from the Akasha of Pisces, that is, from the 'primordial waters'. Aries, because it stands for the initial impulse through which the potential becomes actual, is also related to the dawn and to Spring, and generally to the beginning

of any cycle, process or creation. In Egypt the ram was the symbol
of Amon-Ra, and the god was depicted with ram's horns. As
regards human physiology, Aries controls the head and the brain,
that is to say, the organs which are the centre of the individual's
physical and spiritual energies, as Parabrahman is the centre of
the cosmic forces (40).

Zodiacal sign of Aries.

Ark Both on the material and the spiritual planes the ark
symbolizes the power to preserve all things and to ensure their
rebirth (40). Biologically speaking, it can be regarded as a symbol of
the womb (9) or of the heart (14), there being an obvious connexion
between these two organs. The symbolism of Noah's ark has been
the subject of much discussion beginning as early as St. Ambrose,
De Noe et Arca, and Hugh of Saint Victor, *De arca Noe morali*
and *De arca mystica*. The basic symbolism of the ark is the belief
that the essences of the physical and spiritual life can be extracted
and contained within a minute seed until such time as a rebirth
creates the conditions necessary for the re-emergence of these
essences into external life (14). Guénon has found subtle analogies,
of great symbolic interest, between the ark and the rainbow. The
ark, during the cosmic *pralaya*, floats on the waters of the lower
ocean; the rainbow, in the realm of the 'upper waters', is a sign of
the restoration of the order which is preserved below in the ark.
Both figures together, being complementary, complete the circle of
Oneness. They therefore correspond to the two halves of the ancient
symbol of the 'world egg' (28). As a symbol of the heart (or of the
mind, or of thought) the image of the ark is similar to that of the
drinking-vessel, so frequent in mediaeval mysticism.

Arm In Egyptian hieroglyphs, the sign of the arm stands for
activity in general. Other signs derived from this primary sign
stand for special kinds of activity, such as working, offering,
protecting, donating, etc. The hieroglyph depicting two raised arms
is a symbol of invocation and of self-defence (19), a meaning which
is universally recognized. A frequent motif in heraldic and emblematic devices is that of a weapon held by an arm emerging from a
cloud, or from the surround of a picture. This is the avenging arm
of the Lord of Hosts, or a call from the heavens for vengeance (39).

Arrow The weapon of Apollo and Diana, signifying the light of supreme power (4). In both Greece (8) and pre-Columbian America (39), it was used to designate the sun's rays. But, because of its shape, it has undeniable phallic significance, specially when it is shown in emblems balanced against the symbol of the 'mystic Centre', feminine in character, such as the heart. The heart pierced with an arrow is a symbol of 'Conjunction'.

Arthur, King The hero, king or penteyrn of the Silures of Caerleon in Wales. Around him are built the legends of the Round Table, the earliest known sources of which being the *Brut* (c. 1155) of the Norman, Wace, and the *Historia Regum Britanniae* (c. 1150) by Geoffrey of Monmouth, and the Welsh *Mabinogion* (or *Red Book*) containing the tale of Kuhlwch and Olwen (towards the end of the 9th century). Arthur appears to have been the son of the Breton leader, Uther Pendragon, whom he succeeded in 516. He is credited with deeds of mythic dimensions. For Rhys, he is an avatar of the Gallic god Mercurius Arterius, king of the fabled country Oberon. He is the archetype of the 'mythical king' who synthesizes the hopes of a race and who reflects 'primordial man'. Tradition refuses to accept his death and affirms that he will reappear in the specific shape of Arthur when the English have need of him to triumph over their enemies. Symbols closely connected with King Arthur are such as these: magic or miraculous swords and shields; the 'holy war' or the struggle between good and evil; the twelve knights with their implied relationship with the signs of the zodiac and the idea of totality.

Ascension The symbolism of ascension or ascent has two main aspects: externally a higher level in space signifies a higher value by virtue of its connexion with the symbolism of space and height; and, secondly, it pertains to the inner life, the symbolism of which concerns the 'upward impulse' rather than any actual ascent. As Mircea Eliade has observed: 'Whatever the religious context, and whatever the particular form they may take (shamanist or initiation rites, mystic ecstasy, dream-vision, heroic legend), ascensions of all kinds, such as climbing mountains or stairs or soaring upwards through the air, always signify that the human condition is being transcended and that higher cosmic levels are being attained. The mere fact of "levitation" is equivalent to a consecration. . . .' (17). But, according to a more straightforward interpretation based upon the concept of energy, the action of rising (as, in music, going from bass to treble, or from *piano* to *forte*) expresses an increase in intensity (38), whether it concerns domination or the lust for power, or any other urge whatsoever. All world-axis symbols (the mountain, ladder, tree, cross, liana, rope, the thread of the spider, spear) are connected with the symbolism of ascension (18).

Ashlar In the Egyptian system of hieroglyphs, the sign incorporating the ashlar (or squared stone) symbolizes material which has been worked upon, or the results of creative activity. By analogy, it refers to the trials necessitated by the spiritual evolution which Man must undergo (19) before he can attain to the essential conditions of regularity, order, coherence and continuity. The idea here is the same as that expressed in the alchemic dialectic of the fixed and the volatile principles. The connexion between the ashlar and the human spirit arises from the general symbolism of the stone combined with the notion of humanity as a perfect structure which ensures that every 'saved' man is whole and firm as rock.

Ass This symbolic animal appears as an attribute of Saturn, in his capacity as the 'second sun'. It is always on heat, and hated by Isis (31). The significance of the mock crucifix, with an ass's head, from the Palatine, must be related to the equation of Yahve with Saturn (31), although it may be that it is related to the jester-symbol. In connexion with the latter, the ass's head, frequently found in mediaeval emblems, marks and signs, often stands for humility, patience and courage. Sometimes there is a wheel or a solar symbol between the ass's ears. This symbol, also found on the heads of oxen, always denotes that the animal is a sacrificial victim (4). But the symbolism of the ass involves still further complexities: Jung defines it as *daemon triunus*—a chthonian trinity which in Latin alchemy was depicted as a three-headed monster, one head representing mercury, the second salt and the third sulphur, or, in short, the three material principles of matter (32). In Chaldaea, the goddess of death is depicted kneeling on an ass which is being ferried across the River of Hell in a boat. In dreams, the ass, especially when it appears invested with a solemn and ritual aspect, is usually a messenger of death or appears in connexion with a death, as destroyer of a lifespan.

Aureole A circular or oblong halo surrounding bodies in glory. According to a 12th-century text, attributed to the abbey of St. Victor, the oblong shape derives from the symbolism of the almond, which is identified with Christ. This, however, does not change the general sense of the aureole (6) as a relic of solar cults, and as a fire-symbol expressive of irradiating, supernatural energy (31), or as a manifestation of the emanation of spiritual light (which plays such an important part in Hindu doctrine) (26). The almond-shaped aureole, which usually surrounds the whole of the body, is usually divided into three zones, as an active expression of the Trinity (6).

Axe A symbol of the power of light. The battle-axe has a significance which is equivalent to that of the sword, the hammer and the cross. But much more important and complex is the significance of the twin-bladed axe, related to the sign *tau* (4). This double-headed axe is to be found in a host of works of art from India to

England, and specially in the Mediterranean countries—in Africa and Crete. Very often it is located over the head of an ox, just between its horns, when it comes to symbolize on the one hand the mandorla (related to horns because of its shape), and, on the other, the function of sacrifice in the relationship between the valley-symbol and the mountain-symbol (that is, between earth and heaven) (50). According to Luc Benoist, this twin-bladed axe is the same as the Hindu *vajra* and Jove's thunderbolt, becoming, therefore, a symbol of celestial illumination. Nowadays the double-bladed axe (the *labrys*) is associated with the labyrinth, both being symbols in the Cretan cult. The labyrinth denotes the world of existence—the pilgrimage in quest of the 'Centre' (6). In some paintings in Crete, such as that on a sarcophagus from Hagia Triada, we see a symbol made up of a cone, a double-bladed axe and a bird. The cone alludes to the deity; the axe, like all things dual, is an aspect of the Gemini, that is, of the focal-point of symbolic Inversion; the bird has been recognized as an image of the human soul ever since the time of the Egyptians (Waldemar Fenn). The axe is also symbolic of death ordered by a deity.

B

Babylon   This is a symbol of considerable interest, even if cultural in concept rather than spontaneous or analogical. Like Carthage, Babylon is an image of a fallen and corrupt existence—the opposite of the Heavenly Jerusalem and of Paradise (37). In its esoteric sense, it symbolizes the solid or material world, in which the involution and evolution of the spirit takes place, or, in other words, the pervasion and desertion of matter by the spirit (37).

Balder   A Nordic god killed by the mistletoe, which he himself personifies. Closely connected with various other symbols, such as fire, the sun and the oak (21); he is also related to Odin and the profound symbolism of the Hanged Man (in the Tarot pack).

Bandages   Bandages, bands, sashes or swaddling-bands, in the Egyptian system of hieroglyphs, possess a double symbolism embracing both the swaddling-clothes of the newborn babe and the winding-sheet of the corpse in the tomb. They constitute a determinative sign corresponding to the letter S (a letter which has subsequently been construed as a snake) (19).

Basilisk   A fabulous animal with a snake's body, pointed head and a three-pointed crest. In mediaeval descriptions it was said to be born of a yolkless egg laid by a cock and hatched by a toad on a bed of dung, and to have a three-pointed tail, glittering eyes and a crown on its head. Its glance was believed to be lethal, so that it could only be destroyed while its assailant was watching it in a mirror. This belief is related to the myth of the Gorgon's head. In the East, its body was supposed to be a mixture of cock, snake and toad. According to Diel, this projected image of the human psyche is clearly infernal in character, as is shown by its threefold attributes (its three-pointed crest and trifurcated tail) since they are an inversion of the qualities of the Trinity; and also by the predominance of evil components, such as the toad and the snake. It is one of the many 'keepers of treasure' mentioned in legend.

Basket   For Jung, it stands for the maternal body (31). On Greek coins, the figure of a basket covered with ivy represents the Bacchanalian mysteries. It is said that Semele, while she was bearing Bacchus, was placed in a basket and thrown into the river (the symbolism of water being bound up with the idea of birth) (8).

Bat   Because of its ambiguous nature, the bat is contradictory in implication. In China, for example, it is emblematic of happiness and long life (5). In Western alchemy it had a meaning which was not far removed from that of the dragon and that of the hermaphrodite. Its wings, nevertheless, are an infernal attribute (32).

Bath   The symbolism of immersion in water derives from that of water itself, and signifies not only purification (a secondary symbolism taken from the general concept of water as a clear, cleansing liquid) but, more fundamentally, regeneration through the effect of the transitional powers (implying change, destruction and re-creation) of the 'primordial waters' (the fluid Element). In alchemy, this same meaning received a specialized application: the bath symbolizes the dissolution and also the purification of gold and silver.

Battering-Ram   According to Fr. Heras, a symbol of penetration, that is, of an ambivalent force capable of either fertilizing or destroying.

Bear   In alchemy, the bear corresponds to the *nigredo* of prime matter, and hence it is related to all initial stages and to the instincts. It has consequently been considered a symbol of the perilous aspect of the unconscious and as an attribute of the man who is cruel and crude. Since it is found in the company of Diana it is regarded as a lunar animal (31).

Bee   In Egyptian hieroglyphic language, the sign of the bee was a determinative in royal nomenclature, partly by analogy with the monarchic organization of these insects, but more especially because of the ideas of industry, creative activity and wealth which are associated with the production of honey (19). In the parable of

Samson (Judges xiv, 8) the bee appears in this same sense. In Greece it was emblematic of work and obedience. According to a Delphic tradition, the second of the temples built in Delphi had been erected by bees. In Orphic teaching, souls were symbolized by bees, not only because of the association with honey but also because they migrate from the hive in swarms, since it was held that souls 'swarm' from the divine unity in a similar manner (40). In Christian symbolism, and particularly during the Romanesque period, bees were symbols of diligence and eloquence (20). In the Indo-Aryan and Moslem traditions they have the same purely spiritual significance as in Orphic teaching (50).

Bell Its sound is a symbol of creative power (4). Since it is in a hanging position, it partakes of the mystic significance of all objects which are suspended between heaven and earth. It is related, by its shape, to the vault and, consequently, to the heavens.

Belly The interior of the belly is invariably equated symbolically with the alchemic laboratory, or, in other words, with the place where transmutations are effected. Since these metamorphoses are entirely of a natural order, the belly-laboratory becomes, in a sense, the antithesis to the brain (57).

Belt The belt or girdle is a symbol of the protection of the body and, being an allegory of virginity, implies the 'defensive' (moral) virtues of the person. It is worth noting that the belt, together with gold spurs—doubtless sharing the same significance—was an attribute of the mediaeval knight. On the other hand, when the belt is associated with Venus, it takes on an erotic, fetishistic sense.

Binary Duality is a basic quality of all natural processes in so far as they comprise two opposite phases or aspects. When integrated within a higher context, this duality generates a binary system based on the counterbalanced forces of two opposite poles. The two phases or aspects can be either symmetrical (or in other words identical in extent and intensity) or asymmetrical, successive or simultaneous. Instances of a duality of successive phases would be phenomena such as: day and night; winter and summer; waxing and waning; life and death; systole and diastole; breathing in and out; youth and old age. Examples of duality which can be either successive or simultaneous: wet/dry; cold/hot; male/female; positive/negative; sun/moon; gold/silver; round/square; fire/water; volatile/fixed; spiritual/corporeal; brother/sister, etc. The right hand and left hand, corresponding to the two pillars Jachin and Boaz in Hebrew tradition, and to the gates of heaven and hell which the Latins associated with Janus, can be taken to symbolize a binary system. This is also the case with the King and Queen in alchemy (28). Whether the opposition is one of successive phases or of simultaneous movements of tension, does not affect the nature of

the system, the ultimate expression of which is found in the myth
of the Gemini; in the Manichean and Gnostic doctrines it takes the
form of a moral duality in which evil is given an equal status with
good. Evil and matter, according to Neo-Pythagorean doctrine,
generate the *dyas* (duality), which is female in nature, and depicted in
the Gnosis of Justin as a dual being, with a woman's torso and a
snake's tail. Diel points out that this *dyas*, craving vengeance and
locked in combat with the Pneuma, is the archetype of legendary
figures such as Medea, Ariadne or Yseult (15). The mystery of
duality, which is at the root of all action, is manifest in any opposition of forces, whether spatial, physical or spiritual. The primordial
pairing of heaven and earth appears in most traditions as an image
of primal opposition, the binary essence of natural life (17). As
Schneider has observed, the eternal duality of Nature means that no
phenomenon can ever represent a complete reality, but only one
half of a reality. Each form has its analogous counterpart: man/
woman; movement/rest; evolution/involution; right/left—and
total reality embraces both. A synthesis is the result of a thesis *and*
an antithesis. And true reality resides only in the synthesis (50).
This is why, in many individuals, there is a psychological tendency
towards ambivalence, towards the breaking down of the unitary
aspects of things, even though it may prove to be a source of most
intense suffering. Before Freud, Eliphas Lévi had already suggested
that 'Human equilibrium consists of two tendencies—an impulse
towards death, and one towards life'. The death-wish is therefore as
natural and as spiritual as the life or erotic impulse. The integration
of these symbols within complex patterns of 'correspondences'
reaches its highest pitch of perfection in the East, where cosmic
allegories (such as the Wheel of Transformations, the *Yang-Yin* disk,
the *Shri-Yantra*, etc.) provide a most intense, graphic expression of
these notions of contradiction and synthesis. The basic elements
of such antithesis are the positive principle (male, lucid, active),
and, opposing it, the negative principle (female, obscure, passive);
psychologically speaking, these correspond respectively to the
conscious and unconscious components of the personality; and,
from the point of view of Man's destiny, they correspond to involution and evolution (25). These symbolic figures are therefore
not so much an expression of the duality of the forces involved, but
rather of their *complementary* character within the binary system.
Hindu doctrine asserts that Brahma is *sat* and non-*sat*, what-is and
what-is-not: *satyam* and *asatyam* (reality and non-reality). In the
Upanishads this synthesis is defined in dynamic terms as 'that which
is in motion, yet nevertheless remains still'. Schneider explains these
paradoxes with the suggestion that, in mystic systems, the antithesis is the complement, not the negation, of the thesis (50). It is

in this sense that one should interpret the saying of Lao-Tse that 'he who knows his masculinity and preserves his femininity, is the abyss of the world' (58). Nevertheless, the tendency of opposites to unite in a synthesis is always characterized by stress and suffering, until and unless it is finally resolved by supernatural means. Thus, the step from thesis to ambivalence is painful, and the next step from ambivalence to ecstasy is difficult to achieve. The symbol of the 'Centre', the blue rose, the golden flower, the way out of the labyrinth—all these can allude to the meeting and 'conjunction' of the conscious and the unconscious, as of the union of the lover and the beloved. Metaphors such as 'The wolf also shall dwell with the lamb, and the leopard shall lie down with the kid; and the calf and the young lion and the fatling together; and a little child shall lead them' (Isaiah xi, 6), are references to the final coming of the Heavenly Jerusalem (25), where the binary synthesis is no longer dualistic severance or otherness, difference or separation, nor a balancing of opposing powers, but the assimilation of the lower by the higher, of darkness by light. The symbolism of ascension or ascent alludes not only to the possibility of a superior life for the privileged being, an initiate or saint, a hero or a thinker, but also to the primary and fundamental tendency of the cosmos to strive towards sublimation—to progress from mud to tears, from lead to gold. Rhythms vary, but movement is always in the same direction. Hindu doctrine refers not only to hope of Nirvana but also to the lessons to be learnt from *mâyâ*, or illusion. In the world of *mâyâ*—the world of phenomena—opposites cancel each other out, one opposite being balanced by another through the ceaseless interplay and transmutation of existence—the alternation of creation and destruction (60). The figure of the goddess Kâli, for instance, whose ritual required human sacrifice, is an example of symbolic counterpoise transcending the mere duality of opposing forces. The moral level reached by any religion can in fact be measured by its capacity to show, by means of dogma and imagery, how duality is transcended. One of the most powerfully poetic myths expressing the wish for cosmic unity is that in which it is said that the sun and the moon must be 'united' so that they are made to form a single being (17).

Bird Every winged being is symbolic of spiritualization. The bird, according to Jung, is a beneficent animal representing spirits or angels, supernatural aid (31), thoughts and flights of fancy (32). Hindu tradition has it that birds represent the higher states of being. To quote a passage from the Upanishads: 'Two birds, inseparable companions, inhabit the same tree; the first eats of the fruit of the tree, the second regards it but does not eat. The first bird is *Jivâtmâ*, and the second is *Atmâ* or pure knowledge, free and unconditioned; and when they are joined inseparably, then the one is indistinguishable from the other except in an illusory sense' (26). This interpretation of the bird as symbolic of the soul is very commonly found in folklore all over the world. There is a Hindu tale retold by Frazer in which an ogre explains to his daughter where he keeps his soul: 'Sixteen miles away from this place', he says, 'is a tree. Round the tree are tigers, and bears, and scorpions, and snakes; on the top of the tree is a very great fat snake; on his head is a little cage; in the cage is a bird; and my soul is in that bird' (21). This was given precise expression in ancient Egyptian symbolism by supplying the bird with a human head; in their system of hieroglyphs it was a sign corresponding to the determinative *Ba* (the soul), or the idea that the soul flies away from the body after death (19). This androcephalous bird appears also in Greek and Romanesque art, and always in this same sense (50). But the idea of the soul as a bird—the reverse of the symbolic notion— does not of itself imply that the soul is good. Hence the passage in Revelation (xvii, 2) describing Babylon as 'the hold of every foul spirit, and a cage of every unclean and hateful bird'. According to Loeffler, the bird, like the fish, was originally a phallic symbol, endowed however with the power of heightening—suggesting sublimation and spiritualization. In fairy stories there are many birds which talk and sing, symbolizing amorous yearning (and cognate with arrows and breezes). The bird may also stand for the metamorphosis of a lover. Loeffler adds that birds are universally recognized as intelligent collaborators with man in myths and folktales, and that they are derived from the great bird-demiurges of the primitives—bearers of celestial messages and creators of the nether world; this explains the further significance of birds as messengers (38). The particular colour of a bird is a factor which determines its secondary symbolisms. The blue bird is regarded by Bachelard (3) as 'the outcome of aerial motion', that is, as a pure association of ideas; but in our view, although this may well have been its origin, its ultimate aim is something quite different—to provide a symbol of the impossible (like the blue rose). In alchemy, birds stand for forces in process of activation; here the precise sense is determined by the location of the bird: soaring skywards it expresses volatilization or sublimation, and swooping earthwards it expresses precipitation and condensation; these two symbolic movements joined to form a single figure are expressive of distillation. Winged beings contrasted with others that are wingless constitute a symbol of air, of the volatile principle as opposed to the fixed. Nevertheless, as Diel has pointed out, birds, and particularly flocks of birds —for multiplicity is ever a sign of the negative—may take on evil implications; for example, swarms of insects symbolize forces in process of dissolution—forces which are teeming, restless, indeterminate, shattered. Thus, birds, in the Hercules legend, rising up from the lake Stymphalus (which stands for the stagnation of the soul and the paralysis of the spirit) denote manifold wicked desires (15). The 'giant bird' is always symbolic of a creative deity. The Hindus of Vedic times used to depict the sun in the form of a huge bird—an eagle or a swan. Germanic tradition affords further examples of a solar bird (35). It is also symbolic of storms; in Scandinavian mythology there are references to a gigantic bird called Hraesvelg (or Hraesveglur), which is supposed to create the wind by beating its wings (35). In North America, the supreme Being is often equated with the mythic personification of lightning and thunder as a great bird (17). The bird has a formidable antagonist in the snake or serpent. According to Zimmer, it is only in the West that this carries a moral implication; in India, the natural elements only are contrasted—the solar force as opposed to the fluid energy of the terrestrial oceans. The name of this solar bird is Garuda, the 'slayer of the *nâgas* or serpents' (60). Kühn, in *The Rock Pictures of Europe*, considers a Lascaux cave picture of a wounded bison, a man stricken to death and a bird on a pole, and suggests that, by the late Palaeolithic, the bird may have come to symbolize the soul or à trance-like state.

Birds Birds are very frequently used to symbolize human souls, some of the earliest examples being found in the art of ancient Egypt. Sometimes, they are depicted with human heads, as in Hellenic iconography. In the *Mirach* it is written that, when Mohammed went to heaven, he found, standing in the middle of a great square, the Tree of Life whose fruit restores youth to all those who eat of it. This Tree of Life is surrounded by groves and avenues of leafy trees on whose boughs perch many birds, brilliantly coloured and singing melodiously: these are the souls of the faithful. The souls of evildoers, on the other hand, are incarnated in birds of prey (46). Generally speaking, birds, like angels, are symbols of thought, of imagination and of the swiftness of spiritual processes and relationships. They pertain to the Element of air and, as noted in connexion with the eagle, they denote 'height' and—consequently—'loftiness' of spirit. This general symbolism has sometimes been narrowed down excessively to the particular, as often happens in traditional symbolism. Thus, Odo of Tusculum, in his sermon XCII, describes different kinds of spirituality in men in terms of the characteristics of different kinds of birds. Some birds, he says, are guileless, such as the dove; others, cunning like the partridge; some come to the hand, like the hawk, others flee from it, like the hen; some enjoy the company of men, like the swallow; others prefer solitude and the desert, like the turtle-dove. . . . Low-flying birds symbolize an earth-bound attitude; high-flying birds, spiritual longing (46).

Bite   This, like the great majority of symbols, has a double meaning embracing both the mystic and the psychological planes. On the mystic level, the bite, or, rather, teeth-marks, are equivalent to the imprint or the seal of the spirit upon the flesh (since the teeth are the fortress-walls of the 'inner' or spiritual man). On the psychological level, and especially where animal-bites are concerned, it is symbolic, according to Jung, of the sudden and dangerous action of the instincts upon the psyche (32).

Blacksmith   On some cultural levels, the position of blacksmith is considered to be held under the king's prerogative, and to be sacred (21). There is a close connexion between metallurgy and alchemy: According to Alleau, the blacksmith is equivalent to the accursed poet and the despised prophet. In the Rigveda, the creator of the world is a blacksmith (31); this may be accounted for by the associated symbolism of fire, but also by the fact that iron is associated with the astral world—the first iron known to man was meteoric—and with the planet Mars.

Blood   From the standpoint of the chromatic or biological order, blood, since it corresponds to the colour red, represents the end of a series which begins with sunlight and the colour yellow, the intermediate stage being the colour green and vegetable life. The development from yellow to green and red appears in relation with a corresponding increase of iron. In cases of relationships as close as that between blood and the colour red, it is evident that both are reciprocally expressive: the passionate quality characteristic of red pervades the symbolism of blood, and the vital character of blood informs the significance of the colour red. In spilt blood we have a perfect symbol of sacrifice. All liquid substances (milk, honey and wine, that is to say) which were offered up in antiquity to the dead, to spirits and to gods, were images of blood, the most precious offering of all. Sacrificial blood was obtained from the sheep, the hog and the bull in classical times, and from human sacrifice among Asians, Africans and aboriginal Americans (as well as among the Europeans in prehistoric days). The Arabic saying, 'Blood has flowed, the danger is past', expresses succinctly the central idea of all sacrifice: that the offering appeases the powers and wards off the most severe chastisements which might otherwise befall. The driving-force behind the mechanism of sacrifice, the most characteristic of the symbolic inferences of blood, is the zodiacal symbol of Libra, representing divine legality, the inner conscience of man with its ability to inflict terrible self-chastisement. Wounds, by association, and for the same reason, have a similar function. Similarly with the colour red when its use appears irrational—when it mysteriously invades the object: for example, in alchemy, when matter passes from the white stage (*albedo*) to the red (*rubedo*); or the legendary 'red knight' who expresses the ever-passionate state of him who has mastered steed and monster. The Parsifal of Chrétien de Troyes is a red knight, wreathed in a pattern of images of such beauty and richness that we will quote the whole of the passage: 'A slab of red marble is floating on the water with a sword plunged into it. The knight who proves able to withdraw it will be a descendant of king David. He is clad in a coat of red silk and the aged man accompanying him hands him a cloak of scarlet lined with white ermine. . . . Parsifal meets a knight whose red armour turns all eyes that regard it red. His axe is red, his shield and his lance are redder than fire. In his hand he holds a cup of gold, his skin is white and his hair red.' Lévi, in his penetrating study of this symbol, quotes the following phrase: 'He was clothed in garments stained with blood,' for he had come through war and sacrifice (37). Of great interest, too, heightened by his discussion of the etymological sources, is the quotation supplied by Pinedo; the passage is taken from the commentary upon Isaiah lxiii, 1-2 ('Who is this that cometh from Edom, with dyed garments from Bozrah? . . . Wherefore art thou red in thine apparel?'). Pinedo comments: 'Edom and Bozrah—its capital—stand for all the nations of the Gentiles. The word Edom means "red" and Bozrah means "wine-press", which explains why the Holy Fathers say that he who comes "red" from the "wine-press" is none other than Our Lord Jesus Christ, for, according to them, this is the question which the angels put to him on the day of his triumphal ascension' (46).

Blow, To   For primitives, blowing is a creative act which infuses or enlivens life, increases the force of something or changes its course. Shamans include the act of blowing in their rites.

Boar   The symbolic significance of the boar, as of most other animals, is ambivalent. On the one hand it occurs as a symbol of intrepidness, and of the irrational urge towards suicide (8). On the other hand it stands for licentiousness (15). One of Vishnu's incarnations was in the form of a boar. In Babylonia and other Semitic cultures it was regarded as a sacred animal. In Celtic and Gallic legends there is always a note of distinction and positiveness about it (4). As a hostile force the boar ranks higher than the dragon or primordial monster, but below the lion.

Boat   In the most general sense, a 'vehicle'. Bachelard notes that there are a great many references in literature testifying that the boat is the cradle rediscovered (and the mother's womb) (2). There is also a connexion between the boat and the human body.

Body   For Gichtel, it is 'the seat of insatiable appetite, of illness and death'. In Mithraic thought (according to Evola) the soul, in order to free itself from the body, must cross seven spheres.

Bolt (or **Latch**)   In Egyptian hieroglyphics, this sign represents the link securing the two halves of a double-door, symbolizing by analogy the will to resist any possibility of change (19).

Bone A symbol of life as seen in the character of a seed. The Hebrew word *luz* stands for the mandorla, embracing both the tree and its inner, hidden and inviolable heart. But according to Jewish tradition, it also refers to an indestructible, corporeal particle, represented by a piece of very hard bone; it is, then, symbolic of the belief in resurrection, and is comparable with the symbol of the chrysalis from which the butterfly emerges (28).

Book A book is one of the eight Chinese common emblems, symbolizing the power to ward off evil spirits (5). The book 'written inside and out' is an allegory of the esoteric and exoteric, cognate with the double-edged sword projecting from the mouth (37). Broadly speaking, the book is related—as Guénon has suggested—to the symbolism of weaving. The doctrine of Mohiddin ibn Arabi in this respect may be summarized as follows: 'The universe is an immense book; the characters of this book are written, in principle, with the same ink and transcribed on to the eternal tablet by the divine pen . . . and hence the essential divine phenomena hidden in the "secret of secrets" took the name of "transcendent letters". And these very transcendent letters, or, in other words, all things created, after having been virtually crystallized within divine omniscience, were brought down to lower levels by the divine breath, where they gave birth to the manifest world' (25).

Bottle According to Bayley, the bottle is one of the symbols of salvation (4), probably because of the analogy (of function rather than of shape) with the ark and the boat.

Bow Shiva's bow is, like the *lingam*, the emblem of the god's power (60). Basic to this symbolism is the concept of 'tension', clearly defined by Heraclitus and closely related to the life-force and to spiritual force. Benoist remarks that the bow and arrow, as attributes of Apollo, stand for the sun's energy, its rays and its fertilizing and purifying powers (6). The symbolism of the crossbow is similar, but more complex, including, as it does, the 'conjunction' of the bow and its stock.

Bower Like the tower, the well and the door, it is a common emblem of the Virgin Mary. That powerful painter of female nature, John of Flanders (15th-16th centuries), frequently brings these themes to bear upon his works. Generally speaking, the bower is a feminine symbol (32).

Box Like all receptacles whose basic use is keeping or containing, the box is a feminine symbol which can refer both to the unconscious (15) and to the maternal body itself (31). We do not here refer to spherical objects, which are symbols of Oneness and of the spiritual principle. The myth of 'Pandora's box' appears to allude to the significance of the unconscious, particularly in the special sense of its unexpected, excessive, destructive potentialities. Diel relates this symbol to 'imaginative exaltation' (15). In addition, we would like to point out the analogy—the family resemblance—between Pandora's box and the 'third casket' which figures in so many legends. The first and second contain goods and riches; the third discharges storms, devastation, death. This is clearly an example of a symbol of human life (of the cycle of the year), which is divided into three stages, consisting of two favourable thirds and one adverse. A superb elaboration upon the Pandora theme is to be found in Dora and Erwin Panofsky's *Pandora's Box* (London, 1956). Particularly interesting is the authors' study of the literary heritage of a myth, and the ways in which it may be adapted to serve the visual arts.

Bramble A symbol of virginal purity consumed in its own flame (20). The Biblical burning bush, on the other hand, is symbolically related to the myth of Semele.

Branch When bearing blooms or fruit, it has the same significance as the garland. In the Egyptian system of hieroglyphs it means 'to give way' or 'bend' (19).

Branding or **Marking** The mark, especially when it takes the form of a painting or decoration (insignia) upon the body, is, like the seal, the sign or the signal, cognate with tattooing. Such brands may also have an incidental meaning occasioned by a particular circumstance (mourning, an initiation rite, etc.). But their deepest significance is connected with the symbolism of scars as the marks 'of the teeth of the spirit'. A brand is a distinguishing mark—and this is the original and predominating idea of each and every mark. The individual who wishes to 'belong' accepts the distinctive mark of the group he seeks to belong to; or if he wishes to express his own individuality, he can do so by means of determinative, unrevealed signs. Artistic or spiritual creation of any kind, the development of the personality, the mask, idiosyncrasies of dress or behaviour, are all derived from the essence of mark-symbolism.

Breathing Symbolically, to breathe is to assimilate spiritual power. Yoga exercises place particular emphasis upon breathing, since it enables man to absorb not only air but also the light of the sun. Concerning solar light, the alchemists had this to say: 'It is a fiery substance, a continuous emanation of solar corpuscles which, owing to the movement of the sun and the astral bodies, is in a perpetual state of flux and change, filling all the universe. . . . We breathe this astral gold continuously.' The two movements—positive and negative—of breathing are connected with the circulation of the blood and with the important symbolic paths of involution and evolution (3). Difficulty in breathing may therefore symbolize difficulty in assimilating the principles of the spirit and of the cosmos. The 'proper rhythm' of Yoga-breathing is associated with the 'proper voice' demanded by the Egyptians for the ritual reading of the sacred texts. Both are founded upon imitation of the rhythms of the universe.

Bridge   According to Guénon, the Roman *pontifex* was literally a 'builder of bridges', that is, of that which bridges two separate worlds. St. Bernard has said that the Roman Pontiff, as the etymology of his name suggests, is a kind of bridge between God and Man (*Tractatus de Moribus et Officio Episcoporum*, III, 9). For this reason, the rainbow is a natural symbol of the pontificate. For the Israelites, it was the sign of the Covenant between the Creator and his people, and, in China, the sign denoting the union of heaven and earth. For the Greeks, it was Iris, a messenger of the gods. And there are a great many cultures where the bridge symbolizes the link between what can be perceived and what is beyond perception (28). Even when it lacks this mystic sense, the bridge is always symbolic of a transition from one state to another —of change or the desire for change.

Bucentaur   A monster, half-man and half-ox or bull. In some monuments Hercules is shown fighting a bucentaur or smothering it in his arms. Like the centaur, this mythic animal is symbolic of the essential duality of man, but, in this case, stressing the baser— or animal—part. Hercules' struggle with the bucentaur is the archetype of all mythic combat: Theseus and the Minotaur, Siegfried and the dragon, etc. (8).

Buckle   The buckle implies self-defence and protection, like the fibula on the one hand (which is the shield reduced to its minimal form), and the belt on the other (4). To undo one's belt is symbolically the same as 'letting one's hair down'.

Bucraneum   A decorative motif deriving from the appearance of the remains of the head of the bull or ox, after it had been sacrificed by fire in ancient ritual (41).

Bull   The bull is associated with the symbolism of Taurus (q.v.). It is a highly complex symbol, both from the historical and psychological point of view. In esoteric tradition it is an emblem used by the Hyperboreans as a totem against the dragon of the Negroes, and is equated with the god Thor, the son of heaven and of woodland (49). In principle, this emblematic use symbolizes the superiority of the mammal over the reptile, or of the Aryan over the Negro. The basic dilemma lies between the interpretation of the bull as a symbol of the earth, of the mother, and of the 'wetness' principle (II); and the view that it represents heaven and the father. Mithraic ritual seems to have been founded on the former: the sacrifice of the bull was expressive of the penetration of the feminine principle by the masculine, of the humid by·the igniferous (the rays of the sun, the origin and cause of all fecundity). Krappe, investigating these paradoxes, has pointed to the fact that the bull is the commonest tame animal of the Near East and relates this to the fact that bulls are depicted as lunar as often as solar (that is, they may be subject to either one or the other of the opposed principles we have just outlined). Sin was a Mesopotamian lunar god and he often took the form of a bull; Osiris, also a lunar god, was supposedly represented by the bull Apis. On the other hand, the Vedic god Sûrya is a solar bull. According to the Assyrians, the bull was born of the sun. Krappe explains this disparity not as an internal contradiction but as a consequence of the way in which the lunar and the solar cults succeed one another. The lunar bull becomes solar when the solar cult supplants the more ancient cult of the moon (35). But it may well be that the bull is first and foremost a lunar symbol because it is equated with the moon morphologically by virtue of the resemblance of the horns of the crescent moon, while it must take second place to the solar symbol of the lion. This is the view expressed by Eliade, for example, who suggests that the bull does not represent any of the astral bodies but rather the fecundating sky and that, from the year 2400 B.C. onwards, both the bull and the thunderbolt were symbols connected with the atmospheric deities, the bull's bellow being associated with the rolling of thunder. In all palaeo-oriental cultures, it was the bull which expressed the idea of power. In Accadian, 'to break the horn' signified 'to overpower' (17). According to Frobenius, the black bull is linked with the lower heaven, that is, with death. This belief prevailed in India; and in lands as remote as Java and Bali which fell under the influence of Indian culture, it was the custom to burn the bodies of princes in coffins shaped like bulls. There are Egyptian paintings of a black bull bearing the corpse of Osiris on its back (22). This interpretation is supported by Schneider's observation that, in so far as the bull corresponds to the intermediary zone between the Elements of Fire and Water, it seems to symbolize the communicating link between heaven and earth, a significance which could also apply to the bull of the royal tombs of Ur, which has a head of gold (representing fire) and a jowl of lapis lazuli (water). The ox symbolizes sacrifice, self-denial and chastity, and is also found in association with agricultural cults (50); it is, in other words, the symbolic antithesis of the bull, with its fecundating powers. If we accept that the bull is Uranian in implication, however, then the contradiction is resolved and the bull may be linked with the active, masculine principle, although only in so far as its maternal aspect has been superseded—supplanted, that is, by the son (the Sun or the lion).

This, at least, is what Jung has suggested, together with the idea that
the bull, like the he-goat, is a symbol for the father (31).

Bunch In Christian art, a bunch or cluster always symbolizes
Christ and sacrifice. So, in the book of Numbers (xiii, 23), one
reads: 'and (they) cut down from thence a branch with one cluster
of grapes' (46).

Butterfly Among the ancients, an emblem of the soul and of
unconscious attraction towards the light (8). The purification of the
soul by fire, represented in Romanesque art by the burning ember
placed by the angel in the prophet's mouth, is visually portrayed on
a small Mattei urn by means of an image of love holding a butterfly
close to a flame (8). The Angel of Death was represented by the
Gnostics as a winged foot crushing a butterfly, from which we may
deduce that the butterfly was equated with life rather than with the
soul in the sense of the spirit or transcendent being (36). This also
explains why psychoanalysis regards the butterfly as a symbol of
rebirth (56). In China, it has the secondary meanings of joy and
conjugal bliss (5).

C

Cabiri They are earth-god symbols, personified as little dwarfs,
whose invisibility is implied by the hood covering their head. They
were conceived to be deities watching over shipwrecked men. In
all probability they are symbols of the extraordinary 'powers' held
in reserve by the human spirit (32).

Caduceus A wand with two serpents twined round it, surmounted
by two small wings or a winged helmet. The rational and historical
explanation is the supposed intervention of Mercury in a fight
between two serpents who thereupon curled themselves round his
wand. For the Romans, the caduceus served as a symbol of moral
equilibrium and of good conduct. The wand represents power;
the two snakes wisdom; the wings diligence (8); and the helmet is
an emblem of lofty thoughts. To-day the caduceus is the insignia of
the Catholic bishop in the Ukraine. The caduceus also signifies the
integration of the four elements, the wand corresponding to earth,
the wings to air, the serpents to fire and water (by analogy with the
undulating movement of waves and flames) (56). This symbol is
very ancient, and is to be found for example in India engraved upon
stone tablets called *nâgakals*, a kind of votive offering placed at the
entrance to temples. Heinrich Zimmer traces the caduceus back to
Mesopotamia, detecting it in the design of the sacrificial cup of

king Gudea of Lagash (2600 B.C.). Zimmer even goes so far as to
state that the symbol probably dates back beyond this period, for
the Mesopotamians considered the intertwining serpents as a symbol
of the god who cures all illness, a meaning which passed into Greek
culture and is still preserved in emblems of our day (60). According
to esoteric Buddhism, the wand of the caduceus corresponds to the

Caduceus (Swiss, 1515).

axis of the world and the serpents refer to the force called Kundalini,
which, in Tantrist teaching, sleeps coiled up at the base of the
backbone—a symbol of the evolutive power of pure energy (40).
Schneider maintains that the two S-shapes of the serpents correspond
to illness and convalescence (51). In reality, what defines the essence
of the caduceus is the nature and meaning not so much of its individual elements as of the composite whole. The precisely symmetrical and bilateral arrangement, as in the balance of Libra, or
in the tri-unity of heraldry (a shield between two supporters), is

always expressive of the same idea of active equilibrium, of opposing forces balancing one another in such a way as to create a higher, static form. In the caduceus, this balanced duality is twice stated:

Early Sumerian version of the caduceus.

in the serpents and in the wings, thereby emphasizing that supreme state of strength and self-control (and consequently of health) which can be achieved both on the lower plane of the instincts (symbolized by the serpents) and on the higher level of the spirit (represented by the wings).

Camel Traditionally considered in curious relation with the dragon and with winged serpents, for, according to the Zohar, the serpent in the Garden of Eden was a kind of 'flying camel'. Similar allusions are to be found in the Persian Zend-Avesta (9).

Cancer The fourth sign of the Zodiac. Orphic teaching sees it as the threshold through which the soul enters upon its incarnation. It is governed by the Moon in the performance of its symbolic rôle as mediator between the formal and the informal worlds (40).

Candelabra A symbol of spiritual light and of salvation. The number of its branches has always a cosmic or mystic significance. For example, the Hebraic seven-branched candelabra corresponds to the seven heavens and the seven planets (4).

Zodiacal sign of
Cancer.

Hebraic
seven-
branched
candelabra.

Candle, Lighted Like the lamp, it is a symbol of individuated light, and consequently of the life of an individual as opposed to the cosmic and universal life.

Canopy One of the eight emblems of good luck in Chinese Buddhism. It is also an allegory of regal dignity, and a symbol of protection (5). If it is square, it alludes to the earth; if it is circular, to the sky or the sun; in the latter case it is closely linked with the ritual parasol of so many primitive peoples and of the ancients.

Capricorn The tenth sign of the Zodiac. Its dual nature, expressed allegorically in the form of a goat whose body terminates in a fish's tail, refers to the dual tendencies of life towards the abyss (or water) on the one hand, and the heights (or mountains) on the other; these two currents also signify, in Hindu doctrine, the involutive and evolutive possibilities: the return to or the departure from the 'wheel of rebirth' (that is, the Zodiac).

Zodiacal sign of Capricorn.

Cask, Bottomless A famous Greek symbol which, as in the legend of the Danaides, symbolizes useless labour and, on another level, the apparent futility of all existence (8).

Castle This is a complex symbol, derived at once from that of the house and that of the enclosure or walled city. Walled cities figure in mediaeval art as a symbol of the transcendent soul and of the heavenly Jerusalem. Generally speaking, the castle is located on the top of a mountain or hill, which suggests an additional and important meaning derived from the symbolism of level. Its shape, form and colour, its dark and light shades, all play an important part in defining the symbolic meaning of the castle as a whole, which, in the broadest sense, is an embattled, spiritual power, ever on the watch. The 'black castle' has been interpreted as the alchemists' lair, as well as a rain cloud poised above a mountain-top (50). Its significance as the Mansion of the Beyond, or as the entrance to the Other World, would seem obvious enough. In a great many legends, the Castle of Darkness, inhabited by a 'Black Knight', is symbolic of the abode of Pluto; this is confirmed by Theseus' mythic journey into hell. Charon has his abode in a similar castle which is inaccessible to living men (the 'castle of no return' of folktales). In the legendary heaven of Nordic tradition, the same meaning is to be found. Melwas, the abducter of Guinevere, dwells in a castle surrounded by a deep moat, the only means of access being two bridges difficult to negotiate. According to Krappe, it is very possible that the underlying symbolism of all mediaeval tales and legends about a castle owned by a 'wicked knight' who holds captive all who approach his domain may well be that of the sinister castle of the Lord of the Underworld (35). On the other hand, the 'Castle of Light' is the 'redemption'-aspect of this same image. Piobb explains that the sudden appearance of a castle in the path of a wanderer is like the sudden awareness of a spiritual pattern. 'Before this fascinating vision, all fatigue disappears. One has the clear impression that treasure lies within. The splendid temple is the achieving of the inconceivable, the materialization of the unexpected' (48). The castle, in sum, together with the treasure (that is, the eternal essence of spiritual wealth), the damsel (that is, the anima in the Jungian sense) and the purified knight, make up a synthesis expressive of the will to salvation.

Cat The Egyptians associated the cat with the moon, and it was sacred to the goddesses Isis and Bast, the latter being the guardian of marriage (57). A secondary symbolism is derived from its colour; the black cat is associated with darkness and death.

Catastrophe A general symbol for a change wrought by mutation in a single process, and a frequent sign for the beginnings of psychic transformation (56). A secondary shade of meaning is added by the particular character of the catastrophe: that is, the predominant element, which will be air in the case of a hurricane, fire in the case of conflagrations, water in floods and deluges, and earth in earthquakes. Whether the catastrophe is, in the symbolic sense, positive or negative is, of course, entirely dependent upon the nature of the change wrought in the agent affected by it.

Cauldron Like the skull, a symbol of the receptacle of the forces of transmutation and germination. But whereas the skull, because of its vaulted shape, signifies the higher, sublimated and spiritual aspects of this process, the cauldron, being open at the top, has the opposite meaning of the baser forces of nature. Most of the mythic cauldrons which figure in Celtic tradition are located at the bottom of the sea or of lakes (indicating that the respective symbolisms of the cauldron and of water have coalesced, and that they both relate to the general symbolism of water, which is the vehicle of life and the medial element *par excellence*). We can see, then, that the skull is the receptacle for the 'upper ocean' or the reflection of it in Man, whereas the cauldron—the inversion of the skull—is the vessel for the 'lower ocean'. This is why pots and cauldrons figure so often in legends about magic and in folktales (17). The chalice is a sublimation and a consecration of the cauldron as well as of the cup, which is a pure symbol of containment (Plate IV).

Cave or **Cavern** Broadly speaking, its meaning is probably confined to that of the general symbolism of containment, of the enclosed or the concealed. It underlies certain images such as the mediaeval cave which symbolizes the human heart as the spiritual 'centre' (14). For Jung, it stands for the security and the impregnability of the unconscious. It appears fairly often in emblematic and mythological iconography as the meeting-place for figures of deities, forebears or archetypes, becoming therefore an objective image of Hades, although still expressive of the psychological unconscious (32). Cult sites in prehistory—some caves showing traces of the Ice Age were later made into Christian shrines. Lourdes is a religious cave of the Quaternary. Kühn has found traces of recent offerings in North African sites with prehistoric indications. Caves, with their darkness, are womb-symbols. That the German *Höhle* (cave) and *Holle* (hell) are related is not without significance. (See Herbert Kühn, *The Rock Pictures of Europe*.)

Centaur A fabulous being, half-man, half-horse, supposed by some to be the fruit of the union of Centaurus and the Magnesian mares. From a symbolic point of view the centaur is the antithesis of the knight, that is, it represents the complete domination of a being by the baser forces: in other words, it denotes cosmic force, the instincts, or the unconscious, uncontrolled by the spirit.

Centre To leave the circumference for the centre is equivalent to moving from the exterior to the interior, from form to contemplation, from multiplicity to unity, from space to spacelessness, from time to timelessness. In all symbols expressive of the mystic Centre, the intention is to reveal to Man the meaning of the primordial 'paradisal state' and to teach him to identify himself with the supreme principle of the universe (29). This centre is in effect Aristotle's 'unmoved mover' and Dante's 'L'Amore che muove il sole a l'altre stelle' (27). Similarly, Hindu doctrine declares that God resides in the centre, at that point where the radii of a wheel meet at its axis (51). In diagrams of the cosmos, the central space is always reserved for the Creator, so that he appears as if surrounded by a circular or almond-shaped halo (formed by the intersection of the circle of heaven with the circle of the earth), surrounded by concentric circles spreading outwards, and by the wheel of the Zodiac, the twelve-monthly cycle of labour upon the land, and a four-part division corresponding both to the seasons and to the tetramorph. Among the Chinese, the infinite being is frequently symbolized as a point of light with concentric circles spreading outwards from it. In Western emblems, an eagle's head sometimes carries the same significance (4). In some Hindu mandalas, such as the Shri-Yantra, the centre itself is not actually portrayed, but has to be supplied mentally by the contemplator; the Shri-Yantra is a 'form in expansion' (and a symbol, therefore, of the creation), composed of nine intersecting triangles circumscribed by a lotus flower and a square. A great many ritual acts have the sole purpose of finding out the spiritual 'Centre' of a locality, which then becomes the site, either in itself or by virtue of the temple built upon it, of an 'image of the world'. There are also many legends which tell of pilgrimages to places with character-istics which relate them to Paradise. This Chinese tale, for example, retold by the orientalist Wilhelm in his work on Lao-Tse: 'King Huangti had a dream. He crossed into the kingdom of the Hua Hsü. The kingdom of the Hua Hsü is west of the far West and north of the far North. It is not known how many hundreds of thousands of leagues it is from the Ch'i state. It can be reached neither by boat nor by carriage, nor on foot. It can be reached only by the spirit in flight. This country has no sovereign: everyone acts according to his own dictates; the people have no lawmakers: everyone acts according to his own dictates. The joys of life are not known, nor is the fear of death; so there is no premature death. Self-withdrawal is not known, nor is the shunning of one's fellows; so there is no love and no hate. Revulsion from what is distasteful is not known, nor is the search for pleasure; so there is no profit and no harm. No one has any preference, no one has any dislike. They enter the water and are not drowned, walk through fire and are not scorched... They rise up into the air as others walk on the face of the earth; they rest in space as others sleep in beds; clouds and mist do not veil their gaze. Claps of thunder do not deafen their ears. Neither beauty nor ugliness dazzles their hearts. Neither mountain nor ravine impedes their progress. They walk only in the spirit' (58). This concept of the Centre coincides, of course, with that of the 'Land of the Dead', in which the theme of the *coincidentia oppositorum* of mystic tradition comes to signify not so much 'opposition' as neutralization, in the characteristically oriental sense. The Centre is located at the point of intersection of the two arms of the superficial (or two-dimensional) cross, or of the three arms of the essential, three-dimensional cross. In this position it expresses the dimension of the 'infinite depth' of space, that is, the seed of the eternal cycle of the flux and flow of forms and beings, as well as the dimensions of space itself. In some liturgical crosses, as for example that of Cong in Ireland, the centre is marked by a precious stone.

Centre, Spiritual   In *Le Roi du Monde*, René Guénon speaks of the 'spiritual centre' which was established in the terrestrial world to conserve intact a treasure of 'non-human' knowledge. This, he suggests, is no less than the origin of the concept of 'tradition' from which are derived all the religious, mythical and philosophical customs and explanations of the world. Guénon points out that Saint-Yves d'Alveydre, in a posthumous work (*La Mission de l'Inde*, 1910), places *Agarttha* at the centre. The author connects this symbolic city with the Rosicrucians' 'solar citadel' and Campanella's *City of the Sun*.

Cerberus   A three-headed dog whose throat bristled with serpents. He was the guardian of the abode of Pluto on the banks of the Stygian lake. Neoplatonic doctrine saw in him a symbol of the evil genius. Later he came to be interpreted as the emblem of rotting in the grave, for if Hercules overcame him it was only because his tasks were directed towards the attainment of immortality (8). The three heads of Cerberus are—like the trident—the infernal replica of divine triunity. They are also related to the three Gorgons (40). In all threefold symbols of the baser forces of life, Diel, following his system of moral interpretation, sees the degradation of the three vital 'urges' (of conservation, reproduction and spiritualization), bringing about the death of the soul, which is why Cerberus, the guardian of dead souls in Tartarus, is charged with the task of preventing their return into the world above where atonement and salvation are still possible (15).

Chain   The Egyptian hieroglyphic sign in the shape of a vertical chain of three links formed by two lines intertwining (with a fourth link, left open, at the bottom) holds a dual symbolism: on the one hand, that of the caduceus of Mercury, standing for the dual streams —involution and evolution—of the universe (19); and on the other, implying the general symbolism of the chain, that is, bonds and communication. On the cosmic plane it is the symbol of the marriage of heaven and earth, similar to other symbols such as the cry of pain, the whistle of the stone hurled skywards by the sling, and the arrow (50). On the plane of earthly existence it is the symbol of matrimony: each link actually or potentially corresponding to a blood-relationship: father and mother, sons and daughters, brothers (51). In a wider sense related to the symbolism of bonds and cords, bands and twine, it is a symbol of social or psychic integration along with the secondary but very important characteristic of the toughness of its material. Amongst the Gauls there were comrades in arms who would enter into combat chained together in pairs so that if one died, his companion was bound to fall too. A saying that is power-fully evocative of the spiritual significance of the chain symbol is attributed to Louis XI of France: presenting a golden chain to Raoul de Lannoi as an award for bravery, the king exclaimed: '*Par le Pâque-Dieu*, my friend, thou art so ferocious in battle that thou must be chained up, for I do not wish to lose thee lest I need thy help once more'.

Chalice The chalice of Christian liturgy is the transcendental form of the cup. Related to the Grail, it frequently takes the form of two halves of a sphere placed back to back. In this, the lower part of the sphere becomes a receptacle open to the spiritual forces, while the upper part closes over the earth, which it duplicates symbolically. The chalice has a certain affinity with the Celtic symbolism of the cauldron.

Chaos Realistic philosophy sees chaos as the earliest state of disorganized creation, blindly impelled towards the creation of a new order of phenomena of hidden meanings (22). Blavatsky, for example, asks: 'What is primordial chaos but the ether containing within itself all forms and all beings, all the seeds of universal creation?' Plato and the Pythagoreans maintained that this 'primor-dial substance' was the soul of the world, called *protohyle* by the alchemists. Thus, chaos is seen as that which embraces all opposing forces in a state of undifferentiated dissolution. In primordial chaos, according to Hindu tradition, one also meets Amrita—immortality—and Visha—evil and death (9). In alchemy, chaos was identified with prime matter and thought to be a *massa confusa* from which the *lapis* would arise (32); it was related to the colour black. It has also been identified with the unconscious. But it is better to regard chaos as the state preceding the condition of the unconscious.

Chariot One of the basic analogies in the universal tradition of symbolism is that of the chariot in relation to the human being. The charioteer represents the *self* of Jungian psychology; the chariot the human body and also thought in its transitory aspects relative to things terrestrial; the horses are the life-force; and the reins denote intelligence and will-power. This is a meaning which also appears in Cabalistic writing, where it is given the name ascribed to the chariot itself—*Merkabah* (40, 55). The 'Sun Chariot' is the Great Vehicle of esoteric Buddhism (4); the 'Chariot of Fire', according to René Guénon, may be a symbol of the dynamic and overriding power of the subtle mind (26). Be that as it may, tales about gods or fairies travelling in chariots across land, sea or sky are very frequent and of obvious symbolic interest. The exact details of the vehicle and of the animals drawing it always contribute something to the symbolism of the chariot as a whole.

So Perrault in his literary version of the folktale *La Biche au Bois*, says: 'Each fairy had a chariot of a different material: one was made of ebony drawn by white pigeons; others were of ivory drawn by crows; and others were made of cedarwood. . . . When the fairies became angry, their chariots would be harnessed only to winged dragons or serpents breathing fire out of their mouth and eyes.' The Sun Chariot (or the Chariot of Fire) is, in Loeffler's view, so powerful an archetype that it has found its way into most of the mythologies of the world. When it bears a hero, it becomes the emblem of the hero's body consumed in the service of the soul. The appearance, nature and colour of the team of animals drawing it represent the qualities, good or bad, of the motives driving the chariot onwards in fulfilment of its mission. Hence (for example) the horses of Arjuna (in the Vedic epic) are white, signifying the purity of the driver. A regional Polish tale has it that the Sun Chariot is drawn by three horses, one silver, one gold and one made of diamonds (38). This threefold aspect comes from the well-known significance of the number 3, as in the triple mandorlas and other comparable symbols and emblems.

Chariot, The   The seventh enigma of the Tarot pack. It depicts a youth clad in a cuirass, bearing a sceptre, and riding in a symbolic chariot. He incarnates the higher principles of Man's nature. In the chariot there can be seen an emblem of the Egyptian winged globe, representing the sublimation of matter and its evolutive motion. Furthermore, the chariot has red wheels, which are to be related to the whirlwinds of fire in the vision of Ezekiel. These wheels stand out in contrast to the blue canopy or pallium which covers the chariot, signifying the difference between the absolute and the relative. The allegory of this image is reflected in its smallest details. So, for example, the cuirass of the charioteer represents his defence against the baser forces of life; it is secured with five gold studs, denoting the four elements and the quintessence. On his shoulders there are two crescent moons representing the world of forms. The chariot is drawn by what at first seems to be a pair of sphinxes but which is in fact a two-headed amphisbaena, symbolizing the hostile forces which one must subjugate in order to go forward (in the same way as the two serpents counterbalance one another in the caduceus). Basil Valentine, in his *L'Azoth des Philosophes* (Paris, 1660), illustrates this principle of duality with a serpent coiled round the sun and moon, its extremities bearing the likeness of a lion and an eagle. This Tarot mystery, then, is associated with concepts of self-control, progress and victory (59).

Chequers   Any pattern consisting of squares, lozenges or rectangles, in alternating white and black colours (that is, positive and negative), or, for that matter, in other pairs of colours, stands in symbolic relation to the duality of elements inherent in the extension of time and hence in destiny. Thus, the Romans would mark a happy or an unhappy day with a white or a black stone respectively. The colour of chequer-work changes its meaning according to the particular symbolism of the colours. The significance of chequers, then, embraces concepts of combination, demonstration, chance or potentiality (48), as well as the effort to control irrational impulses by containing them within a given order. All orthogonal forms are symbols of the reason and the intellect, but not of the spirit, because the latter is content *par excellence*, whereas the rational never manages to be more than a system of apprehending things, that is, a container. The heraldic lozenge is a development of the chequer-board, the form of which is such that it represents the dynamic interaction of the two elements which, in all forms of chequer, are opposed and counterpoised one against the other in a pattern of duality. It is significant that the costume of the harlequin (a chthonian deity) is actually chequered or made up of lozenges, which proves beyond doubt that the harlequin is related to the gods of destiny.

Cherubim The cherubim or Kirubi (or Kherebu) which stood at the entrance to Assyrian temples and palaces were, according to Marques-Rivière, nothing less than gigantic pentacles placed there by the priests as 'keepers of the threshold'—a function which in China was fulfilled by griffins and dragons (39). The Egyptian cherub was a figure with many wings, and covered with eyes; it was an emblem of the night sky, of religion and vigilance (8).

Child A symbol of the future, as opposed to the old man who signifies the past (49); but the child is also symbolic of that stage of life when the old man, transformed, acquires a new simplicity—as Nietzsche implied in *Thus Spake Zarathustra* when dealing with the 'three transformations'. Hence the conception of the child as symbolic of the 'mystic Centre' and as the 'youthful, re-awakening force' (56). In Christian iconography, children often appear as angels; on the aesthetic plane they are found as *putti* in Baroque grotesque and ornamentations; and in traditional symbology they are dwarfs or Cabiri. In every case, Jung argues, they symbolize formative forces of the unconscious of a beneficent and protective kind (32). Psychologically speaking, the child is of the soul—the product of the *coniunctio* between the unconscious and consciousness: one dreams of a child when some great spiritual change is about to take place under favourable circumstances (33). The mystic child who solves riddles and teaches wisdom is an archetypal figure having the same significance, but on the mythic plane of the general and collective, and is an aspect of the heroic child who liberates the world from monsters (60). In alchemy, the child wearing a crown or regal garments is a symbol of the philosopher's stone, that is, of the supreme realization of mystic identification with the 'god within us' and with the eternal.

Chimaera A monster born of Typhon and Echidna. It is represented as having a lion's head, the body of a goat and the tail of a dragon. Flames flicker from out of its mouth. Like other teratological beings, the chimaera is a symbol of complex evil (8).

Choice The symbols for choice usually take the form of a cross-roads or a balanced symmetry of two opposing principles. The best-known allegory of choice shows a woman dressed in violet (signifying indecision, according to Otto Weininger, because as a colour it is neither blue nor red), standing at a cross-roads, with a snake crawling along one of the paths; and she is pointing to a verdant tree growing in the other path (8).

Chrism The signographic emblem of Christ, based on the combination of the first two letters of the word Χριστος, X and P. Attention has been drawn to the similarity between this sign, which figured on the Román labarum (banner) from the time of Constantine, and the Egyptian anserated cross.

Chrysalis In the words of Wang Chung: 'The chrysalis precedes the cicada; simply by changing its shape, it becomes the cicada. When the soul leaves the body, it resembles a cicada which leaves its chrysalis in order to become an insect.' In Schneider's view, the mystic function of such a transformation presupposes qualities of balance, regeneration and valour (51). The ritual mask, as well as the theatre-mask, is probably closely connected with the idea of the chrysalis and metamorphosis. For, behind this mask, the transformation of an individual's personality is hidden from view.

Chthonian Demons Various beings mentioned in mythologies come under this heading, such as the Greek harpies and Erinyes, the Hindu Rakshasas, the Arabic djinns, the Germanic elves and valkyries, etc. They are symbols of thanatic forces, of the death-wish in various guises: the subtle fascination of dreams, or the heroic thrill experienced by the man who answers the call to battle (35). The quest for death—extremes meet (because of the curve of the conceptual line)—is apparent in limit-situations, not only in the negative aspect but also—and principally—at the peak of the affirmative. That is, vital optimism and perfect happiness of necessity imply the other extreme, that is, the presence of death.

Circle At times it is synonymous with the circumference, just as the circumference is often equated with circular movement. But although its general meaning embraces both aspects, there are some further details which it is important to emphasize. The circle or disk is, very frequently, an emblem of the sun (and indisputably so when it is surrounded by rays). It also bears a certain relationship to the number ten (symbolizing the return to unity from multiplicity)

(49), when it comes to stand for heaven and perfection (4) and sometimes eternity as well (20). There are profound psychological implications in this particular concept of perfection. As Jung observes, the square, representing the lowest of the composite and factorial numbers, symbolizes the pluralist state of man who has not achieved inner unity (perfection) whilst the circle would correspond to this ultimate state of Oneness. The octagon is the intermediate state between the square and the circle. Representations of the relationship between the circle and the square are very common in

Chinese Yang-Yin, surrounded by the eight trigrams.

the universal and spiritual world of morphology, notably in the mandalas of India and Tibet and in Chinese emblems. Indeed, according to Chochod, in China, activity, or the masculine principle (*Yang*), is represented by a white circle (depicting heaven), whereas passivity, the feminine principle (*Yin*) is denoted by a black square (portraying earth). The white circle stands for energy and celestial influences and the black square for telluric forces. The interaction implicit in dualism is represented by the famous symbol of the Yang-Yin, a circle divided into two equal sections by a sigmoid line across the diameter, the white section (*Yang*) having a black spot within it, and the black (*Yin*) a white spot. These two spots signify that there is always something of the feminine in the masculine and something of the masculine in the feminine. The sigmoid line is a symbol of the movement of communication and serves the purpose of implying—like the swastika—the idea of rotation, so imparting a dynamic and complementary character to this bipartite symbol. The law of polarity has been the subject of much thought among

Chinese philosophers, who have deduced from this bipolar symbol a series of principles of unquestionable value, which we here transcribe: (*a*) the quantity of energy distributed throughout the universe is invariable; (*b*) it consists of the sum of two equal amounts of energy, one positive and active in kind and the other negative and passive; (*c*) the nature of cosmic phenomena is characterized by the varying proportions of the two modes of energy involved in their creation. In the twelve months of the year, for example, there is a given quantity of energy drawn from six parts of *Yang* and six of *Yin*, in varying proportions (13). We must also point to the relationship between the circle and the sphere, which is a symbol of the All.

Circumference   A symbol of adequate limitation, of the manifest world, of the precise and the regular (25), as well as of the inner unity of all matter and all universal harmony, as understood by the alchemists. Enclosing beings, objects or figures within a circumference has a double meaning: from within, it implies limitation and definition; from without, it is seen to represent the defence of the physical and psychic contents themselves against the perils of the soul threatening it from without, these dangers being, in a way, tantamount to chaos, but more particularly to illimitation and disintegration (32). Circumferential movement, which the Gnostics turned into one of their basic emblems by means of the figure of the dragon, the serpent or the fish biting its tail, is a representation of time. The Ouroboros (the circle formed by a dragon biting its own tail) is to be found in the *Codex Marcianus* (of the 2nd century A.D.) and also in the Greek legend *Hen to Pan* (The One, The All), which explains how its meaning embraces all cyclic systems (unity, multiplicity and the return to unity; evolution and involution; birth, growth, decrease, death, etc.). The alchemists took up this Gnostic symbol and applied it to the processes of their symbolic *opus* of human destiny (32). Now, by virtue of its movement as much as by its shape, circular motion carries the further significance of that which brings into being, activates and animates all the forces involved in any given process, sweeping them along with it, including those forces which would otherwise act against each other. As we have seen, this meaning is basic in the Chinese *Yang-Yin* emblem (30). Almost all representations of time have some bearing upon the circle, as for example the mediaeval representations of the year.

Cithara (or **Cithern**)   A symbol of the cosmos, its strings corresponding to the levels of the universe. Being rounded on one side and flat on the other (like the turtle), it comes to signify the synthesis of heaven and earth (14, 50).

City   Up to a certain point it corresponds to landscape-symbolism in general, of which it forms one representational aspect, embracing the important symbols of level and space, that is, height and situation. With the dawning of history there arose, according to René Guénon, a true, 'sacred geography' and the position, shape, doors and gates, and general disposition of a city with its temples and acropolis were never arbitrary or fortuitous, or merely utilitarian. In fact, cities were planned in strict accord with the dictates of a particular doctrine; hence the city became a symbol of that doctrine and of the society which upheld it (28). The city walls had magic powers since they were the outward signs of dogma, which explains and justifies Romulus's fratricide. Ornamental reliefs on capitals, lintels, and tympana of the Middle Ages often depict the outlines of a walled city, although in a way which is more emblematic than symbolic. These ornaments are a kind of prefiguration of the heavenly Jerusalem. An angel armed with a sword is sometimes to be seen at the city gate (46). Jung sees the city as a mother-symbol and as a symbol of the feminine principle in general: that is, he interprets the City as a woman who shelters her inhabitants as if they were her children; that is why the two mother-gods Rhea and Cybele—as well as other allegorical figures derived from them— wear a crown after the pattern of a wall. The Old Testament speaks of cities as women (31).

Climate The analogy between a state of mind and a given climate, as expressed by the interplay between space, situation, the elements and temperature, as well as level-symbolism, is one of the most frequent of all analogies in literature. Nietzsche, for example, embarked upon a passionate quest for the true climate—for the exact geographic location—corresponding to the inner 'climate' of the thinker (3). The universal value of pairs of opposites, such as high/low, dry/wet, clear/dark, is demonstrated in their continued use not only in physical and material but also in psychological, intellectual and spiritual matters.

Cloak Within the symbolism of garments, the cloak is, on the one hand, the sign of superior dignity, and, on the other, of a veil cutting off a person from the world (48). The cloak of Apollonius is an expression of the complete self-possession of the sage, isolating him from the instinctive currents that move the generality of mankind (37). The actual position of the cloak is of great importance in determining the secondary symbolic meanings. For example, the Heddernheim relief of Mithras slaying the bull has a cloak flying out in the wind like wings, thereby equating the hero and the victim with the celebrated alchemic marriage of the volatile with the fixed (31). The material, adornments, colour and shape of the cloak add further shades of meaning. The two colours of the outside and the inside always correspond to a dual significance arising directly out of the symbolism of colours.

Clock Like all circular forms incorporating a number of internal elements, the clock may be interpreted as a kind of mandala. Since the essence of the clock is to tell the time, the predominant symbolism is that of number. As a machine, the clock is related to the notions of 'perpetual motion', automata, mechanism and to the magical creation of beings that pursue their own autonomous existence.

Clothes The wearing of skins by the Roman eagle-bearers appears to be of totemic origin. Without attempting to establish any theoretical connexion between a Sacher-Masoch's concept of 'skins' and their habitual use by women, this possibility must not be forgotten. The spotted skin of an animal (such as a panther) or a multicoloured or shot fabric are symbols of the Whole (the god Pan). In *Aurélia*, which abounds in symbols, Nerval says: 'and the goddess of my dreams appeared before me, smiling, dressed in Indian-style garments. . . . She began to walk among us, and the meadows grew green again and the flowers and plants sprang up over the earth at the touch of her feet.' In another passage, Nerval causes the drapery and designs of his beloved's dress to become so confused with the flowers and plants in a garden that they grow indistinguishable.

Clouds There are two principal aspects to cloud-symbolism: on the one hand they are related to the symbolism of mist, signifying the intermediate world between the formal and the non-formal; and on the other hand they are associated with the 'Upper Waters'— the realm of the antique Neptune. The former aspect of the cloud is symbolic of forms as phenomena and appearance, always in a state of metamorphosis, which obscure the immutable quality of higher truth (37). The second aspect of clouds reveals their family connexion with fertility-symbolism and their analogous relationship with all that is destined to bring fecundity. Hence the fact that ancient Christian symbolism interprets the cloud as synonymous with the prophet, since prophecies are an occult source of fertilization, celestial in origin (46). Hence also the conclusion of Bachelard that the cloud should be taken as a symbolic messenger (3).

Trefoil.

Clover (or **Trefoil**) An emblem of the Trinity. When it is located upon a mountain it comes to signify knowledge of the divine essence gained by hard endeavour, through sacrifice or study (equivalent to ascension) (4). Trifoliate forms, such as the Gothic three-lobed arch, bear the same significance; and, broadly speaking, so do all tripartite forms. In the Middle Ages, triple time in music was regarded in the same light, and it is so used by Scriabin in *Prometheus*.

Clown   Like the buffoon, the clown is a mythic figure, and the inversion of the king—the inversion, that is to say, of the possessor of supreme powers; hence the clown is the victim chosen as a substitute for the king, in accord with the familiar astrobiological and primitive ideas of the ritual assassination of the king. The clown is the last, whereas the king is the first, but in the essential order of things the last comes second. This is confirmed by the folklore custom, mentioned by Frazer, in which village youths, during Spring festivals, would race on horseback up to the tallest mast (symbolizing the world-axis); he who came first was elected Easter king, and the last to arrive was made a clown and beaten (21).

Coal   Like charred wood, the symbolism of coal is closely linked with that of fire. There is a certain ambivalence about it, since it sometimes appears as a concentrated expression of fire, and sometimes as the negative (black, repressed or occult) side of energy. The chromatic relationship between black and red—between coal and flames—can be seen in myths and legends as recounted by Krappe. According to an Australian tradition, the fire-bearing bird (the demiurge) had a red spot on its black back. Similar beliefs existed amongst the Celts, and in America and Asia (35).

√ **Cobweb**   Apart from its association with the spider, the symbolism of the spider's web is identical with that of fabric. Because of its spiral shape, it also embraces the idea of creation and development —of the wheel and its centre. But in this case death and destruction lurk at the centre, so that the web with the spider in the middle comes to symbolize what Medusa the Gorgon represents when located in the centre of certain mosaics: the consuming whirlwind. It is probably a symbol of the negative aspect of the universe, representing the Gnostic view that evil is not only on the periphery of the Wheel of Transformations but in its very centre—that is, in its Origin.

Cock   As the bird of dawn, the cock is a sun-symbol (4), and an emblem of vigilance and activity. Immolated to Priapus and Aesculapius, it was supposed to cure the sick (8). During the Middle Ages it became a highly important Christian image, nearly always appearing on the highest weathervane, on cathedral towers and domes, and was regarded as an allegory of vigilance and resurrection. Davy comments that vigilance in this context must be taken in the sense of 'tending towards eternity and taking care to grant first place to the things of the spirit, to be wakeful and to greet the Sun—Christ—even before it rises in the East'—illumination (14).

Coffer Like all objects whose essential quality is that of containing, it sometimes acquires the symbolic character of a heart, the brain or the maternal womb. The heart, the first of these meanings, is a figure characteristic of the symbolism of Romanesque art (14). In a broader sense, receptacles which can be closed up have, from the earliest times, represented all things that may hold secrets, such as the Ark of the Covenant of the Hebrews, or Pandora's box (48).

Cold In Bachelard's opinion, supported by literary analysis, cold corresponds symbolically to being in the situation of, or longing for, solitude or exaltation. Nietzsche, in his *Human, All Too Human*, makes a call for 'the cold, wild Alpine lands scarce warmed by the Autumn sun and *loveless*'. 'Thanks to the cold, the air gains in attacking virtues, it becomes spiritualized and dehumanized. In the frozen atmosphere, at higher altitudes, one finds another Nietzschean quality: silence' (1).

Colour Colour symbolism is one of the most universal of all types of symbolism, and has been consciously used in the liturgy, in heraldry, alchemy, art and literature. There are a great many considerations bearing upon the meaning of colour which we can here do little more than summarize. To begin with, there is the superficial classification suggested by optics and experimental psychology. The first group embraces warm 'advancing' colours, corresponding to processes of assimilation, activity and intensity (red, orange, yellow and, by extension, white), and the second covers cold, 'retreating' colours, corresponding to processes of dissimilation, passivity and debilitation (blue, indigo, violet and, by extension, black), green being an intermediate, transitional colour spanning the two groups. Then there are the subtle uses to which colour may be put in emblematic designs. The serial order of the colour-range is basic, comprising as it does (though in a somewhat abstract sense) a kind of limited set of definitive, distinct and ordered colours. The formal affinity between, on the one hand, this series of six or seven shades of colour—for sometimes it is difficult to tell blue from indigo, or azure from ultramarine—and, on the other hand, the vowel-series—there being seven vowels in Greek—as well as the notes of the musical scale, points to a basic analogy between these three scales and also between them and the division of the heavens, according to ancient astrobiological thought, into seven parts (although in fact there were sometimes said to be nine). Colour-symbolism usually derives from one of the following sources: (1) the inherent characteristic of each colour, perceived intuitively as objective fact; (2) the relationship between a colour and the planetary symbol traditionally linked with it; or (3) the relationship which elementary, primitive logic perceives. Modern psychology and psychoanalysis seem to place more weight upon the third of these formulas than even upon the first (the second formula acting as a bridge between the other two). Thus, Jolan de Jacobi, in her study of Jungian psychology, says in so many words: 'The correspondence of the colours to the respective functions varies with different cultures and groups and even among individuals; as a general rule, however, . . . blue, the colour of the rarefied atmosphere, of the clear sky, stands for thinking; yellow, the colour of the far-seeing sun, which appears bringing light out of an inscrutable darkness only to disappear again into the darkness, for intuition, the function which grasps as in a flash of illumination the origins and tendencies of happenings; red, the colour of the pulsing blood and of fire, for the surging and tearing emotions; while green, the colour of earthly, tangible, immediately perceptible growing things, represents the function of sensation' (30). The most important of the symbols derived from the foregoing principles are these: red is associated with blood, wounds, death-throes and sublimation; orange with fire and flames; yellow with the light of the sun, illumination, dissemination and comprehensive generalization; green with vegetation, but also with death and lividness (green is therefore the connecting-link between black— mineral life—and red—blood and animal life—as well as between animal life and discomposition and death); light blue with the sky and the day, and with the calm sea; dark blue with the sky and the night, and with the stormy sea; brown and ochre with the earth; and black with the fertilized land. Gold corresponds to the mystic aspect of the sun; silver to that of the moon. The different conclusions reached by psychologists and by traditional, esoteric thinkers, apparent in the above summaries, can be explained by the fact that in the psychologists' view, symbolic impressions formed in the mind may be merely fortuitous, whereas according to esoteric theory, the three series (of shades of colour, of component elements and natural appearances, and of feelings and reactions) are the outcome of a single, simultaneous cause working at the deepest levels of reality. It is for this reason that Ely Star, and others, maintains that the seven colours are severally analogous to the seven faculties of the soul, to the seven virtues (from a positive point of view), to the seven vices (from a negative viewpoint), to the geometric forms, the days of the week and the seven planets (55). Actually this is a concept which pertains more to the 'theory of correspondences' than to the symbolism of colour proper. Many primitive peoples intuitively sense that close links exist between all the different aspects of the real world: the Zuni Indians of Western America, for example, make a yearly offering to their priests of 'corn of seven colours', each colour pertaining to a planetary god. Nevertheless, it is worth while bearing in mind the most essential of these correspondences. For example: fire is represented by red and orange; air by yellow; both green and violet represent water; and black or ochre represent earth. Time is usually symbolized by a sheen as of shot silk. About the various shades of blue, ranging from near black to clear sapphire, there has been a great deal of speculation. The most relevant comments in our opinion are the following: 'Blue, standing for the vertical'—and the spatial, or the symbolism of levels—'means height and depth (the blue sky above, the blue sea below)' (32). 'Colour symbolizes an upward-tending force in the pattern of dark (or gloom and evil) and light (or illumination, glory and good). Thus, dark blue is grouped with black, and azure, like pure yellow, is coupled with white' (14). 'Blue is darkness made visible.' Blue, between white and black (that is, day and night) indicates an equilibrium which 'varies with the tone' (3). The belief that colours may be grouped in respect of their basic essentials, and within the general tendency to place phenomena in antithetical groups, according to whether they are of positive value (associated with light) or of negative (linked with darkness), is echoed even in present-day aesthetics, which bases the colour-system not upon the three primary colours of red, yellow and blue but upon the implied antithesis of yellow (or white) and blue (or black), taking red as the indirect transition between these two colours (the stages being: yellow, orange, red, violet, blue) and green as the direct (or summational) transition, this being the view of Kandinsky and Herbin. To sum up, those interpretations of colour symbolism which in our view have most importance: blue (the attribute of Jupiter and Juno as god and goddess of heaven) (56) stands for religious feeling, devotion and innocence (59); green (the colour pertaining to Venus and Nature) betokens the fertility of the fields (56), sympathy and adaptability (59); violet represents nostalgia and memories, because it is made up from blue (signifying devotion) and red (passion) (59); yellow (the attribute of Apollo, the sun-god) indicates magnanimity, intuition and intellect (56, 59); orange, pride and ambition (56, 59); red (the attribute of Mars), passion, sentiment and the life-giving principle (56, 59); grey, neutralization, egoism, depression, inertia and indifference—meanings derived from the colour of ashes (56, 59); purple (the colour of the imperial Roman paludament, as well as the Cardinal's) provides a synthesis comparable with, yet the inverse of, violet, representing power, spirituality and sublimation (56, 59); pink (the colour of the flesh), sensuality and the emotions (56, 59). One could go on with such interpretations *ad infinitum*, giving more and more exact meanings to more and more precise shades of colour, but to do so would be to fall into one of the traps of symbolism, that is, the temptation to evolve a hard-and-fast system of allegories. It is important, nevertheless, to bear in mind the analogy between the tone (that is, the intensity of a colour, or the degree of its brightness—its place on the scale between the opposite poles of black and white) and its corresponding level-symbolism. It must also be borne in mind that the purity of a colour will always have its counterpart in the purity of its symbolic meaning. Similarly, the primary colours will correspond to the primary emotions, whilst the secondary or tertiary colours will express symbols of like complexity. Children instinctively reject all mixed or impure colours, because they mean nothing to them. Conversely, the art of very advanced and refined cultures has always thrived upon subtle tones of yellowish mauve, near-violet pink, greenish ochres, etc. Let us now consider some of the practical applications of colour-symbolism, by way of clarification of the above. According to Beaumont, colour has a very special significance in Chinese symbolism, for it is emblematic of rank and authority; yellow for instance, because of its association with the sun, is considered the sacred privilege of the royal family (5). For the Egyptians, blue was used to represent truth (4). Green predominates in Christian art because of its value as a bridge between the two colour-groups (37). The mother goddess of India is represented as red in colour (contrary to the usual symbolism of white as the feminine colour), because she is associated with the principle of creation and red is the colour of activity *per se* (60). It is also the colour of blood, and for this reason prehistoric man would stain with blood any object which he wished to bring to life; and the Chinese use red pennons as talismans (39). It is for this reason too that when a Roman general was received in triumph he was carried in a chariot drawn by four white horses which were clad in gilt armour (as a symbol of the sun), and his face was painted red. Schneider, considering the essential bearing of the colour red upon alchemic processes, concludes that it is to be related to fire and purification (51). Interesting evidence of the ominous and tragic character of orange—a colour which in the view of Oswald Wirth is actually a symbol for flames, ferocity, cruelty and egoism—is forthcoming in the following passage taken from Heinrich Zimmer, the orientalist: 'After the Future Buddha had severed his hair and exchanged his royal garments for the orange-yellow robe of the ascetic beggar (those outside the pale of human society voluntarily adopt the orange-yellow garment that was originally the covering of condemned criminals being led to the place of execution) . . .' (60). To wind up these observations upon the psychic significance of colour, let us point to some correspondences with alchemy. The three main phases of the 'Great

Work' (a symbol of spiritual evolution) were (1) prime matter (corresponding to black), (2) mercury (white) and (3) sulphur (red), culminating in the production of the 'stone' (gold). Black pertains to the state of fermentation, putrefaction, occultation and penitence; white to that of illumination, ascension, revelation and pardon; red to that of suffering, sublimation and love. And gold is the state of glory. So that the series black—white—red—gold, denotes the path of spiritual ascension. The opposite or descending series can be seen in the scale beginning with yellow (that is, gold in the negative sense of the point of departure or emanation rather than the point of arrival), blue (or heaven), green (nature, or immediate natural life), black (that is, in the sense of the neoplatonic 'fall') (33). In some traditions, green and black are seen as a composite expression of vegetation manure. Hence, the ascending series of green—white—red, formed the favourite symbol of the Egyptians and the Celtic druids (54, 21). René Guénon also points to the significant fact that Dante, who knew his traditional symbology, has Beatrice appear in clothes coloured green, white and red, expressive of hope, faith and charity and corresponding to the three (alchemic) planes which we have already mentioned (27). The complex symbolism of mixed colours is derived from the primary colours of which they are composed. So, for example, greys and ochres are related to earth and vegetation. It is impossible to give any idea here of all the many notions which may be derived from a primal meaning. Thus, the Gnostics evolved the idea that, since pink was the colour of flesh-tints, it was also the colour of resurrection. To come back to the colour orange, the beautiful explanation of some allegorical figures in the alchemic *Abraham the Jew* contains a reference to orange as the 'colour of desperation', and goes on: 'A man and a woman coloured orange and seen against the background of a field coloured sky-blue, signifies that they must not place their hopes in this world, for orange denotes desperation and the blue background is a sign of hope in heaven.' And finally, to revert to green, this is a colour of antithetical tendencies: it is the colour of vegetation (or of life, in other words) and of corpses (or of death); hence, the Egyptians painted Osiris (the god of vegetation and of the dead) green. Similarly, green takes the middle place in the everyday scale of colours.

Colour (Positive/Negative) The conception of black and white as diametrically opposed symbols of the positive and the negative, either in simultaneous, in successive or alternating opposition, is very common. In our opinion it is of the utmost importance. Like all dual formulae in symbolism, it is related to the number two and the great myth of the Gemini. But some of its particular applications are of great interest; let us begin, for example, with the two sphinxes depicted in the seventh enigma of the Tarot pack. Here, one sphinx

is white and the other black (59). Again: there is a Catalan tale
which relates how some blackbirds which grew up near a magic
waterfall had snowy-white breasts, resembling the habits of Sisters
of Charity (10). In many primitive rites—medicinal dances, for
example—the dancers dress up in white clothes and blacken their
faces (51). The opposition of the two worlds (the subject of the
Gemini-symbol) finds its expression in Indo-Aryan mythology in
the portrayal of one white and one black horse (50). The 'water-
maidens' of Hispanic folklore wear white rings on the fingers of their
right hand and on their left wrist a gold, black-banded bracelet (10).
In Tibet, there are rites in which a man is chosen as the sacrificial
victim, and his face is painted half white and half black (21). Jung
recounts a dream of a man who saw himself as the pupil of a white
magician clothed in black who instructed him up to a certain point
beyond which—he was told in his dream—he would have to be
taught by a black magician dressed in white (34). Struggles between
black and white knights occur often in legends and folktales. There
is a Persian song which tells how a black knight defends a castle
against a white knight who fights valiantly to reach the treasure
within. Grimm has a myth of Lower Saxony which illustrates the
cosmic combat between the positive and the negative principles.
In Jung's version (31), it reads as follows: 'There was once a young
ash-tree that grew unnoticed in a wood. Each New Year's Eve a
white knight riding upon a white horse comes to cut down the
young shoot. At the same time a black knight arrives and engages
him in combat. After a lengthy battle the white knight overcomes
the black knight and cuts down the tree. But one day the white
knight will be unsuccessful, then the ash will grow, and when it is
big enough for a horse to be tethered under it, a mighty king will
come and a tremendous· battle will begin' (implying the destruction of time and the world). Black, in fairly generalized terms, seems
to represent the initial, germinal stage of all processes, as it does in
alchemy. In this connexion, Blavatsky points out that Noah released
a black crow from the ark before he sent out the white dove. Black
crows, black doves and black flames figure in a great many legends.
They are all symbols closely related to the primal (black, occult or
unconscious) wisdom which stems from the Hidden Source (9).
Here, Jung points to the relevance of the 'dark night' of St. John
of the Cross and the 'germination in darkness' of the alchemists'
nigredo. Let us remember too that darkness for both Victor Hugo
and Richard Wagner signifies the maternal, and that light appearing
out of the gloom represents a kind of crystallization (33). Jung also
points out in this connexion that carbon—the predominant chemical
component in Man's organism—is black in so far as it is charcoal or
graphite, but that, in so far as it is a diamond (that is, crystallized

carbon), it is 'crystal-clear water' (32), thus underlining the fact that the profoundest meaning of black is occultation and germination in darkness (32). In this he is supported by Guénon, who maintains that black stands for all preliminary stages, representing the 'descent into hell', which is a recapitulation of (or an atonement for) all the preceding phases (29). Thus, the dark earth-mother—the Diana of Ephesus—was depicted with black hands and face, recalling the black openings of caves and grottos (56). This may also, of course, be concerned with a black woman, such as the one who appears in the Welsh tale of *Peredur* (Parsifal), implying the same sense of inferiority as in the case of the black man or the 'ethiops'. Amongst primitive peoples, black is the colour associated with inner or subterranean zones (9, 21). Black also sometimes comes to symbolize time (60), in contrast to white which represents timelessness and ecstasy. The function of white is derived from that of the sun: from mystic illumination—symbolically of the East; when it is regarded as purified yellow (that is, when it stands in the same relation to yellow as does black to the blue of the deep sea), it comes to signify intuition in general, and, in its affirmative and spiritual aspect, intuition of the Beyond. That is why the sacred horses of Greek, Roman, Celtic and Germanic cultures were white. Even today, in Dithmarschen in the south of Jutland, some people still recall the *Schimmelreiter*, a knight who would ride up on a white horse when the sea-dykes burst and a catastrophe threatened. Most of the words containing the root *alb*—Alberich, the alb-king or elf-king, the river Elbe, the Alps—allude to this shining light of the supernatural (16). According to Guénon, in *Le Roi du Monde*, the colour white represents the spiritual centre, Tula (Thule), the so-called 'white island', which, in India, is identified with the 'land of the living' or paradise. This is the same as mount Meru. Guénon believes that it also explains the etymology of the many geographical names containing *albo* (Alba Longa, the original city of Rome; Albion, Albano, Albany, Albania, etc.). In Greek, Argos has a similar meaning; and from it is derived *argentum*, silver-white. Nevertheless, the colour white, symbolically, does not relate to silver but to gold. Conversely, white, in so far as its negative quality of lividness goes, is (like green and greenish yellow) symbolic also of death (50) and the moon, the latter being the symbolic source of a number of rites and customs. Eliade mentions moonlight dances performed by women with faces painted white (17). This principle of antithetical dualism is illustrated in a great number of allegories and symbols. The night, as the mother of all things, has been portrayed with a veil of stars, carrying two children in her arms, one white and the other black (4). Very common in Slavonic myth were Bielbog and Chernobog, the

white and the black god respectively (35), closely related to the
Gemini. The Ouroboros of the *Codex Marcianus* (of the 2nd century
A.D.) has its top half black and the lower white; this inversion of the
expected order imparts a sense of cyclic movement to the figure,
further emphasized by the circular impulse suggested by the fact of its
biting its tail. It is easy to recognize the bearing this has upon the
binary symbol of the Chinese *Yang-Yin*, and indeed upon every
system of graphic symbolism based upon opposites (32). This,
then, is a question of an inversion-symbol—one of the basic strands
in traditional symbolism—which helps to explain the ceaseless
alternations of life/death, light/darkness and appearance/disappear-
ance which make possible the continued existence of phenomena.
There is a beautiful, double, complex symbol in the Rigveda (III, 7, 3)
which well illustrates this dynamic, alternating dualism: fire,
although clear and bright in the sky (or the air), leaves black traces
on earth (that is a charred object). Rain, although black in the sky
(as rain-clouds), becomes clear on earth (50). This weaving and
unravelling of the strands of all the pairs of opposites is precisely
the import of the positive/negative aspects of white/black, which we
have sought to explain above. The Gemini, a symbol of the necessity
of nature to transmute itself into binary and contradictory aspects,
is represented by both white and black (51). But mankind has
groped towards a way out of the terrible circle divided into two
sections by a sigmoid line (such as that symbolized by the *Yang-Yin*)
and this way is that indicated by the axis white/red or red/gold.
Here we would again recall that the ascending scale of colours is
black—white—red. Loeffler, in his examination of mythic birds in
legend, links those which are black with inspiration of the mind,
those which are white with eroticism and those which are red with
the supernatural. We would also emphasize that in symbolism of
mediaeval Christian art, black stands for penitence, white for
purity and red for charity and love. Through love, then, man can
find the way out of the closed, double circle. Pinedo recounts that
St. Bernard's mother, while she was pregnant, dreamed of a white
dog with a red back. A similar case to this is that of Blessed
Juana of Aza, the mother of St. Dominic Guzman, who went on
a pilgrimage to the tomb of St. Dominic of Silos to beg of him the
favour of a son. The saint appeared to her and promised her that
her wish would be granted, and she looked down and saw at her feet
a white dog with a flaming torch in its mouth (46). In alchemy,
white/red is the conjunction of opposites, or the *coniunctio solis et
lunae*. Two-headed eagles and representations of the Rebis (a
human-being with two heads) are usually coloured white and red,
signifying the sublimation of the black/white antithesis. Also
characteristic of alchemy is the curious white and red rose, symboliz-

ing the union of water with fire. 'My beloved is white and ruddy', so sings the *Song of Songs* (v. 10), and the lily and the rose are essential symbols of white and red implicit in all mystic thought (46). When two colours are contrasted in a given symbolic field, the inferior colour is feminine in character and the superior is masculine. By 'inferior' we mean that which is lower within the alchemic order or series, which runs as follows: yellow, blue, green, black, white, red, gold. So, to take the black/white relationship, black is inferior and feminine; or, in the case of red/gold, gold is superior and masculine (or celestial, as against the terrestrial implications of the feminine principle). Any symbolic composition that, spatially, does not conform with this order presents us with a clear-cut example of Symbolic Inversion (q.v.). For example, in the normal symbolic pattern, white will be placed above black, red above white, and so on.

Column   The single column pertains to the cosmic group of symbols representing the 'world-axis' (such as the tree, the ladder, the sacrificial stake, the mast, the cross), but also it may have a merely endopathic sense deriving from its vertical nature, implying an upward impulse of self-affirmation. Of course, there is a phallic implication too; for this reason, the ancients ascribed a column and a dolphin to Ceres as emblems of love and the sea respectively (8). The isolated column is, in short, as closely related to the symbolic tree as to the ritual erection of the megalithic stone or menhir. In allegories and graphic symbols there are nearly always two columns, not one. When they are situated on either side of a shield, they are equivalent to supporters, representing the balanced tension of opposing forces. They have a similar significance when they act as the supports of a lintel. In a cosmic sense, the two pillars or columns are symbolic of eternal stability, and the space between them is the entrance to eternity. They also allude to Solomon's temple (the image of the absolute and essential principles of building) (4). Variants of this symbol—or rather of its significance—are to be found in esoteric thought; nearly all of them are the result of applying the symbolism of the number two to the dual columns. Taking them as separate symbols, the two units making up the number two are different in kind. For the first unit corresponds to the masculine, affirmative and evolutive principle, whereas the second represents the feminine, negative, passive or involutive. It is for this reason that Saunier gives the particular significance of the two columns rising up at the entrance to temples as that of evolution and involution, or of good and evil (comparable with the Tree of Life and the Tree of Death—or Knowledge—in the Garden of Eden). On occasion, this abstract duality goes hand in hand with the physical duality of the material; thus, in the legendary temple of

Hercules at Tyre, one of the columns was made of gold and the other of a semi-precious stone (49). In Hebrew tradition, the two columns are known as Mercy and Severity (9). To return now to the single column, we cannot fail to see in it a projection of—or an analogous correspondence with—the spinal column; the same kind of correspondence is to be seen in all forms of bilateral symmetry in art, as well as in such organs of the human body as the kidneys or the lungs. The vertebral column may be equated also with the world-axis, in the same way as the skull-image is equated with the sky, within the general relationship of the microcosm and the macrocosm.

Comb According to Schneider the relationship between the comb and the (rowing-) boat is so close that both symbols seem to merge in a way that is suggestive of the reconciliation of fire and water (19). Since the comb is the attribute of some fabulous, female beings, such as lamias and sirens, there is in consequence a relationship between it and the fleshless tail of the fish, in turn signifying burials (or the symbolism of sacrificial remains—for instance the bucraneum—or of devouring).

Compasses An emblematic representation of the act of creation (37), found in allegories of geometry, architecture and equity (8). By its shape, it is related to the letter A, signifying the beginning of all things (4). It also symbolizes the power of measurement, of delimitation.

Concord Concord expresses conformity, reconciliation and harmony in diversity, or the state of peace reached between beings or between the various forces and urges of being; its symbol is the linking of hands or arms, an embrace, or interlacing lines. It is an essential concept in the *Psychomachia* (the Struggle of the Soul) by the Hispanic Latin poet Aurelius Prudentius Clemens (348-410), author also of the *Peristephanon* (the Book of Crowns). On the other hand, the analogy between the pairs: consonance—dissonance and concord—discord, is evident. For that reason, dissonance intensifies all warlike expressions in music, as in Varèse's *Arcana*.

Cone The symbolic significance of the cone is very complex and may be derived from the association of the circle with the triangle. In Byblus it was a symbol of Astarte, but in various parts of Syria, according to Frazer, it was symbolic of the sun—further indication that it can be given no precise meaning. It can also be taken as a symbol deriving from the pyramid (21); it would then signify psychic Oneness.

Conjunction A great many symbols touch upon the great myth of *coniunctio* or unification, representing the *coincidentia oppositorum* and, more particularly, the reconciliation of the separate sexes in an eternal synthesis, after the platonic legend. In Jungian psychology, this conjunction has a purely psychological meaning within the psyche of one individual, as a counterpart of and a substitute for the synthesis achieved through platonic love between two different beings. Mystic longing has its being in the profound yearning for absolute unity of all that is particularized and separate. In conjunction, then, lies the only possibility of supreme peace and rest. The union of heaven and eartl in primitive, astrobiological religions is a symbol of conjunction, as is also the legendary marriage of the princess with the prince who has rescued her (33, 38).

Constellation In Chinese symbolism, it is the third Element. The first is the active, bright force called *Yang*, and the second the passive, dark force called *Yin*. The constellation signifies the connexion between the Upper and the Lower Worlds, or what binds together all that is different. It is one of the imperial emblems (5).

Coral Coral is the aquatic tree. It therefore partakes of and blends together the symbolism on the one hand of the tree as the world-axis, and on the other that of the (lower) ocean or abyss. Hence, it may be equated with the roots of the terrestrial tree. On the other hand, being red in colour, it is also related to blood; hence it has, besides its abyssal connotation, a visceral significance which is well captured in alchemic symbolism (8). According to Greek legend, coral grew out of the drops of blood of the Gorgon Medusa.

Cornucopia In mythology, it was the goat Amalthea who fed the infant Jupiter with milk. Given that the general symbolism of the horn is strength, and that the goat has maternal implications, and in addition that the shape of the horn (phallic outside and hollow inside) endows it with a complex symbolism (including that of the *lingam*, or symbol of generation), it is easy to understand its allegorical use as the horn of abundance. Plobb points out also that the cornucopia is an expression of prosperity deriving from its association with the zodiacal sign of Capricorn (48).

Correspondences The theory of 'correspondences' is basic to symbolist tradition. The implications and scope of this theory are beyond measure, and any valid study into the ultimate nature of the universe must take it into account. But here we can give little more than a brief idea of its scope, with some particular instances. It is founded upon the assumption that all cosmic phenomena are limited and serial and that they appear as scales or series on separate planes; but this condition is neither chaotic nor neutral, for the components of one series are linked with those of another in their essence and in their ultimate significance. It is possible to marshal correspondences by forcing the components of any given scale or scales into a common numerical pattern: for example, it is not difficult to adapt the colour-scale from seven to eight colours, should one wish to equate it with the scale of temperaments laid down by modern character-study, or, for that matter, to reduce it from seven to six colours for some other comparable reason. But it is always preferable to make sure of the correspondences which exist (apparently) only in part between different patterns, rather than to force them into unnatural moulds. The attributes of the ancient gods were really nothing less than unformulated correspondences: Venus, for example, was felt to correspond with the rose, the shell, the dove, the apple, the girdle and the myrtle. There is also a psychological basis for the theory of correspondences, related to synaesthesia. Louis-Claude de St. Martin comments in his *L'Homme du désir*: 'Things were not as they are in our gloomy dwelling, where sounds can be likened only to other sounds, colours to other colours, one substance to another; there everything was of a kind. Light gave out sounds, melody brought forth light, colours had movement because they were alive; objects were at once sonorous, diaphanous and mobile enough to intermix and flow in a line through all space" (3). In Schneider's view, the key to all systems of correspondences is music. He points to a treatise by Sârngadeva in the Indian *Samgîta Ratnâkara* (I, iii, 48) of the 13th century which expounds the mystic relationship between music and animals. He comments that nothing similar is to be found in the West, although he suggests that the capitals of San Cugat del Vallés and those at Gerona (of the 12th century) portray a series of animals which, being disposed in a kind of scale, are somewhat comparable. He points likewise to Jakob Böhme and Athanasius Kircher, both of whom sought to incorporate all these ideas into their systems of mystic correspond- ences (*Musurgia universalis*) (50). Ely Star offers a somewhat crude explanation of correspondences: 'Each of the colours of the prism is analogous to one of the seven faculties of the human soul, to the seven virtues and the seven vices, to geometric forms and to the planets, etc.' (55). Clearly there are certain correspondences of meaning and situation in the physical world itself. For example, sound is the more shrill (or higher) the faster it moves, and vice versa; hence, speed corresponds to height and slowness to lowness, within a binary system. If cold colours are retrogressive, then coldness corresponds to distance, and warmth to nearness; here, then, we have another scientifically demonstrable correspondence. Taking the septenary system, Star suggests some correspondences between colours and musical notes, which we find exact enough: violet (the leading-note); red (the tonic); orange (the super-tonic); yellow (the mediant); green (the sub-dominant); blue (the dominant); indigo (the sub-mediant) (54). The Greeks, the Cabbalists and the Gnostics founded a great deal of their philosophy upon the theory of correspondences. Porphyry mentions the following, between the Greek vowels and the planets: alpha corresponding to the moon; epsilon to Mercury; eta to Venus; iota to the sun; omicron to Mars; upsilon to Jupiter; and omega to Saturn. Again: within the novenary system, he underlines the significance of the Hindu theory of 'modes', that is: the erotic, heroic, odious, furious, terrible, pathetic, marvellous, agreeable, humorous. The symbolism of plants, scents and animals is often based upon the theory of correspondences or derivations of it. To mention a few: the oak (by association with the sun), the walnut (with the moon), the olive tree (with Mercury), the pine (with Saturn); the correspondence may range from the most obvious (such as that of the oak allied with strength, or the palm tree with victory) to the less obvious (47). Among the most important of systems of correspondences is the Zodiac; corresponding to the twelve signs of the Zodiac, one finds the months of the year, the tribes of Israel, the labours of Hercules, and the colour-scale adapted to include twelve colours. Vital also is that relating to the parts of the human body: Aries (corresponding to the head), Taurus (the neck and throat), the Gemini (the shoulders and arms), Cancer (the chest and stomach), Leo (the heart, lungs and liver), Virgo (the belly and intestines), Libra (the backbone and marrow), Scorpio (the kidneys and genitals), Sagittarius (the thighs), Capricorn (the knees), Aquarius (the legs) and Pisces (the feet) (54). The first six signs form an involutive series which corresponds to the 'descending' colour-series of the alchemists, that is, from yellow, through blue and green, down to black. The evolutive series corresponds to the 'ascending' metamorphosis from black, through white and red, up to gold. Schneider, who has made a very useful study of correspondences, refers to Alberuni's *The Book of Instructions in the Elements of the Art of Astrology*, 1934, where the author relates the signs of the Zodiac with the principal elements of landscape: Aries corresponds to the desert, Taurus to the plains, the Gemini to twin mountain-peaks, Cancer to parks, rivers and trees, Leo to a mountain with castles and palaces, Virgo to the homestead, Scorpio to prisons and caves, Sagittarius to quicksands and centres of magic, Capricorn to fortresses and castles, Aquarius to caverns and sewers, Pisces to tombs (50). Piobb has also shown that there are correspondences between the signs of the Zodiac and the processes of the alchemists (48).

Cosmogony The basis of most cosmogonies is the 'cosmic sacrifice', expressing the idea that the creation of forms and matter can take place only by modifying primordial energy. Such a modification, so far as most primitive and protohistoric peoples are concerned, was seen to exist in such painful forms as mutilation, struggle or sacrifice. In Babylonian cosmogony it assumed the form of the killing of the original mother Tiamat (the dragon), whose body was used in the creation of heaven and earth (31). Hindu tradition links the struggle of the gods with a tribe of devils called Asuras, or with monsters of some other kind. According to the Rigveda, the gods would sacrifice a primeval being—the giant Purusha. In Persia it was a bull which was sacrificed by Ahriman or Mithras. In Scandinavia it was the giant Ymir who was dismembered by the Aesir gods and then used as the material for the creation of the world (35). Clearly, then, these cosmogonies have a psychological implication because they express the central idea that there is no creation without sacrifice, no life without death (this being the basis of all inversion-symbolisms and of the Gemini). Here we have the origin of all the bloody sacrifices of the world's religions. It is to the Chinese writer Huai-nan-tzǔ that we owe a more advanced cosmogony which, while incorporating certain of the above ideas, takes its inspiration mainly from the conception of the cosmos as a new order imposed upon primigenial chaos. Here is Wilhelm's version of this interesting passage of Huai-nan-tzǔ (58): 'The collapse of heaven had still taken no definite form. It was floating and swimming and was known as the great light. When the Sense began in the empty chaos of clouds, the cloud-chaos engendered space and time. Space and time engendered force. Force had fixed limits. The pure and clear floated upwards and formed heaven. The heavy and the muddy coagulated below to form earth. . . . The seed of heaven and earth is the union of the clear and the obscure. The concentrated seeds of the obscure and the clear are the four seasons. The scattered seeds of the four seasons is the quantity of things. The heat-force of the clear, when concentrated, engenders fire. The seed of fiery force is the sun. The cold strength of the dark, when concentrated, is water. The seed of water is the moon. . . . The path of heaven is round. The path of the earth is square. The essence of the round is the clear.' Every eschatological process is a partial regeneration of the universe, partaking of the cosmogonic and hence of the sacrificial. Similarly, it is not possible to transform the human soul in any way, except through sacrifice.

Cow   Associated with the earth and with the moon. A great many lunar goddesses wear the horns of a cow on their head. When linked with the primigenial goddess Neith, the cow is a mother-symbol, representing the primal principle of humidity and endowed with certain androgynous—or gynandrous, rather—characteristics (31). In Egypt it was linked with the idea of vital heat (39). *Vac*, the feminine aspect of Brahma, is known as the 'melodious Cow' and as the 'Cow of abundance', the first description stemming from the idea of the world's creation out of sound, while the second—as hardly needs be said—comes from its function of nourishing the world with its milk, the fine dust of the Milky Way. In this we can see also the idea of heaven as a fecundating bull, with its sex inverted; in Hindu belief, the bull and the cow represent the active and the passive aspects of the generating forces of the universe (40).

Crane In cultures ranging from the Chinese to those of the Mediterranean, the crane is an allegory of justice, longevity and the good and diligent soul (51).

Creation In the Egyptian system of hieroglyphics, the whole process of creation is expressed by four signs: the spiral, as the symbol of cosmic energy; the squared spiral, as the symbol of the workings of this energy within the heart of matter; a formless mass, of self-evident meaning; and the square, as a symbol of organized matter (19). There is, then, a duality of the greatest theoretical importance—two paths: that by which abstract energy develops towards energy as an organizing force, and that followed by pure matter towards a state of matter ruled by a given order. Here lies the explanation of the process of all creation in its two most essential aspects: that of energy-content, and that of material form.

Cremation Death at the stake, the consummation of sacrifice through fire, and, from the mystic point of view, any kind of cremation, are all symbols of sublimation, that is, of the destruction of what is base to make way for what is superior; or, in other words, salvation of and through the spirit. This is the significance of the self-sacrifice of Hercules. It was a very common symbol among the alchemists. For example, the 24th emblem in Michael Maier's *Scrutinium Chymicum* (1687) shows a wolf—representing prime matter—burning in the furnace (32).

Crescent There is a dual significance to this symbol. In so far as it pertains to the moon, it stands for the world of changing forms or of phenomena, for the passive, feminine principle, and for things aquatic. Secondly, in mediaeval emblems of the Western world, and especially when associated with a star, it is a symbolic image of paradise (4).

Crest Because of its position on the helmet (linked symbolically with the head), the crest clearly stands for thought, and comes to be a symbol of the predominating theme—the *leitmotiv*—of the knight, which he displays as a token of his beloved (that is, his anima) and so giving tangible expression to his adventures and his combats. The encaged bird of Walter von der Vogelweide (of the 13th century) is probably an emblem of a soul yearning to fly away in freedom.

Crisis Man tends to question his destiny mostly in moments of crisis, that is, when the stream of life (either the stream within him of his feelings and passions, his abnormal urges or sense of inadequacy, or that flowing outside him—the flood of obstacles and failures in communication) goes against him or carries him along farther than he would wish. There is, then, a primordial desire in Man to experience 'inversion', that is, to find the technique whereby everything of a kind can be transmuted into its opposite. So, for example, illness inverted becomes health, hate becomes love, loneliness company, ignorance wisdom, dissension solidarity, rancour forgiveness, sadness happiness, the enemy's victory turns to rout and drought to fertility. Such inversion at first appears as a cross-roads, that is, as a potentiality. Then it takes the form of symbols of sacrifice, expressing the latent—and valid—idea that in every negative situation there is a direct or an indirect sense of guilt. Then, finally, come the symbols of Inversion proper and of rebirth.

Crocodile Two basically different aspects of the crocodile are blended in its symbolic meaning, representing the influence upon the animal of two of the four Elements. In the first place, because of its viciousness and destructive power, the crocodile came to signify fury and evil in Egyptian hieroglyphics (19); in the second place, since it inhabits a realm intermediate between earth and water, and is associated with mud and vegetation, it came to be thought of as an emblem of fecundity and power (50). In the opinion of Mertens Stienon there is a third aspect, deriving from its resemblance to the dragon and the serpent, as a symbol of knowledge. In Egypt, the dead used to be portrayed transformed into crocodiles of knowledge, an idea which is linked with that of the zodiacal sign of Capricorn. Blavatsky compares the crocodile with the Kumara of India (40). Then, finally, come the symbols of Inversion proper and of rebirth.

Cromlech It corresponds to the general symbolism of stone-monuments and is related to fertility cults. Eliade mentions that, in popular European beliefs even today, there are remnants of the ancient faith in the powers of large stones. The space between these rocks or stones, or the holes in the stones themselves, played an important part in fertility and health rites. The cromlech is regarded as a symbol of the Great Mother, whereas the menhir is clearly masculine (17).

Cronos By Cronos we mean here not so much the general symbolism of Saturn as those images of time which originated in oriental thought, and which were so common in the Lower Roman Empire. He is sometimes portrayed with four wings, two of which are outspread as if he were about to take flight, and two are lowered as if he were resting; this is an allusion to the dualism of time: the passage of time, and ecstasy (or transport beyond time). Sometimes he was also depicted with four eyes, two in front and two behind; this is a representation of simultaneity and of the position of the Present between the Past and the Future, a symbolism comparable with the two faces of Janus (8). More characteristic of the general symbolic meaning is the 'Mithraic Cronos', a deity representing infinite time, derived from the Zervan Akarana of the Persians. He has a rigid, human figure, and sometimes is bi-somatic:

a human body with the head of a lion. But when the head is human, then the lion's head is located on the breast. The trunk is enclosed in the five folds of an enormous snake—again denoting the duality of time: the passage of time intertwining with eternity—which, according to Macrobius, represents the path of the god along the celestial ecliptic. The lion, which is generally associated with sun-cults, is here a particular emblem of destructive and all-consuming time. It occurs in this sense in many representations of Roman as well as mediaeval funerals.

Crook The hooked staff is a pastoral attribute in the Church and a symbol of faith (4). By virtue of the sigmoid significance of the hook, it stands for divine power, communication and connexion (50); because of its spiral form it is a symbol of creative power.

Cross The complex symbolism of the cross neither denies nor supplants the historical meaning in Christianity. But in addition to

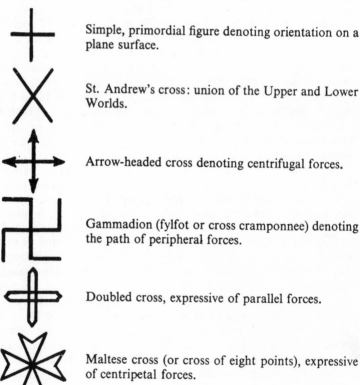

Simple, primordial figure denoting orientation on a plane surface.

St. Andrew's cross: union of the Upper and Lower Worlds.

Arrow-headed cross denoting centrifugal forces.

Gammadion (fylfot or cross cramponnee) denoting the path of peripheral forces.

Doubled cross, expressive of parallel forces.

Maltese cross (or cross of eight points), expressive of centripetal forces.

the realities of Christianity there are two other essential factors: that of the symbolism of the cross as such and that of the crucifixion or of 'suffering upon the cross'. In the first place, the cross is dramatic in derivation, an inversion, as it were, of the Tree of Paradise. Hence, the cross is often represented in mediaeval allegory as a Y-shaped tree, depicted with knots and even with branches, and sometimes with thorns. Like the Tree of Life, the cross stands for the 'world-axis'. Placed in the mystic Centre of the cosmos, it becomes the bridge or ladder by means of which the soul may reach God. There are some versions which depict the cross with seven steps, comparable with the cosmic trees which symbolize the seven heavens (17). The cross, consequently, affirms the primary relationship between the two worlds of the celestial and the earthly (14). But, in addition, because of the cross-piece which cuts cleanly across the upright (in turn implying the symbols of level and of the axis of the world), it stands for the conjunction of opposites, wedding

Cross of the Templars: forces disposed around a circumference.

Teutonic cross: four triangles denoting a centripetal tendency.

Cross of ovals, composed of one continuous line representative of the direction of movement of forces.

Cross with knobbed extremities representing the four Cardinal Points of space.

Lunate cross, representing (according to Piobb) the four tangential circumferences and the phases of the moon.

the spiritual (or vertical) principle with the principle of the world of phenomena. Hence its significance as a symbol for agony, struggle and martyrdom (14). Sometimes the cross is T-shaped, further emphasizing the near-equilibrium of the opposing principles. Jung comments that in some traditions the cross is a symbol of fire and of the sufferings of existence, and that this may be due to the fact that the two arms were associated with the kindling sticks which primitive man rubbed together to produce fire and which he thought of as masculine and feminine. But the predominant meaning of the cross is that of 'Conjunction'. Plato, in *Timaeus*, tells how the demiurge joins up the broken parts of the world-soul by means of two sutures shaped like St. Andrew's cross (31). Bayley stresses the fire-symbolism of the cross, and explains that all the words for 'cross' (crux, cruz, crowz, croaz, krois, krouz) have a common etymological basis in *-ak*, *-ur* or *-os*, signifying 'light of the Great Fire' (4). The cross has been widely used as a graphic emblem, very largely as a result of Christian influence but equally on account of the basic significance of the sign; for it is clear that all basic notions, whether they are ideas or signs, have come about without the prompting of any cultural influence. Hundreds of different shapes of crosses have been summarized in works such as Lehner's *Symbols, Signs and Signets*, and it has been found possible, by the study of graphic symbolism, to elucidate the particular meaning of each one. Many of them take the form of insignias of military orders, medals, etc. The swastika is a very common type of cross (q.v. *Swastika*). The Egyptian, anserated cross is particularly interesting in view of its antiquity. In Egyptian hieroglyphics it stands for life or living (*Nem Ankh*) and forms part of such words as 'health' and 'happiness'. Its upper arm is a curve, sometimes almost closed to form a circle. Enel analyses this hieroglyphic as follows: 'The phonetic significance of this sign is a combination of the signs for activity and passivity and of a mixture of the two, and conforms with the symbolism of the cross in general as the synthesis of the active and the passive principle.' The very shape of the anserated cross expresses a profound idea: that of the circle of life spreading outwards from the Origin and falling upon the surface (that is, upon the passivity of existence which it then animates) as well as soaring up towards the infinite. It may also be seen as a magic knot binding together some particular combination of elements to form one individual, a view which would confirm its characteristic life-symbolism. It may also signify destiny. Judged from the macrocosmic point of view, that is of its analogy with the world, the *Ankh*-cross may represent the sun, the sky and the earth (by reference to the circle, the upright and the horizontal lines). As a microcosmic sign, that is by analogy with man, the circle would represent the human head or reason (or the 'sun' which gives him life), the horizontal arm his arms, and the upright his body (19). In sum, the most general significance of the cross is that of the conjunction of opposites: the positive (or the vertical) with the negative (or horizontal), the superior with the inferior, life with death. The basic idea behind the symbolism of crucifixion is that of experiencing the essence of antagonism, an idea which lies at the root of existence, expressing as it does life's agonizing pain, its cross-roads of possibilities and impossibilities, of construction and destruction. Evola suggests that the cross is a synthesis of the seven aspects of space and time, because its form is such that it both maintains and destroys free movement; hence, the cross is the antithesis of the Ouroboros, the serpent or dragon denoting the primeval, anarchic dynamism which preceded the creation of the cosmos and the emergence of order. There is, thus, a close relationship between the cross and the sword, since both of them are wielded against the primordial monster (Plate V).

Cross-roads According to Jung, it is a mother-symbol. He comments: 'Where the roads cross and enter into one another, thereby symbolizing the union of opposites, there is the "mother", the object and epitome of all union.' Amongst the Ancients, cross-roads were symbols of an ambivalent theophany, since the joining up of three elements always presupposes the existence of the three principles of the active (or beneficent), the neutral (or resultant or instrumental) and the passive (or hurtful). Hence, cross-roads were sacred to the 'triform' Hecate. It was at the crossways that dogs were sacrificed to her, and the bodies of hanged men dumped (31).

Crow Because of its black colour, the crow is associated with the idea of beginning (as expressed in such symbols as the maternal night, primigenial darkness, the fertilizing earth). Because it is also associated with the atmosphere, it is a symbol for creative, demiurgic power and for spiritual strength. Because of its flight, it is considered a messenger. And, in sum, the crow has been invested by many primitive peoples with far-reaching cosmic significance. Indeed, for the Red Indians of North America it is the great civilizer and the creator of the visible world. It has a similar meaning for the Celts and the Germanic tribes, as well as in Siberia (35). In the classical cultures it no longer possesses such wide implications, but it does still retain certain mystic powers and in particular the ability to foresee the future; hence its caw played a special part in rites of divination (8). In Christian symbolism it is an allegory of solitude. Amongst the alchemists it recovers some of the original characteristics ascribed to it by the primitives, standing in particular for *nigredo*, or the initial state which is both the inherent characteristic of prime matter and the condition produced by separating out the Elements (*putrefactio*) (32). An interesting development of crow-symbolism is the representation of it with three legs drawn within a solar disk. In this form it is the first of the Chinese imperial emblems, and represents *Yang* or the active life of the Emperor. The three legs correspond to the sun-symbolism of the tripod: first light or rising sun, zenith or midday sun, and sunset or setting sun. In Beaumont's view, the crow in itself signifies the isolation of him who lives on a superior plane (5), this being the symbolism in general of all solitary birds.

Crowd   The idea of the 'crowd' is symbolically superior to that of 'multiplicity', since it implies a new concept of the numerous as a totality, or of Oneness as a fragmented whole. Thus, Jung's interpretation of the multitude or crowd is well judged; he asserts that, especially when moving or restless, it corresponds to an analogous movement in the unconscious (31). Homer has a well-known simile in which he likens a crowd of warriors in the *agora* (or in battle) to the ocean swell (constituting another symbol of the unconscious).

Crown   The essential meaning of the crown is derived from that of the head, with which it is linked—unlike the hat—not in a utilitarian but in a strictly emblematic manner. By reference to level-symbolism, we may conclude that the crown does not merely surmount the top of the body (and of the human being as a whole), but rises above it and therefore symbolizes, in the broadest and deepest sense, the very idea of pre-eminence. That is why a superlatively successful achievement is spoken of as a 'crowning achievement'. Hence, the crown is the visible sign of success, of 'crowning', whose significance reaches beyond the act to the person who performed it. At first, crowns were made out of the limbs of various trees, hence they are still connected with the symbolism of trees in general and of some trees in particular. They were the attributes of the gods; and they also were once a funeral-symbol (8). The metal crown, the diadem and the crown of rays of light, are symbols of light and of spiritual enlightenment (4). In some books of alchemy there are illustrations showing the planetary spirits receiving their crown—that is, their light—from the hands of their king—that is, the sun (32). The light they received from him is not equal in intensity but graded, as it were, in hierarchies, corresponding to the grades of nobility ranging from the king down to the baron (32). Books on alchemy also stress the affirmative and sublimating sense of the crown. In *Margarita pretiosa*, the six base metals are first shown as slaves, with their uncovered heads bowed low towards the feet of the 'king' (that is, gold); but, after their transmutation, they are depicted wearing crowns on their heads. This 'transmutation' is a symbol of spiritual evolution whose decisive characteristic is the victory of the higher principle over the base principle of the instincts. That is why Jung concludes that the radiant crown is the symbol *par excellence* of reaching the highest goal in evolution: for he who conquers himself wins the crown of eternal life (31). Secondary or more particular meanings sometimes arise from the shape or the material of the crown, on occasion differing considerably from the basic meaning outlined above. The ancient crown of the Egyptian pharaohs is a typical example of unusually shaped crowns with exceptional meanings. Marqués-Rivière here points to the emblematic and near-figurative source of its two basic components: a white and a red crown. The former is similar to the mitre-like bonnets worn in the East through the ages. The latter 'according to de Rochemonteix, is probably a pattern evolved from adapted hieroglyphs. The coif is probably a glass, the curved stem of which represents vegetation and the upright stem the ideogram of the earth. . . . M. E. Soldi sees the curved stem as a "projection of the solar disk, a spiralling flame which fertilizes the seeds" ' (39).

Crucifixion The symbolic meaning of the crucifixion—which does not oppose nor alter the historic fact, but provides further explanations of it—seems to be related to the suffering which is at the root of all contradiction and ambivalence, especially if one bears in mind the practice in mediaeval iconography of showing Jesus on the cross surrounded by symmetrical pairs of objects or beings. These paired items are sometimes, but not always, based upon the actual witnesses of the scene. Thus, the cross may be shown between the sun and the moon, between the Virgin and St. John, the good and the bad thief, the lance and the cup or chalice (or sometimes a stick and the sponge soaked in vinegar), and, of course, between heaven and earth. On occasion, there is the added symbol of the Holy Spirit balancing Adam's skull. These pairs of opposites, then, only serve to emphasize the essential binary system underlying the cross itself. The horizontal limb corresponds to the passive principle, that is, to the world of phenomena. The vertical limb denotes the active principle, that is, the transcendent world or spiritual evolution. The sun and moon are the cosmic representatives of this dualism, echoed also in the symmetrical placing of the Beloved Disciple and the Holy Mother (of opposite sexes) who stand also, respectively, for the outcome and the antecedent of the life and work of Jesus, and hence for the future and the past. The two thieves represent binary symmetry on the moral plane, that is, the two potential attitudes between which Man must choose: penitence leading to salvation and prevarication leading to damnation.

Crutch The symbolic meaning of the crutch derives directly from its literal sense: the invisible, moral or economic means of supporting any other form of existence that may 'lean' upon it. In this sense it has often appeared in Salvador Dali's paintings. It forms one of the Chinese emblems, again with the same significance (5). Frequently the crutch stands for an immoral, hidden or shameful support; this is because the foot is a symbol of the soul (15), and an infirmity or mutilation of the foot is the counterpart of an incurable defect of the spirit. Hence, in legends and adventure-stories, the common appearance of sinister characters, pirates, thieves and immoral hypocrites with crutches that bespeak their symbolic lameness. For a man to seek to revenge himself upon the cause of his mutilation shows that in his spirit he still retains some of his moral strength and that he will endure until he has been vindicated. This is the symbolic background to the famous novel *Moby Dick*, in which the protagonist has his leg torn off by the monster of the deeps, but pursues it dauntlessly to the end.

Crystal Like precious stones, it is a symbol of the spirit and of the intellect associated with the spirit (56). It is interesting to note that mystic and surrealist alike share the same veneration for crystal. The 'state of transparency' is defined as one of the most effective and beautiful conjunctions of opposites: matter 'exists' but it is as if it did not exist, because one can see through it. As an object of contemplation, it offers neither hardness nor resistance nor suffering.

Cube Among solid forms, it is the equivalent of the square. Hence it stands for earth, or the material world of the four Elements. Denis the Carthusian pointed out that cubic objects are not capable of rotation as are spheres, and that therefore they represent stability (14). This explains why the cube frequently forms part of allegories illustrating the solidity and the persistence of the virtues (8). It also explains why, in symbols and emblems, thrones or chariots are sometimes given cubical form.

Curl (or **Loop**) In the Egyptian system of hieroglyphs, the loop is a determinative sign defining the ideas of either binding or unbinding, depending upon the position of the loose ends (19). It corresponds to the general symbolism of bonds and knots. The hair-curl takes its meaning from the symbolism of the hair.

Curtain A symbol of separation, as in the 'veil of the Temple' in Jerusalem. According to Gershom Scholem, 'curtains hanging before the celestial realms of the worlds of the aeons play an important rôle in the Gnostic *Pistis Sophia*, apparently as a result of Jewish influence'. The succession of curtains is related to that of cloaks or veils, or even elements of dress and adornment, as they appear in the Mesapotamic poem of *Ishtar's Descent into Hell*. The action of parting curtains, rending veils or clothing, stripping off diadems, cloaks or bracelets, signifies a move towards an *arcanum* or the penetration of a mystery. Scholem, in *Les Origines de la Kabbale*, says that, among the emanations, similar curtains appear personified in the fountains of Isaac Cohen.

Cybele This goddess, the wife of Saturn, is the personification of the energy animating the earth. The lions drawing her chariot represent the controlled energies necessary for evolution; the chariot in which she is riding is cubic in shape, the cube being a symbol of the earth. Her crown is shaped like a battlemented wall, and this, like the cube, also conveys a sense of building. Associated on occasions with this allegory, is a seven-pointed star (a symbol of cyclic progression) and a lunar crescent (a symbol of the world of phenomena, of the appearance and disappearance of earthly forms in the sublunary world).

Cycle The cyclic character of phenomena—cyclic, that is, because of the tendency of the final stage to curve back towards the initial stage of the process in question—leads to its being symbolized by figures such as the circle, the spiral and the ellipse. All processes are cyclic in this way, embracing movement in space, passage through time, and any change in form or condition, whether they are cycles pertaining to the year, the month, the week, the day, or the span of life of a man, a culture or a race. The symbolism of the Zodiac and the division into twelve (four times three and vice versa) are inextricably linked with the symbolic meaning of the cycle (40, 51). Graphically, the completed cycle is represented by two signs or images facing in opposite directions, symbolic of the acts of going and coming. This can be seen for example in Roman steles, having footprints pointing in opposite directions.

Cyclops A mythological giant, commonly portrayed as having a single eye in the middle of his forehead. This eye does not have the usual symbolism of the 'third' eye, but in this case, appears to symbolize the primary forces of nature.

Cydippe A man with one leg and one foot, found in Romanesque decoration. It is the antithesis of the figure of the two-tailed siren. If the latter is a symbol of femininity, arising out of the number two, the cydippe is symbolic of masculinity arising out of the uneven number one. It may also have some connexion with the figures of Hermes, and perhaps has a phallic significance.

Cypress A tree dedicated by the Greeks to their infernal deity. The Romans confirmed this emblem in their cult of Pluto, adding the name 'funeral' to it, a significance which still clings to it today (8).

Dactyls Mythic dactyls or fingers are related to the Cabiri (q.v.), and correspond to chthonian cults, their function being to link the nether world with the terrestrial (31). Symbolically they may be seen as those forces of the psyche which ordinarily go unheeded but which help as much as hinder the conscious projects of the reason. For Jung they figure among the symbols of 'multiplicity' which form around the essential elements of the psychic structure.

Daena In the ancient Iranian religion, the Daena symbolized the feminine principle (*Anima*) of the human spirit, while at the same time identifying it with the sum of the actions—good and bad—that man performs during his life. On the third day after his death, the just man is greeted on the bridge of Çinvat by a wondrously beautiful young girl, the Daena, who becomes united with him for eternity, thus reconstituting the primordial Androgyne. On a higher plane, the Cabbala needed to give reality to the principle of the eternal feminine and gave the name of Shekhinah to the 'feminine aspect of God'. The Shekhinah is a complex entity—possibly one of Jehovah's angels or Jehovah himself; in every case it is the Loved One referred to in the Song of Solomon. A. E. Waite, in *Secret Doctrine in Israel* (1913), points out that this spiritual principle bears no relation to that represented by the Virgin Mary of Christianity, but is related rather to the Holy Spirit of the Trinity. He observes that the Shekhinah is the angel who comes to the aid of those just men who are suffering, above all if they are suffering for love, and that her work in the soul is analogous to that of the soul in the body. The Daena, as has been stated, does not attain such an elevated position in the hierarchy and should rather be identified with the Jungian *anima*.

Dance   The corporeal image of a given process, or of becoming, or of the passage of time. In Hindu doctrine, the dance of Shiva in his rôle as Natarâjâ (the King of the Cosmic Dance, symbolizing the union of space and time within evolution) clearly has this meaning (6). There is a universal belief that, in so far as it is a rhythmic art-form, it is a symbol of the act of creation (56). This is why the dance is one of the most ancient forms of magic. Every dance is a pantomime of metamorphosis (and so calls for a mask to facilitate and conceal the transformation), which seeks to change the dancer into a god, a demon or some other chosen form of existence. Its function is, in consequence, cosmogonic. The dance is the incarnation of eternal energy: this is the meaning of the circle of flames surrounding the 'dancing Shiva' (60). Dances performed by people with linked arms symbolize cosmic matrimony, or the union of heaven and earth—the chain-symbol—and in this way they facilitate the union of man and wife (51).

Darkness   Equated with matter, with the maternal and germinant, but it pre-exists the differentiation of matter (9). The dualism of light/darkness does not arise as a symbolic formula of morality until primordial darkness has been split up into light and dark. Hence, the pure concept of darkness is not, in symbolic tradition, identified with gloom—on the contrary, it corresponds to primigenial chaos. It is also related to mystic nothingness, and, in consequence, Hermetic language is an *obscurum per obscurius*, a path leading back to the profound mystery of the Origin. According to Guénon, light is the basic principle behind differentiation and hierarchical order. The gloom which preceded the *Fiat Lux* always, in traditional symbolism, represents the state of undeveloped potentialities which give rise to chaos (29). Hence, the darkness introduced into the world, after the advent of light, is regressive; hence, too, the fact that it is traditionally associated with the principle of evil and with the base, unsublimated forces.

Day of Rest Like so many other aspects of existence—both in customs and in utilitarian activities—the concept of the Day of Rest does not arise from material or empirical necessity (even leaving aside the religious implications). According to Erich Fromm, the observance of the Sabbath amongst the Hebrews does not denote mere repose for reasons of health, but rather something much more profound. In effect, because work implies a state of change—of war—between man and the world around him, it follows that rest designates peace between him and Nature. One day a week —a day which, by virtue of the analogy between time and cosmic space, corresponds to the idea of the centre implicit in the position of the sun among the planets or the location of the earth according to the geocentric system—must be set aside for experiencing the spontaneous, perfect harmony of man in Nature. By not working, the human being can break away from the order of change which gives rise to history, and thereby free himself from time and space to return to the state of paradise (23). This symbolism provides the explanation, furthermore, of what Bell called 'the fiery restlessness of the rebel': the instinctive hatred of all forms of rest characteristic of the man of warlike spirit who challenges all Nature and the world as it appears to the senses.

Death Symbolically, death represents the end of an epoch, particularly when it takes the form of sacrifice or the desire for self-destruction in the face of unendurable tension (as with Romeo and Juliet, or Tristan and Isolde). The hero dies young for this same reason: Siegfried, Achilles or Balder for example. The public necessity for a sacrifice of this kind was what lay behind the 'ritual assassination of the king' in which the possibility of his survival was sometimes left open, should he prove victor in combat. As an example of this rite, Frazer cites a festival called 'The Great Sacrifice' in which the king of Calicut was made to hazard his crown and his life. It took place every twelve years, at the time the planet Jupiter turns back towards the constellation of Cancer, since there was a supposed relationship between the planet and the king's destiny (21).

Death, The The thirteenth enigma of the Tarot pack. This playing-card shows the well-known allegory of the skeleton with the difference that here, contrary to custom, he wields his scythe towards the left. And the bones of the skeleton are not grey but pink. The ground is strewn with human remains, but these remains, like

those in legend and folklore, have the appearance of living beings
—heads, for instance, keep their living expression; hands emerging
from the ground seem ready for action. Everything in this enigma-
card tends to ambivalence, underlining the fact that if life is, in
itself, closely bound up with death (as Heraclitus pointed out and as
mediaevalists and modern scientists have corroborated), death is
also the source of life—and not only of spiritual life but of the
resurrection of matter as well. One must resign oneself to dying in a
dark prison in order to find rebirth in light and clarity. In the same
manner as Saturn pruned the tree in order to rejuvenate it, so Siva
(or Shiva) transforms beings by destroying their form without
annihilating their essence. On the other hand, death is the supreme
liberation. In the positive sense, then, this enigma symbolizes the
transformation of all things, the progress of evolution, dematerialization; in the negative, melancholy decomposition, or the end of
anything determinate and therefore comprehended within a period
of time (59). All allegories and images of death have the same
significance. In Greek mythology, death was envisaged as the
daughter of the night and the sister of sleep. Horace depicts death
with black wings and a net for snaring his victims (8), a net which is
identical with that of the Uranian gods as well as that of the Roman
gladiator. Death is related to the Element earth and to the range of
colours from black, through the earth-coloured shades, to green.
It is also associated with the symbolism of manure.

Decapitation Ritual decapitation arose from the discovery in
prehistoric times that the head is the receptacle of the spirit. The
preservation of heads, as practised by certain primitive peoples,
holds the same significance as the separate burial of that part of the
body. The same symbolic meaning is attached to the decorative
use of sculpted heads, set at particular vantage points in many
mediaeval temples, such as Clonfert Cathedral, in Ireland.

Decorations (or **Medals**) The inverse of wound-symbolism.
They denote sublimation and glorification, and are related to the
red/white principle of alchemy.

Defile (or **Gorge**) Within the symbolism of landscape as a whole,
the gorge corresponds to the lower regions and is therefore closely
related to the maternal, the unconscious and, ultimately, to the
forces of evil. If the cavern, or the hollow interior of a mountain,
are authentic illustrations of the unconscious, which remains unknown or enigmatic or is experienced indirectly, then the gorge—
and the fissure—is a symbol of a crack in the conscious life through
which the inner pattern of the individual psyche, or of the world-
soul, may be glimpsed (32). Because of its associations with strategy,
or with other derived ideas, the gorge also incorporates the notion
of danger. By its shape, it implies a sense of inferiority in the face of

overwhelming odds (suggested by the mountains or masses of earth and rock which in effect constitute the gorge). On the other hand, these negative considerations may themselves be negated by the symbolism implicit in the fact that water often runs along the bed of the gorge—and water is always related to birth, regeneration and purification; this is further proof that the gorge has a maternal symbolism.

Deluge   The tradition of the deluge, or of several deluges, is to be found in all parts of the world, with the exception of Africa (35). Science appears to have verified its historical reality. Within the symbolic relationship between the moon and water, the deluge, according to Eliade, corresponds to the three days of the 'death of the moon'. As a catastrophe, the deluge is never represented as final, because it takes place under the sign of the lunar cycle and of the regenerating properties of water. It destroys forms, in other words, but not forces, thus leaving the way open for the re-emergence of life (17). Consequently, apart from its material connotation, the deluge always stands for the final stage of a cycle, coinciding with the zodiacal sign Pisces (9). Torrential rains always retain some of the great symbolic content of the deluge; every fall of rain is tantamount to purification and regeneration, which in turn imply the basic idea of punishment and completion.

Desert   It has a profound and clear-cut symbolism. Berthelot observes that the Biblical prophets, in order to counter the agrarian religions based on fertility rites (related, according to Eliade, to orgies), never ceased to describe theirs as the purest religion of the Israelites 'when they were in the wilderness'. This confirms the specific symbolism of the desert as the most propitious place for divine revelation, for which reason it has been said that 'monotheism is the religion of the desert' (7). This is because the desert, in so far as it is in a way a negative landscape, is the 'realm of abstraction' located outside the sphere of existence (37), susceptible only to things transcendent. Furthermore, the desert is the domain of the sun, not as the creator of energy upon earth but as pure, celestial radiance, blinding in its manifestation. Again: if water is associated with the ideas of birth and physical fertility, it is also opposed to the concept of the everlasting spirit; and, indeed, moisture has always been regarded as a symbol of moral corruption. On the other hand, burning drought is the climate *par excellence* of pure, ascetic spirituality—of the consuming of the body for the salvation of the soul. Tradition provides further corroboration of this symbolism: for the Hebrews, captivity in Egypt was a life held in opprobium, and to go out into the desert was 'to go out from Egypt' (48). Finally, let us point to the emblematic relationship of the desert with the lion, which is a sun-symbol, verifying what we have said about the solar symbolism of the desert.

Destruction   The traditional symbols of destruction are always ambivalent, whether we take the thirteenth mystery of the Tarot, the twelfth sign of the Zodiac (Pisces), the symbolism of water or fire, or of any form of sacrifice. Every ending is a beginning, just as every beginning contains an end; this is the essential idea of the symbols of mystic 'Inversion' which Schneider has subjected to such careful study. All this, then, should be borne in mind when we read such observations as the following by Rudolf Steiner (taken from *La Philosophie de la Liberté*): 'To transform being into an infinitely superior non-being, that is the aim of the creation of the world. The process of the universe is a perpetual combat . . . which will end only with the annihilation of all existence. The moral life of man, then, consists in taking part in universal destruction.' This 'destruction'—like the alchemic process— concerns only phenomena, or what is separate in space (the disjunct or the remote) and in time (the transitory). This is why Steiner entitled a collection of his poems *Destruction or Love*.

Devil, The   The fifteenth mystery of the Tarot pack. It takes the form of Baphomet (of the Knights Templars) portrayed as having the head and feet of a he-goat and the bosom and arms of a woman. Like the Greek sphinx, it incorporates the four Elements: its black legs correspond to the earth and to the spirits of the nether world; the green scales on its flanks allude to water, the undines, and dissolution; its blue wings to sylphs and also to bats (because the wings are membranous); and the red head is related to fire and salamanders. The aim of the devil is regression or stagnation in what is fragmentary, inferior, diverse and discontinuous. Finally, this Tarot mystery-card is related to the instincts and to desire in all its passionate forms, the magic arts, disorder and perversion (59).

Devouring   This symbol, which finds its literal expression in the act, or the fear, of being devoured, is to be found in modified form in the notion of Entanglement, and also, according to Diel, in that of sinking into mud or a swamp. Jung, in connexion with this, quotes the Biblical passage about Jonah and the whale, but Jonah is really better associated with the 'Night Sea-Crossing'. Jung also thinks (31) that fear of incest becomes fear of being devoured by the mother, and that this is then disguised by the imagination in such forms as the witch who swallows up children, the wolf, the ogre, the dragon, etc. On the cosmic plane, the symbol doubtless relates to the final swallowing up by the earth of each human body after death, that is, to the dissolution of the body, so that the symbol may well be related to digestion. In consequence, all those stories which 'have a happy ending', in which children who have been swallowed whole still live inside the animal and eventually escape, refer no doubt to the Christian dogma of the hope of resurrection in the flesh.

Dew All that comes down from the heavens (the thunderbolt, the aerolite, the meteorite, rain or dew) has a sacred character. But dew has a double significance, alluding also to spiritual illumination, since it'is the true forerunner of dawn and of the approaching day (33). The clear, pure water of dew is, according to some traditions, closely connected with the idea of light. There are occasional references in the Far East to the 'tree of sweet dew' situated on mount Kuen-Lun, the equivalent of the Hindu Meru and other sacred mountains symbolizing the world-axis. Light spreads outwards from this tree (25), and, through the process of synaesthesia, it has come to be known as the 'singing tree' of legend and folklore.

Diamond Etymologically, it comes from the Sanskrit *dyu*, meaning 'luminous being'. It is a symbol of light and of brilliance. The word 'adamantine' is connected with the Greek *adamas*, meaning 'unconquerable' (4). In emblems, it often indicates the irradiant, mystic 'Centre' (56). Like all precious stones, it partakes of the general symbolism of treasures and riches, that is, moral and intellectual knowledge.

Diana The goddess of woods, related to nature in general and to fertility and wild animals (21). She bears the Greek name of *Hecate*, meaning 'She who succeeds from afar', and she is therefore linked with the 'Accursed Hunter' (such as Wotan). Accompanied by dogs, she becomes a night-huntress, in turn linked with the demons of chthonian cults (31). It has been pointed out that her characteristics vary with the phases of the moon: Diana, Jana, Janus. This is why some mythological and emblematic designs show her as Hecate with three heads, a famous, triform symbol which—like the trident or the three heads of Cerberus—is the infernal inversion of the trinitarian form of the upper world. According to Diel, these threefold symbolic forms of the underworld allude also to the perversion of the three essential 'urges' of man: conservation, reproduction and spiritual evolution. If this is so, then Diana emphasizes the terrible aspect of Woman's nature. Nevertheless, because of her vows of virginity, she was endowed with a morally good character as opposed to that of Venus, as can be seen in the *Hippolytus* of Euripides.

Digestion A symbol for swallowing, mastery, assimilation and dissolution. What is 'undigested' is what cannot be dissolved, that is, what cannot be conquered or assimilated. The alchemists identified digestion with the dragon and with the colour green (representing the irreducible element of nature, in contrast with those substances which could be sublimated or transformed into spirit, or, in other words, 'digested'). Romanesque iconography is characterized by an extraordinary number of monsters swallowing or carrying in their belly or vomiting up animals, both real and fabulous, which they have devoured whole. The symbolism here must be that which we have just outlined, that is, parallel with yet contrary to the belief of the cannibal that by devouring and digesting the vital organs of his enemy he finally vanquishes him, incorporating within himself the potentialities of his victim.

Dionysos   An infernal deity, and a symbol of the uninhibited unleashing of desire, or of the lifting of any inhibition or repression (15). Nietzsche drew attention to the antithesis between Apollo and Dionysos as symbols of the extreme views of art and of life, drawing man, respectively, towards either order or chaos; or, in other words —in accordance with the Freudian death-wish—towards either existence and eternal life, or self-annihilation. The insatiable character of the Greek god—who is supposed to have come from Asia Minor or from Scythia—is apparent in the attributes commonly ascribed to him, such as the thyrsus surmounted by a phallic pine-cone, or the serpent, the horse, the bull, the panther, the he-goat and the hog. According to Jung, the Dionysos-myth signifies the abyss of the 'impassioned dissolution' of each individual, as a result of emotion carried to the extremes of paroxysm and in relation to the urge to escape from time into 'pre-time', characteristic of the orgy; the myth is therefore representative of an unconscious urge (32).

Disappearance   In many folktales, mediaeval legends and myths, sudden 'disappearances' occur. Sometimes this is as a result of the translation of the vanished object to a distant place, and sometimes as a result of pure and simple annihilation or destruction. Psychologically, this is a symbol of repression, particularly if the vanished object is malign or dangerous. In reality, it is a form of enchantment.

Disk   An emblem of the sun and also of the heavens. In China, the 'sacred disk' is a symbol of celestial perfection (5), and the disk that actually represents the sky (the jade disk called *Pi*) has a hole in the centre. The 'winged disk' is one of the most widespread of ancient symbols, which is still in use today in signs and emblems; in the profoundest sense, it represents matter in a state of sublimation and transfiguration. The two small serpents which are often to be seen next to the disk are those of the caduceus, alluding to the equipoise of opposing forces (59). But in a more esoteric sense, the winged disk signifies the disk in movement—in flight; it is therefore correctly used today in emblems created by an age which has learnt how to dominate the air and space.

Disguise   Disguise—or rather, 'transvestism'—finds its basis in the wearing of clothes belonging to the opposite sex. According to Eliade, this is a rite which is analogous to the symbolism of the orgy and frequently practised in it. Its purport is to resuscitate the hypothetical, primordial, androgynous being referred to by Plato in his Dialogues (17). Zimmer corroborates this symbolism, despite certain discrepancies, pointing out that in India there is a rite carried out every year at the beginning of the rainy season, in which an elephant is escorted in procession by men dressed as women, who in this way pay homage to maternal nature (60).

Disjunction Its simplest symbol is the letter Y, just as the letter X is the simplest symbol of inversion. It corresponds to the idea of a cross-roads, of a duality or multiplicity of divergent paths. In ancient images (14th–18th centuries), the cross of certain crucifixes is sometimes represented in the form of a Y.

Dismemberment An important symbol lies beneath the act of tearing to pieces, or tearing limb from limb. Let us begin with some examples of the way the symbol is used. The best known is the myth of Osiris torn to pieces by Set, who scattered the fragments which Isis then diligently sought out and pieced together again, one piece excepted. There are a great many legends and folktales which tell much the same story: giants' bodies are cut to pieces and then magically put together again. Siegmund's sword, in the Niebelungen saga, is broken in various places beyond repair; only Siegfried, his son, is capable of reforging it. According to Heinrich Zimmer, the dismemberment of the formless dragon Vritra, in Indian mythology, reveals the process whereby multiplicity sprang out of primigenial unity. Indian mythology also maintains that the creation of multiplicity was the outcome of the sin of Indra, whose expiation implies the reintegration of all existence into unity. Coomaraswamy maintains that the meaning of sacrifice is actually this creative and destructive movement—the systole and diastole of reality; present-day theories of cosmogony support this view (60). From the viewpoint of the individual and his spiritual life, it is interesting to note that the Graeco-Russian philosopher Gurdjieff (according to Ouspensky in his *In Search of the Miraculous*) founded his 'Institute for the Harmonic Education of Man' upon the basis of the need to end all dispersal (or 'dismemberment') of the attention and of spiritual Oneness. In their time, the alchemists had already found a way of symbolizing the state of inner separation of the spiritual components by means of the stages of the *opus*, which they called *solutio, calcinatio, incineratio*, portraying them sometimes in such emblems as personal sacrifices or mutilations of the body, such as cutting off the hands of the mother, or the claws of the lion, etc. (33). For Origen, the goal of Christianity was nothing less than the transformation of man into a being of inner Oneness. Conversely, for Jung, to be possessed by the unconscious (that is, by whims, manias and obsessions) is nothing short of being torn up into chaotic multiplicity. He also points out that the idea of displacement or *disiunctio* is the counterfoil to the growth of the child in the maternal womb (as well as to mystic *coniunctio*). In this way, then, every symbol which stands for an involutive, degenerating or destructive process is based upon the changing of unity into multiplicity, as, for example, the breaking of a rock into many fragments. Mutilations of the body, the prising apart of what is united, are so many symbols of analogous situations in the spirit.

Distaff   Like the spindle and the shuttle, the distaff symbolizes time, the beginning and the continuance of creation. Distaffs also have a sexual significance. They are the attributes of the Parcae, who spin the thread of life, and cut it short (56, 38).

Dog   An emblem of faithfulness, and it is in this sense that it appears so often at the feet of women in the engravings on mediaeval tombs; in the same way the lion, an attribute of the male, symbolizes valour (20). In Christian symbolism, the dog has another sense, deriving from the function of the sheep-dog: that of guarding and guiding the flocks, which at times becomes an allegory of the priest (46). In a more profound sense, though still related to the foregoing, the dog is—like the vulture—the companion of the dead on their 'Night Sea-Crossing', which is associated with the symbolisms of the mother and of resurrection. It has a similar significance when it appears in scenes depicting the Mithraic sacrifice of the bull (31). In alchemy, it was used as a sign rather than as a symbol. A dog devoured by a wolf represents the purification of gold by means of antimony.

Doll or Puppet   The doll, as a symbol, appears more often in psychopathology than in the main stream of traditional symbolism. It is well known that in a number of mental diseases the patient makes a doll which he keeps carefully hidden. According to J.-J. Rousseau the personality of the sick person is projected into the toy. In other cases it has been interpreted as a form of erotomania or deviation of the maternal instinct: in short, a hangover from, or regression to an infantile state. Recently, in so-called 'Pop-art', dolls have been included in 'informal' pictorial images. In Spain Modesto Cuixart has produced the most dramatic and profound work of this kind, the obvious symbolism of which is related to the 'putti' of Renaissance art, but, by a reversal of meaning, these dolls are made to appear maimed and soiled as if they were the corpses of children annihilated by bombs and other forces of destruction.

Dolphin   The figure of the dolphin can be seen in many allegories and emblems, sometimes duplicated. When the two dolphins—or even figures representing an indeterminate fish—are pointing in the same direction, the duplication may be obeying the dictates of the law of bilateral symmetry for merely ornamental reasons, or it may be a simple symbol of equipoise. But the inverted arrangement, that is, with one dolphin pointing upwards and the other downwards, always symbolizes the dual cosmic streams of involution and evolution; this is what the 17th-century Spanish writer Saavedra

Fajardo meant by 'Either up or down'. The dolphin by itself is an allegory of salvation, inspired in the ancient legends which show it as the friend of man. Its figure is associated with that of the anchor (another symbol of salvation), with pagan, erotic deities and with other symbols (20). The ancients also held that the dolphin was the swiftest of marine animals, and hence, when, among the emblems of Francesco Colonna, it is shown twined round an anchor, it comes to signify arrested speed, that is, prudence.

Door   A feminine symbol (32) which, notwithstanding, contains all the implications of the symbolic hole, since it is the door which gives access to the hole; its significance is therefore the antithesis of the wall. There is the same relationship between the temple-door and the altar as between the circumference and the centre: even though in each case the two component elements are the farthest apart, they are nonetheless, in a way, the closest since the one determines and reflects the other. This is well illustrated in the architectural ornamentation of cathedrals, where the façade is nearly always treated as if it were an altar-piece.

Double   Every case of duplication concerns duality, balanced symmetry and the active equipoise of opposite forces. Double images, the symmetrical duplication of forms or figures—such as the supporters in heraldry—symbolize precisely that. But any case of duplication based upon a horizontal axis, in which the upper figure is the inverse of the lower, has a deeper meaning arising from the symbolism of level. A dual being is often found in cabbalistic emblems, the upper figure being known as Metatron and the lower Samael; it is said of them that they are inseparable companions for life (57). It may well be that beneath this image there lies a symbol of the essential ambivalence of all phenomena, or, rather, that it refers to the great myth of the Gemini.

Dove   The Slavs believe that, at death, the soul turns into a dove (4). This bird partakes of the general symbolism of all winged animals, that is, of spirituality and the power of sublimation. It is also symbolic of souls, a motif which is common in Visigothic and Romanesque art (46). Christianity, inspired in the Scriptures, depicts the third person of the Trinity—the Holy Ghost—in the shape of a dove, although he is also represented by the image of a tongue of Pentecostal fire (4).

Dragon   A fabulous animal and a universal, symbolic figure found in the majority of the cultures of the world—primitive and oriental as well as classical. A morphological study of the legendary dragon would lead to the conclusion that it is a kind of amalgam of elements taken from various animals that are particularly aggressive and dangerous, such as serpents, crocodiles, lions as well as pre-historic animals (38). Krappe believes that the amazement occasioned by the discovery of the remains of antediluvian monsters may have been a contributory factor in the genesis of the mythic dragon. The dragon, in consequence, stands for 'things animal' *par excellence*, and here we have a first glimpse of its symbolic meaning, related to the Sumerian concept of the animal as the 'adversary', a concept which later came to be attached to the devil. Nevertheless, the dragon—like all other symbols of the instincts in the non-moral religions of antiquity—sometimes appears enthroned and all but deified, as, for example, in the standards and pennons pertaining to the Chinese Manchu dynasty and to the Phoenicians and Saxons (4). In a great many legends, overlaying its deepest symbolic sense, the dragon appears with this very meaning of the primordial enemy with whom combat is the supreme test. Apollo, Cadmus, Perseus and Siegfried all conquer the dragon. In numerous masterpieces of hagiography, the patron saints of knighthood—St. George and St. Michael the Archangel—are depicted in the very act of slaying the monster; there is no need to recall others than the St. George of Carpaccio, or of Raphael, or the St. Michael of Tous by Bermejo. For Dontenville (16), who tends to favour an historicist and socio-logical approach to the symbolism of legends, dragons signify plagues which beset the country (or the individual if the symbol takes on a psychological implication). The worm, the snake and the crocodile are all closely linked with the concept of the dragon in their own particular way. In France, the dragon is also related to the ogre as well as to Gargantua and giants in general. In Schneider's view, the dragon is a symbol of sickness (51). But before going further into its meaning, let us quote some examples to show how wide-spread are the references to this monster. The classics and the Bible very frequently allude to it, providing us with detailed information about its appearance, its nature and habits. But their descriptions point to not one but several kinds of dragon, as Pinedo has noted: 'Some give it the form of a winged serpent; it lives in the air and the water, its jaws are immense, it swallows men and animals having first killed them with its enormous tail. Conversely, others make it a terrestrial animal, its jaws are quite small, its huge and powerful tail is an instrument of destruction, and it also flies and feeds upon the blood of the animals it kills; there are writers who consider it to be amphibious, in which case its head becomes that of a beautiful woman with long flowing hair and it is even more terrible than the previous versions.' In the Bible, there are the following references to the dragon: Daniel xiv, 22, 27; Micah i, 8; Jeremiah xiv, 6; Revelation xii, 3, 7; Isaiah xxxiv, 13, and xliii, 20. There are further mentions by Rabanus Maurus (*Opera*, III), Pliny (VIII, 12), Galen, Pascal (*De Coronis*, IX), and among other characteristics which these writers ascribe to the dragon are the following particu-

larly interesting points: that it is strong and vigilant, it has exception-
ally keen eyesight, and it seems that its name comes from the Greek
word *derkein* ('seeing'). Hence it was given the function, in clear
opposition to its terrible implications, of guarding temples and
treasures (like the griffin), as well as being turned into an allegory of
prophecy and wisdom. In the Bible, it is the negative side of the
symbol which receives emphasis; it is interesting to note that the
anagram of Herod in Syrian—*ierud* and *es*—means 'flaming dragon'
(46). Sometimes the dragon is depicted with a number of heads and
its symbolism then becomes correspondingly unfavourable, given
the regressive and involutive sense of all numerical increase. 'And
behold a great red dragon, having seven heads and ten horns, and
seven crowns upon his heads', in the words of Revelation (xii, 3).
On other occasions, the dragon is used in emblems, in which case it
is the symbolism of the form or shape which takes precedence over
that of the animal, as for example, the dragon biting its tail—the
Gnostic *Ouroboros*, a symbol of all cyclic processes and of time in
particular. The dragon figured quite frequently in alchemy; for the
alchemists, a number of dragons fighting with each other illustrated
the state of *putrefactio* (separating out the Elements, or psychic
disintegration). And the winged dragon represented the volatile
element, while the wingless creature stood for the fixed element
(according to Albert Poison). It is perhaps in China that this monster
has been most utilized and has achieved its greatest degree of transfiguration. Here it becomes an emblem of imperial power. Whereas
the Emperor numbered the five-clawed dragon among his ornaments,
the officials of his court had the right to keep only the four-clawed (5).
According to Diel, the generic dragon of China symbolizes the
mastering and sublimation of wickedness (15), because the implication is that of a 'dragon conquered', like that which obeys St. George
once he has overcome it. Frazer tells how the Chinese, when they
wish for rain, make a huge dragon out of wood and paper and carry
it in procession; but if it does not rain, then they destroy the dragon
(21). Chuang-tzǔ maintains that this arises from the fact that the
dragon and the serpent, invested with the most profound and all-
embracing cosmic significance, are symbols for 'rhythmic life'. The
association of dragon/lightning/rain/fecundity is very common in
archaic Chinese texts (17), for which reason the fabulous animal
becomes the connecting-link between the Upper Waters and earth.
However, it is impossible to generalize about the dragon of Chinese
mythology, for there are subterranean, aerial and aquatic dragons.
'The earth joins up with the dragon' means that it is raining. It plays
an important part as an intermediary, then, between the two extremes
of the cosmic forces associated with the essential characteristics of
the three-level symbolism, that is: the highest level of spirituality;

the intermediary plane of the phenomenal life; and the lower level of inferior and telluric forces. A related and powerful part of its meaning is that of strength and speed. The oldest Chinese images of the dragon are very similar to those of the horse (13). In esoteric Chinese thought, there are dragons which are linked with colour-symbolism: the red dragon is the guardian of higher science, the white dragon is a lunar dragon. These colours derive from the planets and the signs of the Zodiac. In the Middle Ages in the Western world, dragons make their appearance with the throat and legs of an eagle, the body of a huge serpent, the wings of a bat and with a tail culminating in an arrow twisted back upon itself. This, according to Count Pierre Vincenti Piobb, signifies the fusion and confusion of the respective potentialities of the component parts: the eagle standing for its celestial potential, the serpent for its secret and subterranean characteristic, the wings for intellectual elevation, and the tail (because the form is that of the zodiacal sign for Leo) for submission to reason (48). But, broadly speaking, present-day psychology defines the dragon-symbol as 'something terrible to overcome', for only he who conquers the dragon becomes a hero (56). Jung goes as far as to say that the dragon is a mother-image (that is, a mirror of the maternal principle or of the unconscious) and that it expresses the individual's repugnance towards incest and the fear of committing it (31), although he also suggests that it quite simply represents evil (32). Esoteric Hebrew tradition insists that the deepest meaning of the mystery of the dragon must remain inviolate (according to the rabbi Simeon ben Yochai, quoted by Blavatsky) (9). The universal dragon (*Katholikos ophis*) of the Gnostics is the 'way through all things'. It is related to the concept of chaos ('our Chaos or Spirit is a fiery dragon which conquers all things'— Philaletha, *Introitus*) and of dissolution ('The dragon is the dissolution of bodies'). (The quotations are taken from the Pseudo-Democritus.) Regarding symbols of dissolution, Hermetic doctrine uses the following terms: Poison, viper, universal solvent, philosophical vinegar = the potential of the undifferentiated (or the *Solve*), according to Evola. He adds that dragons and bulls are the animals fought by sun-heroes (such as Mithras, Siegfried, Hercules, Jason, Horus, or Apollo) and—bearing in mind the equations woman = dragon, mercury and water; and green = 'what is undigested'—that 'if the dragon reappears in the centre of the "Citadel of Philosophers" of Khunrath, it is still a dragon which has to be conquered and slain: it is that which everlastingly devours its own self, it is Mercury as an image of burning thirst or hunger or the blind impulse towards gratification', or, in other words, Nature enthralled and conquered by Nature, or the mystery of the lunar world of change and becoming as opposed to the world of immutable being governed by Uranus. Böhme, in *De Signatura rerum*, defines a will which desires and yet has nothing capable of satisfying it except its own self, as 'the ability of hunger to feed itself' (Plate VI).

Drum   A symbol of primordial sound, and a vehicle for the word, for tradition and for magic (60). With the aid of drums, shamans can induce a state of ecstasy. It is not only the rhythm and the timbre which are important in the symbolism of the primitive drum, but, since it is made of the wood of 'the Tree of the World', the mystic sense of the latter also adheres to it (18). According to Schneider, the drum is, of all musical instruments, the most pregnant with mystic ideas. In Africa, it is associated with the heart. In the most primitive cultures, as in the most advanced, it is equated with the sacrificial altar and hence it acts as a mediator between heaven and earth. However, given its bowl-shape and its skin, it corresponds more properly to the symbolism of the Element of earth. A secondary meaning turns upon the shape of the instrument, and it should be noted that it is in this respect that there is most variation in significance. The three essential shapes are: the drum in the form of an hour-glass, symbolizing Inversion and the 'relationship between the two worlds' (the Upper and the Lower); the round drum, as an image of the world; and the barrel-shaped, associated with thunder and lightning (50).

Dryness   Dryness is the principle directly opposed to that of organic life. The latter is associated with the fertility of the soil—plants and animal life. Dryness, on the other hand, is an expression of the psychic 'climate'. It is a sign of virility, of passion, of the predominance of the Element of fire (2). The symbol of the 'sea king' as a spirit immersed in the deeps of the unconscious is a clear example, with his cry: 'The man who rescues me from the waters of the ocean and leads me to dry land will be rewarded with everlasting riches.' The waters here symbolize debased existence, subject to time and to things transitory, behaving in accordance with the feminine principle of 'wetness'. Dryness is an image of immortality (32); hence the tendency of individuals anxious to recover their strength of spirit—or to acquire it—to make for the desert, the 'dry landscape' *par excellence*; and hence the fact that a man with a 'dry' personality is, contrary to appearances and common belief, really intensely passionate. Eliade observes that to aspire to be dry is to express the longing for the fleshless, spiritual life, and he quotes Heraclitus' maxim that 'Death, for the soul, is to become as water'. And to quote a fragment of Orphic teaching: 'Water is the death of the soul' (Clement, *Strom.* VI, 2, 17, 1—Kern 226); and Porphyry (*De antro nymph.*, 10-11) explains that the souls of the dead tend towards water because of the desire for reincarnation (17).

Dualism   Dualism is defined as any system which implies a binary pattern, but which is characterized less by a complementary thesis and antithesis tending to resolve into a synthesis than by two opposed principles. The Manichean and Gnostic religions were moral dualisms. Some cosmic forms of division into two parts—such as the Chinese year split into two halves, one (*Yang*) in which the active and benign forces predominate, and the other (*Yin*) in which the passive and malign forces prevail—are binary systems rather than dualisms, because the double, contradictory aspects are synthesized within a system of wider scope. R. Bertrand, in *La Tradition secrète* (Paris 1943), speaking about this *Yang-Yin* symbol, observes: 'The dualism of religion (or of mystic or cosmic philosophy) is theoretical or superficial; in actual fact, there is always something extra—a third term which prevents the two opposing terms from cancelling each other out, forcing both these force-principles to yield, that is, to function alternately and not simultaneously. Thus, the black and white of the *Yin-Yang* bounded by the circle of stability, *t'ai-chi*, combine to form in effect a ternary system, the *Tao*.' However, this solution by means of the 'third term' serves less to 'resolve' the problem than to prolong it indefinitely, since it encourages the persistence of the dualist state by virtue of the inner equilibrium which it implies. It is as if, in the symbolism of alchemy, the twin currents—ascending and descending—of solution and coagulation were kept in perpetual rotation. But this is in fact not the case: the positive forces triumph in the end—they *transmute* matter (that is, the passive, negative or inferior principle), redeem it and bear it upwards. Dual symbols are extremely common. To mention a few: the lash and the crook of Egyptian pharaohs; emblems featuring cattle and agriculture, in which a straight and a curved sword symbolize the 'straight' and the 'oblique' path; the cabbalistic columns Jachin and Boaz; Mercy and Severity.

Duck See **Goose**.

Dumbness A symbol of the early stages of creation, and of the return to this pristine state. Hence legends often allude to someone struck dumb as a punishment for grave sins (which themselves imply just such a regression) (9).

Dummy Like the homuncule and the mandragora, the dummy is an image of the soul, in primitive belief. The same applies to the scarecrow, the doll and any figure that bears a human likeness. Hence the belief in its magic properties.

Duplication In symbolism, this is as common as Inversion. It may appear in the form of a double colour-image (standing for the positive/negative principles), or as a symmetrical pattern of dualism, or as a binary system based upon a common horizontal axis, in which case the symbolic meaning reflects the ambivalence of the form or being in question, since the symbol is able to indicate whether this form or being is located above or below the median level. Duplication is, furthermore, like the reflection in the mirror, a symbol of consciousness—an echo of reality. It corresponds to the symbolism of the number two (31).

Dwarf A symbol of ambivalent meaning. Like dactyls, elves and gnomes, the dwarf is the personification of those forces which remain virtually outside the orbit of consciousness. In folklore and mythology, the dwarf appears as a mischievous being, with certain childish characteristics befitting its small size, but also as a protector like the Cabiri—this being the case with the 'woodland dwarfs' in the tale of Sleeping Beauty. For Jung, they may be regarded as the guardians of the threshold of the unconscious (32). Now, smallness may be taken also as a sign of deformity, of the abnormal and inferior; this is the explanation, then, of the 'dancing Shiva' appearing as an image of a deity dancing upon the prostrate body of a demon-dwarf who symbolizes the 'blindness of life', or the ignorance of man (his 'pettiness'). Victory over this demon signifies true wisdom (60). It is probable that some such idea as this was in the mind of the Renaissance sculptor Leon Leoni when he fashioned the effigy of Charles I subduing Fury.

Eagle A symbol of height, of the spirit as the sun, and of the spiritual principle in general. In the Egyptian hieroglyphic system, the letter A is represented by the figure of an eagle, standing for the warmth of life, the Origin, the day. The eagle is a bird living in the full light of the sun and it is therefore considered to be luminous in its essence, and to share in the Elements of air and fire. Its opposite is the owl, the bird of darkness and death. Since it is identified with the sun and with the idea of male activity which fertilizes female nature, the eagle also symbolizes the father (19). It is further characterized by its daring flight, its speed, its close association with thunder and fire. It signifies, therefore, the 'rhythm' of heroic nobility. From the Far East to Northern Europe, the eagle is the bird associated with the gods of power and war. It is the equivalent in the air of the lion on earth; hence it is sometimes depicted with a lion's head (cf. the excavations at Tello). According to Vedic tradition, it is also important as a messenger, being the bearer of the soma from Indra. In Sarmatian art, the eagle is the emblem of the thunderbolt and of warlike endeavour. In all Oriental art it is often shown fighting; either as the bird Imdugud, who ties the terrestrial and the celestial deer together by their tails, or as Garuda attacking the serpent. In pre-Columbian America, the eagle had a similar symbolism, signifying the struggle between the spiritual and celestial principle and the lower world. This symbolism occurs also in Romanesque art. In ancient Syria, in an identification rite, the eagle with human arms symbolized sun-worship. It also conducted souls to immortality. Similarly, in Christianity, the eagle plays the rôle of a messenger from heaven. Theodoret compared the eagle to the spirit of prophecy; in general, it has also been identified (or, more exactly, the eagle's flight, because of its swiftness, rather than the bird itself) with prayer rising to the Lord, and grace descending upon mortal man. According to St. Jerome, the eagle is the emblem of the Ascension and of prayer (50). Among the Greeks it acquired a particular meaning, more allegorical than properly symbolic in nature, in connexion with the rape of Ganymede. More generally speaking, it was believed to fly higher than any other bird, and hence

Heraldic eagle.

was regarded as the most apt expression of divine majesty. The connexion between the eagle and the thunderbolt, already mentioned above, is confirmed in Macedonian coinage and in the Roman *signum*. The ability to fly and fulminate, to rise so as to dominate and destroy baser forces, is doubtless the essential characteristic of all eagle-symbolism. As Jupiter's bird it is the theriomorphic storm, the 'storm bird' of remotest antiquity, deriving from Mesopotamia and thence spreading throughout Asia Minor (35). On Roman coins it occurs as the emblem of imperial power and of the legions. Its fundamental significance does not vary in alchemy, it merely acquires a new set of terms applicable to the alchemic mystique: it becomes the symbol of volatilization. An eagle devouring a lion is the symbol of the volatilization of the fixed by the volatile (i.e. according to alchemical equations: wings = spirit; flight = imagination, or the victory of spiritualizing and sublimating activity over involutive, materializing tendencies). Like other animals, when in the sign of the Gemini, the eagle undergoes total or partial duplication. Thus arises the two-headed eagle (related to the Janus symbol) which is usually depicted in two colours of great mystical significance: red and white. In many emblems, symbols and allegories, the eagle is depicted carrying a victim. This is always an allusion to the sacrifice of lower beings, forces, instincts and to the victory of the higher powers (i.e. father principle, *logos*) (50). Dante even calls the eagle the bird of God (4). Jung, ignoring the multiple significance of its symbolism, defines it simply as 'height', with all the consequences that flow from a specific location in space. On the other hand the constellation of the Eagle is placed just above the man carrying the pitcher of Aquarius, who follows the bird's movement so closely that he seems to be drawn after it by unseen bonds. From this it has been inferred that Aquarius is to be identified with Ganymede, and also with 'the fact that even the gods themselves need the water of the Uranian forces of life' (40).

Ear of Corn   An emblem of fertility and an attribute of the sun (8). It also symbolizes the idea of germination and growth—of the development of any feasible potentiality. The sheaf has a symbolic significance which confirms that of the individual ear: it adds the ideas of integration and control inherent in the symbolism of a 'bunch' to that of fertility or increase implicit in the single ear. Generally speaking, all sheafs, bunches and sprays stand for psychic forces which are integrated and directed to a proper purpose (Plate VII).

Earth, The   The Northern hemisphere is regarded as that which represents light, corresponding to the positive principle *Yang*; the Southern is linked with that of darkness and corresponds to *Yin*. Hence, cultural movements pass from the Northern to the Southern hemispheres (40).

Earthquake   Most primitive and astrobiological cultures attribute the cause of the earthquake to a theriomorphic demon. In Japan, the earth is supposed to be supported by a huge fish; in Sanskrit literature by a turtle; in North America by a serpent. The earthquake partakes of the general significance of all catastrophes—the sudden change in a given process, which may be either for the better or for the worse. On occasion the earthquake is thought to promote fertility. Basically it is an application of the universal symbolism of sacrifice and of cosmic Inversion (35).

Effigy   Every effigy, as an image of a being, expresses the psychic aspect of that being. Hence, given Jung's contention that the magic and the psychic are practically the same thing, it becomes easy to understand the importance of effigies in magic. The burning of a person in effigy—an ancient practice that has still not been totally banished—does not, then, betoken merely the impotent spite of one who is unable to attack the real person—although this may well be a secondary consideration—but is an act against the image of that person, that is, against the impression that he has made in the minds of others—against his memory and his spiritual presence. One can explain keepsakes and portraits on a similar basis, for they are linked in the mind not so much with the real person they pertain to, as with the *imago* or projection of that person within us. The effigy, consequently, is a symbol of an image rather than of a being.

Effulgence According to Evola, is a symbol of the force of the undifferentiated, or of dissolution.

Egg A great many prehistoric tombs in Russia and Sweden have revealed clay eggs which had been left there as emblems of immortality (17). In the language of Egyptian hieroglyphs, the determinative sign of the egg represents potentiality, the seed of generation, the mystery of life (19). This meaning persisted among the alchemists, who added explicitly the idea that it was the container for matter and for thought (57). In this way was the transition effected from the concept of the egg to the Egg of the World, a cosmic symbol which can be found in most symbolic traditions—Indian, Druidic, etc. (26). The vault of space came to be known as an Egg, and this Egg consisted of seven enfolding layers—betokening the seven heavens or spheres of the Greeks (40). The Chinese believe that the first man had sprung from an egg dropped by Tien from heaven to float upon the primordial waters. The Easter egg is an emblem of immortality which conveys the essence of these beliefs. The golden egg from which Brahma burst forth is equivalent to the Pythagorean circle with a central point (or hole). But it was in Egypt that this symbol most frequently appeared. Egyptian naturalism—the natural curiosity of the Egyptians about the phenomena of life—must have been stimulated by the realization that a secret animal-growth comes about inside the closed shell, whence they derived the idea, by analogy, that hidden things (the occult, or what appears to be non-existent) may actively exist. In the *Egyptian Ritual*, the universe is termed the 'egg conceived in the hour of the Great One of the dual force'. The god Ra is displayed resplendent in his egg. An illustration on a papyrus, in the *Œdipus Ægyptiacus* of Kircher (III, 124), shows the image of an egg floating above a mummy, signifying hope of life hereafter. The winged globe and the beetle pushing its ball along have similar implications (9). The Easter-time custom of the 'dancing egg', which is placed in the jet of a fountain, owes its origin, according to Krappe (who refers only to the Slavs), to the belief that at that time of the year the sun is dancing in the heavens. The Lithuanians have a song which runs as follows: 'The sun dances over a mountain of silver; he is wearing silver boots on his feet'(35).

Egypt A traditional symbol of the animal in man (57). Hence, 'to go out of Egypt' is to abandon the sensual and the material and to progress towards the Promised Land across the Red Sea and the desert: to progress towards a superior, transcendent state (46). The symbol is a Gnostic one.

Elements, The   The four-part distribution of the Elements, which, strictly speaking, corresponds to the three states of matter plus the agent which, through them, brings about the transformation of matter, corresponds to the concept, so often illustrated in symbolism, of the stability of the number four and its derived laws. Earth (or solids), water (or liquids), air (or gas) and fire (the temperature which brings about the transformations of matter) have been conceived in the West from pre-Socratic days onwards as the 'Cardinal Points' of material existence, and, by a close parallel, also of spiritual life. It is for this reason that Gaston Bachelard observes (3): 'Earthly joy is riches and impediment; aquatic joy is softness and repose; fiery pleasure is desire and love; airy delight is liberty and movement.' Jung stresses the traditional aspects: 'Of the elements, two are active—fire and air, and two are passive—earth and water.' Hence the masculine, creative character of the first two, and the feminine, receptive and submissive nature of the second pair (33). The arrangement of the Elements in hierarchal order of importance or priority has varied from age to age and writer to writer; one of the factors influencing this has been the question of whether or not to admit a 'fifth Element', sometimes called 'ether', sometimes freely designated 'spirit' or 'quintessence' in the sense of 'the soul of things'. It will readily be understood that the hierarchical progression must proceed from the most spiritual down to the most material, since creation is involution or materialization. Beginning, then, with the fifth Element at the Origin, identifying it with the power of the demiurge, next comes air (or wind) and fire, next water and lastly earth; or, in other words, deriving from the igniferous or aerial state comes the liquid and finally the solid. The connexion of the fifth Element (considered simply as the beginning of life) with air and fire is self-evident. Schneider, commenting upon Hindu tradition, observes that: 'We can establish tne equation: sound equals breath, wind, the principle of life, language and heat (or fire)' (50). Now, Schneider goes on to say—and his criterion is here mainly psychological—that the *orientation* of the Elements is an important factor always to be held in mind; for example, fire oriented towards earth (or towards water) is an erotic Element, yet pointed towards air it stands for purification. He mentions the four mystic beings of Chinese mythology who express the fusion of two Elements: the phoenix combining fire and air, the green dragon air and earth, the tortoise earth and water, and the white tiger water and fire (50). Bachelard suggests that, within the psychic life (or artistic inspiration), no image is capable of accommodating the four Elements, since such an amalgamation would be tantamount to neutralization or insufferable contradiction. True images, in his view, are unitary or binary; they can mirror monotones of one substance or the conjunction of two (2). By virtue of the theory of correspondences, the Elements may be associated, up to a certain point, with the four ages and the points of the compass.

Elephant Elephant-symbolism is somewhat complex for it embraces certain secondary implications of a mythic character. In the broadest and universal sense, it is a symbol of strength and of the power of the libido (42). Indian tradition has it that elephants are the caryatids of the universe. In processions, they are the bearers of kings and queens. It is interesting to note that, because of their rounded shape and grey colour, they are regarded as symbols of clouds. By a twist of magic thought, there arose first the belief that the elephant can create clouds and then the mythic postulate of winged elephants. A mountain-top or a cloud, elephant-like in outline, could represent an axis of the universe (60), and this idea—clearly primitive in origin—is probably what lies behind the use of the elephant in the Middle Ages as an emblem of wisdom (49), of moderation, of eternity, and also of pity (8).

Emblems When the use of emblems was at its most widespread (16th–18th centuries), it was sometimes the custom to create true variations on an emblem, usually religious, basing them on the symbolic syntax. We have given a few examples of emblems based on the Sacred Heart.

Emperor, The The fourth mystery in the Tarot pack. Here it takes the allegorical form of a figure seated upon a throne which is a cube of gold. Above him is a black eagle. In his hands he holds a globe of the world and a sceptre surmounted by a fleur-de-lis. The crest of his helmet includes four triangles, emblems of the four Elements. The predominantly red colour of his garments signifies invigorating fire, or intense activity. This Tarot mystery is closely related to the image of Hercules holding his club and the golden apples which he has taken from the garden of the Hesperides. The golden cube of the throne represents the sublimation of the constructive and material principle, and the fleur-de-lis on the sceptre, illumination. In sum, then, the symbolism of this card concerns magnificence, energy, power, law and severity; and, on the negative side, domination and subjection (59).

Empress, The The third enigma of the Tarot. She is shown full face, drawing herself up with hieratic stiffness. A smile plays upon her face, framed by fair hair. Her attributes are the sceptre, the fleur-de-lis and a shield with a silver eagle upon a purple background (an emblem of the sublimated soul in the bosom of spirituality). In the positive sense, this playing-card denotes the ideal, sweetness, domination by affective persuasion. In the negative sense, it stands for vanity and seduction (59).

Emptiness   This is an abstract idea, the antithesis to the mystic concept of 'Nothingness' (which is reality without objects and without forms yet nurturing the seed of all things). In the Egyptian system of hieroglyphs, the hollow is defined as 'that place which is created out of the loss of the substance required for the building of heaven', and is thus related to space. On the sarcophagus of Seti I, there is an image of emptiness consisting of the half-full vessel of Nu (or Nou) which forms an inverted semicircle completed by a second semicircle located towards one side of the first (19).

Enchantment   'Enchantment' is a reduction to an inferior state. It is a metamorphosis in a descending direction, appearing in myths, legends and stories as a punishment or as the work of a malign power. It may be the transformation of a person into an animal (as in the case of the story of Circe, related in the *Odyssey*), or into a plant or a stone, as occurs in many folktales. The enchantment of the earth takes the form of a loss of fertility, as in Eliot's *The Waste Land*, which reproduces the situation created by the sin and the wounding of Amfortas in the story of *Parsifal*. Enchantment can also take the form of disappearance, translation to a distant place, or illness (generally: paralysis, dumbness, blindness). In such cases, it represents self-punishment or a punishment from above, as we stated earlier. In 'traditional' tales, if the enchantment is the work of a malign power (necromancer, black magician, sorcerer, dragon, etc.), it will always be lifted by the action of a hero who providentially intervenes with his powers of salvation and liberation.

Enclosure   The walled city is also an image of the 'spiritual centre'. It appears to have been portrayed thus by Domenico di Michelino in his image of Dante; and it also appears frequently in this guise in the Middle Ages as the 'celestial Jerusalem'.

Enigma   In alchemy, the enigma alludes to the relationship between the macrocosm and the microcosm (57). This means that, so far as traditional symbolism goes, the enigmatic aspect of a thing is expressive of its transcendence. Eliade bears out this point with his comment that the surprising thing about kratophanies and theophanies is that they have their origins in primitive societies— and also, we might add, in the All (17). But, more than this, since the enigma is in a way synonymous with the symbol, it also confirms the metaphysical nature of all symbolism. The enigma is also a literary genre (frequently with an esoteric meaning), especially cultivated—along with hieroglyphics and emblems—in the 16th to 18th centuries. Some enigmas that enjoyed great standing in England and Ireland in the 7th and 8th centuries must be considered as antecedents, as Marguerite M. Dubois has shown in *La Littérature anglaise du Moyen Age* (Paris, 1962).

Entanglement   A symbol which is related to that of the net and that of bonds. It has been used as an ornamental motif right from prehistoric times, either in the form of entanglement or of a bunch or knot of ribbons. Sometimes vegetable and animal forms appear to rise—like grotesques—out of a mass of abstract nerve-cords resembling vegetable stalks or animated cords in the form of volutes, or coils or knots or interlacing lines; or sometimes—and this is a more advanced motif—clearly formed beings are shown enmeshed, as it were, in a cage. Entanglement-symbolism takes its place in legends, folklore and myths alongside primitive and Romanesque art. Thus a giant is enmeshed in trees, or the castle in the Sleeping Beauty story is hidden under an inextricable mass of vegetation. Jung has studied the question of entanglement with special care, recalling that Osiris is brought up lying in the branches of a tree which completely cover him. There is also the Grimm tale of a girl imprisoned between the wood and the bark of a tree. Again: while he is travelling by night, Ra's ship is engulfed by the serpent of night, this giving rise to a number of later mediaeval miniatures and tales. Jung also observes that entanglement is often associated with the myth of the sun and its daily rebirth. However, this is nothing more than a variant of the devouring symbol mentioned by Frobenius in connexion with sun-heroes (31). In the key to dreams of the Hindu *Yagaddeva*, one reads: 'He who while dreaming twines round his body lianas, creepers, cords or snakeskins, string or fabrics, dies', or, in other words, he returns to the maternal bosom (31). According to Loeffler, a thing which, on the psychic plane, is entangled, represents the unconscious, the repressed, the forgotten, the past. On the plane of cosmic evolution, it is the collective dream which separates one cycle of life from the other (38) (Plate VIII).

Erinyes, The   In the classical tragedies, the erinyes sometimes appear in the form of dogs or serpents, which is an indication of their infernal character as chthonian demons (31). They personify remorse; that is, they are symbols of guilt turned to destructiveness directed against the guilty one (15).

Eternity   The coins of several Roman emperors bear an allegory of eternity depicted in the figure of a girl holding the sun and the moon in her hands. And, in alchemy, there are comparable images, alluding to the *opus* as a 'conjunction' or a 'marriage of opposites', which illustrate the essential principle that the eternal order can be achieved only with the abolition of antithesis, separateness and change. Eternity has also been represented as infinite time, both in the 'Mithraic Cronos' and in the Ouroboros (the serpent or dragon which bites its own tail). The phoenix is another symbol of eternity (8).

Ethiops   An alchemic symbol representing the *nigredo* or the initial stage of the alchemists' work. It can be seen for example in one of the images of the *Splendor solis* of Solomon Trismosin (1582). The Jungian interpretation of the figures and images of Negroes, Indians, savages, etc—whom he considers as symbols for the shadow or the darker side of the personality—does not contradict the first meaning, for, within the moral approach of alchemy, the *nigredo* is a precise illustration of the initial state of the soul before embarking upon its path of evolution and self-perfection (32).

Euphrates Specific geographical features sometimes form part of traditional symbols; the river Euphrates is an example. It is the equivalent of the fluid cosmos passing across the material world (or Babylon) in the two directions of involution and evolution (57). In a broad sense, the river, and indeed every river in the opinion of Heraclitus—without going into esoteric doctrine—is a symbol of time or of the irreversible nature of processes as they move onward.

Eve A symbol of the material and formal aspect of life, of *Natura naturans*, or mother-of-all-things (57). From the spiritual point of view, Eve is the inversion of the Virgin Mary, or the mother-of-souls. Inversions of this order have sometimes found a parallel expression in the contrasting use of similar names, such as Eros (the god of love) balanced against Ares (war, destruction and hate). This antithesis between Eve and Our Lady has been examined by Antonio de Sousa de Macedo in his *Eva y Ave o Maria triunfante*.

Excrement Gubernatis in his research into folklore, and Freud in his work in experimental psychology, have observed that what is almost worthless is often associated with what is most valued. So, for example, we find in legends and folktales the surprising association between excrement and gold (31), a relationship which occurs also in alchemy, since the *nigredo* and the ultimate attainment of the *aurum philosophicum* form the beginning and the end of the process of transmutation. All this symbolism is contained within Nietzsche's phrase: 'Out of the lowest the highest reaches its peak.'

Eye The essence of the question involved here is contained in the saying of Plotinus that the eye would not be able to see the sun if, in a manner, it were not itself a sun. Given that the sun is the source of light and that light is symbolic of the intelligence and of the spirit, then the process of seeing represents a spiritual act and symbolizes understanding. Hence, the 'divine eye' of the Egyptians —a determinative sign in their hieroglyphics called *Wadza*— denotes 'He who feeds the sacred fire or the intelligence of Man' (28)—Osiris, in fact. Very interesting, too, is the way the Egyptians defined the eye—or, rather, the circle of the iris with the pupil as centre—as the 'sun in the mouth' (or the creative Word) (8). René Magritte, the surrealist painter, has illustrated this same relationship between the sun and the mouth in one of his most fascinating paintings. The possession of two eyes conveys physical normality and its spiritual equivalent, and it follows that the third eye is symbolic of the superhuman or the divine. As for the single eye, its significance is ambivalent: on the one hand it implies the subhuman because it is less than two (two eyes being equated with the norm); but on the other hand, given its location in the forehead, above the place designated for the eyes by nature, it seems to allude to extra-human powers which are in fact—in mythology—incarnated in the Cyclops. At the same time the eye in the forehead is linked up with the idea of destruction, for obvious reasons in the case of the single eye; but the same also applies when there is a third eye in the forehead, as with Siva (or Shiva). This is explained by reference to one of the facets of the symbolism of the number three: for if three can be said to correspond to the active, the passive and the neutral, it can also apply to creation, conservation and destruction. Heterotopic eyes are the spiritual equivalent of sight, that is, of clairvoyance. (Heterotopic eyes are those which have been transferred anatomically to various parts of the body, such as the hands, wings, torso, arms, and different parts of the head, in figures of fantastic beings, angels, deities and so on.) When the eyes are situated in the hand, for example, by association with the symbolism of the hand they come to denote clairvoyant action. An excessive number of eyes has an ambivalent significance which it is important to note. In the first place, the eyes refer to night with its myriads of stars, in the second place, paradoxically yet necessarily, the possessor of so many eyes is left in darkness. Furthermore, by way of corroboration, let us recall that in symbolist theory multiplicity is always a sign of inferiority. Such ambivalences are common in the realm of the unconscious and its projected images. Instructive in this connexion is the example of Argus, who with all his eyes could not escape death. The Adversary (Satan, in Hebrew) has been represented in a variety of ways, among others, as a being with many eyes. A Tarot card in the *Cabinet des Estampes* in Paris (Kh. 34d), for instance, depicts the devil as Argus with many eyes all over his body. Another comparable symbolic device is also found commonly in demonic figures: it consists of taking some part of the body that possesses, as it were, a certain autonomy of character or which is directly associated with a definite function, and portraying it as a face. Multiple faces and eyes imply disintegration or psychic decomposition—a conception which lies at the root of the demoniacal idea of rending apart (59). Finally, to come back to the pure meaning of the eye in itself, Jung considers it to be the maternal bosom, and the pupil its 'child'.[1] Thus the great

---

[1] The Jungian idea is expressed as a pun. 'Niña' means both 'daughter' and 'pupil (of the eye)'. The phrase 'Niña de los ojos' is like the English 'apple of one's eye', which gives something of the feel of the pun.—*Translator.*

solar god becomes a child again, seeking renovation at his mother's bosom (a symbol, for the Egyptians, of the mouth) (31).

Fairies   Fairies probably symbolize the supra-normal powers of the human soul, at least in the forms in which they appear in esoteric works. Their nature is contradictory: they fulfil humble tasks, yet possess extraordinary powers. They bestow gifts upon the newly born; they can cause people, palaces and wonderful things to appear out of thin air; they dispense riches (as a symbol of wisdom). Their powers, however, are not simply magical, but are rather the sudden revelation of latent possibilities. Because of this, it has been possible to link the legendary 'forgotten fairy' with the Freudian 'frustrated act' (38). In a more traditional sense, fairies are, objectively, spinners of thread like the Parcae; they also appear as washerwomen. They have been variously called: White Ladies, Green Ladies, Black Ladies; these are terms which tie up with the epithets applied to mediaeval knights—and for the same reason. Fairies are, in short, personifications of stages in the development in the spiritual life or in the 'soul' of landscapes. Thus, in Mesopotamia, they take the form of the Lady of the Plains, the Lady of the Fountain and the Lady of the Water (or Damgalnunna). They are prone to sudden and complete transformations, and they bear a certain resemblance to other mystic beings such as sirens and lamias (in their evil aspects) (16).

Fall, The   The Fall signifies the incarnation of the spirit. 'Man', observes Jakob Böhme, in *De signatura*, 'died, in so far as he was purely divine essence, because his inner desires, bursting out from the inner fiery centre . . . tended towards external and temporary birth.' Thus (in Evola's transcription), the divine essence or 'inner corporeity' (which nevertheless persists within Man) suffers physical 'death'.

Fan   Its symbolic significance depends on the shape and size. The large flabellate fan is related to air and wind, and is the emblem of Chung-li Chuan, the first of the Eight Chinese Immortals, who is said to have used it to revive the spirits of the dead (5). A fan of this type is usually heart-shaped, and is sometimes decorated with feathers. The feathers stress the association with aerial and celestial symbolism as a whole. It is an attribute of rank among several Asian and African peoples, and is still so used—with a cosmic significance —by the Pope (41). The characteristic Western fan is of the folding type, and hence associated with the phases of the moon, so that its symbolism relates to imagination, change and femininity. The changing pattern of phenomena, as shown in the rhythm of moon-phases (non-being, appearance, increase, full being, decrease), is expressed in terms of erotic, allegorical fan-language. So is the Heraclitean conception of perpetual flux. A fan is used in this latter sense by Max Ernst in one of his paintings.

Farmer Among basic occupations, farming has a very special significance, not only because its activities take place in the sacred world of seeds, buds, flowers and fruits, but also because it follows the cosmic order as illustrated in the calendar. Cyclic sequences of terrestrial events following the pattern of celestial motions express a correlation which is fundamental to astrobiological thought. The farmer is therefore the guardian of agricultural rites, seeing out the 'old year' and seeing in the 'new'. In spiritual terms, this means that the farmer appears as the catalyst of the forces of regeneration and salvation, forces which join every beginning to every end, forging links which bind time together, as well as the successive seasons and renascent vegetation. Farming was essential not only for the development of primitive economy but also for the emergence of a cosmic consciousness in Man. Mircea Eliade puts it most aptly: 'What Man *saw* in the grain, what he *learnt* in dealing with it, what he was *taught* by the example of seeds changing their form when they are in the ground, that was the decisive lesson. . . One of the main roots of soteriological optimism was the belief of prehistoric, agricultural mysticism that the dead, like seeds underground, can expect to return to life in a different form' (17).

Farming See *Agriculture*.

Father The father-image, closely linked with the symbolism of the masculine principle, corresponds to consciousness as opposed to the maternal implications of the unconscious. The symbolic representation of the father is based upon the Elements of air and fire, and also heaven, light, thunderbolts and weapons (56). Just as heroism is a spiritual activity proper to the son, so dominion is the power peculiar to the father (17). Because of this, and also because he stands for the force of tradition (32), he represents the world of moral commandments and prohibitions restraining the forces of the instincts (31) and subversion.

Feather Whether singular or in groups, the feather symbolizes the wind and the creator-gods of the Egyptian pantheon: Ptah, Hathor, Osiris and Amon (41). Feathers correspond to the Element of air—to the realm of the birds (48). And, for the same reason, cultures in which aerial myths predominate, such as those of the American aborigines, make use of feathers as an essential feature of their personal adornment. The feather head-dress of the Indian

chief closely relates him to the demiurgic bird. As a determinative
sign in the Egyptian system of hieroglyphs, the feather enters into
the composition of such words as 'emptiness', 'dryness', 'lightness',
'height', 'flight' (19). According to St. Gregory, feathers symbolize
faith and contemplation, and the quill denotes the Word (50). The
Egyptian sign for the quill signifies 'delineator of all things' (19),
though it may be that this sign really represents a cane-leaf; however, the meaning turns upon the function rather than the material.

Fecundity In allegories, fecundity is usually represented by the

Symbol of the fecundity of sacrifice: the cross bears fruit
(after an engraving dated 1512).

poppy plant, because of its prodigious number of seeds; but it is also symbolized by a grain of barley, and by the bull, the hare and the rabbit (8).

Fertility Symbols of fertility are: water, seeds, phallic shapes. Granet recounts that, in China, the conjugal bed used to be placed in the darkest corner of the room, where the seeds were kept and above the spot where the dead were buried. Eliade maintains that the respective rites pertaining to forebears, harvests and the erotic life are so closely related to each other that it is impossible to distinguish between them (17). In Indian ritual, grains of rice serve to represent the seed of fertility (17).

Fibula The fibula—or clasp—is a minimal form of shield, and, like the belt, a symbol of virginity. In this sense it has found its way into many legends, especially in the *Kalevala* (38).

Fields In the widest sense, they signify spaciousness or limitless potentialities. Into this category come the Uranian gods such as Mithras, called 'the Lord of the Plains'. As lord of the sky, he has the task of conducting souls on their return to heaven (11), like other psychopomps such as Mercury.

Fight All combats are the expression of a conflict of some sort. A great many fights, dances and simulacra are rites, or the vestiges of rites, which express situations of conflict. In Sweden, according to Eliade, combats are enacted on horseback by two sets of riders personifying winter and summer. Usener ascribed a similar meaning to the combat between Xanthos and Melanthos—the fair one and the dark one. On the other hand, the struggle may correspond to the primordial, cosmogonic sacrifice, such as the sacrifice of Tiamat (or Tiawath) by Marduk. Struggles between the gods of vegetation and of drought (such as Osiris and Set) or between good and evil (Ahuramazda and Ahriman or Angramainyu, for example) modify the plane of conflict accordingly. Broadly speaking, the struggle is that of generation or involves antithetically opposed elements (17). For our part, we would suggest that the combats of Roman gladiators reflected an ancestral, mythic and symbolic background with the retiarius (or net-fighter) as the counterpart of Neptune and Pisces (symbolic of the celestial ocean, and the all-embracing god armed with the trident, as a sign of triple power, and with the net); likewise, the *mirmillo* was Cancer (the sun, or the son armed with a sword).

Figures The representational shape of figures is always of a piece with the object, or being, to which they allude. Symbolically speaking, a cock is the same thing as its figure whether painted, engraved or sculpted. When the figure is that of a living being, this being provides the predominant sense, although secondary meanings may be derived from the colour, the form, etc. When the figures are geometric, or when they represent architectural masses, it is

I. Roman sculpture incorporating symbolic *motifs*, throne, lions and
cornucopia.

II. Modesto Cuixart. Painting, 1958.

III. **Architecture.** Portal of the church of San Pablo del Campo, Barcelona
—two columns and tetramorphs.

IV. **Cauldron.** Silver chalice, from Ardagh, Co. Longford, Ireland.

V. **Cross.** 10th-century monument at Clonmacnois, Ireland.

VI. **Dragon.** Chinese version of the cosmic dragon (Pekin).

VII. **Eagle.** A renaissance relief, from the Doge's Palace at Venice,
inspired by Roman 'signs'.

VIII. **Entanglement.** This symbolic *motif* is often found in Romanesque art—capitals, monastery of Santo Domingo de Silos, Spain.

IX. **Fish.** Early Christian symbol—13th-century gravestone, Lérida Museum, Spain.

X. **Fountain.** Gothic fountain—Casa del Arcediano (Archdeacon's House), Barcelona.

XI. **Fracture.** Giorgione, *The Storm*: symbolic elements include shattered columns, lightning, bridge, road, etc.

XII. **Gemini.** Roman statue of the Twins (Prado, Madrid).

XIII. **Grail.** Apparition of the Holy Grail over the Round Table (after a Gothic miniature—detail).

XIV. **Harp.** Detail of *Garden of Delights* by Bosch, in which the dramatic symbolism of the harp may be intuited.

XV. **Head.** Portal of the Romanesque cathedral at Clonfert, Co. Galway, Ireland, decorated with geometric symbols and human heads.

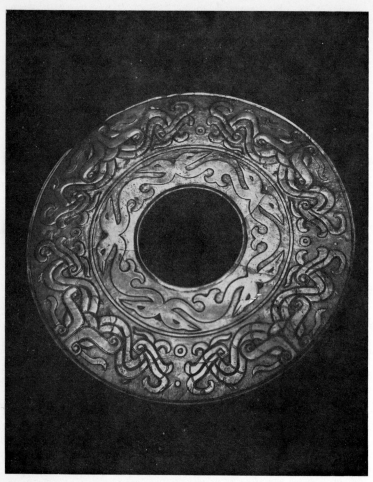

XVI. **Heaven.** Chinese symbol of heaven: the hole in this circular image of space signifies the path of transcendence.

again the symbolism of *form* which comes into play. Schematic figures—marks, signs, tattoos, engravings, prehistoric or primitive inscriptions, magic alphabets, etc—are all related to graphic symbolism, which is founded in the main upon space, number and geometric form. Given the analogy, the possible similarity or inner connexion between Man's works and those of his Creator, invented figures—cultural symbols or instruments—are always related to the natural figures which resemble them. Symbolic or mythic ideas which reveal some influence, resemblance or reminiscence of a natural form or figure, acquire thereby powerful symbolic implications. So, for example, the head of Medusa and the octopus; the swastika and the starfish; the double-bladed axe and the hawk in flight.

Fire   The Chinese, in their solar rites, utilize a tablet of red jade, which they call *Chang*; it symbolizes the Element of fire (39). In Egyptian hieroglyphics, fire is also related to the solar-symbolism of the flame, and associated in particular with the concepts of life and health (deriving from the idea of body-heat). It is also allied with the concept of superiority and control (19), showing that the symbol had by this time developed into an expression of spiritual energy. The alchemists retained in particular the Heraclitean notion of fire as 'the agent of transmutation', since all things derive from, and return to, fire. It is the seed which is reproduced in each successive life (and is thereby linked with the libido and fecundity) (57). In this sense as a mediator between forms which vanish and forms in creation, fire is, like water, a symbol of transformation and regeneration. For most primitives, fire was a demiurge emanating from the sun, whose earthly representative it was; hence it is related on the one hand with the ray of light and the lightning (35), and, on the other, with gold. Frazer lists many rites in which torches, bonfires, burning embers and even ashes are considered capable of stimulating the growth of the cornfields and the well-being of man and of animals. However, anthropological research has furnished two explanations of the fire-festival (as it persists today in the Valencian bonfires on the night of St. John, fireworks and the illuminated Christmas tree): on the one hand, there is the opinion of Wilhelm Mannhardt, to the effect that it is imitative magic purporting to assure the supply of light and heat from the sun, and, on the other, the view of Eugene Mogk and Edward Westermarck that it has as its aim the purification or destruction of the forces of evil (21); however, these two hypotheses are not opposing but complementary. The triumphant power and the vitality of the sun—by analogy, the spirit of the shining Origin—is tantamount to victory over the power of evil (the forces of darkness); purification is the necessary sacrificial means of achieving the sun's triumph. Marius Schneider, however, distinguishes between two kinds of fire, depending upon their direction (or their function): fire as in the axis fire-earth (representing eroticism, solar heat and physical energy), and fire of the axis fire-air (linked with mysticism, purification or sublimation, and spiritual energy). There is an exact parallel here with the ambivalent symbolism of the sword (denoting both physical destruction and determination of spirit) (50). Fire, in consequence, is an image of energy which may be found at the level of animal passion as well as on the plane of spiritual strength (56). The Heraclitean idea of fire as the agent of destruction and regeneration is reproduced in the Indian Puranas and in the Apocalypse (27). Gaston Bachelard recalls the alchemists' concept of fire as 'an Element which operates in the centre of all things', as a unifying and stabilizing factor. Paracelsus demonstrated the parallel between fire and life, pointing out that both must feed upon other lives in order to keep alive. To steal fire like Prometheus, or to give oneself up to fire like Empedocles, are two concepts which point to the basic dualism of the human predicament. The middle way lies in the comfortable solution of simply making material use of the benefits of fire. But fire is ultra-life. It embraces both good (vital heat) and bad (destruction and conflagration). It implies the desire to annihilate time and to bring all things to their end. Fire is the archetypal image of phenomena in themselves (1). To pass through fire is symbolic of transcending the human condition, according to Eliade in *Myths, Dreams and Mysteries* (London, 1960).

Fire-water   Fire-water, like other alcoholic liquors, is a *coincidentia oppositorum* (water and fire) and is therefore related to noumena and to the hermaphrodite. Alcoholism, therefore, may be reckoned an attempt at *conjunctio*.

Fish   In broad terms, the fish is a psychic being, or a 'penetrative motion' endowed with a 'heightening' power concerning base matters—that is, in the unconscious. Because of the close symbolic relationship between the sea and the *Magna Mater*, some peoples have held the fish to be sacred. There were some Asiatic rites that embraced fish-worship, and priests were forbidden to eat it. As Jung has pointed out, the son of Atargatis (Ashtart or Astarte) was named Ichthys (31). Schneider notes that the fish is the mystic Ship of Life, sometimes a whale, sometimes a bird, and at other times simply a fish or a flying fish, 'but at all times it is the spindle spinning out the cycle of life after the pattern of the lunar zodiac' (50). That is to say, the fish incorporates a variety of meanings, reflecting the many essential facets of its nature. Schneider also mentions that for some people the fish has a phallic meaning, whereas for others it has a purely spiritual symbolism. In essence, the character of the fish is twofold: by reason of its bobbin-like shape, it becomes a kind of 'bird of the nether regions', symbolic of sacrifice and of the relationship between heaven and earth. On the other hand, by virtue of the extraordinary number of its eggs, it becomes a symbol of fecundity, imparting a certain spiritual sense (50). In this last sense it is found among the Babylonians, the Phoenicians, the Assyrians (4) and the Chinese (5). There are some fish that have a secondary significance because of their peculiar characteristics: for instance, the sword-fish is associated with the unicorn (32). The Chaldaic peoples used to portray the figure of a fish with the head of a swallow, as a harbinger of cyclic regeneration, an idea directly related to the symbolism of Pisces, the last sign of the Zodiac (40) (Plate IX). The fish became a primitive Christian symbol, principally on the basis of the anagram drawn from the name for fish: ichthys, the initials standing for $'I$-$\eta\sigma o \upsilon\varsigma$ X-$\rho\iota\sigma\tau o\varsigma$ Θ-$\epsilon o \upsilon$ Y-$\iota o\varsigma$ Σ-$\omega\tau\eta\rho$. Then it came to be taken as a symbol of profound life, of the spiritual world that lies under the world of appearances, the fish representing the life-force surging up.

Fish, Cosmic Like the whale and the primordial monster, the cosmic fish symbolizes the whole of the formal, physical universe. The most striking example of this symbol is afforded by the splendid Scythian fish, made of gold, which was part of the Vettersfelde treasure, and which is now in the Museum of Berlin. The cosmic fish can take two different but complementary symbolic forms: The first and more frequent is simply narrative and spatial, for on the upper part of its body, above a heavily marked horizontal line, are four beings of the 'superior stage'—mammals (apparently they are a stag, a horse, a boar and a leopard). Below this line are beings of the 'lower stage'—those of the deeps (fishes and sirens). The second symbolic aspect is the product of morphological collation, based upon paraidolias: so, for instance, the two branches of the tail, reminiscent of two necks, constitute two sheep's heads, while in the middle of the tail there is an eagle spreading out its wings to form an analogous shape. Its eye comes to resemble an octopus, as much in its shape as in the implied comparison between the 'grasping' tentacles and the potentiality for 'grasping' objects apparent in its gaze. This golden fish, then, is a symbol of the progress of the world across the sea of 'unformed' realities (or of worlds dissolved or yet unformed, or of the primordial seas).

Fisher King He belongs to the legend of the Grail. According to Marx, in *Nouvelles Recherches sur la Littérature Arthurienne*, this rôle of the mythical monarch relates him to the apostles or fishermen of the Sea of Galilee. In Robert de Boron's work on this theme, the Fisher King becomes the Rich Fisherman, which Marx regards as confirmation of the thesis. Fishing, symbolically, is not just 'fishing for men' but casting the bait into the depths of one's own inmost nature in order to reach the gnosis.

Fishing 'The path of the Grail was marked by a number of miracles; one of the brothers was called Brous and was also known as "the rich fisherman" because he had succeeded in catching a fish with which he had satisfied the hunger of all round him. Peter is called "the fisher of men" and the fish becomes a symbol of Christ.' This fragment of legend, taken from Waldemar Vedel, affords a clear explanation of the mystic sense of fishing and the fisherman, a sense which has been corroborated by all students of mythology and anthropology, Schneider among them. Fishing amounts to extracting the unconscious elements from deep-lying sources—the 'elusive treasure' of legend, or, in other words, wisdom. To fish for souls is quite simply a matter of knowing how to fish *in* the soul. The fish is a mystic and psychic animal that lives in water (and water is symbolic of dissolution and, at the same time, of renovation and regeneration). The fisherman is able—like the doctor—to work upon the very sources of life because of his knowledge of these founts. This is how it comes about that Parsifal meets the King of the Grail as a fisherman.

Flag Historically speaking, the flag or banner derives from totemistic insignia as found in Egypt and, indeed, in most countries. The Persians carried gilded eagles with outstretched wings on top of long poles; the Medes, three crowns; the Parthians, a sword-blade; the Greeks and Romans had *signa*, standards and banners. The important point about all these symbols is not the kind of figure used, but the fact that it is always placed at the top of a pole or mast. This raised position is expressive of a kind of imperious exaltation, or the will to 'heighten' the spiritual significance of the figure or animal by raising it above the normal level. From this is derived the general symbolism of the banner as a sign of victory and self-assertion (22).

Flame There are certain significant points of contact between the flame and light. For Bachelard, the flame symbolizes transcendence itself (1), whereas light signifies the effect of the transcendental upon the environment. He adds that 'The alchemist attributed the value of gold to the fact of its being a receptacle for the Element of fire (the sun); the quintessence of gold is fire. The Greeks represented the spirit as a gust of incandescent air' (1).

Fleur-de-lis An heraldic flower, non-existent in nature, which has been a symbol of royalty from the earliest times (46). As an emblem, its base is an inverted triangle representing water; above it is a cross (expressing 'Conjunction' and spiritual achievement), with two additional and symmetrical leaves wrapped round the horizontal arm; the central arm is straight and reaches up heavenwards, the symbolism being self-evident (59). During the Middle

Ages the lis was regarded as an emblem of illumination and as an attribute of the Lord (4).

Flight The symbolism of flight comprises a variety of elements. The most basic derives from the pleasurable sensation of movement in a medium that is more subtle than water and unfettered by gravity. But, this apart, flying implies raising oneself and is therefore closely connected with the symbolism of level, not only in connexion with moral values but also with the notion of superiority applied to other qualities, such as power or strength. Diel has pointed out that the importance of the 'rise and fall' image—as illustrated in the myth of Icarus in particular—is corroborated by a great many authors (15). And Bachelard has observed that 'of all metaphors, only those pertaining to height, ascent, depth, descent and fall are axiomatic. Nothing can explain them but they can explain everything.' Flight has also been conceived as the 'transcendence of growth'. According to Toussenel, in *Le Monde des oiseaux*, 'we envy the bird his good fortune and endow with wings the object of our love, for we know by instinct that, in the sphere of complete happiness, our bodies will enjoy the power to wheel through space as the bird flies through the air' (3). Flight is related to space and light; psychologically it is a symbol of thought and of imagination.

Flocks A traditional symbol for the forces of the cosmos, expressive of a state which is neither chaotic nor yet completely ordered (the ordering of chaos is symbolized by the bundle or sheaf). Flocks bear an analogy with constellations and certain stellar groups, since the moon is symbolically a shepherd—at least, this is true of some mythologies. But, at the same time, a flock implies multiplicity—which is a negative quality (40)—and the collapse of a force or an objective.

Flogging In ancient thought, blows, flogging and flagellation do not signify punishment (i.e. vengeance or deterrence) but purification and encouragement. The Arcadian custom of flogging the effigy of Pan when the hunters came back empty-handed was intended to cast out the inhibiting powers (21). In many rites all over the world, flogging is considered necessary to restore possessed or bewitched individuals and, in general, to deal with all situations implying physical or spiritual impotence (51).

Flower Different flowers usually have separate meanings, but, as so often happens, flower-symbolism is broadly characterized by two essentially different considerations: the flower in its essence, and the flower in its shape. By its very nature it is symbolic of transitoriness, of Spring and of beauty. The sixth of the 'Eight Immortals' of China, Lan Ts'ai-ho, is generally depicted clad in blue and carrying a basket of flowers; it is said that he was given to singing of the brevity of life and the ephemeral nature of pleasure (5). The Greeks and Romans, at all their feasts, always wore crowns of flowers. And they would strew flowers over the corpses as they bore them to the funeral pyre and over their graves (not so much as an offering as an analogy) (8). We have, then, another example of an antithetical symbol, like the skeleton which the Egyptians would bring to their banquets, as a reminder of the reality of death and as a stimulus towards the enjoyment of life. Now, because of its shape, the flower is an image of the 'Centre', and hence an archetypal image of the soul (56). 'Celestial flower' is the name given to a meteorite or a shooting star by the alchemists (57), and the flower was, for them, symbolic of the work of the sun (32). The significance would be adapted according to the colour of the flower. So, for example, orange or yellow-coloured flowers represent a reinforcement of the basic sun-symbolism; red flowers emphasize the relationship with animal life, blood and passion. The 'blue flower' is a legendary symbol of the impossible, and is probably an allusion to the 'mystic Centre' as represented by the Grail and other such symbols. The 'golden flower' is a famous parallel in Chinese mysticism, a non-existent flower which is also spoken of in alchemy; in the *Epistola ad Hermannum Arch. Coloniensem* (*Theatr. Chem.* 1622) it is given the name of 'the sapphire-blue flower of the Hermaphrodite' (32).

Flute   The basic meaning of the flute corresponds to erotic or funereal anguish. The complexity of its symbolism derives from the fact that, if, by virtue of its shape, it seems to have a phallic significance, its tone is nevertheless related to inner, feminine intuitive feeling (that is, to the anima) (50). It is also related to the cane and to water.

Fool, The   The final enigma of the Tarot, distinguished from the others because it is un-numbered—all the rest are given numbers from 1 to 21; the significance of this is that the Fool is to be found on the fringe of all orders and systems in the same way as the Centre of the Wheel of Transformations is 'outside' movement, becoming and change. This very fact is in itself a pointer to the mystic symbolism of the Fool, as it is touched upon in the Parsifal legend and others. This figure on the Tarot card is dressed in a costume of many colours denoting the multiple or incoherent influences to which he is subject. The red colour tends to orange, indicating—and this is unequivocal—the colour of the essential fire within him. He carries a bag at the end of his staff, this being symbolic of the mind and its burden. A white lynx is shown in the act of biting his left calf (left being the unconscious side), signifying what remains of his lucidity—that is, his remorse. But this does not deter him, rather does it urge him onward towards the background where may be seen an overturned obelisk—a solar symbol and also symbolic of the Logos—and a crocodile about to devour what must be returned to chaos. There is nothing definite to suggest that the Fool cannot be saved: on the contrary, his predicament, as we have described it, is balanced by the presence of a small, purple-coloured tulip (expressive of active spirituality) and a gold belt adorned with twelve plaques alluding to the Zodiac. This Tarot enigma corresponds, in short, to the irrational, the active instinct capable of sublimation, but related at the same time to blind impulse and the unconscious (59). For Schneider, the mythic and legendary Fool is closely related to the clown. In their medicinal ceremonies and rites, doctor and patient 'act mad', and, through frenzied dancing and 'extravagances', they try to invert the prevailing evil order. The logic of the process is clear enough: when the normal or conscious appears to become infirm or perverted, in order to regain health and goodness it becomes necessary to turn to the dangerous, the unconscious and the abnormal (51). Further, the Fool and the clown, as Frazer has pointed out, play the part of 'scapegoats' in the ritual sacrifice of humans.

Foot In all probability, the foot is to be taken as an ambivalent symbol. For Jung, it is what confirms Man's direct relationship with the reality of the earth, and he considers that it is frequently phallic in significance (31). Ania Teillard points out that, like the hand, it is an essential part of the body and the support of one's entire person; she recalls that in the mythology of a number of countries the rays of the sun are compared with the feet, as witness the figure of the swastika (56). But Diel makes the revolutionary assertion that the foot is a symbol of the soul, possibly because it serves as the support of the body in the sense of keeping man upright. He quotes examples which show that, in Greek legends, lameness usually symbolizes some defect of the spirit—some essential blemish. Jung corroborates this, observing that Hephaestus, Wieland the Blacksmith and Mani all had deformed feet (31). May it not be that certain talents are given to men to compensate for some physical defect? Schneider has indicated the heel as the 'area of vulnerability and of attack' in the foot. It is the heel that scotches the serpent or that is wounded by it (as with Achilles, Sigurd, Krishna) (50). According to Aigremont, 'the shoe, like the foot and the footprint, has also a funereal implication. In a sense, a dying man "is going away". There is no evidence of his going away save his last footmarks. This sombre symbolism is illustrated, possibly, in the monuments characteristic of the Roman Empire, and, beyond question, in primitive Christian art. . . .' (And also, we might add, in Gothic art. The passage is quoted by Stekel.)

Footprints Footprints symbolize the way of gods, saints or demonic spirits, etc. There are footprints of Buddha and Vishnu all over India. Kühn, in *The Rock Pictures of Europe*, says that the footprints of the Virgin Mary may be seen in a chapel in Würzburg; and the footprints of Christ in a hermitage in Rosenstein, Swabia.

Footwear A sign of liberty amongst the ancients, since slaves walked barefoot (46). Its symbolic meaning is linked with that of the foot, from which it acquires its general symbolic characteristics. Given the triple symbolism of the foot—(1) phallic according to the Freudians, (2) symbolic of the soul according to Diel, and (3) signifying, in our opinion, the relationship as well as the point of contact between the body and the earth—it follows that footwear partakes of all three potentialities, together with the general symbolism of level.

Ford This is an aspect of threshold-symbolism (q.v.), denoting the dividing-line between two states or two forms of reality, such as consciousness and unconsciousness, or waking and sleeping. Jung has drawn attention to the highly interesting fact that, in the exploits of Hiawatha, his victims are nearly always in the water or close to it. Every animal that rises out of a ford is a representation of the forces of the unconscious, like some demonic being or metamorphosed magician (31).

Forest Within the general symbolism of landscape, forests occupy a notable place, and are often found in myths, legends and folktales. Forest-symbolism is complex, but it is connected at all levels with the symbolism of the female principle or of the Great Mother. The forest is the place where vegetable life thrives and luxuriates, free from any control or cultivation. And since its foliage obscures the light of the sun, it is therefore regarded as opposed to the sun's power and as a symbol of the earth. In Druid mythology, the forest was given to the sun in marriage (49). Since the female principle is identified with the unconscious in Man, it follows that the forest is also a symbol of the unconscious. It is for this reason that Jung maintains that the sylvan terrors that figure so prominently in children's tales symbolize the perilous aspects of the unconscious, that is, its tendency to devour or obscure the reason (31). Zimmer stresses that, in contrast with the city, the house and cultivated land, which are all safe areas, the forest harbours all kinds of dangers and demons, enemies and diseases (60). This is why forests were among the first places in nature to be dedicated to the cult of the gods, and why propitiatory offerings were suspended from trees (the tree being, in this case, the equivalent of a sacrificial stake) (8).

Fossil Broadly, its symbolic significance corresponds to that of the stone, but, because of its ambivalent character, it embraces the concepts of time and eternity, life and death, the evolution of species, and their petrification.

Fountain (or **Source**) In the image of the terrestrial Paradise, four rivers are shown emerging from the centre, that is, from the foot of the Tree of Life itself, to branch out in the four directions of the Cardinal Points. They well up, in other words, from a common source, which therefore becomes symbolic of the 'Centre' and of the 'Origin' in action. Tradition has it that this fount is the *fons juventutis* whose waters can be equated with the 'draught of immortality'— *amrita* in Hindu mythology (25). Hence it is said that water gushing forth is a symbol of the life-force of Man and of all things (57). For this reason, artistic iconography very frequently uses the motif of the mystic fount; it is also to be found in Mithraism—a Pannonian votive inscription reads: *fonti perenni* (31). There can be no doubt that its significance as the mystic 'Centre' is confirmed and reinforced when it is portrayed in architectural plans: whether in the cloister, the garden or the *patio*, the fountain occupies the centre position, at least in the majority of architectural works built during periods within the symbolist tradition, as in Romanesque or Gothic edifices. Furthermore, the four rivers of Paradise are denoted by four paths which radiate out from the region of the cloister towards a clear space, circular or octagonal in shape, which forms the basin of the fountain; this basin is usually shaped, again, like a circle or an octagon, and sometimes there is a double basin. Jung has devoted much time to the study of fountain-symbolism, specially in so far as it concerns alchemy, and, in view of how much lies behind it, he is inclined to the conclusion that it is an image of the soul as the source of inner life and of spiritual energy. He links it also with the 'land of infancy', the recipient of the precepts of the unconscious, pointing out that the need for this fount arises principally when the individual's life is inhibited and dried up (32). The Jungian interpretation is particularly apt when the symbol concerns a fountain centrally placed in a garden, the central area then being a representation of the *Selbst* or individuality. He mentions as examples: the 'fountain of life' of the Florentine *Codex Spherae*, and the *Garden of Delight* painted by Hieronymus van Aecken (Bosch). He observes that the fountain, in the enclosed garden in the *Ars Symbolica* of Bosch (1702), signifies strength in adversity, and that the central area may be regarded as a *temenos* (a hallowed area) (32) (Plate X).

Fox   A common symbol for the devil during the Middle Ages, expressive of base attitudes and of the wiles of the adversary (20).

Fracture   In general, any state of matter or of form carries a literal symbolism which simply transposes to the mental, spiritual or psychic world the corresponding physical phenomenon. One can see a clear illustration here of the parallel between the two realms of the visible and the invisible. Naturally, the symbolic significance of the object is broadened in consequence. So, for example, a broken column takes its significance from the idea of fracture rather than the notion of the column as such—symbolically, it is the precise equivalent of the stunted tree. Charred wood, rusty iron, lichen-covered rocks are repellent to people of a certain temperament while the same things are attractive to others of a romantic nature precisely because they symbolize the 'conjunction of opposites' or the interplay of positive and negative forces. A fracture may reach the stage of absolute destruction when it becomes symbolic of spiritual ruin or death, as in the case of *The Fall of the House of Usher* by Poe. Giorgione, in his mysterious painting of *The Storm*, portrays two broken columns on a pedestal, which, according to the Freudian interpretation, would signify a critical sexual conflict. But we would rather interpret the picture as an illustration of the break-up of a unified whole (as symbolized by the number two), and this interpretation would seem to be confirmed by the fact that the man is separated spatially from the woman: he is in the left fore-ground of the painting in an attitude expressive of wandering, with the woman on the right, a stream flowing between them, and a flash of lightning, together with two columns, above. Thus, all physical fragmentation is symbolic of destruction and disintegration. Never-theless, there are instances when the break-up may be positive in character in that it symbolizes a possible way of escape. The Roman *Flamen Dialis* was not permitted to wear knots in any part of his garments, nor any bangle that was not split (21). The knots and bangles, bands or necklaces would here symbolize the various kinds of bondage that the priest had to rise above (Plate XI).

Frog   The frog represents the transition from the Element of earth to that of water, and vice versa. This connexion with natural fecundity is an attribute derived from its amphibious character (50), and for the same reason it is also a lunar animal; there are many legends which tell of a frog on the moon, and it figures in many rites invoking rainfall (17). In Egypt, it was an attribute of Herit, the goddess who assisted Isis in her ritual resurrection of Osiris. The little frogs which appeared in the Nile a few days before it overflowed its banks were, therefore, regarded as heralds of fertility (39). According to Blavatsky, the frog was one of the principal beings associated with the idea of creation and resurrection, not only because it was amphibious but because of its alternating periods of appearance and disappearance (phases which likewise characterise all lunar animals). Frog-gods were once placed upon mummies and the early Christians incorporated them into their symbolic system (9). The toad is the antithesis of the frog, as the wasp is of the bee. Jung rounds off all this with his comment that, given its anatomy, the frog, more than any other of the cold-blooded animals, anticipates Man. And Ania Teillard recalls that in the centre of his picture of *The Temptation of St. Anthony*, Bosch places a frog, with

the head of a very aged human being, poised upon a platter held up
by a Negress. Here it represents the highest stage of evolution.
Hence, the frequency of the 'transformation of prince into frog' in
legends and folktales (56).

Fruit Equivalent to the egg, in traditional symbolism, for in the
centre of the fruit is the seed which represents the Origin (29). It is a
symbol of earthly desires.

Garden The garden is the place where Nature is subdued,
ordered, selected and enclosed. Hence, it is a symbol of consciousness
as opposed to the forest, which is the unconscious, in the same way
as the island is opposed to the ocean. At the same time, it is a
feminine attribute because of its character as a precinct (32). A
garden is often the scene of processes of 'Conjunction' or treasure-
hunts—connotations which are clearly in accord with the general
symbolic function we have outlined. A more subtle meaning, depending upon the shape and disposition, or the levels and orientation,
of the garden, is one which corresponds to the basic symbolism
of landscape (q.v.).

Gargoyles Fabulous animals and monsters make their appearance in mediaeval religious art as symbols of the forces of the
cosmos, or as images of the demoniacal and dragon-infested underworld; in the latter case they are captive animals—prisoners under
the sway of a superior spirituality. This is shown by their position
in the hierarchy of the ornamentation: they are always subordinated
to angelic, celestial images (16). They never occupy the centre.

Garland It has been said (37) that everything in the universe is
linked as in a garland; the observation may serve as a pointer to the
actual symbolic significance of the garland. It is related to the
grotesque, to the rosette, to string and all other tokens of bonds or
connexion. The uses to which the garland has been put provide us
with further definitions of its symbolism. The ancients would hang
them at the entrance to their temples on feast-days, as a symbol of
fellowship; and they used also to crown their captives with them (8).
Here, as also in the case of the crowns worn by the guests at
Egyptian, Greek and Roman banquets, it is the symbolism of the
flower which prevails (signifying ephemeral beauty and the dualism
or life and death).

Gazelle This animal is an emblem of the soul. From Primitive
times it has been depicted in iconography in flight from—or in

the jaws of—a lion or a panther. It symbolizes the persecution of the passions and the aggressive, self-destructive aspect of the unconscious.

Gemini, The   As the third sign of the Zodiac, these heavenly twins take on the general significance of all symbolic twins (in that they are both divine and mortal, black and white), but the Gemini acquire the additional significance of a characteristic phase of the cosmic process as symbolized in the Wheel of Transformations: the moment, that is to say, in which pure creative force (Aries and Taurus) is severed into two parts, in such a way that one side of the dualism is elevated but the other descends into the multiplicity characteristic of phenomena. The pillars of Hermes, or those of Hercules, or the so-called Jachin and Boaz columns of the Cabala, are all symbols deriving from the great myth of the Gemini. In the zodiacal symbolism, the third sign is that of the objectivized and reflected intellect (40). Marius Schneider has made a profound study of the Gemini-myth in megalithic culture, showing that it has two tendencies, one white and the other black; one creates, the other destroys; both these characteristics are indicated by the arms of

Zodiacal sign of
the Gemini.

each of the Twins, which, in landscape symbolism, are identical with the river of youth and the river of death. The Gemini represent creative Nature (*Natura naturans*) and created Nature (*Natura naturata*), and this duality is sometimes illustrated in tales by a being that wears a mask, or by a Protean being capable of turning into a giant, a man or an animal. In medicinal rites, the Gemini, by virtue of their double but constant nature, are both the doctor and—more particularly—the invalid, as is borne out in legend and in myth—the Parsifal story, for example (Jean Arthur Rimbaud unknowingly alluded to this duality when he remarked that the poet is both the great invalid and the seer) (51). At times, two different conceptions of the Gemini can be distinguished (as in the parallel myth of the primordial and androgynous being): the 'Heavenly Twin', expressive of opposites, fused together and integrated into Oneness (represented by the spherical or perfect being); and the 'Earthly Twin' displaying the break, the split (as in two-headed Janus, or triform Hecate, etc.), that is, opposites in conflict or at least in dissidence. There is a third aspect, which is that of the individuation or splitting of the 'double being', but this has to do with the existential order and not the mythic. As a result of the dynamic tendencies of all contradictions (white tends towards black, night seeks to become day, the evil man aspires to goodness, life leads to death), the world of phenomena becomes a system of perpetual inversions, illustrated, for example, in the hour-glass which turns upon its own axis in order to maintain its inner movement: that of the sand passing through the central aperture—the 'focal point' of its inversion. The Gemini, in essence a symbol of opposites, is, in its dynamic aspect, then, a symbol of Inversion. According to the megalithic conception—and here we are following Schneider—the mountain of Mars (or Janus) which rises up as a mandorla of the Gemini is the locale of Inversion—the mountain of death and resurrection; the mandorla is another sign of Inversion and of interlinking, for it is formed by the intersection of the circle of earth with the circle of heaven. This mountain has two peaks, and every symbol or sign alluding to this 'situation of Inversion' is marked by duality or by twin heads. Two-headed eagles and cocks are also to be found in this context, the general symbolism of which is that of alternating contradiction: positive/negative, or low/high-pitched. All these are symbols of the harmonious ambiguity of 'thesis and antithesis, paradise and inferno, love and hate, peace and war, birth and death, praise and insult, clarity and obscurity, scorching rocks and swamps, surrounding the fountains and waters of salvation. Here, gay matters are discussed in grave tones, and the most tragic events are joked about' (50). If this cosmic situation were worked out in psychological terms, it would mean that the 'zone of contradiction' would become the threshold of unifying and unified mysticism. This would explain the abundance of contradictory epithets in the most sublime poetry, and the extraordinary richness of paradox in the deepest thinkers, such as Lao-Tse. Also corresponding to the mystery of the Gemini is the morphological fact that in every individual object there are two formal components, one varying, the other unvarying. In other words, one of its faces bespeaks its individuality, the other links it with its species (Plate XII).

Giant The deepest and most ancient meaning of the myth of the giant alludes to the supposed existence of an immense, primordial being, by whose sacrifice creation was brought forth. This cosmogonic myth was very common among primitive and ancient peoples, and it shows how rites involving the sacrifice of humans are an attempt to revive the initial sacrifice and to resuscitate the cosmic forces or to reawaken, at least, their favourable proclivities (17). Now, the giant is, in himself, neither good nor bad, but merely a quantitative amplification of the ordinary; hence, as the case may be, there are some legendary giants who are protectors and others who are aggressive. This sense of the giant as 'that which surpasses' human stature (here symbolic of power and strength), is also indicative of the broad significance of the giant. He may be an image of the 'Terrible Father', arising from childhood memories—children see their parents as giants—or an image of the unconscious, the 'dark side' of the personality menacing the Jungian *Selbst* (21), etc. It is interesting to note that in folklore the giant is tutelar in character: he is usually the defender of the common people against the overlord, upholding their liberties and rights. Without generalizing, one implication of the giant may be said to be the personification of collective Man—as implied in the maxim 'united we stand'—or of the life of a community (16). But the general myth of the giant is far from being confined to this specialized meaning. In nearly all symbolic traditions, he tends to appear as an outcropping of the marvellous and the terrible, even though he always has a certain quality of the inferior or the subordinate about him. The Bible refers to Goliath and to Og, king of Bashan at the time of the exodus (46). Samson has certain characteristics of the giant. In the West, Bodo, Rübezahl, Geryon, Gargantua and Hercules are the most significant in gigantomachy; in Greek tradition, there are the Titans and the Cyclops. Christian tradition has often seen Satan as a giant (50). The tragic hero is intimately linked with the giant, although, at times, in inverse relation as his adversary (60). Frazer describes the numerous cases in which giant figures in wood or wickerwork were set fire to during midsummer festivals, comparable with the Valencian *fallas* (or bonfires). The ancients would fill these figures with animals and even live men, who were burnt with the effigy. They were considered as representatives of the spirit of vegetation, or of the god sacrificed to the world—which brings us back once again to our cosmogonic interpretation. The giant may be a symbol of 'everlasting rebellion', of the forces of dissatisfaction which grow within Man and determine his history and his destiny; it may, that is to say, be a symbol of the Universal Man (Adam Kadmon, 21). Now, according to Jungian psychology, the giant's essence—or his appearance, rather—seems to correspond to the father-symbol, representing the spirit that withstands the instincts, or as the guardian of the treasure (that is, the mother—the unconscious), in which case it is identical with the dragon-symbol. Reviewing all this, Jung quotes the example of Humbaba, the guardian of the garden of Ishtar in the Gilgamesh epic (31).

Globe   The sphere is a whole, and hence it underlies the symbolic significance of all those images which partake of this wholeness, from the idea of the mystic 'Centre' (56) to that of the world and eternity (8), or, more particularly, of the world-soul (4). In neoplatonic philosophy, the soul is explicitly related to the shape of the sphere, and the substance of the soul is deposited as quintessence around the concentric spheres of the four Elements. The same is true of the primordial man of Plato's *Timaeus* (32). In alchemy, the globe, when it is black in colour, is a symbol of prime matter, or it may be depicted with wings to imply spiritual movement or evolution —as, for example, in the *Philosophia Reformata* of Mylius (1622) (32). Another important association is that of perfection and felicity. The absence of corners and edges is analogous to the absence of inconveniences, difficulties and obstacles.

Gloves Gloves, since they are worn on the hands, derive their symbolism from them. Of special interest is the right-hand glove, on account of the ceremonial custom of removing it when one approaches a person of higher rank, or an altar, or the Lord. This custom has twin symbolic roots: in so far as it implies a glove of mail, it signifies disarming oneself before one's superior; at the same time, since the right hand pertains to the voice and to the rational side of Man, it is a custom which suggests candour and the frank disclosure of one's mind.

Goblet (or **Drinking-cup**) In Romanesque times, and especially when, as a chalice, it was furnished with a lid, it was a symbol of the human heart (14). In a broader sense it is, like the coffer and the chest, a notable symbol of containing. To a certain extent it may be seen as a material expression of the surrounds of 'wrapping' around the mystic Centre. An important secondary meaning, in addition to the main symbolism of containing, is derived from the symbolism of the particular liquids which can be contained in goblets, glasses or chalices, and expressive of the non-formal world of possibilities (4). This is the explanation of the fact that hydromancy is practized with crystal or glass vessels which are supposed to have the power of talismans (57).

Gog and Magog They signify respectively the king and the people, as in Ezekiel, where the people of the North-East of Asia Minor are specifically called the enemies of God. This meaning still persists among the Moslems (46).

Gold In Hindu doctrine, gold is the 'mineral light'. According to Guénon, the Latin word for gold—*aurum*—is the same as the Hebrew for light—*aor* (26). Jung quotes the delightful explanation offered by the alchemist Michael Maier in *De Circulo Physico Quadrato* to the effect that the sun, by virtue of millions of journeys round the earth (or conversely) has spun threads of gold all round it. Gold is the image of solar light and hence of the divine intelligence. If the heart is the image of the sun in man, in the earth it is gold (32). Consequently, gold is symbolic of all that is superior, the glorified or 'fourth state' after the first three stages of black (standing for sin and penitence), white (remission and innocence) and red (sublimation and passion). Everything golden or made of gold tends to pass on this quality of superiority to its utilitarian function. Chrysaor, the magic sword of gold, symbolizes supreme spiritual determination. Gold is also the essential element in the symbolism of the hidden or elusive treasure which is an illustration of the fruits of the spirit and of supreme illumination.

Golden Fleece   This is one of the symbols denoting the conquest of the impossible or the ultra-reasonable (32). Since the sheep is symbolic of innocence and gold represents supreme spirituality and glorification, the Golden Fleece signifies that the quest of the Argonauts was for supreme strength of spirit through purity of soul—that quality which distinguished Sir Galahad, the mediaeval Knight of the Holy Grail. It is, in consequence, one of the most advanced forms within the general symbolism of treasure (15).

Goose   Like the duck, gander or swan, the goose is a beneficent animal associated with the Great Mother and with the 'descent into hell'. It is very often found in folktales (Mother Goose, Grimm's tales, etc.). It is linked with destiny as is proven by the 'goose game', a profane offshoot of the symbol in space–time, representing the dangers and fortunes of existence, prior to the return to the maternal bosom.

Gorgon   According to Frobenius, the gorgon is a symbol of the fusion of opposites: the lion and the eagle, the bird and the serpent, mobility and immobility (as in the swastika), beauty and horror (22). Hence it is symbolic of conditions beyond the endurance of the conscious mind, slaying him who contemplates it. Like other fabulous entities, it is also symbolic of the infinite number of forms in which creation can manifest itself.

Grafting   A symbol for artificial interference in the realm of natural order (4). It also has a sexual significance.

Grail, The   The Grail is one of the most beautiful and complex of legendary symbols. Basically, it embraces two different symbols, but it involves others too. The two main symbols are that of the Grail proper, and that of the quest. According to the Western legend (the Fisher King), a mysterious illness (symbolic, like that of Philoctetes) has stricken down the ancient monarch, the keeper of the Grail's secret. And in this rhythm and on this level everything around him is wilting like the peccant King himself (this being the theme of Poe's *Fall of the House of Usher* and of Eliot's *Waste Land*). The animals are declining, the trees bear no fruit, the fountains have ceased to play. Day and night, physicians and knights tend the ailing monarch. Sir Parsifal questions the king forthrightly: Where is the Grail? Instantly, the king rises and Nature is regenerated (18). The Swiss Knight Templar, Wolfram von Eschenbach, the author of

Parsifal, locates the action in Gaul, on the borders of Spain, where the hero Titurel has founded a temple for the preservation of the chalice of the Last Supper (27). It is said that the Grail came from the East and there it must return (32), which is a clear allusion to its significance as the 'source of illumination'. The cup itself has its own symbolism, but there is a legend which tells how it was fashioned by angels from an emerald that dropped from Lucifer's forehead when he was hurled into the abyss. Thus, just as the Virgin Mary redeems the sin of Eve, so the blood of the Redeemer redeems through the Grail the sin of Lucifer. This emerald, as Guénon has shown, is reminiscent of the *urnâ*, the pearl fixed to the forehead which, in Hindu symbolism, is the third eye of Siva (or Shiva), representing the 'sense of eternity'. The loss of the Grail is tantamount to the loss of one's inner adhesions, whether they are religious ties or—in the degraded (that is, the psychological) forms of the mystery—some other 'source of happiness'. Hence, this lapse of memory entails the loss of the primordial or paradisical state, as well as the death and withering up of Nature (that is, of one's own spiritual life). The Grail signifies at once a vessel (*grasale*) and a book (*gradale*). The quest, on the other hand, concerns, broadly speaking, the 'treasure hunt', which is actually the inversion of the endless chase of the 'Accursed Hunter', since the latter pursues phenomenal forms in their constant interplay of being and nonbeing, whereas the Grail implies, above all, the quest for the mystic 'Centre'—the 'unmoved mover', of Aristotle, or the 'unvarying mean' in Far Eastern tradition (28). The appearance of the Grail in the centre of the Round Table, round which are seated the Knights, closely parallels, in the symbolism of its form, the Chinese image of heaven (*Pi*), which is shaped like a circle with a hole (analogous with cup or chalice) in the middle. Ms. Fr. 112 of the Bibliothèque Nationale in Paris, *Lancelot du Lac*, depicts the moment in which the Grail is placed by two angels in the centre of the mystic Round Table (Plate XIII). One of the most widespread legends relates the Grail to the cup or plate in which Joseph of Arimathea caught the blood of Christ nailed to the Cross. The ideas of sacrifice and of self-chastisement (and in part the idea of castration) are associated with the symbolism of the Grail, as A. E. Waite demonstrates in *The Holy Grail* (London, 1933). It is obvious that sublimation of such sacrifice is also connected with the Grail, as in the legends of Parsifal and Sir Galahad.

Grapes Grapes, frequently depicted in bunches, symbolize at once fertility (from their character as a fruit) and sacrifice (because they give wine—particularly when the wine is the colour of blood). In baroque allegories of the Lamb of God, the Lamb is often portrayed between thorns and bunches of grapes.

Graphics We could compile and catalogue an immense repertoire of graphic signs. There is perhaps greater symbolic significance in these signs than in any other aspect of symbolism, because of the clear intention behind them to express an explicit meaning. One

●   Unity: the Origin.

—   Passive, static principle.

| Active, dynamic principle.

☐   Quaternary—material and passive.

◇   Quaternary—material and active.

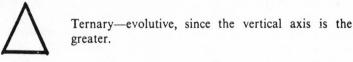 Material generation through the interaction of two opposing principles.

△   Ternary—neutral and successive.

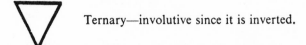 Ternary—evolutive, since the vertical axis is the greater.

▽   Ternary—involutive since it is inverted.

contemporary scholar, Ernst Lehner, tells us that he himself collected 60,000 symbols, signs and marks of different kinds, from varying sources, cultures and periods. The graphic symbol (whether engraved, etched or drawn, or contrived in the form of a diagram,

emblem or plan by any other means, such as that of papermakers'
watermarks) offers a clear illustration of the mystic doctrine of form,
such as it was developed by oriental civilizations in particular. As
Shukrâshârya has said with such lyric fervour: 'The character of the
image is determined by the relationship between the worshipper and

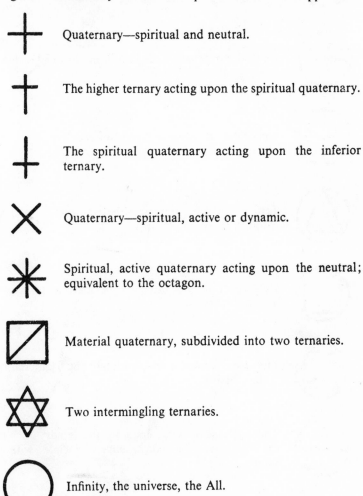

Quaternary—spiritual and neutral.

The higher ternary acting upon the spiritual quaternary.

The spiritual quaternary acting upon the inferior
ternary.

Quaternary—spiritual, active or dynamic.

Spiritual, active quaternary acting upon the neutral;
equivalent to the octagon.

Material quaternary, subdivided into two ternaries.

Two intermingling ternaries.

Infinity, the universe, the All.

the worshipped'; in this he is unconsciously echoing the biologist's
definition of form as 'the diagram between the inner urge of a body
and the resistance of the (physical) medium'. In Hindu doctrine,
beauty is the result not of external characteristics but of the emanation of a spiritual attitude; and the same is true of other aspects of

Centre of infinity: emanation or first cause.

 General movement in the Upper and Lower Worlds.

 Spiritual quaternary in the universe.

 Ternary in the universe: the spiritual principle within totality.

 Quaternary in the universe: the material principle within totality.

 The two quaternaries—spiritual and material—within totality.

 The quaternary acted upon by the ternary within the universe: the constructive principle within totality.

 Sensory, anthropomorphic principle (according to Piobb).

form, such as direction, order, arrangement, or the number of
components. German mystics, as Luc Benoist recalls (6), have also
applied themselves to shape (both in the round and diagrammatically) as a manifestation of the spirit. As Anna Katerina
Emmerich observed: 'Nothing is pure form. Everything is substance
and action, by virtue of signs.' The symbol as crystallized in creative
art involves a high degree of condensation, deriving from its inherent economy of form and allusive power. This, then, is the
psychological basis of the symbolism of graphics (the basis of the
magical interpretation is to be sought in the literal interpretation
of the theory of correspondences). It underlies the graphic symbolism
of amulets, talismans, pentacles and divinatory signs from prehistoric times right up to the present day. Hence the strong and
perfectly justified attraction exerted by certain shapes, emblems,
flags, coats of arms, marks and medals, based not upon convention,
as is usually suggested, but upon inner bonds of symbolic 'common
rhythms' (30). Quite apart from their function as integrating or
synoptic symbols, graphic symbols possess a singular mnemonic
power, as Schneider has shown. He points to the fact that such
figures as the spiral, the swastika, the circle with a central point,
the lunar crescent, the double sigma, etc., were capable of conveying
the most varied of philosophical, alchemical or astronomic data—
a technique of interpretation capable of applying all the information
supplied by these three disciplines to a single plane of significance.
Any one given figure (with its series of multivalencies—that is,
embracing several meanings which are not irrelevant or equivocal)
varies in appearance and in significance with the 'rhythm-symbol'
(that is, the idea and the intended direction) pervading it. Schneider
adds, in connexion with Tanew's *Das Ornament die Elbetiza* (Ipek,
1942), that this constitutes one of the predominant features of
ancient art, which 'is often unfortunately called decorative or
ornamental art' (51). To enumerate some of the fields of activity
which have been profoundly influenced by graphic symbolism:
mythological attributes and figures, signs in astronomy and
astrology, alchemy, magic and primitive mysticism, religions,
heraldry, fabulous figures and monsters, ornaments, signs of
diverse offices, numismatic signs, marks on porcelain, watermarks,
etc. (36). If we pause to consider the prodigious variety offered by
only one of these categories—ornaments, for example—it will
become apparent that even a rough inventory of the symbolic
ramifications would be impracticable here for material reasons.
And we could add further headings: alphabets, for example, or
ideographs, pictographs, metagraphs and mandalas, as well as
graphic artistic compositions, embracing abstract painting for
example, which—like Celtic, Anglo-Saxon and Nordic ornamental

art—provides an unceasing flow of significant forms, expressed willy-nilly, for Man is quite incapable of creating anything which does not bear the marks of his subtle, urgent and all-embracing need for communication. To widen now the scope of this exposition, let us consider the lapidary signs to be found in the stones of many architectural edifices. A great many kinds of different marks have been catalogued, and, without doing violence to their esoteric meaning, we may group them, as follows, into: initial letters, anagrams, astrological, numerical, magic or mystico-Christian signs, or marks pertaining to associations or groups, or to building, or to nationality or race, or to benefactors, etc.

In ornamentation, Greek frets, wavy lines, series of spirals, coils of varying rhythms, sigmas, X-shapes, diamonds, circles, ovals, arrows, triangles, zigzags, triskeles and swastikas are all graphic shapes which, in symbolism, are grouped under the general heading of 'cosmic background', because they are all in effect symbols of the activity of natural forces and of the four Elements (41). In varying degrees, depending upon the period and personal or cultural prejudice, scholars researching into the history and pre-history of art—since few of them have taken any interest in the autonomous doctrine of symbolism—have either lumped these graphic symbols together as sun-symbols, or else as symbols of the hurricane and the heavens. J. Déchelette, for example, says in his *Manuel d'Archéologie préhistorique* that all the signs concerning dual, bilateral symmetry or the irradiating Centre 'were employed as images of the sun from the Bronze Age onwards'. We must not fail to mention one important fact, and that is the connexion of the symbolism of form with divination. The Chinese *Pa Kua*—whose system is described in the *I Ching* (*The Book of Changes*)—the random dots of geomancy, and the innumerable '-mancies' which have come down to us from Antiquity in a great many works upon the subject, are all founded for the most part upon the symbolism of form; this can be seen both in the identification of a given 'matrical shape' with the figure of a particular being (as happens in the case of Rorschach's tests with ink-blots) whose symbolic implications will determine the augury, and in the splitting up of a shape into its numerical components and its tendency towards a particular direction in space, in which case its symbolic sense is determined by the significance of the numbers and the space-zone associated with it. Frazer, for example, describes the Chinese belief that the life and destiny of a city is so influenced by its shape that its fortunes must vary according to the character of the thing which that shape most nearly resembles; and he relates that, long ago, the town of Tsuen-cheu-fu, the outlines of which were like those of a carp, frequently fell a prey to the depredations of the neighbouring city of Yung-chun, which was shaped like a fishing-net (21).

Jung has shown great interest in the question of graphic symbolism, geometric diagrams and numbers determined by the quantitative factor of component elements, without, however, working up his interesting—and valid—findings and conclusions into a comprehensive theory. He observes, for example, that the relationships between number and shape depend not only upon the quantity of the elements but also upon their individual shape and direction, because the direction influences the quantitative factor in the same way as fracture does. By way of illustration, he mentions that in the ninth key of the *Duodecim Claves Fratris Basilii Valentini* (in *Museum Hermeticum*, Frankfurt, 1678) there is an instance of triunity appearing as unity, realized by splitting a Y-sign in the centre, so that it becomes three strokes; and another of duality as a quaternary, by forming a four-armed cross not with four lines but with two independent but counterbalancing right angles, so that they can be said to be two components by virtue of their continuity but four from the point of view of their direction. He comments also upon the fact that irregular quadrilaterals are expressive of the tendency in the equilibrium of the symbolism of the number four to adapt itself in conformity with the direction of the major axis. If the horizontal line is predominant, then it reveals the superiority of the merely rational intellect, whereas if the vertical line prevails then it denotes spiritual non-rationalism. The sign of the conjunction of the quaternary (the cross or the square) with unity is expressed through the union of the numbers four and one, that is, of the square (or the cross) and the circle. The relationship between two intersecting diameters and the circumference is emphasized by sometimes depicting the centre visibly as a small circle symbolic of the mystic 'Centre'. The figure thus arrived at is of great symbolic value: it expresses the original Oneness (symbolized by the centre), the 'way out to the manifest world' (the four radii, which are the same as the four rivers which well up from the *fons vitae* or from the foot of the Cosmic Tree in Paradise), and the return to Oneness (the outer circumference) through the circular movement which 'smooths away' the corners of the square (these corners implying the differentiation characteristic of the multiplicity and the transitoriness of the world of phenomena). By adding a further cross, shaped like an X, to this figure, the wheel is obtained; and the wheel is the commonest symbol of the 'Centre' and of the cycle of transformations. The importance of the relationship between the circle and the square is quite extraordinary; religious and symbolic art as well as profane works provide us with a great variety of shapes incorporating both the circle and the square. But to limit ourselves to religious symbolism, let us quote two instances which are entirely unrelated yet produce the same result: first, the so-called 'pentacle of Laos', a squared figure with a small square at its centre and four circles inside the angles, each divided into four internally; and secondly, the retable in the Cartuja de Miraflores (the Carthusian monastery near Burgos), which is arranged in a similar pattern, but incorporates figures of the Pantokrator and of tetramorphs. The underlying logico-symbolic force of such figures is so strong that, when one has recourse to an abstract image of a cosmic order, capable of expressing the intimate and intense relationship between the 'two worlds', one turns inevitably to this *coniunctio* joining the symbol for earth (the square) with that for heaven (the circle). The fact that figures incorporating the irradiant 'Centre' are cosmic symbols of the ultimate destiny of the spirit accounts for the fact that they are also psychological images of this same destiny, that is, of its presentiment and of the way of fulfilling it—in short, of the mystic idea of consummation (32). Hence, psychoanalysts have noted that the joining of the square with the circle (in such forms as the star, the rose, the lotus, concentric circles, the circle with a visible central point, etc.) is symbolic of the final stage in the process of individuation, or, in other words, of that phase of spiritual development when imperfections (irregular shapes) have been eliminated, as have all earthly desires (represented by malignant, biological symbols of monsters and wild beasts), for the sake of concentrating upon the achievement of Oneness and a vision of Paradise (such as that described by Dante at the end of his masterpiece) (56).

Other conclusions of Jung concerning the psychology of shapes are these: opposites are symbolized by a cross (signifying inner urges) and by a square (standing for the horizon); the process of rising above these urges is symbolized by the circle (33); exact duplication implies confirmation, but when the two symbols face in opposite directions they express the longing for wholeness, that is, the desire not only to explore the two spheres but to conquer all space; to go towards the left is to turn towards the unconscious and the past, to go to the right is to face consciousness and the future. Jung points, as an example, to an illustration in the *Viatorium* of Michael Maier (Rouen, 1651), showing two eagles flying in opposite directions (32).

Concerning graphic compositions proper, and their corresponding symbolic significance, we must not overlook the existence of the theory that they were originally ornamental, a thesis which is upheld by Baltrusàitis among others. He insists upon the *a priori* thesis that artists are faced with a certain area to fill up and the need to achieve certain artistic effects, proceeding from concepts of order, symmetry, logic and clarity. But man's aesthetic urges arose long after his need to express cosmic significances; and the contemporary concept of art as a sign and testimony of a state of mind, rather than as the creation of beauty or of aesthetic pleasure (which would seem automatically to preclude many modern works of art lacking in positive or loveable qualities), appears to favour the view that the primary impulse is to express a symbolic meaning. According to tradition, symmetrical forms in art spring from the same source (the Gemini) as the bilateral symmetry of the human figure, a symmetry which is echoed in the duplication of certain organs; such symmetrical forms include, for instance, the distribution of figures on a Romanesque or Gothic tympanum, or the arrangement of the supporters, the shield and helmet on an escutcheon. But if this idea of a common origin seems unacceptable, then the artistic preference for symmetry may be conceived as a simple anatomic projection, granted that the conviction of primordial rightness can only be experienced when the artificial is felt to be parallel, analogous or corresponding to the natural. A being with two arms at the sides of a body surmounted by a head must tend to formulate primarily an order or pattern in which one principal shape is located in the middle and two secondary shapes are placed at the sides. These elementary notions were first appreciated not—in all probability—in the Palaeolithic Age (an age about which our knowledge is scant, and when man was, in any case, living under constant pressure from the need to exert himself in utilitarian ways), but in the period of the dawning of history, from the latter part of the Neolithic up to the Bronze Age, or, in other words, from 5000 to 3000 B.C. This was the period, then, when cultural factors first appeared or when they reached a definitive stage of development. Ortiz is right to suggest that man not improbably, before arriving at a generic configuration of life, first created ideograms of the tangible realities of life, and specially of those entities, such as the wind, which have no concrete shape. Fire was seen as flame; water as a succession of waves; rain was likened to tears; lightning to the zigzag, and so on (41).

We do not wish to suggest that all pictographs or ideographs, let alone signs, of primitive or astrobiological cultures owe their origins to such motives as these, or that they disclose a similar, morphological process of development. We must here distinguish between: *realistic, imitative images* in the first place (properly, drawings or paintings); in the second place, *diagrammatic, imitative images* (which seek after the inner 'rhythmic' meaning of a given figure, as well as its outer form); and, in the third, *pure, rhythmic images* (such as signs for animals deriving from their tracks). Schneider observes that, in intermediary cultures, animal-symbols are not representations of physical shapes but rhythmic lines determined by the animals' movements. He adds that, in Malacca, the symbolism of a given animal may be applied to one of the four

Elements: so that, for example, the symbol for water is derived from the rhythmic movements of the frog's legs (which, in any case, are comparable with the rhythm of the waves); similarly, ants, as well as centipedes, are signified by the rhythm of their movements (50). This concept of 'rhythm' opens up enormous possibilities when applied to the conception of the light of the spirit. Every man has his own rhythm; and so has every culture. Style or personality are in the last resort simply expressions of rhythm. Germain Bazin, in his *Histoire de l'art* (Paris, 1953), suggests that abstract art is the attempt to externalize the *essential rhythms* of the human, individual and collective soul (the process being closely related to that of endopathy as conceived by Aristotle, Vischer, Kant, Lipps, etc.).

Consequently, in order to decide upon the significance of any graphic figure, we must bear in mind the following factors: (*a*) its resemblance to figures of cosmic beings; (*b*) its shape, whether open or closed, regular or irregular, geometric or biomorphic; (*c*) the number of component elements making up the shape, together with the significance of this number; (*d*) the dominant 'rhythms' as the expression of its elemental, dynamic potential and its movement; (*e*) the spatial arrangement, or the disposition of its different zones; (*f*) its proportions; (*g*) its colours, if any. Factor (*a*)—its resemblance to other figures—is so wide in scope and so obvious in its implications that comment would be superfluous. (*b*) The significance of shape depends upon the relevant geometric symbolism, which we have examined above. (*c*) The number of its components confers an added symbolism to the secondary—though at times very important —consideration of the shape (for example, the seven-pointed star derives its significance as much from the septenary symbolism as from the stellar shape). (*d*) Concerning the 'rhythms', we have already pointed out the connexion with the number of component elements and with animal-movements (Greek frets, and the broken line fashioned after the trapeze are usually said to correspond to earth-symbolism, the wavy line to air-symbolism, a succession of incomplete spirals—or waves—as well as the broken line, to water-symbolism, although fire is also associated with water because of the triangular shape of the tongue of flame). (*e*) Regarding the spatial arrangement: along the vertical axis, it is the symbolism of level which matters most (implying qualities of morality and energy), and on the horizontal axis, the left side is, as we have said, retro-spective (for it is the zone of 'origin', linked with the unconscious and with darkness), and the right side looks to the outcome. Hence, the line running from the left downwards and then upwards towards the right does not indicate a fall but an ascent, the converse also being true. And for this reason, the St. Andrew's cross, with its two intersecting and opposing lines standing for fall and ascent respectively, is symbolic of the intermingling of the 'two worlds', and is therefore comparable with the mystic mandorla. In those figures which feature a centre together with dual, bilateral symmetry, we have two symbolic tendencies: first, that in which the rhythmic movements tend inwards, denoting concentration and also aggression (as, for example, in the classical symbol of the four winds blowing towards the centre); and secondly, that in which rhythms well up from the centre towards the four cardinal points, indicating the defence of 'wholeness" (the cross of St. Ferdinand is related to this) and bearing a certain relationship with the tetramorphs and the 'four archers' of megalithic culture. Irradiating figures denote dispersion, growth and involution. It must also be borne in mind that lines, in addition to their morphological properties, are also means of communication and of conjoining; this is why their significance must always be closely linked with the nature of the zones which they bring into contact. There are, it must be said, some theorists who carry the study of graphics to extremes of prolixity and detail. Ely Star, for example, examines the various shapes suggested by an upright line crossing a horizontal, simply by the process of linking the upright with the active principle and the horizontal with the passive. He comments that straight lines are always expressive of activity, compared with curves which denote passivity (54). To turn now to the way the first ideographic signs were associated with the constellations, it is very important to note that the modern view favours the theory that the constellations were the source of the alphabet. Gattefossé, Fenn and others are quite explicit upon this point. Zollinger shows how the Great Bear is the origin of the sign representing a bond, a link or an item of knowledge, how the Gemini gave rise to the number 8 and the letter H, how the eternal cyclic laws of the sun's orbit or the polar rotation of the earth gave rise to the swastika, the division of the increate into different forms inspired the Chinese Yang-Yin sign, the manifest world inspired the horizontal line, the 'Centre' the cross, and, finally, how the union of the three principles as represented by the signs for the Sun, the Moon and the cross originated the graphic symbol known as the emblem of Hermes. He goes on to mention the family resemblance between forms of bilateral symmetry such as the Yang-Yin sign, the labrys (the twin-bladed axe), the labarum and the cross (61). Bayley found that, among his collection of watermarks, were a large number of graphic signs with a precise meaning to them: three circles, or the clover-leaf and its derivatives stand for the trinitarian; the labyrinth shaped like a cross, denotes both inscrutability and close ties; wheels indicate the sun as the motivating force behind change and cycles (4). Concerning the symbolism of crosses, of which the varieties are numerous, we shall confine ourselves to indicating that they depend upon the shape of their arms and the 'rhythmic direction' which these arms suggest (as in centrifugal, centripetal, neutral or rotatory crosses) (47). The symbols for planets and many other marks which cannot be reduced to a simple geometric figure or explained as a combination of simple component elements, but which disclose a certain complexity of pattern, may nevertheless be interpreted with the help of the principles enumerated above. To give just one example: In alchemy, the sign for 'antimony', representing the intellectual 'soul' alive with all its virtues and faculties, is a cross placed upon a circle; the sign for 'green', denoting the vegetative 'soul' or the physiological world, is a cross inscribed within a circle; the sign for Venus, corresponding to instinctive behaviour or the base urges, is a cross placed below a circle. In short, there is nothing arbitrary about graphic symbolism (59): everything obeys a system which develops out of a single point and expands into more complex forms in which shape, rhythm, quantity, position, order and direction all help to explain and define the pattern.

Great Monarch, The   This is a term which is to be found in some Hermetic writings. According to Piobb, it owes its origin to an incorrect reading of the Greek, mistaking 'he who governs himself alone' for 'he who governs alone' (48). Be that as it may, the symbolism of the king refers, in any case, to him who triumphs over himself, that is, to the hero definitive and victorious (48).

Great Mother, The   The archetype of the Great Mother corresponds to certain feminine deities such as Ishtar in Babylonia, Isis in Egypt, Astarte in Phoenicia, Kâli-Durga in India, Ge and Demeter in Greece (56). It is usually considered to be a symbol of the fertilized earth (51), though the sea also appears in ancient cosmogonies with the same connotation (4). For Jung, the *Magna Mater* represents the objective truth of Nature, masquerading, or incarnate, in the figure of a maternal woman, a sybil, a goddess or a priestess, but sometimes taking the form of a church, for instance, or a city or district. This archetypal image he calls 'mana personality', corresponding to the 'Ancient of Days' who likewise takes such forms as the magician, sorcerer or sage (30).

Great Priest, The   The fifth enigma of the Tarot pack. The card shows him seated upon a throne between the two columns Jachin and Boaz (symbolic of intuition and reason). He wears white gloves to symbolize the purity of his hands. His sceptre terminates in a triple cross, the rounded ends of whose arms give rise to the septenary, alluding to the virtues necessary to combat the seven capital sins: Pride—the Sun; Sloth—the Moon; Envy—Mercury; Wrath—Mars; Lust—Venus; Greed—Jupiter; and Avarice—Saturn. Also depicted in this image are two disciples, both kneeling, one dressed in red (for activity) and the other in black (passivity). On the positive side, this enigma signifies the moral law, duty and conscience (59).

Great Priestess, The   The second enigma of the Tarot, representing Isis as the goddess of the night. She is seated, holding a half-opened book in her right hand and two keys in her left, one of which is golden (signifying the sun, the word, or reason) and the other silver (the moon or imagination). Her throne is situated between two columns—being two in number, they are an allegory denoting the feminine principle—which are in fact the columns called Jachin and Boaz in the Temple of Solomon, joined together by the veil which covers the entrance to the sanctuary. The first (the solar) column is red and corresponds to fire and to activity; the second (the lunar) is blue. The tiara which crowns the head of the Great Priestess has a lunar crescent—a symbol of cyclic phases and of the world of phenomena; this emphasizes the predominance of the passive, reflective and feminine qualities of the figure. She is leaning against the sphinx of the great cosmic questions, and the floor, being composed of alternate white and black tiles, denotes that everything in existence is subject to the laws of chance and of opposites. In the Besançon Tarot, this enigma takes the form of the figure of Juno. On the positive side, the Great Priestess signifies reflection and intuition; on the negative, intolerance (59).

Griffin   A fabulous animal, the front half of which is like an eagle and the rear half like a lion, with a long, serpentine tail. The blending of these two superior solar animals points to the generally beneficent character of this being; it was consecrated by the Greeks to Apollo and Nemesis (8). The griffin, like certain kinds of dragon, is always to be found as the guardian of the roads to salvation, standing beside the Tree of Life or some such symbol. From the psychological point of view it symbolizes the relationship between psychic energy and cosmic force (4). In mediaeval Christian art, from Mozarabic miniatures onwards, the griffin is very common, being associated with signs which tend towards ambivalence, representing, for instance, both the Saviour and Antichrist (20).

Grotesques   A type of ornament serving a largely decorative purpose. Favoured by the Romans, it became very common from the 15th century onwards, especially in the Plateresque style. Some of its characteristics owe their inspiration—like emblems—to Gnosticism which, as is well known, made wide use of the symbolic image in order to spread its doctrines. Bayley has collected a large number of grotesques and similar decorative motifs, among which the following figures predominate: the phoenix, swan, sheep, winged horses, serpents, dragons, gardens, diverse flowers, shrubs, sheaves, garlands, creepers, roses in jars, fruits, baskets of flowers and fruits, vines, pomegranates, trees (especially the evergreen sort), crosses, lilies, caducei, bolts, masks, steps, trophies, rosettes, bows, shields, brackets, swords, lances, cups and chalices, nude children, twins, sowers, fertility goddesses with multiple breasts, caryatids, damsels. All these items have their place in the world of symbolism as component parts of allegories, emblems, Romanesque and Gothic capitals, and so on. But the grotesque in itself, as a form and as a system, emphasizes the close bond between continuity and discontinuity—of ambivalence, that is to say, as expressed, for instance, in the myth of the Gemini. Hence, the grotesque is a general symbol for the world of phenomena and of the coherent unfolding of existence (4).

Guardian Just as the powers of the Earth must be defended, so, by analogy, must all mythic, religious and spiritual wealth or power be protected against hostile forces or against possible intrusion by the unworthy. Hence the familiarity of the 'keeper of the treasure' in legends: almost invariably, this guardian is a griffin or dragon, or else a warrior endowed with superhuman powers. In temples, the idea of defence is implicit in the spatial organization and confirmed by the disposition of the walls, the doors and towers. In the Far East, the guardians are usually fabulous monsters. In Western countries, the same function may be performed by the figures inscribed on doorways. From the psychological point of view, guardians symbolize the forces gathered on the threshold of transition between different stages of evolution and spiritual progress or regression. The 'guardian of the threshold' must be overcome before Man can enter into the mastery of a higher realm.

Gum The term *Gummi arabicum* was one employed by the alchemists to denote the substance of transmutation, for they believed that, once spiritualized, it became endowed with analogous qualities of spiritual adhesion. It is a symbol for the seminal substance (32).

Hair (Body-Hair) Whereas hair on the head, because it grows on the top of the human body, symbolizes spiritual forces and can be equated, within the symbolism of water, with the 'Upper Ocean', body-hair is equivalent to the 'Lower Ocean', that is to say, it denotes the proliferation of the irrational power of the cosmos and of the instinctive life. This explains why the priests of many religions, the Egyptians among them, shaved off all their hair. And it also explains why the god Pan—a prefiguration of the devil—was depicted with hairy legs. Despite the above generalization, there are some traditions in which the hair of the head as well as on the body takes on a malign significance (8).

Hairs In general, hairs represent energy, and are related to the symbolism of levels. That is, a head of hair, being located on the head, stands for higher forces, whereas abundant body-hair signifies the prevalence of the baser forces. Sometimes these two meanings have coalesced: on a Romanesque capital at Estibaliz, Adam is depicted beardless before the Fall and with long hair and bushy beard after he has fallen into sin (46). Hairs also signify fertility. Origen used to say: 'The Nazirites do not cut their hair because all that is done by just men prospers and their leaves to not fall' (46). In Hindu symbolism, hairs, like the threads of a fabric, symbolize the 'lines of force' of the universe (25). A full head of hair represents *élan vital* and *joie de vivre*, linked with the will to succeed (42). Again, hairs correspond to the element of fire, signifying the burgeoning of primitive forces (50). A highly important secondary meaning is derived from the colour of hair. Brown or black hair reinforces the symbolism of hair in general, that is, dark, terrestrial energy; golden hair is related to the sun's rays (31, 38) and to the whole vast sun-symbolism; copper-coloured hair implies a Venusian or demoniacal characteristic (32). Hairs, then, come to symbolize the concept of spiritualized energy. Phaldor, in his *Libro d'oro del sogno*, comments that they 'represent the spiritual assets of Man. Abundant, beautiful hair, for both man and woman, signifies spiritual development. To lose one's hair signifies failure and poverty' (56). Now, the reverse of loss brought about by forces outside Man's control is, in part, willing sacrifice. For this reason, Zimmer points out that all who renounce and defy the principles of procreation and multiplication of life, in order to embark upon the path of total asceticism, are bound on principle to cut their hair short. They must simulate the sterility of the aged and hairless who form the last link in the chain of generations. Some religions, as for example that of the ancient Egyptians, used to prescribe total depilation (60). Hair, wigs and beards were used by the Sumerians to ward off evil spirits (as was smoke).

Halo The aureole, nimbus or halo is a luminous circle like a crown with which the ancients invested their deities and which Christians accord to the holy (8). It is a visual expression of irradiating, supernatural force, or, sometimes, more simply, of intellectual energy in its mystic aspect; the fact that the Ancients almost invariably equated intelligence with light is proof enough of this. Other kinds of halos are spherical in form: the Moslems, for example, often made use of the pearl to represent paradise and their belief was that the blessed, each one united with his houri, live in pearls. The halo is equated with the cage and, in particular, with the sphere itself (46). Jurgis Baltrusaitis, in *Le Moyen Age fantastique*, has collected a host of mediaeval drawings and paintings of beings enclosed in transparent spheres apparently made of glass. Many of the works of Hieronymus van Aecken (Bosch) contain examples of this. The halo, in this case, is a simple visual expression of a kind of determinism enveloping each man within his mode of being and his destiny, whether it is favourable and paradisiac, or adverse and infernal.

Hamlet Although literary myths do not normally enter into the scope of this work, we have decided to make an exception in the case of *Hamlet, Prince of Denmark*. This famous Shakespearian tragedy has its origins in a Nordic legend. Apart from the Renaissance dramatist's explanation of its 'obvious contents', it also lends itself to other explanations of latent contents, or, better, to disclosures on other planes. One of these interpretations, the psychoanalytic, would tend towards the belief that Hamlet really becomes mad, and that the assassination of his father by his uncle is mere fiction, an invention of his mind intended to help him to accept more easily the Oedipus complex which is so powerful in him. His satisfaction on killing Polonius, which foreshadows the moment when he kills his step-father, seems to bear out this explanation. So do his rejection of Ophelia (which may be interpreted in a different way), and his complete forgiveness of his mother, who in *Electra* (a Greek tragedy along similar lines) is implacably assassinated by her avenging offspring. A second explanation of *Hamlet*, which is more profound and symbolic, results from applying Gnostic doctrine to his story. Hamlet hates the world and considers it to be the work of the evil god, of the demiurge (the husband of his mother, who is the material and whom he pardons because he judges her to be the merely passive agent of Evil). He dreams of the good god, of the Father, who seems rather to be his own projection, his autodivination in a transcendent situation. The rejection of the world has a 'necrophiliac' explanation in the scene in the graveyard with Yorick's skull and an absolute manifestion in his spurning of Ophelia (woman = guilt). There is an angelism in Hamlet which causes us to consider him to be the symbol and archetype of Oedipal man, who suffers from being tied to the world, from being a material entity and from owning his existence to a being whom he would kill and by whom he might possibly be killed (cf. the slaying of the firstborn by the primitive father, according to Freud). As a case of anguish and repressions leading to a series of crimes which can only be resolved by his own self-destruction, Hamlet is a symbol of man in rebellion against the 'filial' situation, a humanized (and Christianized?) symbol, successor to Aeschylus' 'Prometheus' and predecessor to Milton's 'Satan'. I owe these ideas to seeing the cinematographic *Hamlet*, directed and interpreted by Sir Laurence Olivier, whose intensity suggested to me all that I express here in the form of a hypothesis.

Hammer An instrument proper to the smith, endowed with the mystic power of creation (51). The two-headed hammer is, like the twin-bladed axe, an ambivalent symbol of the mountain of Mars and of sacrificial Inversion.

Hand In the Egyptian tongue, the term designating the hand was related to that for the pillar (or a support, or strength) and for the palm (4). In esoteric doctrine, the position of the hand in relation to the body, and the arrangement of the fingers, convey certain precise symbolic notions (48). According to the Egyptian system of hieroglyphs, the hand signifies manifestation, action, donating and husbandry. An eye in association with a hand—as for example in some oriental mythic beings—symbolize 'clairvoyant action' (19). Schneider concedes a major rôle to the hand 'because it is the corporeal manifestation of the inner state of the human being' and because 'it expresses an attitude of mind in terms other than the acoustic'—or, in other words, a gesture. It follows, then, that the raised hand is the symbol of the voice and of song; the hand placed on the breast indicates the attitude of the sage; placed on the neck it denotes sacrifice; two hands joined signifies mystic marriage— the Jungian individuation; the hand covering the eyes represents clairvoyance at the moment of death (50). Of great importance is the fact that the hand has five fingers, firstly, because of its broad analogy with the human figure (composed of four extremities plus the head), and, secondly, by reason of the symbolism of the number five (denoting love, health and humanity) (40). In Egyptian hieroglyphics, the open hand signifies any specificially human task as well as magnetic force (19)—an idea also characteristic of pre-Columbian America. And a very similar belief lies behind the widespread use of the hand as an amulet in Islamic cultures. According to Berber thought, the hand signifies protection, authority, power and strength; the *manus* had the same meaning for the Romans, symbolizing in particular the authority of the *pater familias* and of the emperor, and is sometimes to be seen surmounting the *signum* of the legions in place of the imperial eagle. In the Islamic amulets mentioned above, the figure of the hand undergoes various modifications or appears in association with other symbols, as, for instance, the star, the dove, the bird, the fan, the zigzag and the circle, forming emblems comparable with those of the Christian West (12). The familiar emblem of the 'linked hands' is expressive of a virile fraternity, or solidarity in the face of danger (49). In Jung's opinion, the hand is endowed with a generative significance (31). The difference between the right hand and the left is usually ignored, but when the distinction is made it appears merely to serve the purpose of enriching the basic significance with the additional implications of space-symbolism, the right side corresponding to the rational, the conscious, the logical and the virile; the left side representing the converse (33). There are alchemic images which represent a King clasping in his own left hand the left hand of the Queen. Jung suggests that this may refer to the unconscious character of their union but that it may also be indicative either of affection or of suspicion (33).

Hanged Man   This figure has a profound and complex symbolism. It is enigma number twelve of the Tarot pack of cards, but its fundamental significance has wider implications. Frazer noted that primitive man endeavours to keep his deities alive by isolating them between heaven and earth, thereby placing them in a position which is immune to ordinary influences (21), especially terrestrial ones. This and every other kind of suspension in space implies, then, a mystical isolation which is doubtless related to the idea of levitation and to dream-flight. On the other hand, the inverted position is in itself a symbol of purification (because it inverts, analogically, the natural, terrestrial order) (50). Both the legend of the Hanged Man as a figure endowed with magic powers, and the Odin myth, belong to this symbolic system. Of Odin it was said that he had sacrificed himself by hanging. The relevant verses of *Havamal* read: 'I know that I have been hanging from the stormy tree for nine consecutive nights, wounded by the spear, as an offering to Odin: myself offered to myself.' Similar sacrifices are part of normal cult-practice in many parts of the world (21). Jung explains this symbolism in purely psychological terms, saying that 'hanging . . . has an unmistakable symbolic value, since swinging (hanging and suffering as one swings) is the symbol of unfulfilled longing or tense expectation' (31). The Tarot card mentioned above depicts a figure like the Minstrel hanging by one foot from a rope tied to a crossbar supported by two leafless trees. The interpretation is that the Hanged Man does not live the ordinary life of this earth, but, instead, lives in a dream of mystical idealism. The strange gallows from which he hangs is yellow in colour to indicate it consists of concentrated light, i.e. concentrated thought. Thus it is said that the Hanged Man hangs from his own doctrine, to which he is attached to such an extent that his entire being hangs upon it. The two trees between which he hangs are related—like anything that is connected with the numerical symbolism of 2—to the Boaz and Jachin pillars of the Cabala. They are coloured green tending to blue (natural or terrestrial nature tending towards heaven). The Hanged Man's clothing is red and white, these being the mystical colours of the two-headed eagle of the alchemists. His arms are tied together, and hold half-opened bags out of which gold coins are tumbling, this being an allegory of the spiritual treasures to be found in the being who performs this self-sacrifice. According to Wirth, the mythological hero closest to this symbolic character is Perseus, the personification of thought in action, who—in his flight—overcame the forces of evil in order to free Andromeda, who symbolizes the soul chained to the dull rock of matter, rising from the waves of the primeval ocean. In the positive sense, number twelve of the Tarot pack stands for mysticism, sacrifice, self-denial, continence. In the negative sense it denotes a Utopian dream-world (59).

Hare In the Egyptian series of hieroglyphs, the hare is a determinative sign defining the concept of being, and symbolic in consequence of elemental existence (19). Among the Algonquin Indians, the Great Hare is the animal-demiurge. The myth was also known to the Egyptians. In Greece, the lunar goddess, Hecate, was associated with hares. The German equivalent of Hecate, the goddess Harek, was accompanied by hares (35). In general, the hare is a symbol of procreation; it is ambivalent in that it may be considered as naturally amoral or moral. The Hebrews regarded it as an 'unclean' animal (Deuteronomy xiv, 7). For Rabanus Maurus, it symbolized lasciviousness and fecundity. However, it had also become, by Gothic times, an allegorical figure of fleetness and of diligent service, for it is to be found on many Gothic sepulchres as an emblem in this particular sense—a sense subsidiary to that outlined above (46). A feminine character is inseparable from the fundamental symbolization of the hare; hence it is not surprising to find that it was the second of the twelve emblems of the Emperor of China, symbolic of the *Yin* force in the life of the monarch (5). The Chinese conceived the hare as an animal of augury and it was said to live on the moon.

Harp Equated with the white horse (4) and the mystic ladder. It acts as a bridge between heaven and earth. This is why, in the Edda, heroes express their desire to have a harp buried with them in their grave, so as to facilitate their access to the other world. There is also a close connexion between the harp and the swan (50). It might also be regarded as a symbol of the tension inherent in the strings with its striving towards love and the supernatural world, a situation of stress which crucifies man in every moment of the anguished expectation of his earthly life. This would explain the detail of Bosch's *Garden of Delights*, where a human figure hangs crucified on the strings of a harp. Music being a symbol of pure manifestation of the Will (Schopenhauer), the harp would seem to be a particularly intense and characteristic embodiment of sound as the carrier of stress and suffering, of form and life-forces (Plate XIV).

Harpies Fabulous beings, daughters of Neptune and the sea, usually regarded as allegories or personifications of vice in its twin aspects of guilt and punishment (8). At a deeper level, they have been defined as a representation of the 'evil harmonies of cosmic energies' (48). Sometimes the emphasis is entirely on their dynamic nature, in which case they are depicted in the well-known attitude of 'swift movement', reminiscent of the swastika. This is also the case with the Erinyes and the Gorgons (41). In mediaeval decorative art they sometimes occur merely as emblems of the sign of Virgo in its musical aspects. In heraldry, the figure of the harpy has no sinister associations (48).

Harpist   The symbolism of the harpist follows from that of his instrument. He frequently occurs in literature, one of the most famous examples being in Goethe's *Wilhelm Meister*. In a German poem—*Die Krone*—Guinevere arouses her husband's jealousy by telling him of a knight who rides past every night, singing. . . . Celtic folklore tells how Yseult was abducted by a harp-player. The tale of the Pied Piper describes how the children follow him as he plays a tune on his pipe. All these figures are personifications of the fascination of death, that is, Freud's death-wish. Also, in Greek mythology the psychopomp Hermes is the inventor of the lyre and the flute (35).

Hat   According to Jung, the hat, since it covers the head, generally takes on the significance of what goes on inside it: thought. He recalls the German saying 'to put all ideas under one hat', and mentions that in Meyrink's novel *The Golem*, the protagonist thinks the thoughts and undergoes the experiences of another man whose hat he has put on by mistake (32). Jung also points out that, since the hat is the 'crown' and summit of an individual, it may therefore be said to cover him, an idea which carries a special symbolic significance. By its shape, the hat may be invested with specific significance; for example, that of the Minstrel in the Tarot pack (56). To change one's hat is equivalent to a change of mind or of ideas. The choice of a hat—associated with a particular social order —denotes the desire to be admitted to that set or to partake of its inherent characteristics. There are hats, like the Phrygian cap, that have a special phallic significance, and others that can confer invisibility (symbolic of repression).

Hawk   An emblem of the soul in ancient Egypt, with the im-plication of solar transfiguration (57). Nevertheless, Pinedo maintains that it may have been a mediaeval allegory of the evil mind of the sinner. In the cloister at Silos there is an illustration of hawks tearing hares to pieces, and it appears to carry this significance (46) although, given the negative significance of the hare, (it symbolizes fecundity, but also lasciviousness), the hawk might be taken as a symbol of victory over concupiscence (since it destroyed the lascivious hares). But this kind of struggle is better represented by the mythic and legendary motif—also frequent in folklore—of the griffin composed of various parts all struggling one against the other, so that it appears at once as executioner and victim.

Head In the Zohar, the 'magic head' stands for astral light (9); in mediaeval art it is a symbol for the mind (46) and for the spiritual life, which explains the frequency with which it appeared in decorative art. On the other hand, Plato in *Timaeus* asserts that 'the human head is the image of the world'. In corroboration of this, Leblant points out that the skull, the semi-spherical crown of the human body, signifies the heavens. Clearly, the head-symbol here coalesces with that of the sphere as a symbol of Oneness. It had the same significance in Egyptian hieroglyphics (19). The eagle's head has been used as a solar symbol and an emblem of the centre-point of emanation—that is, of the cosmic flame and the spiritual fire of the universe (4). Two, three or four heads shown in juxtaposition symbolize a corresponding intensification of a given aspect of head-symbolism. Thus, the Gemini, a symbol of the duality of Nature, or of the integrating (but not unifying) link between the two principles of creation, are represented by beings with two heads or two faces, like the Roman Janus for example. Hecate is depicted with three heads—she is called triform for this reason—a symbolism which may be related to the 'three levels' of heaven, earth and hell, as well as to Diel's three 'urges of life' (15). The juxtaposition of four heads or faces, as in the image of Brahma the Supreme Lord, stems from the same symbolism as that of the tetramorph (60). A factor of major importance bearing upon the symbolism of the head is mentioned by Herbert Kühn, in his *L'Ascension de l'humanité* (Paris, 1958). He makes the point that the decapitation of corpses in prehistoric times marked Man's discovery of the independence of the spiritual principle, residing in the head, as opposed to the vital principle represented by the body as a whole. Kühn adds that Neolithic thought was very close to the mediaeval in its conviction that an eternal and invisible essence underlies all appearances (Plate XV).

Head-dress and Throne In ancient, oriental cultures, and especially in Mesopotamia and India, there is always a formal and significant relationship between all the objects and edifices related to any one particular cult. For example, as Eliade notes, there is an inner and outer analogy between head-dress, thrones and palaces in Babylonian traditions: all three refer to the 'Centre' (17). And Luc Benoist has observed of Hindu cults that the altar, the temple, the throne, the palace, the city, the kingdom and the world are all by implication images of the 'Centre', their direct model being mount Meru (the centre of the world). The processional carriage is a temple-on-wheels (6), with all the 'correspondences' implied.

Heart In the vertical scheme of the human body, the focal points are three in number: the brain, the heart and the sexual organs. But the central point is the heart, and in consequence it comes to partake of the meanings of the other two. The heart was the only part of the viscera left by the Egyptians in the mummy, since it was regarded as the centre indispensable to the body in eternity; for all centres are symbols of eternity, since time is the motion of the periphery of the wheel of phenomena rotating around the Aristotelian 'unmoved mover'. In traditional ways of thought, the heart was taken as the true seat of intelligence, the brain being merely instrumental (25); hence, in ancient attempts to explain the profound and continuing analogies between concepts, the moon was said to correspond to the brain and the sun to the heart. All representations of the 'Centre' have been related in some way to the heart, either through correspondences or through substitution, as in the case of the goblet, the coffer and the cavern. For the alchemists, the heart was the image of the sun within man, just as gold was the image of the sun on earth (32). The importance of love in the mystic doctrine of unity explains how it is that love-symbolism came to be closely linked with heart-symbolism, for to love is only to experience a force which urges the lover towards a given centre. In emblems, then, the heart signifies love as the centre of illumination and happiness, and this is why it is surmounted by flames, or a cross, or a fleur-de-lis, or a crown (4).

Hearth A form of 'domestic sun', a symbol of the home, of the conjunction of the masculine principle (fire) with the feminine (the receptacle) and, consequently, of love (49).

Heat For Jung, heat is an image of the libido (31). Any representation—or even the mere mention—of heat always bears a symbolic relation to maturation, whether biological or spiritual (32). In emblems of the sun, it is portrayed as wavy lines alternating with the straight lines representing light. We should also bear in mind all the correspondences which exist between heat and tones, sounds, colours, the seasons, etc.

Heaven Here is Luc Benoist's version of a passage about heaven taken from the *Chândogya Upanishad*: 'In the beginning, all the universe was non-being. It became being. It grew and formed an egg, which remained unbroken for a year. Then it broke open. Of the two halves of the shell, one was of silver and the other of gold.' The latter was heaven, while the former became earth. In Hindu architecture, these two halves are represented by the altar and the *stupa* (6). One can clearly see in all this how the myth arose from converging formal analogies. Heaven has always been considered, except in Egypt, as part of the masculine or active principle, associated with things of the spirit and with the number three, whereas the earth is related to the feminine, passive or material principle, and the number four. Mircea Eliade has something to say about the symbolism of heaven which is rather less abstract and therefore fails to be so cosmogonic: the azure of the sky, he suggests, is the veil which hides the divine face. The clouds are his garments. The light of heaven is the ointment with which he anoints· his immense body. The stars are his eyes (17). Again: among oriental peoples, the dome of heaven is associated with the nomad's tent— quite apart from the usual heaven/earth association—as if they had a presentiment that three-dimensional space is only a kind of lid which prevents Man from penetrating into the mystery of the other world. Celestial space, then, ceases to be a container and becomes content of hyperspace, or rather, of trans-space. A terrible aspect of heaven can be seen in the myth of the cosmic catastrophe which William Blake appears to have had in mind when he wrote of 'the angry religion of the stars' (3). We must also remember that, from the earliest times, heaven has been thought of as consisting of several heavens, owing to the tendency of primitive logic to assign a separate, cellular space to each celestial body or group of bodies, a tendency which anticipates the theory of gravitation, the gravitational field and the laws of organic structures, and which illuminates the very essence of the relationship between the qualitative (the discontinuous) and the quantitative (the continuous) (Plate XVI).

Hecate A symbol of the Terrible Mother, appearing as the tutelar deity of Medea or as a lamia who devours men. She is a personification of the moon, or of the evil side of the feminine principle, responsible for madness, obsession and lunacy. Her attributes are the key, the lash, the dagger and the torch (31).

He-Goat The he-goat is a kind of scape-goat—a symbol of the projection of one's own guilt upon someone else, and of the consequent repression of one's conscience. Hence the traditional significance of the he-goat as an emissary, and its evil association with the devil (15). It is also, like the bull, a father-symbol (50).

Helios Helios signifies the sun in its astronomic aspect, just as Apollo symbolizes it in its spiritual aspect. In ancient cults, he appears as a god who presides over the seasons, vegetation, fecundity and the fruitfulness of the earth (15).

Helmet In heraldic symbolism, it is an emblem of lofty thoughts, or of hidden thoughts if the vizor is lowered. This latter aspect corresponds to the general symbolism of invisibility, which is thus equated with the hood and the hat (38), although this seems to be a clear case of undue emphasis upon one meaning at the expense of all the others. The inevitable and intimate association of the helmet with the head has an important bearing upon the relation between two symbols: thus, a helmet with a strange crest may be a symbol of highly imaginative or restless exhilaration. The hat, the hood and the mantilla have the same intimate, symbolic association with the head: their colour usually denotes the wearer's prevailing shade of thought.

Hemispheres In Egyptian hieroglyphics, the semicircle with the diameter as the base is a sign representing the sun's orbit and also the hemisphere. It symbolizes the Origin counterbalanced by the End—or birth counterbalanced by death. Grammatically, this hieroglyph expresses the feminine principle balancing the masculine (19).

Herald at Arms Like Egyptian and Chaldean scribes, heralds at arms are repositories of hermetic wisdom and, therefore, 'keepers of secrets', according to Alleau in *De la Nature des symboles* (Paris, 1958). Heralds at arms are related to shield-bearers and to the standard-bearers of ancient armies (e.g. the Roman *aquilifer*, or eagle-bearer).

Heraldic Symbols The outward components of heraldry (crowns, helmets, mantles, lambrequins, supporters, chains), like the inner elements (or arms: colours, metals, furs, parties, noble quarterings, figures), apart from their literal or anecdotal senses, have a symbolic significance, according to Cadet de Gassicourt and the Baron du Roure de Paulin, in *L'Hermétisme et l'art héraldique* (Paris, 1907). (Piobb supports their opinion in his review of the book in *L'Année occultiste et psychique*, 1907.) Metals and colours may be 'read' in terms of their own particular symbolism; parties and noble quarterings by spatial and graphic symbolism, as well as by their implicit 'correspondences'. Heraldic art recognizes five colours or enamels and two metals: gold (the Sun), silver (the Moon), gules (red—Mars), sinople (green—Venus), azure (Jupiter), purple (Mercury) and sable (Saturn). The symbolic meanings of colours, metals and parties are considered as products of the active (or spiritual) principle of the shield-of-arms working upon the passive, quaternary material symbolized by the surface of the shield. City coats-of-arms may be explained along similar lines, according to Gérard de Sède who, in *Les Templiers sont parmi nous* (Paris, 1962), suggests that the ship in the shield of the City of Paris may derive from the myth of the Argonauts, the quest for the Golden Fleece and the alchemical Work.

Herbs Herbs sometimes have the symbolic significance of human beings. This is suggested by the etymology of the Greek *neophytos* ('new herb') (17). They are also related to the idea of natural forces, both of good and evil. Because they can be both medicinal and poisonous, herbs are very commonly featured in legends and folktales, as well as in magic. The business of cataloguing the different characteristics of each herb or plant is clearly a matter for specialized study.

Hercules As a hero, Hercules became a symbol of the individual freeing himself in the quest for immortality, expiating his sins and errors through suffering and 'heroic striving'. In this way he was able, for his own sake and for that of his brother (whose existence relates Hercules to the Gemini-myth), to conquer, exterminate or master all monsters (symbolic of plagues, vices and the forces of evil) within the ordered and gradual process of the evolutionary struggle (15). His attributes are the club (a symbol of overwhelming force, of annihilation—not merely of victory) and the Nemean lion's skin (a solar symbol) (8). Hercules was unable to undertake a new task until after he had brought his previous trial to a successful conclusion. Hence alchemists, from Antiquity to the Middle Ages, would interpret the myth of Hercules-the-hero as a configuration of the spiritual struggle which leads to the 'conquest of the golden apples in the Garden of the Hesperides'—or immortality. Piobb has linked the twelve trials of Hercules with the signs of the Zodiac—thus confirming his character as a solar hero recognized by mythologists —as follows: his victory over the giants such as Geryon and Cacus with Aries; the Cretan bull with Taurus; the pillars with the Gemini; the hydra of Lerna and the birds of lake Stymphalus with Cancer; the lion of Nemea with Leo; the Amazons with Virgo; the walls of Troy and the Augean stables with Libra; the boar of Erymanthus with Scorpio; the centaurs and the mares of Diomedes with Sagittarius; the stag of the golden horns with Capricorn; the eagle and Prometheus with Aquarius; and the monster which attacked Hesione with Pisces (48).

Hermaphrodite Hermaphrodite deities, connected with the myth of birth (19), are found on many Egyptian monuments: for example, the pedestal of one of the colossi at Memnon. The hermaphrodite is a consequence of applying the symbolism of the number two to the human being, creating a personality which is integrated despite its duality. In India, this dual being—two sexes united in a single personality—was the primal force, the light from which life emanates (49), that is to say, the *lingam* (60). The myth of the hermaphrodite was also known in pre-Columbian Mexico, in the figure of Quetzalcoatl, the god in whom the laws of opposites and of the separate sexes are finally united. The hermaphrodite is, above all, a god of procreation (41), closely linked, and ultimately identified, with the Gemini archetype. Plato, in the *Symposium*, states that the Gods first created Man in the form of a sphere incorporating two bodies and both sexes. This shows to what extent he subjected reality to symbolic and conceptual patterns and how—in a characteristically Greek manner—he permitted mortals to partake of such qualities as hermaphroditism, which were generally regarded as exclusive to the more primitive gods (8). Psychologically, it must not be overlooked that the concept of hermaphroditism represents a formula (which, like most mythic formulas, is only an approximation) of 'totality', of the 'integration of opposites' (17). In other words, it expresses in sexual—and hence very obvious—terms the essential idea that all pairs of opposites are integrated into Oneness. For Eliade, hermaphroditism is, therefore, simply an archaic form

ARDANARI ISWARA.

One of many representations of the Hermaphrodite, with symbolic coiling snake and lotus
(from C. J. W. Olliver, *An Analysis of Magic and Witchcraft*).

of divine bi-unity. Magic-religious thinking first stated this concept in biological terms, before clothing it in metaphysical (*esse non esse*) or theological language (the revealed or non-revealed world). The androgynous divinity was also known in China and in many other countries (Persia, Palestine, Australia, etc.) (17). In the androgynous myth we see, however, not only an expression of the cause but also of the controlling spiritual energy. This is very clearly brought out by Ely Star when he says that no happiness, unless it be one of the exceptions mentioned by St. Paul, can prove satisfying until it is made whole by marriage (which is an imperfect image of hermaphroditism), since the spirit always manifests itself as a segregated form in the world of existence, and this is a source of suffering and restlessness (54). Thus, the Hermaphrodite is not only linked to the remote Platonic past, but also projected into the future. In addition, it is clearly a symbol of an intellectual activity which is not in itself connected with the problem of the sexes. Blavatsky says that all peoples regarded their first god as androgynous, because Primitive humanity knew that he had sprung from 'the mind', as is shown by many traditions such as that of Minerva springing from the head of Jupiter (9). In alchemy, the Hermaphrodite plays an important rôle as Mercury; he is depicted as a two-headed figure, often accompanied by the word *Rebis* (double thing).

Hermit, The   The ninth enigma of the Tarot pack. It is an allegory of an old man carrying in his right hand a lantern partially covered by one of the folds of his cloak, which is dark outside (signifying withdrawal and austerity) but with a blue lining (representing aerial nature). If he finds the serpent of the instincts in his path, he does not destroy it but simply charms it into twining itself round his staff, as Aesculapius did. He is a master of the invisible. On the positive side, the hermit signifies tradition, study, reserve, patient and profound work. On the negative, he stands for all that is taciturn, tedious and meticulous (59).

Hero, The   The cult of the hero has been found necessary not only because of the exigencies of war, but because of the virtues inherent in heroism—virtues which have surely been apparent to Man from prehistoric times and which he has felt the need to exalt, emphasize and record. The magic, the apparatus and the splendour of the very appurtenances of the ancient warrior proclaim the truth of this, as does the custom of according an acclamation worthy of kings to the conquering hero. The relationship between the 'little holy war', that is the struggle with the material enemies outside, and the 'Great Holy War', or combat with the spiritual enemies inside the personality, inevitably gave rise to the same relationship being drawn between the hero of the 'little war' and the champion of the 'Great War'. Every heroic characteristic finds its analogy among the virtues necessary to vanquish chaos and overcome the temptations offered by the forces of darkness. This explains why, in many myths, the sun was identified with the hero *par excellence*. Hence, Alexander the Great is pictured on coins with the horns of Jupiter Ammon, that is, he is identified with the awakening sun of Spring under the sign of Aries. And this leads Jung to state that the most widely accepted of all the symbols of the libido—and he could equally well have said 'the spirit'—is the human figure as the hero— the subject of so many myths, legends and traditional tales. He adds that in the life destined for the hero, the historical and the symbolic are one and the same thing. The first object of the hero is to conquer himself; and this is the reason why the heroes of Germanic legends are usually portrayed with the eyes of a snake. The mythic hero, Cecrops, is half-man and half-serpent (31). A hero turned Christian is a hero turned knight, with the aid of the saintly warriors such as St. George and St. Michael (Plate XVII).

Heron   Among the Egyptians, a symbol of the morning and of the generation of life. Together with the ibis and the stork, it carried a favourable significance (4).

Hesperides, The   They are the daughters of Atlas and Hesperis. They lived in a garden with trees bearing golden apples, watched over by a dragon. Hercules took possession of these apples, following upon his victory over the guardian dragon. Vossius explained this myth by an astronomical analogy, whereby the Hesperides become eventide, the garden becomes the firmament, the golden apples the stars, the dragon the Zodiac and Hercules the sun (8). But this interpretation does not invalidate the psychology implicit in all the other symbols connected with this myth, in particular that of the hero and the treasure acquired only after great exertions.

Hieroglyphics   Under this heading are grouped representative ideographs, i.e. comprising schematic images of objects, to which may be added others, more simple or more abstract. In itself, the basic concept of hieroglyphics is similar to that of the enigma. By antonomasia, hieroglyphics are confined to those of the Egyptian civilization (which recognized three forms of writing: hieroglyphic, hieratic and demotic). The hieroglyphic system attained a total of 900 signs (representative of ideas, syllables, words and letters, or their complements = determinatives). Because of its complexity, it was mastered only by the priestly caste, and, by Roman times, people were already beginning to forget how to decipher it. Hora-pollo Niliacus attempted to restore it in the 2nd and 3rd centuries of our era, taking symbolism as his basis. The subject was forgotten for centuries, until Father Athanasius Kircher revived it during the 17th century. Anybody interested in this subject should consult the work by Madeleine V.-David, *Le Débat sur les écritures et l'hiéroglyphe aux XVIIe. et XVIIIe. siècles* (Paris, 1965), which is a modern, symbolic, profound interpretation, based on that of Enel in *La langue sacrée*.

Hippalectryon A fabulous animal, half-horse and half-cock, and probably a sun-symbol.

Hippogryph A fabulous animal, half-horse and half-griffin, which Ariosto and other authors of books of chivalry gave to their heroes for a steed. It is a kind of supercharged Pegasus, a blend of the favourable aspects of the griffin and the winged horse in its character as the 'spiritual mount' (8).

Hippopotamus In the Egyptian system of hieroglyphs, it represents strength and vigour. It is also related to the ideas of fertility and water, and, consequently, to the mother-principle (19).

Hog A symbol of impure desires, of the transmutation of the higher into the lower and of the amoral plunge into corruption (15).

Hole A very important symbol, with two main aspects: on the biological level, it has fertilizing power and is related to fertility rites; on the spiritual plane, it stands for the 'opening' of this world on to the other world. Worship of 'perforated stones' in one form or another is very common all over the world. Eliade notes that, in the region of Amance, there is just such a stone in front of which women kneel to pray for the health of their children. To this day, in Paphos, barren women crawl through the hole of such a stone. Primitive Indian peoples were mainly concerned with its symbolism at the physical level, identifying the hole with the female sexual organs, although they too had an intuitive awareness of the fact that holes could stand for the 'gateway of the world', which the soul has to cross in order to be released from the cycle of *karma* (17). In the *Brihadaranyaka Upanishad* it is said that 'when a human being leaves this world, he makes his way through the air, and the air opens up for him as wide as a cartwheel' (50). The artistic expression of this symbol is found in the Chinese *Pi*, i.e. the representation of heaven. It is a jade disc with a hole in the middle; measurements vary from case to case, but according to the Chinese dictionary *Erh Ya*, the relation between the outside ring and the central hole remains constant. This hole is the Hindu 'gateway', also the Aristotelian 'unvarying mean' or 'unmoved mover'. The origins of the *Pi* are exceedingly remote, and carved and decorated *Pi* have also been found (39). As a symbol of heaven, the hole also stands specifically for the passage from spatial to non-spatial, from temporal to non-temporal existence, and corresponds to the zenith (52). The strange and roughly hewn door-openings of some neolithic stone-structures have been interpreted by some scholars as symbolic holes in the above sense; the laborious nature of these holes could otherwise have been avoided by means of the simple and well-known pillar-and-lintel method of construction. An outstanding example of this kind of door is that at Hagiar Kim (Malta). It is interesting to note, in this connexion, that the initiation ceremony among the Pomo Indians of Northern California includes a ritual blow from a grizzly bear paw, which is supposed to make a hole in the neophyte's back, on account of which he 'dies' and is reborn to a new stage of life. It is probable that, from the earliest times, the visual aspect of wounds helped to strengthen the association between the concept of the hole and that of passing into the other life. All this seems to be corroborated by the fact that in many symbolist pictures, e.g. in Gustave Moreau's *Orpheus*, the background landscape includes perforated rocks which are evidently invested with a transcendental significance. It is also worth recalling Salvador Dali's frequent practice, amounting almost to an obsession, of painting holes (regular in shape, like windows) on the backs of some of his figures.

Hollow   A hollow is the abstract aspect of the cavern, and the inverse of the mountain. There are many symbolic significances superimposed upon the basic sense of the hollow, such as that of the Abode of the Dead, of Memories and of the Past, with further allusions to the mother and also to the unconscious (15), as the link between all these different aspects.

Honey   In Orphic tradition, honey is a symbol of wisdom. The occult maxim 'the bees are born from the oxen' finds its explanation in the astrological relationship between Taurus and Cancer (40) and in the symbolic use of the ox as a sign for sacrifice, expressive of the idea that there is no higher knowledge without suffering. Honey was also credited with other meanings: rebirth or change of personality consequent upon initiation; and, in India, the superior self (comparable with fire). Given that honey is the product of a mysterious and elaborate process, it is easy to understand how it came by analogy to symbolize the spiritual exercise of self-improvement (56).

Hood   The hood or cone-shaped hat often figures in ancient and mediaeval iconography. It is to be related with the Phrygian cap and other similar forms of headgear which are to be seen in Greek and Roman art. A relief of the 14th century shows Parsifal armed with two lances and wearing the cone-shaped cap characteristic of the Cabiri. It seems that the hood unites and blends together the two separate meanings of the cape and the hat; in addition, its shape and its colour contribute further to the symbolism as a whole (32). In Jung's view, the hood, since it envelopes practically the whole of the head and is almost spherical in shape, comes to symbolize the highest sphere, that is, the celestial world (represented symbolically by the bell, the vault, the upper part of the sand-bag and the double-pumpkin, as well as by the skull) (32). Furthermore, covering one's head signifies invisibility, that is, death. For this reason, the initiated appear in some scenes in ancient mystery plays with their heads covered by a cloak. Jung rounds off the presentation of his evidence with this piece of information: 'Among the Nandi, of East Africa, the newly-circumcised, the initiates, have to go about for a long time dressed in queer cone-shaped grass hats, which envelop them completely and reach to the ground. The circumcised have become invisible, i.e., spirits. The veil has the same significance among nuns' (31). Diel confirms this interpretation, taking the hood as a symbolic agent of repression or that which renders the psychic content invisible (15).

Horns Some of the unfavourable interpretations of horn-symbolism are due to the all-too-common association with the ancient symbol of the ox (standing for castration, sacrifice and persistent toil), or perhaps also as a result of 'symbolic inversion'. For, in fact, all primitive traditions prove that the horn is a symbol of strength and power. Hides and battle-helmets were adorned with horns from prehistoric times right up to the Middle Ages. The horn played its part in the decorative art of Asiatic temples; like the bucraneum (representing sacrificial remains), the horn was considered sacred. The precise meaning of the horn-symbol was understood as far back as Egyptian times. In their system of hieroglyphs, the sign of the horn indicates 'what is above the head' and, by extension, 'to open up a path for oneself' (in which it is comparable with the ram's head, Aries and the battering-ram). It is a striking fact that the signs which initiate the cycle of the Zodiac (Aries and Taurus) are both represented by horned animals (19). The relevant Egyptian hieroglyph also enters into composite words signifying elevation, prestige, glory, etc. (19). The single horn pertains in essence—apart from its employment in the emblem of the cornucopia or as a musical instrument—to the fabulous unicorn and the rhinoceros. The horn of the latter, carved out in the form of a cup, is one of the 'common emblems' of China, and stands for prosperity (and therefore for strength) (5). The same belief is found among the Gnostics, who expressly state that the horn symbolizes the 'principle which bestows maturity and beauty upon all things'. Jung offers the explanation that the horn is a dual symbol: from one point of view it is penetrating in shape, and therefore active and masculine in significance; and from the other, it is shaped like a receptacle, which is feminine in meaning (32). As a musical instrument, it figures in emblems symbolizing the spiritual call to join the Holy War. This particular meaning is corroborated by the crosses, trefoils, circles and fleurs-de-lis associated with the horn (4). Horns are the attributes of the Cilician god of agriculture. He holds handfuls of corn, symbolizing fertility.

Horse   The symbolism of the horse is extremely complex, and beyond a certain point not very clearly defined. Eliade finds it an animal associated with burial-rites in chthonian cults (17), whereas Mertens Stienon considers it an ancient symbol of the cyclic movement of the world of phenomena; hence the horses, which Neptune with his trident lashes up out of the waves, symbolize the cosmic forces that surge out of the Akasha—the blind forces of primigenial chaos (39). Applying this latter concept to the biopsychological plane, Diel concludes that the horse stands for intense desires and instincts, in accordance with the general symbolism of the steed·and the vehicle (15). The horse plays an important part in a great number of ancient rites. The ancient Rhodians used to make an annual sacrifice to the sun of a four-horse quadriga, which they would hurl into the sea (21). The animal was also dedicated to Mars, and the sudden appearance of a horse was thought to be an omen of war (8). In Germany and England, to dream of a white horse was thought to be an omen of death (35). It is very interesting to note that the great myth and symbol of the Gemini, illustrated in pairs or twins, in two-headed beasts or in anthropomorphic figures with four eyes and four arms, etc., appears, too, in horse-symbolism, especially in the form of a pair of horses, one white and one black, representing life and death. The Indian Asvins—the probable source of Castor and Pollux—would depict themselves as horsemen. In mediaeval illustrations of the Zodiac, the sign for the Gemini is sometimes portrayed in this way, as for example in the Zodiac of Notre Dame de Paris (39). Considering that the horse pertains to the natural, unconscious, instinctive zone, it is not surprising that, in Antiquity, it should often have been endowed with certain powers of divination (8). In fable and legend, horses, being clairvoyant, are often assigned the task of giving a timely warning to their masters, as in the Grimms' fable, for example. Jung came to wonder if the horse might not be a symbol for the mother, and he does not hesitate to assert that it expresses the magic side of Man, 'the mother within us', that is, intuitive understanding. On the other hand, he recognizes that the horse is a symbol pertaining to Man's baser forces, and also to water, which explains why the horse is associated with Pluto and Neptune (56). Deriving from the magical nature of the horse, is the belief that the horse-shoe brings luck. On account of his fleetness, the horse can also signify the wind and sea-foam, as well as fire and light. In the *Brihadaranyaka Upanishad* (I, 1), the horse is actually a symbol of the cosmos (31) (Plate XVIII).

Hour-Glass   A symbol denoting the inversion of the relations between the Upper and Lower Worlds—an inversion encompassed periodically by Shiva (or Siva), the lord of creation and destruction. Connected with it are the drum—similar in shape—and the cross of St. Andrew; the symbolic significance of all three is identical (51).

Hours, The   In the *Iliad*, the hours are personifications of the atmospheric moisture: they open and close the gates of Olympus, form and disperse the clouds, govern the seasons and human life. While they were performing these duties, they were regarded as daughters of Zeus and Themis, bearing such names as Eunomia, Dike and Irene, representing Law, Justice and Peace. All twelve constitute the retinue of Eos and are depicted ranged around the sun-throne or busily coupling the horses to the sun-chariot. We must observe, therefore: (*a*) that they are expressive of cosmic forces; (*b*) that they personify *moments* of these forces and therefore create the *opportunities* for human action. Their position, surrounding the sun, is analogous to the way angels (red and blue—positive and negative) are depicted encircling the mandorla of God in Christian iconography.

House   Mystics have always traditionally considered the feminine aspect of the universe as a chest, a house or a wall, as well as an enclosed garden. Another symbolic association is that which equates the house (and the above, related forms) with the repository of all wisdom, that is, tradition itself (4). In architectural symbolism, on the other hand, the house carries not only an overall symbolism but also particular associations attached to each of its component parts. Nevertheless, the house as a home arouses strong, spontaneous associations with the human body and human thought (or life, in other words), as has been confirmed empirically by psychoanalysts. Ania Teillard explains this by pointing out that, in dreams, we employ the image of the house as a representation of the different layers of the psyche. The outside of the house signifies the outward appearance of Man: his personality or his mask. The various floors are related to the vertical and spatial symbols. The roof and upper floor correspond to the head and the mind, as well as to the conscious exercise of self-control. Similarly, the basement corresponds to the unconscious and the instincts (just as sewers do, in symbols pertaining to the city). The kitchen, since this is where foodstuff is transformed, sometimes signifies the place or the moment of psychic transmutation in the alchemical sense. The intercommunicating rooms speak for themselves. The stairs are the link between the various planes of the psyche, but their particular significance depends upon whether they are seen as ascending or descending. Finally, there is, as we have said, the association of the house with the human body, especially regarding its openings, as was well understood by Artemidorus Daldianus (56).

Hunter In Ludovico Dolce's *Le Transformationi*, the following scene is described: In a clearing in a wood there is a small lake, with a man, kneeling, gazing into the surface of the water—a symbol of contemplation. In the background, a hunter on horseback, with a pack of dogs, is in pursuit of his prey—a symbol of action for its own sake, of repetition, of the pursuit of transitoriness, of the will to remain (as the Hindu phrase has it) on the 'wheel of reincarnations'. Lao-Tse (58) taught that racing and hunting only serve to madden the heart of Man, thus revealing that the enemy is within: that it is desire itself. Similarly, Zagreus—another name for Dionysos—means 'the Great Hunter' and stands for the insatiable incontinence of desire (15), according to the moral interpretation of Diel. For those who prefer a cosmic interpretation, the myth of the infernal hunt, in which colour and form are mixed together without rhyme or reason, alludes to the howling wind (3). The Arabs identify this wind with both the hunter and death (35). The figure of the accursed hunter is one which is to be found in a great many mythologies, traditions, legends and folktales. The following passage taken from Julio Caro Baroja will illuminate many aspects of the myth, and clarify what we have already said: 'A Basque tradition (*Abade chacurra*: the abbot's dogs) has it that an abbot or priest, much drawn to hunting, was saying Mass just as a hare happened to run past. The Abbot's dogs caught its scent and rushed out, howling, after it; the abbot deserted the Most Holy Sacrament, and hastened out of the temple after his dogs in pursuit of the prey. Henceforth, as a punishment, he was condemned to an endless chase, whirling across the plains behind his howling dogs, never to run down the quarry he so bootlessly pursues.' This is clearly a case of a symbol for a 'limiting situation', that is, of a falling away from the centre—or the tendency to do so—towards the endlessly turning periphery of the wheel of phenomena: unending because self-delusion is a perpetual incitement to the sterile urge of the pursuit of worldly things. In other versions the hare is the devil disguised. This theme of the accursed hunter is to be found called, variously, 'The Black Hunter', 'The Wicked Hunter' or 'The King's Dog'. It is derived from the myth of Odin, the god of souls. Amongst the so-called Celtic peoples, Odin has been replaced by King Arthur or Arthus, as is shown by the 'chasses du roi Arthus', traditional in Normandy. There are other similar traditions, such as the 'chasse Annequin' in Normandy, 'Manihennequin' in the Vosges, the 'chasse Saint Hubert' and 'du Grand Veneur' (10). In Dontenville's view, an important mythic precedent is to be found in Meleager and the boar (16).

Hurricane Anthropologists have found that many graphic symbols owe their origin to the hurricane—especially in America.

This is true, for instance, of the sigma, the double sigma and the swastika. But at the same time, the hurricane has a symbolic meaning of its own. Ortiz observes that the hurricane, like celestial bodies, has two characteristic motions: rotary and sideways. In its sidewise motion, there is an intermediary point of absolute calm: the so-called 'eye of the hurricane'. For American aborigines, the hurricane is cosmic synergy, since it contains three Elements within itself (fire or light-rays, air or wind, water or rain) and disturbs the fourth—earth. It was worshipped as a deity of the winds and waters, and also of the heavens (41). This latter aspect of its correspondences brings us once again to the celebrated and persistent celestial symbol of the 'hole' in the disc of Chinese jade, representing the concept of the zenith as a void through which one may pass out of the world of space and time into spacelessness and timelessness.

Hyle   Hyle is protomatter, a symbol of the passive, feminine, primordial principle. According to Nicomachus of Gerasa, the pristine state of chaos of the hyle was fecundated by Number. Hildegard of Bingen (1098-1179), the abbess of Rupertsberg, in *Scivias*, describes cosmogonic visions in which *Nous* blends and harmonizes with the monster chaos (14).

Ibis   The ibis is related to Thoth, the Egyptian god of wisdom. According to the Greek scholar Aelian, in his *De Natura Animalium*, this bird was chosen because it tucks its head under its wing when it sleeps, so that it comes to resemble the shape of the heart; and also because of the fact that the stride of the ibis measures exactly a cubit (which was the measure used in the building of temples), and because it destroyed harmful insects (19). There were two kinds of ibis: the white bird (associated with the moon) and the black. The belief was that Thoth hovered over the Egyptian people in the form of an *Ibis religiosa*, and that he taught them the occult arts and sciences (9).

Ice   Given that water is the symbol of communication between the formal and the informal, the element of transition between different cycles, yielding by nature, and also related to the ideas of material, earthly fecundity and the Heraclitean 'death of the soul', it follows that ice represents principally two things: first, the change induced in water by the cold—that is, the 'congelation' of its symbolic significance; and, secondly, the stultification of the potentialities of water. Hence ice has been defined as the rigid dividing-line between consciousness and the unconscious (or between any other dynamic levels) (56). Although the negative sense is predominant, it is not lacking in a positive sense in so far as the solidification is tantamount to toughness, and the coldness implies resistance to all that is inferior; in this latter sense it corresponds to Nietzsche's freezing and 'hostile' air of mountain-peaks.

Identities Many symbols can, like the gods of old, be equated, relatively speaking, one with another. For example: the Ship of Fools and the Endless Chase (of the Accursed Hunter); or the 'centre' of the cross and the Holy Grail; or the centaur and the Gemini; or Pandora's box and effulgence. In the proper application of identities lies much of the true science of symbolism.

Image A pattern of forms and figures endowed with unity and significance. It is implied in the theory of form—and is true, also, of melody—that the whole is greater than the sum of its parts being, in a sense, their origin and justification. If for Sartre the image is a degraded awareness of knowing, for other psychologists the image is, in fact, the highest form that knowing can assume, for all knowledge tends towards a visual synthesis. Also to be borne in mind is the theory propounded by Sir Herbert Read in *Icon and Idea*, according to which every creation in the visual arts—and, in fact, every kind of pattern—is a form of thought and therefore corresponds to an intelligible mental concept. This leads us towards an intuition of the world as a vast repertoire of signs that await being 'read'. We may note here that some of the works of Trithemius and Athanasius Kircher tend towards this interpretation.

Image, Pictorial Every pictorial creation gives rise to an image, whether imitative or invented, with or without figuration. Alongside the symbolic meaning which subjects or figures may have, they possess, in a pictorial image, a symbolic background: spatial zones, colours, geometric or non-geometric forms, predominant axes, rhythms, composition and texture. In the most recent type of art, known as 'informalism', expression and symbolization are achieved through texture and lineal rhythm in particular, with colour taking a secondary rôle. To find the 'meaning' of a given work, one must think in terms of putting its elements in the order of their importance, assessing each kind of element within the pictorial system. Exactly the same thing occurs in architecture and sculpture.

Imago Ignota From about the middle of the last century, the tendency of poetry and the visual arts has been towards a mode of expression whose antecedents go back through the ages—but received a particular impetus, around the year 1800, from the works of William Blake—and which might, with justification, be termed hermetic. This movement was characterized by the quest for the obscure as a self-sufficient goal, and by the representation of 'harmonious wholes' whose fascination lies in their remoteness. There is an illuminating definition of poetry in this sense by the German poet Gottfried Benn: 'The writing of poetry is the elevation of things into the language of the incomprehensible.' It is this type of unfamiliar pattern that constitutes the 'unknown image'—a pattern of words, shapes or colours that has no correspondence with the normal, either in the world of exterior reality or in that of normal, human feelings. These 'unknown images' create their own kind of reality and express the spiritual need of particular individuals to live within this created reality. They symbolize, in sum, the unknown, the antecedents and the aftermath of man, or that which surrounds him and which his senses and his intelligence are incapable of apprehending or of appropriating. The scope of the unknown is immense, for it encompasses the Supreme Mystery or the Mystery of mysteries (the secret of the cosmos and of creation and the nature of Being), and also the psychological—and, indeed, existential —mystery of the 'unexplored'. What is unknown is that which is unformed. The 'unknown image' is also related to death and to the thread which connects death with life (Plate XIX).

Impossibilities This theme of the 'impossible' is one which appears very frequently in legends and folktales, embracing, for example, the life of the unborn, or the fruit of one tree growing upon another, etc. Some refrains reflect the same ideas, such as the well-known Spanish saying: 'Over the sea run the hares, over the mountain the sardines.' They may well be symbols of Inversion, but it seems clear that they are more likely to pertain to subversion. There is a possible relationship between such impossibilities, as well as errors or comedies of mistaken identity—likewise owing their origin to folklore—and the belief in the existence of beings, imps and goblins bent upon creating disorder. Father La Peña, in his work *El ente dilucidado*, has discussed the problem of whether men can live without eating, whether they can fly, and so on. In short, all these examples may be interpreted as a 'call to chaos': symbols of the regressive, orgiastic desire (10), comparable with certain aspects of surrealism.

Incest Whereas the union of analogous matter is a symbol of incest—in music, for example, the idea of a concerto for harp and piano—incest in itself symbolizes, according to Jung, the longing for union with the essence of one's own self, or, in other words, for individuation. This explains why the gods of antiquity very frequently engendered offspring through incestuous relationships (33).

Instruments Symbolically, they are objective portrayals of potentialities, actions and desires. Each instrument, therefore, possesses a purely literal meaning, as well as a further significance when it is applied to the psychological and spiritual plane.

Intersection   The intersection of two lines, objects or paths is a sign of 'Conjunction' and communication, but also of symbolic Inversion, that is, of that point or zone where a transcendental change of direction is induced or sought. This is what lies behind the superstitious crossing of fingers or of objects. In medicinal dances, swords and iron bars are crossed in order to encourage a change (that is, a cure), or, to put it another way, to alter the course of a process so that it does not reach its ordinary or expected outcome (51).

Intestines   An Egyptian determinative sign defining the concept of circulation (19). In a broader sense, intestines carry the same symbolism as the alembic. They are also connected with the labyrinth and with death (the return to the interior of the earth = mother, along the 'curved way' = Saturn's scythe).

Inversion   According to Schneider, the continuity of life is assured by the mutual sacrifice which is consummated on the peak of the mystic mountain: death permits birth; all opposites are for an instant fused together and then inverted. What is constructive turns to destruction; love turns to hate; evil to good; unhappiness to happiness; martyrdom to ecstasy. Corresponding to this inner inversion of a process is an outer inversion of the symbol pertaining to it. This gives rise to a reversed arrangement of the symbolic structure. When the symbol has two aspects, the inversion of one determines that of the other. So, for example, if what is below is black and it seeks to ascend, it may do so by turning white. Or, conversely, if what is black is below and seeks to turn to white, then let it ascend and white it will be. This 'symbolic logic' of Inversion is, it hardly needs to be said, closely bound up with the myth of sacrifice. The more terrible the situation, the more urgent the need to transform and invert it (as in a public calamity or an unsuccessful war) and the greater must be the sacrifice; this explains the sacrifice of the Carthaginians and the pre-Columbian Mexicans. There is a psychological basis to this, since the mind, through the process of sublimation, is always promoting inversions and metamorphoses of this order. Ambivalence, contrast, paradox, or the *coincidentia oppositorum*, are capable, on account of their transcendent implications, of pointing the way to the other world, or of pointing, in a more practical way, to the focal point of Inversion. Jung observes that this is why the alchemists would express the unknowable by means of contrasts (33); and Schneider notes that, since the world is a duality, each phenomenon or thesis is denoted by its opposite. The closer phenomena come to the focal point of Inversion, the more they tend to collide with one another. The numerical expression of Inversion seems to be two and eleven. Symbols of Inversion are: the double-spiral, the hour-glass, the drum shaped like an hour-glass, St. Andrew's cross, the letter X, the quiver of arrows, and, in general, all that is X-shaped. Hence, the superstitious act of crossing the fingers is tantamount to tempting Fate; and, similarly, crime is a feature of many desperate rites, while primitives often insult the dead, because the insults, after passing through the focal point, are inverted—like rays of light—and changed into praise (50). Also symbolizing Inversion are all those beings or objects which are depicted upside down, such as the figure of the Hanged Man in the Tarot pack, the bat or vampire hanging from rock or branch, the acrobat on the trapeze, and so on. Still other examples of Inversion are those which tend to take the form of an antithesis; for example, according to L. Charbonneau Lassay in *Le Bestiaire du Christ* (Bruges, 1940), the malevolent animals—the toad, the scorpion, the rhinoceros and the basilisk— are the natural enemies respectively of the beneficent animals—the frog, the scarab, the unicorn and the cock. Similarly, the wasp is the antithesis of the bee, the he-goat of the crow. There are some inversions of symbols which owe their origins to racial or national factors, or to a change in the predominant caste: in Islam, politeness demands that the man should not remove his headgear, the opposite being the case in Christian countries. An instance of positive, historical sublimating inversion might be some humiliating situation —such as that in which the Roman army was made to pass under the yoke at Caudium—transformed into one of glory (with its characteristic expression of the triumphal arch, which was a particular obsession of the Romans). The custom among certain layers of society of turning the head of a saint downwards, or against a wall, is less an intended 'punishment' for the holy image than a consequence of the symbolism of Inversion: by inverting the physical position of the effigy, the faithful hope to invert his attitude towards them, and by virtue of the change in his attitude, to induce a change in their destiny.

Invisibility To become or to be invisible, psychologically corresponds to repression or to what is repressed. On the other hand, to become invisible is also, for the unconscious, an image of dissolution. Related to this symbol are the Night Sea-Crossing, Devouring and the *sol niger* of the alchemists (32).

Iopode A man with horse's hoofs, a feature of Romanesque decoration. It is undoubtedly related to the symbolism of the centaur, of which it may be a simplified version.

Ishtar Ishtar is pictured in many Western images and books of magic, as well as in esoteric thought, with a ring in her left hand and a cup or chalice in her right; or else armed like Minerva. These attributes denote the continuity of life, the power of invigorating liquids such as water, milk, blood and soma (related to the draught which Isolde gives to Tristan to drink), and the hardships of existence. Her weapons announce quite clearly that Ishtar loves the hero and despises the coward (59).

Island A complex symbol embracing several different meanings. According to Jung, the island is the refuge from the menacing assault of the 'sea' of the unconscious, or, in other words, it is the synthesis of the consciousness and the will (33). Here he is following the Hindu belief that—as Zimmer notes—the island is to be seen as the area of metaphysical force where the forces of the 'immense illogic' of the ocean are distilled (60). At the same time, the island is also a symbol of isolation, of solitude, of death. Most island-deities have something funereal about them—Calypso for instance. One could perhaps postulate an equation (of counterpoise and identity) between island and woman on the one hand, and monster and hero on the other.

Island, Accursed In the *Lai de Joseph d'Arimathie*, of the Romanesque period, the existence of an Accursed Island, which harboured infernal apparitions, enchantments, tortures and dangers, was postulated along with that of a Happy Island. This is the equivalent of the black castle in other legends. In both cases, it expresses the law of polarity which contrasts the Lower and the Upper Worlds, either on opposite sides of the earth, or above and below it.

Island of the Blessed Hindu doctrine tells of an 'essential island', golden and rounded, whose banks are made of pulverised gems, giving rise to its name of the 'island of the gems'. Sweet-smelling trees flourish on the land, and in the centre is a palace—the oriental equivalent of the *lapis philosophorum*. Inside the palace, in a jewelled pavilion, is the enthroned *Magna Mater* (60). According to Krappe, the 'Island of the Blessed' in its Greek version was the Land of the Dead (35), that is, a symbol, albeit a negative one, of the 'Centre' itself. Krappe goes on to speak of the perennial validity of the symbol, recalling how the Spanish nobleman Juan Ponce de León set off in search of Bimini and discovered Florida. The belief in the existence of the Island, or Islands, of the Blessed is something which one comes across in the most varied of sources. Blavatsky observes that 'Tradition says, and the records of the Book of Dzyan explain, that . . . where now are found but salt lakes and desolate barren deserts, there was a vast inland sea, which extended over middle Asia . . . (and) an island (of) unparalleled beauty' and this island was an exact copy of the island situated in the midst of the zodiacal wheel in the Upper Ocean (or the Ocean of the heavens). The signs of the Zodiac are themselves conceived as twelve islands (9). Finally, the Island of the Blessed (or the Happy Island) seems to be symbolic of earthly paradise for most classical writers. Schneider mentions the island visited by St. Brendan, according to mediaeval legend, where there was a huge tree growing near a fountain, and on its branches lived many birds. Two rivers flowed across the island: one was the river of youth and the other that of death (51). Here we have the clearest possible example of landscape-symbolism in which the terrestrial substance is integrated into a cosmic pattern by means of the essential elements of traditional symbolism.

Ivy Consecrated by the Phrygians to their god Attis. The eunuch-priests tattooed themselves with patterns of ivy leaves (21). It is a feminine symbol denoting a force in need of protection.

J

Jade The traditional Chinese symbolism of jade with its peculiar characteristics is derived from the broader universal symbolism of lithophanies. According to the Chinese tradition, jade possesses an essential quality of immortality as of right. Hence, it figured in rites and invocations from the 3rd millennium before our era: in figures of dragons and tigers, for example, which were intended to represent the cycle of decrease and increase in natural forces. This symbolism is dealt with in the *Chou Li*, dating from the 12th century B.C. It lists six ritual implements of jade: *Pi, Ts'ung, Hu, Huan, Kuei, Chang*. The *Pi*-symbol is a disk with a central hole signifying heaven, which is, as it were, a zone of perfect emptiness. *Hu* is a jade tiger. *Huan* is like a *Pi*, but is of black jade broken into two or three pieces; it is used in Chinese magic, particularly in the practices of necromancy. *Ts'ung* is the symbol of the earth; rounded inside and square outside, it is usually made of yellow jade (39). Generally speaking, jade corresponds to the masculine, *Yang* principle and to the dry Element.

Janus A Roman deity who is represented with two faces joined along the line from ear to jaw, the two faces looking in opposite directions. Like all symbols facing right and left at the same time, Janus is a symbol of wholeness—of the desire to master all things. Because of its duality, it may be taken to signify all pairs of opposites— that is, to be equivalent to the myth of the Gemini. It seems that the Romans associated Janus essentially with destiny, time and war. His faces were turned towards the past and the future, denoting both awareness of history and foreknowledge (the two-headed eagle has a comparable significance). But, as Guénon has rightly pointed out, two heads are, in fact, hindrances to the knowledge of true destiny, which lies in the 'eternal present' (25). This explains why many peoples (those of Northern Europe for example) invented similar symbols but with three heads arranged in the form of a rotating triangle, after the fashion of Janus, but with a third head facing forward. Triform Hecate is represented in this way (59). Janus also symbolizes the union of the powers of priest and monarch (28). Marius Schneider has suggested to us that Janus may also be identified with the two-peaked Mountain of Mars and, consequently, with all symbols of Inversion and mutual sacrifice.

Jerusalem, The Celestial   'And (the city) had a wall great and high, and had twelve gates, and at the gates twelve angels, and names written thereon, which are the names of the twelve tribes of the children of Israel. On the east three gates; on the north three gates; on the south three gates; and on the west three gates. And the wall of the city had twelve foundations, and in them the names of the twelve apostles of the Lamb' (Revelation xxi, 12-14). 'And he shewed me a pure river of water of life, clear as crystal, proceeding out of the throne of God and of the Lamb. In the midst of the street of it, and on either side of the river, was there the tree of life, which bare twelve manner of fruits, and yielded her fruit every month: and the leaves of the tree were for the healing of the nations' (Revelation xxii, 1-2). The celestial Jerusalem is usually described as a city in which the mineral element is predominant, whereas the lost Paradise is portrayed as a garden which is mostly vegetable in composition. Guénon, in noting this, has posed the question of whether we should 'say that the vegetation represents the proliferation of the seeds in the sphere of vital assimilation, whereas the minerals represent the results definitively "fixed"—"crystallized" as it were—at the close of a cyclic process of growth' (27). He links the twelve gates with the signs of the Zodiac, deducing that in this symbol a temporal cycle is transformed into a spatial one, upon the world's ceasing to rotate (28). St. John's apocalyptic vision, then, apart from its prophetic value, is a description, in terms of symbolic logic, of the all-embracing, unifying, 'saved' character of the paradise-to-be, seen as a 'new city'.

Jester   The jester is the symbolic inversion of the king, and hence, in certain rites of the period immediately preceding history, it appears in association with the sacrificial victim. According to Schneider, he is the terrestrial counterpart of the Gemini, that is to say that the jester is an expression of duality and not a comic figure. The jester or clown says pleasant things harshly and terrible things jokingly (50). Certain deformed or abnormal beings, such as dwarfs, are closely related to, and even identical with, the figure of the jester.

Frazer relates of Asia Minor in the 6th century B.C. how 'when a city suffered from plague, famine, or other public calamity, an ugly or deformed person was chosen to take upon himself all the evils which afflicted the community. He was brought to a suitable place, where dried figs, a barley loaf and cheese were put into his hand. These he ate. Then he was beaten seven times upon his genital organs with squills and branches of the wild fig and other wild trees while the flutes played a particular tune. Afterwards he was burned on a pyre built of the wood of forest trees; and his ashes were cast into the sea' (21). This passage illustrates the 'inverted' function of the victim and shows how, by way of suffering and sacrifice, the inferior creature could be sublimated into a superior being.

Jewels and Gems In most symbolic traditions, jewels signify spiritual truths (4); the precious stones in the garments of princesses, or in necklaces and bracelets, as well as gems shut away in hidden rooms, are symbols of superior knowledge (38). In the case of jewels belonging to princesses or ladies-in-waiting, they are clearly a symbol closely connected with the Jungian 'anima'. Treasures guarded by dragons allude to the difficulties of the struggle for knowledge— knowledge not as science in the sense of an impersonal erudition, but as the sum of experiences, and inextricably bound up with living and with evolution. Gems hidden in caves refer to the intuitive knowledge harboured in the unconscious. Another interesting connotation sometimes appearing in mythic form and still alive today in superstitions is that which associates the gem, symbolic of knowledge as such, with the snake, representing energy which tends towards a given end. The best example is the legend of the 'snake's stone'. There are many folklore traditions which illustrate the belief that precious stones once fell from the head of snakes or dragons. This gave rise to the idea that the diamond is poisonous and that it was once to be found in the jaws of serpents (according to the Hindu, Hellenistic and Arabic belief), or that all precious stones originated in their saliva (according to a belief widespread in primitive cultures from the Far East to England). These myths express the maximum degree of proximity possible between 'protector' and 'adversary'—between, that is, the guarding 'monster' and the guarded 'treasure'. They constitute a synthesis of opposites, an amalgam in which the antitheses become all but identical within an ambivalent psychological zone marking out a common fund of significance between the antithetical meanings. Eliade notes that metaphysical emblems, watched over by serpents or dragons, come to be represented by specific objects located in the forehead, the eyes or mouth of these ophidia (17). At the same time, precious stones incorporate the general symbolism of lithophanies, sub- limated in the perfection and beauty of the gems. This is why

Gougenot des Mousseaux, in his *Dieu et les Dieux*, emphasizes the important part always played by stones. The aerolite, in particular, because of its connexion with the celestial sphere, represents the mansion and the vestments of a god descended upon earth. Shooting stars are related to angels. There is another tradition which imparts an infernal shade of meaning to the precious stone, by reason of the 'obscure' nature of the knowledge which it connotes. Plainly, in this case it is the feeling of aversion towards the material richness of the stone that prevails over—or is allied with—admiration for its hardness, colour and transparency. In this connexion, Baron Guiraud, in *La Philosophie de l'histoire*, comments that, when Lucifer fell, angelic light was given corporeal form in the shining stars and glittering gems. Jewels have also been equated with metals, as a kind of 'subterranean astronomy', and in fact, through the application of the theory of correspondences, with every other order of existence. All kinds of glistening specks of colour, too, may contain some of the symbolic sense of particular precious stones, but only as secondary meanings and by association with the essential symbolism of the stone itself. The Hebrews were well aware of the symbolic significance of jewels and made use of it in their liturgy. Lévi, in *Les Mystères du Rational d'Aaron*, recalls that 'The Rational, consisting of twelve precious stones (representing the twelve months of the year, and the signs of the Zodiac), was arranged as four lines with three stones in each, and the type and colour of the stones, from left to right and from top to bottom were: sardonyx (red), emerald (green), topaz (yellow), ruby (red tending to orange), jasper (deep green), sapphire (deep blue), jacinth (lilac), amethyst (violet), agate (milky), chrysolite (golden blue), beryl (darkish blue), and onyx (pink). Each one of these stones had a given magic ability. The order in which they appear is based upon their colour and luminosity, decreasing, as in a tongue of flame, from top to bottom and from the outside to the centre' (59).

Journey From the spiritual point of view, the journey is never merely a passage through space, but rather an expression of the urgent desire for discovery and change that underlies the actual movement and experience of travelling. Hence, to study, to inquire, to seek or to live with intensity through new and profound experiences are all modes of travelling or, to put it another way, spiritual and symbolic equivalents of the journey. Heroes are always travellers, in that they are restless. Travelling, Jung observes, is an image of aspiration, of an unsatisfied longing that never finds its goal, seek where it may (31). He goes on to point out that this goal is in fact the lost Mother; but this is a moot point, for we might equally well say that, on the contrary, its journey is a flight from the Mother. Flying, swimming and running are other activities which may be equated with travelling; and so also are dreaming, day-dreaming and imagining. Crossing a ford marks the decisive stage in the passage from one state to another (56). There is a connexion between the symbolism of the journey, in its cosmic sense, and the symbolism of the essential landscape of megalithic cults (or that seen by the shamans in their visions). Travelling may also be related to the complete cycle of the year or to the attempt to escape from it, depending upon certain secondary characteristics of the journey. But the true Journey is neither acquiescence nor escape—it is evolution. For this reason Guénon has suggested that ordeals of initiation frequently take the form of 'symbolic journeys' representing a quest that starts in the darkness of the profane world (or of the unconscious—the mother) and gropes towards the light. Such ordeals or trials—like the stages in a journey—are rites of purification (29). The archetype of the journey is the pilgrimage to the 'Centre' or the holy land—or the way out of the maze. The Night Sea-Crossing, equivalent to the Journey into Hell, illustrates certain basic aspects of journey-symbolism which still call for elucidation. Primarily, to travel is to seek. The Turkish Kalenderi sect require their initiates to travel ceaselessly, since, as we have suggested, travelling is often invested with a higher, sublimatory significance.

Journey into Hell   Dante's descent into the inferno was anticipated by that of Aeneas in the *Aeneid* of Virgil, as well as by the journey of Orpheus. Asín Palacios, in his *Escatología musulmana de la Divina Comedia* (Madrid, 1919)—quoted by Guénon—has suggested that the Florentine poet based the path which he traced, as well as the pattern of the three worlds that he draws, upon the two works of Mohiddin ibn Arabi (who preceded him by more than eighty years), entitled *The Book of the Journey by Night* and *Revelations of Mecca* (27). From the symbolic point of view, and leaving aside the otherworldly implications of the two complementary universes—the 'central level of manifestation' and the terrestrial— the Journey into Hell symbolizes the descent into the unconscious, or the awareness of all the potentialities of being—cosmic and psychological—that are needed in order to reach the Paradisiac heights, except, that is, the divinely chosen few who attain to these heights by the path of innocence. Hell fuses together the ideas of 'crime and punishment', just as purgatory embraces the notions of penitence and forgiveness.

Journey of the Soul   According to Hindu belief, the individual, upon freeing himself from the shackles of the manifest world, follows a route which is the inverse of that path which he took when entering into it. Within this system of thought there are two possible paths which he may take: either that of the liberated (*dêva-yâna* or the 'way of the gods') or else that followed by those who still have further states of individuation to pass through (*pitri-yâna* or the 'way of the ancestors'). As the *Bhagavad-Gítâ* observes: 'At this juncture, those who tend towards union, without having actually achieved it, leave manifest existence behind them, some to return to it later, others never to return. . . . Fire, light, day, the crescent moon, the half-year of the sun's ascendence and its northerly course—these are the luminous signs which lead to Brahma those who acknowledge Brahma. Smoke, night, the waning moon, the half-year when the sun descends towards the south— such are the signs that lead to lunar light and immediately to the return to states of manifestation' (26).

Judgement, The Day of   The twentieth enigma of the Tarot pack, representing the resurrection of the dead in the valley of Jehoshaphat, when the angel of the Apocalypse sounds the last trump. This angel has a sun-symbol on his forehead and his golden hair further emphasizes his sun-symbolism. Death, in the symbolic sense, is equivalent to the death of the soul—to ignoring the transcendental aim of Man. The tomb is the body and fleshly desires. The angel, by means both of his light and of his trumpet-call, 'awakens' the latent desire for resurrection in the man who has fallen into iniquity. The constellation which shows the closest affinity with this enigma is the Swan of Leda, the harbinger of the final 'Conjunction'. On the positive side, this card stands for illumination, regeneration, healing and resurrection. On the negative side, for hot-headedness and Dionysiac ecstasy (59).

Juice   Juice or sap represents life-giving liquid. It is a sacrificial symbol connected with blood and also with light as the distillation of igniferous bodies, suns and stars.

Jupiter   Among the Graeco-Roman gods, he corresponds to the supreme virtues of the judgement and the will. As the lord of the sky, his infernal counterparts are Pluto, the lord of the chthonian world, and Neptune as the lord of the deeps (symbolizing the unconscious). Jupiter's attributes are the thunderbolt, the crown, the eagle and the throne (8).

Justice   The eighth enigma of the Tarot, this is an allegory of the idea of justice personified as an image rather like that of the Empress, depicted full-face and symmetrical (this being symbolic of exact, bilateral equilibrium) with a red tunic and a blue cloak. In one hand, she holds up a pair of scales (symbolic of the equilibrium of good and evil), and in the other a sword (for psychic decisiveness, and the Word of God). Her throne is like the Emperor's, massively stable. A crown with fleurons shaped like iron lances surmounts the head-dress of this allegorical figure. The enigma is related to Libra, the sign of the Zodiac, and, like it, represents not so much external justice or social legality as inner judgement setting in motion the entire psychic (or psychosomatic) mechanism involved in the process of determining guilt; the idea behind this is basically the same as Weininger's concept of sin as intrinsically indistinct from punishment. Astronomically speaking, Justice is Astrea. In the positive sense, this enigma denotes harmony, a strict code of behaviour and firmness; in the negative sense, restriction, pettiness and craft (59).

K

Key As an attribute, it pertains to several mythic characters, including Hecate (31). It is symbolic of mystery or enigma, or of a task to be performed, and the means of carrying it out. It sometimes refers to the threshold of the unconscious (32). The key to knowledge corresponds, within the cycle of the year, to the month of June (healing). The conjunction of the symbols of the male dove and the key signifies the spirit opening the gates of heaven (4). The emblem formed by two keys, sometimes placed over a heart, relates to Janus (4). In legend and folklore, three keys are often used to symbolize a like number of secret chambers full of precious objects. They are symbolic representations of initiation and knowledge. The first key, of silver, concerns what can be revealed by psychological understanding; the second is made of gold, and pertains to philosophical wisdom; the third and last, of diamond, confers the power to act (38). The finding of a key signifies the stage prior to the actual discovery of the treasure, found only after great difficulties. Clearly there is a morphological relationship between the key and the *Nem Ankh* sign (or 'Eternal Life')—the anserated cross of the Egyptians; their gods are sometimes shown holding this cross by the top as if it were a key, especially in ceremonies concerning the dead. But it should perhaps be pointed out that, in this case, it is the keys that derive from the anserated cross, the archetype of the key of Eternal Life that opens up the gates of death on to immortality.

King In the broadest and most abstract sense, the king symbolizes universal and archetypal Man. As such, according to animistic and astrobiological ways of thought widespread from India to Ireland (21), he possesses magic and supernatural powers. He also expresses the ruling or governing principle, supreme consciousness, and the virtues of sound judgement and self-control (56). At the same time, a coronation is equivalent to achievement, victory and consummation (33). Hence any man may properly be called a king when he achieves the culminating point in the unfolding of his individual life. Deriving from, and equated with the king-symbolism are the symbols for gold, the sun and Jupiter. These symbols imply in essence the idea that the king is Man transposed to the solar plane, to the ideal or 'golden' situation—that is, 'saved' and made eternal. The idea of immortality was passed from god to monarch, and only later was it vouchsafed to the hero and later still to ordinary mortals in so far as they merited the 'crown' of success, having overcome certain obstacles (usually of a moral order). The king, quite apart from all this, may also symbolize the 'royalty'—'or grandeur—of Man. In this case, he may be subjected to a period of unfavourable or painful circumstances; when this is so, the particular symbol becomes that of the 'sick king' (like Amfortas in *Parsifal*), or of the 'sea-king' (signifying the negative aspect of humanity) (32). Love also plays a highly important part in the symbolism of royalty, since love is held to be one of the most obvious of culminating points in the life of Man. This is why the bride and bridegroom in the Greek marriage-ceremony wear crowns made of some precious metal. The king and queen together comprise the perfect image of the *hieros gamos*, of the union of heaven and earth, sun and moon, gold and silver, sulphur and mercury; and—according to Jung— they also signify the spiritual 'conjunction' that takes place when the process of individuation is complete, with the harmonious union of the unconscious and consciousness. The title of king is bestowed upon the most outstanding specimen in every species or type: so, the lion is the king of beasts, as is the eagle of birds or gold among the metals (57). To come back to the symbolism of the 'sick king', he— like such afflicted heroes as Philoctetes—signifies, on the one hand, the punishment which pursues sin as the shadow follows the body (given the existence of the light of consciousness), and, on the other, sterility of spirit. A particularly significant instance of the symbolic process is implied by the king's projecting his spiritual state on to nature around him, as happens with Amfortas in *Parsifal*, in the *Waste Land* of Eliot, and, to some extent, the *Fall of the House of Usher* by Poe. As for the 'sea-king', he is symbolic of the ocean (another version of Neptune) and therefore personifies the deeps of the unconscious in their regressive and evil form as opposed to the waters of the 'Upper Ocean' (the clouds, rain or fresh water) which are fecund (32). The 'aged king'—such as Dhritarashtra, the aged monarch of Vedic epics, or king Lear, or all those aged kings of legends and folktales—is symbolic of the world-memory, or the collective unconscious in its widest and most all-embracing sense (38). The king often exhibits, in concentrated form, the character- istics of the father and the hero, and there is a touch of the Messianic about him; by inversion of the temporal order of things, what is past becomes 'what is to pass' and the dead king is supposed by his subjects to be living a strange existence as a ghost, later to return to his country when it is in great danger. This legend tends to accrue to the names of historical monarchs who have fallen in strange or unhappy circumstances, as in the case of the Portuguese dom Sebastian or that of don Rodrigo, the last of the Gothic kings. The supreme example is the mythic king Arthur, called by Malory *Arthurus, rex quondam, rexque futurus* (q.v.) (16).

Knife A symbol which is the inversion of sword-symbolism. It is associated with vengeance and death, but also with sacrifice (8). The short blade of the knife represents, by analogy, the primacy of the instinctive forces in the man wielding it, whereas the long blade of the sword illustrates the spiritual height of the swordsman.

Knight A symbol which confirms what we have suggested concerning the steed. He is the master, the *logos*, the spirit which prevails over the mount (that is, over matter). But this is possible only after a lengthy period of apprenticeship, which may be seen, historically speaking, as a real attempt to create in the knight a human type superior to all others. As a consequence, the education of the knight was directed in part to strengthening him physically, but in particular to developing his soul and spirit, his affections (that is, his morals) and his mind (that is, his reason) in order to prepare him adequately for the task of directing and controlling the real world, so that he might take his proper place in the hierarchies of the universe (that is, in the feudal hierarchy, ordered after the celestial pattern, ranging from the baron up to the king). We also find mounted monks, priests and laymen skilfully controlling their steed, thereby demonstrating their allegiance to the spiritual (or symbolic) order of knighthood in deliberate competition with the historico-social order of knights. This is why in the bas-reliefs on the capitals in the cloister at Silos, knights are shown bestriding goats. Now, goats are symbolic of superiority, because of their association with high peaks, and Rabanus Maurus points out that knights mounted on goats must therefore be interpreted as saints (46). Of course, the purpose of the assimilation of saint with knight is to magnify the symbolic worth of the knight, as in the case of St. Ignatius Loyola. More profound examples of such assimilation are to be seen in that of the king and knight (King Arthur), or the king, knight and saint (St. Ferdinand III of Spain or St. Louis IX of France). This knight-symbolism is common in all symbolic traditions. Ananda Coomaraswamy observes that 'the "horse" is a symbol of the bodily vehicle, and the "rider" is the Spirit: when the latter has come to the end of its incarnations, the saddle is unoccupied, and the vehicle necessarily dies' (60). By taking account of certain other orders of things analogous with chivalry, including (particularly) alchemy (which was in fact a mediaeval technique of spiritual-

Knight Errant, after an early 16th-century engraving.

ization) and also certain aspects of colour-symbolism, we have been
able to arrive at a system of analogies which we believe to be very
helpful in explaining some of the more recondite aspects of the
symbolism of knighthood. Mediaeval tales and legends often refer to
a green, white or red knight, but most frequently of all to a black
knight. Should we regard this as merely a matter of aesthetic
appreciation of the colour in a literal and decorative sense? Or does
the choice of colour proceed necessarily from a highly significant

cause? The latter, we think. In alchemy, the rising scale of colours (the progressive, evolutive scale) is: black, white, red (corresponding to prime matter, mercury, sulphur), with gold representing the hypothetical, final stage. Conversely, it can be said that the descending scale would be from blue to green, that is, descending from heaven to earth. These two colours stand for the celestial, and the natural or terrestrial factors. Furthermore, black is associated with sin, penitence, the withdrawal of the recluse, the hidden, rebirth in seclusion, and sorrow; white with innocence (natural as well as that regained through expiation), illumination, openheartedness, gladness; and red with passion (moral or material—love or pain), blood, wounds, sublimation and ecstasy. We may therefore surmise that the Green Knight is the pre-knight, the squire, the apprentice sworn to knighthood; the Black Knight stands for him who undergoes the tribulations of sin, expiation and obscurity in order to attain to immortality by way of earthly glory and heavenly beatitude; the White Knight (Sir Galahad) is the natural conqueror, the 'chosen one' of the Evangelists, or the 'illuminated one' re-emerging from a period of *nigredo*; the Red Knight is the knight sublimated by every possible trial, bloodied from every possible sacrifice, supremely virile, the conqueror of all that is base, who, having completed his life's work, is fully deserving of gold in its ultimate transmutation—glorification. Knighthood should be seen, then, as a superior kind of pedagogy helping to bring about the transmutation of natural man (steedless) into spiritual man. An important part was played in this symbolic tradition by prototypes such as the famous, mythical knights of the court of King Arthur or patron saints such as St. George, Santiago of Compostela, or the archangel Michael. The practical means of achieving the knight's ultimate goal consisted of corporeal exertions, which were, in effect, not merely physical or material since the knight practised with *all* kinds of arms, and these arms stood for symbolic potentialities; these practical exertions, then, led eventually to the inversion of the world of desire through the ascetic denial of physical pleasure—the very essence of knighthood—and the almost mystic cult of the beloved. The knight's relative shortcomings while carrying out his sworn duties provide the explanation of the colour black which we have just examined. Nevertheless, other explanations have also been advanced, as for example that the knight is the 'guardian of the treasure', supplanting the monster he has conquered (the serpent or dragon). Clearly this symbolism is not opposed to that which we have proposed, rather does it support it by emphasizing the essential mission of the knight's service. Another interesting aspect of knight-symbolism—though, in a way, a negative one—can be seen in the use of the epithets 'wandering' and 'errant' in mediaeval tales, legends and folklore. At times, the adjective has a precise meaning, at other times it is much more imprecise. In every case, the wandering (or 'errantry') of the knight implies an intermediate position between the 'saved' knight and the accursed hunter, with the difference that the knight errant, so far from being caught up in the pursuit of his desires, is of course striving to master them—and this is what we had in mind when we observed that this aspect 'in a way, is a negative one'. Needless to say, this symbolism of one who takes the dark and lonely path of expiation, verifies our observation that the Black Knight is a symbol of withdrawal, penitence and sacrifice.

Heraldic knot.

Knot A complex symbol embracing several important meanings all of which are related to the central idea of a tightly closed link. It implies also the symbolism of the spiral and the sigmoid line (41). The sign for infinity—the horizontal figure 8—as well as the number 8 itself, are at once interlacing and also knotted, and this emphasizes the relationship of the knot with the idea of infinity—or, rather, with the manifestation of the infinite. It is comparable with the net, the loop and the plait, in that it expresses the concept of binding and fettering—a concept which is generally expressive of an unchanging psychic situation, however unaware of his predicament the individual may be: for example, that of the unliberated man who is 'tied down' by the Uranian god. This is why the *Flamen Dialis* of the ancient Romans could not wear knots in his habits; and this is also true of the Moslems on their pilgrimages to Mecca (21). These magic associations of binding, which form part of the symbolism of the knot, are sometimes given literal expression in magical practices, such as those of fishermen in the Shetland Islands who still believe that they can control the winds by the magic use of knots (21). A knotted cord forms a kind of closed ring, or a circumference, and hence it possesses the general significance of an enclosure, and of protection. The 'slip-knot' is a determinative sign in the Egyptian language, entering into the composition of words such as calumny, oaths, or a journey. The meaning must have originated in the idea of keeping in touch with someone who is far away, and there is unquestionably some connexion with the enigma of the Hanged

Man in the Tarot pack (19). The 'endless knot' is one of the eight
Emblems of Good Luck of Chinese Buddhism, representing
longevity (5); the symbolism here has taken one aspect of the
concept of the knot—that of pure connexion—and applied it to the
biological and phenomenal planes. Finally, the famous 'Gordian
knot' cut by Alexander the Great, by virtue of his determination
and his sword, is a long-standing symbol of the labyrinth, arising
out of the chaotic and inextricable tangle of the cords with which
it was tied. To undo the knot was equivalent to finding the 'Centre'
which forms such an important part of all mystic thought. And to
cut the knot was to transfer the pure idea of achievement and
victory to the plane of war and of existence.

L

Labyrinth An architectonic structure, apparently aimless, and
of a pattern so complex that, once inside, it is impossible or very
difficult to escape. Or it may take the form of a garden similarly
patterned. Ancient writings mention five great mazes: that of
Egypt, which Pliny located in lake Moeris; the two Cretan
labyrinths of Cnossus (or Gnossus) and Gortyna; the Greek maze
on the island of Lemnos; and the Etruscan at Clusium. It is likely
that certain initiatory temples were labyrinthine in construction for
doctrinal reasons. Ground-plans, sketches and emblems of mazes
appear fairly frequently over a very wide area, but principally in
Asia and Europe. Some are believed to have been conceived with
the purpose of luring devils into them so that they might never
escape. It is to be supposed, therefore, that, for the Primitive, the
maze had a certain fascination comparable with the abyss, the
whirlpool and other phenomena (8). Nevertheless, Waldemar
Fenn suggests that some circular or elliptical labyrinths in prehistoric
engravings—those at Peña de Mogor, for example—should be
interpreted as diagrams of heaven, that is, as images of the apparent
motions of the astral bodies. This notion is not opposed to the
previous one: it is independent of it and, up to a point, complementary, because the terrestrial maze, as a structure or a pattern, is
capable of reproducing the celestial, and because both allude to the
same basic idea—the loss of the spirit in the process of creation—
that is, the 'fall' in the neoplatonic sense—and the consequent need
to seek out the way through the 'Centre', back to the spirit. There is
an illustration in *De Groene Leeuw*, by Goosse van Wreeswyk

(Amsterdam, 1672), which depicts the sanctuary of the alchemists' *lapis*, encircled by the orbits of the planets, as walls, suggesting in this way a cosmic labyrinth (32). The emblem of the labyrinth was widely used by mediaeval architects. To trace through the labyrinthic

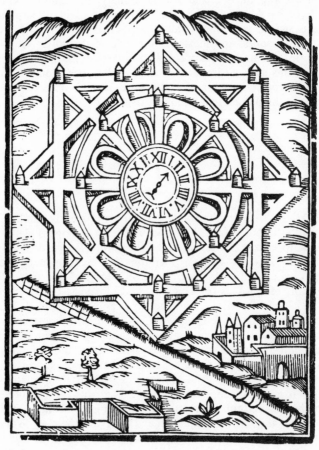

Labyrinth—the clock implies juxtaposition of time and space.
(After an old engraving.)

path of a mosaic patterned on the ground was once considered a symbolic substitute for a pilgrimage to the Holy Land (28). Some labyrinths shaped like a cross, known in Italy as 'Solomon's knot', and featured in Celtic, Germanic and Romanesque decoration, are a synthesis of the dual symbolism of the cross and the labyrinth; they are known, for this reason, as the 'emblem of divine inscrutability'. It is not difficult to make out, in the centre of the pattern, the figure of the swastika, which adds to the basic symbolism a suggestion of rotating, generating and unifying motion (4). For Diel, the maze signifies the unconscious, and also error and remoteness from the fount of life (15). Eliade notes that the essential mission of the maze was to defend the 'Centre'—that it was, in fact, an initiation into sanctity, immortality and absolute reality and, as such, equivalent to other 'trials' such as the fight with the dragon. At the same time, the labyrinth may be interpreted as an apprenticeship for the neophyte who would learn to distinguish the proper path leading to the Land of the Dead (17).

Lake In the Egyptian system of hieroglyphs, the schematic figure of a lake expresses the occult and the mysterious, probably by allusion to the underground lake which the sun has to pass over during its 'night-crossing' (but also simply by associating it with the symbolism of level, given that water always alludes to the 'connexion between the superficial and the profound'; a lake becomes, then, a fluid mass of transparency). In the temple of the god Amon, at Karnak, there was an artificial lake symbolizing *hyle*—or the 'lower waters' of protomatter. And, at certain times during the year, a procession of priests would cross the lake in boats, in this way re-enacting the 'night-crossing' of the sun mentioned above (19). The symbolism here is the same, broadly speaking, as that of the watery deeps. The Irish and Breton belief that the Land of the Dead is at the bottom of the ocean or of lakes may be derived from watching the sun setting over the water; and the death of human beings, and therefore by analogy the setting of the sun, was interpreted as passing over into the nether world. But, as we have suggested, the structure of lake-symbolism may have arisen directly out of the symbolism of level; for this latter symbolism, so deeply rooted in the psyche of man, equates all that is on a low level spatially with what is low in a spiritual, negative, destructive, and hence fatal, sense. The fact that water-symbolism is closely connected with the symbolism of the abyss serves to corroborate the fatal implications of the lake-symbol, for the part played by the liquid Element is to provide the transition between life and death, between the solid and the gaseous, the formal and the informal. At the same time, the lake– or, rather, its surface alone—holds the significance of a mirror, presenting an image of self-contemplation, consciousness and revelation.

Lamb The origins of the symbolism of the lamb are to be found in the Book of Enoch (32). It signifies purity, innocence, meekness (as well as unwarranted sacrifice). In allegories, it lies at the root of representations of either pure thought, or a just man, or the Lamb of God (4). Pinedo, however, points to the interesting relationship between the lamb and the lion, by inversion of their respective symbolic meanings. Examples of this are common in Christian symbolism, especially during the Romanesque period; a good instance is that of a tympanum in the church at Armentia, where the *Agnus Dei* is shown inside a circle (symbolizing the All, or perfection) accompanied by the epigraph: '*Mors ego sum mortis. Vocor Agnus, sum Leo fortis*' (I am the death of death. I am called a lamb, I am a strong lion) (46) (Plate XX). Its etymology suggests other symbolic meanings: Alleau, in *De la Nature des symboles* (Paris, 1958), proposes that *agnus* is related to the Greek *agnos* and therefore symbolizes the unknown; and that it is also related to *ugni* (fire) and so is a sacrificial symbol of the periodic renovation of the world.

Lamia   The mythic queen Lamia, celebrated for her beauty, was turned into a wild beast because of her cruelty. Ancient writings refer to lamias, in the plural, as beings similar to sirens, found in the company of dragons in caves and deserts. In 1577, Johann Wier published an entire treatise upon these beings, entitled *De Lamiis Liber*. According to Caro Baroja, this belief in lamias still persists in Gascony. Their attribute is the gold comb—a fish skeleton perhaps? —with which they comb their hair (10). Legend has it that lamias are devourers of children (8). Jung has pointed out that the fact that 'lamia' is also the word used for a huge and very voracious fish (from 'lamos'—an abyss) verifies the connexion between the devouring lamias and the dragon-whale of the kind studied by Frobenius in *Zeitalter des Sonnengottes* (31).

Lamp   A symbol of intelligence and the spirit (56). It appears in this sense in the Greek myth of Psyche, in the legend of Diogenes and in the hermit (the ninth enigma) of the Tarot pack (40). The lamps of the ancients were shaped according to their function— profane, religious or funereal—and to suit the nature of the god to whom they were dedicated. There were lamps with twelve wicks, symbolizing the Wheel of the Zodiac. And there were perpetually burning lamps such as that kept alight by the vestal virgins, or that of the temple of Venus noted by St. Augustine (8).

Lance   A symbol of war, and also a phallic symbol (8). It is a weapon of earthly character, in contrast to the celestial implications of the sword. It is connected with the symbolism of the cup or chalice. Generally speaking, the lance is comparable from the symbological point of view with the branch, the tree, the cross, and all symbols pertaining to the valley-mountain axis. In the *Libro del orden de caballería*, Raymond Lull expresses the belief that the lance is given to a knight as a symbol of rectitude. The 'bleeding lance', which appears in the legend of the Grail, has sometimes been interpreted as the lance of Longinus, relating it to that of the Passion. There are authors who reject this interpretation and see it rather as a general sacrificial symbol.

Landscape Logically speaking it may be deduced that the country-side—landscapes of all kinds—is the mundane manifestation of a dynamic complex which in origin was non-spatial. Inner forces are liberated to unfold as forms which disclose in themselves the qualitative and quantitative order of their inner tensions. Thus a mountain crest becomes a graphic sign. Let us take, by way of illustration, landscapes as they appear in dreams. Leaving aside the phenomenon of memory, reminiscence, or the complex association of various sense-data, the scenes and towns which figure in dreams are neither arbitrary and indeterminate nor objective: they are symbolic—that is, they well up in order to illuminate certain momentary experiences called forth by varying combinations of influences in varying degrees of intensity. Landscape-scenes arising in the imagination in this way are sustained solely by the validity, duration and intensity of the feelings which aroused them. Form—just as in physical morphology—is the diagram of force. Now, what we have said about landscapes in dreams can be applied also to an actual landscape, seen and selected by an automatic response of the unconscious, which detects in it an affinity that gives us pause and makes us return to it again and again. This, then, is a question not of a projection of the mind but of an analogy whereby the landscape is adopted by the spirit in consequence of the inner bond linking the character of the scene with the spirit of the observer himself. Subjectivism concerns only the act of choosing. The intellection of the significance of a landscape is, then, wholly objective, as is the grasping of the symbolic values of colours and numbers. The Chinese saw this with the utmost clarity: as Luc Benoist has observed, Chinese art has always placed more emphasis upon landscape than upon man (as a figure, that is to say), and upon the macrocosm rather than the microcosm. 'If the superior man loves the country-side,' to quote the words of Kuo Hsi, 'why is this so? Hills and gardens will always be the haunts of him who seeks to cultivate his original nature; fountains and rocks are a constant joy to him who wanders whistling among them. . .' (6). It is a well-established tradition of symbology that the different worlds (or zones) are strictly only different states of being. Hence the fact that the 'chosen site' is the enshrining image which arises out of it. The 'trysting place', when it truly possesses that character, and is not merely arbitrary or fortuitous, signifies a meeting or 'conjoining' in precisely this same sense—that is, transposed into topographical or spatial terms (26). However revolutionary these assertions may seem, they are nevertheless confirmed by the findings of the psychology of form and by isomorphism, since it has been shown that it is not possible to distinguish between psychic and physical formal processes—other than externally. In support of all this, there is the

comment of Mircea Eliade that 'In point of fact, man never chooses
a site, he simply "discovers it". . . . One of the means of discovering
one's situation is by orientation' (17). Now, in order to grasp the
symbolic sense of a landscape it is necessary to distinguish between
the predominant elements and the merely incidental, and between
the character of the whole and the character of the component
elements. When the predominant element is a cosmic one, its
effect is to bind all the other components together, and it is this
cosmic ingredient which makes its influence felt over and above
that of the individual features of the landscape. Instances of such
cosmic features are the sea, the desert, the icy wastes, the mountain-
peak, clouds and sky. It is when the ingredients of landscape-
symbolism are varied and evenly balanced that symbolic interpretation is most needed. The interpreter must, then, look for the following: (a) a spatial pattern organized within particular limits which
endow it with a structure after the manner of a building or a work
of art. By spatial symbolism we mean, in the first place, the symbolism of level, that is, the disposition of the zones of the landscape
according to the three levels of the normal, the lower and the higher;
and secondly the symbolism of orientation, that is, the position of
the accidental elements in relation to the north-south and the
east-west axes. He must then bear in mind (b) the form—the pattern
or the shape of the terrain, whether it is undulating or broken,
steeply sloped or flat, soft or hard; (c) the positional relationship of
the particular area chosen to the region as a whole or to the zone
surrounding it—whether it is lower or higher, more open or more
enclosed; and finally (d) the natural and artificial elements which
make up the organized pattern: trees, shrubs, plants, lakes, springs,
wells, rocks, sandy shores, houses, steps, benches, grottoes, gardens,
fences, doors and gates. Also important is the predominating colour,
or the clash of colours, or the general feeling of fecundity or barren-
ness, of brightness or gloom, of order or disorder. Roads and
cross-roads are of great significance, and so are streams. About the
objective meaning of each of the factors we have listed above there
is much that we could say; however, since the more important
factors—such as the symbolism of level—are dealt with under
separate headings, we will here add no more than a few notes.
Steepness indicates primitiveness and regression; flat country
denotes the apocalyptic end, the longing for power and for death.
There is a Persian tradition that, when the end of the world has
come—when Ahriman is vanquished for ever, the mountains will be
levelled and all the earth will become one great plain. Ideas cognate
with this are to be found in certain traditions of Israel and France
(35). It would not be hard to point to the history of architecture and
town-planning as evidence of the subconscious application of these

principles. Furthermore, there are some aspects of landscapes which have a symbolic air about them that is very difficult to analyse intellectually. For instance, the following descriptive passage from Dante's *Commedia* has always seemed to us to evoke an atmosphere of profound mystery: 'Around this little island, in its lowest reaches, there, where it is lashed by the waves, reeds grow in the soft mud' (*Purgatorio* I, 100). Independent of the cosmic significance of landscape, there may also be a sexual implication. It is also essential to bear in mind that this is not strictly a matter of symbols as such but of complex, symbolic functions. For instance, in scenes depicting low-lying topographical features, the following factors may be at work: (*a*) depth in the sense of what is base, comparable therefore with the wicked and infernal; (*b*) depth in the sense of what is symbolically profound; (*c*) depth as it pertains to the material earth itself, implying a chthonian and maternal symbolism. Only the context can help us to tell the essence from the accessory—as is true also of the vast majority of symbols. Here we must bear in mind the primitive concept of the archetypal 'ideal countryside'. Schneider has observed that the fact of there being so many identical names for rivers and mountains in different parts of the world, suggests that megalithic ways of thought must have led to the custom of naming the topographical features of different regions after some ideal model. This model, it may be argued, could be the product of the lasting impression made upon the mind of Primitive Man by a particular environment endowed with such unity and variety as to prevent him from ever wishing to leave it; but it could also be explained as the projection of a psychic order founded upon laws comparable with those governing quaternary patterns, or the mandala, etc. Man's attention was first drawn to the contraposition of heaven and earth by topographical features, and he gave expression to this in the struggle between gods and Titans, angels and demons, and in the opposition of mountain and valley. Next, he set out to explain the earth's surface by means of the laws of orientation, taking the four points of the compass from the apparent orbit of the sun as well as from the human anatomy, and identifying them as ambivalent forces—ambivalent because they are at once hostile to things external and the defenders of their limits. As Schneider adds: 'To preserve cosmic order, the gods fought with the giants and the monsters which had from the very beginning of creation sought to devour the sun. They stationed the heroic lion on the celestial mountain. Four archers'—the tetramorphs—'are continuously on guard day and night against anyone who attempts to disrupt the order of the cosmos' (50). The stockade, the wall or stone enclosure, comments Eliade, are among the oldest known parts of the structure of temples, appearing as early as in proto-Indian civilizations such as that of Mohenjo-Daro and also in Crete (17). They owe their origins to the same basic, primordial idea of the symbolism of landscape—its representation of cosmic order. The mountain with one peak is symbolic of the One—of transcendent purpose; the two-peaked Mountain of Mars stands for the Gemini, the world of appearances and the dualism of all forms of life. Both these symbolic mountains find their symbolic complement in the general pattern of archetypal landscape—also, incidentally, an image of the year; this pattern is composed of the river of life (denoting the positive phase) and the river of oblivion (the negative phase) which flow through the sea of flames (expressing infirmity) and well up from a single source (birth or the Origin). According to this scheme, every landscape has a disastrous and a felicitous tendency, corresponding on the temporal plane with the self-evident distinction between 'coming' and 'going' which in turn is analogous to the two halves of human existence. But, quite apart from all this, the symbolic interpretation of a landscape may be determined according to the laws governing diverse and individual correspondences, as well as the overall significance derived from the complex of meanings afforded by its separate features. By way of an illustration of the many possibilities of interpreting the significance of a landscape, we will conclude with some comments on Vallcarca with its characteristic low-lying features. The gardens are at a lower level than the city proper, and screened from it by the vegetation, which has something of the archaic and oriental about it. The main street leads north towards an open plain, signifying the process of disintegration. On the other hand, those streets which lead towards the mountain are on the favourable axis. In this case, the interpretation is obvious enough, as it is in all instances of scenes where it is possible to identify the essential features of archetypal landscape.

Lantern Like all 'lights' that are independent of the Light—that which, in other words, is severed—the lantern symbolizes individual life in the face of cosmic existence, transitory fact in the face of eternal truth, 'distraction' in the face of essence. This explains the magic use of lanterns. Because of its psychological interest, we quote here a passage taken from a Chinese work of the Tang dynasty: 'On the mid-Autumn feast-day, the devil turned himself into a man, ingratiated himself with women and children and led them off to secret places whence they could not escape (a death-symbol). Seeing that this demon was greatly persecuting the people, the jurisconsult Bao-Cong informed the king of the matter and persuaded him to issue a decree to the effect that paper lanterns, shaped like fishes, should be hung at the entrances of the houses. In this fashion would the carp-demon, deceived by these images, leave the Hundred Families in peace' (13).

Laurel A tree sacred to Apollo and expressive of victory. Laurel leaves were used to weave festive garlands and crowns. The crowning of the poet, the artist or conqueror with laurel leaves was meant to represent not the external and visible consecration of an act, but the recognition that that act, by its very existence, presupposes a series of inner victories over the negative and dissipative influence of the base forces. There is no achievement without struggle and triumph. Hence the laurel expresses, the progressive identification of the hero with the motives and aims of his victory. An associated idea is the generic implication of fecundity pertaining to all vegetation-symbols.

Lead A metal associated with Saturn. The alchemists employed the image of a white dove contained in lead to express their central idea that matter was the receptacle of the spirit (32). The specific symbolism of lead is the transference of the idea of weight and density on to the spiritual plane.

Leaf One of the eight 'common emblems' of Chinese symbolism, it is an allegory of happiness. When several leaves appear together as a motif, they represent people; in this sense it is closely related to the significance of herbs as symbols of human beings (5).

Leg In the Egyptian system of hieroglyphs, the figure of a leg is symbolic of erecting, lifting and founding (19). The symbolic significance is related to that of the foot, and both symbols emphasize the fundamental difference, from the merely biological point of view, of the human form as compared with other animals, in that humans stand erect. The leg is also equivalent to the pedestal, and in Cabbalistic thought it denotes qualities of firmness and splendour.

Lemures The Romans gave this name to disembodied spirits. According to Ovid, the festival of the Lemuralia was a commemoration of the dead. It is likely that the *umbra*—the ghost or apparition —is closely linked with the lemur, and that both are symbolic of certain states of psychic dissociation (47).

Zodiacal sign of Leo.

Leo The fifth sign of the Zodiac. It corresponds to solar power, the will, fire, and the clear, penetrating light which passes from the threshold of the Gemini into the realm of Cancer. It is connected with feelings and emotions (40).

Leopard An attribute of Dionysos, the leopard has been equated with Argus-of-the-thousand-eyes (4). It is a symbol of ferocity and of valour (5). The leopard, like the tiger and panther, expresses the aggressive and powerful aspects of the lion without his solar significance.

Letters of the Alphabet   Letters, in all cultures, have a symbolic significance, sometimes in a twofold sense corresponding to both their shape and their sound. Letter-symbolism probably derives from Primitive pictograms and ideographs—quite apart, that is, from the theory of cosmic 'correspondences' which prescribes that each component of a series must correspond to another given component of a parallel series. Enel, in *La Langue sacrée*, has subjected the Egyptian alphabet to a profound and scrupulous study, selecting those that have a phonetic value from the vast repertory of syllabic and ideographic signs. He recalls that Horapollo Niliacus in antiquity, and Kircher and Valeriano in the Renaissance, tried unsuccessfully to analyse the meaning of these symbolic signs; it is only the work of Champollion, Maspero, Mariette, etc., which has made a true understanding possible. The significance of many Egyptian signs can best be understood by grasping the import of the so-called 'determinative' signs, governing groups of phonetic signs. We cannot here give any idea of this complex Egyptian system, which was a mixture of ideographic signs and phonetic signs, abstract allusions and concrete pictograms in the form of visual patterns, such as the sign for combat (two arms holding an axe and a shield) or figures denoting geographical places (Lower Egypt was represented by plants characteristic of the Delta). We must limit ourselves, then, to the so-called Egyptian alphabet, which Enel sees closely linked, in its development, with the idea of creation itself. Here is his explanation: 'Thus the divine principle, the essence of life and the reason for creation, is represented by the eagle, but, within the microcosm, this same sign expresses reason—the faculty which brings Man into proximity with the godhead, raising him above all other created beings. The creative manifestation of the reason-principle is action, depicted by an arm, a sign which is symbolic of activity in all its aspects, and is opposed to that for passivity—represented by a broken line as the image of the primary element. The nature of the action, and the vital movement, convey the divine word—represented as a schematic image of a mouth—as the first manifestation of the world's beginning. . . . The creative action irradiated by the word continues and develops into all the varied manifestations of life; its sign is a curving spiral—a pattern of the universe, representing the cosmic forces in action. From the point of view of the microcosm, as an expression, that is, of man's labours, the sign corresponding to the cosmic spiral is the squared spiral—a sign of construction. By his own efforts, and by utilizing the forces of nature susceptible to his will, Man can transform brute matter—denoted by a kind of irregularly formed rectangle—into organized matter: a rectangle, or a stone, with which he builds his home or a temple for his god (this being a schematic sign also pertaining to the temple). But the development of the creative forces of the macrocosmos, like that of human labour, is subject to the law of equilibrium (expressed by a semicircle based upon its diameter). There are two aspects to this equilibrium: (1) the swing of the needle of the scales through 180 degrees, and (2) the daily trajectory of the sun across the sky from East to West—the alpha and omega of St. John—represented by the bird of day (the eagle) and the night-bird (the owl), and corresponding respectively to life and death, dawn and sunset. . . . The connexion between the two opposite poles of these constant alternations is symbolized by the distinction between the "upper waters" and the "lower waters", and represented by a sign which is equivalent to the Hebrew *mem*. Through this connexion, day is transformed into night and life is born of death. This ceaseless flux forms the cycle of life which is symbolized by a snake which ceaselessly rears and undulates. The bonds uniting life with death, where man is concerned, are represented by swaddling clothes (echoed by the bandages that swaddle a corpse). . . . The forces which animate every manifestation of life are the dual streams of the evolutive/involutive principle, or descent and ascent, represented by the leg as a sign of upward movement. This hieroglyph has the same meaning, also, in relation to man's activities, since it is by means of his legs that he can go where he will: towards failure as well as towards success. The relationship between the dual streams is symbolized by a plaited cord. . . .' Other signs follow the same pattern: the tie or loop signifies the connexion between the Elements; the bolt, the fixed state of a mixture; the cane-leaf, human thought, etc. (19).

The letters of the Hebrew alphabet are characterized by a similar system with symbolic and semantic meanings; the system has two aspects: the Cabbalistic, and that which corresponds to figures on the cards of the Tarot. For example, the letter *aleph* denotes will-power, man, the magician; *beth*, science, the mouth, the temple door; *ghimel*, action, the grasping hand; etc. (48). In alchemy, too, letters are significant: A expresses the beginning of all things; B, the relation between the four Elements; C, calcination; G, putrefaction; M, the androgynous nature of water in its original state as the Great Abyss, etc. (57). But this is really a case of the fusing of true symbolism with purely conventional connotations—although the significance of the letter M is symbolic in the true sense. As Blavatsky observes, M is the most sacred of letters, for it is at once masculine and feminine and also symbolic of water in its original state (or the Great Abyss) (9). It is also interesting to note the relationship of the letter S with the moon by virtue of the symbolism of form; the S can be said to consist of a waxing and a waning moon counterbalancing each other.

Letters of the alphabet played a very important part among the Gnostics and in the mysteries of Mithraic cults; equivalents ascribed to them were taken from the symbolism of numbers, as well as from the signs of the Zodiac, the hours of the day, etc. One of the early Fathers of the church, Hippolytus, quotes the remark attributed to Marcus the Pythagorean that: 'The seven heavens . . . pronounced severally their vowels and all these vowels together formed a single doxology, the sound of which, transmitted below, became the creator. . .' (9). Similarly, each vowel was related to a colour (11). The seven letters also corresponded to the seven Directions of space (that is, the six extremities of the three-dimensional cross plus the centre) (39).

Among the Arabs, too, letters had a numerical value: the number of the letters in the alphabet was twenty-eight, like the days of the lunar month. Given the importance traditionally attached to the word—the Element of air—it is easy to understand why Man, in every system ever formulated, has always tried to prove the divine power of letters by making them dependent upon mystic and cosmic orders. Saint-Yves d'Alveydre, in *L'Archéometre* (1911), has made a broad study of letter-symbolism, although, in our opinion, he comes to somewhat arbitrary conclusions concerning the relationship between the alphabet, colour, sound, planets, the signs of the Zodiac, virtue, the element of nature, and so on. As an example, here is what he says about the letter M: 'It corresponds to the natural Origin, which gives rise to all temporal forms of existence. Its number is 40. Its colour, sea-green; its sign, Scorpio; its planet, Mars; its musical note, Re.' Of greater symbolic authenticity is the summary which Bayley makes, drawing upon a variety of sources of information to arrive at a synthesis of the intrinsic significance of the letters which now comprise our Western alphabet. Clearly, there are some letter-symbols of more obvious meaning than others. Here are some of the less obvious suggested by Bayley: A is related to the cone, the mountain, the pyramid, the first cause; B, (?); C, the crescent moon, the sea, the *Magna Mater*; D, the brilliant, the diamond, the day; E is a solar letter; F signifies the fire of life; G, the Creator; H, Gemini, the threshold; I, number one, the axis of the universe; L, power; M and N, the waves of the sea and the undulations of the snake; O is a solar disk, denoting perfection; P, R, the shepherd's crook, the staff; S, the snake or serpent; T, the hammer, the double-headed axe, the cross; U, the chain of Jupiter; V, a receptacle, convergence, twin radii; X, the cross of light, the union of the two worlds—the superior and the inferior; Y, three in one, the cross-ways; and Z, the zigzag of lightning (4). As an interesting sidelight, here are Bayley's conclusions concerning the ideas—merely conventional in this instance—related to initials most commonly figuring in mediaeval and 16th-century emblems: A (combined with V) signifies *Ave*; M is the initial letter of the Virgin Mary, and also a sign of the *Millennium*, that is, of the end of this world; R stands for *Regeneratio* or *Redemptio*; Z for *Zion*; S for *Spiritus*; SS for *Sanctus Spiritus*; T for *Theos*, etc.

Any study of letter-symbolism must be closely related to the examination of words. Loeffler recalls that, among the Aryans and also among the Semites, M has always been the initial letter of words related to water and to birth of beings and the worlds (Mantras, Manu, Maya, Madhava, Mahat, etc.) (38). Concerning the connexion between M and N, we believe that the latter is the antithesis of the former, that is: if M corresponds to the regenerating aspect of water, N pertains to its destructive side, or to the annihilation of forms. Letters, because of their associations, were one of the techniques used by the Cabbalists.

We cannot here do more than mention the study of the 'tifinars'; or prehistoric symbolic signs, made by R. M. Gattefossé in *Les Sages Ecritures* (Lyon, 1945). Also very interesting is the philosophy of letters—and of grammar—in their symbolic context worked out by M. Court de Gebelin in his *Du Génie allégorique et symbolique de l'antiquité* (Paris, 1777). Basing his study upon a primitive tongue, he draws conclusions concerning the mental attitudes which inspired the symbolism of proper names, linguistic roots, sacred fables, cosmogonies, symbolic pictures, escutcheons, hieroglyphs, etc., as well as of letters. For example, Λ, he suggests, can be: a cry, a verb, a preposition, an article, an initial letter—apart from its character in oriental tongues, etc. For a profound analysis of the Cabbalistic significance of the symbolism of letters, the work of Knorr de Rosenroth, *Le Symbolisme des lettres hébraïques . . . selon la Kabbala Denudata* (Paris, 1958), may be consulted. An important general review of the symbolism of letters and graphic signs is given by Alfred Kallir in his book, *Sign and Design* (London, 1961).

Level This is a term which refers to that aspect of the symbolism of space which is concerned with the simple moral pattern deriving from the notions of height and—ultimately—of centre. Hindu doctrine describes the three fundamental states of the human spirit as *sattva*, which is 'loftiness' of spirit; *rajas*—manifestation, struggle and dynamism; and *tamas*, or obscurity and brute instinct; and these three states are located on three vertical levels. Strictly speaking, there are five zones or levels: the absolute low level and the absolute high level, plus the central area divided into three zones merging into each other and at the same time bringing the outer extremes into progressive relationship. When the baser levels concern not the intellectual but the moral—which is in essence infinitely more complex and mysterious—then the precise significance of the symbolism is not nearly so hard-and-fast. There is always the possibility of symbolic Inversion, in which case the two opposing directions have something in common in that both partake of the idea of depth. Hence the saying: 'Deep calls to deep.' The temptations endured by the chosen few find their counterpart in the abysses of salvation which may be opened up for the reprobate. Dostoievski has spoken eloquently about this. Finally, here is a quotation from *L'Art chinois* by M. Paléologue, written in 1888: 'Under the Chinese Chou dynasty (11th century B.C.), the dead of the lower classes were buried in the plains; princes, on hills of moderate height; and emperors in tombs built on a mountain-top. The head of the corpse would be turned to face North.' In virtually every work of art whose composition is of an ideological rather than a naturalistic character, the vertical line locates the Three Worlds of the infernal, terrestrial (with its own, internal orders—the marine, the animal and the human) and celestial. Thus, in the Mesopotamian stele (or *Kudurru*), the illustrations are arranged on several levels, divided off by lines to suggest their relative values: the most primitive beings are placed at the lowest level (since they are closest to the 'primordial monster') while astral bodies and symbols of the godhead are situated on the highest plane. The same principles are true of Romanesque art.

Leviathan   A huge, fabulous fish which bears the weight of the waters upon its back and which the Rabbis claimed was destined for the Supper of the Messiah (8). In Scandinavian mythology, the oceans are the creation of a great serpent or dragon which swallows the waters only to regurgitate them: this being is called Midgardorm (35). The Leviathan is an archetype of things inferior—of the primordial monster connected with the cosmogonic sacrifice, such as the Mesopotamian Tiamat (or Tiawath). Sometimes it is in all respects identical with the world—or, rather, with the force which preserves and vitalizes the world.

Liberation of the Damsel   Of mythological origin (Siegfried waking Brunhild, the story of the Sleeping Beauty), it appears in pagan and Christian legends, and in books of knight-errantry. Perseus liberating Andromeda is possibly the archetype, though we must not forget St. George and the princess. In the 'matière de Bretagne', there are numerous instances of knights liberating damsels, and this could almost be regarded as their essential mission. As a symbol of the search for the *anima* and its liberation from the subjugation in which it is held by malign and inferior powers, it seems to be of mystical origin.

Libra The seventh sign of the Zodiac, Libra, is, like the cross and the sword, related to the symbolism of the number seven, and the sign for equilibrium, on both the cosmic and the psychic planes, and concerning both social and inward legality and justice. It is said, therefore, that the balance or scales designates the equilibrium between the solar world and planetary manifestation, or between the spiritual ego of Man (the *Selbst* of Jungian psychology) and the external ego (or the personality). It likewise indicates the equilibrium between good and evil; for, like Man, the scales has two tendencies, symbolized by the two symmetrically disposed pans, one tending towards the Scorpion (denoting the world of desires) and the other towards the sign of Virgo (sublimation). Man must, after the model of the scales, balance out his inner tendencies. According to traditional astrology, the sign of the balance rules the kidneys. The seventh sign pertains to human relations and to the union of the spirit within itself, that is to say, to spiritual and mental health. As an allegory of justice, it refers to the intimate and moderating influence of self-chastisement (40). As a symbol of inner harmony and of intercommunication between the left side (the unconscious, or matter) and the right (the consciousness or spirit), it represents 'Conjunction' (Plate XXI).

Zodiacal sign of Libra.

Life All things that flow and grow were regarded in early religions as a symbol of life: fire represented the vital craving for nourishment, water was chosen for its fertilizing powers, plants because of their verdure in spring-time. Now, all—or very nearly all—symbols of life are also symbolic of death. *Media vita in morte sumus*, observed the mediaeval monk, to which modern science has replied *La vie c'est la mort* (Claude Bernard). Thus, fire is the destroyer, while water in its various forms signifies dissolution, as suggested in the Psalms. In legend and folklore, the Origin of life —or the source of the renewal of the life forces—takes the form of caves and caverns where wondrous torrents and springs well up (38).

Light Light, traditionally, is equated with the spirit (9). Ely Star asserts that the superiority of the spirit is immediately recognizable by its luminous intensity. Light is the manifestation of morality, of the intellect and the seven virtues (54). Its whiteness alludes to just such a synthesis of the All. Light of any given colour possesses a symbolism corresponding to that colour, plus the significance of emanation from the 'Centre', for light is also the creative force, cosmic energy, irradiation (57). Symbolically, illumination comes from the East. Psychologically speaking, to become illuminated is to become aware of a source of light, and, in consequence, of spiritual strength (32).

Lightness The sonorous, the transparent and the mobile constitute a trilogy which is related to the sensation of lightness within (3). Air is the Element which corresponds primarily to this sensation. From the oneirocritic and literary points of view, the desire for lightness is depicted by the symbol of the dance—as in Nietzsche— rather than by flight. If the latter is in essence expressive of the will to rise above oneself and above others, the former concerns the urge to escape.

Lilith Lilith, in Hebrew legend, was the first wife of Adam. She was a night-phantom and the enemy of childbirth and of the new-born. In mythic tradition she was regarded as a satellite invisible from the earth (8). In Israelite tradition, she corresponds to the Greek and Roman Lamia. She may also be equated with Brunhild in the saga of the Niebelungen, in opposition to Kriemhild (or Grimhild, or Eve). She is symbolic of the Terrible Mother. All these characteristics relate her closely to the Greek figure of Hecate, with her demands for human sacrifice. Lilith personifies the maternal *imago* in so far as she denotes the vengeful mother who reappears in order to harry the son and his wife (a theme which, in some respects, is transferred to the Stepmother and to the Mother-in-Law). Lilith is not to be related literally to the Mother, but with the idea of the mother venerated (that is, loved and feared) during childhood. Sometimes she also takes the form of the despised mistress, or the 'long forgotten' mistress, as in the case of Brunhild mentioned above, or of the temptress who, in the name of the maternal *imago*, seeks and brings about the destruction of the son and his wife. There is a certain quality of the virile about her, as there is about Hecate, the 'accursed huntress'. The overcoming of the threat which Lilith constitutes finds its symbolic expression in the trial of Hercules in which he triumphs over the Amazons.

Ioannis da Sylveira, *Comentariorum in Textum Evangelicum.* Lugduni, 1670.

Lily An emblem of purity, used in Christian—and particularly mediaeval—iconography as a symbol and attribute of the Virgin Mary (46). It is often depicted standing in a vase or jar, which is, in its turn, a symbol of the female principle. Félix de Rosnay, in *Le Chrisme, les lys et le symbolisme de Paray* (Lyon, 1900), points to the connexion between the fleur-de-lis, in respect of the symbolism of its form, and the chrism or cross of St. Andrew intersected by the *rho*, and the ancient cross of the Aeduan Gauls (a cross with a vertical line traced through the centre), which is quite clearly a symbol of inversion; it was worn on the sword-guard. The lily, in Byzantium and among the Christianized Franks, was a sign of royalty.

Lingam The lingam is not just a sign for the phallus, but for the integration of both sexes, symbolizing the generating power of the universe (8). It is very commonly found in Hindu temples. A comparable symbol is that of the Tree of Life of the Persians whose seeds when mixed with water preserve the fertility of the earth (31). All symbols of 'conjunction' of this kind allude to the *hieros gamos*, without which the continuous process of creation and preservation of the universe would be inconceivable; hence they find their way into fecundity and fertility rites. In China, the lingam is called *Kuei*; it is an oblong piece of jade terminating in a triangle. The seven stars of the Great Bear are often engraved on the *Kuei* (39), probably symbolizing space and time (that is, the Seven Directions and the seven days of the week).

Lion The lion corresponds principally to gold or the 'subterranean sun', and to the sun itself, and hence it is found as a symbol of sun-gods such as Mithras. In Egypt, it used to be believed that the lion presided over the annual floods of the Nile, because they

Heraldic lion, 18th century.

coincided with the entry of the sun into the zodiacal sign of Leo during the dog-days. The lion-skin is a solar attribute (8). The equation of the sun and the lion, borne out by primitive and astrobiological cultures, persisted into the Middle Ages and found its way into Christian symbolism (14), although the significance of the lion is enriched by a variety of secondary symbolisms. In alchemy, it corresponds to the 'fixed' element—to sulphur. When counter-balanced by three other animals, it represents earth (although elsewhere it has been said that it stands for 'philosophical fire') (57), while gold is given the name of 'lion of metals'; the red-coloured lion is more strictly applicable to the latter (56). But, apart from these considerations, which lie more in the province of the theory of correspondences than in symbology proper, the lion, the 'king of beasts', symbolizes the earthly opponent of the eagle in the sky and the 'natural lord and master'—or the possessor of strength and of the masculine principle. As Frobenius notes, the motif of the solar lion which tears out the throat of the lunar bull is repeated intermin-ably in Asiatic and African ornamentation (22). According to Schneider, the lion pertains to the Element of earth and the winged lion to the Element of fire. Both are symbolic of continual struggle, solar light, morning, regal dignity and victory. As a symbol of the Evangelists, the lion came to be associated with St. Mark in particular. Naturally, other meanings may be derived from the location or the context in which the lion appears. The young lion corresponds to the rising sun, the old or infirm lion to the setting sun. The lion victorious represents the exaltation of virility; the lion tamed carries, on the symbolic plane, the obvious significance which it has in real life (50). For Jung, the lion, in its wild state, is broadly speaking an index of latent passions; it may also take the form of a sign indicating the danger of being devoured by the unconscious (32). But this latter sense goes beyond lion-symbolism as such, being related to the general symbolism of devouring (which in turn is related to the symbolism of time). The wild lioness is a symbol of the *Magna Mater* (35).

Loaves of Bread As with grains of corn, loaves are symbols of fecundity and perpetuation, which is why they sometimes take on forms that are sexual in implication.

Locusts In Christian symbolism, locusts represent the forces of destruction (20), a symbolism which can be traced back to the Hebrew tradition of the 'plagues of Pharaoh'. To quote the words of the Bible (Revelation ix, 1-10): 'And the fifth angel sounded, and I saw a star fall from heaven unto the earth: and to him was given the key of the bottomless pit. And he opened the bottomless pit; and there arose a smoke out of the pit, as the smoke of a great furnace; and the sun and the air were darkened by reason of the smoke of the pit. And there came out of the smoke locusts upon the earth; and unto them was given power, as the scorpions of the earth have power. And it was commanded them that they should not hurt the grass of the earth, neither any green thing, neither any tree;

but only those men which have not the seal of God in their foreheads. And to them it was given that they should not kill them, but they should be tormented five months: and their torment was as the torment of a scorpion, when he striketh a man. And in those days shall men seek death, and shall not find it; and shall desire to die, and death shall flee from them. And the shapes of the locusts were like unto horses prepared unto battle; and on their heads were as it were crowns like gold, and their faces were as the faces of men. And they had hair as the hair of women, and their teeth were as the teeth of lions. And they had breastplates, as it were breastplates of iron; and the sound of their wings was as the sound of chariots of many horses running to battle. And they had tails like unto scorpions, and there were stings in their tails: and their power was to hurt men five months.'

Logos   The Logos is the light and the life, at once spiritual and material, which combats both death and night (7). It is the antithesis of disorder and chaos, of evil and darkness. It is also cognate with the word and with thought.

Loops and **Bonds**   In mythology and iconography, the symbolism of loops and knots has an endless number of variants, both as images of connexion and as forms of ornamental art, appearing as plaited links, rosettes, knots or ties, ribbons, cords or string, ligaments, nets and whips. In the broadest sense, loops and knots represent the idea of binding. It would seem that, if modern man —according to the 'existentialist' approach—feels himself to be 'thrown' into the world, the primitive, oriental and astrobiological man perceived that he was 'bound' to the world, to the creator, to the order and society of which he was part. Jurgis Baltrusaitis, in his *Etudes sur l'art mediéval en Géorgie et en Arménie*, distinguished the following types cf rosette in Romanesque ornamentation: intersecting, intertwining, connecting and linking. He comments that intertwining plaits pertain to the most ancient of forms created by man, for they cannot be accounted a product of either barbarian art or of any particular Asiatic influence. Entangled in the knots, nets or cords, very commonly one finds monsters, animals or human figures. In the Egyptian system of hieroglyphs, the loop or tie was a sign corresponding to the letter T, and equivalent grammatically to the possessive (such as 'to bind', 'to dominate' or 'to possess') (19). A related symbol is that of Entanglement (q.v.). But there are particular aspects of this symbol which present it in a favourable light: the 'golden thread', for example, identical with the 'silver cord' in Hindu tradition, and with 'Ariadne's thread', and symbolic of the path leading to the creator. The mystic sense comes about by inversion: instead of the symbol representing external bonds, it comes to stand for inner links. The cordons which are such a constant feature of heraldry also pertain to these 'inner links', sometimes in the form of knots, or of ribbons bunched together to form the letter S or the number 8 (4), representing linkage or dependence in the feudal system of hierarchies (ratified in the oath of allegiance), or the sublimation of the idea of being 'in bondage' to one's superior (36). On the other hand, the external net which envelops and immobilizes should be related in significance to the words of the Bible (quoted by Pinedo): 'Upon the wicked he shall rain snares' (Psalms xi, 6) (46). Mircea Eliade has made a special study of the symbolism of knots and ties as they concern the tangle of thread which has to be unravelled in order to solve the essential basis of a problem. Some gods, such as Varuna or Uranus, are shown holding a length of rope, signifying their prerogative of supreme power. Eliade notes that there is a symbolic relationship between loops and bonds on the one hand and threads and labyrinths on the other. The labyrinth may be regarded as a knot to be untied, as in the mythic undertakings of Theseus and Alexander. The ultimate aim of mankind is to free himself from bonds. The same thing is to be found in Greek philosophy: in Plato's 'cave', men are fettered and unable to move (*Republic*, VII). For Plotinus, the soul 'after its fall, is imprisoned and fettered . . . but when it turns towards (the realm of) thought, it shakes off its bonds' (*Enneads* IV, 8). Eliade has also studied the morphology of bonds and knots in magic cults, distinguishing two broad divisions: (*a*) those which are beneficent and a protection against wild animals, illness and sorcery, and against demons and death; (*b*) those which are employed as a form of 'attack' against human enemies— symbolically the inverse of severing ropes or bonds (18). This latter practice is carried to the extent of tying up dead bodies to prevent them from performing the injurious acts which they were supposed to have indulged in (17, 18). Sometimes symbolic loops and ropes appear in vegetable form as foliage which inextricably envelops bodies that fall into it; this is a theme which is related to the symbolism of devouring, as well as to grotesques.

Lorelei A siren in Germanic mythology who appears on a rock bearing her name in the Rhine, and whose song is the perdition of mariners, for when they hear her singing they forget to watch out for the reefs and are dashed to pieces. The Lorelei is also related to the legend of the treasure of the Niebelungen.

Loss On the one hand, the sense of loss is bound up with the feeling of guilt together with a presentiment of ultimate purification or pilgrimage and journeying. On the other hand, the idea of losing and of rediscovering oneself, or the notion of the 'lost object' that is missed very painfully, are concepts parallel to that of death and resurrection (31). To feel lost or neglected is to feel dead, and hence, even though the blame for, or cause of, this feeling may be projected onto circumstantial matters, the true cause always lies in forgetfulness of the Origin and severance of the individual's attachment to it (as expressed in the thread of Ariadne). Within the twofold structure of the spirit (symbolized by the Gemini twins), loss corresponds to the equation of consciousness with the merely existential aspect of life, ignoring the eternal aspect of the spirit; and it is this which lies behind the 'lost feeling', or purposelessness, or the symbolic lost object.

Lotus There is a certain parallel between the symbolism of the lotus and that of the rose in Western culture. In Egypt, the lotus symbolizes nascent life, or first appearance (19). Saunier regards it as a natural symbol for all forms of evolution (49). In the Middle Ages it was equated with the mystic 'Centre' and, consequently, with the heart (56, 14). As an artistic creation it is related to the mandala, its significance varying according to the number of its petals: the eight-petalled lotus·is considered in India as the Centre where Brahma dwells and as the visible manifestation of his occult activity (26). The figure eight is like the mandorla of Romanesque art, signifying the intersection of the earth (four, or the square) with heaven (the circle). The 'thousand-petalled' lotus symbolizes the final revelation; in the centre there is usually a triangle and inside the triangle is the 'great emptiness' symbolic cf formlessness. René Guénon has examined lotus-symbolism at great length, observing that 'The potentialities of being are realized by means of an activity which is always internal' (this is the 'growth' of Father Gratry) 'since it is exercised from the centre of each plane; furthermore, from the metaphysical point of view, it is impossible for external action to be brought to bear upon the total being, for such action is possible only on a relative and a particular plane. . . . This realization of potentialities is depicted in various symbolisms as the unfolding of a flower on the surface of the "waters"; generally, in oriental traditions, it is a lotus, and a rose or lis in the West. There is a further relationship between these flowers and the circumference as a symbol of the manifest world, as well as with the cosmic Wheel. This symbol finds other forms of expression in many different ways, but always related to the symbolism of numbers, that is, depending upon the number of petals' (25). From the remotest days of antiquity, the lotus was the unanimous choice of the Chinese, the Japanese, the Hindus, the Egyptians and the Aryans. The lotus flower growing out of the navel of Vishnu, symbolizes the universe growing out of the central sun—the central point or the 'unmoved mover'. It is the attribute of many deities (9). In lotus symbolism, the idea of emanation and of realization predominated over that of the hidden Centre, which is a Western accretion.

Love Traditional symbols of love always express a duality in which the two antagonistic elements are, nevertheless, reconciled. Thus, the Indian *lingam*, the Chinese *Yang-Yin*, or even the Cross, where the upright beam is the world-axis and the cross-beam the world of phenomena. They are, in other words, symbols of a conjunction, or the expression of the ultimate goal of true love: the elimination of dualism and separation, uniting them in the mystic 'centre', the 'unvarying mean' of Far Eastern philosophy. The rose, the lotus flower, the heart, the irradiating point—these are the most frequent symbols of this hidden centre; 'hidden' because it does not exist in space, although it is imagined as doing so, but denotes the state achieved through the elimination of separation. The biological act of love itself expresses this desire to die in the object of the desire, to dissolve in that which is already dissolved. According to the *Book of Baruch*: 'Erotic desire and its satisfaction is the key to the origin of the world. Disappointment in love and the revenge which follows in its wake are the root of all the evil and the selfishness in this world. The whole of history is the work of love. Beings seek and find one another; separate and hurt one another; and in the end, comes acute suffering which leads to renunciation.' Or to put it another way: Maya as opposed to Lilith, illusion balanced by the serpent.

Loved One, The The woman loved, in the light of the Gnostic idea of the beloved as a mediator personified in Sophia (q.v.) and the Catharist view of human love as a form of mysticism, ceases to be a vessel for the perpetuation of the species and becomes a profoundly spiritual and spiritualizing entity, as in Dante, the paintings of Rossetti, the most exalted of the romantics, or in André Breton (*L'Amour fou*). The earliest and purest expression of this conception of the beloved seems to have occurred in Persia.

Lover, The The sixth enigma of the Tarot pack. It is related to the legend of Hercules which tells how he was given the choice of two women, the one personifying Virtue (or decisive activity, vocation, sense of purpose, and struggle) and the other Vice (passiveness, surrender to base impulses and to external pressures). The Lover, faced like Hercules with these two opposite modes of conduct, hesitates. He has parti-coloured clothes divided vertically: one half is red (for activity) and the other green (neutral—for indecision). On the positive side, this mystery-card implies the making of the right choice and represents moral beauty or integrity; on the negative side it alludes to uncertainty and temptation (59).

Lozenge One of the eight 'common emblems' of the Chinese, symbolic of victory. In graphics, the lozenge is simply a rhomb elongated along the vertical axis (5). The rhomb is a dynamic sign, as in St. Andrew's cross, and denotes the intercommunication between the inferior and the superior.

Luz The Hebrew word *luz* has a number of meanings: city-centre, like Agarttha; 'mandorla', or place of the apparition; and, according to Guénon (*Le Roi du Monde*), it also means 'an indestructible corporeal particle, symbolized by an extremely hard bone to which a part of the soul remains attached from the time of death to that of resurrection'. In *Le Mystère de la vie et de la mort d'après l'enseignement de l'ancienne Égypte*, Enel agrees with this interpretation.

Lycanthrope A legendary man whom the devil covers with a wolf's skin and forces to roam howling over the countryside (8), and symbolic of the irrationality latent in the baser part of man and the possibility of his awakening. Hence, it is similar in meaning to all evil monsters and fabulous beings.

Lyre A symbol of the harmonious union of the cosmic forces, a union which, in its chaotic aspect, is represented by a flock of sheep (40). The seven strings of the lyre correspond to the seven planets. Timotheus of Miletus raised the number of strings to twelve (corresponding to the signs of the Zodiac). A serial development of a similar kind is that effected by Arnold Schoenberg in our day by giving the same value to chromatic notes as to the notes of the diatonic scale, creating in place of the old scale of seven notes, a new one of twelve. Schneider draws a parallel between the lyre and the fire, recalling that in the temple of Jerusalem (according to Exodus xxxviii, 2) there was an altar with horns 'overlaid with brass' on either side, and the smoke of sacrifice rose up between them. The lyre, similarly, produces its sounds through the horns forming the sides of its structure, and representing the relationship between earth and heaven (50).

Mace A determinative sign in the Egyptian system of hieroglyphs, governing the ideas of the creative Word and achievement (19). It is related to the oar, the sceptre, the staff and the club, all of them symbolic instruments of one morphological family. In Egypt the oar was also linked with the idea of creating. As a weapon, the mace denotes a crushing blow or utter destruction and not simply victory over the adversary; it is therefore used as the insignia denoting the annihilation of the subjective, assertive tendency in Man, and also of the monsters symbolizing this tendency; for the same reason it is the attribute of Hercules (15).

Machines The symbolism of machines is founded upon the shape of their components and the rhythm and direction of their movement. Broadly speaking, this symbolism finds its inspiration in the obvious analogy with the physiological functions of ingestion, digestion and reproduction.

Macrocosm—Microcosm This relationship is symbolic of the situation in the universe of man as the 'measure of all things'. The basis of this relationship—which has occupied the minds of thinkers and mystics of all kinds in all ages—is the symbolism of man himself, particularly as the 'universal man' together with his 'correspondences' with the Zodiac, the planets and the Elements. As Origen observed: 'Understand that you are another world in miniature and that in you are the sun, the moon and also the stars' (33).

Maize One of the eight 'common emblems' of China, maize is symbolic of prosperity and is widely used in ornamental art (5). Almost all cereals have a common meaning in that they are spermatic images. Peruvians represent fertility by means of the figure of a woman made out of stalks of maize which they call 'the mother of the maize' (17).

Makara An Indian mythic monster, part-fish and part-crocodile. It is also to be found in the ornamental art of the Indonesians.

Man Man comes to see himself as a symbol in so far as he is conscious of his being. Hallstatt art, in Austria, shows fine examples of animal-heads with human figures appearing above them. In India, in New Guinea, in the West as well, the bull's or ox's head with a human form drawn between the horns is a very common motif. Since the bull is a symbol for the father-heaven, man comes to be seen as both his and the earth's son (22), also, as a third possibility, the son of the sun and the moon (49). The implications of Origen's remark: 'Understand that you are another world in miniature and that in you are the sun, the moon and also the stars', are to be found in all symbolic traditions. In Moslem esoteric thought, man is the symbol of universal existence (29), an idea which has found its way into contemporary philosophy in the definition of man as 'the messenger of being'; however, in symbolic theory, man is not defined by function alone (that of appropriating the consciousness of the cosmos), but rather by analogy, whereby he is seen as an image of the universe. This analogical relationship is sometimes expressed explicitly, as in some of the more ancient sections of the *Upanishads*—the *Brihadaranyaka* and the *Chandogya* for instance—where the analogy between the human organism and the macrocosmos is drawn step by step by means of correspondences with the organs of the body and the senses (7). So, for example, the components of the nervous system are derived from fiery substance, and blood from watery substance (26). These oriental concepts first appear in the West during the Romanesque period: Honorius of Autun, in his *Elucidarium* (12th century) states that the flesh (and the bones) of man are derived from the earth, blood from

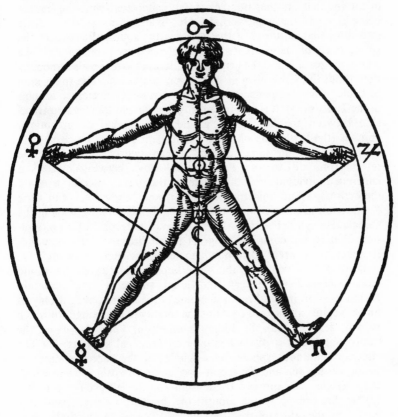

Man the microcosm (after Agrippa of Nettesheim).

water, his breath from air, and body-heat from fire. Each part of the body relates to a corresponding part of the universe: the head corresponds to the heavens, the breath to air, the belly to the sea, the lower extremities to earth. The five senses were given analogies in accordance with a system which came to Europe, perhaps, from the Hebrews and the Greeks (14). Thus, Hildegard of Bingen, living in the same period, states that man is disposed according to the number five: he is of five equal parts in height and five in girth; he has five senses, and five members, echoed in the hand as five fingers. Hence the pentagram is a sign of the microcosmos. Agrippa of Nettesheim represented this graphically, after Valeriano, who drew the analogy between the five-pointed star and the five wounds of Christ. There is a relationship, too, between the organic laws of Man and the Cistercian temple (14). Fabre d'Olivet, following the Cabala, maintains that another number closely associated with the human being is nine—the triple ternary. He divides human potentialities into three planes: those of the body, of the soul or life and of the spirit. Each of these planes is characterized by three modes: the active, the passive and the neutral (43). In the Far East, also, speculation about the symbolism of man began very early. The same kind of triple ternary organization is to be seen in the ancient teachings of the Taoists (13). It is also interesting to note that there is a relationship between the human being and the essential or archetypal animals (the turtle, the phoenix, the dragon and the unicorn) who appear to bear the same relation to man—who is central—as the tetramorphs do to the Pantokrator. Now, between man as a concrete individual and the universe there is a medial term—a mesocosmos. And this mesocosmos is the 'Universal Man', the King (*Wang*) in Far Eastern tradition, and the *Adam Kadmon* of the Cabala. He symbolizes the whole pattern of the world of manifestation, that is, the complete range of possibilities open to mankind. In a way, the concept corresponds to Jung's 'collective unconscious'. According to Guénon, Leibniz—perhaps influenced by Raymond Lull—conceded that every 'individual substance' must contain within itself an integral reproduction of the universe, even if only as an image, just as the seed contains the totality of the being into which it will develop (25). In Indian symbolism, *Vaishvânara*, or the 'Universal Man', is divided into seven principal sections: (1) The superior, luminous spheres as a whole, or the supreme states of being; (2) the sun and the moon—or rather, the principles to which they pertain—as expressed in the right and the left eye respectively; (3) the fire-principle—the mouth; (4) the directions of space—the ears; (5) the atmosphere—the lungs; (6) the intermediary zone between earth and heaven—the stomach; (7) the earth—the natural functions or the lower part of the body. The heart is not mentioned, because, being the 'centre' or dwelling-place of Brahma, it is regarded as being beyond the 'wheel' of things (26). Now, this concept of the 'Universal Man' implies hermaphroditism, though never specifically. For the concrete, existential human being, in so far as he is either a man or a woman, represents the dissected 'human' whole, not only in the physical sense but also spiritually. Thus, to quote the *Upanishads*: 'He was, in truth, as big as a man and a woman embracing. He divided this *atman* into two parts; from them sprang husband and wife.' In Western iconography one sometimes finds images which would seem to be echoes of this concept (32). A human couple, by their very nature, must always symbolize the urge to unite what is in fact discrete. Figures which are shown embracing one another, or joining hands, or growing out of roots which bind them together, and so on, symbolize 'conjunction', that is, *coincidentia oppositorum*. There is a Hindu image representing the 'joining of the unjoinable' (analogous to the marriage of fire and water) by the interlinking of Man and Woman, which may be taken to symbolize the joining of all opposites: good and bad, high and low, cold and hot, wet and dry, and so on (32). In alchemy, Man and Woman symbolize sulphur and mercury (the metal). In psychology, level-symbolism is often brought to bear upon the members of the body, so that the right side corresponds to the conscious level and the left to the unconscious. The shapes of the parts of the body, depending upon whether they are positive or negative—whether they are protuberances or cavities—should be seen not only as sex-symbols but also in the light of the symbolism of levels. The head is almost universally regarded as a symbol of virility (56). The attitudes which the body may take up are of great symbolic importance, because they are both the instrument and the expression of the human tendency towards ascendence and evolution. A position with the arms wide open pertains to the symbolism of the cross. And a posture in the form of the letter 'X' refers to the union of the two worlds, a symbol which is related to the hour-glass, the 'X' and all other symbols of intersection (50). Another important posture is that of Buddha in the traditional iconography of the Orient, a posture characteristic also of some Celtic gods such as the so-called 'Bouray god' or the famous Roquepertuse figure. This squatting position expresses the renunciation of the 'baser part' and of ambulatory movement and symbolizes identification with the mystic centre.

Mandala This is a Hindu term for a circle. It is a kind of *yantra* (instrument, means or emblem), in the form of a ritual geometric diagram, sometimes corresponding to a specific, divine attribute or to some form of enchantment (*mantra*) which is thus given visual expression (6). Cammann suggests that mandalas were first brought to Tibet from India by the great guru Padma Sambhava in th' 8th century A.D. They are to be found all over the Orient, and always as a means towards contemplation and concentration—as an aid in inducing certain mental states and in encouraging the spirit to move forward along its path of evolution from the biological to the geometric, from the realm of corporeal forms to the spiritual. According to Heinrich Zimmer, mandalas are not only painted or drawn, but are also actually built in three dimensions for some festivals. One of the members of the Lamaist convent of Bhutia Busty, Lingdam Gomchen, described the mandala to Carl Gustav Jung as 'a mental image which may be built up in the imagination only by a trained lama'. He maintained that 'no one mandala is the same as another': all are different because each is a projected image of the psychic condition of its author, or in other words, an expression of the modification brought by this psychic content to the traditional idea of the mandala. Thus, the mandala is a synthesis of a traditional structure plus free interpretation. Its basic components are geometric figures, counterbalanced and concentric. Hence it has been said that 'the mandala is always a squaring of the circle'.

The expanding centre
—a concept exemplified in the Shri-Yantra mandala.

There are some works—the *Shri-Chakra-Sambhara-Tantra* is one— which prescribe rules for the better imagining of this image. Coinciding in essence with the mandala are such figures as the Wheel of the Universe, the Mexican 'Great Calendar Stone', the lotus flower, the mythic flower of gold, the rose, and so on. In a purely psychological sense it is feasible to identify the mandala with all figures composed of various elements enclosed in a square or a circle—for instance, the horoscope, the labyrinth, the zodiacal circle, figures representing 'The Year' and also the clock. Ground-plans of circular, square or octagonal buildings are also mandalas. As for the three-dimensional form, there are temples built after the pattern of the mandala with its essential counterbalancing of elements, its geometric form and significant number of component elements. The stupa in India is the most characteristic of these temples. Again, according to Cammann, there are some Chinese shields and mirror-backs which are mandalas. In short, the mandala is, above all, an image and a synthesis of the dualistic aspects of differentiation and unification, of variety and unity, the external and the internal, the diffuse and the concentrated (32). It excludes disorder and all related symbolisms, because, by its very nature, it must surmount disorder. It is, then, the visual, plastic expression of the struggle to achieve order—even within diversity—and of the longing to be reunited with the pristine, non-spatial and non-temporal 'Centre', as it is conceived in all symbolic traditions. However, since the preoccupation with ornamentation—that is, with unconscious symbolism—is in effect a concern for ordering a certain area—that is, for bringing order into chaos—it follows that this struggle has two aspects: firstly, the possibility that some would-be mandalas are the product of the simple (aesthetic or utilitarian) desire for order, and secondly, the consideration that the mandala proper takes its inspiration from the mystic longing for supreme integration. In Jung's view, mandalas and all con-comitant images—prior, parallel or consequent—of the kind mentioned above, are derived from dreams and visions corresponding to the most basic of religious symbols known to mankind—symbols which are known to have existed as far back as the Palaeolithic Age (as is proved, for example, by the Rhodesian rock engravings). Many cultural, artistic or allegorical works, and many of the images used in numismatics, must have sprung from this same primordial interest in the psychic or inner structure (with its external counterpart to which so many rites pertaining to the founding of cities and temples, to the divisions of heavens, to orientation and the space-time relationship, bear eloquent testimony). The juxtaposition of the circle, the triangle and the square (numerically the equivalents of the numbers one and ten; three; and four and seven) plays a fundamental rôle in the most 'classic' and authentic of oriental mandalas. Even though the mandala always alludes to the concept of the Centre—never actually depicting it visually but suggesting it by means of the concentricity of the figures—at the same time it exemplifies the obstacles in the way of achieving and assimilating the Centre. In this way, the mandala fulfils its function as an aid to man in his efforts to regroup all that is dispersed around a single axis—the Jungian *Selbst*. It is of interest to note that the same problem occupied the alchemists, except that a very different aspect of being was under investigation. Jung suggests that the mandala represents an autonomous psychic fact, or 'a kind of nucleus about whose intimate structure and ultimate meaning we have no direct knowledge' (32). Mircea Eliade, speaking as an historian of religions and not as a psychologist, sees the mandala chiefly as an objective symbol, an *imago mundi* rather than a projection of the mind, without, however, discrediting the latter interpretation. The structure of a temple—the Borobudur temple for instance—in the form of a mandala has as its aim the creation of a monumental image of life and the 'distortion' of the world to make it a suitable vehicle for the expression of the concept of supreme order which man—the neophyte or initiate—might then enter as he would enter into his own spirit. The same is true of the great mandalas traced on the ground with coloured threads or coloured dust. Here, rather than serving the purposes of contemplation, they have a ritual function in which a man may move gradually towards the inner area, identifying himself with each stage and each zone as he goes. This rite is analogous to that of entering into the labyrinth (denoting the quest for the Centre) (18), and the psychological and spiritual implications are self-evident. There are some mandalas which counterbalance not enclosed figures but numbers arranged in geometric discontinuity (for instance: four points, then five, then three), and are then identified with the Cardinal Points, the Elements, colours, and so on, the significance of the mandala being wonderfully enriched by these additional symbolisms. Mirrors of the Han dynasty depict the numbers four and eight balancing each other and disposed round the centre in five zones which correspond to the five Elements (that is, the four material Elements plus the spirit or quintessence). In the West, alchemy made quite frequent use of figures having a definite affinity with the mandala, composed of counterpoised circles, triangles and squares. According to Heinrich Khunrath, the triangle within the square produces the circle. There are, as Jung has pointed out, 'distorted' mandalas different in form from the above and based upon the numbers six, eight and twelve; but they are comparatively rare. In all mandalas in which numbers are the predominant element, it is number-symbolism which can best plumb its meaning. The interpretation should be such that the superior (or the principal) elements are always those nearest the centre. Thus, the circle within the square is a more developed structure than the square within the circle. And the same relationship to the square holds good for the triangle; the struggle between the number three and the number four seems to represent that between the central elements of the spirit (corresponding to three) and the peripheral components, that is, the Cardinal Points as the image of ordered externality (corresponding to four). The outer circle, on the other hand, always fulfils the unifying function of overriding the contradictions and the irregularities of angles and sides by means of its implicit movement. The characteristics of the Shri-Yantra, one of the finest mandala-instruments, have been explained by Luc Benoist. It is composed around a central point which is the metaphysical and irradiating point of primordial energy; however, this energy is not manifest and therefore the central point does not actually appear in the drawing, but has to be visualized. Surrounding it is a complex pattern of nine triangles—an image of the transcendent worlds; four of these triangles have the apex pointing upwards and the other five downwards. The intermediate—or subtle—world is suggested by a triple aureole surrounding the triangles. An eight-petalled lotus (signifying regeneration), together with others of sixteen petals, and a triple circle, complete this symbolic representation of the spiritual world. The fact that it exists within the material world is suggested by a triple-lined serrated surround, signifying orientation in space (6).

The mandorla symbolizes the intersection of the two spheres of heaven and earth.

Mandorla   Although the geometric symbol of the earth is the square (or the cube) and the symbol of heaven is the circle, two circles are sometimes used to symbolize the Upper and the Lower worlds, that is, heaven and earth. The union of the two worlds, or the zone of intersection and interpenetration (the world of appearances), is represented by the mandorla, an almond-shaped figure formed by two intersecting circles. In order that, for the purposes of iconography, the mandorla might be drawn vertically, the two circles have come to be regarded as the left (matter) and the right (spirit). The zone of existence symbolized by the mandorla, like the twin-peaked Mountain of Mars, embraces the opposing poles of all dualism (51). Hence it is a symbol also of the perpetual sacrifice that regenerates creative force through the dual streams of ascent and descent (appearance and disappearance, life and death, evolution and involution). Morphologically, it is cognate with the spindle of the *Magna Mater* and with the magical spinners of thread (50).

Mandragora (or **Mandrake**) A plant which was supposed to have various magic properties, a belief arising out of the likeness of its roots to the human form. Mandragora was also the name of the ghost of a devil, who appeared as a tiny black man, beardless and with unkempt hair (8). For the primitive mind, the mandrake represented the soul in its negative and its minimal aspects.

Man-Eating Monster A monster, dragon or sea-serpent with a human being in its jaws, symbolizes the danger of being devoured by the destructive forces of the unconscious, a fate to which only the most noble of man's faculties, such as his reason or his morals, are susceptible. In mediaeval iconography, this monster's head is an allegory of the gates of hell.

Manicora A fabulous being which figures in Romanesque decoration, a quadruped covered in scales and with the head of a woman wearing a kind of Phrygian cap. Its significance may be compared with that of the siren; scales always allude to the ocean —to the primordial, Lower Waters.

Marriage In alchemy, a symbol of 'Conjunction', represented symbolically also by the union of sulphur and mercury—of the King and the Queen. Jung has shown that there is a parallel between this alchemic significance and the intimate union or inner conciliation —within the process of individuation—of the unconscious, feminine side of man with his spirit.

Mars The primitive and astrobiological conception of creation is that it can take place only through 'primordial sacrifice'; similarly, what has been created can only be preserved through sacrifice and war. The image of Janus, or the twin-peaked mountain of Mars, are symbols of inversion, that is, of the intercommunication between the Upper, non-formed World of future potentialities, and the Lower World of materialized forms. Schneider insists upon this principle as characteristic of the primordial order, commenting that 'its rigid law demands a death for each life, sublimates the criminal instinct to serve good and humanitarian ends, and fuses love and hate in the interests of the renewal of life. In order to preserve the order of existence, the gods struggled with the giants and monsters who from the beginning of creation sought to devour the sun'—the Logos (50). Mars is the perennial incarnation of this necessity for the shedding of blood, apparent in all orders of the cosmos. Hence, early cults of Mars embraced vegetation: it was to Mars that the Roman farmer appealed for the prosperity of his harvest (21). His attributes are weapons, and specially the sword.

Marsh According to Schneider, marshlands are a symbol of the 'decomposition of the spirit'; that is, they are the place in which this occurs because of the lack of the two active elements (air and fire) and the fusion of the two passive elements (water and earth). Therefore, in legends, novels of chivalry, etc., marshes appear with this meaning. In the story of Gawain, knight of the Round Table, the protagonist finds himself in a marsh, and this implies his inability to bring his enterprise to a successful conclusion, just as when he is unable to mend the 'broken sword'. In *The Lovers*, by Leslie Stevens, the protagonist finds himself obliged to defend marshlands from a tower which has been profaned, premonitory signs of his downfall and death.

Mask   All transformations are invested with something at once of profound mystery and of the shameful, since anything that is so modified as to become 'something else' while still remaining the thing that it was, must inevitably be productive of ambiguity and equivocation. Therefore, metamorphoses must be hidden from view —and hence the need for the mask. Secrecy tends towards trans-figuration: it helps what-one-is to become what-one-would-like-to-be; and this is what constitutes its magic character, present in both the Greek theatrical mask and in the religious masks of Africa or Oceania. The mask is equivalent to the chrysalis. Frazer has noted some very peculiar types of masks used in the initiation ceremonies of some Oceanian peoples: the youths keep their eyes closed and

Mask of Mithras—Persian image of the Sun.

cover their faces with a mask of paste or fuller's earth, and pretend not to hear the orders shouted out by their elders. But they gradually recover, and on the following day they wash themselves clean of the crust which had covered their faces (as well as their bodies); and their initiation is then complete (21). Apart from this—the most essential—symbolic meaning, the mask also constitutes an image bearing another symbolic meaning which derives directly from it. The mask, simply as a face, comes to express the solar and energetic aspects of the life-process. According to Zimmer, Shiva created a lion-headed, slender-bodied monster, expressive of insatiable appetite. And when this creature demands of his creator a victim to devour, the god tells him to eat of his own body, which the monster does so that it is reduced to a mere mask itself (60). There is a Chinese symbol, T'ao T'ieh—the 'mask of the ogre'—which may well be similar in origin (5).

Matron   A form of personification very common in all symbolic images bearing upon the feminine principle; she appears not as spirit but as mother-protector: the Night, the Earth, the Church or the Synagogue, for example. Cities too are very often personified as matrons wearing a mural crown. Their attributes and features add the finishing touches to the symbolic content of the image (32). Psychologically speaking, the matron seems to express the domineering side of the mother.

Matter   According to Evola, matter is equivalent to the moon, and form to the sun.

Maya   'The lesson may be read psychologically, as applying to ourselves, who are not gods but limited beings. The constant projection and externalization of our specific shakti (vital energy) is our "little universe", our restricted sphere and immediate environment, whatever concerns and affects us. We people and colour the indifferent, neutral screen with the movie-figures and dramas of the inward dream of our soul, and fall prey then to its dramatic events, delights, and calamities. The world, not as it is in itself but as we perceive it and react upon it, is the product of our own maya or delusion. It can be described as our own more or less blind life-energy, producing and projecting demonic or beneficent shapes and appearances. Thus we are the captives of our own Maya-Shakti and of the motion picture that it incessantly produces. . . . The Highest Being is the lord and master of Maya. All the rest of us . . . are the victims of our own individual Maya. . . . To liberate man from such a spell . . . is the principal aim of all the great Indian philosophies.' (60)

Meadow   Bachelard has pointed out that the meadow, being nourished by the waters of a river, is in itself a subject of sadness and that, in the true meadow of the soul, only asphodels grow. The winds find no melodious trees in the meadow—only the silent waves of uniform grass. Bachelard also mentions Empedocles' description of 'the meadow of ill fortune' (2).

Melusina   A fairy occurring in legends, sometimes in the form of a siren. Jean d'Arras dealt specifically with this fabulous being in *La Noble Hystoire de Luzignen* (1393). When a great disaster was about to befall she would give voice to a scream thrice repeated. 'Melusina it was who caused mysterious buildings to be set up in a single night by swarms of workers who would disappear without trace once the work had been completed. When she marries, all her children have some physical abnormality; in the same way, her magic buildings all have some defect, like those bridges of the devil which always have one stone missing' (16). Melusina seems to be the archetype of intuitive genius, in so far as intuition is prophetic, constructive and wondrous, and yet at the same time is infirm and malign.

Menhir Like all stones, the menhir embraces the idea of lithophany. In particular, because it stands erect, it is symbolic of the masculine principle and vigilance. It is further related to the sacrificial stake and, in consequence, to the world-axis (with all its related symbols: the cosmic tree, the steps, the cross, etc.) (50). There are also phallic as well as protective implications, as Eliade has noted (17).

Mephistopheles He represents the negative, infernal aspect of the psychic function which has broken away from the All to acquire independence and an individual character of its own (32).

Mercury The planetary god and the metal bearing his name. In astronomy, he is the son of heaven and light; in mythology, he was engendered by Jupiter and Maia. In essence he is the messenger of heaven. His Greek name of Hermes signifies 'interpreter' or 'mediator'. Hence it is his task to conduct the souls of the dead to the Lower World. Like Hecate, he is often triform, that is, represented with three heads. He epitomizes the power of the spoken word—the emblem of the word; and for the Gnostics he was the *logos spermatikos* scattered about the universe, an idea which was taken up by the alchemists who equated Mercury with related concepts of fluency and transmutation (9). At the same time, he was seen as a god of roads (that is, of potentialities) (4). In astrology he is defined as 'intellectual energy'. The nervous system is controlled by him, for the nerves are messengers on the biological plane (40). Probably it was the alchemists, with their lofty speculations, who penetrated farthest into the archetypal structure of Mercury. In many cases they identified their transmutation-substance with the 'lively planet', that is, with the god whose metal is white and decidedly lunar. However, since Mercury is the planet nearest to the sun (related to gold), the resultant archetype has a double nature (of a chthonian god and a celestial god—a hermaphrodite) (32). Mercury (the metal) symbolizes the unconscious because of its fluid and dynamic character; it is essentially *duplex* for, in one way, it is an inferior being, a devil or monster, but in another sense it is the 'philosophers' child' (33). Hence, its unlimited capacity for transformation (as in the case of all liquids) came to be symbolic of the essential aim of the alchemist to transmute matter (and spirit) from the inferior to the superior, from the transitory to the stable. Mercury was also credited with an unlimited aptitude for penetration (32). Its synonyms of *Monstrum hermaphroditus* and *Rebis* ('something double') reveal its close connexion with the Gemini myth (Atma and Buddhi); its representation as a feminine figure and *Anima mundi* (32) is more frequent and significant than its absorption by the masculine principle alone. In this connexion René Alleau recalls that the essential stages of the alchemic process were: prime matter, Mercury, Sulphur, *Lapis*. The first phase corresponds to indifferentiation; the second to the lunar and feminine principle; the third to the masculine and solar, the fourth to absolute synthesis (which Jung identifies with the process of individuation). The attributes of Mercury are the winged hat and sandals, the caduceus, the club, the turtle and the lyre (which he invented and gave to Apollo) (8).

Metals In astrology they are called 'terrestrial' or 'subterranean planets', because of the analogous correspondences between the planets and the metals (57). For this reason astrologers consider that there are only seven metals (influenced by the same number of spheres), which does not mean that mankind during the astrobiological period did not recognize more. As Piobb has pointed out, some engineers have noted that the seven planetary metals make up a series which is applicable to the system of the twelve polygons (48). But, apart from the theory of correspondences, the metals symbolize cosmic energy in solidified form and, in consequence, the libido. On this basis, Jung has asserted that the base metals are the desires and the lusts of the flesh. Extracting the quintessence from these metals, or transmuting them into higher metals, is equivalent to setting creative energy free from the fetters of the sense world (33), a process identical with what esoteric tradition and astrology regard as liberation from the 'planetary influences'. The metals can be grouped within a progressive 'series' in which each metal displays its hierarchical superiority over the one preceding it, with gold as the culminating point of the progression. This is why, in certain rites, the neophyte is required to divest himself of his 'metals'—coins, keys, trinkets—because they are symbolic of his habits, prejudices and characteristics, etc. (9). We, for our part, however, are inclined to believe that in each particular pairing of planet with metal (as Mars with iron) there is an essential element of the ambitendent, in that its positive quality tends one way and its negative defect tends the other. Molten metal is an alchemic symbol expressing the *coniunctio oppositorum* (the conjunction of fire and water), related to mercury, Mercury and Plato's primordial, androgynous being. And at the same time, the solid or 'closed' properties of matter emphasize its symbolism as a liberator—hence the connexion with Hermes the psychopomp mentioned under 'Mercury' above (32). The correspondences between the planets and the metals, from inferior to superior, are: Saturn—lead, Jupiter—tin, Mars—iron, Venus—copper, Mercury —mercury, Moon—silver, Sun—gold.

Metamorphosis The transformation of one being or of one species into another generally relates to the broad symbolism of Inversion, but also to the essential notion of the difference between primigenial, undifferentiated Oneness and the world of manifestation. Everything may be transformed into anything else, since nothing is really anything. Transmutation is quite another matter: it is metamorphosis in an ascending direction, carrying all appearances away from the moving rim of the Wheel of Transformations along the radial path to the 'Unmoved mover'—the non-spatial and timeless Centre. 'The duplicity of Mercurius', writes Jung, 'his simultaneously metallic and pneumatic nature, is a parallel to the symbolization of an extremely spiritual idea like the Anthropos by a corporeal, indeed metallic substance (gold). One can only conclude that the unconscious tends to regard spirit and matter not merely as equivalent but as actually identical, and this in flagrant contrast to the intellectual one-sidedness of consciousness, which would sometimes like to materialize matter and at other times to materialize spirit. . . .'

Minaret The minaret is a symbolic torch of spiritual illumination, since it embraces the symbols of the tower (on account of its height) and the belvedere or watch-tower (signifying the consciousness). Hence it appears as a figure emblematic of the city of the Sun—or Camelot, where King Arthur held his court. The same symbolic sense is sometimes represented by a skyline with towers and pinnacles (4).

Minotaur A fabulous monster the lower half of which was a man and the upper a bull. It was in order to contain the minotaur that the Cretan Labyrinth was constructed. The monster was carnivorous, and the vanquished Athenians were obliged every seven years to deliver up seven youths and seven maidens for it to eat. This tribute was paid three times, but on the fourth occasion Theseus slew the minotaur with the aid of Ariadne and her magic thread (8). Every myth and legend which alludes to tributes, monsters or victorious heroes illustrates at once a cosmic situation (embracing the Gnostic ideas of the evil demiurge and of redemption), a social implication (for example, of a state oppressed by a tyrant, or a plague, or by some other hostile force) and a psychological significance pertaining either to the collective or the individual (implying the predominance of the monster in man, and the tribute and sacrifice of his finer side: his ideas, sentiments and emotions). The minotaur all but represents the last degree in the scale of relations between the spiritual and the animal sides in man. The predominance of the spiritual is symbolized by the knight; the prevalence of the monstrous is denoted by the centaur with the body of a horse or bull. The inversion of this, where the head is animal-like and the body human, implies the dominance of base forces carried to its logical extreme. The symbolism of the number seven (as in seven-headed dragons, or a period of seven years, or the sacrifice of seven youths) always denotes a relationship with the essential series (namely: the days of the week, the planetary gods, the planets, and the Vices and Cardinal Sins together with their corresponding Virtues). To vanquish a seven-headed monster is to conquer the evil influences of the planets (in consequence of the equation of the planets with the instincts and the baser forces).

Minstrel, The The first enigma of the Tarot pack, this figure of a minstrel is a symbol of the original activity and the creative power of Man. He is depicted on the Tarot card wearing a hat in the form of a horizontal eight (the mathematical sign for infinity); he holds up a magic wand ('clubs') in one hand, and the other three symbols of the card-pack are on the table facing him; these are the equivalent of diamonds, spades and hearts, which, together with the wand ('clubs'), correspond to the four Elements (as well as the points of the compass). These attributes symbolize mastery over a given situation. The minstrel's garb is multi-coloured, but the predominant colour is red—denoting activity. In its transcendental implications, the enigma is related to Mercury (59).

Mirabilia During Antiquity and the Middle Ages, this name was given to strange and amazing incidents (the hidden powers of animals, plants and stones, natural phenomena, 'miracles', and the sympathies or antipathies which unite or separate such beings or incidents). The literature of the 'Mirabilia' obtained a great success, especially in Hellenistic Egypt, whence it passed to the mediaeval Western world via the Arabs. Strange or amazing incidents are frequently traditional symbols and were sometimes connected with magic and alchemy. According to the Rev. Fr. Festugière O.P. in *La Révélation d'Hermès Trismégiste*, Bolus the Democritean (*c.* 200 B.C.), Pseudo-Manetho (2nd–1st centuries B.C.), Nigidius Figulus (1st century B.C.), Demetrius and Apollodorus (1st century A.D.) greatly contributed to the upsurge of this literature. It continued to evolve, tinged with hermetism, and found its fullest expression in the *Book of the Things of Nature*, written in Syria at the beginning of the 7th century. The general symbolic meaning of the 'Mirabilia' doubtless corresponds to the equation orgy = chaos, established by Eliade. They express a nostalgia for the era of animist indifferentism, which, in part, can also be seen to take refuge in contemporary poetry, especially that of the symbolist movement. On the other hand, the belief in 'powers' and even in a personal psychology of all beings, their aspects and qualities, became well rooted in the Western world, down through the Lower Middle Ages, the Renaissance, and the baroque period. For example, Father J. E. Nieremberg's book, *Oculta filosofía de la Sympatia y antipatia de las cosas, Artificio de la Naturaleza y noticia naturel del mundo*, published in Barcelona in 1645, belongs to this ideological stream.

Mirror   As a symbol, it has the same characteristics as the mirror in fact; the temporal and existential variety of its function provides the explanation of its significance and at the same time the diversity of its meaningful associations. It has been said that it is a symbol of the imagination—or of consciousness—in its capacity to reflect the formal reality of the visible world. It has also been related to thought, in so far as thought—for Scheler and other philosophers—is the instrument of self-contemplation as well as the reflection of the universe. This links mirror-symbolism with water as a reflector and with the Narcissus myth: the cosmos appears as a huge Narcissus regarding his own reflections in the human consciousness. Now, the world, as a state of discontinuity affected by the laws of change and substitution, is the agent which projects this quasi-negative, kaleidoscopic image of appearance and disappearance reflected in the mirror. From the earliest times, the mirror has been thought of as ambivalent. It is a surface which reproduces images and in a way contains and absorbs them. In legend and folklore, it is frequently invested with a magic quality—a mere hypertrophic version of its fundamental meaning. In this way it serves to invoke apparitions by conjuring up again the images which it has received at some time in the past, or by annihilating distances when it reflects what was once an object facing it and now is far removed. This fluctuation between the 'absent' mirror and the 'peopled' mirror lends it a kind of phasing, feminine in implication, and hence —like the fan—it is related to moon-symbolism. Further evidence that the mirror is lunar is afforded by its reflecting and passive characteristics, for it receives images as the moon receives the light of the sun (8). Again, its close relationship to the moon is demonstrated by the fact that among the primitives it was seen as a symbol of the multiplicity of the soul: of its mobility and its ability to adapt itself to those objects which 'visit' it and retain its 'interest'. At times, it takes the mythic form of a door through which the soul may free itself 'passing' to the other side: this is an idea reproduced by Lewis Carroll in *Alice Through the Looking Glass*. This alone is sufficient explanation of the custom of covering up mirrors or turning them to face the wall on certain occasions, in particular when someone in the house dies (21). All that we have said so far by no means exhausts the complex symbolism of the mirror: like the echo, it stands for twins (thesis and antithesis), and specifically for the sea of flames (or life as an infirmity) (50, 51). For Loeffler, mirrors are magic symbols for unconscious memories (comparable with crystal palaces) (38). Hand-mirrors, in particular, are emblems of truth (4), and in China they are supposed to have an allegorical function as aids to conjugal happiness as well as a protection against diabolical influences (5). Some Chinese legends tell of 'the animals in the mirror'.

Mist Mist is symbolic of things indeterminate, or the fusing together of the Elements of air and water, and the inevitable obscuring of the outlines of each aspect and each particular phase of the evolutive process. The 'mist of fire' is that stage of cosmic life which follows upon the state of chaos (9) and corresponds to the three Elements which existed prior to the solid Element—earth.

Mistletoe A parasitic plant associated with the oak. Celtic druids once used to gather it to use in their fertility rites (8). It symbolizes regeneration and the restoration of family-life (49). Frazer has equated it with the 'golden bough', of which Virgil wrote: 'A wondrous tree shimmering with a golden light among the green foliage. Just as, throughout the cold winter, the mistletoe, guest of a tree that never engendered it, unfailingly displays its fresh greenery, flecking the sombre trunk with the yellow of its berries, just so do golden leaves show among the green foliage of the oak, and so would these golden leaves whisper to the gentle breeze' (*Aeneid*, VI). The yellow colour of the withered mistletoe-branch was thought—by a process of sympathetic magic—to be endowed with the power to discover buried treasure (21).

Monkey The simians generally symbolize the baser forces, darkness or unconscious activity, but this symbolism—like that of legendary fabulous beings—has two sides to it. If, on the one hand, this unconscious force may be dangerous, while it may degrade the individual, nevertheless it may also prove a boon—like all unconscious powers—when least expected. This is why, in China, the monkey is credited with the power of granting good health, success and protection, being related in this way to sprites, sorcerers and fairies (5).

Monolith In the Egyptian system of hieroglyphs, the monolith is a determinative sign associated with the name of the god Osiris and signifying 'to last'. In the myth, Osiris was slain by Set (or Typhon) and put together again by Isis. The ceremony performed in commemoration of this event included the erection of a monolith (a symbol of lithophanic unity) as a sign of resurrection and life

eternal (19), or of unity counterbalancing multiplicity, fragmentation and disintegration (this, in turn, being a symbol of the world
of phenomena 'fallen' into the multiplicity of the diverse—space—
and the transitory—time). The monolith, because of its shape and
position, possesses other secondary meanings alluding—as in the
case of the menhir—to the masculine, the solar and the procreative
principle.

Monsters They are symbolic of the cosmic forces at a stage one
step removed from chaos—from the 'non-formal potentialities'. On
the psychological plane, they allude to the base powers which
constitute the deepest strata of spiritual geology, seething as in a
volcano until they erupt in the shape of some monstrous apparition
or activity. Diel suggests that they symbolize an unbalanced psychic
function: the affective whipping up of desire, paroxysms of the
indulged imagination, or improper intentions (15). They are, then,
par excellence, the antithesis—or the adversary—of the 'hero' and
of 'weapons'. For weapons are the positive powers granted to man
by the deity, and this is the explanation of the mysterious, miraculous
or magical context of weapons wielded by heroes in myth and
legend. Weapons, then, are the symbolic antithesis to monsters.
Diel has pointed out that, paradoxically, the chimerical enemy—
perversion, the fascination of madness or of evil *per se*—is the
fundamental adversary in the life of Man. On the social plane, the
motif of the monster ravaging a country is symbolic of the ill-fated
reign of a wicked, tyrannical or impotent monarch (15). The fight
against a monster signifies the struggle to free consciousness from the
grip of the unconscious. The hero's deliverance corresponds to the
sunrise, the triumph of light over darkness, of consciousness or the
spirit over the affective strata of the unconscious (31). In a less
negative sense, the monster may be equated with the libido (56).
Monsters are closely connected in symbolism with fabulous beings,
which afford a wider range of meanings embracing some that are
wholly favourable and positive such as Pegasus, the phoenix, etc.
Some of the principal monsters known to tradition and perpetuated
by art are the following: the sphinx, the griffin, the siren-fish, the
siren-bird, the lamia, the bird with the head of a quadruped, the
bird-serpent, the winged bull, the dragon, the giant fish, the giant
sea-serpent, the chimaera, the Gorgon, the minotaur, the triton,
the hydra, the salamander, the merman, the harpy, the hippogryph,
the sea-demon and the Fury (36). The head of a monster, dragon or
sea animal, with one or more human heads in its mouth, is a
mediaeval symbol of hell. Psychologically it represents the danger
of being devoured by the destructive forces of some species, a danger
which may affect only the more noble parts of the human being,
such as his moral sense or his reason. For Walter Abell, in *The*

Collective Dream in Art (Cambridge, 1957), monsters also symbolize the latent and dangerous forces, in a greater or lesser state
of freedom, of the human unconscious in its aggressive and ugly
aspect. He points out that monsters are the principal characters in
the 7th-century Anglo-Saxon poem, *Beowulf.* He establishes an
interesting comparison and asserts that, in later prehistory (the
Neolithic Age, the Age of Metals), the monsters dominated the
gods; between Antiquity and the Romanesque period, the gods
succeeded in counterbalancing the monsters, who, nevertheless, still
played an important rôle (as revealed, for example, in miniatures
and capitals of the time); and in the Gothic period, the angelic spirits
triumphed over the monsters. In more than one aspect, contemporary art, especially since Blake and Goya, might be taken as
pointing to a certain 'resurrection of the monsters' and of the
monstrous, as seen particularly in the surrealist movement.

Montsalvat In the legend of the Grail, it is the *mons salvationis*,
the peak situated 'on distant shores which no mortal may approach',
similar to the Hindu mount Meru, the polar mountain. It is the
symbol of supreme spiritual fulfilment.

Montserrat There are some prehistoric paintings that depict a
squatting man in such a way that his outline resembles the jagged or
'serrated' skyline of a mountain. And—although it is mere coincidence—the significance of Montserrat (the 'Serrated Mountain'
near Barcelona) is precisely that it presents Man as occupying,
through sacrifice, a marginal position at the point of intersection
of the circles of heaven and earth (corresponding to the cross-
symbolism). At the same time, some mediaeval representations of
the siren are entitled *Serra.*

Moon The symbolism of the moon is wide in scope and very
complex. The power of this satellite was noted by Cicero, when he
observed that 'Every month the moon completes the same trajectory
executed by the sun in a year. . . . It contributes in large measure to
the maturation of shrubs and the growth of animals.' This helps to
explain the important rôle of the lunar goddesses such as Ishtar,
Hathor, Anaitis, Artemis. Man, from the earliest times, has been
aware of the relationship between the moon and the tides, and of the
more mysterious connexion between the lunar cycle and the physiological cycle of woman. Krappe believes—with Darwin—that this
follows from the fact that animal life originated in the watery deeps
and that this origin imparted a rhythm to life which has lasted for
millions of years. As he observes, the moon thus becomes the
'Master of women'. Another essential fact in the 'psychology of the
moon' is the apparent changes in its surface that accompany its
periodic phases. He postulates that these phases—especially in
their negative sense of partial and gradual disappearance—may

have been the source of inspiration for the Dismemberment myth (Zagreus, Pentheus, Orpheus, Actaeon, and Osiris for example). The same might be said of the myths and legends of the 'spinners' (35). When patriarchy superseded matriarchy, a feminine character came to be attributed to the moon and a masculine to the sun. The *hieros gamos*, generally understood as the marriage of heaven and earth, may also be taken as the union of the sun and the moon. It is generally conceded nowadays that the lunar rhythms were utilized before the solar rhythms as measures of time, and there is also a possible equation with the resurrection—spring follows upon winter, flowers appear after the frost, the sun rises again after the gloom of night, and the crescent moon grows out of the 'new moon'. Eliade points to the connexion between these cosmic events and the myth of the periodic creation and recreation of the universe (17). The regulating function of the moon can also be seen in the distribution of the waters and the rains, and hence it made an early appearance as the mediator between earth and heaven. The moon not only measures and determines terrestrial phases but also unifies them through its activity: it unifies, that is, the waters and rain, the fecundity of women and of animals, and the fertility of vegetation. But above all it is the being which does not keep its identity but suffers 'painful' modifications to its shape as a clear and entirely visible circle. These phases are analogous to the seasons of the year and to the ages in the span of man's life, and are the reasons for the affinity of the moon with the biological order of things, since it is also subject to the laws of change, growth (from youth to maturity) and decline (from maturity to old age). This accounts for the mythic belief that the moon's invisible phase corresponds to death in man, and, in consequence, the idea that the dead go to the moon (and return from it—according to those traditions which accept reincarnation). 'Death', observes Eliade, 'is not therefore an extinction, but a temporal modification of the plan of life. For three nights the moon disappears from heaven, but on the fourth day it is reborn. . . . The idea of the journey to the moon after death is one which has been preserved in the more advanced cultures (in Greece, India and Iran). Pythagorean thought imparted a fresh impulse to astral theology: the "Islands of the Blessed" and all mythic geography came to be projected on to celestial planes—the sun, the moon, the Milky Way. It is not difficult to find, in these later formulas, the traditional themes of the moon as the Land of the Dead or as the regenerating receptacle of souls. (But) . . . lunar space was no more than one stage in the ascension; there were others: the sun, the Milky Way, the "supreme circle". This is the reason why the moon presides over the formation of organisms, and also over their decomposition (as the colour green). Its destiny consists of reabsorbing forms and of recreating them. Only that which is beyond the moon, or above it, can transcend becoming. Hence, for Plutarch, the souls of the just are purified in the moon, whilst their bodies return to earth and their spirit to the sun.' The lunar condition, then, is equivalent to the human condition. Our Lady is depicted above the moon, thereby denoting that eternity is above the mutable and transitory (17). René Guénon has confirmed that, in 'the sphere of the moon', forms are dissolved, so that the superior states are severed from the inferior; hence the dual rôle of the moon as Diana and Hecate—the celestial and the infernal. Diana or Jana is the feminine form of Janus (26, 17). Within the cosmic order, the moon is regarded as a duplication of the sun, but in diminished form, for, if the latter brings life to the entire planetary system, the moon influences only our own planet. Because of its passive character— in that it receives its light from the sun—it is equated with the symbolism of the number two and with the passive or feminine principle. It is also related to the Egg of the World, the matrix and the casket (9). The metal corresponding to the moon is silver (57). It is regarded as the guide to the occult side of nature, as opposed to the sun which is responsible for the life of the manifest world and for fiery activity. In alchemy, the moon represents the volatile (or mutable) and feminine principle, and also multiplicity because of the fragmentary nature of its phases. These two ideas have sometimes been confused, giving rise to literal interpretations which fall into the trap of superstition. The Greenlanders, for example, believe that all celestial bodies were at one time human beings, but the moon in particular they accuse of inciting their women to orgies and for this reason they are not permitted to contemplate it for long (8). In pre-Islamic Arabia, as in other Semitic cultures, the cult of the moon prevailed over sun-worship. Mohammed forbade the use of any metal in amulets except silver (39). Another significant aspect of the moon concerns its close association with the night (maternal, enveloping, unconscious and ambivalent because it is both protective and dangerous) and the pale quality of its light only half-illuminating objects. Because of this, the moon is associated with the imagination and the fancy as the intermediary realm between the self-denial of the spiritual life and the blazing sun of intuition. Schneider has drawn attention to a highly interesting morphological point with his observation that the progressive change in the shape of the moon— from disk-shape to a thin thread of light—seems to have given birth to a mystic theory of forms which has influenced, for example, the manner of constructing musical instruments (51). At the same time, Stuchen, Hommel and Dornseif have demonstrated the influence of the lunar shapes upon the characters of the Hebrew and Arabic alphabets, in addition to their profound effect upon the morphology of instruments. Eliade quotes Hentze's comment to the effect that all dualisms find in the moon's phases, if not their historical cause, at least a mythic and a symbolic model. 'The nether world—the world of darkness—is represented by a dying moon (horns = quarter moon; the sign of a double volute = two quarter moons facing in opposite directions; two quarters superimposed back to back = lunar change representing a decrepit, bony old man). The upper world—the world of life and of the nascent sun—is symbolized by a tiger (the monster of darkness and of the new moon) with the human being, represented by a child, emerging from its jaws' (17). Animals regarded as lunar are those which alternate between appearance and disappearance, like the amphibians; examples are the snail which leaves its shell and returns to it; or the bear which vanishes in winter and reappears in spring, and so on. Lunar objects may be taken as those of a passive or reflecting character, like the mirror; or those which can alter their surface-area, like the fan. An interesting point to note is that both objects are feminine in character.

Moon, The The eighteenth enigma of the Tarot. It shows an image of the moon dimly lighting up the objects of the world with its uncertain light. Beneath the moon there is a huge, red crab resting upon the mud. The allegory also shows two watchdogs guarding the orbit of the sun and barking at the moon. Behind them, to the left and right, are two castles in the form of square towers, flesh-coloured and edged in gold. The moon is represented by a silvered disk bearing the outlines of a woman. Long, yellow rays stream out from this disk, intermixed with other shorter, reddish rays. Inverted drops of water are floating in the air, as if attracted by the moon. It is a scene which illustrates the strength and the dangers of the world of appearances and the imagination. The visionary sees things in a lunar light. The crab, like the Egyptian scarab, has as its function that of devouring what is transitory—the volatile element in alchemy —and of contributing to moral and physical regeneration. The watchdogs are a warning to the moon to stay away from the realm of the sun (the logos); the towers, on the other hand, rise up as a warning that the approach to the domain of the moon is beset by very real dangers (the 'perils of the soul' of primitive man). As Wirth describes it, behind the towers is a steppe-land, and behind that, a wood (the 'forest' as it appears in legends and folklore) full of ghosts. Beyond that there is a mountain (Schneider's 'twin-peaked mountain') and a precipice bordering a stream of purifying water. This seems to suggest the route followed by the shamans on their ecstatic journeys. There is another ancient Tarot card depicting a harpist singing, in the moonlight, to a young girl loosening her hair at a window. The image here alludes to the mortal characteristics of the moon, for the harpist is a widespread symbol of death (and of the death-wish), and the girl is unquestionably a symbol of the soul. This Tarot enigma, in sum, seeks to give instruction upon the 'lunar way' (of intuition, imagination and magic) as distinct from the 'solar way' (of reason, reflection, objectivity); but at the same time it is pregnant with negative and fatal significance. In the negative sense, it alludes to error, arbitrary fantasy, imaginative sensitivity, etc. (59).

Mother Mother-symbols are characterized by an interesting ambivalence: the mother sometimes appears as the image of nature, and vice-versa; but the Terrible Mother is a figure signifying death (31). For this reason, Hermetic doctrine held that to 'return to the mother' was equivalent to dying. For the Egyptians, the vulture was a mother-symbol, probably because it devours corpses (19); it also stood for the means whereby Hammamit (the universal soul) was split up into separate parts to form individual souls (19). For the same reason, the maternal sentiment has been said to be closely bound up with the nostalgic longing of the spirit for things material (18), or with the subjection of the spirit to the unformulated but implacable law of destiny. Jung mentions that in Jean Thenaud's *Traité de la Cabale* (of the 16th century) there is a mother-figure actually represented in the form of a god of destiny (32). He mentions further that the Terrible Mother is the counterpart of the *Pietà*, representing not only death but also the cruel side of nature—its indifference towards human suffering (31). Jung also notes that the mother is symbolic of the collective unconscious, of the left and nocturnal side of existence—the source of the Water of Life. It is the mother, he argues, who is the first to bear that image of the *anima* which the man must project upon Woman passing from the mother to the sister and finally to the beloved (32). A predominantly maternal social pattern—a matriarchal society—is characterized, according to Bachofen, by special emphasis upon blood relationships, telluric allegiances, and the passive acceptance of natural phenomena. Patriarchies are distinguished by a respect for man-made laws, the favouring of works of art and craft, and obedience to the hierarchy (23). Even now that matriarchal societies, sociologically speaking, no longer exist in the West, psychologically man is nevertheless passing through a phase when he is in all essentials dominated by the feminine principle. To come triumphantly through this stage and to reinstate the masculine principle as the guiding-rule of life—bringing to the fore the characteristically patriarchal qualities noted above—would signify an achievement of the kind that was once symbolized by the transformation of the 'lunar work' into the solar, or by the transmutation of mercury into sulphur. To quote Evola: 'Symbols of the earth-mother are: water, the mother of the waters, stone, the cave, the maternal home, night, the house of depth, and the house of strength or of wisdom.'

Mound of Earth   A sign in the Egyptian system of hieroglyphs in the form of a rectangle with two sides incomplete. It symbolizes the intermediate stages of matter, and is related to the symbols of primordial waters and of slime (19).

Mountain   The different meanings which have been attached to the symbolism of the mountain stem not so much from any inherent multiplicity as from the various implications of each of its component elements: its height, verticality, mass and shape. Deriving from the first idea (height) are interpretations such as that of Teillard, who equates the mountain with inner 'loftiness' of spirit (56), that is, transposing the notion of ascent to the realm of the spirit. In alchemy, on the other hand, the reference is nearly always to the hollow mountain, the hollow being a cavern which is the 'philosophers' oven'. The vertical axis of the mountain drawn from its peak down to its base links it with the world-axis, and, anatomically, with the spinal column. Because of its grandiose proportions, the mountain came to symbolize, for the Chinese, the greatness and generosity of the Emperor; it is the fourth of the twelve imperial emblems (5). But the profoundest symbolism is one that imparts a sacred character by uniting the concept of mass, as an expression of being, with the idea of verticality. As in the case of the cross or the Cosmic Tree, the location of this mountain is at the 'Centre' of the world. This same profound significance is common to almost all traditions: suffice it to recall mount Meru of the Hindus, the Haraberezaiti of the Iranians, Tabor of the Israelites, Himingbjör of the Germanic peoples, to mention only a few. Furthermore, the temple-mountains such as Borobudur, the Mesopotamian *ziggurats* or the pre-Columbian *teocallis* are all built after the pattern of this symbol. Seen from above, the mountain grows gradually wider, and in this respect it corresponds to the inverted tree whose roots grow up towards heaven while its foliage points downwards, thereby expressing multiplicity, the universe in expansion, involution and materialization. This is why Eliade says that 'the peak of the cosmic mountain is not only the highest point on earth, it is also the earth's navel, the point where creation had its beginning'—the root (18). The mystic sense of the peak also comes from the fact that it is the point of contact between heaven and earth, or the centre through which the world-axis passes, binding the three levels together. It is, incidentally, also the focal point of Inversion—the point of inter-section of the immense St. Andrew's cross, which expresses the relationship between the different worlds. Other sacred mountains are Sumeru of the Ural-Altaic peoples (17) and Caf in Moslem mythology—a huge mountain the base of which is formed by a single emerald called *Sakhrat* (8). Mount Meru is said to be of gold and located at the North Pole (8), thus underlining the idea

of the Centre and, in particular, linking it with the Pole Star—the
'hole' through which all things temporal and spatial must pass in
order to divest themselves of their worldly characteristics. This
polar mountain is also to be found in other symbolic traditions,
always bearing the same symbolism of the world-axis (25); its
mythic characteristics were, in all probability, based upon the fixed
position of the Pole Star. It is also called the 'white mountain', in
which case it embraces both the basic mountain-symbolism with all
the implications outlined above and that of the colour white
(intelligence and purity). This was the predominating characteristic
of Mount Olympus (49), the supreme, celestial mountain which
Schneider sees as corresponding to Jupiter and equivalent to the
principle of the number one. There is another mountain, relevant
to the symbolism of the number two, and that is the mountain of
Mars and Janus—that is, as the Gemini; basically, they represent
two different aspects of the same mountain, but blending together
the symbolism of the 'two worlds' of *Atma* and *Buddhi*, or the two
essential, rhythmic aspects of manifest creation—light and darkness,
life and death, immortality and mortality. This mountain has two
peaks, in order to give visual expression to its dual or ambivalent
meaning. It occurs constantly in traditional, megalithic culture,
particularly in the form of a landscape, illustrating yet again the
Protean myth of the Gemini, which bursts out in so many different
forms in primitive thought and art. This mountain is also a form of
mandorla consisting of the intersection of the circle of the heavens
with that of the earth, and this mandorla is, as it were, the crucible
of life, containing the opposite poles of life (good and bad, love and
hate, fidelity and treachery, affirmation and negation, the numbers
2 and 11—both equal to one plus one—and finally construction
and destruction). Incidentally, the animals which correspond to
this all-embracing significance of the mandorla are the whale and the
shark (51). In Hindu legend, the castle of Indra was built on this
mountain; whereas in Roman legend it was the castle of Mars, and
the home of the thunderbolt, the two-headed eagle and the Gemini.
It has been called the 'mountain of stone' and is at once the abode
of the living (the exterior of the mountain) and of the dead (the
hollow interior) (50). Krappe has borne this out with the observation
that 'The interior of a mountain has frequently been taken as the
location of the Land of the Dead: the derivation of the Celtic and
Irish fairy-hills, and of the legend, widespread in Asia and Europe,
of a demiurge or hero asleep inside a mountain, one day to emerge
and renew all things sublunar' (35). This myth has obvious connexions with the myth of Entanglement—of the castle inextricably
entangled in a wood and also with the story of the 'Sleeping
Beauty'. All such myths are concerned with the mystery of a dis-

appearance between appearance and reappearance. Schneider lists the following trades and professions as being associated with Mars: those of the king, physician, warrior and miner, as well as the martyr (51). In Western tradition, the mountain-symbol appears in the legend of the Grail, as Montsalvat (the 'mountain of salvation' or 'of health')—just as much a 'polar mountain' as it is a 'sacred island', according to Guénon; but always it is inaccessible or difficult to find (like the 'centre' of the labyrinth) (28). In general, the mountain, the hill and the mountain-top are all associated with the idea of meditation, spiritual elevation and the communion of the blessed. In mediaeval emblems, the symbolism of the 'mountain of salvation' is further defined by a complementary figure surmounting it, such as the fleur-de-lis, the star, the lunar crescent, the cross, steps, the crown, the circle, the triangle, or the number three. The letter Z sometimes occurs, standing for *Zion*; similarly, an R is short for *Regeneratio* (4). Some of these symbols have lent themselves to a poetic treatment that is well worth examination. From the moment when the mountain, so to speak, divests itself of its terrestrial and material character and becomes the image of an idea, the more numerous the component elements pertaining to this idea, the greater will be its clarity and force. Hence, mount Meru of India is considered to have the shape of a pure, seven-sided pyramid (corresponding to the seven planetary spheres, the seven essential virtues and the seven Directions of space) and each face has one of the colours of the rainbow. Seen as a whole, the mountain is a shining white, by which token it may be equated with the 'polar mountain' and the all-embracing image of totality (also symbolized by the pyramid-symbol), tending towards Oneness (symbolized by the peak)—to avail ourselves of the concepts of Nicholas of Cusa.

Mouth In the symbolism pertaining to the body, the most elementary association is the one between the organ or member and its function. It is, then, self-evident that, in Egyptian hieroglyphs, the mouth should stand for the power of speech and hence for the creative word. In this sense it stands for the pristine emanation of creative power. Very closely connected with this hieroglyph is another showing a mouth with a solar disk inside. This disk, primarily standing for the sun, is connected, but not identical, with the eye. (In hieroglyphs which are coloured, the eye is wholly blue, while the sign under discussion consists of a blue mouth with a little red circle inside) (19). Guénon supports this interpretation of the sign (29), pointing to the example of the *Mândûkya Upanishad* where, apropos the state of deep sleep, the mouth is said to represent integral consciousness (26). In the Old Testament, the concepts of mouth and fire are frequently associated; epithets such as 'devouring' or 'consuming', frequently applied to the latter, are descriptive of the functions of the former. Hence the fire-breathing animals of legend. Jung explains these associations by synaesthesia and suggests that they are connected with Apollo, the sun-god who is depicted with a lyre as his characteristic attribute. The common link between the symbolisms of sounding, speaking, shining and burning finds a physiological parallel in the phenomenon known as 'coloured hearing' whereby some individuals experience sounds as colours. Furthermore, it is hardly a coincidence that the two main characteristics that set Man apart from all other beings are the power of speech and the use of fire. Both are, in fact, the product of *mana* (psychic energy) (31). In consequence, mouth-symbolism, like fire-symbolism, has two aspects: creative (as in speech) and destructive (devouring). And, of course, the mouth is the point of convergence between the external and the inner worlds. This explains the frequent symbol of the 'monster's mouth', with sets of upper and lower teeth that are expressive of the 'interlocking' of the two worlds: heaven and earth or, more often, hell and earth (50). There are, in mediaeval iconography, abundant examples of the mouths of dragons or large fishes affording access to the inner world or to the underworld.

Mud   Mud signifies the union of the purely receptive principle (earth) with the power of transition and transformation (water). Mud is regarded as the typical medium for the emergence of matter of all kinds (17). Plasticity is therefore one of its essential characteristics, and it is related, by analogy, with biological processes and nascent states.

Multiplicity   Given the mystic and emanatistic character of the philosophy of symbolism whereby—as in Neoplatonism—the One is identified with the Creator, it follows that multiplicity must represent the farthest point from the Source of all things. If the image of the circle is taken to express the relationship between unity and multiplicity, then the centre corresponds to unity and the outer circumference or rim relates to multiplicity (as in the Buddhist Wheel of Transformations) (25). Jung has corroborated this principle from the psychologist's point of view, observing that multiplicity is always regressive in character, and recalling that when the protagonist of the *Hypnerotomachia Poliphili* appears surrounded by a bevy of women, this is an indication of the nature of the unconscious —but of the unconscious revealed as in a state of fragmentation. Hence the Greek maenads, Erinyes, Bacchantes, harpies and sirens all express a situation in which man's inner wholeness is torn to shreds (32). This is something which greatly concerned the alchemists, and one part of their work was directed to transforming the volatile (or the transitory and multiple) into the fixed (the stable, or the unified). Another way in which multiplicity is induced is by the creation of hierarchies. But, in addition to all this, we must note that multiplicity, and its consequence, diversity, may be products of division as well as of multiplication. For symbolic purposes, the essence of multiplication is division. As an example, we might suggest that in contrast to a unitary fruit like the apple, the pomegranate is a perfect illustration of multiplicity because it is internally subdivided into a multitude of cells. Hence the negative character of multiplicity, and hence the symbolic doctrine that the totality of the individual has no value until it has become transmuted—that is, until the individual has destroyed in himself the desire for dispersal in space (corresponding to multiplicity) and in time (corresponding to transitoriness) so that ultimately he may be transformed into an image of the One and so be assimilated into the eternal principle. This is a mystic tendency which does not fail to make its mark on the plane of existence, particularly where the moral issues of love are involved. Legends such as that of the Flying Dutchman afford a precise illustration of just such a pilgrimage of the spirit in its quest for the unique soul, searching through all those imperfect forms that lie in its path. The 'temptations' of Parsifal likewise correspond to this same symbolism. Symbolic jewels, when they come to lose their unitary significance as 'treasure' conceived as an integrated whole, and fall into multiplicity, acquire negative and distracting implications.

Multiplicity of a Common Element A dream that occurs quite often among certain abnormal types of subjects involves a multitude —of objects or of people—all with the same characteristics, that is, the multitude comprises the multiplication of one single phenomenon instead of a collection of many different ones. This is a symbol alluding to the secret and, at root, terrible unity of all things. Now, the anguish which nearly always attends this symbol is a psychological consequence of 'repetition' (as studied by Kierkegaard) and of the fact that in this world it seems to be the law of diversification that prevails. Or, to put it another way, diversity justifies multiplicity. Multiple monsters imply the multiplicity of their own symbolism as images of disintegration, dissociation, dispersion and separation. For this reason it is a characteristically pathological symbol.

Music The symbolism of music is of the greatest complexity and we cannot here do more than sketch out some general ideas. It pervades all the component elements of created sound: instruments, rhythm, tone or timbre, the notes of the natural scale, serial patterns, expressive devices, melodies, harmonies and forms. The symbolism of music may be approached from two basic standpoints: either by regarding it as part of the ordered pattern of the cosmos as understood by the ancient, megalithic and astrobiological cultures, or else by accepting it as a phenomenon of 'correspondence' linked with the

business of expression and communication. Another of the fundamental aspects of music-symbolism is its connexion with metre and
with number, arising out of the Pythagorean theory (27). The cosmic
significance of musical instruments—their allegiance to one particular
Element—was first studied by Curt Sachs in *Geist und Werden der
Musikinstrumente* (Berlin, 1929). In this symbolism, the characteristic shape of an instrument must be distinguished from the timbre,
and there are some common 'contradictions' between these two
aspects which might possibly be of significance as an expression of
the mediating rôle of the musical instrument and of music as a
whole (for an instrument is a form of relationship or communication,
substantially dynamic, as in the case of the voice or the spoken word).
For example, the flute is phallic and masculine in shape and feminine
in its shrill pitch and light, silvery (and therefore lunar) tone, while
the drum is feminine by virtue of its receptacle-like shape, yet
masculine in its deep tones (50). The connexion of music-symbolism
with self-expression (and even with graphic art) is well in evidence
in primitive music-making, which often amounted to almost literal
imitations of the rhythms and movements, the features and even the
shapes of animals. Schneider describes how, hearing some Senegalese
singing the 'Song of the Stork', he began to 'see as he was listening',
for the rhythm corresponded exactly to the movements of the bird.
When he asked the singers about this, their reply confirmed his
observation. Given the laws of analogy, we can also find cases of the
expressive transferred to the symbolic: that is, a melodic progression
as a whole expresses certain coherent emotions, and this progression corresponds to certain coherent, symbolic forms. On the
other hand, alternating deep and high-pitched tones express a
'leap', anguish and the need for Inversion; Schneider concludes
that this is an expression of the idea of conquering the space between
the valley and the mountain (corresponding to the earth and the
sky). He observes that in Europe the mystic designation of 'high
music' (that is, high-pitched) and 'low music' (low-pitched) persisted
right up to the Renaissance. The question of relating musical notes
to colours or to planets is far from being as certain as other symbolic
correspondences of music. Nevertheless, we cannot pass on without
giving some idea of the profound, serial relationship which exists
in phenomena: for instance, corresponding to the pentatonic scale
we usually find patterns grouped in fives; the diatonic and modal
scale, since it has seven notes, is related to most of the astrobiological systems, and is unquestionably the most important of all
the series; the present-day tendency towards the twelve-note series
could be compared to the signs of the Zodiac. But, so far, we have
not found sufficient evidence for this particular facet of music-
symbolism. All the same, here are the correspondences as set down

by Fabre d'Olivet, the French occultist: Mi—the Sun, fa—Mercury, sol—Venus, la—the Moon, ti—Saturn, do—Jupiter, re—Mars (26). A more valid series of relationships, at least in the expressive aspect, is that which links the Greek modes with the planets and with particular aspects of the *ethos*, as follows: the mi-mode (the Dorian) —Mars (who is severe or pathetic); the re-mode (the Phrygian)— Jupiter (ecstatic): the do-mode (the Lydian)—Saturn (pained and sad); the ti-mode (the Hypodorian)—the Sun (enthusiastic); the la-mode (the Hypophrygian)—Mercury (active); the sol-mode (the Hypolydian)—Venus (erotic); the fa-mode (the Mixolydian)—the Moon (melancholy) (50). Schneider's profound investigations into the symbolism of music seem to us well-founded. The tetrachord formed by the notes do, re, mi, fa, he considers, for instance, to be a mediator between heaven and earth, the four notes corresponding respectively to the lion (signifying valour and strength), the ox (sacrifice and duty), man (faith and incarnation) and the eagle (elevation and prayer). Conversely, the tetrachord formed by sol, la, ti, do, could represent a kind of divine duplicate of the previous tetrachord. Fa, do, sol, re are regarded as masculine elements corresponding to the Elements of fire and air and to the instruments of stone and metal, whereas la, mi, ti, are feminine, and pertain to the Elements of water and earth. The interval fa-ti, known to musicologists as a tritone (or augmented fourth), expresses with its dissonance the 'painful' clash between the Elements of fire and water —a clash occurring in death itself (50). We have been able to suggest here only a few outlines of the music-symbolism developed by Schneider in his work *The Musical Origin of Animal-Symbols*, the scope of which is so wide that, as he has privately intimated to us, he believes all symbolic meanings are at root musical or at least to do with sounds. This becomes easier to understand when we recall that singing, as the harmonization of successive, melodic elements, is an image of the natural connexion between all things, and, at the same time, the communication, the spreading and the exaltation of the inner relationship linking all things together. Hence Plato's remark that the character of a nation's music cannot be altered without changing the customs and institutions of the State (26).

Musician   The musician is a common symbol of the fascination of death (personified by the Greeks as a youth). The Pied Piper of Hamelin in the well-known tale, the harpist and the citharist in legends and folktales, all allude to this one symbol. Music represents an intermediate zone between the differentiated or material world, and the undifferentiated realm of the 'pure will' of Schopenhauer. Hence its use in rites and liturgies (together with fire and smoke).

Names In esoteric thought, names are an integrating expression of the horoscope (49). There has been a great deal of speculation about the symbolic elements entering into the composition of names: letters in their graphic or phonetic aspects, similes, analogies, and so on. Piobb, for instance, has suggested that the name Napoleon is Apollo in the Corsican pronunciation of *O'N'Apolio* (48). The question of why a given name should determine the destiny of one individual but not of another is something which lies beyond the scope of this work. Here we must limit ourselves to describing the rational basis of the symbolism of names and its connexion with the Egyptian idea of the 'power of words' (as described in a poem by Edgar Allan Poe). Given the symbolic nature of the Egyptian language, it follows that a name could never be a product of chance but only of the study of the characteristics of a given thing, whether the name in question was common or proper. The name RN (signifying a mouth over the surface of water) represented the action of the 'word' upon passivity. Concerning personal nomenclature, the Egyptians believed that their names were a reflection of their souls. This gave rise to the belief that a name could have a magical effect upon some other person. The equation of name with character (and destiny) had its repercussions also in descriptive names, such as that of Osiris, which means 'he who is at the top of the steps' (the steps, that is, of evolution); or that of Arabia, signifying 'he who walks in silence'. Onomatopoeia was another highly important source in the genesis of language and its ideographic representation, whereby a given being is characterized by one of its essential aspects—as the lion by its roar, for example: or RW in Egyptian (19). Popular works on occultism which suggest symbolic implications for certain proper names, as in other cases of vulgarized interpretation, have some roots in authentic symbolism but they may also fall into the trap of being too hard-and-fast about the true scope of symbolism. Language has, in the last century or two, reached such a complex stage of development that the applied symbolism of etymology is subject to innumerable errors.

Narcissus Joachim Gasquet sees the Narcissus-myth as a primordial illustration not on the sexual but on the cosmic level, commenting that 'the world is an immense Narcissus in the act of contemplating itself', so that Narcissus becomes a symbol of this self-contemplative, introverted, and self-sufficient attitude (quoted by Bachelard, 2).

Nature The 12th-century writer Alan of Lille, in his *De planctu naturae*, describes Nature as an allegorical figure wearing a diadem set with jewels in imitation of the stars: twelve stones symbolize the signs of the Zodiac and seven stand for the Sun, the Moon and the five planets (14). This concept is wholly astrobiological in character, since it partakes of the tendency to bring the discipline of numbers to bear upon living things, and to infuse the astral, the mineral and the abstract with the vital forces of plant and animal life.

Necklace Broadly speaking, the threaded bead-necklace stands for the unifying of diversity, that is, it represents an intermediate state between the inherent disintegration of all multiplicity—always a negative state—and the state of unity inherent in continuity. Regarded as a string, the necklace becomes a cosmic and social symbol of ties and bonds. Because it is usually worn on the neck or breast, it acquires a symbolic relation with those parts of the body and with the signs of the Zodiac pertaining to them. Since the neck has an astrological association with sex, the necklace also betokens an erotic link.

Negro The image of the Negro always alludes to the baser part of man—to the substrata of the passions. This psychological fact, empirically proven by psychoanalysis, finds its parallel—or its origin—in traditional symbolic doctrine, according to which coloured people are the children of darkness and the white man is the child of the sun or of the white, polar mountain (49).

Neptune In primitive thought, he was the deity of heaven in its symbolic aspect of the 'Upper Waters', that is, the god of clouds and of rain. Later he became the god of fresh and fertilizing water. Finally, he was seen as the god of the sea. In this development we can trace not only a chronological and historical line of progress but, more especially, a spiritual projection of the myth of the 'fall', which finally became absorbed into the character of Neptune. The trident, seen from this point of view of 'descent'—of the 'fall'—can be equated with the thunderbolt. Charles Ploix, in *La Nature et les dieux*, on the other hand, identifies the trident with the magic wand used in water-divining (2). For the alchemists, Neptune was quite simply a symbol for water. Apart from the trident, his attributes are sea-horses (8), signifying the cosmic forces and the swelling rhythm of the foamy waves. The discovery of psychoanalysts that the ocean is a symbol of the unconscious has, at the same time, proved beyond question the relationship of Neptune with the deepest layers of the individual, and the universal, soul. Diel, therefore, is able to conclude that Neptune, like Pluto, symbolizes the negative aspect of the spirit. He is king of the deeps of the subconscious and of the turbulent waters of life; it is he who unleashes storms—representing the passions of the soul—particularly in his extreme rôle as the destroyer. Diel regards the trident as an emblem of the threefold sin arising from the corruption of the three 'vital impulses' of the spirit (conservation, reproduction and evolution), adding that the trident is also an attribute of Satan (15).

Net The net is the extreme form of expression of the symbolic bunch of ribbons, the bow and the bond, and hence it is closely bound up with the symbolisms of Entanglement and Devouring. It is the weapon of the Uranian gods, such as Varuna (18) and of those who fish in the waters of the unconscious. Ea, god of water and wisdom, did not fight the primordial monsters face to face but ensnared them by craft. The weapon of Marduk in his combat with Tiamat was again a net, a symbol of magic authority (17). The connexion between the net and heaven is explained in the following passage taken from the *Tao Te Ching*: 'The net of heaven', that is, the network of stars and constellations, 'is wide-meshed but lets nothing through' (58). The symbolism here strikingly illustrates the idea that it is not possible for the individual, by his own efforts (nor, of course, by suicide), to escape from the universe. God has bound us with his power and it is beyond our capacity to withdraw or leave.

Night Night is related to the passive principle, the feminine and the unconscious. Hesiod gave it the name of 'mother of the gods', for the Greeks believed that night and darkness preceded the creation of all things (8). Hence, night—like water—is expressive of fertility, potentiality and germination (17); for it is an anticipatory state in that, though not yet day, it is the promise of daylight. Within the tradition of symbology it has the same significance as death and the colour black.

Night-Sea Crossing This expression, frequent in works of symbology, originates in the ancient notion of the sun, in its nightly course through the lower abyss where it suffers death (which is sometimes conceived as a real death followed by resurrection, and at other times as purely figurative). This abyss was associated with the watery deeps of the third—or infernal—level, either in the sense of a lower ocean or of a subterranean lake. According to Leo Frobenius, in *Das Zeitalter des Sonnengottes*, all the sea-faring gods are solar symbols. For their passage they are shut up in a chest, hamper or trunk (symbolizing the maternal bosom) and exposed to a variety of perils. The direction of their journey is always contrary to the visible, daily course of the sun. Here is the account given by Frobenius of the archetypal avatars of this essential journey: 'A hero is swallowed by a sea-monster in the West. The animal journeys with him in its belly to the East. During the journey, the hero lights a fire in the belly of the monster and, feeling hungry, cuts off a

slice of its heart. Shortly afterwards he observes that the fish has
reached land; he then begins to cut away the flesh of the animal
until he can slip out. In the belly of the fish it was so hot that his hair
fell out. Often the hero sets free those who have been swallowed
before him and they escape with him' (31). This basic situation
takes on a variety of forms in a great many legends and folktales,
but the essential features of devouring, confinement, enchantment
and escape are always present. For Jung, this symbol is a kind of
Journey into Hell comparable with the journeys described by Virgil
and Dante, and also a sort of journey to the Land of Spirits, or, in
other words, a plunge into the unconscious (33). But he goes on to
add that darkness and watery deeps, in addition to being symbolic
of the unconscious, also signify death—not in the sense of total
negation but as the other side of life (or life in its latent state) and
as the mystery which exerts its fascination over the consciousness
from its abode in the abyss. The journey's end is expressive of
resurrection and the overcoming of death (and the same applies to
the end of a dream or of an illness). Related in symbolism to this
is the story of Joseph cast into the pit by his brothers, and Jonah in
the belly of the whale (32) (Plate XXX).

Nothingness The Upanishads laid down several different states
of consciousness, ranging from wakefulness—peopled by objective
forms—or daydreams—ordered in accordance with profound,
subjective impulses—to the deepest state of consciousness experienced in dreams of the most intense character, devoid of images.
This latter state is directly related to the mystic idea of nothingness.
In order properly to grasp the notion of Nirvana, and to understand
the ecstasy of self-annihilation, it is very important to recognize
that this oriental 'nothingness' is not absolute negation—not the
death of all things—but indifferentiation or, in other words, the
absence of conflicts and contrasts and hence, the banishment of pain
and dynamism. Guénon, in his explanation of this Hindu doctrine,
comments: 'In this state the different objects of manifestation,
including those of individual manifestation, external as well as
internal, are not destroyed, but subsist in principal mode, being
unified by the very fact that they are no longer conceived under the
secondary or contingent aspect of distinction; of necessity they find
themselves among the possibilities of the Self and the latter remains
conscious in itself of all these possibilities, as "non-distinctively"
beheld in integral Knowledge' (26). This concept of nothingness as
'non-objective reality'—and hence ineffable—probably reached the
Hebrew mystics by way of the Middle East and Persia. According
to Rabbi Joseph ben Shalom, living in Barcelona in the 13th century,
more than to any other of the symbolic descriptions of the revelation
of God, special attention should be devoted to that concerning the

mystic nothingness, which is apparent in every abysmal crevice of existence. He suggests that in each transformation of reality, in each crisis, or moment of suffering, each metamorphosis or change of form, or on every occasion when the state of a thing is altered, then the abyss of Nothingness is spanned and made visible for a mystic instant, for nothing can change without making contact with that region of absolute being which the oriental mystics call Nothingness (the relevant passage is quoted by G. G. Scholem in *Major Trends in Jewish Mysticism*). There is a Cabbalistic anagram which serves to corroborate this by demonstrating that 'nothing' in Hebrew is *Ain*, and that the same letters form the word for 'I'—*Ani*.

Nudity The distinction between *nuditas virtualis* (purity and innocence) and *nuditas criminalis* (lasciviousness and vain exhibition) was already clearly established by Christians in the Middle Ages. Hence every nude must always have an ambivalent meaning and imply an ambiguous emotion: on the one hand, it lifts one's thoughts towards the pure peaks of mere physical beauty and (in a Platonic sense) towards the understanding of, and identification with, moral and spiritual beauty; but, on the other hand, it can never lose altogether its all too human ballast—its irrational attraction rooted in urges beyond the control of the conscious mind. Clearly, the human form revealed, whether in nature or in art, induces either one attitude or the other in the contemplator.

√ **Numbers** In symbolism, numbers are not merely the expressions of quantities, but idea-forces, each with a particular character of its own. The actual digits are, as it were, only the outer garments. All numbers are derived from the number one (which is equivalent to the mystic, non-manifest point of no magnitude). The farther a number is from unity, the more deeply it is involved in matter, in the involutive process, in the 'world'. The first ten numbers in the Greek system (or twelve in the oriental tradition) pertain to the spirit: they are entities, archetypes and symbols. The rest are the product of combinations of these basic numbers (44). The Greeks were much preoccupied with the symbolism of numbers. Pythagoras, for example, observed that 'Everything is disposed according to the numbers'. Plato regarded number as the essence of harmony, and harmony as the basis of the cosmos and of man, asserting that the movements of harmony 'are of the same kind as the regular revolutions of our soul' (24). The philosophy of numbers was further developed by the Hebrews, the Gnoptics and the Cabbalists, spreading to the alchemists as well. The same basic, universal notions are found in oriental thought—Lao-tse, for example: 'One becomes two; two becomes three; and from the ternary comes one'—the new unity or new order—'as four' (Maria Prophetissa) (32). Modern symbolic logic and the theory of groupings go back to the idea of the quantitative as the basis for the qualitative. Pierce suggests that the laws of nature and of the human spirit are based on these same principles, and that they can be ordered along these same lines (24). Apart from the basic symbols of unity and multiplicity, there is another general symbolism attached to the even numbers (expressing the negative and passive principle) and the uneven numbers (the positive and active). Furthermore, the numerical series possesses a symbolic dynamism which it is essential not to overlook. The idea that

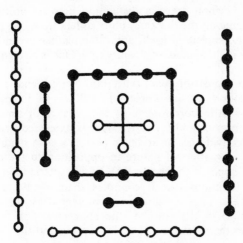

Oriental talisman based upon numbers.

one engenders two and two creates three is founded upon the premiss that every entity tends to surpass its limits, or to confront itself with its opposite. Where there are two elements, the third appears as the union of the first two and then as three, in turn giving rise·to the fourth number as the link between the first three, and so on (32). Next to unity and duality (expressing conflict, echo and primordial duplication), the ternary and the quaternary are the principal groupings; from their sum comes the septenary; and from their multiplication the dodecanary. Three is the more direct derivation of seven (since both are uneven) and four more closely related to twelve (both being even numbers). The usual symbolisms are as follows: The ternary represents the intellectual or spiritual order; the quaternary the terrestrial order; the septenary the planetary and moral order; the dodecanary the universal order. Here now are the most generally accepted symbolic meanings of each number, which will serve as a basis for a brief summary of the psychological theory of Paneth.

Zero Non-being, mysteriously connected with unity as its

opposite and its reflection; it is symbolic of the latent and potential and is the 'Orphic Egg'. From the viewpoint of man in existence, it symbolizes death as the state in which the life-forces are transformed (40, 55). Because of its circular form it signifies eternity.

One   Symbolic of being (40) and of the revelation to men of the spiritual essence. It is the active principle which, broken into fragments, gives rise to multiplicity (43), and is to be equated with the mystic Centre (7), the Irradiating Point and the Supreme Power (44). It also stands for spiritual unity—the common basis between all beings (55). Guénon draws a distinction between unity and one, after the Islamic mystic thinkers: unity differs from one in that it is absolute and complete in itself, admitting neither two nor dualism. Hence, unity is the symbol of divinity (26). One is also equated with light (49).

Two   Two stands for echo, reflection, conflict and counterpoise or contraposition; or the momentary stillness of forces in equilibrium (43); it also corresponds to the passage of time—the line which goes from behind forward (7); it is expressed geometrically by two points, two lines or an angle (44). It is also symbolic of the first nucleus of matter, of nature in opposition to the creator, of the moon as opposed to the sun (55). In all esoteric thought, two is regarded as ominous (9): it connotes shadow (49) and the bisexuality of all things, or dualism (represented by the basic myth of the Gemini) in the sense of the connecting-link between the immortal and the mortal, or of the unvarying and the varying (49). Within the mystic symbolism of landscape in megalithic culture, two is associated with the mandorla-shaped mountain, the focal point of symbolic Inversion, forming the crucible of life and comprising the two opposite poles of good and evil, life and death (51), Two, then, is the number associated with the *Magna Mater* (51).

Three   Three symbolizes spiritual synthesis, and is the formula for the creation of each of the worlds. It represents the solution of the conflict posed by dualism (43). It forms a half-circle comprising: birth, zenith and descent (7). Geometrically it is expressed by three points and by the triangle (44). It is the harmonic product of the action of unity upon duality (55). It is the number concerned with basic principles (41), and expresses sufficiency, or the growth of unity within itself (9). Finally, it is associated with the concepts of heaven (51) and the Trinity.

Four   Symbolic of the earth, of terrestrial space, of the human situation, of the external, natural limits of the 'minimum' awareness of totality, and, finally, of rational organization. It is equated with the square and the cube, and the cross representing the four seasons and the points of the compass. A great many material and spiritual forms are modelled after the quaternary (43). It is the number associated with tangible achievement (55) and with the Elements (41). In mystic thought, it represents the tetramorphs.

Five   Symbolic of Man, health and love, and of the quintessence acting upon matter. It comprises the four limbs of the body plus the head which controls them, and likewise the four fingers plus the thumb (43) and the four cardinal points together with the centre (7). The *hieros gamos* is signified by the number five, since it represents the union of the principle of heaven (three) with that of the *Magna Mater* (two). Geometrically, it is the pentagram, or the five-pointed star (44). It corresponds to pentagonal symmetry, a common characteristic of organic nature, to the golden section (as noted by the Pythagoreans) (24), and to the five senses (55) representing the five 'forms' of matter.

Six   Symbolic of ambivalence and equilibrium, six comprises the union of the two triangles (of fire and water) and hence signifies the human soul. The Greeks regarded it as a symbol of the hermaphrodite (33). It corresponds to the six Directions of Space (two for each dimension) (7), and to the cessation of movement (since the Creation took six days). Hence it is associated with trial and effort (37). It has also been shown to be related to virginity (50), and to the scales.

Seven   Symbolic of perfect order, a complete period or cycle. It comprises the union of the ternary and the quaternary, and hence it is endowed with exceptional value (43). It corresponds to the seven Directions of Space (that is, the six existential dimensions plus the centre) (7), to the seven-pointed star, to the reconciliation of the square with the triangle by superimposing the latter upon the former (as the sky over the earth) or by inscribing it within. It is the number forming the basic series of musical notes, of colours and of the planetary spheres (55), as well as of the gods corresponding to them; and also of the capital sins and their opposing virtues (41). It also corresponds to the three-dimensional cross (38), and, finally, it is the symbol of pain (50).

Eight   The octonary, related to two squares or the octagon (44), is the intermediate form between the square (or the terrestrial order) and the circle (the eternal order) and is, in consequence, a symbol of regeneration. By virtue of its shape, the numeral is associated with the two interlacing serpents of the caduceus, signifying the balancing out of opposing forces or the equivalence of the spiritual power to the natural (55). It also symbolizes—again because of its shape—the eternally spiralling movement of the heavens (shown also by the double sigmoid line—the sign of the infinite) (9). Because of its implications of regeneration, eight was in the Middle Ages an emblem of the waters of baptism. Furthermore, it corresponds in mediaeval mystic cosmogony to the fixed stars of the firmament, denoting that the planetary influences have been overcome.

Nine The triangle of the ternary, and the triplication of the triple. It is therefore a complete image of the three worlds. It is the end-limit of the numerical series before its return to unity (43). For the Hebrews, it was the symbol of truth, being characterized by the fact that when multiplied it reproduces itself (in mystic addition) (4). In medicinal rites, it is the symbolic number *par excellence*, for it represents triple synthesis, that is, the disposition on each plane of the corporal, the intellectual and the spiritual (51).

Ten Symbolic, in decimal systems, of the return to unity. In the *Tetractys* (whose triangle of points—four, three, two, one—adds up to ten) it is related to four. Symbolic also of spiritual achievement, as well as of unity in its function as an even (or ambivalent) number or as the beginning of a new, multiple series (44). According to some theories, ten symbolizes the totality of the universe—both metaphysical and material—since it raises all things to unity (9). From ancient oriental thought through the Pythagorean school and right up to St. Jerome, it was known as the number of perfection (50).

Eleven Symbolic of transition, excess and peril and of conflict and martyrdom (37). According to Schneider, there is an infernal character about it: since it is in excess of the number of perfection —ten—it therefore stands for incontinence (50); but at the same time it corresponds, like two, to the mandorla-shaped mountain, to the focal point of symbolic Inversion and antithesis, because it is made up of one plus one (comparable in a way with two) (51).

Twelve Symbolic of cosmic order and salvation. It corresponds to the number of the signs of the Zodiac, and is the basis of all dodecanary groups. Linked to it are the notions of space and time, and the wheel or circle.

Thirteen Symbolic of death and birth, of beginning afresh (37). Hence it has unfavourable implications.

Fourteen Stands for·fusion and organization (37) and also for justice and temperance (59).

Fifteen is markedly erotic and is associated with the devil (59).

Other Numbers Each of the numbers from sixteen to twenty-two is related to the corresponding card of the Tarot pack; and sometimes the meaning is derived from the fusion of the symbols of the units composing it. There are two ways in which this fusion may occur: either by mystic addition (for example, $374 = 3 + 7 + 4 = 14 = 1 + 4 = 5$) or by succession, in which case the right-hand digit expresses the outcome of a situation denoted by the left-hand number (so 21 expresses the reduction of a conflict— two—to its solution—unity). These numbers also possess certain meanings drawn from traditional sources and remote from their intrinsic symbolism: 24, for example, is the sacred number in Sankhya philosophy, and 50 is very common in Greek mythology—there were fifty Danaides, fifty Argonauts, fifty sons of Priam and of Aegyptus, for example—as a symbol, we would suggest, of that powerful quality of the erotic and human which is so typical of Hellenic myths. The repetition of a given number stresses its quantitative power but detracts from its spiritual dignity. So, for example, 666 was the number of the Beast because 6 was regarded as inferior to seven (37). When several kinds of symbolic meaning are contained within a multiple number, the symbolism of that number is accordingly enriched and strengthened. Thus, 144 was considered very favourable because its sum was 9 $(1+4+4)$ and because it comprises multiples of 10 and 4 plus the quaternary itself (37). Dante, in the *Divine Comedy*, has frequent recourse to the symbolism of numbers (27).

The work of Ludwig Paneth upon numbers concerns not so much symbolism as such, but rather the normal interpretation of numbers from the psychologist's point of view as they appear in obsessions and dreams of average people. His conclusions are as follows:

One rarely appears, but where it does occur it alludes to the paradisiac state which preceded good and evil—which preceded, that is to say, dualism.

Two significs counterpoise, or man's experience of separate existence, with its concomitant problems, inevitable analysis, dividing up, inner disintegration and struggle.

Three stands for biological synthesis, childbirth and the solution of a conflict.

Four, as a kind of double division (two and two), no longer signifies separation (like the number two) but the orderly arrangement of what is separate. Hence, it is a symbol of order in space and, by analogy, of every other well-ordered structure. As Simonides, the Greek poet, observed: 'It is difficult to become a superior man, tetragonal in hand, foot and spirit, forming a perfect whole.'

Five is a number which often occurs in animate nature, and hence its triumphant growth corresponds to the burgeoning of spring. It signifies the organic fullness of life as opposed to the rigidity of death. There is an erotic sense to it as well.

Six is, like two, a particularly ambiguous number: it is expressive of dualism $(2 \times 3$ or $3 \times 2)$. However, it is like four in that it has a normative value as opposed to the liberating tendencies of five and the mystic (or conflicting) character of seven.

Seven is, like all the prime numbers, an irreducible datum, and an expression of conflict or of a complex unity (the higher the prime number the greater the complexity). It is sometimes associated with the moon (since $7 \times 4 =$ the 28 days of the month).

Ten, in its graphic form as 10, is sometimes used to express marriage.

Nought, as the decimal multiplier, raises the quantitative power of a numerical symbol. A number of repeated noughts indicates a passion for grand things.

General Characteristics of Numbers Paneth draws a distinction between the arithmetical number and the symbolic number: the former defines an object by its quantity but says nothing about its nature, whereas the latter expresses an inner link with the object it defines by virtue of a mystic relationship between what is enumerated and the number itself. In arithmetic, the addition of 1 and 1 and 1 gives 3, but not triunity; in symbolism the second and third of these ones are intrinsically different from the first because they always function within ternary orders which establish the first term as an active element, the second as passive and the third as neuter or consequent. Aristotle spoke of the 'qualitative structure' of the numbers as opposed to the amorphous character of the arithmetical unity. Concerning the higher numbers, Paneth has this to say: 'The multiplication of a number simply increases its power: thus, 25 and 15 are both symbols of eroticism. Numbers composed of two digits express a mutual relationship between the individual digits (reading from left to right). For example, $23=2$ (conflict) and 3 (the outcome).' Numbers made up of more than two digits may be broken down and analysed in a number of different ways. For example, 338 may equal 300 plus 2×19, or else 3 and 3 and 8. The dynamism and symbolic richness of the number three is so exceptional that it cannot be over-emphasized. The reconciling function of the third element of the ternary, we would add, may appear in either a favourable or an adverse light. For instance, when in myths and legends there are three brothers or sisters, three suitors, three trials, three wishes, and so on (42), the first and second elements correspond broadly to what is already possessed, and the third element represents the magic or miraculous solution desired and sought after; but this third element may—as we have said— also be negative. Thus, just as there are legends where the first and the second fail and the third succeeds—sometimes it is the first six followed by the successful seventh—so there are others where the inversion of the symbolism produces the opposite result: the first two are favourable (and the second usually more so than the first) but then comes the third which is destructive or negative. The Three Kings, for example, offer the Infant Jesus gifts of gold, frankincense (both positive) and myrrh (negative). In almost all those myths and tales about three chalices, three chests or three rooms, the third element corresponds to death, because of the asymmetrical division of the cycle of man's life, composed of two parts which are ascending (infancy-adolescence, youth-maturity) and the third and last which is descending (old age-death). There is a Hebrew tale, called 'True Happiness', which exactly expresses the symbolic significance of this 'third element'. Here it is in Loeffler's exemplary version: 'A peasant and his wife, dissatisfied with their lot, envied those who dwelt in palaces, imagining their existence to be an unending flow of delights. While he was working in the fields, the man came across three iron chests. On the first was an inscription which said: "He who opens me will become rich." On the second he read: "If gold makes you happy, open me." On the third: "He who opens me, loses all that he possesses." The first chest was at once opened up and with the silver it contained the couple gave a sumptuous banquet, purchased splendid garments and slaves. The contents of the second chest enabled the couple to discover the luxury of refined living. But with the opening of the third, a terrible storm destroyed all their belongings' (38). The symbolism bears a relationship to the asymmetrical cycle of the year (Spring—Summer—Autumn followed by Winter) and to all symbols of the 'superior'—for superiority is always perilous.

Finally, there are also visual interpretations of number-symbols, derived from the shape of the digits; but such interpretations are of a specialized nature and are not always well-founded.

Numismatic Symbols   Coins have, from Antiquity, had a certain talismanic meaning, gradually lost with the passing of time: the power of a city, of a king, of a magistrate. Symbols, *signa* (ensigns), allegories and personifications have been stamped on them, clearly reflecting the cultural ethos of the day. Swastikas, tripods, tridents, labyrinths, chariots, winged horses, roses, tortoises, eagles, griffins, shields, crowns, bulls, cornucopias, etc., are frequently found on Greek coins. And on Roman coinage: military trophies, *signa* (standards) of the legions, ships' prows, heads of gods (especially double-headed Janus), eagles, votive crowns, chariots, temples, etc. It is worth noting that from the 4th to the 2nd centuries B.C. in the coinage of Luceria (Apulia) there appear geometric symbols such as ovals, triangles and series of dots, alongside Jupiter's thunderbolts, and also the cross-potent as it was later to appear in the Christian escutcheon of Jerusalem. Strictly speaking, mediaeval coinage dates from Carolingian times and displays crosses, anagrams, triple enclosures and very schematic temples. Byzantine coins are characterized above all by emperors' heads and figures of Christ, the Virgin and saints, as well as crosses and schematic ladders or steps. Mediaeval coinage in the West has a wide range of motifs, embracing various forms of cross, triple enclosures, roses, fleurs-de-lis, crowns, angels, armed knights, swords, hands raised in benediction, castles and shrines, lions, eagles, etc. On the reverse side of some coins there are veritable mandalas formed by the juxta-position of lobular enclosures, circles and crosses. From Renais-sance times onwards, money, by now secularized, takes on the standardized characteristics of Imperial Rome, with the face of a monarch on the obverse and heraldic shields on the reverse. But in many of the more imaginative stampings symbolic implications are still to be found in the form of 'wild men', solar symbols, religious or alchemical themes, etc. Islamic coins are usually based on calli-graphy, but they sometimes portray stars, figures and conjunctions of the square and the circle. Another topic, allegorical rather than symbolic, but nevertheless of great beauty, is found on mediaeval gold pieces and portrays the king standing, sword in hand, on a ship. A history of numismatic motifs in geography and in chronology has yet, we believe, to be written.

Nymphs   The Greek word νύμφη means 'bride' and also 'doll'. The nymphs accompanying some of the mythic deities are symbolic of the concomitant ideas of those deities (48). According to Mircea Eliade, nymphs correspond in essence to running water, fountains, springs, torrents and waterfalls. The best known of the nymphs are the sisters of Thetis, the Nereides, who figure in the expedition of the Argonauts. By virtue of their association with the Element of water, their significance is ambivalent and they may preside equally over birth and fertility or dissolution and death (17). Jung, from the psychological standpoint of his theory of individuation, regards the nymph as an independent and fragmentary expression of the feminine character of the unconscious. He concludes, therefore, that what Paracelsus called the *regio nymphidica* corresponds to a relatively undeveloped stage of the process of individuation, a stage which he relates to the notions of temptation, transitoriness, multiplicity and dissolution (32).

Oak   A tree sacred to Jupiter and Cybele, standing for strength and long life. Hercules' club, according to legend, was made of oak (8). Its consecration to Jupiter may derive from the ancient belief that the oak tree attracts the lightning more than any other. The oak had this symbolic and allegorical meaning throughout the Aryan cultures of Russia, Germany, Greece and Scandinavia (17). Like all trees, it represents a world-axis.

Oar   In ancient rites connected with the founding of temples, the king would make the round of the site, an oar in his hand. Virgil mentions this ceremony in connexion with the rebuilding of Troy. It is a symbol of creative thought and the Word, the source of all action (19).

Obelisk A symbol of the sun-ray, by virtue of its shape. Because of its substance, it is bound up with the general symbolism of stone. It is further related to the myths of solar ascension and of light as the 'penetrating spirit', in consequence of its upright position and the pyramidal point in which it terminates.

Object The symbolism of objects varies with the kind of object in question. But, broadly speaking, every object consists of a material structure with certain unconscious elements adhering to it (31). The fact that these forgotten or repressed constituents should reappear in a new medium—the object—enables the spirit to accept them in a form different from the original. Utensils in particular are possessed of a mystic force which helps to strengthen the intensity and the rhythm of human volition. Thus, Schneider maintains that such instruments fulfil a triple rôle: they are cultural instruments, instruments of labour and finally reflections of the harmonious soul of the universe. The drinking-vessel, for instance, is a sacrificial vessel and also a drum. The blow-pipe is both a flute and a magic whistle, etc. (50). Such ideas as these, concerned with the primitive notion of an object, have lately been resuscitated by artistic movements such as Dadaism and surrealism. By depicting objects in common use as if they were works of art, Marcel Duchamp removed them from the context of their merely utilitarian function (their only function according to Western ways of thinking) and showed them in the light of their true essence, since that essence is revealed only in their uselessness (freed from the necessity to serve some useful purpose). He showed that it was possible to see in a bottle-stand, for instance, the very mystic structure that governed the Gothic spires rising in the form of a cage, or the lamps in Islamic mosques with their multiple, descending hoops; and that all the foregoing are related to the hollow pyramid of the Primitives (a symbol of the 'conjunction' of earth—or the mother—with fire— or the spirit), and also to the artificial mountain and the geometric temple. The form of the object, then, fulfils an essential rôle in determining the symbolism; thus, all those symbols which take the form of a twin bell, with the upper bell placed upside down on the lower—for example, the twin drum or the hour-glass—are closely related to the corresponding graphic symbol: the letter X, or the cross of St. Andrew (symbolic of the intercommunication between the Upper and the Lower Worlds). Objects that are simple in form and function usually correspond either to the active or to the passive groups; in other words, they represent either the contents or the receptacle. For instance: the lance (which is made to pierce) and the cup or chalice (whose sole function is to contain). The parallel between this classification and the division of the sexes is self-evident; but to limit the symbolic relevance of a given object to this sexual implication is to mutilate seriously its true symbolism. The 'conjunction' of the feminine and masculine principles within a complex object, specially if this object is—as in the case of a machine —endowed with movement, enables us to carry the sexual parallel a stage further and to characterize it as a kind of secularized lingam. The 'objects of symbolic function' of the surrealists were nothing but the practical illustration of this allusive reality, strengthened by the fetishistic character of the objects illustrated in their compositions. It was Lautréamont in *Les Chants de Maldoror* who best described this shifting of the symbolic significance of objects towards their generic grouping in his remark: 'beautiful as the chance-finding of an umbrella and a sewing-machine on a dissecting table'. As always, a symbol of integration such as this can be taken either on the cosmic plane or at the existential and sexual level. In the latter case, the umbrella would be a merely phallic representation, the machine would stand for the *cteis*, and the dissection-table would be an illustration of the bed. On the cosmic plane, the umbrella is the cosmic serpent, the machine is the jaguar, and the table is the universe. At the same time, objects owe part of their significance to their origins: objects fallen from heaven, such as aerolites and meteorites for example, partake of the sacred character of Uranus and constitute a symbol of the power of the celestial deities (17). Submarine objects, on the other hand, possess a viscous and abysmal quality betokening their irrational nature and their aptness for the expression of all that is base and unconscious. Sacred objects are so by virtue of their associations—as in the case of attributes or emblems for instance, or their origins—such as the legendary palladium of Troy, the Salian shields of Rome, the Hebrew Ark of the Covenant, etc. (28). To come back now to the broadest of generalizations, alongside their specific symbolism deriving from their form, function, character, origin, colour and so on, objects in themselves are always symbols of the world: that is, they are particular expressions of a material order which expounds both the blind irrational force of continuity and the structural pattern defining the object as opposed to the subject. Finally we would mention that an elaborate application of the theory of correspondences would demonstrate the serial structure of objects and suggest a way of reconciling their 'character' with the principles governing the two essential prototypes of the serial arrangement of the universe: that based upon the number seven, or the planetary prototype; and twelve, or the zodiacal model. The incomplete character of such forms of symbolic expression has been apparent to man since the earliest times, and for this reason the attempt was made to discover objects which could be invested with great symbolic power by means of the combination and juxtaposition of various ingredients, which were usually 'noble' in character, but were occasionally bizarre or even base—as was the case, for example, with the alchemic preparation known as 'prime matter'. The aim was to endow the object with all the powers inherent in the several planes of cosmic reality. An example of a 'complete object' of this kind is the sword in the Grail legend: its pommel was a precious stone of many colours, each colour representing a particular virtue; its haft was composed of the bones of strange beasts.

Objects, Marvellous Objects which are marvellous because of their rarity, beauty, splendour, or magical or miraculous qualities, frequently appear in myths, legends, folktales and books of knight-errantry. They are invincible weapons, talismans; on another plane, however, they are also purely and simply works of art, giving pleasure to their owner. The 'marvellous objects' *par excellence* are relics, or the ancestral symbols which sometimes become identified with them: the Grail, the bleeding lance, the Celtic cauldron, etc. Occasionally, the marvellous object is the motive for a symbolic 'test', such as the Sphinx's question to Oedipus; this is the case with the broken sword, which, in the legends of the Round Table, is given to Gawain and Parsifal for mending, and which Siegfried successfully achieves in the *Niebelungen*.

Ocean According to Piobb, the Graeco-Roman conception of the ocean encompassing the earth was a graphic representation of the current of energy induced by the terrestrial globe (48). Setting aside its grandeur, the two most essential aspects of the ocean are its ceaseless movement and the formlessness of its waters. It is a symbol, therefore, of dynamic forces and of transitional states between the stable (or solids) and the formless (air or gas). The ocean as a whole, as opposed to the concept of the drop of water, is a symbol of universal life as opposed to the particular (38). It is regarded traditionally as the source of the generation of all life (57), and science has confirmed that life did in fact begin in the sea (3). Zimmer observes that the ocean is 'immense illogic'—a vast expanse dreaming its own dreams and asleep in its own reality, yet containing within itself the seeds of its antitheses. The island is the opponent of the ocean and symbolic of the metaphysical point of irradiating force (60). In keeping with the general symbolism of water, both fresh and salt, the ocean stands for the sum of all the possibilities of one plane of existence. Having regard to its characteristics, one may deduce whether these potentialities are positive (or germinant) or negative (destructive) (26). The ocean, then, denotes an ambivalent situation. As the begetter of monsters, it is the abysmal abode *par excellence*, the chaotic source which still brings forth base entities ill-fitted to life in its aerial and superior forms. Consequently, aquatic monsters represent a cosmic or psychological situation at a lower level than land-monsters; this is why sirens and tritons denote a sub-animal order. The power of salt water to destroy the higher forms of land-life means that it is also a symbol of sterility, so confirming the ambivalent nature of the ocean—its contradictory dynamism (32). The ocean is also to be found as a symbol of woman or the mother (in both her benevolent and her terrible aspects) (56). As Frobenius comments in *Das Zeitalter des Sonnengottes*: 'If the blood-red sunrise is interpreted as the "birth" of an astral body, then two questions arise: Who is the father? And how did the mother come to conceive? And since she, like the fish, is a sea-symbol, and since our premiss is that the sun plunges into the sea and yet is born in it, the answer must be that the sea previously swallowed up the old sun and the appearance of a "new sun" confirms that she has been fecundated. The symbolism here coincides with that of Isis whose twin lunar horns embrace the sun.' This appearance of the sun and its disappearance back into the deeps of the ocean confirm that the 'Lower Waters' signify the abyss out of which forms arise to unfold their potentialities within existence. Thus, the ocean is equated also with the collective unconscious, out of which arises the sun of the spirit (32). The stormy sea, as a poetic image or a dream, is a sign of an analogous state in the lower depths of the affective unconscious. A translucent calm, on the other hand, denotes a state of contemplative serenity.

Octagon Embellishments, architectonic structures, and different dispositions based on the octagon (in ground-plan or elevation in the case of a building or structure such as a baptistry, fountain, etc.) symbolize spiritual regeneration, because the eight-sided figure is connected with this idea as the intermediary between the square and the circle. It is not surprising, therefore, that the majority of baptistries have a definite octagonal shape. However, twelve is sometimes used for baptismal fonts (the sum of the facets of the semi-polyhedron), because it symbolizes totality.

Octopus It has the same significance as the dragon-whale myth (31). As a decorative motif it appears most frequently in Cretan art. It is related to the spider's web and the spiral, both being symbolic of the mystic Centre and of the unfolding of creation. It has also been credited with a merely existential significance (41).

Ogre The origins of the ogre, a common feature in legend and folklore, go back to Saturn, who would devour his children as soon as Cybele gave them birth (38). If the core of the Saturn-myth is the idea that destruction is the inevitable outcome of creation (since

creation takes place in time), then the ogre seems to be a personification of the 'Terrible Father'. Henri Dontenville derives the word
'ogre' from the definition of the Latin poet Ennius: *Pluto latine est
Dis Pater, alii Orcum vocant*. Orcus was the lord of the underworld,
with his mother Orca, and both are characterized by the Saturnian
practice of eating little children (16). It is beyond doubt that these
legends are also closely bound up with other ancient myths founded
upon the most savage aspects of pre-human life and that, like other
kinds of legend, they serve the cathartic function of issuing a
warning.

Ojancanu   This is the name given to the Cyclops in the folklore
of Northern Spain. According to Caro Baroja, the *Ojancanu* is
regarded as a giant with red hair (and therefore Satanic), tall and
stout, with one bright and evil-looking eye. If two eyes are an
expression of normality, and three denote the superhuman (as in the
case of Shiva), a single eye is a clear allusion to what is base. The
Cyclops-myth appears in different versions throughout Europe and
Asia Minor, but it is not known in the Far East (10). The *Ojancanu*
is, in sum, a symbol of the evil and destructive forces behind the
primary or regressive side of Man.

Old Man   In the Cabala, the Old Man is the symbol of the
occult principle (like the holy or silver palace). In the modern study
of symbols, the Old Man is regarded as the personification of the
age-old wisdom of humanity, or of the collective unconscious. The
Old Men (Elders) of the Apocalypse are the twelve prophets and the
twelve apostles. The 'Ancient of Days' is a similar symbol, sometimes
identified with the creative principle, the Cabbalistic *Ain-Soph* and
the *Atum* of Egyptian religion (19). According to Jung, the Old
Man, particularly when invested with special powers or prestige, is
the symbol of the 'mana' personality, i.e. the spirituality of the
personality which emerges when consciousness is overburdened
with clarified, apprehended and assimilated matter welling up
from the unconscious (30).

Olive Tree   A symbol of peace, consecrated by the Romans to
Jupiter and Minerva. It carries the same symbolic significance in
many oriental and European countries (8).

Omphalos   To quote Pausanias (X, 16, 2): 'What the inhabitants
of Delphi call *omphalos* is made of white stone and is considered
to be at the centre of the earth', and Pindar, in one of his odes,
confirms this opinion. It is, then, one of the many symbols of the
cosmic 'Centre' where intercommunication between the three worlds
of man, of the dead, and of the gods, is effected (17). W. H. Roscher
(according to René Guénon) collected a number of documents in a
work entitled *Omphalos* (1913) which prove that this symbol was in
existence among the most diverse of races. By locating it in one

particular spot, man made of it a sacred zone around the 'centre of the world'. The material image of the *Omphalos* (the 'navel' in Greek) was known as the Bethel, which was made of stone and shaped like a pilaster. It has been suggested that the menhir may have had a similar significance. Another image of the omphalos may have been the ovoid stone as it sometimes appears in Greek designs encircled by a snake or serpent. In all these images we can descry the attempt to express the sexual principles of the cosmos: the pilaster is related to the masculine and active factor, the Egg of the World is connected with the feminine principle, and the egg encircled by the serpent suggests the synthesis of both principles in the *lingam*. More abstract and therefore spiritually superior ways of depicting this 'Centre' (at once cosmic, temporal and spatial, physical and metaphysical) are to be found in China: the hole in the middle of the disk of jade known as *Pi*, for instance, where the centre is identified as the non-being of mystic Nothingness, or the quadrangular pyramid rising up in the centre of each feudal domain where each face of the pyramid corresponds to one of the cardinal points and the summit represents the centre. These pyramids were also known in Ireland, according to J. Loth in his *Brehon Laws* (28).

One   The number one is equivalent to the 'Centre', to the non-manifest point, to the creative power or the 'unmoved mover'. Plotinus equates one with moral purpose, and multiplicity with evil—a distinction which is in complete accord with symbolist doctrine.

Orchestra   Symbolic of the activity of a corporate whole. This is the idea behind Schneider's remark that when the high and the low orchestras (that is, heaven and earth) perform the counterpoint of the cosmos, these two antithetical voices are 'descanting'. But when one of the voices imposes its own rhythm upon the other, then that voice is 'enchanting' its opponent (50).

Orgy   Orgies, characterized by drunkenness, sexual licence, excesses of all kinds and occasional transvestism, always correspond to a 'call to chaos' as a result of a weakening of the will to accept the norm in the ordinary way. Hence, as Eliade has pointed out, the orgy is a cosmogonic equivalent of Chaos and of supreme, ultimate fulfilment, as well as of the eternal moment and of timelessness. The Roman Saturnalia—whose origins go back to prehistoric times—or Carnival were expressions of the orgiastic urge. In these uninhibited festivities the tendency is to 'confuse forms' by means of the inversion of the social pattern, the juxtaposition of opposites and the unleashing of the passions—even in their destructive capacity. All this is a means not so much towards pleasure as to bring about the dissolution of the world in a momentary disruption—although the moment seems definitive while the orgy lasts—of the reality-principle, alongside the corresponding restoration of the primigenial *illud tempus* (17).

Orientation In Islamic thought, orientation is the materialization of intent. The Orient, since it is the point where the sun rises, symbolizes illumination and the fount of life; to turn towards the east is to turn in spirit towards this spiritual focal point of light. Orientation plays its due part in rites and ceremonies all over the world, particularly in those to do with the founding of temples and cities. The orientation of Graeco-Latin temples and mediaeval churches was inspired by the same idea (28). However, not all mystic orientations take the east as their point of reference: there is an alternative point in the geography of the sky, symbolic of the 'hole' in space-time and of the 'unmoved mover'—and that is the North Star. The Etruscans located the abode of the gods in the north, and hence their soothsayers, when about to speak, would turn to face the south—that is, they would take up a position which identified them, ideologically, with the gods (7). To face the north is to pose a question. To turn westwards is to prepare to die, because it is in the watery deeps of the west that the sun ends its journey. The notion of orientation, taken in conjunction with the concept of space as a three-dimensional whole, plays a powerful part in the symbolic organization of space. The human anatomy itself, with its quasi-rectangular, symmetrical and bilateral pattern, in distinguishing between the front and the back thereby designates two corresponding points of orientation. The natural position of the arms and shoulders completes this quadrangular scheme—a symbolic pattern which, interpreted according to strictly anthropological and empirical criteria, would perhaps provide us with the key to the original conception of orientation as quaternary on the surface but septenary three-dimensionally (embracing north, south, east and west, together with the zenith, the nadir and the centre). Also closely linked with the symbolism of the cardinal points and orientation are the gestures and movements of the body, as symbolic expressions of the will applying itself in one direction or another. All attitudes of concentration denote the enshrining of the 'Centre' within the heart.

Ornamentation This is a symbol of cosmic activity, of development in space and of the 'way out of chaos' (chaos being denoted by blind matter) (13). Ornamentation by virtue of graduated motifs— its progressive reconciliation with order—signifies the gradual stages in this evolutive development of the universe. The principal elements in ornamentation are the spiral, the sigma, the cross, waves, the zigzag; these are discussed in their appropriate place. Some of the basic principles behind these ornamental motifs concern graphic and spatial symbolisms. Negatively speaking, the art of

ornamentation is opposed to figurative art, particularly when the
ornaments are geometric forms or stylizations of plants. 'Beware of
representation, whether it be of the Lord or of man, and paint
nothing except trees, flowers and inanimate objects'; so spoke
Mohammed according to the oral traditions or *Hadith*. For Moslems,
consequently, art is a kind of aid to meditation, or a sort of mandala
—indefinite and interminable and opening out onto the infinite, or
a form of language composed of spiritual signs, or handwriting;
but it can never be a mere reflection of the world of existence. In
Islamic ornamentation—which we may regard as one of the basic
prototypes—the essential constituents are as follows: plaits, foliage,

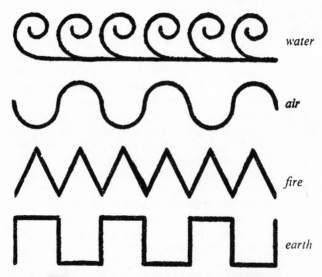

Ornamental symbols of the Elements.

polygons, arabesques, inscriptions, the twenty-eight letters of the
alphabet, five or six stylized flowers (such as the hyacinth, the tulip,
the eglantine, the peach-blossom), certain of the fabulous animals
and the seven smalts in heraldry. Patterns such as these are blended
into a vast symbolic network reminiscent of polyphonic music and
the aspiration towards the harmony of infinity (6). In figurative
ornamentation—Romanesque for instance—every item represented possesses its own symbolic sense, while the pattern as a whole
constitutes a veritable symbolic syntax.

Ouroboros   This symbol appears principally among the Gnostics
and is depicted as a dragon, snake or serpent biting its own tail. In
the broadest sense, it is symbolic of time and of the continuity of
life (57). It sometimes bears the caption *Hen to pan*—'The One, the

All', as in the *Codex Marcianus*, for instance, of the 2nd century A.D. It has also been explained as the union between the chthonian principle as represented by the serpent and the celestial principle as signified by the bird (a synthesis which can also be applied to the dragon). Ruland contends that this proves that it is a variant of the symbol for Mercury—the *duplex* god. In some versions of the Ouroboros, the body is half light and half dark, alluding in this way to the successive counterbalancing of opposing principles as illustrated in the Chinese *Yang-Yin* symbol for instance (32). Evola asserts that it represents the dissolution of the body, or the universal serpent which (to quote the Gnostic saying) 'passes through all things'. Poison, the viper and the universal solvent are all symbols of the undifferentiated—of the 'unchanging law' which moves through all things, linking them by a common bond. Both the dragon and the bull are symbolic antagonists of the solar hero. The ouroboros biting its own tail is symbolic of self-fecundation, or the primitive idea of a self-sufficient Nature—a Nature, that is, which, *à la* Nietzsche, continually returns, within a cyclic pattern, to its own beginning. There is a Venetian manuscript on alchemy which depicts the Ouroboros with its body half-black (symbolizing earth and night) and half-white (denoting heaven and light).

Oven or **Furnace** A mother-symbol. The alchemists' crucible is symbolic of the body, and the alembic is expressive of the *vas Hermetis* (31). But it has a further significance as a symbol of pure, spiritual gestation; it is in this sense that the glowing furnace makes its appearance in so many alchemic treatises, such as Michael Maier and the *Museum Hermeticum* (1678).

Oviparous Animals In India, birds, reptiles and all oviparous beings receive the name of 'twice born'. With this in mind we can conclude that the laying of the egg is equivalent to the birth of man, and the breaking out from the egg symbolizes his second birth or initiation (18).

Owl In the Egyptian system of hieroglyphs, the owl symbolizes death, night, cold and passivity. It also pertains to the realm of the dead sun, that is, of the sun which has set below the horizon and which is crossing the lake or sea of darkness (19).

Ox Broadly speaking, the ox is a symbol of the cosmic forces (40). In Egypt and in India, a more specialized symbolism was evolved for the ox, contrasting it with the lion on the one hand and with the bull on the other. For obvious reasons it became a symbol of sacrifice, suffering, patience and labour. In Greece and in Rome it was regarded as an attribute of agriculture and of foundation-laying (and so, by extension, was the yoke). Roman generals who had been granted the honour of a triumph would sacrifice white oxen to the Capitoline Jupiter as part of the ceremony (8). In

Herrad of Landsberg's *Hortus Deliciarum*, the moon's chariot is
drawn by oxen (14), which points to the emasculated character of
the animal (14). In mediaeval emblems, the ox is frequently found
symbolizing patience, submissiveness and the spirit of self-sacrifice
(20). Very often the ox-head, without its body, is shown with one of
the following signs between its horns: a crown, a snake coiled round
a staff, a chalice, a circle, a cross, a fleur-de-lis, a crescent moon
or the Gothic 'R' (standing for *Regeneratio*) (4). The ox (because
of its connexion with the moon) is also a symbol of darkness and
night in contrast to the lion, which is a solar animal (50).

Palace   In Cabbalistic symbolism, the sacred palace, or the
'inner palace', is located at the junction of the six Directions of
Space which, together with this centre, form a septenary. It is,
consequently, a symbol of the occult Centre—of the 'unmoved
mover' (28). It is also known as the 'silver palace', the 'silver thread'
being the hidden bond which joins man to his Origin and to his
End (28). This concept of the Centre embraces the heart and the
mind; hence, in legends and folktales, the palace of the old king
contains secret chambers (representing the unconscious) which
hold treasure (or spiritual truths). Loeffler suggests that palaces
made of glass or of mirrors, and also those which suddenly appear
as if by magic, are specially symbolic of the ancestral memories
of mankind—of the basic, primitive awareness of the Golden Age
(38).

Palafitte   The architectural pillar and lintel owe their origin to the
palafitte or lake-dwelling. Paul Sarrasin has shown that the classic
Greek temple derives directly from lacustrine structures (22). The
palafitte came about not just because of topographical necessity but
as a consequence of motives of a mystic order: the urge to raise
one's dwelling above the general level. Now, lake-dwellings acquire
greater symbolic interest still by virtue of their connexion with three
of the Elements: earth, since the lake-dwelling is a home—and the
home is always associated in turn with the cave and the mountain;
air, since it is elevated; and water, because the piles which support
it are immersed in this Element. The palafitte is, then, a symbol of
the world: it is both the Tree of Life and a mystic vessel, for its
'masts' touch the water, and its roof, sickle-shaped, is representative
of the mandorla (q.v.) (50).

Palm A classic emblem of fecundity and of victory (8). For Jung, it is also symbolic of the anima (32).

Pan The god Pan is a symbol of nature, and is usually represented with horns (expressive of the sun's rays and of the aggressive force of Aries) and with legs covered with hair (denoting the vitality of base forces, earth, shrubs and the instincts) (8). In astrology, Pan is one aspect of Saturn, and is also equated with Satan and with life in its involutive, and, in particular, its base, aspects (39).

Pandora According to Diel, Pandora is symbolic of the wicked temptations besetting humankind—the rebellious Promethean beings who have risen up against the divine order (15). She is also at times a representation of the irrational, wild tendencies of the imagination.

Pansy In Spanish,[1] this flower is called 'thought' precisely because it is thought which it symbolizes by virtue of its clearly pentagonal pattern: five being the number that symbolizes man (48).

Papyri In the Egyptian system of hieroglyphs, a rolled papyrus is a determinative sign defining the concept of knowledge. The fact that the papyrus is rolled signifies progress, efflorescence and omniscience. The unfolding of life itself is also symbolized by a roll of papyrus, though more frequently by a mat or carpet; in the words of Themistocles to Artaxerxes: 'Human life is like a rolled-up carpet slowly unfolding', an idea which Stefan George incorporated in one of his poems. In every case the symbolic significance corresponds not so much to the object or material in question as to the process of its manifestation (19).

Paradise Lost Symbolic of the mystic 'Centre'—or, rather, of its manifestation in space. The Chinese locate it in central Asia, referring to it as a garden inhabited by 'dragons of wisdom', with the four essential rivers of the world—the Oxus, Indus, Ganges and Nile—rising out of a common source which is termed the 'lake of the dragons' (9). Leaving aside the Christian dogma, there are a host of Western and oriental legends dealing with the lost Paradise. It is found in symbolic traditions all over the world, and it is here that its true beginnings should be looked for. As a symbol of the spirit, it corresponds to that state which is above all queries and quibbles. The fall of man from the paradisiac state and his return to it find varied manners of symbolic expression, the most characteristic being the labyrinth. As Saunier has observed: 'When man comes to ponder this mysterious problem, he knows no more peace,

---

[1] *Pensamiento* in Spanish is the common name for 'thought' and the popular word for 'pansy'. The English word 'pansy' derives, of course, from the French *'pensée'*; and our synonym, 'heart's ease', is perhaps another pointer to the symbolic interpretation.—*Translator.*

for his mind, faced with a series of insurmountable obstacles, is shattered, filling his heart, his soul and his body with rage and despair. . . . Man, urged on by his desire . . . bent his mind to a rigorous investigation into the smallest particles of the cosmos, enshrined his intelligence in matter, and strove by hard and constant work to rediscover himself in the labyrinth of science. Only once he had grasped the worlds of the infinitely small and the infinitely large could man once again vibrate in sympathy with the cosmic harmonies and blend in ineffable communion with all the beings and things in earth and heaven' (49). The 'weekly day of rest' is a temporal image of Paradise, comparable with the Islands of the Blessed and El Dorado, etc., in geographical symbolism. The 'lost' characteristic, which gives the symbol of Paradise its particular symbolic direction, is connected with the general symbolism of the feeling of abandonment and fall, recognized by modern existentialism as an essential part of human make-up.

Parakeet Related to other members of the parrot family in its faculty for pronouncing words. Maurice Bouisson, in *Le Secret de Schéhérazade* (Paris, 1961), comments on the *Tuti nameh*, a Persian translation of Nakchabi's *Book of the Parrot*. He comes to the conclusion that it is a messenger-symbol, like the crow, and also a symbol of the soul (the Egyptian *ba*), like other birds. In *The Conference of the Birds*, by the 13th-century Persian poet Farid Ud-Din Attar, the parrot seeks the water of immortality.

Partridge The partridge is very common in Romanesque ornamentation—in the southern gallery of the cloister at Silos, for instance. Pinedo has noted how Aristotle, Theophrastus, Pliny and other ancient and mediaeval writers all have something to say about the characteristic habit of the partridge, succinctly expressed by St. Jerome as follows: 'Just as the partridge lays eggs and hatches young birds who will never follow it, so the impious man possesses wealth to which he is not entitled, and which he must leave behind when he is least inclined.' It is this idea that underlies the symbol of the partridge. Another symbolic function comes from the bird's capacity for deception. In the words of St. Ambrose: 'The partridge, taking its name from the word *perdendo* and in Hebrew called *kore* (to call and shout), is Satan tempting the multitudes with his voice' (46).

Paste According to Bachelard, the notion of matter is very closely related to that of paste. Water is here a predominant constituent, imparting cohesion. Hence it has been said that 'matter is the unconscious of form'. Mud is the 'dust' of water, just as ash is the 'dust' of fire. Bachelard goes on to suggest that mud, dust and smoke afford images which, in a changed and shadowy form, imply the matter from which they arise—they are the residue of the four Elements (2). They correspond to a quasi-aquatic state, and hence come into the symbolisms of dissolution and regeneration: ash and dust are expressive of an ending, but all ends are beginnings.

Peacock On Roman coins, the peacock designates the apotheosis of princesses, just as the eagle does of victors (8). The peacock's tail, in particular, appears in the eighty-fourth emblem of the *Ars Symbolica* of Bosch as a symbol for the blending together of all colours and for the idea of totality (32). This explains why, in Christian art, it appears as a symbol of immortality (20) and of the incorruptible soul (6). The common *motif* of the two peacocks symmetrically disposed on either side of the Cosmic Tree or *hom* —a feature which came to Islam from Persia and subsequently reached Spain and the West—denotes the psychic duality of man (related to the myth of the Gemini) drawing its life-force from the principle of unity (6). In the mystic horology, the peacock corresponds to dusk (50). In Hindu mythology, the patterns on its wings, resembling innumerable eyes, are taken to represent the starry firmament (50).

Pearl One of the eight 'common emblems' of Chinese tradition. It symbolizes 'genius in obscurity' (5), doubtless after the rather less categorical observation of Lao-tse that, 'Hence, the chosen one wears coarse garments, but in his breast he hides a precious stone' —by allusion to the pearl hidden inside its oyster. Because of all this, psychoanalysts have recognized that the function of the pearl is to represent the mystic Centre and sublimation (seen here as the transfiguration of an infirmity, or of some abnormality) (56). The Moslems often have recourse to the pearl as a symbol of heaven, since their belief is that the blessed are enclosed in a pearl, each one with his houri (46); there is an obvious connexion here with Plato's androgynous 'spherical man' who is both primordial and final. They also believe—and this confirms the parallel with the Platonic spherical man—that the pearl is the product of the 'conjunction' of fire and water. It has also been identified as the human soul (18). Pearls in large numbers take on a different character: despite their high value, they come to be mere beads: when joined they correspond to the symbol of the necklace, and when scattered they relate to the symbol of dismemberment, like all things that are dispersed.

Pegasus A winged horse which sprang from the blood of Medusa, the Gorgon, when Perseus cut off her head with the aid of the magic weapons given him by the gods. Bellerophon rode upon Pegasus in his fight with the chimaera. A similar being finds its way into mediaeval legends under the name of hippogryph. It symbolizes the heightening power of the natural forces—the innate capacity for spiritualization and for inverting evil into good.

Pelican   An aquatic bird which, as legend has it, loved its young so dearly that it nourished them with its own blood, pecking open its breast to this end (8). It is one of the best-known allegories of Christ, and it is in this form that it figures as the seventieth emblem of the *Ars Symbolica* of Bosch (32). Also one of the principal symbols in alchemy, it is to some extent the antithesis of the raven.

Perfume   As Gaston Bachelard has shrewdly observed (3), scent or perfume in its association with the general symbolism of the air is tantamount to the wakes or tracks that mark the passage of solid bodies through the atmosphere, and consequently symbolic of memories or reminiscences. Whereas the pure, cold air of mountain heights is associated with heroic and solitary thought—in St. John of the Cross quite as much as in Nietzsche—a scent-laden atmosphere is expressive of the mind saturated with emotion and with nostalgia. The over-enthusiastic application of the laws of correspondences has led some people to lay down hard-and-fast symbolisms for every particular smell. It is feasible, however, to pick out some of the basic and characteristic significances attaching to particular smells and to arrange them in serial order so that they constitute a scale of values equivalent to those of colours, textures, shapes and all phenomena that are characterized by both continuity and discontinuity and that express the graduated differentiations of Oneness.

Persephone   A personification of earth and of spring. The myth tells how the goddess was gathering flowers when the earth opened up and Pluto, the god of the underworld, appeared and carried her off to be his queen in hell. Her mother, Demeter, obtained this concession—that Persephone should spend two-thirds of the year with her (spring to autumn) and only one-third with her ravisher (winter). Folklore in many European countries preserves the archetypes of Persephone and Demeter in the figures of the 'Harvest Maiden' and the 'Mother of the Corn' (21).

Personification   This may be defined as the attribution of human properties to an object, and as the embodying of an idea. The urge to personify objects or ideas is a peculiar characteristic of mythic thought, but it played a particularly important part during the period from the latter days of pre-history up to the rise of Christianity, which was the age of elaboration and crystallization of abstract ideas. Personification results from a synthesis of animism and of the anthropomorphic view of the world. The Ancients personified the great themes of destiny (life, death, good, evil), of the cosmic and elemental entities (heaven, earth, ocean, rivers, springs), man's emotions and impulses (fear, laughter, love and desire), the virtues (fortune, liberty, constancy, victory, fecundity), the collective entities (town or city) and the cultural fields (history and astronomy).

These themes came to constitute allegories once certain symbolic elements and attributes had accrued to them, so giving formal expression to their inherent reality or adapting irrational nature to more intelligible forms in which human conversation—the original form of analytic thought—was feasible. It hardly needs to be said that mythological deities can be explained, in part, as products of personification—apart, that is to say, from the fact that they correspond to the basic truths, to the basic 'series', and to the diversified meaning, of the universe.

Petrifaction   The myth of Deucalion, who made men out of stones, as well as lithophany, find their inversion in legends about petrifaction. This is clearly a question of the antithetical tendencies of evolution and involution. To petrify is to detain or to enclose. The glance of Medusa the Gorgon, so it was said, was sufficient to turn men to stone. There are many folktales and mediaeval legends which tell of similar cases of petrifaction or enchantment. Fairies, sometimes, instead of sending people to sleep—although the symbol is the same—turn them to stone and leave them looking like statues. In *Beauty and the Beast*, the two wicked sisters of the heroine are turned into statues. The words the author puts into the mouth of the good fairy illuminate the symbolic meaning: 'Become two statues, but retain your reason beneath the stone which envelops you. You shall stay by the door of your sister's palace and I shall inflict no other punishment upon you but to require you to witness her happiness. You may not return to your original state until you recognize the error of your ways' (38). Petrifaction, then, is the detention of moral progress—of the evolution of the soul. Sin forces this spiritual evolution from its proper course and, even if it does not plunge into the abyss, at least it arrests ('petrifies') and stagnates it. This is what happens in the case of Lot's wife, and this is the peril which Ulysses resolutely surmounts in his journey back to Ithaca (a symbol of the celestial homeland—of eternity assuming the aspect of temporal existence).

Phallus   A symbol for the perpetuation of life, of active power and of the propagation of cosmic forces (57).

Pheasant   Similar in symbolism to the cock. In China, it was the allegorical animal of light and of day (17).

Phoenix   A mythical bird about the size of an eagle, graced with certain features of the pheasant. Legend has it that when it saw death draw near, it would make a nest of sweet-smelling wood and resins, which it would expose to the full force of the sun's rays, until it burnt itself to ashes in the flames. Another phoenix would then arise from the marrow of its bones (8). Turkish tradition gives it the name of *Kerkés*, and Persian *Simurgh*. In every respect it symbolizes periodic destruction and re-creation (38). Wirth suggests a psychological interpretation of the fabulous bird as a symbol of the 'phoenix' which we all keep within ourselves, enabling us to live out every moment and to overcome each and every partial death which we call a 'dream' (59) or 'change'. In China, the phoenix is the emperor of birds and a sun-symbol (5). In the Christian world, it signifies the triumph of eternal life over death (20). In alchemy, it corresponds to the colour red, to the regeneration of universal life (57) and to the successful completion of a process.

Phonetics We quote the definition of phonetic symbolism as it appears in the *Rituale mitriaco*, bearing the stamp of traditional Egyptian ideas mentioned in the Book of the Dead: 'And the word, which *is* fundamentally an acoustic phenomenon, has greater value as a sound than as an expression of an idea, since the sound contained in it, and emanating from it as certain given vibrations, is the modulation of the cosmic breath; to sound a word, tuning it in, as it were, to the varied rhythms of the cosmos, is tantamount to restoring its elemental power' (11). Hindu tradition often alludes to the meaning, as sound, of letters, syllables and words. So, for example, the sound of each letter of the words *Makara* and *Kumara* is given a precise value as part of the general meaning of the word: the trilled 'r' is onomatopoeic, alluding to thunder as the symbol of creative power (it is for this reason that most verbs in almost all languages contain the letter 'r'), and the syllable '*Ma*' refers to matter, etc. (40). The tradition is that the entire essence of the universe is contained in the syllable '*Om*' (or *Aum*) of the Hindu or Tibetan languages: *A*=the beginning, *U*=transition, *M*=the end, or deep sleep. This mystic belief in the power of phonetics *per se* led the Gnostics and the followers of Mithras to insert passages entirely devoid of any literal sense into parts of their ritual chants, as a kind of symbolic music effective only by virtue of the power of their phonetic significance.

Phrygian Cap In part it is a phallic symbol. The fact that, being an item of headgear, it corresponds in symbolism to the head, ensures that its significance will embrace eroticism in its superior and sublimated—and at times obsessive—form. Hence, the Trojan Paris, being a pure type of Venusian man, who is destined in times of fortune and misfortune always to be at the mercy of Eros, is depicted with a Phrygian cap. Its red colour may also imply a sacrificial significance—either of self-immolation (as in the case of Cybele's priests) or of the immolation of others (as in the case of the French revolutionaries in 1789). In principle, every red bonnet has a similar meaning. The cap worn by the Venetian Doge (*il corno*) is a stylized version of the fisherman's bonnet—for the dignitary and the fisherman are symbolically alike—and, like the Phrygian cap, ends in a point.

Physical Processes Changes or transformations in matter may afford a symbolic significance comparable with the marks used by Rorschach in his tests. It was, in fact, upon the symbolism pertaining to processes of elaboration of 'prime matter' that the alchemists founded their entire practice, since they aspired to pass beyond the stages of combination of mercury with sulphur in order to produce, not the *aurum vulgi*, but the philosophers' gold; all of which is a clear indication of the spiritual nature of alchemy or, in other words, of its affinity with symbolism. As René Alleau has said, 'the material technique was only an apprenticeship, preparing the neophyte for the understanding of truths'. If we were to take works of art and ignore the material result, we would then see the genesis of the artist's work as a long process of self-education and of groping towards the ideals of truth and beauty.

Pictorial Image Every pictorial creation gives rise to an image, either imitated or invented, figurative or non-figurative. In any such image, alongside the symbolic significance attached to the subject or figure, there are also implications arising from the spatial distribution, the colours, the inclusion or absence of geometric shapes, the signs, predominant axes, rhythms, composition and texture. In the most recent, so-called 'informalist' style of art, the expression and symbolization is realized primarily by means of texture and line-rhythm, colour being of secondary significance. In order to grasp the 'meaning' of any particular work, it is first necessary to classify its component elements and to estimate the significance of each class of such components according to their prominence within the pictorial whole. Exactly the same is true of architecture and sculpture.

Pilgrim The concept of man as a pilgrim and of life as a pilgrimage is common to a great many peoples and traditions (4), for it accords with the great myth of the celestial origin of man, of his 'fall' and his hopes of being restored to the celestial realm, since the effect of all this is to make him something of a stranger during his stay on earth and to imprint the mark of the transitory upon his every step. Man leaves and returns to his place of origin—*exitus* and *reditus*. It is precisely this view of life as a pilgrimage that lends the Christian pilgrimage its special value (14). The following are the attributes associated with the symbolism of the pilgrim: the shell, the crook or staff, the well of the water-of-salvation which he finds in his path, the road, the cloak, etc. The idea is cognate with that of the labyrinth: to go on a pilgrimage is to come to understand the nature of the labyrinth, and to move towards the mastery of it as a means to the 'Centre'.

Pillar The solitary pillar is related to the world-axis, as are the post, the mast and the tree. The Egyptian hieroglyphic sign *zed* is interpreted both as a pillar and as the spinal column (there is no symbolic contradiction here) (39). Frobenius says that Africans interpret pillars as caryatids shorn of their human likeness, that is, as indirect images of man (21). When there are two pillars, the symbolism corresponds to that of the cabbalistic columns of Jachin and Boaz.

Pine-tree Like other evergreen trees, the pine is a symbol of immortality. Conifers, by virtue of their shape, also partake of the symbolism corresponds to that of the Cabbalistic columns of Jachin sacred tree, associating it with the cult of Attis. Pine-cones were regarded as symbols of fertility (4, 21).

Zodiacal sign
of Pisces.

Pisces The last sign of the Zodiac, closely bound up with the symbolism of water and of the 'dissolution of forms' which takes place in the Akasha. Neptune whipping up the waves with his trident, and calling forth bulls and horses out of them, is a symbolic expression of the resurgence of cosmic energy from the watery deeps of the primordial ocean. If Capricorn marks the beginning of the process of dissolution, Pisces denotes the final moment which, for this very reason, contains within itself the beginning of the new cycle. Related to Pisces are the avatar in the form of the fish of Vishnu in India, and the Chaldean myth of Oannes the man-fish. This twelfth house of the Zodiac, when transposed, by analogy, to the existential and psychic plane, denotes defeat and failure, exile or seclusion, and also mysticism and the denial of the self and its passions (40). The dual aspect of this symbol is well expressed by the zodiacal sign itself, composed of two fishes arranged parallel to one another but facing in different directions: the left-hand fish indicates the direction of involution or the beginning of a new cycle in the world of manifestation, while the fish that faces the right points to the direction of evolution—the way out of the cycle (52).

Plait Like bunches of ribbons, rosettes, ties and knots, the plait is symbolic of intimate relationship, intermingling streams and interdependence (19).

Planetary Gods They are personifications of idealized qualities of Man: 'modes' of existence and the range of the essential possibilities in behaviour and knowledge. Since these gods are endowed with enviable powers and disport themselves upon a delectable

field of action, they have come to symbolize the triumph of the
particular principle pertaining to each one of them; hence they
frequently appear in mythology in association with ideas of justice
and the underlying laws governing life (15). Through the process of
catasterism, the major gods were projected into the heavens and
identified with the sun, the moon and the five nearest planets. This
can be clearly seen in the beginnings of astrobiological thought (7)
in Mesopotamia. For the Chaldeans, the astral bodies were living
but divine beings, an idea which persists in clear though fragmentary form in Aristotle and throughout the Middle Ages in the
Western world, as Seznec has shown (53). The respective names of
the gods among the Chaldeans, the Greeks and the Romans were
these: *Shamash*, the Sun, Helios, Apollo; *Sin*, the Moon, Artemis,
Diana; *Marduk*, Zeus, Jupiter; *Ishtar*, Aphrodite, Venus; *Nabu*,
Hermes, Mercury; *Nergal*, Ares, Mars; *Ninib*, Cronos, Saturn. By
virtue of the theory of correspondences, the relationships stemming
from these gods embrace the whole—or almost the whole—of
the pattern of the universe.

Planets The planets constitute a particular order within the
cosmos. It is the business of the science of astronomy to study them
from a naturalistic and mathematical point of view, upon the basis
of the system which Copernicus established with his *De Revolutionibus
Orbium Coelestium* of 1543, according to which the sun is the centre
around which are set the orbits of the planets: Mercury, the nearest,
followed by Venus, Earth, Mars, the Asteroids, Jupiter, Saturn,
Uranus, Neptune (and Pluto). But astrology and traditional symbolism owe their inspiration not to the Copernican system but to that
which had been accepted by the Ancients. Since the validity of the
symbolism here depends exclusively upon a process of catasterism
(that is, the projection of a given mental order into the celestial
order, or the interpretation of a 'series' capable of explaining
phenomena in the psychological and spiritual world) it is unnecessary
for us to examine the complex question of how far the Ptolemaic
system (in part confirmed by the Theory of Relativity) can be
reconciled with the Copernican. At the same time, the fact of there
being seven planets responds to the idea of the seven planetary
heavens, which in turn tallies with that of the seven Directions or
areas in space (which in turn, when transposed into terms of time,
becomes the origin of the seven days of the week). The relationship
of the planets to the seven points in space is as follows: Sun—the
zenith, Moon—the nadir, Mercury—the centre, Venus—the West,
Mars—the South, Jupiter—the East, and Saturn—the North (54).
The order in which astrology places the planets—counting the Sun
and the Moon also as planets—is as follows, taking the Earth as the
centre and then proceeding from the nearest to the farthest: Moon,

Mercury, Venus, the Sun, Mars, Jupiter, Saturn (Uranus and Neptune, although these two are not generally counted). The sex of these entities is clearly established so far as Venus, Mars, Jupiter and Saturn are concerned. Mercury appears as both masculine and androgynous. The Sun and the Moon have interchanged their sex through the ages, according to the culture of the period. The mystic basis of the planetary myth is to be sought in the generalization of Varro to the effect that the planets are celestial bodies and, at the same time, generators of life (7). Each of these generating powers has a characteristic sphere of action, which is its 'heaven', and the influence of this 'heaven' spreads out through the interpenetrating zones of space. Planetary symbolism reaches its highest degree of complexity in its relationship to the Zodiac; whereas the Zodiac symbolizes the grades and phases of a given cycle of creation, the planetary 'series' expresses rather the pattern of the moral world. The theory of 'correspondences', applied to the planets, educes a complex system wherein each planet is seen as a particular 'mode' endowed with a specific characteristic, and related to one particular Sense, or a metal, a perfume, or a plant, for example. It is more important, however, to grasp the connexion of each planet with a given virtue or tendency: thus, the Sun is related to the will and to activity, the Moon to imagination and the world of forms, Mars to action and destruction, Mercury to intuition and movement, Jupiter to good judgement and direction, Venus to love and relationships, Saturn to endurance and reserve. However, the fundamental tendencies of these qualities are sometimes negative and sometimes positive. Ely Star suggests the following arrangement, in accordance with the principles of evolution and spiritualization: Sun—potential good, Moon—potential evil, Mercury—duality and, consequently, free will, Venus—objective good, Mars—objective evil, Jupiter—subjective good, Saturn—subjective evil. The planets are thus divided into two zones, one luminous and the other dark, both of them necessary to the cycle of existence; these zones correspond to the clear and dark sections respectively of the Chinese symbol of universal flux—the *Yang-Yin* (54). Mertens-Stienon has studied the planetary powers in their theogonic aspect, proceeding from the outside inward, so that the most distant becomes the oldest and the most 'primitive' of the gods: Uranus engenders Saturn (celestial space creates time), and the reign of Saturn is succeeded by the constructive order of Jupiter; next comes the offspring of Jupiter—Mars (the active principle), Venus (the passive) and Mercury (the neutral) (40). From the symbolic point of view, this evolutive series draws the inquirer inwards, concentrating itself within the human spirit, since the spirit is the microcosm which reflects the macrocosmic universe. The importance of the planetary archetypes is apparent in the persistent influence of Graeco-Roman mythology, for it was the classic myths that most clearly and forcibly expressed their inner meaning; as Jean Seznec (53) has shown, these myths continued in popularity throughout the Christian culture of the Middle Ages and the Renaissance unopposed by the Church, since it perceived their symbolic and psychological truth. Waldemar Fenn maintains that there are certain prehistoric engravings which contain groups of four and of three component elements and that these drawings correspond to planetary configurations. The popular art of the Nordic races, of course, keeps to this division of the spheres—essential from the psychological viewpoint—into two groups: an inner group of three factors and an outer one of four. Given the equation of the planets with the seven Directions of Space (as we have previously outlined), then the inner group (disposed along the vertical axis) would comprise the series of Sun-Mercury-Moon, while the outer, equivalent to the cardinal points, relates to Venus-Mars-Jupiter-Saturn. This suggests that, as components of the human spirit, the three central ingredients have more importance and greater influence than the outer four, since the latter concern the square and the symbolism of situation and limitation (as with the tetramorphs), whereas the former constitute the very psychic dynamism of the ternary order, comprehending the active, the passive and the neuter.

Plants   An image of life, expressive of the manifestation of the cosmos and of the birth of forms. Aquatic plants, in particular, are symbolic of the 'nascent' character of life. In India, cosmic images are depicted as emerging from the lotus flower (17). At the same time, man, conscious that biologically he was related to the animals, could not but be aware that his upright posture was more closely related to that of the tree, the shrub and the very grass, than to the horizontal posture of all animals (other than the celestial birds). Thus, whereas totemism drew up relationships between man and certain animals, the astrobiological era was characterized by frequent connexions and equations between mythic beings and plants. In particular, lives which had come to a violent end were supposed to carry on a metamorphosed existence in vegetable form. Osiris, Attis, Adonis, to name only a few deities, are closely related to plants. Another aspect of plant-symbolism is the annual cycle, in consequence of which they sometimes symbolize the mystery of death and resurrection (17). The fertility of the fields affords the most powerful image of cosmic, material and spiritual fecundity.

Playing-cards   The entire pack of playing-cards is symbolic in origin. It finds its fullest expression in the twenty-two major enigmas of the Tarot pack (each card representing an integral allegory which is, up to a certain point, complete in itself), followed by the fifty-six lesser enigmas. The latter comprise fourteen figures in each of the four suits: gold—equivalent to diamonds (made up of circles, disks and wheels), clubs (truncheons and sceptres), spades (swords) and cups—equivalent to hearts. The gold symbolizes the material forces; the club or staff the power of command; the cup or chalice varies somewhat in significance but generally concerns the receptacle as such: the chalice or the chest, for instance; the sword is an emblem, in this particular instance, of discrimination between error and justice. The number inscribed on each card implies the symbolism pertaining to that particular number, *see* TAROT.

Pleiades The constellation of the Pleiades comprises the central group in sidereal symbolism. Both Hebrew and Hindu traditions see in these stars the image of the septenary as applied to space, to sound and to action (40).

Plough Symbol of fertilization. In an Aryan legend, Rama, the hero, marries Sita (the furrow). Because the earth is female in nature, ploughing is a symbol of the union of the male and the female principle. The former Chinese custom of ceremonial plough-ing by the emperor at the beginning of his reign is connected with this symbolism (33).

Point The point signifies unity, the Origin and the Centre. It also represents the principles of manifestation and emanation, and hence in some mandalas the centre is not actually shown but must be imagined by the initiate. There are two kinds of point to be considered: that which has no magnitude and is symbolic of creative virtue, and that which—as suggested by Raymond Lull in his *Nova Geometria*—has the smallest conceivable or practicable magnitude and is a symbol of the principle of manifestation. Moses of Leon defined the nature of the original Point as follows: 'This degree is the sum total of all subsequent mirrors, that is, of all external aspects related to this one degree. They proceed therefrom because of the mystery of the point, which is in itself an occult degree emanating from the mystery of the pure and awe-inspiring ether. The first degree of all is absolutely occult, that is, not manifest, and cannot be attained' (25). This explains why the Centre—identical with the mystic point of Moses of Leon—is usually represented as a hole.

Pole The mystic 'Centre', or the 'unvarying mean', is the fixed point which all symbolic traditions concur in designating as the 'pole', since the rotation of the earth takes place around it (28). On the other hand, the pole is also identified with the zenith. In ancient China, it was represented by the hole in the centre of the jade disk known as *Pi* (7). The 'unvarying mean' is, nevertheless, the cause of all change. The Chinese *Book of Changes* shows that the continuous metamorphoses of matter are generated by the great pole—a Oneness located far beyond all duality, beyond all occurence, and equated with the 'unmoved mover' of Aristotle (58). This contradiction between the immobile and the cause of all movement was expressed metaphorically by the alchemists in the saying: 'At the pole lies the heart of Mercury, which is true fire' (32).

Pomegranate The Greeks believed that the pomegranate sprang from the blood of Dionysos. There are similar beliefs linking anemones with Adonis and violets with Attis (21). But the predominating significance of the pomegranate, arising from its shape and internal structure rather than from its colour, is the reconciliation of the multiple and diverse within apparent unity. Hence, in the Bible, for example, it appears as a symbol of the Oneness of the universe (37). It is also symbolic of fecundity.

Poplar In addition to the general symbolism attached to trees, wood and vegetable life, the poplar has a special allegorical significance connected with the fact that the two sides of the poplar leaf are of a different shade of green. Thus, it becomes the tree of life, bright green on the side of water (moon) and a darker green on the side of fire (sun) (50). The poplar also has a place within the general range of bipolar symbols (positive-negative) (32).

Potion Generally a love-potion, frequently mentioned in Roman antiquity, where it is said, for example, that the poet Lucretius' madness was caused by a potion. It appears with still greater frequency in mediaeval legends and is related to the Celtic *geis*, according to Jean Marx (*Nouvelles Recherches sur la littérature Arthurienne*). A potion symbolizes love's ill-fortune. Whoever drinks it can no longer observe the feudal laws, nor the duties incumbent on his position, and can even be driven to death by this plight, as exemplified by Tristan.

Potne Theron This is the name given by the Greeks to compositions depicting the figure of a man between two animals; they were much used in ancient and mediaeval art (for example, the harp of Ur in Mesopotamia; the capital at Estany; Cappadocian seals, or Sumerian ivories). Sometimes this feature attached itself to legendary or historic figures: Gilgamesh in Mesopotamia, or Daniel and the lions in the Christian, Biblical tradition. But, for the Greeks, this composition was a symbol of the union of man with nature, or of the equilibrium of forces necessary to bring this union about. Now, in the view of Shekotov, the Russian art critic, 'the symmetrical disposition of figures around a single centre denotes, both in an artistic context and in religious or profane ceremonies, the idea of triumph'.

Power The symbolism of power has been subjected to an extensive study by Percy Ernst Schramm in his *Herrschaftszeichen und Staatssymbolik* (Stuttgart, 1954). Power, as a symbol, represents irradiating force, but it is only latterly that it has acquired this significance, for in totemistic and primitive times it was generally understood more in the sense of an image of the forces of nature (and of the animal world in particular) than as an expression of abstract or temporal dominion. Hence, the principal attributes of a superior power are simply magnified versions of totemic emblems or of adornments derived from them, such as necklaces of teeth and claws, hides, head-dresses, horns, and various kinds of standards exhibiting these objects. It was probably with the dawning of the solar cult that the diadem—the original form of the crown—came to be adopted as another attribute of power. The immediate effect of the assumption of power upon the body and the attitude of mind is to confer impassivity, indifference—either real or affected—and serenity and, equally, a tendency to 'swell with pride'. Hence the fascination of the hieratic gesture and its use on solemn occasions. Dynamic movements such as stretching out the arms or nodding or turning the head may also be executed in a rhythm suggestive of hieratic strength and calm. Ancient art gave expression to a basically similar attitude towards the powers of the world. Height above ground-level, and the situation of a particular symbolic element at the centre of a symmetrical pattern—the Greek *Potne Theron* for instance—are further illustrations of power-symbolism, deriving from the symbolisms of level and of the 'Centre'. Differentiated expressions of power give rise to the king, the priest and the military leader, each one characterized by his respective attributes. The synthesis of power is denoted by ternary symbols such as the triple crown. Certain other symbols embracing the threefold power, such as the trident, are generally reckoned to pertain to the infernal regions, but this has come about rather through the influence of traditional, mythological ideas than by true symbolic logic. Magic power—a corrupt form of religious power—is symbolized by the wand and sometimes by the sword. There are also certain other objects linked with the idea of power, but they are attributes or instruments rather than symbols proper.

Of great interest is the complex symbolic system behind the emblems of the Egyptian pharaoh. The double crown denotes Upper and Lower Egypt, but it also expresses the ideas of the masculine and feminine principles, and of heaven and earth. Sceptres —straight (the lash) and curved (the crook)—are probably attributes of cattle-raising and of agriculture respectively; yet at the same time they denote the straight path (or the solar, diurnal, logical course) and the crooked path (the lunar, nocturnal and intuitive). The Uraeus beyond doubt symbolizes the sublimated serpent—raised, that is to say, in height (the *kundalini*), so as to become a symbol of strength transformed into spirit or an aspect of power. In itself, the idea of power embraces the notions of extreme self-awareness and integrity, defensive concentration of forces, appropriation and domination of the environment, and effulgence. Hence, to take these ideas in turn, the symbols of power are names, seals, marks, standards and signs; masks, helmets, head-dresses, swords and shields; sceptres, crowns, *pallia* and palaces; and effulgence is expressed by gold and precious stones. Domination also finds expression in such forms of the quaternary as four-headed sceptres, *hermae* or thrones alluding to the cardinal points. The crown, in its most highly developed form, embraces the diadem or circle and the hemisphere or image of the vault of heavens; and sometimes it denotes the four points of the compass—or suggests them by means of four bands which rise up from the diadem to meet higher up, in the middle, surmounted by another symbolic motif. The idea of royalty is, of course, linked with sun-symbolism, and therefore the animals associated with it are such as the eagle and the lion, and on occasion the dragon. Once Christianity had become the official religion of the Roman Empire, various Christian symbols of sublimation accrue to the symbolism of power, notably the crucifix and the fleur-de-lis. The latter symbol is found in Byzantium, whence it reached Central Europe, Germany, France and the Western world by the 1st millennium A.D.

Precinct All images to do with the precinct—an enclosure, a walled garden, a city, a square, a castle, a *patio*—correspond to the idea of the *temenos*, or a sacred and circumscribed space which is guarded and defended because it constitutes a spiritual entity. Such images as this may also symbolize the life of the individual and in particular the inner life of his thoughts (32). It will be recognized that a square or a circle is the tactical formation commonly adopted as a means of defence in a critical situation against a more powerful adversary. This in itself would suffice to explain the meaning of the mandala, or any one of the innumerable symbols that are based upon the notion of the precinct or the protection of a given space, identified with the self. Circular dances, such as the maypole dance, or the *sardana* of Catalonia; or the prehistoric stone-circles (sometimes known as cromlechs); or emblems featuring fences or people formed in a circle—all carry this same symbolic meaning, this same notion of self-protection, as Adama van Scheltema has noted in *Documents* VII (Paris, 1930) in connexion with the *Centre féminin sacré*.

Prester John The realm of the fabulous Prester John, like certain other mythic 'lands', is, in fact, a symbol of the supreme, spiritual 'centre' (28).

Prime Matter This represents the basic stage out of which grew the alchemic process with its quest for the transmutation of gold, that is, for perfect and definitive sublimation, or the consolidation of the spirit itself. The alchemists gave a host of names to this unidentified prime matter: quicksilver, lead, salt, sulphur, water, air, fire, earth, blood, *lapis*, poison, spirit, sky, dew, shade, mother, sea, moon, dragon, chaos, microcosm, etc. The *Rosarium* terms it 'root of itself', and elsewhere it is named 'earth of paradise'. This explains why prime matter was thought to come from the mountain where distinctions are still unknown and where all things are one, neither distinguished nor distinguishable (32). It is also regarded as associated with the unconscious.

Prince The prince, or the son of the king, is a rejuvenated form of the paternal king, as the nascent sun is a rejuvenation of the dying sun. The prince often figures as the hero in legends; his great virtue is intuition and it is by no means rare for him to possess the powers of a demiurge (32).

Procession This word, expressive of the idea of marching, finds its truest expression in the liturgical procession. Davy points out that it takes its meaning from the idea of a pilgrimage and indicates the need for constant progress unfettered by earthly things, although making progressive use of them. The idea of the procession is also reminiscent of the Exodus of Israel and of the desert-crossing (14). As Schneider has noted, the movements of claustral processions imply a symbolism related to space-time: the hymns which are sung last the length of the procession; the return to the cloister is equivalent to the passage of a year by virtue of the correspondence of the four sides with the cardinal points and the seasons. But, speaking more generally, every procession is a rite which gives substance to the concept of the cycle and passage of time, as is proved by the fact of its returning to the point of departure. Various symbolic and allegorical figures are attached to it: the Chinese dragons, for instance, or the Roman eagles (since a military march-past is a form of procession). Christianity has incorporated some early aspects of the symbol into its rites; for example, there is a book upon St. Macarius that contains some allegorical chariots with all the principal symbolic animals drawing them, from the bear and the rhinoceros to the unicorn and the phoenix. Those festivals which have incorporated elements of folklore have likewise assimilated the symbolic implications of folk art. From prehistoric times, giants, carnival grotesques, dwarfs, dragons, vipers, lions, oxen, have all figured in processions. The famous *tarasque*[1] of Tarascon, has been seen as the Great Whore of Babylon. The eagle may correspond to St. John; the viper and the dragon allude to the legend of St. George. According to esoteric thought, giants,

---

[1] The figure of a huge serpent or dragon carried in Corpus Christi processions.—*Translator*

dwarfs, salamanders and nymphs are elemental spirits pertaining respectively to air, earth, fire and water. To carry them in procession is to display man's dominion over them, for although they are borne in triumph, they are really exhibited as captives; and it was in this sense that the Romans incorporated them into their grand march-past at the end of a campaign.

Professions   Schneider has noted the sober and artisan character of mystic thought, with its belief that an individual's profession or calling is what basically determines his mythic and cosmic situation. This is not to invalidate common-sense ways of thinking, but to substantiate them by rooting them firmly in the plane of transcendence. Were we to envisage an ideal landscape with a valley, a mountain with its corresponding cave, and the sea, we would find that the sea is the haunt of seamen and fishermen, the valley corresponds to labourers and gardeners, the mountain-side to shepherds, the cave to blacksmiths and perhaps also to potters, and the mountain-peak to the ascetic and the lofty-minded sages. Schneider suggests that, by analogy, the mountain is also the dwelling-place of warriors, miners, doctors and martyrs (50, 51). In order to determine the appropriate grade of each profession it is necessary only to apply the laws of the symbolism of level. If the symbolic significance of any profession lies in the translation of its practical aspects to the realm of the spiritual or the psychological, the sailor's calling symbolizes the coming to grips with the unconscious and with the passions, or the struggle at the level of the chaotic. The fisherman draws symbolic tokens out of the deeps. The farmer is in close contact with fecund nature and contributes with his labours to the fertility of the soil. The gardener fulfils the same function on a higher spiritual and intellectual plane, for the garden is a symbol of the soul, and he works upon his garden in order to improve it. Blacksmiths and potters are creators of forms, masters of matter. The miners' work is analogous to that of fishermen, since they extract what is valuable from one of the Elements. The ascetic and the sage direct the pattern of life, virtually without action. Doctors purify existence and combat what is harmful. The martyr suffers and triumphs over life by his sacrifice. Other callings related to the demiurge are those of the weaver and the spinner (who spin and sever the threads of existence). There were certain professions which, about the 4th millennium before our era, characterized the period of the profoundest development in man. As Berthelot has observed, the devising of the calendar, the development of metallurgy and the production of the first of the alloys (bronze), seem to have been the causes of the change from primitive to civilized cultures (in Mesopotamia and Egypt in the first place). Berthelot has also drawn an interesting parallel between the development of certain cults and the corresponding growth of the professions which determined and demanded them as the level of civilization rose. The hunters, fishermen and weavers of the Palaeolithic Age limited their cults to the animals which provided them with their subsistence; the shepherd and seafarer of Neolithic and early historical times based their cults upon the moon and the stars, which were their means of orientation; the blacksmith, metallurgist and early chemist, with whom the era of recorded history opens, exalted fire in their cults, since it played a decisive part in their work. And finally, the agricultural worker, or the prevalence of his conception of the world, ensured the predominance of the solar cult, since the sun is the creator of the cycle of the year and of the seasons. In the above observations, then, we have attempted to show how men's callings are graduated from the most primitive to the most recent, with their corresponding symbolism (7). The caste-system may also be related to this.

Prometheus The Prometheus myth, according to Piobb, is an illustration of sublimation—by virtue of the family resemblance between the vulture and the eagle—which confirms the alchemic relationship between the volatile and the fixed principles. At the same time, suffering (like that of Prometheus) corresponds to sublimation because of its association with the colour red—the third colour in the alchemic *Magnum Opus*, coming after black and white. The rescue of Prometheus by Hercules expresses the efficacy of the process of sublimation, and its outcome (48).

Promised Land, The The Promised Land—the Holy Land— was, for the alchemists, with their concept of the three worlds as 'states' and of landscapes as 'expressions', the 'final stage of an experiment'. Where, within the order of time, peace and perfection is the goal, within the order of space it becomes the Promised Land, whether it is Canaan for the Jews wandering in the desert, or Ithaca for Ulysses sailing the seas (57). The Israelites identified their spiritual 'Centre' with Mount Sion, known to them as the 'heart of the world'. Dante described Jerusalem as the 'pole of the spirit' (28).

Pumpkin or **Gourd, Double** A Chinese emblem of Li T'ieh-kuai, the second of the Eight Immortals. Like the hour-glass, twin drums, St. Andrew's cross or the letter X, it is a symbol of the link between the two worlds—the upper and the lower—and of the principle of inversion regulating the ordered pattern of events of cosmic phenomena, that is, night and day, life and death, infamy and sublimity, sorrow and joy. Li T'ieh-kuai was, in effect, a mythic figure whose essential characteristic was his ability to leave his body and visit heaven. He was also symbolized by a column of smoke (5). But this symbol of the twin pumpkin is very far from being limited to the Far East; it was also common in the West. Among other representations, the frontispiece of Book II of Maier's work on alchemy, *Symbola*

Aureae Mensae (1617) shows us the twin pumpkin in the form of two amphorae, with the top one up-ended. The surprising thing is that this image also incorporates the above-mentioned symbol of the column of smoke joining the interior of the lower amphora with the upper; in this case there is not just a single column, but a ring of smoke circulating between the mouths of the two amphorae.

Pun Schneider (50) has summed up one of the most profound of all symbolic questions with his remark that 'to create a poetic pun is to jump over or annihilate the distance between two logical or spatial elements—to place under one yoke two elements which are naturally discrete'. This is the explanation too of the mystic sense of modern poetry derived from Rimbaud and Reverdy. In the words of the latter: 'The image is a pure creation of the spirit. It is born not of a comparison, but of the reconciliation of two more or less distinct realities. The more distant and apt the two realities so reconciled, the stronger will be the image, and the greater emotive force and poetic reality will it possess'—symbolic reality, we would rather say. In consequence, what is equivocal tends towards the orgiastic disruption of the 'given order' to make way for the 'new order'. Hence the fact that 'the art of equivocal phrases' always expresses, in a cultural sense, the need to invert one style in order to attain the opposite (as, for instance, from the Gothic to the Renaissance, or from 19th-century realism to the formalist style of the 20th century).

Putrefaction The alchemic symbolism of *putrefactio*, with its graphic representation as black crows, skeletons, skulls and other funereal signs, embraces the concept of life renewed—like the zodiacal sign of Pisces. Hence it has been said that it signifies 'rebirth of matter after death and the disintegration of the residue' (57). From the psychological point of view, putrefaction is the destruction of the intellectual impediments in the way of the evolution of the spirit. Certain rites and folkloristic customs seem to be derived from the alchemic concept; at least, they appear in a similar symbolism. Thus in Corella (Navarre), the Good Friday procession is headed by a skeleton which, in ancient times, had bunches of grapes hanging from its back. This conveys the idea of the new life, which arises from *putrefactio*, and which was in reality already present in the Orphic mysteries and in all beliefs in the value of sacrifice as the generator of new forces.

Pyramid There is an apparent contradiction in the symbolism of the pyramid. In the first place, in megalithic culture and in European folklores which have preserved its memory, it is symbolic of the earth in its maternal aspect. Pyramids with Christmas decorations and lights, moreover, express the twofold idea of death and immortality, both associated with the Great Mother. But this concerns the pyramid only in so far as it is a hollow mountain, the dwelling of ancestors and an earth-monument. The pyramid of stone, of regular geometrical shape, corresponds to fire, at any rate in the Far East (4). Marc Saunier has suggested the right approach to a more precise understanding of the problem. He regards the pyramid as a synthesis of different forms, each with its own significance. The base is square and represents the earth. The apex is the starting-point and the finishing-point of all things —the mystic 'Centre' (Nicholas of Cusa, in his disquisitions, concurs with this interpretation). Joining the apex to the base are the triangular-shaped faces of the pyramid, symbolizing fire, divine revelation and the threefold principle of creation. In consequence, the pyramid is seen as a symbol expressing the whole of tne work of creation in its three essential aspects (49).

Quadriga A variant of the square (q.v.). It carries the inherent symbolism of the quaternary, here implied in the four horses drawing the chariot. With this in mind, Dio Chrysostom worked out the following analogies: the charioteer corresponds to the Pantokrator and the chariot to the halo (indicating two different levels of the manifest world through the intersection of the circles of heaven and earth); and the four horses relate to the four Elements and the tetramorphs. The symbolic relationship of the horses with the Elements is the key to the following passage: 'The first horse is very fleet. His coat is shining and bears the signs of the planets and the constellations. The second horse is slower and is lit up on only one side. The third goes slower still and the fourth twists round and round. But there comes a time when the hot breath of the first sets fire to the mane of the second, and the third drowns the fourth with his sweat.' The four horses correspond to fire, air, water and earth respectively, beginning with the most energetic of the Elements and ending with the most material or *lento*. The quadriga, then, becomes a symbol of the universe of space-time (31).

Quaternary The quaternary bears the same relationship to the number-series as does the tetramorph on the mystic plane; if they are not identical they are certainly related or analogous. It is based, of course, upon the number four. In the words of Plato: 'The ternary is the number pertaining to the idea; the quaternary is the number connected with the realization of the idea.' Hence within the septuple pattern of space, the ternary is situated on the vertical line because it is associated with the vertical division into three worlds on three levels, whereas the quaternary is located on the surface, that is, on the intermediate of the three planes, or, in other words, it is situated in the world of phenomena. The quaternary, then, corresponds to earth, to the material pattern of life; and the number three to moral and spiritual dynamism. The human anatomy confirms this concept of the number four. The spatial or surface-symbolism of the number four is described by the Renaissance writer, Cartari, in *Les Images des dieux des anciens*: 'The square figures representing Mercury, possessing only a head and a phallus, signified that the sun is the lord of the world, the sower of all things; furthermore, the four sides of the square represented what the four-stringed sistrum portrayed as an attribute of Mercury, that is, the four regions of the world, or, in other words, the four seasons. . . .' (32). There is a clear connexion between these 'herms' and the Indian figures of Brahma with four faces (60), corresponding to the four Kumaras (who were four angels in Persian tradition), related to the four so-called 'royal' stars (Aldebaran, Antares, Regulus and Fomalhaut) and represented by the four fixed signs of the Zodiac, in turn related to the tetramorphs. Another obvious connexion is the symbol of the four rivers of paradise which rise at the foot of the Tree of Life (or the world-axis) (40). This fourfold orientation conforms with the cardinal points which, according to the Zohar, correspond to the four Elements (9) and to all quaternary forms. The most interesting of these correspondences are these: East corresponding to spring, air, infancy, dawn and the crescent moon; South, to summer, fire, youth, midday and full moon; West, to autumn, water, middle-age, evening and the waning moon; North, to winter, earth, old age, night and the new moon. As is the case with symbols based upon seven (the week or the planets, for example) or upon twelve (the year or the Zodiac), analogies with the symbolism for four may extend to cover every possible process in life (55). The Elements correspond to the so-called elemental beings as follows: Air—sylphs and giants; fire—salamanders; water—undines and mermaids; earth—gnomes and dwarfs. Gaston Bachelard considers that the four temperaments are related to the Elements (1), in which case the pattern of correspondences might be seen as follows: Air linked with the sanguinary; fire with the nervous; water with the lymphatic; earth with the bilious (55). Bachelard, in his psychoanalytic work upon the significance of the Elements, studies the significant way in which dynamic images are related with a particular Element, such as the image of fire in Hoffmann, water in Edgar Allan Poe, air in Nietzsche. To return to the question of the cardinal points, there is not complete accord about which of them—West or North—is the most negative, but there is complete agreement that the East is the luminous source of the spirit (14, 31, 48). In China, the Emperor once used to perform a strange rite whereby he identified himself with the annual course of the sun, embracing also the points of the compass. This he did by living in one quarter of his square-shaped palace at a time, depending upon the season and the compass-point corresponding to that season (in accordance with the pattern we have just mentioned) (7). The mystic animals corresponding to the cardinal points are: East, blue dragon; South, red bird; West, white tiger; North, black tortoise (6). But in the Western world, according to Schneider, these animals become: East (or the morning)—lion; South (or midday)—eagle; West (or the evening)—peacock; North (or the night)—ox (50). The importance of the number four is borne out statistically: the square is the shape most frequently used by man, or, where necessary, the rectangle. According to a Hindu belief—comparable with the Platonic—completeness has four angles and is supported on four feet (60). Jung has shown profound interest in the symbolism of the quaternary, and upon its basis he has built up the pattern of the human psyche as one endowed with four functions: sensing, intuiting, feeling and thinking. These four functions he relates to the four ends of a cross, postulating that the three placed respectively at the left, the right and the top are conscious, while the fourth is unconscious (or repressed). But the placing of the functions varies according to the individual personality (34). These four functions cluster around the essential component of volition or judgement, just as the tetramorphs are ranged around the Pantokrator. Jung adds that the principal components—the archetypes—of the human being are disposed similarly in quaternary order; they are: the anima, shadow, ego and personality forming around the *Selbst* or 'the God within' (32). The phases of the alchemic process may also be placed in quaternary order, from lowest to highest: black, white, red, gold. Diel's 'life-urges' may be similarly ordered, for although Diel mentions only three (conservation, reproduction and spiritualization or evolution) this is because the hidden function, in this case, is thanatism.

Quinary This is a group of five elements. It is represented formally by the pentagon and the five-pointed star, and also by the square together with its central point. Traditionally, the number five symbolizes man after the fall, but, once applied to this order of earthly things, it signifies health and love (44). Esoteric thinking sees this, not as the effect but, in fact, as the cause of man's five extremities with the number five inscribed also on each hand and foot (54). This association of the number five with the human figure, common during the Romanesque period, is found all over the world, from England to the Far East. Agrippa of

Nettesheim depicted the image of man with arms and legs apart and
related to the pentagram. Many amulets and talismans are based
upon the number five, not only because of the associated ideas of the
human figure, health (or physical integrity) and love, but because
the quinary is symbolic of the whole of the material world (denoted
by the quaternary) plus the centre or quintessence. In Morocco, for
example, to protect oneself against the evil eye one repeats the
phrase *hamsa fi ainek* ('five in your eye'). Certain Islamic rites and
concepts were patterned after the quinary: there are five religious
duties, five keys to secret knowledge, five daily prayers and a solemn
oath is repeated five times (12). For the Chinese, five is the most
important of all the numbers. The quinary, in sum, represents the
natural rhythm of life, the order of the cosmos. The following
groups (among others) are based upon the quinary 'model': the
five planets (Mercury, Venus, Mars, Jupiter, Saturn); the five
elemental forms (metal, vegetable, water, fire, earth); the five
colours (white, black, blue, red, yellow); the five musical timbres (of
bronze, stone, silk, wood and clay); the five essential landscapes (of
mountains and woods, rivers and lakes, hills, fertile plains, springs
and swamps) (13). In the Near East and in the West the number five
has been used solely as an expression of the human figure as a whole,
and of eroticism; here the predominant model-numbers have been
four and seven, and it is according to these numbers that the cosmic
components of the universe and of man have been ordered.

Radiance Bachelard (3) has suggested that there is an interesting
connexion between radiance, the human glance and starlight. In
itself, a brightness or radiance is always felt to be supernatural, like
a message standing out clearly against a negative or neutral background. Brightness is, of course, related to fire and to daylight both
in their positive and in their destructive aspects.

Rags and Tatters They are symbolic of wounds and gashes in
the soul. More precise meanings are derived from the actual garment
which is in tatters.

Rahab This priestess symbolizes primordial chaos mastered by
God in the beginning of time, comparable with Tiamat vanquished
by Marduk in Chaldean tradition (7). She represents the essential
idea of all cosmogonies.

Rain Rain has a primary and obvious symbolism as a fertilizing
agent, and is related to the general symbolism of life (26) and water.

Apart from this, but for the same reason, it signifies purification, not only because of the value of water as the 'universal substance'—as the mediating agent between the non-formal or gaseous and the formal or solid, an aspect which is common to all symbolic traditions (29) —but also because of the fact that rainwater falls from heaven (7). Hence it is also cognate with light. This explains why, in many mythologies, rain is regarded as a symbol of the 'spiritual influences' of heaven descending upon earth (28). In alchemy, rain symbolizes condensation or albification—further proof that, for the alchemists, water and light were of the same symbolic family.

Rats   The rat occurs in association with infirmity and death. It was an evil-doing deity of the plague in Egypt and China (35). The mouse, in mediaeval symbolism, is associated with the devil (20). A phallic implication has been superimposed upon it, but only in so far as it is dangerous or repugnant.

Rectangle   Of all geometric forms, the most rational, the most secure and regular; this is explained empirically by the fact that, at all times and in all places, it has been the shape favoured by man when preparing any space or object for immediate use in life: house, room, table, bed, for example. The square implies tense domination born of an abstract longing for power, whereas the circle avoids all earthly associations by virtue of its celestial symbolism. Less regular shapes than the rectangle, such as the trapezium or the trapezoid, are abnormal or dolorous forms, expressive of suffering and inner irregularity (42).

Red Sea   In alchemic symbolism 'crossing the Red Sea' is symbolic of the most dangerous part of an undertaking or of a stage in a man's life. To leave Egypt for the Promised Land implies the act of crossing this sea bloodied with wounds and sacrifice; hence the crossing is a symbol of spiritual evolution (57) and also of death seen as the threshold between the worlds of matter and of the spirit. The man who sacrifices himself, in a sense dies.

Reefs   Reefs and shoals were, in antiquity, the object of religious awe and were personified as giants and aquatic monsters (8). Sandbanks and even islands were looked upon in the same way. Here we can see the great myth of regression or petrifaction (that is, stagnation of the spiritual flow of evolution) which the ancient mind considered the worst of all crimes. Hence, in the *Odyssey*, reefs, islands, complete with their enchantress (Calypso or Circe), and quicksands, are all symbols of every kind of enchantment and obstruction of destiny.

Regard or **Glance**   To regard some object, or simply to see it, is traditionally identified with acquaintance or awareness (and also with the possession of knowledge or simply with possession) (26). On the other hand, the glance is symbolically comparable with the teeth in representing the defensive barrier put up by the individual against the world round him—the towers and the city wall, respectively, of the 'city within'.

Reins Reins enter into the symbolism of the chariot and of horses. Since the chariot is symbolic of the body and horses signify the forces of life, the reins bespeak the relationship between the soul and the body—the nerves and willpower. To cut the reins is equivalent, symbolically, to dying (38).

Relief The depth of a relief, in general corresponding to the vividness of the forms depicted rather than to their intensity, is connected with the ideas of truth and material reality. A relief which is lacking in force symbolizes futility, falsity, equivocation and utter lack of persuasive power or of attractive 'values' of any kind. An intensely expressive relief, on the other hand, denotes the powerful surge of an emotion or of an idea in all its nascent power.

Return The return home, or the return to the material home or to the motherland or birthplace, is symbolic of death, not in the sense of total destruction but of reintegration of the spirit into the Spirit. As the Chinese thinker Lieh-tzŭ observed, 'when the soul leaves the form, both are restored to their true essence, and that is why they are said to have returned home' (58).

Rhomb According to Hentze (*cit.* Eliade, 17), the rhomb is emblematic of the female sexual organ. This would seem to confirm the Greek definition of the rhomb as an instrument of magic which, when brandished, was supposed to excite and inflame the passions of men (8)—an analogous and related idea, fetishist in character.

Ribbons Ribbons knotted together to form a circle (worn by Romans as a kind of diadem in the same way as they wore garlands of flowers) are symbols of immortality by virtue of their circular shape. They also carry a heroic significance, like all crowns or garlands, for the very act of 'crowning' an undertaking fulfilled is so called because of the symbolic relationship between the crown and the concept of absolute fulfilment.

Ring Like every closed circle, the ring is a symbol of continuity and wholeness. This is why (like the bracelet) it has been used both as a symbol of marriage and of the eternally repeated time-cycle. Sometimes it occurs in animal form, as a snake or an eel biting its tail (Ouroboros); sometimes as a pure geometrical form (8, 20, 32). It is interesting to note that, in some legends, the ring is regarded as the only remaining link of a chain. Thus, it is told that when Jupiter allowed Hercules to rescue Prometheus, it was on condition that the latter should thereafter wear an iron ring, set with a piece of rock from the Caucasus, as a symbol of submission to his punishment (8). Another type of ring is found in the circle of flames surrounding the dancing Shiva as he performs the cosmic dance; this flame-ring can be related to the Zodiac. Like the Zodiac and the Ouroboros of the Gnostics, it has an active and a passive half (evolution, involution), and stands for the life-cycle of both the universe and each individual being: the circular dance of nature in eternal process of creation and destruction. At the same time, the light radiated by the ring of flames symbolizes eternal wisdom and transcendental illumination (60).

Rite   In essence, every rite symbolizes and reproduces creation (17). Hence, rites are connected with the symbolism of ornaments (38). The slow-moving ritual, characteristic of all ceremonies, is closely bound up with the rhythm of the astral movements (3). At the same time, every rite is a meeting, that is, a confluence of forces and patterns; the significance of rites stems from the accumulated power of these forces when blended harmoniously one with the other.

River   An ambivalent symbol since it corresponds to the creative power both of nature and of time. On the one hand it signifies fertility and the progressive irrigation of the soil; and on the other hand it stands for the irreversible passage of time and, in consequence, for a sense of loss and oblivion (8, 60).

Rock   The Chinese attribute to the rock a symbolism denoting permanence, solidity and integrity (5), and this may be taken as generally valid. Like the stone, it is held in many traditions to be the dwelling-place of a god. As a Caucasian tradition has it: 'In the beginning, the world was covered with water. The great creator-god then dwelt inside a rock' (35). It seems, then, that man intuitively regards stones (as in the myth of Deucalion) and rocks as the source of human life, while the soil (inferior because more disintegrated) is the mother of vegetable and animal life. A mystic significance is attributed to this mineral, arising from the sound it makes when struck and because of its unity—that is, its solidity and cohesion.

Room   A symbol of individuality—of private thoughts. The windows symbolize the possibility of understanding and of passing through to the external and the beyond, and are also an illustration of any idea of communication. Hence, a closed room lacking windows may be symbolic of virginity, according to Frazer, and also of other kinds of non-communication. Many rites involving the enclosure-image are performed to mark the reaching of puberty, all over the world. The legend about Danae, shut up by her father in a bronze tower, pertains to this particular symbolism. There is a Siberian legend concerning a 'dark house of iron' which is also relevant to it (21). We might also mention the 'vase with a lid', one of the eight emblems of good luck in Chinese Buddhism, and a symbol of wholeness, of the idea with no 'exit', or, in other words, of supreme intelligence triumphant over birth and death (signified respectively by the doors and windows of the room) (5). This explains why the hermetically sealed room may possibly be a variant form of the 'vase with a lid'.

Rope Like the chain, it is a general symbol for binding and connexion. Knotted cord, in Egyptian hieroglyphics, signifies a man's name. Since the knot is a symbol for the individual's existence, there are various hieroglyphic signs related to the name of a person in the shape of a knot or a bow or a belt or a crown and so on. The seal has the same significance (19). The silver cord in Vedic teaching has a significance which goes still deeper: it expresses the sacred, inner path which binds the outer consciousness of man (his intellect) with his spiritual essence (the 'centre' or 'silver palace') (38).

Rose The single rose is, in essence, a symbol of completion, of consummate achievement and perfection. Hence, accruing to it are all those ideas associated with these qualities: the mystic Centre, the heart (14), the garden of Eros, the paradise of Dante (4), the beloved (31), the emblem of Venus (8) and so on. More precise symbolic meanings are derived from the colour and number of its petals. The relationship of the white rose to the red is in accordance with the relationship between the two colours as defined in alchemy (q.v.). The blue rose is symbolic of the impossible. The golden rose is a symbol of absolute achievement. When the rose is round in shape, it corresponds in significance to the mandala. The seven-petalled rose alludes to the septenary pattern (that is, the seven Directions of Space, the seven days of the week, the seven planets, the seven degrees of perfection). It is in this sense that it appears in emblem DCCXXIII of the *Ars Symbolica* of Bosch and in the *Summum Bonum* of Robert Fludd (32). The eight-petalled rose symbolizes regeneration (46).

Rotation For Roux, in *Les Druides* (Paris, 1961), rotation (the dynamic determining of circumference in rites or in art) generates a magic force, particularly of a defensive order, since it marks out a sacred precinct—the circle—which calls for the projection of the self. For Blavatsky, David's dance round the Ark, like that of the Sabean star-worshippers, was a circular dance or at least a dance that followed a closed curve.

Round Table The Round Table is equated, by its shape, with the Chinese disk of jade, *Pi*, which represents the sky. The appearance of the Grail in the centre of the table completes the symbolism, for the concave shape of the sacred chalice corresponds to the central hole in the Chinese *Pi*. The twelve knights are related to—but not identical with—the signs of the Zodiac, expressing in particular a parallel tendency, the struggle for the triumph and the establishment of 'paradise regained', or, in other words, of the 'unvarying mean'.

The tasks allotted to the knights implied the perfection of the circle of the sun, and involved succouring the weaker sex, the chastisement of tyrants, the liberation of the bewitched, the outwitting of giants, and the destruction of all evil men and noxious animals (4); and this programme was but the prelude to the establishment of the reign of the 'Centre'. Similar institutions are the 'round council' of the Dalai Lama (consisting of the twelve great *Namshans*) and the Twelve Peers of France. The model which is composed of twelve parts is the most important of all (the next being the ternary division, and then the quaternary and septenary) since it is equated with the circle and, in consequence, with the idea of totality (which is at times also expressed by the number ten). It was for this reason that the Etruscan state was divided into twelve parts and Romulus created twelve lictors (28). The evil that afflicted the Round Table, through the love of Queen Guinevere for Lancelot and the frailties of other knights, was sufficient cause for the failure of the community of knights to achieve their mystic ends; only Sir Galahad of the pure heart could come near to fulfilment once he had been granted the divine gifts of the shield and the sword.

Rudder   In ancient representations of ships, the rudder frequently plays an important part as an allegory expressive of the ideas of safety and the steering of a straight course. It figures with the same significance in mediaeval and Renaissance emblems.

Ruins   The symbolic sense of ruins is self-evident and derived directly from the literal sense: they signify desolation and life defunct. They are tantamount to sentiments, ideas or bonds which are no longer animated by the breath of life but which nevertheless persist shorn of any use or function relevant to thought and existence, but saturated with the past and redolent with a sense of the destruction of its reality wrought by the passage of time. Ruins are symbolically equivalent to biological mutilation.

Sacrifice   The central idea of cosmogonies is that of 'the primordial sacrifice'. Inverting the concept, we can deduce that there is no creation without sacrifice. To sacrifice what is esteemed is to sacrifice oneself, and the spiritual energy thereby acquired is proportional to the importance of what is lost. All forms of suffering can be sacrificial, if fully and wholeheartedly sought and accepted. The physical and negative signs—of mutilation, chastisement, self-abasement and severe penalties or tribulations—are all symbolic of the obverse tendencies in the spiritual order. This is why the majority of legends and folktales, stories of heroes, saints and exceptional men commonly tell not only of suffering but also of strange situations of inferiority such as that so vividly illustrated in the story of Cinderella. (*See illustration* p. 103.)

Zodiacal Sign
of Sagittarius.

Sagittarius According to Subba Rao, this is a cosmic symbol expressive of the complete man—he who is at once animal, spiritual and worthy of his divine origin. Man thus constitutes a link between heaven and earth, implying a state of tension which finds its symbolic expression in the arc (or rainbow). Sagittarius, the Centaur, or the Archer signify this triple nature of the symbol; the horse symbolizes the instinctive organism, the human part denotes the three higher principles embracing the monad as expressed by the arrow. In the Babylonian epic of Gilgamesh, Sagittarius is represented by 'scorpion-men' who are 'no more than two-thirds divine' (40).

Sails In Egyptian hieroglyphs, a determinative sign symbolizing the wind, the creative breath and the spur to action (19). It corresponds to the Element of air. In some mediaeval emblems it appears as an allegory of the Holy Spirit (4).

Salamander A mythological fire-spirit, a kind of lizard which was supposed to inhabit the Element of fire (57, 8). In graphic symbolism, and also in alchemy, the salamander signifies fire—which in fact constitutes its general significance.

Salvation In numerous legends and stories, and in many myths, situations are recounted in which 'salvation' should occur and frequently does occur. Obviously, this adventure is a profanation of the avatar of the soul on its return journey after its 'fall' from the paradisiac state. The salvation *par excellence* is that occasioned by the Passion of the Lord. However, an association between the ideas of sacrifice and salvation is found in many religions.

Sandals, Winged An attribute of Mercury, and a symbol of 'loftiness' of spirit in Greek mythology, with the same significance as Pegasus. Perseus put on winged sandals in order to slay Medusa the Gorgon (15).

Sarcophagus Symbolic of the feminine principle and, at the same time, of the earth as the beginning and end of material life. Its significance corresponds to that of the receptacle, the amphora and the boat (9). Hence, in alchemy, it is known as the 'philosophical egg' (or the vessel of transmutation).

Saturn Saturn symbolizes time which, with its ravenous appetite for life, devours all its creations, whether they are beings, things, ideas or sentiments. He is also symbolic of the insufficiency, in the mystic sense, of any order of existence within the plane of the temporal, or the necessity for the 'reign of Cronos' to be succeeded by another cosmic mode of existence in which time has no place. Time brings restlessness—the sense of duration lasting from the moment of stimulus up to the instant of satisfaction. Hence, Saturn is symbolic of activity, of slow, implacable dynamism, of realization and communication (15); and this is why he is said to have 'devoured his children' (32) and why he is related to the Ouroboros (or the

Saturn (from *Poeticon astronomicon*, Venice, 1485).

serpent which bites its own tail). Other attributes of his are the oar (standing for navigation and progress in things temporal), the hour-glass and the scythe (8). In the scythe we can detect a double meaning: first, its function of cutting, parallel to and corroborating the symbolism of devouring; and, secondly, its curved shape, which invariably corresponds to the feminine principle. This is why the alchemists, masters in the spiritual science of symbolism, named Saturn '*Mercurius senex*': given the androgynous character of Mercury, Saturn takes on the same characteristic ambiguity of gender and sex, and is related to the earth, the sarcophagus and putrefaction, as well as to the colour black. Mertens Stienon suggests that Saturn is, in every case, a symbol of the law of limitation which gives shape to life, or the localised expression in time and space of the universal life (40).

Saturnalia A characteristic of ancient mythology is the idea that each reign must give way to another, even on the plane of the divine; it was an idea which was inextricably bound up with the notion of life as continuity and succession, and of sacrifice as the sole source of re-creation. The successive cosmic reigns of Uranus, Saturn and Jupiter provided a model for earthly government, for the 'ritual assassination of the king' at certain astral conjunctions or at the end of certain periods, and later for the displacement of this bloody ceremony by its simulacra. In Rome, the Saturnalia was the most outstanding example of such sacrifice and simulacra. Frazer notes that it was a general practice in ancient Italy to elect a man to play the part of Saturn and enjoy all the prerogatives of the god for a while before dying either by his own hand or by sacrifice. The principal figure in the Carnival festival is a burlesque image and a direct successor of the old king of the Saturnalia. The 'King of the Bean', the mediaeval 'Bishop of Fools', the 'Abbot of Unreason' and the 'Lord of Misrule' are all personifications of one and the same thing and may well stem from a common source. In every case they are symbolic of the ideas of duration and sacrifice, whereby, by means of inversion and transformation, the brevity and intensity of life may be contrasted with its vulgar mediocrity (21). The Carnival itself is, in its brevity, a symbol of this desire to concentrate into a given period of time all the possibilities of existence, apart from the fact that, in its orgiastic sense, it is an invocation of primordial chaos and a desperate quest for the 'way out of time'.

Scales This instrument, of Chaldaean origin (7), is the mystic symbol of justice, that is, of the equivalence and equation of guilt and punishment. In emblems, marks and allegories it is often depicted inside a circle crowned by a fleur-de-lis, a star, a cross or a dove (4). In its most common form, that is, two equal scales balanced symmetrically on either side of a central pivot, it has a secondary meaning—subservient to the above—which is, to a certain extent, similar to other symbolic bilateral images, such as the double-bladed axe, the Tree of Life, trees of the Sephiroth, etc. The deepest significance of the balance derives from the zodiacal archetype of Libra, related to 'immanent justice', or the idea that all guilt automatically unleashes the very forces that bring self-destruction and punishment (40).

Scales (of the Fish)   On the one hand, they signify protection and defence. On the other, water and the nether world. And also, by extension, the previous persisting into the subsequent, the inferior into the superior. The story of the Apostles (Acts ix, 18) tells how, when Paul was called by the voice of God, there fell from his eyes 'as it had been scales' (50). The scaly pattern on the lower parts of some beings such as mermaids, mermen and Baphomet of the Knights Templar serves to emphasize their association with level-symbolism, expressing in visual form the cosmic (or moral) inferiority of what, from the viewpoint of vertical 'height', appears below.

Scars   Certain elements of reality which are not in themselves symbols, or which have not *yet* been analysed for symbolic significance, nevertheless evidently possess such significance. This is sometimes brought to light by the conjunction of several separate events. The author once dreamed of an unknown damsel (*anima*) whose beautiful face was marked by scars and burns which in no way disfigured her features. Milton says that Satan's face 'deep scars of thunder had intrenched'. Lacroix, in *Rostros de la Fe*, states that 'it is certain that the stigmata of original damnation can sometimes be read in the beautiful faces of these coveted objects'. Moral imperfections, and sufferings (are they one and the same?) are, therefore, symbolized by the wounds and scars caused by fire and sword.

Sceptre   Related to the magic wand, the club, the thunderbolt and the phallus, as well as to Thor's hammer. The symbolism of all these falls within the general group of signs and emblems of fertility (31), but it could be linked also to that of the 'world-axis'. In allegories containing the sceptre, the form, colour and material of the object all play their part in enriching the basic symbolism. One of the most common representations of a sceptre terminates in a fleur-de-lis, which is a symbol of light and purification.

Scissors   Like the cross, a symbol of 'conjunction' (51); but it is also an attribute of the mystic spinners who cut the thread of life of mortal Man. It is, then, an ambivalent symbol expressive of both creation and destruction, birth and death.

Scorpio   The eighth sign of the Zodiac. It corresponds to that period of the span of man's life which lies under the threat of death (that is, the 'fall'). It is also related with the sexual function (40). In the Middle Ages the scorpion makes its appearance in Christian art as an emblem of treachery and as a symbol for the Jew (20). In the symbolism of megaliths it is the antithesis of the bee whose honey succours Man. Finally, its symbolism is equivalent to that of the hangman (51).

Zodiacal sign
of Scorpio.

Scythe An attribute of Saturn and, in general, linked with allegories of death; it is also associated with Attis and the priests of Cybele, in which case the allusion is to self-mutilation (8). In some images of these deities it is not a large agricultural scythe that is portrayed but a small dagger curved in shape and called *harpe*. Broadly speaking, all curved weapons are lunar and feminine symbols, whereas straight ones are masculine and solar. Straightness signifies penetration and forcefulness, curves suggest the means to an end and passivity. For this reason, the *harpe* has been linked with the 'indirect way', that is, with the secret path which leads to the beyond. According to Diel, the scythe is also symbolic of the harvest—of renewed hopes for rebirth. Hence, like Pisces in the Zodiac, the scythe-symbol incorporates the ambiguity of the beginning as the end, and vice versa (15). Both these senses—of mutilation and of hope—are, despite their contradictory nature, related to the idea of sacrifice inherent in all images of weapons.

Sea The symbolic significance of the sea corresponds to that of the 'Lower Ocean'—the waters in flux, the transitional and mediating agent between the non-formal (air and gases) and the formal (earth and solids) and, by analogy, between life and death. The waters of the oceans are thus seen not only as the source of life but also as its goal. 'To return to the sea' is 'to return to the mother', that is, to die.

Seal Like other marks or brands, the seal is a sign of ownership and individuality—of differentiation. And, in the form of a seal of beeswax or sealing-wax, it is symbolic of virginity, of narrow-mindedness and of repression.

Seal of Solomon This consists of two triangles superimposed and interlaced so as to form a six-pointed star. Wirth terms it the 'star of the microcosm', or a sign of the spiritual potential of the individual who can endlessly deny himself. In reality it is a symbol of the human soul as a 'conjunction' of consciousness and the unconscious, signified by the intermingling of the triangle (denoting fire) and the inverted triangle (water) (59). Both of these are, according to alchemic theory, subject to the principle of the immaterial, called Azoth by the philosophers, and represented in the

Seal of Solomon by a central point which is not actually portrayed but which has to be seen in the imagination alone, as in some of the mandalas of India and Tibet.

Seasons, The They consist of the four 'phases' of the sun's orbit and hence correspond to the phases of the moon as well as to the four stages of a man's life. The Greeks represented the seasons by the figures of four women: Spring was depicted wearing a floral crown and standing beside a shrub in blossom; Summer, with a crown of ears of corn, bearing a sheaf in one hand and a sickle in the other; Autumn carries bunches of grapes and a basket full of fruit; Winter, bare-headed, beside leafless trees. They have also been represented by the figures of animals: Spring as a sheep, Summer as a dragon, Autumn as a hare, Winter as a salamander (8). The four-part division of the seasons enables them to be related also to the points of the compass and to the tetramorphs.

Sea-urchin Called 'serpent's egg' in Celtic tradition, it is one of the symbols for the life-force (26) and the primordial seed.

Secret All secrets symbolize the power of the supernatural, and this explains their disquieting effect upon most human beings. Jung is emphatic about this, pointing out that, for the same reason, it is very helpful for the individual so affected to unburden himself of his secrets (31). On the other hand, the ability to master this state of tension within oneself confers an awareness of unfailing superiority —a sensation which is common in individuals who live outside the law and in spies and privy counsellors to kings and magnates. This same notion supplies part of the basic attraction of esoteric thought and of all forms of Hermetic science in literature and art.

Seed Symbolic of latent, non-manifest forces, or of the mysterious potentialities the presence of which, sometimes unsuspected, is the justification for hope. These potentialities also symbolize the mystic Centre—the non-apparent point which is the irradiating origin of every branch and shoot of the great Tree of the World (26).

Sefiroth The sum of the ten sefirah, or emanations of God, according to the Cabbala (which, in itself, constitutes a mystical and symbolic explanation of the Creation). The sefirah are: Crown, Wisdom, Understanding, Mercy, Justice, Beauty, Firmness, Splendour, Victory, and Kingdom or Shekhinah. There have been attempts to identify these aspects of the divine power with the mythological deities which, even in the days of the Roman Empire, were already symbols for the Stoics, the Neo-Pythagoreans and the Neoplatonists. The most important books of historical investigation into the Cabbala (whose principal work, the *Zohar*, was written in Spain during the 13th century by Moisés de León) are those of Gershom G. Scholem, Professor at the University of Jerusalem. In another sense, the syntheses of A.-D. Grad are interesting.

Septenary This is an order composed of seven elements. Ultimately, it is founded upon the seven Directions of Space: two opposite directions for each dimension, plus the centre. This spatial order of six dynamic elements, plus one which is static, is projected into the week as a model of the septenary in the passage of time. Three is, in many cultures, the number pertaining to heaven (since it constitutes the vertical order of the three-dimensional spatial cross) and four is associated with the earth (because of the four directions—comparable with the cardinal points—of the two horizontal dimensions). Hence, seven is the number expressing the sum of heaven and earth (as twelve is the expression of their multiplicative possibilities) (22). In religion, the septenary is expressed or alluded to by means of ternaries such as the three theological virtues plus the quaternary of the cardinal virtues; the septenary of the capital sins (59), in particular, is seen in traditional symbolist theory as deriving from the influence of—or analogy with—the spiritual principles of the seven planets, or the ancient mythological deities. In the heavens, seven finds particular expression in the constellation of the Pleiades, the daughters of Atlas (six of whom are visible and one hidden) (9). Seven, with its characteristic quality of synthesis, is regarded as a symbol of the transformation and integration of all hierarchical orders as a whole (32); hence there are seven notes in the diatonic scale, seven colours in the rainbow, and seven planetary spheres together with their seven planets. Sometimes it is taken as being split into—or alternatively as the union of—the numbers two and five (the Sun and Moon; and Mercury, Venus, Mars, Jupiter and Saturn), or three and four (the Sun, Moon and Mercury; and Venus, Mars, Jupiter and Saturn). Seven is represented graphically by the joining of the triangle and the square, the triangle being either superimposed upon or inscribed within the square. This septenary pattern is often employed in extensive architectural layouts, for it has a quality of the mandala about it, comparable with the notion of 'squaring the circle'. It would be impossible to name, even in brief or in sum, all the innumerable applications of the septenary, or the ways in which this cosmic 'model' figures in myths, legends, folktales and dreams, or in historical events, works of art, and so on. At times the seven-scheme takes on a complex symbolism—the planetary gods in their evil guise, or the days of the week conceived in terms of spiritual peril (in the configuration of the seven-headed dragon); and sometimes it gives expression to the reigning celestial order (as with the seven-branched candelabra in the Temple of Solomon. Schneider notes that, in the Scottish sword-dance, St. George conquers the dragon in the company of seven saints (the seven-heads theme inverted in order to ensure victory) (51). It was from its use as a symbol for the

complete musical scale (as in Orpheus' lyre) that the number seven
came to acquire such widespread application: there were seven
Hesperides, seven kings who attacked Thebes and seven who defended
it, seven sons and seven daughters of Niobe (38); and Plato conceived
of a celestial siren singing in each of the seven spheres, and these
'seven Sirens of the Spheres' correspond to the seven virgins in
Cinderella (4) and the seven fairies of legend and folklore (one
each for each Direction of space and time). For Loeffler, these
fairies correspond to the seven *Lipiki* of Hindu esoteric thought,
that is, the spirits relative to each plane of the human consciousness:
sensation, emotion, reflective intelligence, intuition, spirituality, will
and intimations of the divine (38). Hence the esoteric conclusion
that the human being is composed of seven spheres after the pattern
of the heavens. The Jewish Cabbala provides a link between the
mythological deities, in so far as they are creative and beneficient,
and the seven celestial hierarchies: the Sun—the angel of light—
Michael; the Moon—the angel of hope and dreams—Gabriel;
Mercury—the civilizing angel—Raphael; Venus—the angel of love
—Anael; Mars—the angel of destruction—Samael; Jupiter—the
administering angel—Zachariel; Saturn—the angel of solicitude—
Oriphiel. Lévi has drawn a number of parallels based on the
septenary, exactly corresponding to certain elements on all planes
of the cosmos. To quote only the emblems which he attributes to
particular deities: the Sun—a serpent with a lion's head; the Moon
—a globe divided into two half-moons; Mercury—the Hermetic
caduceus; Venus—the lingam; Mars—a dragon biting the hilt of a
sword; Jupiter—a flaming pentagram in the claws of an eagle;
Saturn—an aged man with a scythe (37). It is not too difficult to
grasp the significance of numbers based on the septenary. The vast
majority of symbols containing seven elements all over the world
originate from the celestial prototype of the seven spheres. Cola
Alberich refers to a number of examples of the number seven
appearing as a characteristic feature of tattoos and amulets. He
quotes Hippocrates, for example: 'The number seven, because of its
occult virtues, tends to bring all things into being: it is the dispenser
of life and the source of all change—for the moon itself changes its
phase every seven days. This number influences all sublime beings.'
And Cola Alberich comments that 'combs with seven points were
magic symbols in Susa; among the Chinese, the "fox with seven
tails" is the evil genius; the saints and sages have "seven holes" in
their heart; the animal spirits are seven in number; there are seven
fairies of seven colours; on the seventh day of the seventh month,
great popular festivals were held all over China, and the most favoured
of amulets is the lotus with seven leaves. In Tibet, there are seven
emblems of Buddha. . . . In the sacred pyramids of Mocha, on the

Peruvian coast, the *guaca* (Indian tomb) of the sun has seven steps. In Islam, the number seven enjoys great popularity: there are seven heavens, seven earths, seven seas; pilgrims walk seven times round the temple of Mecca; there are seven days of ill-omen; man is composed of seven substances; seven is the number of the foods gathered from the fields. . . .' (12).

Seriality Serial order dèrives from the separate existence of a certain number of elements in discontinuity, disclosing minor differences when opposed to or contrasted with other orders or scales. Serial orders are, then, composed of the differentiation of one entity, or the diversification of what is unitary or the unification of what is relatively diverse. Hence we should distinguish in any given series: (*a*) the *limits* or poles of the series; (*b*) a limited number of *elements* included in the series by virtue of their ability to fall into place between the two poles; (*c*) an inner *graduation* which obtains between two or more of these elements. This graduated scale expresses the relationship between the qualitative and the quantitative (that is, the potentiality of either to be transformed into the other) as exemplified by the vibratory phenomena of the notes of the musical scale and the colours of the spectrum. The arrangement of a series in time is equivalent to defining or constituting a *process*, and this process will be evolutive if it is ascending, and regressive if it is descending or recurring.

Serpent (or **Snake**) If all symbols are really functions and signs of things imbued with energy, then the serpent or snake is, by analogy, symbolic of energy itself—of force pure and simple; hence its ambivalence and multivalencies. Another reason for its great variety of symbolic meaning derives from the consideration that these meanings may relate either to the serpent as a whole or to any of its major characteristics—for example, to its sinuous movements, its common association with the tree and its formal analogy with the roots and branches of the tree, the way it sheds its skin, its

Serpent (after an Inca image).

threatening tongue, the undulating pattern of its body, its hiss, its resemblance to a ligament, its method of attacking its victims by coiling itself round them, and so on. Still another explanation lies in its varying habitat: there are snakes which inhabit woods, others which thrive in the desert, aquatic serpents and those that lurk in lakes and ponds, wells and springs. In India, snake cults or cults of the spirit of the snake are connected with the symbolism of the

waters of the sea. Snakes are guardians of the springs of life and
of immortality, and also of those superior riches of the spirit that
are symbolized by hidden treasure (17). As regards the West,
Bayley has suggested that the snake, since its sinuous shape is
similar to that of waves, may be a symbol of the wisdom of the
deeps (4) and of the great mysteries. Yet, in their multiplicity and
as creatures of the desert, snakes are forces of destruction, afflicting
all those who have succeeded in crossing the Red Sea and leaving
Egypt (57); in this sense, they are connected with the 'temptations'
facing those who have overcome the limitations of matter and have
entered into the realm of the 'dryness' of the spirit. This explains
why Blavatsky can say that, physically, the snake symbolizes the
seduction of strength by matter (as Jason by Medea, Hercules by
Omphale, Adam by Eve), thereby providing us with a palpable
illustration of the workings of the process of involution; and of how
the inferior can lurk within the superior, or the previous within the
subsequent (9). This is borne out by Diel, for whom the snake is
symbolic not of personal sin but of the principle of evil inherent in
all worldly things. The same idea is incorporated into the Nordic
myth about the serpent of Midgard (15). There is a clear connexion between the snake and the feminine principle. Eliade observes
that Gresmann (*Mytische Reste in der Paradieserzahlung*, in *Archiv
f. Rel.* X, 345) regarded Eve as an archaic Phoenician goddess of
the underworld who is personified in the serpent (although a better
interpretation would be to identify it with the allegorical figure of
Lilith, the enemy and temptress of Eve). In support of this, Eliade
points to the numerous Mediterranean deities who are represented
carrying a snake in one or both of their hands (for example, the
Greek Artemis, Hecate, Persephone), and he relates these to the
finely sculpted Cretan priestesses in gold or ivory, and to mythic
figures with snakes for hair (Medusa the Gorgon, or the Erinyes).
He goes on to mention that in Central Europe there is a belief that
hairs pulled out from the head of a woman under the influence of
the moon will be turned into snakes (17). The serpent (or snake)
was very common in Egypt; the hieroglyph which corresponds
phonetically to the letter Z is a representation of the movement of
the snake. Like the sign of the slug, or horned snake (phonetically
equivalent to F), this hieroglyph refers to primigenial and cosmic
forces. Generally speaking, the names of the goddesses are determined by signs representing the snake—which is tantamount to
saying that it is because of Woman that the spirit has fallen into
matter and evil. The snake is also used, as are other reptiles, to
refer to the primordial—the most primitive strata of life. In the
Book of the Dead (XVII), the reptiles are the first to acclaim Ra
when he appears above the surface of the waters of Nou (or Nu or

Nun). The demonic implications of the serpent are exemplified in Tuat, whose evil spirits are portrayed as snakes; however, these—like the vanquished dragon—may also take on a beneficent form as forces which have been mastered, controlled, sublimated and utilized for the superior purposes of the psyche and the development of mankind, and in this sense they correspond to the goddesses Nekhebit and Uadjit (or Buto). They also become an Uraeus—the same thing happens in the symbolism of the Kundalini—constituting the most precious ornament of the royal diadem (19).

As we have said, it is the basic characteristics of the snake which have determined its symbolic significances. To quote Teillard's definition of the snake, it is: 'An animal endowed with magnetic force. Because it sheds its skin, it symbolizes resurrection. Because of its sinuous movement' (and also because its coils are capable of strangling) 'it signifies strength. Because of its viciousness, it represents the evil side of nature' (56). Its ability to shed its skin greatly impressed ancient writers: Philo of Alexandria believed that when the snake shakes off its skin it likewise shakes off its old age, that it can both kill and cure and that it is therefore the symbol and attribute of the aggressive powers, positive and negative, which rule the world. (This is a Gnostic and Manichean idea of Persian provenance.) He decided finally that it is the 'most spiritual of animals'. Jung has pointed out that the Gnostics related it to the spinal cord and the spinal marrow, an excellent image of the way the unconscious expresses itself suddenly and unexpectedly with its peremptory and terrible incursions (31). He adds that, psychologically, the snake is a symptom of anguish expressive of abnormal stirrings in the unconscious, that is, of a reactivation of its destructive potentiality. This is directly comparable to the significance of the serpent of Midgard in Norse mythology. In the *Völuspa* it is proclaimed that the deluge will commence when the serpent awakens to destroy the universe (31). For Zimmer, the serpent is the life-force which determines birth and rebirth and hence it is connected with the Wheel of Life. The legend of Buddha tells how the serpent wound itself round his body seven times (as in the effigies of the Mithraic Cronos), but, since it could not crush him, it turned into a youth bowing low before Gautama (60).

The connexion of the snake with the wheel is expressed in graphic form in the Gnostic symbol of the Ouroboros, or serpent biting its own tail; half of this mythic being is dark and the other half light (as in the Chinese *Yang-Yin* symbol), which clearly illustrates the essential ambivalence of the snake in that it pertains to both aspects of the cycle (the active and the passive, the affirmative and the negative, the constructive and the destructive). Wirth comments that the 'ancient serpent is the prop of the world, providing it with both materials and energy, unfolding as reason and imagination, and also as a force of the darkness' (59). The snake was an important symbol for the Gnostics, and especially for the so-called Naassene sect (from *naas*—snake). Hippolytus, criticizing this doctrine, asserted that the snake was said to live in all objects and in all beings. This brings us to the Yoga concept of the Kundalini or the snake as an image of inner strength. Kundalini is represented symbolically as a snake coiled up upon itself in the form of a ring (*kundala*) (29), in that subtle part of the organism corresponding to the lower extremity of the spinal column; this, at any rate, is the case with the ordinary man. But, as a result of exercises directed towards his spiritualization—Hatha Yoga, for instance—the snake uncoils and stretches up through wheels (*chakras*) corresponding to the various plexuses of the body until it reaches the area of the forehead corresponding to the third eye of Shiva. It is then, according to Hindu belief, that man recovers his sense of the eternal (28). The symbolism here probably relates to an ascending force, rising up, that is, from the area governed by the sexual organ up to the realm of thought—an interpretation which it is also possible to justify by simple reference to the symbolism of level, taking the heart as central. In other words, the symbol denotes 'sublimation of the personality' (Avalon, *The Serpent Power*). Jung has noted that the custom of representing transformation and renovation of figures of snakes constitutes a well-documented archetype; and he suggests that the Egyptian Uraeus is the visible expression of the Kundalini on a higher plane (32). There are also various rites which accord with this concept of progressive elevation. The progress through the six *chakras*—there is in fact a seventh, but it is unnamed and (like the central point of certain mandala-like patterns) is not represented visually—may be regarded as analogous to climbing up the terraces of the *ziggurat* or mounting the steps pertaining to the seven metals in the Mithraic ritual (11). Apart from the circular (and cosmic) position it tends to take up, and the quality of completeness which this implies, the snake is frequently related to other symbols. The most common of these is the tree, which, being unitary, may be said to correspond to the masculine principle, in which case the ophidian would represent the feminine. The tree and the serpent are, in mythology, prefigurations of Adam and Eve. Furthermore, by analogy, we also have here a situation of symbolic Entanglement—the snake curled round the tree (or round the staff of Aesculapius)—and a symbolic image of moral dualism. Diel, who tends to favour this kind of interpretation, suggests that the snake coiled round the staff or club of the god of medicine recalls the basic, Biblical symbol of the Tree of Life encircled by the snake and signifying the principle of evil; the pattern here points to the close relationship between life and corruption as the source of all evil. Diel goes on to suggest that it is this subversion of the spirit that brings about the death of the soul, and that this is what medicine must, in the first place, set out to combat (15).

Now, the opposite to the encircling (or triumphant) snake is the crucified snake, as it is to be found among the figures included in *Abraham le Juif* (Paris, Bibl. Nat. Ms. Fr. 14765, of the 16th century) (32). This figure of the reptile nailed to a cross—or the chthonian and feminine principle vanquished by the spirit—is also represented mythically by the victory of eagle over serpent. Heinrich Zimmer recalls that, in the *Iliad*, an eagle appears to the Greeks, carrying a wounded snake in its claws. The seer Calchas saw this as an omen portending the triumph of the Greeks (the masculine and patriarchal order of the Aryans subduing the predominantly feminine and matriarchal principle of Asia) (60). Since all struggle is a form of 'conjunction' and therefore of love, it is hardly surprising that man should have created a synthesis of opposing powers—heaven and earth—in the image of the 'plumed serpent', the most notable symbol of pre-Columbian America. This serpent has feathers on its head, in its tail and sometimes on its body. Quetzalcoatl is another androgynous symbol of this kind (41). The symmetrical placing of two serpents, as in the caduceus of Mercury, is indicative of an equilibrium of forces, of the counterbalancing of the cowed serpent (or sublimated power) by the untamed serpent, so representing good balanced by evil, health by sickness. As Jung has shrewdly observed, this much-used image is an adumbration of homoeopathy—a cure effected by what caused the ailment. The serpent therefore becomes the source of the healing of the wound caused by the serpent. This is why it could serve as a symbol of St. John the Evangelist (32) and appear in association with a chalice.

The different forms which the serpent may take are not numerous. The sea-serpent seems simply to emphasize the integration of the symbolism of the unconscious with that of the abyss (9). If it has more than one head, this merely serves to add to the basic symbolism, the extra significance corresponding to the particular number of heads it is given. The dragon or the serpent with seven heads occurs often in legends, myths and folktales simply because seven represents multiplication of unity and locates the reptile among the essential orders of the cosmos. The seven-headed serpent partakes of the symbolism of the seven Directions of Space, the seven days of the week, and the seven planetary gods, and has a bearing upon the seven sins (9). The three-headed serpent refers to the three principles of the active, the passive and the neutral. In alchemy, the winged serpent represents the volatile principle, and the wingless the fixed principle. The crucified serpent denotes the fixation of the volatile and also sublimation (as in the Prometheus myth). Alchemists also saw in the serpent an illustration of 'the feminine in Man' or his 'humid essence', relating the reptile to Mercury (57) as the androgynous god who—like Shiva—was doubtless endowed with a tendency towards both good and evil (an aspect also portrayed by the Gnostics in their twin serpents called *Agathodaemon* and *Kakodaemon*) (9). There are also serpents of unusual aspect—the snake with a sheep's head, for instance, in reliefs on certain Gallo-Roman sepulchres. In view of the favourable symbolic sense of the sheep (connected with Aries, spring, initiation and fire), this adaptation implies a degree of spiritualization (16). Finally, according to Schneider, the sacrificed serpent is the symbolic equivalent of the swan's neck and of the swan itself (and it is by the swan that the hero is wafted heavenwards, plucking away upon his harp) (50). That is to say, the sacrifice of the serpent (as a life-force) makes it possible to accept death gratefully (like the swan) and to soar up to higher regions. Father Heras has suggested that the snake is symbolic of fertility and destruction and that it is in this sense that it appears on the menhir of Kernuz (Finistère). It appears in opposition to the arrow in the effigy of the horned god of Cerdeña (with another head on top alluding to the symbolism of the Gemini).

Sexes, The   Plato, in *Timaeus*, speaks of the sexes as 'living', as if in some way they were independent of the beings to which they pertain. This is visually symbolized by the ventral faces given to some of the fabulous mediaeval figures, as well as by the paws added to the heads of the *gryces*, deriving from ancient Carthaginian and Gnostic images. Now, orthodox Freudians have reduced the great majority of objects, depending upon whether their predominant characteristic is that of the container or the contained, to either feminine or masculine sexual implications; but there is nothing new in this, for implicit in the ancient Chinese *Yang-Yin* symbol is the notion of a classification whereby all things fall within a system which locates the genders at opposite poles, corresponding to the duality of the sexes. We must not overlook that the sexes may symbolize spiritual principles; consciousness and the unconscious, heaven and earth, fire and water. The sexual *conjunctio* is the most graphic and impressive of all images expressive of the idea of union, and hence alchemists used it to represent initiatory truths which transcend the laws of biology, as Jung has demonstrated, particularly in *Psychology of the Transference*.

Shadow   As the Sun is the light of the spirit, so shadow is the negative 'double' of the body, or the image of its evil and base side. Among primitive peoples, the notion that the shadow is the *àlter ego* or soul is firmly established; it is also reflected in the folklore and literature of some advanced cultures (35). As Frazer has noted, the primitive often regards his shadow, or his reflection in water or in a mirror, as his soul or as a vital part of himself (21). 'Shadow' is the term given by Jung to the primitive and instinctive side of the individual.

Shape (or **Form**) Certain branches of science, such as the Psychology of Form, Isomorphism and Morphology, have arrived at conclusions which coincide with those of traditional symbolism. The most comprehensive and valid definition of the significance of form is that which appears in the legendary *Tabula Smaragdina*: 'What is above is like what is below', which Goethe confirmed and bettered by adding: 'What is within'—the idea—'is also without'—form. Hence, Paul Guillaume has been able to declare that 'the terms of shape, structure and organization pertain not only to the language of biology (that is, forms) but also to psychology (that is, thought or ideas) . . .' and that 'isomorphism, propounding a theory of form which revives the ancient tradition of parallelism (or magic analogy), refuses to draw a dividing line between spirit and time'. This

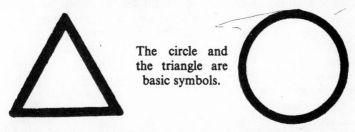

The circle and the triangle are basic symbols.

observation is rounded off with the observation that 'shapes correspond, in our perception and thought, to comparable forms in the nervous processes'; hence, what is circular is equivalent both to the circle and to the cyclic, and the square is identical with things quaternary and also with the number four (50), so that form takes its place as the 'intermediary between spirit and matter' (57). In the broadest sense, then, we may conclude that a preference for regular shapes indicates 'regulated' or well-ordered sentiments, whereas irregular forms suggest 'unregulated' sentiments. Oval shapes are related to things biomorphic; cubes with the artificial and the constructional; simple shapes with what is straightforward; and complex shapes with what is complicated. The same applies to rhythms, structures and compositions. There are other general principles too, such as that which equates symmetry with equilibrium and with the static; asymmetry with dynamism; absolute regularity and, likewise, absolute irregularity with chaos, in so far as they are both expressions of the undifferentiated: differentiation is brought about by ritual, that is, by the organization of regularized irregularity. Examples of morphological analyses may be taken over and applied to the symbolic; to take one example: in the phenomenon of growth, the circular or irradiating form signifies, in symbolic terms, the regular force of diffusion, the existence of a centre as the 'Origin', and a uniform pattern of resistance. These laws are equally true of the spirit. Forms which, within a given system or group, are different one from the other may be ordered in a series or in a scale (or within orders of analogies and correspondences). So, the trapezium, the rectangle, the square, the circle represent a series which progresses from irregularity to regularity, a series which could equally well apply to moral evolution. Jung touches upon this question, commenting that the square, as the minimal composite number (symbolizing a situation), represents the pluralist or inner state of the man who is not yet at one with himself. And yet the square is superior to the trapezium, just as the trapezium is superior to the trapezoid. The octagon is the 'intervening figure' (or the intermediary) between the square and the circle. It is unnecessary to emphasize that the meaning of a symbol varies from plane to plane, notably on the psychological and cosmic planes. So, for example, from the psychological point of view, the triangle, in its natural position with the apex uppermost, when placed between the square and the circle, is expressive of communication. But, objectively speaking, these three figures symbolize the relationship (represented by the triangle) between earth (the square) and heaven (the circle, the wheel, or rose-window); this explains why these are the essential symbols of so many Cistercian and Gothic façades. Another law to be taken into account is that forms explain objects, and objects forms; that is to say, the symbolic meaning of a being or figure is usually confirmed and emphasized by the significance of its shape, the converse also being true. Gothic spires are related to the pyramid, therefore the pyramid is related to Gothic spires. In India, geometric forms have the following cosmic implications: The sphere is associated with the ether or heaven; the crescent with air; the pyramid, fire; the cube, earth (4). The analysis of the symbolism of geometric shapes has been carried to excess by some writers—Piobb among them. Star, for example, proposes the following correspondences: the sphere, intellectual life, pure thought, and abstraction; the cone, a synthesis of all other shapes and a symbol for psychic wholeness; the cylinder, material thoughts and the mechanistic intellect (55). In general, flat shapes have a more spiritual character than shapes with bulk, but the latter are linked more closely with the macrocosmos. It is unnecessary to emphasize that, in the symbolism of shape—even when three-dimensional—the diagrammatic cross-section or ground-plan is of the essence. Thus, to take the cathedral as an example, the figure of the cross, that is, of the ground-plan, takes precedence over the temple/mountain symbolism deriving from the irregularly ascending pyramid-shape without neutralizing its effect. Another factor of importance is number-symbolism: for example, two towers, over and above the inherent symbolism of towers, of prisms and cylinders, embrace a meaning which springs from their duality. For this reason, most religious edifices shun the number two (since it implies conflict) and turn to the number three (implying resolution, quite apart from the fact that it is the image of the Trinity), and the two bell-towers of the façade are completed by the cimborrio above the transept. The circle and the square stand for limitlessness and limitation respectively.

Sheaf In Egyptian hieroglyphics, a determinative sign defining the concept of limitation (19).

Sheaf (or **Bundle**) Eliade points out that the Latin *fascis* (sheaf or bundle) and *fascia* (band, sash, or bandage) are related to *fascinum* (fascination or evil-doing); they are words which fall within the vast symbolic group composed of bindings, knots, bows, plaits, ropes and cords, all of which allude to 'being tied to' existence (18). But this is to explain only the negative side of the symbol. Like most symbols, it tends to ambivalence, and in the positive sense, the sheaf symbolizes unification, integration and strength.

Shekhinah This is not a symbol but a Cabbalistic sefirah. It represents the feminine aspect of the Supreme Being, i.e., to quote Jungian terminology, his *anima*, of which all such souls as the young woman, the stranger, the beloved, are mirrors. The never-ending search for the *ideal* through a multiplicity of women must represent the search for the Shekhinah, either through the images of the *anima* or simply through women's powers of carnal seduction which, according to the Book of Henoch, even tempted some of the angels themselves. The rejection of the woman—as exemplified by Hamlet's spurning of Ophelia—might, in such a context, represent a longing to return to the angelic state, to escape from the merely human condition by an opposite route to that of *conjunctio*. Gershom G. Scholem, in *On the Kabbalah and its Symbolism* (London, 1965), says that the Shekhinah may contain aspects which are negative, occult and destructive, and this leads one by another path to the Hindu trinity, in which Siva (or Shiva) symbolizes the destructive side of the deity. It should not be forgotten that, in this case, destruction is only concerned with the phenomenic side of beings, and, in reality, it is transformation, renovation and rebirth.

Shell One of the eight emblems of good luck in Chinese Buddhism, found in allegories about royalty, and also a sign for a prosperous journey (5). This favourable implication is the result of the shell's association with water, the source of fertility. According to Eliade, shells are also related to the moon and to Woman. Pearl-symbolism also is very closely linked with the shell. The mythic birth of Aphrodite from a shell is of obvious relevance (18). In Schneider's view, the shell is the mystic symbol of the prosperity of one generation rising out of the death of the preceding generation (5). In all probability, its favourable meaning is—as in the case of the well and the bottle—a consequence of the thirsty traveller or pilgrim linking the shell in his mind with the presence of water; this would explain its significance in mediaeval allegories.

Shepherd The title given to the lunar god Tammuz (or Thammuz) as the shepherd of the 'flocks' of the stars. According to Krappe, this idea is closely bound up with the passion of Tammuz (as Adonis) for Aphrodite (or Ishtar), because of the relationship between the phases of the moon and dismemberment (35). The shepherd is also the conductor of souls to the Land of the Dead—the psychopomp, and a symbol of supreme power, since flocks are representative of the cosmic forces.

Shield The symbolic significance of the shield amounts to a simple transposition of its defensive function to the spiritual plane. The fact that coats-of-arms were generally emblazoned upon shields yields an additional meaning which may be interpreted as implying that the knight defends himself by displaying his identity and invoking it in the hour of peril.

Ship On coins, a ship ploughing through the seas is emblematic of joy and happiness (8). But the most profound significance of navigation is that implied by Pompey the Great in his remark: 'Living is not necessary, but navigation is.' By this he meant that existence is split up into two fundamental structures: living, which he understood as living for or in oneself, and sailing or navigating, by which he understood living in order to transcend—or what Nietzsche from his pessimistic angle called 'living in order to disappear'. The *Odyssey* is, basically, nothing but a navigation-myth in the sense of victory over the two essential perils of all sailing: destruction (or the triumph of the ocean—corresponding to the unconscious) and withdrawal (regression or stagnation). Yet Homer reserves the end of the periplus of Odysseus for a triumphant but affectionate 'return' to his wife, his hearth and home. This is a mystic idea analogous to the mystery of the 'fall' of the soul into the material plane of existence (by the process of involution) and to the necessity of its returning to the starting-point (evolution)—a mystery which has been expounded by Platonic idealism and by Plotinus in particular. This law of the returning soul corresponds to the belief in the concept of a 'closed' universe (like that of the Eternal Return) or the conception of all phenomena as a cyclic organization. Navigation, as envisaged in any philosophy of the absolute, would deny even the hero his triumphant return to the homeland and would make of him a perpetual explorer of oceans, under endless skies. But to come back to the symbolism of the ship, every vessel corresponds to a constellation (48). The ship-symbol has been related to the holy island, in so far as both are differentiated from the amorphous and hostile sea. If the waters of the oceans are symbolic of the unconscious, they also can allude to the dull roar of the outside world. The notion that it is essential first to learn to sail the sea of the passions in order to reach the Mountain of Salvation is the same as the idea mentioned earlier in connexion with the perils of exploring the oceans. For this reason Guénon suggests that 'the attainment of the Great Peace is depicted in the form of sailing the seas'; hence, in Christian symbolism, the ship represents the Church (28). Some of the less clearly defined aspects of the symbolism of the ship—comparable here with the small boat and the carriage—are related to symbols of the human body and of all physical bodies or vehicles; in addition to this, there is a cosmic implication deriving from the age-old comparison between the sun and the moon on the one hand, and, on the other, two ships floating upon the celestial ocean. The solar ship frequently appears on Egyptian monuments. In Assyrian art, too, ships shaped like cups are clearly solar in character; this cup-shape narrows down still further the scope of the meaning (35). Another meaning, sometimes quite independent of the foregoing, derives not so much from the idea of the ship as such but rather from the notion of sailing; this is the symbolism of the Ship-of-Death. Hence, many primitive peoples place ships on the end of a pole or on the roof of a house. On occasion, it is the roof itself (of the temple or house) which is made to resemble a ship. Always the implication is the desire to transcend existence—to travel through space to the other worlds. All these forms, then, represent the axis valley-mountain, or the symbolism of verticality and the idea of height. An obvious association here is with all the symbols for the world-axis. The mast in the centre of the vessel gives expression to the idea of the Cosmic Tree incorporated within the symbolism of the Ship-of-Death or 'Ship of Transcendence' (50).

Ship of Fools This symbol is fairly common in mediaeval iconography and is related to the Biblical 'foolish virgins'. It expresses the idea of 'sailing' as an end in itself, as opposed to the true sense of 'sailing', which is transition, evolution and salvation, or safe arrival at the haven. Hence, illustrations of *stultifera navis* usually showed a naked woman, a wine-glass and other allusions to terrestrial desires. The Ship of Fools is, then, a parallel symbol to that of the Accursed Hunter.

Shoes According to Swedenborg, shoes symbolize the 'lowly nature', in the sense both of the humble and the despicable (4). Shoes are also a symbol of the female sex organ and may have this implication in the story of Cinderella. For the ancients, they were a sign denoting liberty.

Sieve In the Egyptian system of hieroglyphs, the sign representing a cribble or sieve symbolizes the means of selecting the particular forces needed to reach a required synthesis. The deepest significance of this symbol alludes—like all alchemic experiments—to work carried out upon oneself. The concepts here involved fall within the ambit of the Greek maxim 'know thyself', but the criterion is concerned more with action than with speculation (19). To sieve is to purify and to perfect, to garner the useful, and to discard the useless.

Sigma The S-shape, both vertical and horizontal, together with all its derived forms known generically in the art of ornamentation as scrolls, symbolize relationship and movement or the underlying rhythm of apparently continuous motion. As Ortiz has noted, sigmoid signs, like the spiral, have been utilized as symbols of the wind, but they are more properly related to the whirlwind or whirlpool. The double, symmetrical spiral (like the Ionic volute) may, according to a suggestion of Breuil, be a stylized image of the bull's horns. The curved swastika is composed of two intersecting sigmas (41). A different, wider and deeper implication of the sigma (closely connected, however, with the symbolism of the whirlwind and the hurricane as a synthesis of the Elements and as the supreme cosmic 'moment') is afforded by Schneider's suggestion that the sigma, especially in its vertical position, is a representation of the stream winding its way down the mountain-side and so constituting a characteristic symbol of the valley-mountain axis (or earth-heaven, or, in other words, the *hieros gamos*). He further suggests that this S-shape seems to be formed by one waning moon plus another waxing: the symbols for the two alternating phases of the evolutive and involutive processes which govern the sacrificial relationship of earth and heaven. He believes that this is the explanation of the frequency of the sigma in primitive ornamentation (50).

Sign According to Raymond Lull, 'meaning is the revelation of secrets through the sign', a thesis which puts the emphasis upon the sign as a fact, as a reality. On the other hand, for Stanislas de Guaita (*Essais de Sciences maudites*, II, Paris, 1915) the sign is the 'point of reference needed by the will (or conscience) in projecting itself towards a predetermined goal'. The sign, then, is the concrete form, the symptom, of an invisible, an inner reality and, at the same time, the means whereby the mind is reminded of that reality. Determination and meaning are immanent in the sign. The occult theory of 'signatures' conceives everything that exists as a sign and holds that everything has a feasible 'reading' (the shape of a tree, the position of three or more rocks on a plain, the colour of some eyes, marks

XVII. **Hero.** Archetypal image of the Archangel triumphant over the Adversary (15th-century painting).

XVIII. **Horse.** Celtic candelabra incorporating symbolic horse and solar wheel. (Museo Arqueológico Nacional, Madrid).

XIX. Antonio Tapies. A painting (1958) that illustrates the *imago ignota*.

XX. Lamb. Door to the sanctuary of the church of San Plácido (Madrid), by Claudio Coello.

XXI. **Libra** and other signs of the Zodiac—a 15th-century mural by Fernando Gallego, Salamanca University.

XXII. Night Sea Crossing. Ship and whale, as symbols at once related and opposed—Gothic miniature.

XXIII. **Siren** in its most characteristic form of 'bird-woman'—relief in Barcelona cathedral.

XXIV. The number two is an essential element in the symbolism of the twin-tailed siren. (From a Roman painting).

XXV. **Sphinx.** Greek, 5th century B.C.

XXVI. **Steps.** Jacob's dream (after an old engraving).

XXVII. **Supporter.** 'Wild Men' are the commonest type of heraldic
supporters—College of San Gregorio, Valladolid.

XXVIII. **Tetramorphs** surrounding the mandorla of the Pantokrator—
Romanesque painting, San Isidoro de León.

XXIX. **Tree and Serpent.** In this Roman composition the two symbols are associated with the story of Adam and Eve.

XXX. **Virgo.** The sixth sign of the Zodiac. Part of a 15th-century mural by Fernando Gallego in Salamanca University.

XXXI. **Window.** Detail of a painting by Pedro Berruguete (*c.* 1500), with symbolic vase with lilies.

XXXII. **Year.** Circular representation of the signs of the Zodiac, corresponding to the year's labours (from a medieval miniature).

made by natural forces on a natural or artificial terrain, the structure of a landscape, the pattern of a constellation, etc.). Auguste Rodin, a realist who was always hovering on the borders of symbolism, in his *Conversations* collected by Paul Gsell, places all art within this realm of occult meaning, with the words: 'lines and shades are for us nothing more than the signs of a hidden reality. Beyond the surface, our gaze plunges into the spirit'. The painter Gustave Moreau expressed himself in similar terms when referring to 'the evocation of thought by line, arabesque and plastic means'. In the present century, Max Ernst and Dubuffet, among other artists, have explained their pictorial and graphic experiments as an immersion in the psychic projected onto the material. At the same time, C. G. Jung gives a similar explanation of the quest of the alchemists.

Twin-tailed siren (15th century).

Siren A symbolic figure which usually takes one of two main forms: as a bird-woman or as a fish-woman. The sirens in Greek mythology were supposed to be daughters of the river Achelous by the nymph Calliope; and Ceres turned them into birds. They inhabited mountainous places. Legend attributed to them a song of such sweetness they could entice the wayfarer, only to devour him. Latterly, the myth arose of sirens with fish-tails whose haunts were rocky islands and cliffs and who behaved in the same manner as did their sisters inhabiting the Element of air. The siren-myth is one of the most indestructible of all myths; among some marine peoples it has persisted even into the present day (8). Material concerning these sirens is to be found in Aristotle, Pliny, Ovid, Hyginus, the *Physiologus* (2nd century A.D.) and mediaeval bestiaries. Dating from before the 10th century are the two-tailed sirens on the tympanum of the chapel of St. Michael d'Aiguilhe at Le Puy, and the siren-birds at Saint-Benoît-sur-Loire. These and the French viper-fairies—as exemplified by Melusina in particular—are complex figures and we are not satisfied that a merely literal interpretation is the right one. They may well be representations of the inferior forces in woman, or of woman as the inferior, as in the case of lamias; or they could also be symbolic of the corrupt imagination enticed towards base ends or towards the primitive strata of life; or of the torment of desire leading to self-destruction, for their abnormal bodies cannot satisfy the passions that are aroused by their enchanting music and by their beauty of face and bosom. It seems that they are largely symbols of the 'temptations' scattered along the path of life (or of symbolic navigation) impeding the evolution of the spirit by bewitchment, beguiling it into remaining on the magic island; or, in other words, causing its premature death. The twin-tailed siren (a fine example of which may be seen on a capital in the apse of San Cugat monastery) can be explained psychologically as a simple amalgamation: the two legs of woman applied to the single tail of the fish giving the twin-tail of the woman-fish; but it may also be interpreted symbolically by reference to the profound significance of the Gemini. It seems to us that the twin tail is an infernal replica of the classical attitude of adoration in which both arms are raised—an attitude characteristic, for example, of the Cretan statuettes of priestesses. Given that the sea is the lower abyss and an image of the unconscious, then the twin fish-tail, pertaining to the sea, must express a duality (or conflict) within the watery deeps. Wirth maintains that the siren is quite simply a symbol of woman, and that woman is a true incarnation of the spirit of the earth, as opposed to the man, who is the son of heaven. He expresses his concept of transmigration as follows: 'Life entices the souls of those deprived of it. Why does the other world not retain once and for all those spiritual entities that aspire towards reincarnation? The daughters of men ensnare the sons of heaven with their beauty, dragging them irresistibly down. The spell thus cast is attributed to the siren whose song so captivates the listener that he falls into the ocean' (of the lower waters and of nascent forms) 'teeming with multitudinous life. This temptress owes her powers to the changing forms governed by the moon, the crescent of which shines upon her forehead' (59) (Plates XXIII and XXIV).

Skeleton In the majority of allegories and emblems it is the personification of death. In alchemy it is a symbol of the colour black and of the putrefaction or 'disjunction' of the component elements.

Skin Skin is associated with the ideas of birth and rebirth. In the Egyptian system of hieroglyphs there is a determinative sign comprising three skins knotted together, signifying 'to be born'; it comes into the composition of words such as 'to engender', 'to bring up', 'child', 'to form'. The amulet which the Egyptians used to present to the newly-born comprised, like the hieroglyph, three animal pelts which were attached to a solar globe. The number of the skins here refers to the essentially threefold nature of the human being—the body, the soul and the spirit—while the globe denotes his incorporation into the All. The symbolism of skin is borne out by the rite known as 'the passage through the skin' which pharaohs and priests used to carry out in order to rejuvenate themselves; this rite was later replaced by a simulacrum, and then latterly it became just a panther's tail which kings wore knotted round their waist. This notion that an individual may assume the characteristics of an animal, with its totemic implications, also comes into skin-symbolism (19). There is a basic analogy here with the sacrificial rite once practised by the priests of pre-Columbian Mexico in which human victims were clad in skins; similarly with the wearing of skins by the bearers of the *signum* in Roman legions.

Skull Broadly speaking, it is an emblem of the mortality of man, as in the literary examples of Hamlet and Faust. However, like the snail's shell, it is in truth 'what survives' of the living being once its body has been destroyed. It therefore comes to acquire significance as a receptacle for life and for thought, it is with this symbolic meaning that it figures in books on alchemy, where it is represented as the receptacle used in the processes of transmutation (32). A great many forms of superstition, ritual and—indeed—of cannibalism, are derived from this idea.

Sleeping Beauty On the one hand she may be regarded as a symbol of the anima in the Jungian sense. On the other she symbolizes, rather than the unconscious proper, the ancestral images which lie dormant in the unconscious, waiting to be stimulated into action. As Loeffler points out, in fairy-tales and legends princesses lie dreaming in their palaces, like memories and intuitions deep down in our unconscious. The princesses in their palaces, though not always asleep, are invariably outside the world of action, so that every sleeping, or otherwise secluded, princess stands for a passive potential (38).

Slug The sign denoting the slug—sometimes also interpreted as a small snake—symbolizes the male seed, the Origin of life, the silent tendency of darkness to move towards light; this concept is well expressed in Chapter 17 of the Book of the Dead (19).

Smoke The antithesis of mud, since mud combines the Elements of earth and water, whereas smoke corresponds to air and fire. There are some folklore traditions which attribute a beneficent power to smoke, which is supposed to possess the magic ability to ward off the misfortunes that beset men, animals and plants (21). On the other hand, the column of smoke is a symbol of the valley-mountain antithesis, that is, of the relationship between earth and heaven, pointing out the path through fire to salvation (17). According to Geber, the alchemist, smoke symbolizes the soul leaving the body.

Snail In Egyptian hieroglyphics the snail is associated with the action of the microcosmic spiral upon matter (19). Modern scientific research in morphology tends to verify this intuition, not only in this particular case but also in all cases where the spiral scheme appears in nature.

Sophia Woman as *anima* (the soul of man) and as spiritual guide. According to the Gnostic Ptolemaeus, in his *Letter to Flora*, Sophia is the intermediary between the soul of the world (the demiurge) and ideas (pleroma) or plenitude, a mass of aeons opposed to the world of phenomena. For the 17th-century mystics Jakob Böhme and Georg Gichtel, Sophia, the divine virgin, was originally found in 'primordial man' (see Eliade, *Méphistophélès et l'androgyne*, Paris, 1962). She abandoned him, and man cannot be saved until he finds her again. This idea, which is related to the Persian idea of the loved one (Daena), was taken up by the Catharists; it also colours romantic thought (as in Novalis, Hölderlin, Poe, Wagner). A brutally figurative allegory of the idea is furnished by the Greek myth of Athene born from the head of Zeus (i.e. the virgin = thought).

Sorcerer Like the giant and the magician, he is a personification of the Terrible Father, of the 'evil demiurge' of the Gnostics, prefigured in Saturn (31).

Sound In India, the sound of Krishna's flute is the magical cause of the birth of the world. The pre-Hellenic maternal goddesses are depicted holding lyres, and with the same significance (56). There are other traditional doctrines which hold that sound was the first of all things to be created, and that which gave rise to all others, commencing with light, or, alternatively, with air and fire. An instance of this is the lament quoted in the *Poimandres* of Hermes Trismegistos (31).

Space In a manner of speaking, space is an intermediate zone between the cosmos and chaos. Taken as the realm of all that is possible, it is chaotic; regarded as the region in which all forms and structures have their existence, it is cosmic. Space soon came to be associated with time, and this association proved one of the ways of coming to grips with the recalcitrant nature of space. Another—and the most important—was the concept of space as a three-part organization based upon its three dimensions. Each dimension has two possible directions of movement, implying the possibility of two poles or two contexts. To the six points achieved in this way, there was added a seventh: the centre; and space thus became a logical structure. The symbolisms of level and of orientation were finally brought to bear in order to complete the exegesis. The three dimensions of space are illustrated by means of a three-dimensional cross, whose arms are oriented along these six spatial directions, made up of the four points of the compass plus the two points of the zenith and the nadir. According to René Guénon, this symbolism—because of its structural character—is identical with that of the Sacred Palace (or the inner palace) of the Cabala, located at the centre-point from which the six directions radiate. In the three-dimensional cross, the zenith and the nadir correspond to the top and the bottom, the front and back to East and West, the right and left to the South and North. The upright axis is the polar axis, the North-South axis is the solstitial line, the East-West the equinoctial. The significance of the vertical or level-symbolism concerns the analogy between the high and the good, the low and the inferior. The Hindu doctrine of the three gunas—sattva (height, superiority), rajas (intermediate zone of the world of appearances, or ambivalence) and tamas (inferiority, or darkness)—is in itself sufficient to explain the meaning of the symbolism of level up and down the vertical axis. It is, in consequence, the intermediate plane of the four-directional cross (that which incorporates the cardinal points and which implies the square) which represents the world of appearances. Taking next the East-West axis, traditional orientation-symbolism associates the East—being the point of sunrise—with spiritual illumination; and the West—the point where the sun sets—with death and darkness. Passing next to the North-South axis, there is no one definite interpretation. In many oriental cultures, the zenith coincides with the mystic 'Hole' through which transition and transcendence are effected, that is, the path from the world of manifestation (spatial and temporal) to that of eternity. But it has also been identified with the centre of the three-dimensional cross, taken as the heart of space. Reduced to two dimensions—those of the contrasting horizontal and vertical arms—the cross comes to represent harmony between extension (associated with width) and exaltation (with height). The horizontal arm concerns the implications of a given gradation or moment in an individual's existence, and the vertical pertains to moral elevation (25). William of Saint-Thierry, describing the seven gradations of the soul, observes that it ascends these steps in order to reach the celestial life (14). If we seek an interpretation which will justify the four points of the horizontal plane's being reduced to two (the left and right), we can find a basis for it in Jung's assertion that the rear part coincides with the unconscious and the front with the manifest or consciousness; and since the left also can be equated with the unconscious and the right with consciousness, the rear then becomes equivalent to the left and the front to the right (32). Other equivalents are: left side with the past, the sinister, the repressed, involution, the abnormal and the illegitimate; the right side with the future, the felicitous, openness, evolution, the normal and the legitimate (42). In all this, there is an apparent contradiction with the corresponding number-symbolisms: Paneth observes that, in most cultures, the uneven numbers are considered to be masculine and the even numbers to be feminine. Since the left side is the *zone of origin* and the right that of the *outcome*, the corresponding number-symbolisms would seem to be one (the uneven or masculine number) for the left side (that is, the past) and two (the even or feminine number) for the right side (the subsequent or outcome). The solution is to be found in the fact that the number one (unity) never corresponds to the plane of the manifest world or to spatial reality: it is the symbol of the centre, but not in the sense of occupying any situation in space which might imply a sequel. Hence we must conclude that two is the number corresponding to the left side and three is that related to the right. Guénon explains the way in which the cosmic order conforms with all this in a lucid exposition of the relevant Hindu doctrines to the effect that the right hand zone is the solar region; the left-hand the lunar. 'In the aspect of this symbolism which refers to the temporal condition, the Sun and the right eye correspond to the future, the Moon and the left eye to the past; the frontal eye corresponds to the present which, from the point of view of the manifested, is but an imperceptible moment, comparable to the geometrical point without dimensions in the spatial order; that is why a single look from the third eye destroys all manifestation (which is expressed symbolically by saying that it reduces everything to ashes), and that is also why it is not represented by any bodily organ; but when one rises above this contingent point of view, the present is seen to contain all reality (just as the point carries within itself all the possibilities of space), and when succession is transmuted into simultaneity, all things abide in the "eternal present", so that the apparent destruction is truly a "transformation"' (26). Now, the seven aspects that define space have been regarded as the origin of all septenary groups, and in particular of the seven planets, the seven colours and the seven kinds of landscape (50). Hence Luc Benoist can assert that the Christian Church, by building on earth a mighty, three-dimensional cross of stone, has created for the entire world the co-ordinate lines of a supernatural geometry. Benoist then quotes Clement of Alexandria as saying that the six directions of space symbolize—or are equivalent to—the simultaneous and eternal presence of the six days of the Creation, and that the seventh day (of rest) signifies the return to the centre and the beginning (6). Once the cosmic sense of spatial symbolism has been demonstrated, it is simple to deduce its psychological applications. And once the static laws have been determined, it is easy to grasp the dynamic·implications, always bearing in mind the symbolism of orientation. Here, we must point out that the swastika—a solar and polar symbol—implies a movement from right to left, like the apparent movement of the sun; and that Clotho—one of the Parcae—spins her 'wheel of destiny' in the same direction, that is, the opposite way to existence, so destroying it. Right-handedness is characteristic of all symbols of natural life (28); hence, in the Egyptian system of hieroglyphs, to enter is to go towards the right and to go out is to go towards the left (19); orienting these hieroglyphs, we have the right corresponding with the rise and the left with the setting of the sun. Similarly, the right side takes on an extra implication of birth and life, while the left side acquires an association with death (17). Another consequence, apparent in allegories and emblems, is that the right side corresponds to the higher virtues— if one may put it that way—such as compassion, and the left side to justice. All of the above conclusions are logical deductions drawn from the study of oriental tradition, supported by the findings of experimental psychology. But they are conclusions which have also been verified by anthropologists and sociologists in their studies of the habits of diverse peoples. Ania Teillard, for example, has collated a mass of facts; she quotes J. J. Bachofen as asserting (in his *Mutterrecht und Urreligion und Grabersymbolik der Alten*) that, in the important and very common equation 'right hand=masculinity', the left hand harbours magic powers and the right hand the force of reason, and also that in matriarchal societies one always finds the idea of superiority attributed to the left side, and conversely. To turn to the left is to look back upon the past, the unconscious, implying introversion; to turn to the right is to look upon the outside world, implying action and extraversion. At the same time, ethnologists are agreed that during the first stage of any period of sun-worship, the right side becomes pre-eminent, whereas in lunar cults it is the left side which prevails (56). In paintings, reliefs and other artistic creations of man, the left side is characterized by a more vivid projection of the self (that is, by identification) and the right side is more extravert.

Spark   An image of the spiritual principle which gives birth to each individual, related also to the Cabbalistic (emanatist) concept of souls scattering from the centre outwards into the world in the form of sparks (32). For Jung, it is therefore a symbol of the heavenly father.

Sparrowhawk   Like the eagle, this bird was consecrated to the sun by the Egyptians, the Greeks and Romans, who attributed to it all the powers associated with the sun (8).

Sphinx   A fabulous being composed of several parts of the human being and four of various animals. The sphinx at Thebes had the head and breasts of a woman, the body of a bull or dog, the claws of a lion, the tail of a dragon and the wings of a bird (8). Being the supreme embodiment of the enigma, the sphinx keeps watch over an ultimate meaning which must remain for ever beyond the understanding of man. Jung sees in it a synthesis of the 'Terrible Mother', a symbol which has left its mark on mythology as well (31). The mask of the sphinx pertains to the mother-image and also to nature-symbolism; but beneath the mask lie the implications of the myth of multiplicity or of the enigmatic fragmentation of the cosmos. According to esoteric tradition, the Gizeh sphinx is a synthesis of all the science of the past. It is shown contemplating the rising sun and seems to embrace both heaven and earth in its meaning. It is, of course, a symbol which unites, in the midst of the heterogeneity of existence, the four Elements (corresponding to the tetramorphs) with the quintessence or the spirit (signified by the human part of the figure) (49) (Plate XXV).

Spider The spider is a symbol with three distinct meanings; sometimes they merge or overlap, sometimes one or the other predominates. The three meanings are derived from: (i) the creative power of the spider, as exemplified in the weaving of its web; (ii) the spider's aggressiveness; and (iii) the spider's web as a spiral net converging towards a central point. The spider sitting in its web is a symbol of the centre of the world, and is hence regarded in India as Maya, the eternal weaver of the web of illusion (32). The spider's destructive powers are also connected with its significance as a symbol of the world of phenomena. As Schneider points out, spiders, in their ceaseless weaving and killing—building and destroying—symbolize the ceaseless alternation of forces on which the stability of the universe depends. For this reason, the symbolism of the spider goes deep, signifying, as it does, that 'continuous sacrifice' which is the means of man's continual transmutation throughout the course of his life. Even death itself merely winds up the thread of an old life in order to spin a new one (51). The spider is a lunar animal because the moon (owing to its passive character, in the sense that it merely *reflects* light, and because of its waxing and waning phases, taking these in the positive and negative sense) is related to the world of phenomena, and, on the psychic level, to the imagination. Thus the moon, since it holds sway over the whole phenomenal world (for all phenomenal forms are subject to growth and death), weaves the thread of each man's destiny. Accordingly, the moon is depicted as a gigantic spider in many myths (17).

Spindle or **Bobbin** The spindle and the distaff, and likewise the act of sewing, are symbols of life and the temporal; they are therefore related to the moon, a symbol expressing the transitoriness of life

or all that goes in phases. Hence, deities incorporating the characteristics of the moon, the earth or vegetation usually have the spindle
or the distaff as attributes; this is the case with Ishtar, Atargatis,
etc. (17). Schneider supports this with his definition of the spindle
as a symbol of the *Magna Mater* who is sewing with it inside a
mountain of stone or on top of the Tree of the World. In shape, the
spindle is a mandorla and so acquires the symbolism of two intersecting circles which stand for heaven and earth, that is, of the
sacrifice which renews the generating force of the universe. All
spindle-shaped symbols signify the broad idea of mutual sacrifice
and the power of inversion (50).

Spinning Spinning—like singing—is equivalent to bringing
forth and fostering life. Hence Schneider's comment 'unhappy is the
poor spinner who leaves her skeins (that is, her offspring) to dry on
the river-bank and finds them gone' (51). The Parcae, like fairies,
are spinners. Likewise, a host of figures of legend and folklore.

Spiral A schematic image of the evolution of the universe. It
is also a classical form symbolizing the orbit of the moon (50), and a
symbol for growth, related to the Golden Number (32), arising (so
Housay maintains) out of the concept of the rotation of the earth.
In the Egyptian system of hieroglyphs the spiral—corresponding to
the Hebrew *vau*—denotes cosmic forms in motion, or the relationship between unity and multiplicity. Of especial importance in
relation to the spiral are bonds and serpents. The spiral is essentially
macrocosmic (19). The above ideas have been expressed in mythic
form as follows: 'From out of the unfathomable deeps there arose a
circle shaped in spirals. . . . Coiled up within the spirals, lies a snake,
a symbol of wisdom and eternity' (9). Now, the spiral can be found
in three main forms: expanding (as in the nebula), contracting (like
the whirlwind or whirlpool) or ossified (like the snail's shell). In
the first case it is an active sun-symbol, in the second and third cases
it is a negative moon-symbol (17). Nevertheless, most theorists,
including Eliade, are agreed that the symbolism of the spiral is fairly
complex and of doubtful origin. Its relationship with lunar animals
and with water has been provisionally admitted (18). Going right
back to the most ancient traditions, we find the distinction being
made between the creative spiral (rising in a clockwise direction, and
attributed to Pallas Athene) and the destructive spiral like a whirlwind (which twirls round to the left, and is an attribute of Poseidon)
(51). As we have seen, the spiral (like the snake or serpent and the
Kundalini force of Tantrist doctrine) can also represent the potential
centre as in the example of the spider's web. Be that as it may, the
spiral is certainly one of the essential motifs of the symbolism of
ornamental art all over the world, either in the simple form of a
curve curling up from a given point, or in the shape of scrolls, or

sigmas, etc. Parkin observes in his *Prehistoric Art* that 'no ornamental motif seems to have been more attractive than the spiral'. Ortiz (41) suggests that, from a semantic point of view, the spiral is an emblem of atmospheric phenomena and of the hurricane in particular; but the fact is that the hurricane in its turn is a symbol of secession from the creative (as well as destructive) functions of the universe, that is, of the suspension of the provisional but pacific order of the universe. He also points to the connexion between breathing and the creative breath of life. He goes on to suggest that the volute in ancient cultures was a spiral form symbolizing the breath and the spirit. It is for this reason that the Egyptian god Thoth is represented with a large spiral on his head. Finally, by virtue of its significance in connexion with creation, with movement and progressive development, the spiral is an attribute of power, found in the sceptre of the Egyptian pharaoh, in the *lituus* of Roman augurs and in the present-day walking-stick. In addition to the above, it is also possible that the spiral may symbolize the relationship between the circle and the centre. For the spiral is associated with the idea of the dance, and especially with primitive dances of healing and incantation, when the pattern of movement develops as a spiral curve. Such spiral movements (closely related to the pattern of the mandala and to the spiral form that appears so frequently in art from the Mesolithic Age onwards—particularly in France, Ireland and England) may be regarded as figures intended to induce a state of ecstasy and to enable man to escape from the material world and to enter the beyond, through the 'hole' symbolized by the mystic Centre. Striking examples of such spirals are those of Gravinias (Morbihan), New Grange (Leinster), Carnwath (Scotland) and Castle Archdall (Ulster).

Spiral, Double The double spiral represents the completion of the sigmoid line, and the ability of the sigmoid line to express the intercommunication between two opposing principles is clearly shown in the Chinese *Yang-Yin* symbol. Two double spirals intersecting form the swastika with curved arms, a motif which is fairly common although not so frequent as the arrangement of a series of double spirals in a continuous rhythm. It has been suggested that this motif first appeared in Danubian culture, whence it spread outwards to the north and south of Europe and across Asia to the Far East. Whereas the architectural meander of straight lines and right angles is a symbol of earth, the double spiral is closely linked with water. Given that water is the Element of transition, transformation and regeneration, the double spiral is capable of fully representing its symbolic significance. Hence, it is of common occurrence in the Cretan and other markedly marine cultures. From a cosmic point of view, the double spiral may be regarded as the flattened projection of the two halves of the egg of the world, or of the primordial hermaphrodite separated into two halves, or of the Upper and Lower Waters (8). Hence, together with the St. Andrew's cross, and the drum shaped rather like an hour-glass, it constitutes a symbol of Inversion and of the relationship between opposites (6, 50).

Spur   The spur is a symbol of active force. It is attached to the heel like the wings of Mercury, and protects the legendary Achilles' heel. The spur of gold, together with the belt, symbolized, in the Middle Ages, the 'defensive' (or moral) virtues of the knight.

Square   The square, as the expression of the quaternity, is a symbol of the combination and regulation of four different elements. Hence, it corresponds to the symbolism of the number four and to all four-part divisions of any process whatsoever. Psychologically, its form gives the impression of firmness and stability, and this explains its frequent use in symbols of organization and construction. For Jung, the four-part division of movements and forms is of greater value than the three-part. Whether or not this is so, what is certain is that, as against the dynamism of the odd numbers and their related geometric forms (such as: three, five, the triangle or the pentagon), the even numbers and forms (for example: four, six, eight, the square, the hexagon, the octagon) are characterized by the qualities of stability, firmness and definition. Hence, ternary symbolism tends to illustrate activity and dynamism (or pure spirit), whereas the quaternary alludes predominantly to things material (or the merely rational intellect). The four Elements, the four seasons, the four stages of Man's life, and specially the four points of the compass, are all sources of the order and the stability of the world. This does not contradict the feminine character which Chinese, Hindu and other traditions ascribe to the square, since it corresponds to the earth, in contrast to the masculine character of the circle (and the triangle) (32). In Egyptian hieroglyphs the square signifies achievement and the square-shaped spiral denotes constructive, materialized energy (19). However, the square resting upon one of its corners acquires a dynamic sense which is quite new, implying a change in its fundamental symbolism: during the Romanesque period, it was used as a symbol of the sun, comparable with the circle (51).

Squaring the Circle   The ancient Mesopotamians used to place a circle between two squares in order to find out its area. And the idea of equating the circle with the square also grew out of the concept of the rotating square. But our concern is not with the mathematical but the symbolic problem. 'Squaring the circle', like the *lapis* or the *aurum philosophicum*, was one of the preoccupations of the alchemists; but whereas the latter two were symbols of the quest for the evolutive goal of the spirit, the former problem concerned the equating of the two great cosmic symbols of heaven (or the circle) and earth (or the square). It is to do, then, with the union of two opposites; not juxtaposition as in the *coniunctio* of the two arms of the cross, for example, but the equation and cancelling out of two components in a higher synthesis. The square was seen to correspond to the four Elements. The aim of 'squaring the circle', then (which strictly ought to be called 'circling the square'), was to obtain unity in the material world (as well as in the spiritual life) over and above the differences and obstacles (the static order) of the number four and the four-cornered square. We have already suggested that the rotated square was reckoned an important part of this project, and Heinrich Khunrath comments in his *Von hylealischen Chaos*: 'By means of circumrotation or circulatory revolution, the quaternary is restored to purest simplicity and innocence' (32). Another means of getting an *ersatz* 'squaring' was to superimpose two squares, inscribing a circle within them, in such a way as to form an octagon. The octagon can indeed be considered, in both a geometric and a symbolic sense, as the intermediary form between the square and the circle. For this reason it never symbolized the *opus* itself (that is, the mystic consummation of the synthesis of opposites), but it did stand for the path indicated by things quaternary (such as the earth, the feminine element, matter or reason) towards the circle (representing perfection, eternity and spirit). That is why many mediaeval baptisteries, fonts and cupolas are octagonal in shape.

Staff The staff has a double symbolism, as a support and as an instrument of punishment. As regards the first, Frazer notes that the ancient Egyptians held a festival after the Autumn Solstice which they called the 'Nativity of the Sun-Stick', because they supposed that, as the day grew shorter and the sunlight weaker, the sun needed a stick for support (21). Dalí has revived the mythic staff in the form of crutches, which are a recurrent theme in his paintings. The use of staff-symbolism, both among the ancient Egyptians and in a modern artist such as Dalí, exemplifies an elementary principle of symbolism: the correlation and interchangeability of the material and spiritual aspects of a given situation. As a weapon it is symbolically identical with the club, the royal weapon (15) (Oedipus kills Laius, whom he does not know to be his father, with a blow of his staff).

Stag Its symbolic meaning is linked with that of the Tree of Life, because of the resemblance of its antlers to branches. It is also a symbol of the cycles of regeneration and growth, as Henri-Charles Puech has observed. The stag, in several cultures of Asia and pre-Columbian America, came to be thought of as a symbol of regeneration because of the way its antlers are renewed. Like the eagle and the lion, it is the secular enemy of the serpent, which shows that, symbolically, it was viewed favourably; it is closely related to heaven and light, whereas the serpent is associated with night and subterranean life (18). Hence, in the Milky Way, on both sides of the Bridge of Death and Resurrection are figures of eagles, stags and horses acting as mediators between heaven and earth (50). In the West, during the Middle Ages, the way of solitude and purity was often symbolized by the stag, which actually appears in some emblems with a crucifix between its horns (thus providing the last link in the chain of relationships: tree/cross/horns) (4). It has also been considered as a symbol of elevation (20). The Greeks and Romans perceived certain 'mystical' gifts in the stag, which they exaggerated through psychic projection. One of these supposed gifts was the ability instinctively to recognize medicinal plants, which is what lies behind the assertion in ancient bestiaries that 'the stag can recognize the dictamnus plant'. His prestige is in part a consequence of his appearance: his beauty, grace, agility (46). Because of his rôle as messenger of the gods, the stag may be considered as the antithesis of the he-goat.

Stains The symbolism of blots or stains—like that of the wall-flakings which so impressed Piero de Cosimo and Leonardo da Vinci—is a combination of the symbolisms pertaining to the shapes of these stains and their texture or material. A related symbol is that of clouds, in so far as both clouds and blots suggest imaginary shapes which, by analogy, may be identified with other shapes. Proof of this has been afforded by the Rorschach test. These blots or stains are often associated with the passage of time, in which case they allude to ideas of the transitory and death. At the same time, stains and areas of discoloration or imperfection of all kinds may also be explained by reference to the symbolism of the abnormal, for, according to the alchemists, such 'infirmities' in objects or materials actually constitute 'prime matter', the basis for the creation of philosophical gold (equated with spiritual evolution). As the *Rosarium Philosophorum* says: 'Our gold is not common gold. You, nevertheless, have asked about the green assuming that the mineral is a leprous body because of the green which grows in it. It is for this reason that I tell you that what is perfect in the mineral is solely this green, because very soon it will be transformed by our craft into the truest gold.' Relevant to this is Nietzsche's remark, in *Thus Spake Zarathustra*, that 'Out of the lowest the highest reaches its peak' (32).

Star As a light shining in the darkness, the star is a symbol of the spirit. Bayley has pointed out, however, that the star very rarely carries a single meaning—it nearly always alludes to multiplicity. In which case it stands for the forces of the spirit struggling against the forces of darkness. This is a meaning which has been incorporated into emblematic art all over the world (4). For this reason, 'identification with the star' is possible only to the chosen few. Jung recalls the Mithraic saying: 'I am a star which goes with thee and shines out of the depths' (31). Now, individual stars are often seen in graphic symbolism. Their meaning frequently depends upon their shape, the number of points, the manner of their arrangement, and their

Five-pointed and six-pointed stars.

colour (if any). The 'flaming star' is a symbol of the mystic Centre—of the force of the universe in expansion (4). The five-pointed star is the most common. As far back as in the days of Egyptian hieroglyphics it signified 'rising upwards towards the point of origin', and formed part of such words as 'to bring up', 'to educate', 'the teacher', etc. (19). The inverted five-pointed star is a symbol of the infernal as used in black magic (37).

Stars Being nocturnal, their symbolism is associated with that of night; they are also linked with the idea of multiplicity (or with disintegration) because they appear in clusters, and with order and destiny because of their disposition and location (according to Horapollo Niliacus).

Stars, The The seventeenth enigma of the Tarot, depicting an allegorical image of a naked girl kneeling down beside a pool, as, from a golden jar, she pours a life-giving liquid into the still waters. In her left hand she holds a silver jar from which she pours fresh water on to the dry earth, encouraging the growth of the vegetation—signified most often by a sprig of acacia and a rose in full bloom, an emblem of immortality and of love. Above this figure are a bright star and several lesser ones. The ultimate meaning of this symbol seems to be expressive of intercommunication of the different worlds, or the vitalization by the celestial luminaries of liquids contained in certain vessels, and implying, furthermore, the transference of these celestial characteristics to the purely material Elements of earth and water. For this reason, Oswald Wirth concludes that this enigma represents the soul uniting spirit with matter (59).

State of Mind The symbolist idea that the different worlds are so many different states of being (crystallized into different orders of matter and form with their corresponding, expressive characteristics), and that they can be systematized, in their diversity, within a scale or series, after the manner of the regular figures of geometry, colours or sounds, can equally well be taken the other way round. In which case, the states of being, which, from the psychological point of view, are represented as corresponding emotional states, that is, as varying 'states of mind' (comparable with the emotional expressions peculiar to each one of the musical modes: severe, ecstatic, anguished, enthusiastic, active, erotic, melancholic)—these states of being, then, come to be represented as certain definite kinds of landscape, in which the additional symbolisms of level, of symmetry, of light and colour, all play a definite part.

State of Preservation A symbol whose meaning is almost literal, or analogous to the physical, by simple transference of the physical characteristics of a thing on to the spiritual and psychological plane. So, for example, fracture symbolizes fragmentation, disintegration and mutilation on the spiritual level; wear stands for weariness of spirit, poor health and a worn-out sentiment or idea; corrosion for destruction, infirmity and suffering. We have here the age-old concept of the parallel between the physical and the psychic worlds, an idea which gave rise to the alchemists' postulate that a series of operations upon matter must have repercussions upon the spirit— and indeed this was true by virtue of the force of their *intention*. Nevertheless, one must guard against accepting the above symbological interpretation as the only possible one, for it is a very generalized conclusion; there are, in fact, other symbolic meanings, sometimes, in particular cases, of greater importance than this, deriving from the agent which is bringing it about. The action of each of the Elements, for instance, always imparts a strong flavour of its own symbolic character. Fire, water or earth, if they burn or soak an object, or cause it to putrefy, in addition to altering its physical identity and changing its state also inject into it some part of their own mode of behaviour.

Steed A symbol of the animal in man, that is, of the force of the instincts. As a riding-mount, it is also a symbol of the body. That is why most mythological figures, quite apart from their other attributes, are linked with one particular mount (Wotan mounted on Sleipnir, Ahuramazda on Angramainyu, Mithras on the bull, Men on a horse with human feet, Freyr on the boar with bristles of gold) (31). The arrangement of the symbol is like that of the centaur, but the hierarchical order is reversed: whereas the centaur stands for the superior force of the instincts (or even for intuition, a gift attributed by some primitive peoples to animals in general and to the horse in particular), the steed in itself symbolizes control of baser forces. In India, the mount is seen as *vahana* (materialization). The pedestal plays a similar rôle, its shape always being symbolic. In this way, the goddess Padmâ, for example, is associated with the lotus (60).

Steel According to Evola in *La tradizione ermetica*, steel denotes the transcendent toughness of the principle of the all-conquering spirit.

Steps This is a symbol which is very common in iconography all over the world. It embraces the following essential ideas: ascension, gradation, and communication between different, vertical levels. In the Egyptian system of hieroglyphs, steps constitute a determinative sign which defines the act of ascending; it forms part of one of the appellations of Osiris, who is invoked as 'he who stands at the top of the steps'. Ascending, then, can be understood both in a material and in an evolutive and spiritual sense. Usually, the actual number of steps involved in the symbol is of symbolic significance. In Egyptian images, the number tends to be nine: the triple ternary which symbolizes the gods of the ennead who, together with Osiris, make up the symbolic number ten which stands for the completed cycle or the return to unity (19). A great many Egyptian tombs have yielded up amulets in the shape of ladders. The Book of the Dead says: 'My steps are now in position so that I may see the gods.' Eliade has pointed out parallel images, such as the following: Among many primitive peoples, mythic ascension is indicated by means of a rope, a stake, a tree or a mountain (symbolizing the world-axis). Or, according to an Oceanian myth, the hero reaches heaven by means of the fantastic hyperbole of a chain of arrows. And in Islamic tradition, Mohammed saw a ladder which the just climbed up to reach God (17). To refer again to primitive belief, Schneider observes that in order to 'reach' the mountain of Mars and reap its benefits, one must ascend the ladder of one's forebears —suggesting a biological and historical source for the mystic symbol of the ladder. Hence steps are also one of the most notable symbols in ancestral rites (50). Images specifically connected with the steps are the mountain, and architectural structures incorporating steps, such as the Egyptian pyramid of Sakkara, the Mesopotamian ziggurats, or the teocallis of America of pre-Columbian days; we have then a synthesis of two symbols—that of the 'temple-mountain' and that of the steps—signifying that the entire cosmos is the path of ascension towards the spirit. In Mithraism, the ceremonial steps were seven in number, each step being made of a different metal (as was each different plane of the ziggurat in a figurative sense). According to Celsus, the first step was of lead (corresponding to Saturn). The general correspondence with the planets is self-evident. Now, this idea of gradual ascent was taken up particularly by the alchemists from the latter part of the Middle Ages onwards; they identified it sometimes with the phases of the transmutation process. In Stephan Michelspacher's work *Die Cabala, Spiegel der Kunst und Natur* (1654), the following graded scale is given: Calcination, Sublimation, Solution, Putrefaction, Distillation, Coagulation, Tincture, leading to a kind of shrine inside a mountain (32). According to the Zohar, the ladder which Jacob is said to have seen in his dreams had seventy-two rungs and its top disappeared into the clouds (39). Broadly speaking, in emblems and allegories throughout the Middle Ages, it is the ascending (affirmative) aspect of the steps which predominates, emphasized by the signs and symbols clustering round the ladder. Bayley points out that many steps are surmounted by a cross, the figure of an angel, a star or a fleur-de-lis (4) located on the border itself. In Romanesque art, and generally in the thought characteristic of the period, the steps are the symbol of the 'relationship between the worlds' (14, 20), but it must not be forgotten that, within the spatial symbolism of level, there are not two grades indicating two different worlds (the terrestrial or intermediary and the celestial or upper) but three (through the addition of a third: the infernal or lower world). This is why Eliade (for reasons of psychology as well) states that the steps are a vivid image of 'breaking through' the levels of existence in order to open up the way from one world to another, establishing a relationship between heaven, earth and hell (or between virtue, passivity and sin). Hence, steps located beneath the level of the earth are always a symbol for an opening into the infernal regions. In Bettini's *Libro del monte santo di Dio* (Florence, 1477), steps are shown superimposed upon a mountain; to emphasize the parallel—and indeed identical—symbolism of the mountain and the ladder, the former is portrayed as if it were terraced and the terraces are shown to be the rungs of the ladder. On these rungs are the names of the virtues: Humility, Prudence, Temperance, Fortitude, Justice, Awe, Mercy, Science, Counsel, Understanding and Wisdom. The steps are portrayed as if chained to the mountainside. On the peak of the mountain is a mandorla formed of angels with Christ in the centre. (Plate XXVI).

Stick   A material symbol of the valley-mountain axis, comparable with steps, the cross and the artificial stake. The post has the same symbolic sense, largely because it stands erect. A burnt stick represents death and wisdom (50).

Stone   Stone is a symbol of being, of cohesion and harmonious reconciliation with self. The hardness and durability of stone have always impressed men, suggesting to them the antithesis to biological things subject to the laws of change, decay and death, as well as the antithesis to dust, sand and stone splinters, as aspects of disintegration. The stone when whole symbolized unity and strength; when shattered it signified dismemberment, psychic disintegration, infirmity, death and annihilation. Stones fallen from heaven served to explain the origin of life. In volcanic eruptions, air turned to fire, fire became 'water' and 'water' changed to stone; hence stone constitutes the first solid form of the creative rhythm (51)—the sculpture of essential movement, and the petrified music of creation (50). The mythic and religious significance is only one step removed from this basic symbolic sense, a step which was taken by the immense majority of peoples during the animistic era. Meteorites, in particular, came in for worship; the most celebrated are the Kaaba meteorite in Mecca and the Black Stone of Pessinus, an aniconic image of the Phrygian Great Mother taken to Rome during the last of the Punic Wars (17). Here is a description of the Mohammedans' stone, taken from Marques-Rivière: 'Inside the Kaaba, which is nothing more than a dark hall, there are three columns holding up the roof which has a number of silver and gold lamps hanging down from it. The floor is of marble tiles. In the eastern corner, some five feet above floor-level, not far from the door, is the famous black stone (al hadjar alaswad) sealed off, composed of three great sections. . . . In colour it is reddish black with red and yellow patches; in appearance it recalls lava or basalt' (39). Among the stones venerated by the ancients, we must not overlook the Greek omphaloi; Guénon maintains that they are really bethels, a word derived from the Hebrew Beith-El (or the House of God), related to the biblical 'And this stone which I have set for a pillar, shall be God's House' (Genesis xxviii, 22), even though its sense is magic and not architectonic (28). There are numerous legends dealing with stones: the so-called Abadir which Saturn devoured, mistaking it for Jupiter; or the stones of Deucalion and Pyrrha; or those in the myth of Medusa the Gorgon (6); or that which contained Mithras until his birth (11). There are other stones in folktales, but these seem to be invested with rather more modest powers: the Lapis lineus, for example, as it was called by the Romans, which was supposed to be able to prophesy by changing its colour; or the Irish stone Lia-Fail, associated with coronations (8). As for the philosophers' stone in alchemy, it represents the 'conjunction' of opposites, or the integration of the conscious self with the feminine or unconscious side (or in other words, the fixing of volatile elements); it is, then, a symbol of the All (33). As Jung rightly says, the alchemists approached their task obliquely—they did not seek the divine in matter but tried to 'produce' it by means of a lengthy process of purification and transmutation (32). According to Evola, the touchstone is symbolic of the body, since it is 'fixed', as opposed to the 'wandering' characteristic of thought, the spirits and desires. But only the resuscitated body—in which 'two will be one'—can correspond to the philosophers' stone. Evola points out that, for the alchemist, 'between eternal birth, reintegration, and the discovery of the philosophers' stone, there is no difference whatsoever'.

Stone-Circle Often called a 'cromlech', and popularly known as 'the giant's circle'. Diodorus Siculus had in mind the great stone-circle of Stonehenge when he referred to the existence, on an island off Gaul 'as big as Sicily', of 'the circular temple of Apollo' where the Hyperboreans sang the praises of god-the-sun. The sun-symbolism connected with the stone-circle is obvious (16). It also partakes of circle-symbolism (that is, of the cyclic process, Oneness and perfection), of disk-symbolism (representing the sun), and of stone-symbolism (or, in the eyes of most primitive peoples, theophany—a manifestation of the divine which they associated with fertility-cults). Often standing in the midst of the circle of monoliths is the 'hyrmensul' or sun-stone.

Stork This bird, dedicated to Juno by the Romans, was a symbol of filial piety. It is also an emblem of the traveller (8). In the allegory of 'Great Wisdom', two storks are shown facing each other and flying within a circle formed by the figure of a snake (4).

Storm The myth of the creative storm (or creative intercourse between the Elements) is universal: among the Nordic peoples it appears in connexion with Thor, in Assyrio-Babylonian mythology with Bel, in the Germanic with Donar, in the Greek with Zeus, among the Slavs with Peroun, and so on (38). The storm, like everything else that occurs in heaven or descends therefrom, has a sacred quality about it.

Stranger In myths, legends, folktales and in literature as a whole, the 'stranger' is frequently 'the one destined to replace' the reigning power in a country or locality. He stands for the possibility of unseen change, for the future made present, or for mutation in general. Frazer tells us how Lityerses, a son of King Midas, was wont to challenge people to a reaping match, and if he vanquished them he used to thrash them; but one day he met with a stranger who, proving himself to be a stronger reaper, slew him (21).

Strength The eleventh enigma of the Tarot pack. The image shows a queen who, without apparent effort, overcomes a lion, holding his jaws wide open. The allusion to the Zodiac is clear enough—Leo vanquished by Virgo—and the subject finds its mythological counterpart in Hercules overcome by Omphale. Wirth points to a highly interesting detail in the allegory: the queen does not slay the lion, but clasps it to her bosom having stunned it with her club, signifying that one must not despise the inferior, but master it and put it to good use. There is an echo here of the alchemists' belief that what is base must not—and indeed cannot—be destroyed, it must be transmuted into what is superior. In the affirmative sense, this enigma symbolizes the triumph of intelligence over brutality; in the negative, it denotes insensibility and fury (59).

String (or **Cord**) All types of string, cord or rope are forms of binding, and this forms the basis of their symbolic meaning. It is what lies behind the sacred cord worn by all high-caste Hindus. The *Jâbâla-Upanishad* makes it clear that the sacred cord is the external symbol of the *Sûtrâtma*, or the spiritual thread binding together all things in existence, as the thread of a necklace binds together all the pearls (60). This is an idea of such clarity that expressions of it are to be found everywhere. The cords worn by soldiers and by officials, sashes and bows, braid and stripes, are all nothing but emblems of cohesion and binding, although in a form referring to a particular social status. In our view, this and no other is the significance of the neck-tie, despite the Freudian tendency to interpret it as a phallic symbol.

Struggles between Animals Animals symbolize different stages of instinct and can therefore be placed along an ideal vertical axis (for example, in ascending order: bear, lion, eagle). Accordingly, a struggle between different animals—between a lion and a griffin, a serpent and an eagle, an eagle and a lion, etc.—represents the struggle between widely-differing instinctive inclinations. The victory of a winged animal over a wingless one is always a positive symbol, comparable to sublimation. The struggle of an eagle with a lion involves a vector of lesser intensity than that between an eagle and a serpent, because the distance separating the latter pair is greater. The struggle between real and fabulous animals may represent the conflict between realistic instincts or tendencies and fanciful or misleading ones. But this must be decided by the context, for it may also represent a reduction in the power of the imagination (that is, in the creative fantasy), to the benefit of material, direct and realistic activity.

Styx, The A subterranean spring or lake in Greek mythology—corresponding to the underground sea in Egyptian belief—which the sun crosses every night. By analogy, therefore, the lower waters of the Styx pertain to death, just as every sunrise points to resurrection (8).

Subterranean Chambers Symbolic of the body's inside, the viscera. Verne's 'journey to the centre of the earth', through caves, passages and wells, is a return to the maternal body, to the earth.

Sulphur Symbolic of the desire for positive action, and of vital heat (57). In the complex symbolism of alchemy, sulphur represents one of the stages of the evolution of matter (and of the psyche). According to René Alleau, the various stages, from the lowest to the highest, can be classified as follows: prior elements, denoting the inherent possibilities of the cosmos, or of man; prime matter, or the elementary organization of inherent possibilities, equi~ perhaps to the unconscious, or the instincts; mercury, or the ..... purification, feelings, imagination, the dominant female principle; sulphur, or more profound purification, reason and intuition, the male principle; and the Great Work, or transcendence.

Sun In theogony, the Sun represents the moment (surpassing all others in the succession of celestial dynasties) when the heroic principle shines at its brightest. Thus, after Uranus, Saturn and Jupiter, comes Helios Apollo. On occasion, the Sun appears as the direct son and heir of the god of heaven, and Krappe notes that he inherits one of the most notable and moral of the attributes of this deity: he sees all and, in consequence, knows all. In India, as Sûrya, it is the eye of Varuna; in Persia, it is the eye of Ahuramazda; in Greece, as Helios, the eye of Zeus (or of Uranus); in Egypt it is the eye of Ra, and in Islam, of Allah (35). With his 'youthful' and filial characteristic, the Sun is associated with the hero, as opposed to the father, who connotes the heavens, although the two (sun and sky) are sometimes equated. Hence, the weapon of heaven is the net (the pattern of the stars) or the power of binding; while the hero is armed with the sword (symbolically associated with fire). And it is for this reason that heroes are promoted to solar eminence and even identified with the Sun itself. In a given period of history and at a certain cultural level, the solar cult is the predominant if not the only one. Frazer, however, as Eliade has noted, brought out the divergencies of the solar elements in the sacred rites of Africa, of Australia and Oceania as a whole, and of North and South America. The cult of the Sun reached an advanced stage of development only in the New World, and—most advanced of all—in Mexico and Peru. Eliade concludes that, since these were the only countries in pre-Columbian America to evolve a viable political system, it may be concluded that there is a parallel between predominantly solar cults and 'historical' forms of human existence. We must not overlook the fact that Rome, the most powerful political force of Antiquity, and the originator of the historical sense, upheld solar hierophany, which, during the Empire, dominated all other cults in the form of Mithraic ritual (17). An heroic and courageous force, creative and guiding—this is the core of solar symbolism; it may actually come to constitute a religion complete in itself, as is shown by the 'heresy' of Ikhnaton in the 18th dynasty of Egypt; here the hymns to the sun are, setting aside their profound lyrical interest, expressions of theories about the beneficent activity of the king of astral bodies. The sun on the horizon had long served the Egyptians of the Ancient Empire as a means of defining 'brightness' or 'splendour'. They were also forcibly struck by the analogy between the daily disappearance of the Sun and the winter solstice (19). At

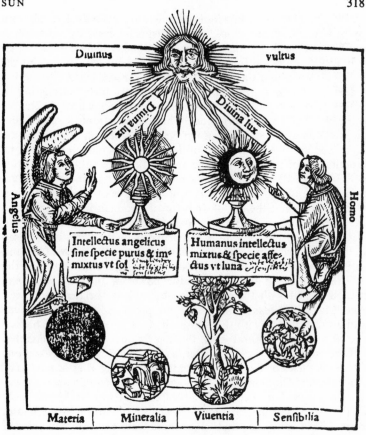

The Sun and the Moon, symbols of the active and the passive
principles of the universe as 'Intellectus angelicus' and 'Humanus
intellectus' respectively. (Engraving from Bovillus, *De Intellectu*,
Paris, 1510.)

the same time, there was, for the primitive, astrobiological mind, an
essential connexion between the Sun and Moon, analogous to that
between heaven and earth. It is well known that, for the vast majority
of peoples, the sky is symbolic of the active principle (related to the
masculine sex and to the spirit), while the earth symbolizes the
passive principle (cognate with the feminine sex and with matter);
these equations, nevertheless, are occasionally transposed. And the
same thing happens with the Sun and Moon: solar 'passion', so to
speak, with its heroic and fierce character, clearly had to be
assimilated to the masculine principle, and the pale and delicate

nature of lunar light, with its connexion with the waters of the ocean (and the rhythm of woman), obviously had to be classified as feminine. These equations are certainly not constant; but the exceptions do not invalidate the essential truth of this symbolism. Even physically speaking, the Moon merely fulfils the passive rôle of reflecting the light which the Sun actively diffuses. Many primitive tribes hold that the eyes of heaven are the Sun and the Moon located on either side of the 'world-axis', and there are prehistoric drawings and engravings which may be interpreted after this fashion. Eliade notes that, for the Pigmies and Bushmen, the sun is the eye of the supreme god. The Samoyeds see the Sun and the Moon as the eyes of heaven, the Sun being the good eye, and the Moon the evil eye (one can see here an unequivocal instance of the symbolism of dualism expanded by the assimilation of that of moral polarity). The idea of the invincible character of the sun is reinforced by the belief that whereas the Moon must suffer fragmentation (since it wanes) before it can reach its monthly stage of three-day disappearance, the Sun does not need to die in order to descend into hell; it can reach the ocean or the lake of the Lower Waters and cross it without being dissolved. Hence, the death of the Sun necessarily implies the idea of resurrection and actually comes to be regarded as a death which is not a true death. For this reason, too, ancestor-worship is associated with the cult of the sun, in order to offer the symbolic promise of protection and salvation. Megalithic monuments are based upon the amalgamation of these two cults (17). Thus, the broadest and most authentic interpretation sees the sun as the cosmic *reductio* of the masculine force, and the Moon of the feminine (49). This implies that the active faculties (of reflexion, good judgement or will power) are solar, while the passive qualities (imagination, sentiment and perception) are feminine, with intuition possibly androgynous (26). The 'correspondences' of the Sun are chiefly gold, among the metals, and, of the colours, yellow. Alchemists regarded it as 'gold prepared for the work' or 'philosophical sulphur', as opposed to the Moon and mercury (the metal), which is lunar (57). Another alchemic concept, that of the *Sol in homine* (or the invisible essence of the celestial Sun which nourishes the inborn fire of Man) (57), is an early pointer to the way the astral body has latterly been interpreted by psychoanalysts, narrowing its meaning down to that of heat or energy, equivalent to the fire of life and the libido. Hence Jung's point that the Sun is, in truth, a symbol of the source of life and of the ultimate wholeness of man (32). But here there is probably some inexactitude, for totality is in fact uniquely symbolized by the 'conjunction' of the Sun and the Moon, as king and queen, brother and sister (32). In some folklore-traditions, the urge to allude in some way to the supreme good, which, by definition, is incapable of definition, is met by the saying 'to join the Sun and the Moon'.

Now, having established the principal terms of solar symbolism—as an heroic image (*Sol invictus, Sol salutis, Sol iustitiae*) (14), as the divine eye, the active principle and the source of life and energy—let us come back to the dualism of the Sun as regards its hidden passage—its 'Night Sea-Crossing'—symbolic of immanence (like the colour black) and also of sin, occultation and expiation. In the *Rigveda*—Eliade reminds us—the Sun is ambivalent: on the one hand it is 'resplendent' and on the other it is 'black' or invisible, in which case it is associated with chthonian and funereal animals such as the horse and the serpent (17). Alchemists took up this image of the *Sol niger* to symbolize 'prime matter', or the unconscious in its base, 'unworked' state. In other words, the Sun is then at the nadir, in the depths out of which it must, slowly and painfully, ascend towards its zenith. This inevitable ascent does not relate to its daily journey, although this is used as an image, and hence it is symbolized by the transmutation of prime matter into gold, passing through the white and red stages, like the Sun itself in its orbit. Of undoubted interest, as an indication of the intensity of man's attitude towards the Sun, is the reference by Tacitus and Strabo to the 'sound' made by the Sun as it rises in the East and drowns in the oceans of the West. The sudden disappearance of the Sun below the horizon is related to the sudden death of heroes such as Samson, Hercules and Siegfried (35).

Sun, The The nineteenth enigma of the Tarot pack. The allegory shows the disk of the astral king surrounded by alternating straight and flamelike rays, golden and red, symbolizing the twofold activity of the Sun in giving out warmth and light. Beneath the Sun, from which a golden spray is falling, are a young couple in a green field, and in the background there is a wall. This couple symbolize the Gemini under the beneficial influence of spiritual light. The Sun is the astral body of immutable constancy, and hence it reveals the reality of things—not their changing aspects as the Moon does. It is related to purification and tribulation, the sole purpose of which is to render transparent the opaque crust of the senses so that they may perceive the higher truths. But the Sun, apart from providing light and heat, is the source of supreme riches, and this is symbolized, in the allegory, by the golden drops which, as in the myth of Danae, rain down upon the human couple. On the positive side, this enigma symbolizes glory, spirituality and illumination. On the negative side, it stands for vanity or an idealism incompatible with reality (59).

Sun-shade A solar symbol, an emblem of authority and dignity, and one of the eight allegories of good fortune in Chinese Buddhism

(5). It incorporates the symbolic concepts of irradiation and protection.

Superiority In certain Babylonian rites, the *hieros gamos* was represented by an act of erotic consummation between a priestess of Ishtar and a slave, who was afterwards put to death. This was not an act of cruelty, but the inevitable consequence which attended the act of the slave, as the shadow pursues the body. For if he had been left alive, the remainder of his existence would have been a living death, since he had experienced contact with the Superior. The same may be said of Lazarus; and this is the meaning of the myth of Semele, consumed by the fiery radiance of Jupiter whom she sought to see in all his true and essential glory. The superior destroys— burns up—the inferior. But, for this very reason, the recipient of any such token of the supra-normal who is not destroyed by the gift but proves himself capable of retaining it, establishes thereby his own (comparable) superiority. Hence, anything of value surpassing the ordinary and the commonplace is a sign of special favour and a symbol of absolute transcendence. He who dares to desire the superior, thereby invites comparison with it; if he succeeds in entering into the domain of this superiority and withstands it, then he is invested with it, but should he prove unworthy then he must needs be destroyed. Every limiting situation, every extreme trial—such as placing one's hand in boiling water, for instance— denotes this same idea. The knight conquered and devoured by the dragon is thereby proved inferior. Only the knight capable of vanquishing the dragon is worthy to confront it. Aspiring to the hand of the 'princess' is another expression of the same idea. As Plato observes in the *Republic*: 'All great things are fraught with danger.'

Coat of arms with supporters in
the form of Wild Men.

Supporters In heraldic or decorative compositions, human, animal or fabulous beings that support the coat of arms or the central figure or element. These supporters, nearly always two in

number, one on either side, symbolize those base forces which, once
hostile and aggressive, have been obliged to become the servants and
defenders of the central element, symbolizing the victorious power
(Plate XXVII).

Swallow A bird sacred to Isis and to Venus (8), and an allegory
of spring. The poet Bécquer makes use of this symbol to convey
the pathos and the inexorable nature of time, drawing analogies
with other symbols.

Swan A symbol of great complexity. The dedication of the swan
to Apollo, as the god of music, arose out of the mythic belief that it
would sing sweetly when on the point of death (8). The red swan is a
symbol of the sun (2). But almost all meanings are concerned with
the white swan, sacred to Venus, which is why Bachelard suggests
that in poetry and literature it is an image of naked woman, of chaste
nudity and immaculate whiteness. But Bachelard finds an even
deeper significance: hermaphroditism, since in its movement and
certainly in its long phallic neck it is masculine yet in its rounded,
silky body it is feminine. In sum, then, the swan always points to
the complete satisfaction of a desire, the swan-song being a particular
allusion to desire which brings about its own death (2). This
ambivalent significance of the swan was also well known to the
alchemists, who compared it with 'philosophical Mercury' (57), the
mystic Centre and the union of opposites, an interpretation entirely
in accord with its archetypal implications (56). Now, in Schneider's
view, the swan, by virtue of its relationship with the harp and the
sacrificial serpent, also pertains to the funeral-pyre, because the
essential symbols of the mystic journey to the other world (apart
from the death-ship) are the swan and the harp. This would afford
another explanation of the mysterious song of the dying swan. The
swan also has a bearing upon the peacock, although the situation is
reversed. The swan/harp relationship, corresponding to the axis
water/fire, denotes melancholy and passion, self-sacrifice, and the
way of tragic art and martyrdom. Conversely the peacock/lute
relationship, linked with earth/air, is possibly a representation of
logical thought (50). As Jacques de Morgan has shown in *L'Humanité
préhistorique*, if it was the horse that pulled the Sun-god's chariot by
day, it was the swan that hauled his bark over the waters by night.
The relevance to this myth of the Lohengrin legend is self-evident.

Swastika This graphic symbol is to be found in almost every
ancient and primitive cult all over the world—in Christian catacombs,
in Britain, Ireland, Mycenae and Gascony; among the Etruscans,
the Hindus, the Celts and the Germanic peoples; in central Asia
as well as in pre-Columbian America. The implications of the
swastika are very wide, for it is a synthesis of two symbols of
independent force: the (Greek) cross with arms of equal length and

the cross with four arms appearing to rotate in the same direction. The tetraskelion, or swastika with four arms at right angles, is also called the *gammadion* because it can be formed by joining up four gamma letters. According to Ludwig Müller, the swastika, during the Iron Age, represented the supreme deity (39). For Mackenzie, it is associated with agriculture and with the points of the compass. Colley March sees the swastika as a specific sign denoting rotation about an axis. There are in fact two swastikas: the right-handed *Swastika* and the left-handed *Swavastika* (41). The shape of the swastika has been interpreted as a solar wheel with rays and feet sketched in at the extremities (56). By the Middle Ages, the most general interpretation was that it symbolized movement and the power of the sun (14); but, at the same time, it was seen as an obvious symbol of the quaternary, in the particular sense of the 'configuration of a movement split up into four parts', related to the poles and the four cardinal directions (16). The latter view is one held by René Guénon, for whom the swastika is the 'sign of the pole'. Since it is widely accepted that the pole and the zenith coincide with the mystic Centre, it follows, then, that the swastika would signify the action of the Origin upon the universe (25). Schneider has suggested a very different meaning: that the swastika is the symbol of the succession of the generations, and that the hooks on the ends of its arms are the ships of life, or, put another way, the different stages of life (51).

Sword   The sword is in essence composed of a blade and a guard; it is therefore a symbol of 'conjunction', especially when, in the Middle Ages, it takes on the form of a cross. Among many primitive peoples it was the object of much veneration. The Scythians used to make an annual sacrifice of several horses to the blade of a sword, which they conceived as a god of war. Similarly, the Romans believed that iron, because of its association with Mars, was capable of warding off evil spirits (8). The belief still persists in Scotland (21). Founders of cities, in the ancient *Che-King* tales of China, wear swords (7). As a religious symbol, it is still in use as part of the ceremonial dress of oriental bishops. Its primary symbolic meaning, however, is of a wound and the power to wound, and hence of liberty and strength. Schneider has shown that, in megalithic culture, the sword is the counterpart of the distaff, which is the feminine symbol of the continuity of life. The sword and the distaff symbolize, respectively, death and fertility—the two opposites which constitute the basic symbolism of the mountain (Schneider suggests that in the animal world the equivalents are the phallic fish and the frog) (50). Furthermore, given the cosmic sense of sacrifice (that is, the inversion of the implied realities of the terrestrial and the celestial orders), the sword is then seen as a symbol of physical extermination and psychic decision (60), as well as of the spirit and the word of God, the latter being a particularly common symbol during the Middle Ages (4). In this connexion, Bayley draws attention to the interesting relationship between the English words *sword* and *word*. There can be no doubt that there is a sociological factor in sword-symbolism, since the sword is an instrument proper to the knight, who is the defender of the forces of light against the forces of darkness. But the fact is that in rites at the dawning of history and in folklore even today, the sword plays a similar spiritual rôle, with the magic power to fight off the dark powers personified in the 'malevolent dead', which is why it always figures in apotropaic dances. When it appears in association with fire and flames—which correspond to it in shape and resplendence—it symbolizes purification. Schneider bears this out with his comment that whereas purification goes with fire and the sword, punishment goes with the lash and the club (51). In alchemy, the sword is a symbol for purifying fire. The golden sword—Chrysaor in Greek mythology—is a symbol for supreme spiritualization (15). The Western type of sword, with its straight blade, is, by virtue of its shape, a solar and masculine symbol. The Oriental sword, being curved, is lunar and feminine. Here one must recall the general meaning of weapons, which is the antithesis of the monster. The sword, because of its implication of 'physical extermination', must be a symbol of spiritual evolution, just as the tree is of involution; that is, the tree stands for the development of life within matter and activity. This dualism between the spirit on the one hand and life on the other was resolved by Ludwig Klages, for his part, by opting for life, but Novalis has well expressed the contrary opinion with his observation that 'life is an infirmity of the spirit'. It is a duality which is well illustrated by the opposing characteristics of wood (which is feminine) and metal. If the tree corresponds to the process of proliferation, then the sword represents the inverse. At least Conrad Dinckmut's *Seelen Wurzgarten* (Ulm, 1483), like many other similar works, has a 15th-century illustration of Christ with a branch or a tree on the left side of his face, whereas symmetrically opposite there is a sword. This association of the sword with the tree is of great antiquity: we ourselves have seen a prehistoric Germanic relief depicting two figures, one being feminine and bearing a branch, the other masculine, with a sword. One may also see here an allegory of War and Peace; certainly the mediaeval illustration may allude to the olive branch, but there is nothing of this in the Germanic relief. Evola maintains that the sword is related to Mars, but with additional vertical—and horizontal—symbolisms, alluding, that is, to life and death. It is also linked with steel as a symbol of the transcendent toughness of the all-conquering spirit. To quote from Emilio Sobejano, *Swords of Spain*, in *Arte Español*, XXI (1956): 'Among the Germanic races, as Livy observed, the sword was at no time very common; on the contrary, it served as a symbol befitting high command and the loftiest rank; one only has to think of the dignity and pomp which characterized the institution of the *Comes Spatharius*, created by the Emperor Gordian the Younger around the year 247. . . . The sword is almost exclusively the prerogative of high dignitaries. There is an Arabic tradition to the effect that it was the Hebrews who invented the sword, and that the place where it was first made—a tragic sign of how the idea first came into the world—was mount Casium, on the outskirts of Damascus, which was to become famous throughout Islam on account of its steel, and where, according to the ancient belief, Cain slew his brother. There, by an accident of fate, settled the first artificers of the newly invented weapon.' The sword of fire bears testimony to the intrinsic relationship between the symbols of the sword, steel (or iron), Mars and fire, all of which have a 'common rhythm'. On the other hand, it emphasizes the heat of the flame and the coldness of the bare metal; hence, the sword of fire is a symbol implying an ambivalent synthesis, like the volcano (*gelat et ardet*), and also a symbol of the weapon which severs Paradise (the realm of the fire of love) from earth (the world of affliction).

Sword, Broken Because the sword symbolizes spiritual aggression or a hero's courage, the broken sword is a symbol of those qualities being in a state of destruction. Nevertheless, like the 'buried sword', it is more likely to appear in mediaeval legends as an inheritance which has to be reconquered by personal valour. Thus, as a youth, Siegfried discovers the pieces of the sword Balmunga, which Odin was said to have given to his father Siegmund. Mime, the blacksmith, was unable to reforge it, but Siegfried succeeds in doing so. In the epic entitled 'Gawain-poems' in the Arthurian cycle (Jean Marx, *Nouvelles Recherches sur la littérature Arthurienne*, Paris, 1965), Gawain is given a broken sword which he is unable to repair completely, symbolizing his inability to penetrate to the 'centre' of his undertaking.

Sybil A figure of antiquity, which reappears in mediaeval literature and iconography, symbolizing the intuiting of higher truths and prophetic powers.

Symbolism, Phonetic When, about 1870, Rimbaud wrote his famous sonnet on the vowels, assimilating each one to a colour, he doubtless yielded to a presentiment rather than to a true intuition and formulated a possibility rather than a certitude: A (black), E (white), I (red), U (green), O (blue). The idea of placing vowels into correspondence with colours is essential to the penetration of the symbolism of phonemes (syllables), but the identifications proposed by Rimbaud do not appear correct to us. Also, as the critics have pointed out, he defines, for example, the U by a line in which the I predominates. But there is another feat in the sonnet in question, and that is its boldness in altering the apparently sacred order of the vowels: A, E, I, O, U.

Anybody who has penetrated the world of symbolism will know that the theory of 'correspondences' is one of its corner-stones. This theory postulates that one phenomenon alone takes place and that its appearances are resonances of the same thing on different planes of reality (sounds, colours, letters, planets in the solar system, mythological gods, prime metals, etc.). In Marius Schneider's books—especially in *El origen musical de los animales-símbolos en la mitología y escultura antiguas*, as the very title indicates—he based his entire symbolic system on sounds. He proposes correspondences which may appear strange, arbitrary and fantastic to one who has not delved deeply into the analyses of this eminent ethnologist, professor at Cologne University and student *in situ* of African symbolic thought. He goes so far as to identify musical intervals with types of landscape (a major fifth = fountain, pool, marsh, etc.). He suggests a symbolism of the vowels which seems correct. In general, he classifies them in two groups: A, O (affirmative vowels) and U, I (negative, dissolvent vowels). The E would seem to occupy an intermediate position. Taking into account the fact that the scales of many systems have seven elements (for example, the directions of space, the days of the week, the planetary gods, the colours, the notes of the diatonic scale, etc.), one must form a group of seven vowels (which, indeed, do exist in many languages) in order to establish exact correspondences. But before indicating what these relationships might be, let us transcribe the definition of the term 'symbolic correspondence' as found in Schneider's work. For him, 'such correspondences are based on the idea of the indissoluble unity of the universe in which each phenomenon has its own particular cosmic position and receives its mystical meaning through the plane which it occupies in the world and through the analogous relationship which it maintains with a specific "corresponding" element, which may be a heavenly body, a colour, a substance, an element of nature, an animal, a part of the human body, an era in human life, etc.' According to Schneider, this symbolist philosophy flourished during the Megalithic period and then spread throughout most of the world, even including Indonesia. It appears that in many languages which do not belong to the same 'family', there are still to be found phonemes which have exactly the same or a similar meaning, and which must be derived from the language-universal concept of both that period and the one immediately preceding it. Gustav Zollinger, in *Tau oder Tau-t-an*, explains this point and makes some interesting connexions. Working from the opposite side, that of the symbolism of letters as signs, Alfred Kallir, in *Sign and Design*, also reaches similar conclusions.

If we arranged a series of seven vowels according to the logic of symbolism, we would have the scale: A, O, OE, E, I, Ü, and U, which corresponds perfectly to the series of colours: Red, orange, yellow, green, blue, indigo and violet; and to the diatonic scale of C minor: C, D, E flat, F, G, A flat, B. The reason why this scale has to be minor and not major is that in this way the distances between the intervals correspond better to the 'distances' separating the colours and the sounds. The meaning of each vowel is easy to find in accordance with the meaning of the corresponding colour and musical sound. From the very start, we may see the perfect correspondence between the warm colours (red, orange and yellow) and the affirmative sounds (A, O, and OE, or AE), while the correspondence of the E, as the intermediate sound between the affirmative and the dissolutive groups, with green, the transitional tone between the warm and cold colours, is unquestionable.

The organization of consonants within a similar system is difficult. Apart from the lucubrations of the Cabbala, and the definitions of the symbolism of letters to be found within it, it is extremely difficult to find other sources from which to derive such a system. But there are a few facts which have been proved as certain: for example, Schneider and other authors of treatises on symbolism point out the opposition between the M and the N (fecundating, maternal waters, and the dissolvent waters of the Nothingness), the contrast between the F and the T (affirmation and sacrifice), and between the B and the Z (body or house and lightning). This last contrast appears in the sixteenth enigma of the Tarot (The Tower Struck by Lightning). Thus, it may be seen that, if one eliminates from the consonants all those which repeat sounds, and arranges them in two scales (each one of them is the middle of the whole series inverted), one meets these correspondences of opposites face to face. Thus the first half is: B, D, F, G, K, L, M, and the second half: N, P, R, S, T, X, Z, each scale consisting of seven consonants, which give the following symbolic oppositions: B–Z, D–X, F–T, G–S, K–R, L–P, and M–N. Provisionally, as the symbolism of the letter as a sign has already been studied (by Kallir and other authors), this knowledge should be applied and then, when one knows the symbolism of one consonant, one knows that of its opposite number (its antithesis). Then, one only has to confirm this symbolism by the sound impression in order to attribute it to the letter as a phoneme. Once the symbolism of the vowels and consonants has been established, they can be placed in relation in order to analyse the meaning of different syllables or words. The consonants to be omitted are the following: W (= U), Y (= I), J (= G), Q (= K) and H.

All this may seem superficial, artificial, or, worse still, useless. But nothing in investigation is useless, and even the most superficial is important in a field which no one has explored in detail as yet. We only wish that this type of linguistic and literary analysis might have the necessary repercussion so that one day we may establish a basis of authentic phonetic symbolism—in which many linguists believe, but without passing judgement on the substance.

Symmetry   This is equivalent to achievement, crowning triumph and supreme equipoise (as in the caduceus, the reliefs of Naksh-i-rustam, and in heraldic shields).

Tarot Pack, The   Present-day psychology has confirmed the conclusions of Eliphas Lévi, Marc Haven and Oswald Wirth that the Tarot cards comprise an image (comparable to that encountered in dreams) of the path of initiation (56). At the same time, Jung's view, coinciding with the secular, intuitive approach to the Tarot enigmas, recognizes the portrayal of two different, but complementary, struggles in the life of man: (*a*) the struggle against others (the solar way) which he pursues through his social position and calling; and (*b*) against himself (the lunar way), involving the process of individuation. These two ways correspond to reflexion and intuition—to practical reason and pure reason. A person of lunar temperament first creates, then studies and verifies what he already knew; the man of solar temperament studies first and then produces. These two approaches also correspond, up to a point, to the concepts of introversion (which is lunar) and extraversion (which is solar)—or to contemplation and action (34). The complete pack of cards, known by the name of *Tarocco*, is made up of 22 major enigmas, with images that together comprise a synthesis and, up to a point, an entity; and 56 minor images, incorporating 14 figures in four series: gold—corresponding to the English 'diamonds'—bearing figures of circles, disks and wheels; clubs (maces and sceptres); swords ('spades') and goblets ('hearts'). The gold suit symbolizes the material forces, the club the power of command, the goblet sacrifice, and the sword, discernment and the meting out of justice. The 22 major cards correspond to the letters of the Hebrew alphabet. Included in each of the suits of the minor cards are the King, the Dame (Queen), the Knight (Horse) and the Knave (Jack) (48). These suits have been equated with the powers that reign on earth and, in consequence, with the controlling or higher professions, as follows: government with clubs; the military career with spades (swords); the priesthood with goblets; intellectual activity with gold —for all forms of treasure are always symbolic of the riches of the spirit and the mind (54). According to Saunier, the images of the major enigmas derive from the symbolic paintings in the Egyptian Books of Thoth-Hermes, representing the knowledge of the universe (49). However, Oswald Wirth, whose interpretations of the symbolism of the Tarot we shall, in the main, follow, points out that archaeology has never unearthed the least trace of anything that might conceivably be an Egyptian, Arabic or Graeco-Arabic Tarot pack. But he indicates that the Cabala must have been well known to the authors of the Tarot, because they fixed the number of major enigmas at 22, which is the same as the number of letters in the Hebrew alphabet, every one of them pregnant with symbolism, and the same, also, as the number of the *teraphim*, the hieroglyphs used by the Hebrews in divination. Wirth, arguing from the fact that Italy was undeniably the first country to develop playing-cards, maintains that these allegorical images grew up in that country. The earliest representation known to us of the major enigmas dates from 1392. To quote Eliphas Lévi: 'The Tarot is a monumental and singular work, simple and strong as the architecture of the pyramids, and, in consequence, as durable; it is a book which is the sum of all the sciences and whose infinite permutations are capable of solving all problems; a book which informs by making one think; it is perhaps the greatest masterpiece of the human mind, and certainly one of the most beautiful things handed down by Antiquity.' The 22 mysteries are: I, The Minstrel; II, The Archpriestess; III, The Empress; IV, The Emperor; V, The Archpriest; VI, The Lover; VII, The Chariot; VIII, Justice; IX, The Hermit; X, The Wheel of Fortune; XI, Strength; XII, The Hanged Man; XIII, Death; XIV, Temperance; XV, The Devil; XVI, The Tower Struck by Lightning; XVII, The Stars; XVIII, The Moon; XIX, The Sun; XX, The Judgement; XXI, The World; XXII or 0, The Fool. The cards from I to XI comprise the solar way—active, conscious, reflective and autonomous. Cards XII to XXII denote the lunar way—passive, unconscious, intuitive and 'possessed'. We cannot here explain the relationships which can be drawn, or the patterns of meanings which can be derived from these relationships, without going beyond the bounds of strict symbolism; an examination of the particular meaning of each card will be found under its appropriate heading. Nevertheless, we will quote the broadest meanings of these 22 enigmas suggested by Eliphas Lévi: I signifies The Being, the spirit, creation; II, sanctuary, the law, knowledge, woman, the mother, the church; III, the Word, fecundity, generation in all three worlds; IV, the door, initiation, power, the cubic stone or its base; V, information, proof, philosophy and religion; VI, enmeshment,

union, antagonism, equilibrium, combination; VII, the weapon, the
sword, triumph and majesty; VIII, the scales, attraction and
repulsion, the path or way, promise and threat; IX, good, morality,
wisdom; X, manifestation, fecundity, the paternal sceptre; XI, the
hand in the act of taking and sustaining; XII, an example, teaching,
a public lesson; XIII, domination and strength, rebirth, creation
and destruction; XIV, the seasons, the flux and flow of life, always
different yet always the same; XV, magic, eloquence, commerce,
mystery; XVI, sudden subversion, weakness; XVII, effusion of
thought, the moral influence of the idea upon forms, immortality;
XVIII, the Elements, the visible world, reflected light, material
forms, symbolism; XIX, the head, the summit, the prince of heaven;
XX, vegetation, the generative virtues of the soil; XXI, the senses,
the vehicle, the body, transitory life; XXII, the microcosm, the
sum of All-in-All. Each of these images comprises a fusion of
certain ideas relative to the outer and inner worlds, disposed according to the forms and patterns of the mind. The intention is to create,
by means of these images, an order more comprehensive even than
that comprising the twelve divisions of the Zodiac, and to design a
wheel which would embody all the archetypal potentialities of the
existence and evolution of mankind.

Our aim has been simply to sketch in an idea of how the Tarot
pack functions as a symbolic instrument. In order to grasp the full
range of its significance, it is necessary to study not only the basic
commentaries written upon it but also the cards themselves,
observing all the combinations and implications—a field so vast as
to constitute a special branch of symbolism as wide-ranging as that
of dreams.

Tattooing Tattooing and ornamentation may be regarded as
falling within one generic symbolic group, for both are expressions
of cosmic activity. But since tattoos are applied to the body, other
important meanings accrue to it—sacrifice, the mystical and magical.
E. Gobert, in *Notes sur les tatouages des indigènes Tunisiens*, suggests
that tattooing is connected with the Arabic proverb 'blood has
flowed, the danger has passed'. Since sacrifice has the power to
store up latent forces which later may be made use of, each sacrifice
tends to invert a given situation. A mystic purpose lies at the root of
the mark or sign of identification: he who brands himself seeks to
display his allegiance to that which is signified by the mark. (Lovers'
marks carved on tree-trunks, and initials and heart-shapes pricked
out on the skin, are clear illustrations of this.) In the last analysis,
the attitude of allegiance is reversed: the sign is expected to
'reciprocate' this display of sacrifice and subservience on the part of
the individual who has so marked himself; and this is the magic
property of the tattoo as a defensive talisman. Apart from these

three meanings of the tattoo, ethnologists have noted two others: it may serve as a sign designating sex, tribe and social status (v. Robert Lowie's *Cultural Anthropology*), in which case it is simply a profane version of the mystic symbolism; and, also, as a personal adornment. This latter purpose seems to us over-simplified, but we cannot go into the matter here. In particular, tattooing is a 'rite of entry' or of initiation which alludes to the turning-points in the span of a man's life and in the development of his personality. Cola has pointed out that some of the most ancient monuments of pre-history, in particular those of Egypt, suggest that tattooing was practised in ancient times, for the priestess of the goddess Hathor displayed three lines on her lower belly. He also enumerates the principal techniques of tattooing: incision, stitching, wounding by cutting or burning, and pseudo-tattoos or paintings on the face or body (in which case the motives are the same although the effect is transitory). Among primitive races, the principal forms of tattoos are as follows: stripes, dots, combinations of both, or numbers expressed through either, chains, knots and rosettes, crosses, stars, triangles, rhombs, circles, combinations of any two or more of these, and also, highly stylized anthropomorphic figures either complete or fragmentary (just the limbs), etc. Cola also notes that tattoos have been used in imitative magic. For instance: the tattooed figure of a scorpion is credited with the power of warding off the actual scorpion's sting; and the image of a bull is a guarantee of numerous progeny (12).

Zodiacal sign of Taurus.

Taurus   The second sign of the Zodiac expresses the evolutionary force of Aries—that is, the spring-time pugnacity of the ram—in an intensified form. It also denotes the functions of fecundation and creation in both aspects, victorious and sacrificial—related, that is, to the primordial sacrifice; an example of this is the myth of Mithras, 'for out of his body grow all the plants and herbs that adorn the earth with verdure, and from his seed spring all the animal species' (Cumont, *Les Mystères de Mithra*). This basic idea of the bull as the force which animates forms of all kinds is deeply rooted in a great many myths. At the same time, the fact that the sign of Taurus corresponds to the number two relates it to the principle of duality composed of the masculine (*Viraj*, or *Yang*) and the feminine (*Vac*, or *Yin*). There is also a morphological relationship between the bull, on account of its head and horns, and the waxing and waning aspects of the moon, which is further evidence of the bull's symbolic function of invigoration, at least in the sublunary sphere. The sign of Taurus governs the throat and voice, and is in turn dominated by Venus (40).

Teeth According to Allendy, teeth are the primigenial weapons of attack, and an expression of activity. Loss of one's teeth, then, signifies fear of castration or of complete failure in life, or inhibition (56); it represents an attitude which is the inversion of that of the Primitive, who, according to the findings of anthropology, commonly adorned himself with the teeth and claws of conquered animals. Some interpretations underline the significance of teeth in respect of the sexual aspect of energy. But of greater importance is the Gnostic concept—for which we are indebted to Leisegang's *Die Gnosis*—in which the teeth constitute the battlements, the wall and the fortifications of the inner man, from the material or energetic point of view, just as the eyes and the glance are the defence of the spirit. This explains the negative symbolism of the loss or fracture of the teeth.

Temperance The fourteenth enigma of the Tarot pack, this card contains the image of a winged being, clad in a red tunic and a cloak with a lining of greenish-blue, who is pouring water out of a silver vessel into a golden one. In itself, this hermaphroditic—or gynandrous—figure has a favourable significance, since it is expressive of the *coniunctio oppositorum*. The act of pouring denotes the transformation of water as it passes from the lunar order (of silver) to the solar order (of gold), that is, from the world of transient forms and of feeling to the world of fixed forms and of reason; the water here is that of the 'Upper Ocean'—or vital fluid. This enigma suggests universal life, and ceaseless circulation through formation, regeneration and purification (59).

Temple The word 'temple' derives from the root *tem*—'to divide'. Etruscan soothsayers made a division of the heavens by means of two straight lines intersecting at a point directly above the head, the point of intersection being a projection of the notion of the 'Centre', and the lines representing the two 'directions' of the plane; the north-south line was called *cardo* and the east-west *decumanus*. Phenomena were interpreted according to their situation within this division of space. Hence, the earthly temple is seen as an image of the celestial temple and its basic structure is determined by considerations of order and orientation (7). The temple affords a particular and additional meaning to the generic symbolism of architectonic structures. Broadly speaking, it is the mystic significance of the 'Centre' which prevails; the temple and, in particular, the altar, being identified with the symbol of the mountain-top as the focal point of the intersection of the two worlds of heaven and earth. Solomon's temple, according to Philo and Flavius Josephus, was a figurative representation of the cosmos, and its interior was disposed accordingly: the incense table signified thanksgiving; the seven-branched candelabra stood for the seven planetary heavens; the holy table represented the terrestrial order. In addition to this, the twelve loaves of bread corresponded to the twelve months of the year. The Ark of the Covenant symbolizes the intelligibles (14). Romanesque, Gothic and Renaissance architects, each in their own way, sought to imitate this superior archetype. For example, between 1596 and 1604, imaginary reconstructions of the Temple of Solomon appeared in various works published in Rome and based upon holy writ, and the illustrations they contained deeply influenced the architects of the period. Another fundamental significance of the temple derives from its being a synthesis of the various symbols for the world-axis, such as the hollow mountain, steps and the sacrificial mountain-peak mentioned above. In certain astrobiological cultures the temple or altar is in fact built upon an artificial mountain—the *teocalli* of Mexico is an example. A more advanced concept can be seen in the architectural portrayal of those essential elements of the inner pattern of the universe founded upon the numbers three, seven, ten and twelve in particular. Seven is basic to the representation of the planets and their derived symbolisms, and hence the Mesopotamian temple-mountains—or *ziggurats*—were constructed after the fashion of a seven-terraced pyramid. Each of the terraces was dedicate to a particular planet. The Babylonian *ziggurat* known as *Etemenanki* ('the house of the seven directions of heaven and earth') was built of crude bricks overlaid with others that had been fired. A tablet in the Louvre records that in plan it measured 2,200 feet long by 1,200 wide. The first level was black in colour and dedicated to Saturn, the second orange-coloured and sacred to Jupiter, the third red and consecrated to Mars, the fourth golden and sacred to the Sun, the fifth yellow (to Venus), the sixth blue (to Mercury), the seventh silver (to the Moon) (39). This order is not always observed, for sometimes the Moon is situated in the sixth heaven and the Sun in the seventh (17). Berthelot, however, suggests that the *ziggurat* not only embraces the mystic aspects of the Mountain and the Centre (by virtue of its mass and situation) and of Steps (because of its shape), but also constitutes an image of paradise, since vegetation appears to flourish on its terraces (7). The origins of this type of structure are Sumerian (7), and examples are to be found in Egypt, India, China and pre-Columbian America. Eliade, in confirming this, adds that the climb to the top of the Mesopotamian or of the Hindu temple-mountain was equivalent to an ecstatic journey to the 'Centre' of

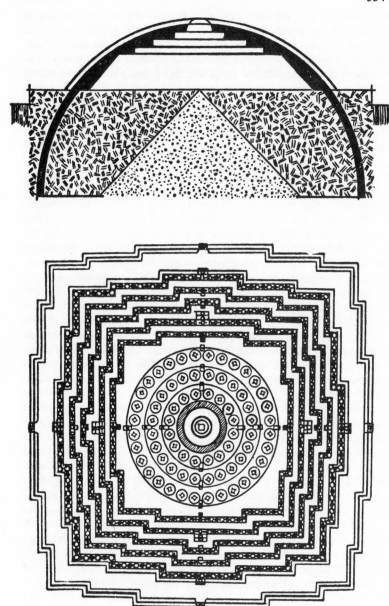

Borobudur temple.
Elevation and ground-plan, illustrating the mandala pattern.

the world; once the traveller has reached the topmost terrace, he breaks free from the laws of level, transcends profane space and enters a region of purity (18). It is hardly necessary to observe that climbing mountains implies ultimately the same mystic tendency, as can be seen in the fact that mountain heights are the chosen abode of the recluse. And the favourable symbolic significance of the goat derives solely from his predilection for heights. Another important example of the temple-mountain, a product of Hindu culture, comes from Indo-China—the temple of Borobudur built in the centre of the island of Java in the 8th century of our era. Basically it consists of four levels of square-shaped galleries, with four more circular platforms on top surmounted by an enclosed belvedere. In form, then, it is similar to the Egyptian *ziggurat*, or, in the Khmer language, a *Phnom*, signifying a temple-mountain comparable with Meru, the Hindu Olympus. Four flights of steps up the centre of each pyramid face lead directly from the base to the top. It would appear that the profoundest meaning attached to this temple is of a supernatural character. Its name—Borobudur—signifies 'the seat of secret revelation'. All graduated edifices such as steps concern the symbolism of discontinuous spiritual evolution, that is, the separate but progressive stages of evolution (6). At the same time, the ground-plan of the Borobudur temple is diagrammatically a true *yantra*, and its various square and round-shaped levels constitute a mandala related to the symbolism of 'squaring the circle' (6). The symbolic structure of the Greek temple is fundamentally the same as that of the lake-dwelling: that is, it symbolizes the intercommunication between the Three Worlds—the Lower (represented by the water and the piles on the one hand and earth and the subterranean part on the other), the Terrestrial (the base and columns) and the Upper (suggested by the pediment). Christian cathedrals are related less to the macrocosm than to the microcosm, the human figure being depicted in terms of the apse (representing the head), the cross and transepts (the arms), the nave and side aisles (the body) and the altar (the heart). In the Gothic temple, the upward sweep, the vital rôle of the vertical axis—and indeed the structure as a whole—embrace the idea of the temple-mountain with its implied synthesis of the symbolism of both macrocosm and microcosm. According to Schneider, the two towers usually placed at the western face correspond to the twin-peaked 'mountain of Mars' in primitive megalithic cultures (and linked with the Gemini myth), while the cimborrio over the transept is expressive of a higher synthesis, an image of heaven. Both the synthesis and the crux of the matter are established by Gershom G. Scholem, in *Les Origines de la Kabbale* (Paris, 1966). He recalls that God lives in his reason or that God is the absolute Reason and logos of the world, and that the temple 'is the house' or abode of God, and thus identifies *temple* with *reason*.

Tent   In the Egyptian system of hieroglyphs this is a determinative sign relating to that division of the soul which is known as 'body of glory' and which surrounds the spirit like a tent (19). Deriving from this hieroglyph is the broad symbolic meaning of the tent as something which 'envelops'. In our view, this symbolism is closely connected with the symbolisms of weaving and of clothes. For the Greeks, the physical world—and space itself—were 'the vestments of the gods', or, in other words, comparable with the tent as something which envelops and hides them from sight. To tear aside the temple-veil, or to rend one's garments, represents a desperate attempt to achieve, by force of analogy, the tearing aside of the veil that enshrouds the mystery of the other world. Berthelot suggests two other symbolic meanings of the tent: one related to its function as a nomadic dwelling, and the other arising from the mystic significance of the desert (7).

Ternary   The ternary system is created by the emergence of a third (latent) element which so modifies the binary situation as to impart to it a dynamic equilibrium. As Jung has observed, Plotinus with his characteristic combination of philosophical precision and poetic allusiveness compared Oneness (the creative principle) with light, intellect with the sun, and the world-soul with the moon. Unity is split internally into three 'moments'—the active, the passive and the union or outcome of these two (31). Undoubtedly, the vital, human significance of the number three and the ternary embraces the multi-secular origins of biological evolution. The existence of two (father and mother) must almost inevitably be followed by three (the son) (42). As Lao-Tse says: 'One engenders two, two engenders three, three engenders all things' (58). Hence three has the power to resolve the conflict posed by dualism; it is also the harmonic resolution of the impact of unity upon duality. It symbolizes the creation of spirit out of matter, of the active out of the passive (55). Besides the triangle, there are a number of symbols relevant to the ternary, since, in a sense, it may be said to be the 'inner structure of unity'. Hence, many infernal beings that are base counterparts of the ternary are three-headed like Cerberus or Hecate, or else wield three-pronged weapons such as the trident. The notion of the 'three suns'—the East, the zenith and the West—is related to this symbolism and, according to Dontenville, the form of the tripod is derived from it. If the number four has been found the most fitting 'model' to symbolize exterior or situational quantitative values, three has proved itself the number attached to the interior or vertical order of things. Hence, disposed in accordance with the essential points pertaining to the symbolism of level—the high, the middle and the low—it comes to be related to the 'Three Worlds' (the celestial, terrestrial and infernal), in turn closely connected with the three-part division of man into spirit (the impalpable or the mind), the soul (sentiments) and body (the instincts), and with the moral categories of the good, the indifferent and the bad. There are some writers who analyse the ternary structure of man in terms of intuition (or moral light), thought (intellectual light) and instinct (animal light) (54). Also corresponding to this division, modified by the influence of a particular ruling force, are the well-known stages of mystic perfection: the unitive, illuminative and purgative; in alchemy these stages are symbolized by the colours red, white and black. In Hindu thought the three levels are termed *sattva* (the highest state or that of the predominance of the spirit), *rajas* (the intermediate, dynamic and transforming state) and *tamas* (the instinctive or inferior state). Eliade suggests that the image of the three levels as three cosmic divisions carved out by moral precepts and diffused by human thought is very ancient, for it is present among the pigmies of the Semang tribe in Malaya and among other races at the very earliest stage of cultural development (18). In Ireland this idea is symbolized by a three-storied tower (4). For Diel, the essential functions of man are three in number: conservation, reproduction and spiritualization, and the deformation or perversion of these three functions is represented by the three traditional 'enemies' of the soul—the world, the flesh and the devil, in turn representing the inversion of the three theological Virtues. Guénon, dealing with the 'three worlds' described by Dante in the *Commedia*, suggests the following interesting ternary correspondences: *Sattva, rajas* and *tamas* related respectively to the sky, the atmosphere and the earth's surface or interior; to the future, the present and the past; and to the superconscious, the conscious and the unconscious (27).

Tetrachord According to Schneider, the tetrachord *do, re, mi, fa* may be regarded in the mystic sense as the mediator between heaven and earth; while the tetrachord *sol, la, ti, do* could be taken to represent the divine order. The common note—*do*—relates the symbol to the eagle (of the tetramorphs) (50).

Tetramorphs This is an illustration of the quaternary principle, linked with the concept of situation (just as the ternary is connected with that of activity) and with the intuitive sense of spatial order. It is to the Christian tetramorphs, with their synthesis of the four symbols of the Evangelists, that we are bound to look for the purest and truest expression of this ancient and universal idea. Megalithic culture, possibly reflecting some obscure tradition of remote antiquity, was given to expressing the struggle of the gods against the monsters that, from the beginnings of creation, sought to devour the sun. When they formed the cosmos out of chaos, the gods, in order to safeguard what they had created, placed the lion on the celestial mountain and posted four archers (at the Cardinal Points) to ensure that none might disrupt the cosmic order (50). This proves that the four Cardinal Points, besides representing the extremities of the four horizontal Directions of Space (which, since they pertain to the earth as the zone of manifestation, denote the superficial and the tangible, whereas the nadir and the zenith relate to heaven), may also denote autonomous, spatial zones, as worlds in themselves. This idea is expressed in graphic symbolism by those forms of crosses whose four limbs are rounded (to imply circular motion) or hammer-headed. These personified, autonomous zones may take on a beneficent or a malign character. As a defence against the latter influence stand the four archers already mentioned. In the tetramorphs, the beneficent aspects of the spatial 'order' are all equidistant from the 'Centre'. Schneider relates the animals of the tetramorph to the notes of the tetrachord. The relatively common habit of dividing a country into four provinces implies the same basic idea. Ireland used to be called the 'Island of the Four Kings', these Kings corresponding to four regions, with a fifth in the centre where the High King reigned, like the Pantokrator among the four symbols. This analogy vividly expresses the strength and cohesion of a spatial order derived intuitively, according to Jung, from spiritual and psychological principles and modelled either upon three or upon four depending upon whether those principles pertain to the notions of activity and inner structure or to passivity and situation. This pattern is completed by the number five: four plus the central point, sometimes denoted by a circle or almond-shaped mandorla; or else by the number seven: four outside and three inside. This scheme finds expression in a great many monuments designed upon the basis of a square, walled-in space with three towers in the centre—the Escorial, for instance. Before coming back to the Christian tetramorphs, let us consider some comments of Schneider about the quaternary order in China: 'In the *Ta-tai-li*, the philosopher Tsêng-tse distinguished, as was the custom, four animals destined for the service of a saint; two of these animals (those covered with hair and feathers) proceed from *Yin* (the feminine and passive principle) and two others are depicted bearing a hide, a cuirass or scales.' In this way they clearly reflect the four Elements (with the 'Centre' corresponding to the quintessence, or the spirit) —air, fire, water and earth. Another four-part grouping of animals is to be found in Sumerian art, composed of a lion, an eagle and a peacock mounted on the back of an ox. *The Book of the Dead*, on the other hand, mentions a group of three beings with the heads of animals and a fourth being with a long-eared human head (like the heads in some Romanesque paintings). Likewise, Ezekiel's vision contains the lion, the eagle, the ox and man. Oriental iconography

must have had a great influence upon Ezekiel's vision—and
Egyptian images must have been specially influential. The four
mystic beings in Christian tradition are usually the lion, the eagle,
the ox and the (winged) man. A 4th-century mosaic in the apse of
Santa Pudenziana in Rome groups them in pairs on either side of the
crucifix. Biblical illustrations do not always follow the order laid
down in the holy writ. St. Jerome suggested the following correspondences: the lion corresponding to resurrection, the eagle to ascension, the man to incarnation, the ox to passion. By comparing the
four-part grouping of ancient Mesopotamia (of the lion, the eagle,
the ox and the peacock) with that of Ezekiel (the lion, eagle, ox and
man), we arrive at the equation peacock=Man' (50). According to
Chochod, the equivalent Chinese animals afford the following
correspondences: the dragon corresponding to the lion, the unicorn
to the bull, the turtle to Man, the phoenix to the eagle (13). The
spatial arrangement set out in Ezekiel (i, 10) is: the lion on the
right with the man above him, the ox on the left and, above him, the
eagle (50). Applying the principles of spatial symbolism, whereby,
psychologically speaking, the superior is always a sublimation of the
inferior, and the right side invariably appertains to the consciousness
while the left side concerns the unconscious, we arrive at the conclusion that the winged man is the sublimation of the lion and the
eagle of the ox. In esoteric thought the four beings can be interpreted
symbologically as follows: the eagle is air, intelligence and action;
the lion is fire, strength and movement; the ox is earth, labour,
forbearance and sacrifice; and the winged man is an angel symbolizing the intuitive knowledge of truth. According to Lévi, certain
'disciples of Socrates' substituted the cock for the eagle; the horse
for the lion; the sheep for the ox (the latter substitution being
explained by the proximity of the two zodiacal signs of Aries and
Taurus, while that of the cock for the eagle would follow from the
aerial character of both animals) (37, 59). Correspondences such
as these, we repeat, are not identical relationships but analogies—
that is, close affinities, or relationships between component elements
of separate 'series', resulting from their analogous situation within
the series. Consequently, all the various meanings attributed to
the tetramorphs help to suggest the range of their allusions, as well
as the complex mechanism governing the pattern of their properties.
In Christian symbolism, the symbolic associations of the four
Evangelists (as the archers defending truth and the order of Christ
—the 'Centre') are: Matthew, the winged man; Mark, the lion;
Luke, the ox; John, the eagle (49) (Plate XXVIII).

Texture   The symbolism of texture has received scant attention
nor has it even been recognized as a problem. But certain trends of
contemporary art indicate that the material quality of a work of

art, or the relationship between the apparent surface—space—and the surface proper—the inter-relationship of points in space—is once again being accorded that recognition it formerly enjoyed in ornamental and even in figurative art. We may see in texture two essential component elements: one that produces a pattern of lateral concurrences and one which, so to speak, thrusts upwards. The first—the lateral—factor gives rise to features which are sometimes pre-formal—nascent, symbolic forms only to be glimpsed after careful study, related to the paradoxical 'informal forms' (symbolic blots, klexographies, paper-transfers, and so on), to the so-called 'buried symbolism' of some works of art—which has been seen as a kind of infra-configuration produced by the play of light and shade, by the brush-strokes or by the background patterns—and associated also with the symbolism of composition in so far as this creates an effect of perspective. But texture proper is determined by the quality and thickness of the impasto, of the material, and by the structure of this material as it is understood in mineralogy, producing textures which are caked or fibrillar or pearlitic or porous or cellular, and so on. Broadly speaking, textures may be divided into the hard and smooth and the soft and porous. Since the impression of smoothness (or continuity) is increased in proportion to the distance from which it is viewed, all smooth textures may be regarded as symbolic of remoteness and, by analogy, of cold colours. Conversely, porous textures symbolize nearness and warm colours, expressing a greater degree of inner dynamism in the material and in the corresponding tactile sensation. More detailed conclusions than the above could be educed only after a closer study of the problem of texture.

Theatre An image of the world of phenomena, for both the theatre and the world are 'stages'. Guénon has noted that the theatre is not limited to representing the terrestrial world alone: in the Middle Ages it stood for both this world and the next. The author symbolizes the demiurge; the actors stand in relation to their parts as the Jungian *Selbst* stands to the personality (29).

Theogony According to Diel, the successive reigns of Uranus, Saturn and Jupiter express the progressive stages of the mind, equivalent to unconscious, conscious and superconscious (15). Primeval Neptune, as the ancient Uranian god (associated with the Upper Waters), also symbolized the unconscious, like all aged kings and like the sea-king himself, standing, that is, both for the historical aspect of the unconscious—man's ancestral memory—and for its cosmic aspect, or the latent seeds of thought which did not burgeon until the reign of Saturn (signifying time and, consequently, man as an existential being). By superconsciousness is meant intuition of the supernatural and recognition of the celestial sphere.

Thighs In the Egyptian system of hieroglyphs they express strength (19), a significance which corresponds exactly to their function as the dynamic support of the body. This symbolism was preserved by the Cabala, laying special emphasis upon the firmness and majesty of the thighs.

Thirst Symbolized by the dragon, and denoting the blind appetite for life, according to Evola.

Thorn The thorn of the acacia, in particular, was regarded by the Egyptians as an emblem of the mother-goddess Neith. It is also related to the world-axis, and therefore to the cross (4). The thorn on the rose-bush helps to emphasize the counterpoise or 'conjunction' between thesis and antithesis, that is, between the ideas of existence and non-existence, ecstasy and anguish, pleasure and pain; this again is related to the symbolism of the cross. The crown of thorns adds to the basic symbolism of the thorn the evil characteristics of all things multiple and also the cosmic symbolism of the circle (by virtue of the shape of the crown).

Thread According to the Zohar, thread is one of the most ancient of symbols (like hair). It denotes the essential connexion between any of the different planes—the spiritual, the biological, social, etc. (38).

Threshold A symbol of transition and transcendence. In architectural symbolism, the threshold is always given a special significance by the elaboration and enrichment of its structure by means of porches, perrons, porticoes, triumphal arches, battlements, etc., or by symbolic ornamentation of the kind which, in the West, finds its finest expression in the Christian cathedral with its sculpted mullions, jambs, archivolts, lintels and tympana. Hence the function of the threshold is clearly to symbolize both the reconciliation and the separation of the two worlds of the profane and the sacred. In the East, the function of protecting and warning is effected by the 'keepers of the threshold'—dragons and effigies of gods or spirits. The Roman god Janus also denoted this dualism characteristic of the threshold, which can be related analogically to all other forms of duality (6). Hence the tendency to speak of the threshold between waking and sleeping.

Throne In Asiatic symbolism, the throne stands midway between the mountain and palace on the one hand and the head-dress on the other, for they are all rhythmic variants of one and the same morphological family that symbolize—or, rather, allude to—the 'Centre'. They are also signs expressive of synthesis, stability and unity (37). In the Egyptian system of hieroglyphs, the throne is a determinative sign embracing the concepts of support, exaltation, equilibrium and security (19).

Thule This mythic realm derives its name from *Tula*—or the

'Peerless Land'—which Guénon considers more ancient than *Paradêsha*. It is found in many languages from Russia to Central America. In Sanskrit, *Tulâ* signifies 'scales' and is related to the zodiacal sign of Libra. But there is an ancient Chinese tradition which suggests that the antique 'scales' were related to the Great Bear. This would seem to point to the conclusion that Thule is identical with the polar region, that is, with the 'Centre' *par excellence*. Thule has also been called the 'white island'—identical with the 'white mountain'—or the symbol for the world, as well as with the Blessed Islands of Western tradition. Guénon has also mentioned that whiteness, in relation to topographical features, is always an allusion to these paradisiac isles which man has lost and to which he returns again and again in his legends and folktales. Guénon adds that Latin *albus* (white) corresponds to the Hebrew *Lebanah*, signifying the moon, and points to the examples of Albania, Albion and Alba Longa as places signifying 'whiteness'. The equation of island with mountain is explained by him by the fact that both express ideas of stability, superiority and of refuge from prevailing mediocrity. The island, rising unscathed in the midst of the swirling ocean (representing the outer world—the 'sea of the passions'), corresponds to the biological symbol of the mountain, as the 'mount of salvation' which towers above the transient 'stream of forms' (28).

Thunderbolt The thunderbolt (or lightning) is celestial fire as an active force, terrible and dynamic. The thunderbolt of Parabrahman, the fire-ether of the Greeks, is a symbol of the supreme, creative power. Jupiter possesses this attribute by way of emphasizing his demiurgic nature. At the same time, the flash of lightning is related to dawn and illumination. Because of these parallels, lightning is connected with the first sign of the Zodiac, symbolic of the spring-principle and of the initial stage of every cycle (40). The thunderbolt is held to be an emblem of sovereignty. The winged thunderbolt expresses the ideas of power and speed (8). Jupiter's three thunderbolts symbolize chance, destiny and providence—the forces that mould the future (8). In the majority of religions we find that the godhead is hidden from man's gaze, and then suddenly the lightning-flash reveals him momentarily in all his active might. This image of the Logos piercing the darkness is universal (9). The *vajra*, the Tibetan symbol for both 'thunderbolt' and 'diamond', is also connected with the world-axis (22); but, if the cross or crucifix, the steps and the sacrificial stake, are all symbols of man's longing for the higher world, the thunderbolt expresses the inverse: the action of the higher upon the lower, It is also related to the glance from the third eye of Shiva (or Siva), the destroyer of all material forms.

Tiger Two interpretations of the tiger have been offered which are easily reconciled: 'It is associated with Dionysos, and is a symbol of wrath and cruelty' (8); 'In China, it is symbolic of darkness and of the new moon' (17). For darkness is always identical with the darkness of the soul, and corresponds to that state which the Hindus term *tamas* and which falls within the general symbolism of level, and also denotes the unbridled expression of the base powers of the instincts. Now, in China the tiger seems to play a rôle comparable with that of the lion in African and Western cultures: both animals —like the dragon—take on two different characters—as the wild beast and as the tamed animal. This is what lies behind the tiger as an allegorical expression of strength and valour in the service of righteousness. Five mythic tigers together constitute a symbol which is invested with the same meaning as the tetramorphs in Christian tradition, in so far as they are the defenders of the spatial order against the forces of chaos. The Red Tiger reigns in the south, his season being summer and his Element fire; the Black Tiger reigns in the north—winter is his season, and his Element water; the Blue Tiger reigns in the East, in the spring and amidst vegetation; the White Tiger predominates in the west, in autumn and among the metals; and, finally, the Yellow Tiger (solar in colour) inhabits the earth and reigns supreme over all the other tigers. This Yellow Tiger is located in the 'Centre', as the Emperor was situated in the heart of China and as China lies at the centre of the world (13). This quaternary division plus the centre as the fifth Element is, as Jung has shown, of archetypal significance in the symbolism of situation. When the tiger appears in association with other animals, his symbolic significance varies according to the relative status of the animals within the hierarchy: for instance, the tiger struggling with a reptile stands for the superior principle, but the converse applies if it is locked in combat with a lion or a winged being.

Time Berthelot has noted that the time-pattern usually follows from the division of space, and this applies most particularly to the week (7). It was indeed the awareness of the seven Directions of Space (that is, two for each of the three dimensions plus the centre) that gave rise to the projection of the septenary order into time. Sunday—the Day of Rest—corresponds to the centre and, since all centres are linked with the 'Centre' or the Divine Source, it is therefore sacred in character. The idea of rest is expressive of the notion of the immobility of the 'Centre', whereas the other six Directions are dynamic in character. At the same time, the 'Centre' of space and time also retains a spiritual significance. As Elkin has said, 'It must not be thought that the mythic era is now past: it is also the present and the future, as much a state as a period.' Corresponding, in the strictest sense, to this zone within the circle, the 'Centre', is spacelessness and timelessness, or the non-formal, or, in short, the 'mystic nothingness' which, in oriental thought, is the hole in the Chinese disk of jade called *Pi*, representing heaven. As Eliade notes, *in illo tempore* everything was possible—species and forms were not fixed but 'fluid'. He goes on to point out that a return to this state implies the cessation of time (17). The idea that time—the week—derives from the space-pattern ought strictly to be discarded in favour of the notion that both time and space are the outcome of one and the same principle.

Titans   They signify the wild and untamable forces of primeval Nature (15). The astrobiological and mythic mind—rightly—found it impossible to accept the idea that there was no intermediate stage between the state of chaos and the creation of a cosmic order by man-the-conqueror-of-darkness. Antediluvian monsters and pre-Cromagnon Man were intuited as fabulous animals, Titans, giants and Cyclops, who struggled initially with the gods, and eventually suffered defeat at the hands of the hero—the representative of the 'true man', *not, that is, of the 'mass man' but of the individual who stands out as the mark of the progressive evolution of the species and of the spirit.* In the psychology of the individual this myth still persists in the shape of monsters and of certain other base beings that allude to the 'shadows'—the 'dark' or inferior side. The beginning of Calderón's play *Life is a Dream* is symbolic in this way: the cave stands for the unconscious; the imprisoned Cyprian lamenting his loss of liberty represents the 'dark side' of the dramatist—his baser part—mastered and rendered powerless by the sound judgement and will-power of his 'conscious side' schooled in intellectual and moral disciplines.

Toad   The inverse and infernal aspect of the frog-symbol; that is to say, the symbolic significance is the same though in a negative sense. Or, as the traditional language of esoteric thought puts it: 'There are also certain animals whose mission it is to break up the astral light by a process of absorption peculiar to them. There is something fascinating about their gaze: they are the toad and the basilisk.'

Tomb   Symbolic of the body as matter (57), of transformation and of the unconscious (56). It is also sometimes a maternal and feminine symbol of a generic kind.

Torch   Identified with the sun (14), it is the symbol of purification through illumination. It was the weapon wielded by Hercules against the hydra of Lerna; its fire cauterizes wounds. It occurs in many allegories as the emblem of truth (15).

Tower   In the Egyptian system of hieroglyphs, the tower is a determinative sign denoting height or the act of rising above the common level in life or society (19). Basically, then, the tower is symbolic of ascent. During the Middle Ages, towers and belfries held the significance of watch-towers, but also, by the simple application of the symbolism of level (whereby material height implies spiritual elevation), they expressed the same symbolism as the ladder— linking earth and heaven. The tower-symbol, given that it is enclosed and walled-in, is emblematic of the Virgin Mary, as can be seen in a great many allegorical designs and litanies (14). Since the idea of elevation or ascent, implicit in the tower, connotes transformation and evolution, the athanor (the alchemists' furnace) was given the shape of a tower to signify inversely that the metamorphosis of matter implied a process of ascension. Another symbol usually mentioned in this connexion is the bronze tower in which Danae, the mother of Perseus, was imprisoned (48). Finally we would point to the analogy between the tower and man: for just as the tree is closer to the human figure than are the horizontal forms of animals, so, too, is the tower the only structural form distinguished by verticality: windows at the topmost level, almost always large in size, correspond to the eyes and the mind of man. It is in this sense that the Tower of Babel acquired special symbolic point as a wild enterprise bringing disaster and mental disorder (31). And, for the same reason, the sixteenth enigma of the Tarot denotes catastrophe by the image of a tower struck by lightning. However, it is possible to discover a dual tendency in the symbolism of the tower. Its upward impulse may be accompanied by a deepening movement; the greater the height, the deeper the foundations. Nietzsche talked of descent during ascent. Nerval (in *Aurélia*, to be precise) refers to the symbolism of the tower and says: 'I found myself in a tower, whose foundations were sunk so deep into the earth and whose top was so lofty, reaching up like a spire into the sky, that my whole existence already seemed bound to be consumed in climbing up and down it.'

Tower Struck by Lightning The sixteenth enigma of the Tarot pack, this card is an allegory showing a tower half-destroyed by a flash of lightning which strikes the top (symbolically equivalent to the head). This tower should be identified with the first of the two columns known as Jachin and Boaz, that is, as a symbol of individual power and life. To emphasize that the structure is an image of the living human being, the bricks are flesh-coloured. Pieces of the tower that have fallen away are shown to have struck, first, a king and, secondly, the architect of the tower. The evil implications of the allegory are connected with Scorpio, and allude to the dangerous consequences of over-confidence—or the sin of pride, with its related symbolism of the Tower of Babel. Megalomania, the wild pursuit of fanciful ideas, and small-mindedness form the context of this symbol (59).

Toys Toys are symbols of temptation. According to Diel, this is the meaning when, in Greek mythology, the Titans offer toys to the infant Dionysos (15). A similar trial confronted Achilles when he was given a choice of jewels and valuables, among them a sword, which the hero chose without hesitation.

Trapezium This geometric form unites the shape of the ox's head with that of the primitive stone axe. It is a symbol of sacrifice (50), and also of irregularity or abnormality since geometric figures must, by analogy, express notions of degrees of perfection depending upon how regular are their shapes. The scale of regularity would run as follows: circle, square, trapezium, trapezoid.

Treasure Treasure represents a sublimated form of the symbolism of the colour gold, a solar attribute, as opposed to gold as coins, which signifies exaltation of and corruption by earthly desires (15). In myths, legends and folktales, the treasure is usually found in a cave; there is a double image here embracing the idea of the cave, as the mother-image or the unconscious, containing 'the elusive treasure'. This is an allusion to one of the fundamental mysteries of life (31)—to nothing less than the mystic 'Centre' within the spirit of man, which Jung has dubbed the *Selbst*, to distinguish it from the mere 'ego'. The trials and tribulations that attend the quest for treasure may, up to a point, be equated with the experiments of the alchemists in their pursuit of transmutation (32). Jung maintains that the treasure which the hero wins only after painful effort is nothing less than himself reborn in the cave in which introversion or regression has confined him. The hero, in so far as he remains bound to the mother-principle, is himself the dragon, but in so far as he is reborn of the mother, he is the conqueror of the dragon (and therefore of his former self) (31). In truth, all striving and all suffering are steps along the path of moral progress. And it is possible to equate the one with the other, for as Eliphas Lévi—rightly, in our view—asserts, 'to suffer is tó strive'. The truth of his remark is borne out by Rorschach's discovery that colour and movement are expressions respectively of feeling and of activity, denoting quantities that are analogous and yet opposed, as it were the two 'balance-pans' of the psyche. But it is only when born of conscious choice that work and suffering contribute to progress in its profoundest sense of self-awareness, virtue and superiority.

The dragon in the cave may also represent the sevenfold malignity of the seven planets (as the seven deadly sins), whereas the hero's weapons are the god-given powers which make victory possible. Gold coins, however, and all other derived concepts such as, for example, a bulging wallet, symbolize 'treasure easily come by' (that is, earthly desires, the sensual pleasures, love in so far as it is selfish love) and in consequence 'easily lost'.

Tree The tree is one of the most essential of traditional symbols. Very often the symbolic tree is of no particular genus, although some peoples have singled out one species as exemplifying *par excellence* the generic qualities. Thus, the oak was sacred to the Celts; the ash to the Scandinavian peoples; the lime-tree in Germany; the fig-tree in India. Mythological associations between gods and trees are extremely frequent: so, Attis and the pine; Osiris and the cedar; Jupiter and the oak; Apollo and the laurel, etc. They express a kind of 'elective correspondence' (26, 17). In its most general sense, the symbolism of the tree denotes the life of the cosmos: its consistence, growth, proliferation, generative and regenerative processes. It stands for inexhaustible life, and is therefore equivalent to a symbol of immortality. According to Eliade, the concept of 'life without death' stands, ontologically speaking, for 'absolute reality' and, consequently, the tree becomes a symbol of this absolute reality, that is, of the centre of the world. Because a tree has a long, vertical shape, the centre-of-the-world symbolism is expressed in terms of a world-axis (17). The tree, with its roots underground and its branches rising to the sky, symbolizes an upward trend (3) and is therefore related to other symbols, such as the ladder and the mountain, which stand for the general relationship between the 'three worlds' (the lower world: the underworld, hell; the middle world: earth; the upper world: heaven). Christian symbolism—and especially Roman-esque art—is fully aware of the primary significance of the tree as an axis linking different worlds (14). According to Rabanus Maurus, however, in his *Allegoriae in Sacram Scripturam* (46), it also sym-bolizes human nature (which follows from the equation of the macrocosm with the microcosm). The tree also corresponds to the Cross of Redemption and the Cross is often depicted, in Christian iconography, as the Tree of Life (17). It is, of course, the vertical arm of the Cross which is identified with the tree, and hence with the 'world-axis'. The world-axis symbolism (which goes back to pre-Neolithic times) has a further symbolic implication: that of the central point in the cosmos. Clearly, the tree (or the cross) can only be the axis linking the three worlds if it stands in the centre of the cosmos they constitute. It is interesting to note that the three worlds of tree-symbolism reflect the three main portions of the structure of the tree: roots, trunk and foliage. Within the general significance of the tree as world-axis and as a symbol of the inexhaustible life-process (growth and development), different mythologies and folklores distinguish three or four different shades of meaning. Some of these are merely aspects of the basic symbolism, but others are of a subtlety which gives further enrichment to the symbol. At the most primitive level, there are the 'Tree of Life' and the 'Tree of Death' (35), rather than, as in later stages, the cosmic tree and the tree of the knowledge of Good and Evil; but the two trees are merely two different representations of the same idea. The *arbor vitae* is found frequently, in a variety of forms, in Eastern art. The—

apparently purely decorative—motif of *hom* (the central tree), placed between two fabulous beings or two animals facing each other, is a theme of Mesopotamian origin, brought both to the West and to the Far East by Persians, Arabs and Byzantines (6). In Romanesque decoration it is the labyrinthine foliage of the Tree of Life which receives most emphasis (the symbolic meaning remaining unchanged, but with the addition of the theme of Entanglement) (46). An important point in connexion with the 'cosmic tree' symbol is that it often appears upside down, with its roots in heaven and its foliage on earth; here, the natural symbolism based on the analogy with actual trees has been displaced by a meaning expressing the idea of involution, as derived from the doctrines of emanation: namely, that every process of physical growth is a spiritual *opus* in reverse. Thus, Blavatsky says: 'In the beginning, its roots were generated in Heaven, and grew out of the Rootless Root of all-being. . . . Its trunk grew and developed, crossing the plains of Pleroma, it shot out crossways its luxuriant branches, first on the plane of hardly differentiated matter, and then downward till they touched the terrestrial plane. Thus . . . (it) is said to grow with its roots above and its branches below' (9). This concept is already found in the Upanishads, where it is said that the branches of the tree are: ether, air, fire, water and earth. In the Zohar of Hebrew tradition it is also stated that 'the Tree of Life spreads downwards from above, and is entirely bathed in the light of the sun'. Dante, too, portrays the pattern of the celestial spheres as the foliage of a tree whose roots (i.e. origin) spread upwards (Uranus). In other traditions, on the other hand, no such inversion occurs, and this symbolic aspect gives way to the symbolism of vertical upward growth. In Nordic mythology, the cosmic tree, called Yggdrasil, sends its roots down into the very core of the earth, where hell lies (*Völuspâ*, 19; *Grimnismâl*, 31) (17).

We can next consider the two-tree symbolism in the Bible. In Paradise there were the Tree of Life and the tree of the knowledge of good and evil. Both were centrally placed in the Garden of Eden. In this connexion, Schneider says (50): 'Why does God not mention the Tree of Life to Adam? Is it because it was a second tree of knowledge or is it because it was hidden from the sight of Adam until he came to recognize it with his new-found knowledge of good and evil—of wisdom? We prefer the latter hypothesis. The Tree of Life, once discovered, can confer immortality; but to discover it is not easy. It is "hidden", like the herb of immortality which Gilgamesh seeks at the bottom of the sea, or is guarded by monsters, like the golden apples of the Hesperides. The two trees occur more frequently than might be expected. At the East gate of the Babylonian heaven, for instance, there grew the Tree of Truth and the Tree of Life.' The doubling of the tree does not modify the symbol's fundamental significance, but it does add further symbolic implications connected with the dual nature of the Gemini: the tree, under the influence of the symbolism of the number two, then reflects the parallel worlds of living and knowing (the Tree of Life and the Tree of Knowledge). As is often the case with symbols, many more specialized meanings have been developed on the basis of the general tree-symbolism already outlined. Here are a few: firstly, the triple tree. According to Schneider, the Tree of Life, when it rises no higher than the mountain of Mars (the world of phenomena) is regarded as a pillar supporting heaven. It is made up of three roots and three trunks—or rather one central trunk with two large boughs corresponding to the two peaks of the mountain of Mars (the two faces of Janus). Here the central trunk or axis unifies the dualism expressed in the two-tree symbolism. In its lunar aspect, it is the Tree of Life and emphasizes the moon's identification with the realm of phenomena; in its solar aspect it relates to knowledge and death (which, in symbolism, are often associated). In iconography, the Tree of Life (or the lunar side of a double or triple tree) is depicted in bloom; the tree of death or knowledge (or the solar side of a double or triple tree) is dry, and shows signs of fire (50). Psychology has interpreted this symbolic duality in sexual terms, Jung affirming that the tree has a symbolic, bisexual nature, as can also be seen in the fact that, in Latin, the endings of the names of trees are masculine even though their gender is feminine (31). This *conjunctio* confirms the unifying significance of the cosmic tree. Other symbols are often brought into association with the tree, sometimes by analogy with real situations, sometimes through the juxtaposition of psychic images and projections. The resulting composite symbolism is, of course, richer and more complex, but also more specific, and consequently less spontaneous and of less scope. The tree is frequently related to the rock or the mountain on which it grows. On the other hand, the Tree of Life, as found in the celestial Jerusalem, bears twelve fruits, or sun-shapes (symbols of the Zodiac, perhaps). In many images, the sun, the moon and the stars are associated with the tree, thus stressing its cosmic and astral character. In India we find a triple tree, with three suns, the image of the Trimurti; and in China a tree with the twelve suns of the Zodiac (25). In alchemy, a tree with moons denotes the lunar *opus* (the Lesser Work) and the tree with suns the solar *opus* (the Great Work). The tree with the signs of the seven planets (or metals) stands for prime matter (protohyle), from which all differentiations emerge. Again, in alchemy, the Tree of Knowledge is called *arbor philosophica* (a symbol of evolution, or of the growth of an idea, a vocation or a force). 'To plant the philosophers' tree' is tantamount to stimulating the creative imagination

(32). Another interesting symbol is that of the 'sea-tree' or coral, related to the mythic sea king. The fountain, the dragon and the snake are also frequently related to the tree. Symbol LVII of Bosch's *Ars Symbolica* shows the dragon beside the tree of the Hesperides. As regards the symbolism of levels, it is possible to establish a vertical scale of analogies: dragons and snakes (primal forces) are associated with the roots; the lion, the unicorn, the stag and other animals expressing the ideas of elevation, aggression and penetration, correspond to the trunk; and birds and heavenly bodies are brought into relation with the foliage. Colour correspondences, are: roots/black; trunk/white; foliage/red. The snake coiled round the tree introduces another symbol, that of the spiral. The tree as world-axis is surrounded by the sequence of cycles which characterizes the revealed world. This is an interpretation applicable to the serpent watching at the foot of the tree on which the Golden Fleece is suspended (25). Endless instances could be quoted of such associations of symbols, full of psychological implications. Another typical combination of symbols, extremely frequent in folktales, is that of the 'singing tree'. In the *Passio S. Perpetuae XI* (Cambridge, 1891) we read that St. Saturius, a martyr alongside St. Perpetua, dreamed on the eve of his martyrdom 'that, having shed his mortal flesh, he was carried eastward by four angels. Going up a gentle slope, they reached a spot bathed in the most beautiful light: it was Paradise opening before us', he adds, 'like a garden, with trees bearing roses and many other flower-blooms; trees tall as cypresses, singing the while' (46). The sacrificial stake, the harp-lyre, the ship-of-death and the drum are all symbols derived from the tree seen as the path leading to the other world (50) (Plate XXIX). Gershom G. Scholem, in *Les Origines de la Kabbale*, speaks of the symbolism of the tree in connexion with hierarchical, vertical structures (such as the 'sefirothic tree' of the Cabbala, a theme that we cannot develop here). He asks himself whether the 'tree of Porphyry', which was a widespread symbol during the Middle Ages, was of a similar nature. In any case, it is reminiscent of the *Arbor elementalis* of Raymond Lull (1295), whose trunk symbolizes the primordial *substance* of Creation, or *hyle*, and whose branches and leaves represent its nine *accidents*. The figure ten has the same connotation as in the sefiroth, the 'sum of all the real which can be determined by numbers'.

Trees and Flowers In Chinese symbology, they usually symbolize longevity and fertility. Predominantly popular are the bamboo, the cherry-tree and the pine, called 'the three friends' because all three are evergreen. In painting they frequently appear together (2).

Triangle The geometric image of the ternary and, in the symbolism of numbers, equivalent to the number three. In its highest sense it concerns the Trinity. In its normal position with the apex uppermost it also symbolizes fire and the aspiration of all things towards the higher unity—the urge to escape from extension (signified by the base) into non-extension (the apex) or towards the Origin or the Irradiating Point. Nicholas of Cusa said of the triangle that, truncated (without its apex), it served the alchemists as a symbol of air; inverted (with apex pointing downwards) it symbolizes water; and inverted but with the tip cut off, it symbolizes earth. Two complete triangles, one in the normal position and one inverted—representing, respectively, fire and water—superimposed so as to form a six-pointed star (called Solomon's seal), constitute a symbol of the human soul. A triangle surmounted by horns was the Carthaginian symbol for Tanit (or Tanith) (12).

Trident Various interpretations of the trident or three-pointed spear have been advanced, ranging from Eliade's suggestion that originally it was a representation of the teeth of sea-monsters (17), to Diel's explanation which we will discuss below. It is an attribute of Neptune and of Satan. According to Bayley, it is a corrupt form of the cross (4), adapted, that is, in such a way as to suggest a vicious character. More precisely, every instrument, object or being having three members or parts where one would normally suffice realizes a trebling of its symbolic force or potentiality (8). This is born out by Zimmer's comment that the trident denotes threefold hostility. The third point might well correspond to the third eye of Shiva (or Siva) the Destroyer, since the trident is also an attribute of this god. The fact that the trident was the weapon of the Roman *retiarius* is highly significant, for the net which he also used relates him to the Uranian deity, whereas the sword wielded by the *mirmillo* gladiator suggests the heroic, solar son. Hence, the trident, in the hands of the *retiarius*, would seem to be an attribute of archaic, paternal power opposed to the unique heroism of the solar son. Diel, with his moralist approach, carries the negative implication of the trident to its logical conclusion, suggesting that it symbolizes triple sin, corresponding to the perversion of the three 'vital urges' of nutrition or preservation (transformed into possession, property and authority); reproduction (lust); and spiritualization or evolution (which, in its negative aspect, becomes vanity). Hence it is an attribute of the god of the unconscious and of sin—Neptune, whose realm is the haunt of monsters and base forms of life. The triple character of the trident is an 'infernal replica of the Trinity', comparable with the three heads of Cerberus or of triform Hecate (17). On the other hand, a favourable interpretation has also been ascribed to the trident; Charles Ploix, in *La Nature et les dieux*, associates it with the wand used in water-divining (2), although this interpretation seems to rest on somewhat dubious grounds. According to Father Heras, the trident was, in the proto-Indian era, an attribute of god.

Triform   A second name of Hecate, who, with her three heads, presided, according to Servius, over birth, life and death (representing the past, the present and the future). This is a teratological application of the principle of triplicity or triunity (8). Similar in significance is the *Trimurti* (embracing creation, preservation and destruction) formed by Brahma, Vishnu and Shiva (60). Triform symbolism conforms to the general symbolism of ternary forms, in its depiction of power as holiness, science and armed might, in turn clearly corresponding to the spirit, the intellect and vitality (28).

Triple Enclosure   A schematic pattern of various forms (three squares or concentric circles, combinations of both or combinations with polygons) which, according to Louis Charbonneau-Lassay in *L'Ésotérisme de quelques symboles géométriques chrétiens*, symbolizes the ternary or triple make-up of man: body, soul, spirit; or of the world: physical universe, intelligible or intellectual universe, spiritual or transcendental universe. This symbol, in the form of squares, has been found engraved on some stelae such as that of Suèvres (Orléannais, France), dating back roughly to the Druidic or Gallo-Roman period. Similar symbols have been found engraved in bone, attributed to the Merovingian period, and in the *graffiti* of the Knights Templars in the castle of Chinon (1308). The reverse of English coins in the 14th and 15th centuries and the obverse of Castilian 'anagram' coins are triple enclosures in pattern and perhaps in significance.

Triple enclosure

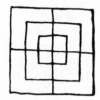

Tripod   Dontenville regards this as a solar symbol, not because it has a circular top but because of the three supports which can be said to correspond to the three solar 'moments'—the rising, the zenith and the setting (16). The symbolic figure of the triskeles—three legs joined together to form a kind of swastika—is similar in meaning according to Dontenville (16), but Ortiz holds that it is expressive of 'swift movement' (41).

Triumph   The symbols of triumph are related to those of power. In addition, there are elements of exhibition and exaltation; and thereby they become connected with the symbols of verticality, ascension and radiance, and with the solar symbols (crown, palm, gold, purple, chariot, white horses, stepped temples). It was probably the Romans who created the most perfect form of triumphal symbolism for the glorification of their *imperatores* and Caesars. The standards of the legions and cohorts, with an eagle or a phoenix on the point of a lance, are themselves another example of triumphal symbols.

Trumpet Since it is a metal instrument, it corresponds to the Elements of fire and water and also to the twin-peaked Mountain of Mars. Metallic instruments pertain to nobles and warriors, whereas wooden instruments, from their associations with the valley, are more properly related to the common folk and to shepherds (50). The trumpet symbolizes the yearning for fame and glory (8). On the other hand, the horn, because of its shape, is connected with the symbolism of the animal-horn (50).

Tunic Whereas the cloak symbolizes the outer bounds of the personality or the 'mask' which envelops the Jungian *Selbst*, the tunic may denote the self or the soul, that is, the zone in most direct contact with the spirit. An individual clothed in an orange-coloured tunic is 'afire', since orange is the colour symbolizing fire and passion. The tunic of Nessus, which was the cause of Hercules' death by burning, was of this same colour. Holes in the tunic (or a suit), or tatters, are equivalent to scars and symbolic of the wounds in the soul. Concerning the orange-coloured tunic, Zimmer relates that in India this was the garment in which criminals were clothed when condemned to death for terrible crimes (60).

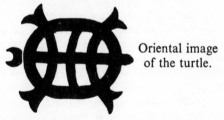

Oriental image of the turtle.

Turtle The turtle has a variety of meanings, all of which are organically related. In the Far East its significance is cosmic in implication. As Chochod has observed: 'The primordial turtle has a shell that is rounded on the top to represent heaven, and square underneath to represent the earth' (13). To the Negroes of Nigeria it suggests the female sex organ (12) and it is in fact taken as an emblem of lubricity. In alchemy it was symbolic of the '*massa confusa*' (32). These disparate senses have, nevertheless, one thing in common: in every case, the turtle is a symbol of material existence and not of any aspect of transcendence, for even where it is a combination of square and circle it alludes to the forms of the manifest world and not to the creative forces, nor to the Origin, still less to the irradiating Centre. In view of its slowness, it might be said to symbolize natural evolution as opposed to spiritual evolution which is rapid or discontinuous to a degree. The turtle is also an emblem of longevity. An engraving in the *Hypnerotomachia Poliphili* (p. 79) depicts a woman holding a pair of outspread wings in one hand and a turtle in the other. The counterbalancing of one with the other would suggest that the turtle is the inversion of the wings; that is, that since the wings signify elevation of the spirit, the turtle would denote the fixed element of alchemy although only in its negative aspect. In short, then, it would stand for turgidity, involution, obscurity, slowness, stagnation and highly concentrated materialism, etc. Perhaps this is the explanation of the turtles in Moreau's painting of *Orpheus* with their disquieting negativeness.

Turtle Dove A symbol of fidelity and of affection among human beings (8). It is to be found in many allegories and is sometimes confused with the dove.

Twelve Strictly, of all the numbers, twelve is the broadest in scope, for the Tarot formulas are such that they contain two groups of eleven and four of fourteen, but the components of these numbers have no archetypal significance. Given that the two essential proto-types of quantity are the numbers three and four (signifying respectively dynamism or inner spirituality, and stability or outer activity), it can be argued that their sum and their multiplication give the two numbers which are next in importance: seven and twelve. The latter corresponds to the geometrical dodecagon; but it may also be associated with the circle, since their symbolic meaning is practically identical. For this reason, systems or patterns based upon the circle or the cycle tend to have twelve as the end-limit. Even when structures are made up of less than twelve elements at first, they later tend towards the superior number of twelve, as, for example, in music, where the seven-note modal scale has developed into the twelve-note system of the Arnold Schoenberg school. Other examples are: the twelve hours on the clock-face; the twelve months of the year; the twelve major gods of many mythologies, as a kind of amplification of the seven planets; and the markings of the wind-rose (corresponding to Eurus, Solanus, Notus, Auster, Africus, Euroauster, Zephyrus, Stannus, Ireieus, Boreas, Aquilo, Volturnus). All these examples, then, prove the existence of an order founded upon patterns of twelve, which can be split up either into the 'inner' three-part division of the 'outer' or circumstantial pattern of four, or else into the 'outer' four-part division of the 'inner' and actual pattern of three. For the Vedic Indians, the twelve middle days of winter (from Christmas to Epiphany) were an image and a replica of the entire year; and a similar tradition exists in China (17). In our view, the symbolism of the Zodiac lies at the root of all these systems based upon the number twelve, that is, the idea that the four Elements may appear in three different ways (levels or grades), giving twelve divisions. It is for these reasons that Saint-Yves draws the sociological conclusion that, among groups of human beings in the line of symbolic tradition, 'the circle which comes highest and nearest to the mysterious centre, consists of twelve divisions representing the supreme initiation (the faculties, the virtues and knowledge) and corresponding, among other things, to the Zodiac'. Guénon (who quotes the above) adds that the twelve-formula is to be found in the 'circular council' of the Dalai Lama, and (quite apart from the twelve apostles) in the legendary knights of the Round Table and the historical Twelve Peers of France. Similarly, the Etruscan state was subdivided into twelve minor states; and Romulus created twelve lictors (28).

Twilight (or **Half-light**) The half-light of morning or evening is a symbol of dichotomy, representing the dividing-line which at once joins and separates a pair of opposites. Frazer relates an Indian legend which embodies a curious mythic stratagem: 'Indra swore to the demon Namuci that he would slay him neither by day nor by night. . . . But he killed him in the morning-twilight' (21). Half-light is characterized by lack of definition and ambivalence, and is therefore closely related to the space-symbolism of the Hanged Man or of any object suspended between heaven and earth. Evening-light is associated with the West, symbolizing the location of death. Dontenville suggests that it is, therefore, not by chance that Perseus goes westward in his quest for the Gorgon's head. And the same may be said of Hercules in his journey to the garden of the Hesperides, since the place and the time of sunset imply the end of one cycle (corresponding to the zodiacal sign of Pisces) and the beginning of another. According to legend, Merlin buried the sun in Mount Tombe. King Arthur fell mortally wounded in the West, and there he was healed by Morgana the Fairy (a name deriving from *Morgen* —morning) (16).

Twins In representations of the *sacrificium mithriacum*, the two dadophori, Cautes and Cautopates, are very frequently shown, one with his torch pointing upwards and the other with his turned downwards: the one is alight, the other extinguished. Cumont considers that they symbolize life and death. Sometimes one dadophorus has the head of a bull and the other that of a scorpion, confirming Cumont's conclusion. They also signify the two essential aspects of the sun: its alternate appearance and disappearance— day and night (31). A careful study of Primitive traditions and of the mythologies of the more advanced cultures has enabled us to draw the conclusion that most of them incorporate the symbol of the twins, such as the Vedic Asvins (or Ashwins), Mitra and Varuna, Liber and Libera, Romulus and Remus, Isis and Osiris, Apollo and Artemis, Castor and Pollux, Amphion and Zethus, or

Arion and Orion. On some occasions the addition of a third figure (brother or sister) permits of further associations, as, for example, Castor and Helen, or Osiris and Set. They are always mythic beings born of an immortal father and a mortal mother. The respective characteristics of their parents—expressed in landscape-symbolism by the dualism of the mountain (representing heaven) and the valley or water (representing earth)—are not fused in their offspring, but discrete. Thus, one brother may be a fierce hunter, another a peaceful shepherd (50). In sum, these beings are usually beneficent deities (17). Through the influence of totemism or of animalistic symbolism, they appear fairly often in the symbolic guise of animals: as birds (35)—the myth of oviparous human birth is a parallel manifestation of this; or as lions (that is, the wild lion and the tame lion, or day and night) (4); or as horses, one white or chestnut, the other black. The twin Indian Ashwins (or Asvins) are depicted in this latter form, one in light and the other in darkness, as if the chariot they draw is ever running along the borderline of dusk. But most commonly one of the twins signifies the eternal side of man, his inheritance from his celestial father (as a reflection of the *hieros gamos*), or, in short, his soul, and the other twin indicates the mortal side (40). However, they also symbolize the counterbalancing principles of good and evil, and hence the twins are portrayed as mortal enemies. This is what lies behind the Egyptian myth of Osiris and Set and the Persian myth of Ahuramazda and Angra-mainyu (or Ahriman) as well as the Iroquois myth of Hawneyn and Hanegoasegeh and the Slav myth of Bielbog and Chernobog (or Zcernoboch) (the 'white god' and the 'black god') (35). Since the life-principle is usually allied with evil, the principle of good has to fall back upon ascetic spirituality; it follows then, that, in order to achieve immortality, it is essential to accept the maxim 'Deny thyself'. In India, such duality is precisely exemplified in the two names of *Atman* (or individual soul) and *Brahman* (world-soul); up to a point, they are pantheistic in tendency. Friedrich Nietzsche exactly described the mystic message implied in this partial negation necessary for the salvation of the spiritual essence of Man, with his advice: 'Cast into the abyss that which lies most heavily upon you. Let man forget. . . . Divine is the art of forgetting. If you would raise yourself—if you yourself would dwell among the heights, cast into the sea that which lies most heavily upon you'; yet Nietzsche, as a Westerner, does not succeed in escaping from self.

Twisted Shapes These fall within the broad group of symbolic abnormalities, in so far as they deviate from the norm in shape and significance (where, for example, the normal shape is straight or curved).

U

Umbrella This symbol is invariably related to the sun-shade, which is a solar emblem of the monarchs of certain peoples. But its mechanism has tended to lend it a phallic significance. It is a father-symbol for this reason and because of its implications of protection and of mourning (42).

Undines Water-nymphs, or undines, are symbolically the inverse of sirens: in the latter, the fishy part of their body refers to the relationship between the waters (and the moon) and woman; with undines, it is the feminine—or perilous—nature of the waters which is symbolized. Krappe notes that these nymphs are usually wicked in so far as they represent the treacherousness of rivers, lakes and torrents.

Unicorn Symbolic of chastity and also an emblem of the sword or of the word of God (20, 4). Tradition commonly presents it as a white horse with a single horn sprouting from its forehead, but according to esoteric belief it has a white body, a red head and blue eyes. Legend has it that it is tireless when pursued yet falls meekly to the ground when it is approached by a virgin (59). This seems to suggest that it is symbolic of sublimated sex. In China, the animal known as Ch'i-lin is identified by some writers with the unicorn, whereas there are others who dispute this because it has two horns. It is an attribute of high-ranking army officers and an emblem of uprightness and high birth. Its skin is of five colours—red, yellow, blue, white and black; its cry is like the sound of bells. In legend it is reputed to live for a thousand years and to be the noblest of animals (5). Jung, in his work on the relationships between psychology and alchemy, has studied a great many aspects of this fabulous animal, concluding that, broadly speaking, it has no one definite symbolic character but rather many different variants embracing single-horned animals, both real and fabulous, such as the sword-fish or certain types of dragon. He notes that the unicorn is at times transmuted into a white dove, offering the explanation that on the one hand it is related to primordial monsters while on the other it represents the virile, pure and penetrating force of the *spiritus mercurialis*. He quotes the remark of Honorius of Autun in his *Speculum de Mysteriis Ecclesiae*, as follows: 'The very fierce animal with only one horn is called unicorn. In order to catch it, a virgin is put in a field; the animal then comes to her and is caught, because it lies down in her lap. Christ is represented by this animal, and his invincible strength by its horn. He, who lay down in the womb of the Virgin, has been caught by the hunters; that is to say, he was found in human shape by those who loved him.' However, in Antiquity the unicorn appears on occasion with certain evil characteristics. The *Physiologus Graecus* comments that it is 'an animal fleet of foot, single-horned and harbouring ill will towards men'. As Jung has observed, the Church does not recognize this negative side of the unicorn. On the other hand, the alchemists made use of its ambivalent implications in order to symbolize the *Monstrum Hermaphroditum*. The universality of this symbolic being, non-existent in nature, is indeed surprising; it is, for instance, in the Vedas. Regarding its iconography, of special interest are the 15th-century tapestries in the Cluny Museum in Paris, with their illustrations of *La Dame à la Licorne* (32).

Urn A symbol of containment which, like all such symbols, corresponds to the world of things feminine. The urn of gold or silver, associated with a white lily, is the favourite emblem of the Virgin in religious iconography. The urn with a lid is one of the eight emblems of good luck in Chinese Buddhism, and signifies Oneness, or that state of supreme intelligence which triumphs over birth and death (5).

Utensils Generally speaking, their symbolic significance amounts to a simple transference to the spiritual plane of their practical and utilitarian function (56). Secondary implications are prompted by the particular shape, material and colour of the utensil.

Valley Within the symbolism of landscapes, the valley, which, because it is low-lying, is considered to lie at the level of the sea, represents a neutral zone apt for the development of all creation and for all material progress in the world of manifestation. Its characteristic fertility stands in contrast to the nature of the desert (symbolically a place of purification), of the ocean (which represents the Origin of life but which, in relation to man's existence, is sterile), and of the mountain (the region characterized by snows and the ascetic, contemplative life, or by intellectual illumination). In short, the valley is symbolic of life itself and is the mystic abode of shepherd and priest (51).

Vase In the Egyptian system of hieroglyphs, this is a determinative sign corresponding to Nu (or Nun or Nou), the god of repose, immanence and acceptance (19), The 'full vase' is associated with the Plant of Life and is an emblem of fertility (17). The golden vase or pot filled with white lilies is the common emblem of the Virgin Mary.

Vault   According to Leo Frobenius, in prehistoric and proto-historic thinking, every vault represents the union of the sky-god with the earth-goddess. The separation of the two deities created the void (22).

Vegetation   Vegetation, in all its forms, has two main implications: firstly, pertaining to its annual cycle, whence its symbolism of death and resurrection following the pattern of winter and spring; and, secondly, that of its abundance, giving rise to its significance in connexion with fertility and fecundity. Vegetation rites are celebrated in many different regions, and on dates ranging from Carnival (Shrove-tide) to the feast of St. John (24th June) (17). In every case, the aim is to encourage the cosmic forces to continue to bring about the annual regeneration of life.

Vehicles   The various ancient and modern vehicles are corruptions of the essential symbol of the chariot. Those that possess some individual characteristics are connected with existence itself; those that are generic in character pertain to the collective life (56). According to Jung, the particular type of vehicle that appears relates to the individual's characteristic movement—whether lively or slow, regular or irregular—or the character of his inner life or his mind, or whether his ideas are his own or borrowed, and so on (32). Every vehicle is an expression of the body (including the mind and thought) or, in other words, of the spirit in its existential aspect. Thus, from the symbolic point of view, to see in the imagination, or in dreams, a chariot or a car on fire has the same significance as the vision of a man in an orange-coloured tunic (since orange is the colour of fire).

Veil   In addition to partaking of the generic symbolism of fabrics, the veil signifies the concealment of certain aspects of truth or of the deity. Guénon draws attention to the double meaning of the verb 'to reveal' ('re-veil'), which may mean either to pull back the veil or to cover again with a veil. The Bible tells us that when Moses came down from mount Sinai 'the skin of his face shone' so that he had to cover his face with a veil while he spoke with the people because they were unable to look upon his shining face (Exodus xxxiv, 29-35) (28).

Venus   The planet Venus is, in alchemy, related to the goddess of love and also to copper. In astrology, it is associated with the Moon in particular and with Mars. Its spiritual significance has two aspects: that of spiritual love and that of mere sexual attraction, so that some writers have come to regard its true symbolic significance as physical and mechanical in character.

Verbs   Every verb denotes an action, a passion or an operation, and its symbolism is a direct consequence of the transference of this material sense to the spiritual plane. For example, to take food is symbolic of receiving spiritual or intellectual nourishment; to kill is to eradicate a given being from the mind; to travel is to move, by exercise of the imagination and awareness, away from one world and towards another; and so on.

Verticality   Since all symbolism is, in essence, dynamic, the idea of verticality is closely related to upward movement, which, by analogy with the symbolism of space and with moral concepts, corresponds symbolically to the tendency towards spiritualization (dealt with in connexion with the symbolism of Levels—q.v.). Symbolic theory attaches such importance to the level or height of a given figure (in relation to the norm) that it can even define the significance of this form or being solely by reference to its vertical 'height'. Bachelard corroborates this and even goes so far as to say that 'it is impossible to ignore the vertical axis in expressing moral values' (3).

Vessel   In the Egyptian system of hieroglyphs, a determinative sign corresponding to the idea of receptacles in general. It is a symbol whose immediate significance is that of the context in which the intermingling of forces takes place, giving rise to the material world. From this sense arises a secondary symbolism—that of the female matrix (19).

Victory   The crown as an expression of fulfilment, and the palm in the sense of elevation and exaltation, are the two outward attributes of victory. When Victory is personified as a winged figure, the allusion is to its spiritual worth. Whether, as in the Mithraic mysteries, the victory is over the bull, or whether it is over the dragon or some other such monster, as in the exploits of Hercules, Perseus, Bellerophon and St. George, the significance of the act of conquering lies in the disarming of the adversary and his subjugation to the will of the victor. In addition to the objective and cosmic sense of victory, there is also a psychological implication: confrontation with another force presupposes resemblance, and therefore the conquered force is the very inferiority of the conqueror himself.

Vine   Just as the grape has an ambivalent symbolism, pertaining to sacrifice and to fecundity, so wine frequently appears as a symbol both of youth and of eternal life. In the earliest times, the supreme ideogram of life was a vine-leaf. According to Eliade, the Mother-Goddess was known by the Primitives as 'The Goddess of the Vines', representing the unfailing source of natural creation (17).

Virgo   The sixth sign of the Zodiac. For the Egyptians it was identical with Isis. Since it is governed by Mercury and corresponds

to the number six, it is symbolic of hermaphroditism, or that state
which is characterized by dual—positive and negative—forces.
Hence Virgo is sometimes depicted with the symbol of the soul or
the Seal of Solomon (two triangles, representing fire and water,

Zodiacal sign
of Virgo.

superimposed and intersecting to form a six-pointed star) (40). In
mythology and in religions generally, this symbol is always associated
with the birth of a god or a demigod, as the supreme expression of
the dynamic consciousness (52) (Plate XXX).

Volcano   In mythology, the volcano is invested with antithetical
powers: on the one hand there is the extraordinary fertility of the
volcanic earth in such regions as Naples, California or Japan; but
on the other hand the destructive fire of the volcano is linked with
the idea of evil. This accounts for the variety of ideas associated
with the volcano. For the Persians, for instance, it was quite simply
the Great Adversary, Ahriman, who, in the form of a huge dragon
or serpent, was shackled (as in the comparable myth of Prometheus)
to mount Demâvand, the volcano of Elburz, there to await the
Day of Judgement (35). The volcano is symbolic not only of the
primary force of nature and of the fire of life (representing creation
and destruction) (4), but also of the original 'site' of the 'descent' of
the Elements—involution, that is to say; here, in the bowels of the
volcano, the Elements of air, fire, water and earth are intermingled
and transformed (50). Hence it becomes feasible to relate the
volcano to Shiva, the god of creation and destruction. As a psychological symbol, the volcano represents the passions which, according
to Beaudoin, become the sole source of our spiritual energy once
we have managed to master and transform them. An examination
of the 30th symbol of the *Ars Symbolica* of Bosch in relation to
the legendary motto *Gelat et ardet*, points to the conclusion that
there is a profound significance of the volcano touching upon the
coincidentia oppositorum. Another important sense of the volcano
arises from its peculiar characteristic whereby a long period of
latent, enclosed and occult labour is followed by a sudden and
terrible eruption. By analogy between this process and many other
similar processes in the lives of individuals and social groups, the
word 'volcano' has come to be used as an image of this dual tendency
of tension and distension (31).

Vulcan   Vulcan, as a symbol, is related to the smith who has his forge in the mountain-cave, and hence to the demiurge. Indeed, the ancients explained volcanoes by reference to underground forges and supernatural smiths. The cult of the Hephaestia festival was connected with the volcanic activity of the Aegean islands (35). But Vulcan, the demiurge, is characterized by negative qualities as ascribed to him by the Gnostics and the doctrine of Mani. He is lame and this is symbolic of his weak or corrupt soul. According to Diel, he bears a family relationship to the Christian devil. His deformity was a consequence of his defiance of Jupiter—the spirit—who punished him by hurling him down from mount Olympus. Diel also suggests that Vulcan, Icarus and Prometheus are symbolic of the intellect—understood almost in its technical and 'merely human' sense—in open rebellion against the spirit (15).

Vulture   In Egyptian hieroglyphs, the sign of the vulture—like the wavy line which is the sign for water—stands for the idea of the Mother (19). According to Jung, the 'mother'-symbolism of the Egyptian vulture is probably derived from its necrophagous habits (31). It was believed that the vulture, because it fed upon corpses, was related to Mother Nature (and to death). The Parsees place their dead in specially built towers so that vultures will consume them, believing that this facilitates rebirth (56). A sublimation of this meaning—mythic rather than symbolic in nature—is found in India, where the vulture is the symbol of the tutelary spirits which watch over the individual in lieu of the parents, denoting abnegation and spiritual counsel (38).

Wall   Its significance is diverse, depending upon which of its different characteristics is taken as fundamental. In the Egyptian system of hieroglyphs, the wall is a determinative sign conveying the idea of 'rising above the common level' (19); clearly the predominant sense here is that of its height. A wall enclosing a space is the 'wall of lamentations', symbolic of the sensation of the world as a 'cavern'—of the doctrine of immanentism or the metaphysical notion of the impossibility of reaching the outside. It expresses the ideas of impotence, delay, resistance, or a limiting situation. Now, the wall seen from within as an enclosure has a secondary implication of protection which, according to its function and the attitude of the individual, may even be taken as its principal meaning. Psychoanalysts frequently regard it in this light and hence have classified it as a mother-symbol, comparable with the town and the house or home (56). Bayley sums up the two essential features of the wall as follows: Like the house, it is a mystic symbol representing the feminine element of mankind. This enables us to understand the (otherwise absurd) assertion of the Shulamite in the *Song of Songs*: 'I am a wall'. At the same time, this image has another term of comparison, that of matter as opposed to spirit (4). It should be noted that the symbolism in the latter case remains unchanged, since matter corresponds to the passive or feminine principle, and spirit to the active or masculine.

Wallowing Rolling on the ground, and especially wallowing in mud or swamp, form part of primitive therapy all over the world. The custom also figures in some rites involving rain or fertility, and is also to be found in magic practices where a man is required to roll on the ground in order to rise up again transformed into a wolf (51). The myth of Antaeus is connected with this belief. In all this, the supposition is that contact with the earth instigates certain latent possibilities either in the cosmos or in the individual or his spirit. The desire to be cured, or for metamorphosis or rain, corresponds to the general longing for 'Inversion'—the upsetting of a given order so that it may be replaced by its opposite. To roll on the ground is, then, one of those sacrificial acts that are supposed to encourage or facilitate inversion, a change in circumstances or in the broad stream of life.

Wand, Magic Alongside the 'technical' symbolism implied by its material or its colour, its significance derives from the magic power attributed to it, which in turn derives from the concept of every stick or wand as a straight line, embodying implications of direction and intensity. Derived, or related, forms are the royal sceptre, the marshal's baton, the battle-club, the mayor's staff and the conductor's baton (48).

Wandering Jew The legend of Ahasuerus, the Wandering Jew, is believed to be of Western origin. Underlying it is the symbolic idea of the man who cannot die, or who, after his apparent death (King don Rodrigo, or don Sebastian, or King Arthur, for example) appears again. The tradition can be related also to that of the Eternal Youth—the oriental Jadir. In Jung's opinion they are but one symbol alluding to the imperishable side of Man, such as in the myth of the Dioscuri or the Gemini (31).

War In a cosmic sense, every war concerns the struggle of light against darkness—of good against evil. In mythology, there are copious examples of such struggles between the powers of light and the forces of darkness: Jupiter's combat with the Titans, Thor versus the giants, Gilgamesh and other heroes versus monsters (4). The particular field of action is symbolic of the plane of reality on which the action takes place. In Islamic tradition, material war is merely the 'little holy war', whereas the 'great Holy War' is that which liberates man from the enemies within. The more just the war, the more faithful the image of it. Guénon specifically states that the only justification for war is the reducing of multiplicity to unity—disorder to order. In this way, war can be seen as the means of reinstating the original order, or as a kind of 'sacrifice' which echoes the cosmogonic sacrifice. Exactly the same applies to the psychic plane: Man must seek to achieve inner unity in his actions, in his thoughts, and also between his actions and his thoughts. Unity of purpose is symbolized by ritual orientation, in which the terrestrial 'centres' (the North star, or the East) become visual images of the one true 'Centre' (25).

Warriors They symbolize forebears, or the latent forces within the personality ready to come to the aid of the consciousness. If the warriors are hostile, then they signify antagonistic forces, but still within the framework of the personality. This symbolism is similar to that of the four archers who defend the cardinal points; the 'spaces' rendered independent of the 'centre' are illustrations of the forces which may rise up, as it were, against the integrity of the individual. Defenders and attackers then become, respectively, forces for and against the personality.

Water In Egyptian hieroglyphs, the symbol for water is a wavy line with small sharp crests, representing the water's surface. The same sign, when tripled, symbolizes a volume of water, that is, the primaeval ocean and prime matter. According to hermetic tradition, the god Nu was the substance from which the gods of the first ennead emerged (19). The Chinese consider water as the specific abode of the dragon, because all life comes from the waters (13). In the Vedas, water is referred to as *mâtritamâh* (the most maternal) because, in the beginning, everything was like a sea without light. In India, this element is generally regarded as the preserver of life, circulating throughout the whole of nature, in the form of rain, sap, milk and blood. Limitless and immortal, the waters are the beginning and the end of all things on earth (60). Although water is, in appearance, formless, ancient cultures made a distinction between 'upper waters' and 'lower waters'. The former correspond to the potential or what is still possible, the latter to what is actual or already created (26). In a general sense, the concept of 'water' stands, of course, for all liquid matter. Moreover, the primaeval waters, the image of prime matter, also contained all solid bodies before they acquired form and rigidity. For this reason, the alchemists gave the name of 'water' to quicksilver in its first stage of transmutation and, by analogy, also to the 'fluid body' of Man (57). This 'fluid body' is interpreted by modern psychology as a symbol of the unconscious, that is, of the non-formal, dynamic, motivating, female side of the personality. The projection of the mother-*imago* into the waters endows them with various numinous properties characteristic of the mother (31). A secondary meaning of this symbolism is found in the identification of water with intuitive wisdom. In the cosmogony of the Mesopotamian peoples, the abyss of water was regarded as a symbol of the unfathomable, impersonal Wisdom. An ancient Irish god was called Domnu, which means 'marine depth'. In prehistoric times the word for abyss seems to have been used exclusively to denote that which was unfathomable and mysterious (4). The waters, in short, symbolize the universal congress of potentialities, the *fons et origo*, which precedes all form and all creation. Immersion in water signifies a return to the pre-formal state, with a sense of death and annihilation on the one hand, but of rebirth and regeneration on the other, since immersion intensifies the life-force. The symbolism of baptism, which is closely linked to that of water, has been expounded by St. John Chrysostom (*Homil. in Joh.*, XXV, 2): 'It represents death and interment, life and resurrection. . . . When we plunge our head beneath water, as in a sepulchre, the old man becomes completely immersed and buried. When we leave the water, the new man suddenly appears' (18). The ambiguity of this quotation is only on the surface: in this particular aspect of the general symbolism of water, death affects only Man-in-nature while the rebirth is that of spiritual man. On the cosmic level, the equivalent of immersion is the flood, which causes all forms to dissolve and return to a fluid state, thus liberating the elements which will later be recombined in new cosmic patterns. The qualities of transparency and depth, often associated with water, go far towards explaining the veneration of the ancients for this element which, like earth, was a female principle. The Babylonians called it 'the home of wisdom'. Oannes, the mythical being who brings culture to mankind, is portrayed as half man and half fish (17). Moreover, in dreams, birth is usually expressed through water-imagery (*v.* Freud, *Introduction to Psycho-Analysis*). The expressions 'risen from the waves' and 'saved from the waters' symbolize fertility, and are metaphorical images of childbirth. On the other hand, water is, of all the elements, the most clearly transitional, between fire and air (the ethereal elements) and earth (the solid element). By analogy, water stands as a mediator between life and death, with a two-way positive and negative flow of creation and destruction. The Charon and Ophelia myths symbolize the last voyage. Death was the first mariner. 'Transparent depth', apart from other meanings, stands in particular for the communicating link between the surface and the abyss. It can therefore be said that water conjoins these two images (2). Gaston Bachelard points to many different characteristics of water, and derives from them many secondary symbolic meanings which enrich the fundamental meaning we have described. These secondary meanings are not so much a set of strict symbols, as a kind of language expressing the transmutations of this ever-flowing element. Bachelard enumerates clear water, spring water, running water, stagnant water, dead water, fresh and salt water, reflecting water, purifying water, deep water, stormy water. Whether we take water as a symbol of the collective or of the personal unconscious, or else as an element of mediation and dissolution, it is obvious that this symbolism is an expression of the vital potential of the psyche, of the struggles of the psychic depths to find a way of formulating a clear message comprehensible to the consciousness. On the other hand, secondary symbolisms are derived from associated objects such as water-containers, and also from the ways in which water is used: ablutions, baths, holy water, etc. There is also a very important spatial symbolism connected with the 'level' of the waters, denoting a correlation between actual physical level and absolute moral level. It is for this reason that the Buddha, in his Assapuram sermon, was able to regard the mountain-lake—whose transparent waters reveal, at the bottom, sand, shells, snails and fishes—as the path of redemption. This lake obviously corresponds to a fundamental aspect of the 'Upper Waters'. Clouds are another aspect of the 'Upper Waters'. In *Le Transformationi* of Ludovico Dolce, we find a mystic figure looking into the unruffled surface of a pond, in contrast with the accursed hunter, always in restless pursuit of his prey, implying the symbolic contrast between contemplative activity—the *sattva* state of Yoga—and blind outward activity—the *rajas* state. Finally, the upper and lower waters communicate reciprocally through the process of rain (involution) and evaporation (evolution). Here, fire intervenes to modify water: the sun (spirit) causes sea water to evaporate (i.e. it sublimates life). Water is condensed in clouds and returns to earth in the form of life-giving rain, which is invested with twofold virtues: it is water, and it comes from heaven (15). Lao-Tse paid considerable attention to this cyclic process of meteorology, which is at one and the same time physical and spiritual, observing that: 'Water never rests, neither by day nor by night. When flowing above, it causes rain and dew. When flowing below, it forms streams and rivers. Water is outstanding in doing good. If a dam is raised against it, it stops. If way is made for it, it flows along that path. Hence it is said that it does not struggle. And yet it has no equal in destroying that which is strong and hard' (13). When water stands revealed in its destructive aspects, in the course of cataclysmic events, its symbolism does not change, but is merely subordinated to the dominant symbolism of the storm. Similarly, in those contexts where the flowing nature of water is emphasized, as in the contention of Heraclitus that 'You cannot step twice into the same river; for fresh waters are ever flowing in upon you.' Here the reference is not to water-symbolism as such, but to the idea of the irreversible flow along a given·path. To quote Evola, in *La tradizione ermetica*: 'Without divine water, nothing exists, according to Zosimus. On the other hand, among the symbols of the female principle are included those which figure as origins of the waters (mother, life), such as: Mother Earth, Mother of the Waters, Stone, Cave, House of the Mother, Night, House of Depth, House of Force, House of Wisdom, Forest, etc. One should not be misled by the word "divine". Water symbolizes terrestrial and natural life, never metaphysical life.'

Water-Maidens These are mythic beings in Hispanic folklore, diminutive figures with a star in their forehead, shimmering, straw-coloured bodies and golden locks. On the fingers of their right hand they wear white rings and on the left wrist a gold band with black stripes. Legend has it that yellow flowers spring up in their footprints, bringing happiness to the person who finds them (10). These endearing creatures exactly illustrate the functioning of symbolic mechanism: the antithesis of black and white reflects the theme of symbolic inversion; and gold is an emblem of power. In short, these water-maidens are endowed with the power to stir up and invert the order of things, bringing happiness to the wretched—that is, to everyone.

Waves There is a Chinese tradition that the waves are the abode of dragons, and that they are also symbolic of purity (5). The apparent contradiction here arises from the fact that the ocean swell offers two different aspects: because of their rhythmic undulations they are reminiscent of dragons, and by virtue of their white foam they suggest purity. There is thus no question of dual tendencies here—only juxtaposition.

Weapons Within the general symbolism of the hero's struggle, his weapons are, in a way, the counterpart of the monsters he has to fight. Just as there are different kinds of monsters, so there are different kinds of weapons. Hence, the weapon used in mythic combat has a deep and specific significance: it defines both the hero and the enemy whom he is trying to destroy. Since, in a purely psychological interpretation of the symbol, the enemy is simply the forces threatening the hero from within, the weapon becomes a genuine representation of a state of conflict. (The wings of Icarus, the sword of Perseus, the club of Hercules, the staff of Oedipus, Neptune's trident, Hades and Satan) (15). Jung summarizes this by saying that 'weapons are an expression of the will directed towards a certain end' (56). Paul, giving advice on how the Christian should meet the enemy, says, in the Epistle to the Ephesians (vi, 10-17):

'Finally, my brethren, be strong in the Lord, and in the power of his might. Put on the whole armour of God, that ye may be able to stand against the wiles of the devil. For we wrestle not against flesh and blood, but against principalities, against powers, against the rulers of the darkness of this world, against spiritual wickedness in high places. Wherefore take unto you the whole armour of God, that ye may be able to withstand in the evil day, and, having done all, to stand. Stand therefore, having your loins girt about with truth, and having on the breastplate of righteousness; and your feet shod with the preparation of the gospel of peace; above all, taking the shield of faith, wherewith ye shall be able to quench all the fiery darts of the wicked. And take the helmet of salvation, and the sword of the Spirit, which is the word of God' (46). According to St. Ephraem, the allegorical interpretation of Paul's symbolism is as follows: the helmet—hope; the girding of the loins—charity; shoes —humility; the shield—cross; the bow—prayer; the sword—the word of God (46). Díel's interpretation of the symbolism of weapons also stresses their moral significance; he observes that, with 'the weapons lent by the deity'—it will be recalled that in myths, mediaeval legends and folklore weapons are often miraculously given to the hero—man must struggle against the urge of his irrational desires, against the beguiling monster, thus serving the higher aims of the spirit and of the species. Arms therefore symbolize the powers and functions of sublimation and spiritualization, in contrast to monsters, which stand for the baser forces (15). This is why myths and legends stress the almost autonomous power of the weapons, attributes and objects belonging to heroes, saints and demigods, such as Roland's oliphant, Thor's hammer and the rod of Moses (4). In addition to this general significance, the symbolism of some arms is enriched by the associations of the Element to which they pertain. Thus, the bolas of South American Indians and *gauchos*, and the sling, have associations with the air; the spear, with earth; the sword, with fire; the trident, with the watery deeps (41). Further connotations follow on from certain groupings of arms in connexion with status or character: the sceptre, the mace, the staff and the whip are attributes of royalty; the spear, the dagger and the sword are the weapons of the knight; the knife and the poniard are secret weapons and, to a certain extent, base; the thunderbolt and the net are the arms of the Uranian gods, and so on. A comparison between the different symbolic grades of arms and the Jungian archetypes would give the following correlations: Shadow (knife, dagger), Anima (spear), Mana (mace or club, net, whip), Self (sword). On the basis of this correlation, Schneider states (50) that the combat of spear against sword is that of earth against heaven. On the other hand, a further specific meaning pertains to the sword as the 'weapon of salvation', in connexion with medicinal rites (51) and with ceremonies more exalted in implication. Crushing weapons, such as the club, stand for destruction rather than victory (15).

Weaving The act of weaving represents, basically, creation and life, and particularly the latter in so far as it denotes accumulation and multiplication or growth. In this sense it was known, and put to magic and religious use, in Egypt and the pre-Columbian cultures of Peru (40). Beigbeder recalls that weaving was an attribute of the Parcae, and also of the Virgin in Byzantine iconography. The weaving symbol is universal, and of prehistoric origin.

Week The pattern of the week is related to that of the seven Directions of Space: two days are associated with each of the three dimensions, while the centre, as the 'unvarying mean' or the image of the Aristotelian 'unmoved mover', corresponds to the day of rest. The fact that this space-time prototype, founded upon the number seven, embraced also the planetary spheres and the principal deities of each pantheon, can be seen in the way each of the planets (including the sun and the moon) gave its name to one of the weekdays. As a consequence of this influence of the planetary gods (comparable in their negative aspect with the seven deadly sins), the seven-headed monster of myth, legend and folklore also refers to the dangers of temptation growing day by day as the week progresses.

Well In Christian symbolism the well falls within the group of ideas associated with the concept of life as a pilgrimage, and signifies salvation (4). The well of refreshing and purifying water is symbolic of sublime aspirations, or of the 'silver cord' which attaches man to the function of the Centre. Demeter and other deities were shown standing beside a well (15). But this symbol is found not only in the higher cultures of Antiquity but also among the primitives. Schneider has noted that, in the medicinal rites of peoples at the animistic level, the centre of the scene is taken up by a lake or well in whose water the sick wash their hands, breast and head. At the water's edge, reeds grow and shells are to be found, and both are signs of the waters of salvation (51). In particular, the act of drawing water from a well is—like fishing—symbolic of drawing out and upwards the numinous contents of the deeps (31). To look into the waters of a lake or well is tantamount to the mystic attitude of contemplation. Finally, the well is also a symbol of the soul, and an attribute of things feminine (32).

West For the Egyptians and the Greeks, the West—where the sun sets—is where the kingdom of the spirits is to be. St. Jerome sites the devil here. The East symbolizes the kingdom of Christ and the West the kingdom of the devil (the death of the sun). In the High Middle Ages, the Nordic peoples located the poisoned sea of destruction and the abyss in the West.

Wetness Although its value may be positive on the plane of natural life, it has an entirely negative effect on spiritual life. Dryness and heat correspond to the predominance of fire, the active element; but wetness corresponds to that of water, the element of passivity and dissolution.

Whale Symbolic of the world, the body and the grave (20), and also regarded as an essential symbol of containing (and concealing). Rabanus Maurus (*Operum*, III, *Allegoriae in Sacram Scripturam*) lays particular stress on this aspect (46). Nowadays, however, the whale seems to have acquired more independence as a symbolic equivalent of the mystic mandorla, or the area of intersection of the circles of heaven and earth, comprising and embracing the opposites of existence (51).

Wheel This is a symbol, wide in scope, much used in the ornamental arts and in architecture, complex and enclosing several layers of meaning. Some of the disagreement about its symbolic sense may be due to confusion of the disk (which is immobile) with the wheel (which rotates). There is, however, no objection to the fusion of the two symbols with a view to reconciling the two ideas of the disk and the wheel. One of the elementary forms of wheel-symbolism consists of the sun as a wheel, and of ornamental wheels as solar emblems (14). As Krappe has pointed out, the concept of the sun as a wheel was one of the most widespread notions of antiquity. The idea of the sun as a two-wheeled chariot is only at one remove from this. These same ideas can be found among the Aryans and also among the Semites (35). Given the symbolic significance of the sun as a source of light (standing for intelligence) and of spiritual illumination, it is easy to understand why the Buddhist doctrine of the solar wheel has been so widely admired (31). 'Catherine-wheels', and the 'wheel of fire' rolled down the hillside in popular festivals of the summer-solstice; and the mediaeval processions in which wheels were mounted on boats or carts, as well as the torture-on-the-wheel; and such traditions as the 'Wheel of Fortune' or the 'Wheel of the Year', all point to a deeply rooted solar or zodiacal symbolism. The function of the wheel-of-fire was, in essence, to 'stimulate' the sun in its activity and to ward off winter and death (17). It is, therefore, a symbolic synthesis of the activity of cosmic forces and the passage of time (57). There is, it must be admitted, a discrepancy between the interpretation of those who see the wheel particularly as a solar symbol, and those who relate it to the symbolism of the pole (although basically both allude to the mystery of the rotational tendency of all cyclic processes). The swastika, being an intermediate sign between the cross and the wheel, is similarly regarded by some as a solar and by others as a polar sign. Guénon tends towards the latter hypothesis

(28). But, in any case, the allusion is, in the last resort, to the splitting up of the world-order into two essentially different factors: rotary movement and immobility—or the perimeter of the wheel and its still centre, an image of the Aristotelian 'unmoved mover'. This becomes an obsessive theme in mythic thinking, and in alchemy it takes the form of the contrast between the volatile (moving and therefore transitory) and the fixed. The dual structure of the wheel is usually indicated by characteristic patterns which tend to confine geometric ornamentation—either stylized or figurative—to the periphery, while the round, empty space in the middle is either left vacant, or a single symbol is inscribed therein—a triangle, for instance, or a sacred figure. Guénon notes that the Celtic wheel-symbol persisted into the Middle Ages, and adds that the ornamental *oculi* of Romanesque churches and the rose-windows of Gothic architecture are versions of this wheel. He also shows that there is an indubitable connexion between the wheel and such emblematic flowers as the rose (in the West) and the lotus (in the East) (28)—in other words, figures patterned after the mandala. The rim of the wheel is divided into sectors illustrating phases in the passage of time. In alchemy, there are numerous symbolic representations of the wheel, denoting the circulatory process: the ascending period is shown on one side, the descending on the other. These alchemic stages are also represented as birds soaring heavenwards or swooping down to earth, denoting sublimation and condensation, in turn corresponding to evolution and involution, or spiritual progress and regression (32). The 'Wheel of Law, Truth and Life' is one of the eight emblems of good luck in Chinese Buddhism. It illustrates the way of escape from the illusory world (of rotation) and from illusions, and the way towards the 'Centre' (5). The wheel which is divided up into sectors by radii drawn from its outer perimeter to the circumference of an inner circle, is a graphic symbol sometimes seen in water-marks of mediaeval times over a plant-stem located between the horns of an ox (symbolizing sacrifice); Bayley opines that this wheel represents the 'communion of saints', or the reunion of the faithful in the mystic Centre (4). René Guénon says, in relation to Taoist doctrine, that the chosen one, the sage, invisible at the centre of the wheel, moves it without himself participating in the movement and without having to bestir himself in any way. He quotes, among others, the following Taoist passages: 'The sage is he who has attained the central point of the Wheel and remains bound' to the "Unvarying Mean", in indissoluble union with the Origin, partaking of its immutability and imitating its non-acting activity'; 'He who has reached the highest degree of emptiness, will be secure in repose. To return to the root is to enter into the state of repose', that is, to throw off the bonds of things transitory and contingent (25).

Wheel of Fortune, The   The tenth enigma of the Tarot pack. It is an allegory which turns upon the general symbolism of the wheel. Based upon the symbolism of the number two, it expresses the equilibrium of the contrary forces of contraction and expansion— the principle of polarity. The wheel is set in motion by a handle— fateful because it is irreversible—and it is floating on a figurative representation of the ocean of chaos, supported by the masts of two boats which are joined one to the other; in each boat there is a snake, symbolizing the two principles of the active and the passive. The ascending half of this wheel has an effigy of Hermanubis and his caduceus, while the descending portion displays a Typhon-like monster with its trident; the two halves symbolize respectively the constructive and destructive forces of existence, the first figure being related to the constellation of Canis, and the second to Capricorn (denoting, within the symbolism of the Zodiac, the principle of dissolution initiated in Pisces). Above the wheel, this allegorical card has a motionless sphinx, alluding to the mystery of all things and the intermingling of the disparate (59).

Whip   The symbolism of the whip is a mixture of that of the knot or bow and that of the sceptre, both of them signs for domination, mastery and superiority. It expresses the idea of punishment, like the truncheon and the club—counterbalanced by the sword as a symbol of purification—and also the power to encircle and over- whelm (51). In Egypt, the lash, because of its morphological associa- tion with lightning, was the attribute of *Min*, the god of the wind, and, in general, of certain deities reigning over storms (41). The Dioscuri carried whips; and bronze whips figured in the cult of Zeus in Dodona (35). The Egyptian Pharaohs used the whip as an emblem of power. The Romans used to hang their whips in their triumphal chariots (8). Logically, the whip ought also to be related to rites of flagellation (or fecundity) (8). It is, furthermore, an attribute of the 'Terrible Mother' (31).

Whirlwind   Characterized by spiral or helicoid movement, this symbol expresses the dynamism of the three-dimensional cross— that is, of space itself. It is, therefore, symbolic of universal evolution.

Whistling   Whistling is, to follow Jung, like clacking the tongue in so far as both are archaic ways of calling to and attracting the attention of theriomorphic deities—or totemic or deified animals (31). This explains the social taboo upon whistling.

Wild Man   The image of the Wild Man or savage, covered only with a loin-cloth, or a garment of leaves or skins, is a common one in the folklore of almost every country. It is related to, but not identical with, such mythic beings as the 'snowman', the ogre, giants, etc. In heraldry, the image takes the form of the supporter of an escutcheon, when its significance becomes analogous to that of the animals that normally fulfil this function—that is, they express, by virtue of their bilateral symmetry, the counterbalancing of base forces, while sustaining certain spiritual and sublimating elements (the heraldic symbols themselves). Sometimes one finds Wild Women of similar aspect and similar significance. Frazer has described some folklore customs which are unquestionably related to this fabulous woman. Some regions of Germany, during Whitsuntide, hold a festival called 'the Expulsion of the Wild Man', in which the part of the savage is played by a youth, covered in leaves and moss, who hides in the woods. The others then begin a chase which ends with his figurative death. Next day they make a stretcher and place on it a straw puppet resembling the Wild Man. This they carry in procession to a lake where the executioner throws it into the water (21). In Bohemia, the 'king' makes his appearance clothed in grass and flowers. The Wild Man seems to coincide with the 'Scapegoat' in the ritual assassination of the king. Jung suggests that this myth symbolizes the primitive or baser part of the personality, or the unconscious in its perilous and regressive aspect, which he has termed the 'shadow' (56). It is also connected with fabulous islands such as the island of St. Brendan or the land of Prester John.

Wind   The wind is air in its active and violent aspects, and is held to be the primary Element by virtue of its connexion with the creative breath or exhalation. Jung recalls that in Arabic (and paralleled by the Hebrew) the word *ruh* signifies both 'breath' and 'spirit' (31). At the height of its activity, the wind gives rise to the hurricane (a synthesis and 'conjunction' of the four Elements), which is credited with the power of fecundation and regeneration. It was taken up in this sense by the alchemists, as can be seen for example in Jamsthaler's *Viatorium Spagyricum* (Frankfort, 1625) (31). The winds were numbered and brought into correspondence with the cardinal points and the signs of the Zodiac, so as to bring out their cosmic significance. In Egypt and Greece the wind was reckoned to possess certain evil powers; but for the Greeks, this menacing implication, which they associated with Typhon, was reversed from that moment when the fleet of Xerxes was destroyed by a tempest (41).

Window   Since it consists of an aperture, the window expresses the ideas of penetration, of possibility and of distance, and because it is square in shape, its implications are rational and terrestrial. It is also symbolic of consciousness (32), especially when it is located at the top of a tower, by analogy with the head of the human figure. Divided windows carry a secondary significance, which may at times even be the predominant sense, deriving from the number of openings or lights and from the inter-relationships between the relevant number-symbolism and the general symbolism of the window (Plate XXXI).

Wine An ambivalent symbol like the god Dionysos himself. On the one hand wine, and red wine in particular, symbolizes blood and sacrifice; on the other, it signifies youth and eternal life, like that divine intoxication of the soul hymned by Greek and Persian poets which enables man to partake, for a fleeting moment, of the mode of being attributed to the gods (17).

Wine-skin An attribute of the satyr and of Silenus. In Greek, the phrase 'to untie the wine-skin' meant to indulge in Venusian delights (8). The phrase itself is suggestive of the lingam in the conjunction of a masculine, phallic element (the feet of the goat) and a feminine element (the skin as a receptacle). This idea was taken up by Christians who linked it with the idea of sin, and the wine-skin thereby came to symbolize evil-mindedness or a heavy conscience. Pinedo has pointed out that the wine-skin carried by various figures in Rómanesque designs—such as that on the *Porta Speciosa* of the sanctuary at Estibaliz—bears precisely this meaning, and he quotes the Psalms in support: 'He gathereth the waters of the sea together as in a wine-skin[1]: he layeth up the depth in store-houses' (Psalms xxxiii, 7) (46). Analogous in significance are the haversack, the shepherd's pouch, and also the horn-pipe and the bladder of the buffoon (though, because of his sacrificial character, the buffoon alludes to the sins of others).

Wings In the more general sense, wings symbolize spirituality, imagination, thought. The Greeks portrayed love and victory as winged figures, and some deities, such as Athena, Artemis and Aphrodite were at first—though not later—also depicted with wings. According to Plato, wings are a symbol of intelligence, which is why some fabulous animals are winged, depicting the sublimation of those symbolic qualities usually ascribed to each animal. Pelops' horses, and Pegasus, as well as Ceres' snakes, have this attribute. Wings are also found on certain objects such as heroes' helmets, the caduceus and the thunderbolt in the cult of Jupiter (8). It follows that the form and nature of the wings express the spiritual qualities of the symbol. Thus, the wings of night-animals express a perverted imagination, and Icarus' wax wings stand for functional insufficiency (15). In Christian symbolism it is said that wings are simply the light of the sun of justice, which always illuminates the mind of the righteous. Since wings also signify mobility, this meaning combines with that of enlightenment to express the possibility of 'progress in enlightenment' or spiritual evolution (46). In

---

[1] The English Authorised version reads: 'He gathereth the waters of the sea together as *an heap . . .*' The Septuagint gives 'wine-skin'.—*Translator.*

alchemy, wings are always associated with the higher, active, male principle; animals without wings are related to the passive female principle (33). It should also be recalled that, since the foot is regarded as a symbol of the soul (15), the wings on the heels of some deities, especially Mercury, stand for the power of spiritual elevation comparable in essence with cosmic evolution. Jules Duhem, in his thesis on the history of flight, remarks that, in Tibet, 'Buddhist saints travel through the air wearing a special kind of shoes known as "light feet"' (3).

Withdrawal Every withdrawal, retreat or concealment—like the moon and like sleep—symbolizes that period of life before and after its involution as matter, that is, before and after the manifest life of appearances.

Wolf Symbolic of valour among the Romans and the Egyptians. It also appears as a guardian in a great many monuments (8). In Nordic mythology we are told of a monstrous wolf, Fenris, that would destroy iron chains and shackles and was eventually shut up in the bowels of the earth. It was also said that, with the twilight of the gods—the end of the world—the monster would break out of this prison too, and would devour the sun. Here, then, the wolf appears as a symbol of the principle of evil, within a pattern of ideas which is unquestionably related to the Gnostic cosmogony. Nordic mythology presupposes that cosmic order is possible only through the temporary shackling of the chaotic and destructive potential of the universe—a potential which (through the process of Symbolic Inversion—q.v.) must triumph in the end. The myth is also connected with all other concepts of the final annihilation of the world, whether by water or by fire.

Woman In anthropology, woman corresponds to the passive principle of nature. She has three basic aspects: first, as a siren, lamia or monstrous being who enchants, diverts and entices men away from the path of evolution; second, as the mother, or *Magna mater* (the motherland, the city or mother-nature) related in turn to the formless aspect of the waters and of the unconscious; and third, as the unknown damsel, the beloved or the anima in Jungian psychology. In his *Symbols of Transformation*, Jung maintains that the ancients saw Woman as either Eve, Helen, Sophia or Mary (corresponding to the impulsive, the emotional, the intellectual, and the moral) (33). One of the purest and all-embracing archetypes of Woman as anima is Beatrice in Dante's *Commedia* (32). All allegories based upon the personification of Woman invariably retain all the implications of the three basic aspects mentioned above. Of great interest are those symbols in which the Woman appears in association with the figure of an animal—for example, the swan-woman in Celtic and Germanic mythology, related to the woman with the hoof of a goat in Hispanic folklore. In both cases the woman disappears once her maternal mission has been completed and, similarly, the virgin *qua* virgin 'dies' in order to give way to the matron (31). In iconography it is common to find parts of the female figure combined with that of a lion. The Egyptian goddess Sekhmet, characterized by her destructiveness, had the body of a woman and the head (and therefore the mind) of a lion. Conversely, a figure with a lion's body and a woman's head appears in the *Hieroglyphica* of Valeriano as an emblem of the hetaira (39). The inclusion of feminine, morphological elements in the composition of traditional symbols such as the sphinx always alludes to a background of nature overlaid with the projection of a concept or of an entire complex of cosmic intuitions. In consequence, the Woman is an archetypal image of great complexity in which the decisive factor may be the superimposed symbolic aspects—for example, the superior aspects of Woman as Sophia or Mary determine her function as a personification of science or of supreme virtue; and when presented as an image of the anima, she is superior to the man because she is a reflection of the loftiest and purest qualities of the man. In her baser forms as Eve or as Helen—the instinctive and emotional aspects—Woman is on a lower level than the man. It is here, perhaps, that she appears at her most characteristic—a temptress, the *Ewig Weibliche*, who drags everything down with her, and a symbol comparable with the volatile principle in alchemy, signifying all that is transitory, inconsistent, unfaithful and dissembling. See also *The Loved One* and *Sophia*.

Woman, Dead The image, vision or dream of a dead young woman in her tomb, is a direct symbol of the death of the *anima*. The French legend of Queen Blanche, quoted by Gérard de Sède in *Les Templiers sont parmi nous* (Paris, 1962), tells of this. Sède, in this context, links the names of Isis, a legendary Yse of the Knights Templars, and Yseult or Isolde. Georg Gichtel, a disciple of Jakob Böhme, refers to this symbol of the dead maiden or queen (dead in fact or in appearance, that is to say, sleeping, as in the well-known fairy tale) as one that relates 'to the corruption of the shining Paradisiac body' (cf. Evola, *La Tradizione ermetica*, Bari, 1948).

Wood A mother-symbol (31). Burnt wood signifies wisdom and death (50). The magic and fertilizing propensities of the wood burnt in sacrificial rites are supposed to be transmitted to the ashes and the charcoal. Cremation is regarded as a return to the 'seed'-state; this has given rise to many rites and folklore customs, related in turn to fire-symbolism (17).

World Symbolically, the world is the realm in which a state of existence is unfolded (25), comprising many component parts adhering together. Used in the plural, the term pertains, in a sense, to space-symbolism, but the 'worlds' are really only different modes of the spirit (26). The explanation of the cosmic and moral significance of the three worlds (the infernal, the terrestrial and the celestial) is to be sought in the symbolism of level. The inferior must not always be equated with the subterranean, for, in megalithic cultures, the latter was usually located high up, or in the hollow interior of mountains (conceived as the dwelling-place of the dead). Guénon has pointed out that references to the 'subterranean world' are found in a large number of cultural traditions, in which the 'cult of the cavern' or cave is linked with that of the 'centre'. One must also bear in mind the equation of the cavern with the cave of the heart, the latter being considered as the Centre of being or the Egg of the World (28).

World, The The twenty-first enigma of the Tarot pack. The fact that the series consists of ternaries and septenaries is further proof that the number 21 implies a synthesis, or the totality of the manifest world, that is, the world of space as a reflection of permanent creative activity. This idea is represented in the allegorical image of this playing-card by a young girl running with two small sticks inside a garland which is surrounded by the cosmic quaternary or tetramorphs. The sticks are symbolic of polarization inducing the rotational motion of all things in the entire cosmos. According to Wirth, this girl also represents major Fortune, whereas minor Fortune corresponds to the tenth card of the Tarot. The quaternary is connected with the Elements, and the garland with the cosmic process (59).

World-image The host of possibilities opened up by the very word 'world', points to the great number of symbolic images capable of reflecting its multiple aspects. All the great symbols are really images of the world: The septenary, for example, in the form of candelabra with seven branches, reflecting the arrangement of the planets; and bilateral symmetry as, for example, in the caduceus of Mercury, is the image of the world in so far as it is an equilibrium of hostile forces; and all forms of wheel symbols, such as the Zodiac, mandalas, or the Tarot pack, correspond to the world in so far as it appears as a cycle or succession of changes. But the essence of the world is the conflict between time and eternity, matter and spirit, or the conjunction of opposites which yet remain separate on the plane of existence—a conflict, that is, between continuity and discontinuity, usually conveyed by means of images reconciling the square with the circle, sometimes simply by 'squaring the circle' as in alchemic practice, and sometimes by multiplying one of the component elements by four, as in the oriental pentacle of Laos. The arrangement of the tetramorphs as a spiritual quaternary, keeping the centre as an image of the Origin (that is, heaven) which is counterbalanced by the world of manifestation, is sometimes represented as a city with four towers and four gates, always with an image of paramount significance in the centre (32). Frobenius recounts the history of a group of interesting symbols of this kind bearing upon the ritual cups or chalices of Ethiopia (inspired in the ceramics of Susa) in the fourth millenary before our era. In the middle of these cups there is a cross or some other symbol either of the swastika or of the damero type; this may be a representation of earth, for on the edges there is a motif sketched in, which might be an image of water. An African cup from Benin has a sea-serpent in the same position; here the symbol may be related to the dragon biting his own tail as in the Gnostic *Ouroboros*. A wooden disc from Morka shows an image of the sun in the centre, then a double chain suggesting the ocean, and finally an outer corona divided into four parts to accord with the four cardinal points (corresponding in turn with the seasons and the four Elements). But Frobenius also speaks of three-dimensional images of the world. He relates how, in 1910, he happened to be in the Yoruba (West Africa), where he made his way to the holy city of Ife, and there, in a place sacred to the god Ejar, he found an object like a kind of platform with a cone at each of its four corners and another larger one in the centre, surmounted by a cup or chalice. The central cone is the Mountain of the World (the mystic mandorla); and the four others correspond to the cardinal points. He notes the relationship between this image and certain thrones with five supports (22). Quite apart from the pictorial images of the Pantokrator and the tetramorphs, which are comparable to the above, Christianity too has an example of the same kind of pattern, depicted three-dimensionally, in the baptismal font at Estibaliz. Pinedo describes it as follows: The base is a heavy column, with four smaller ones close to it (analogous with the Centre and the four cardinal points); above it, a lotus flower is shown opening its corolla (a symbol of the world made manifest, and of nativity). Above this corolla, there is a colonnade with arches on which are inscribed other smaller, trefoiled arches. In the spaces there are diverse symbolic beings (connoting the plane of cosmic life, that is, of existence). Above the arches, there is a pattern representing the battlements of the celestial Jerusalem—paradise regained (46). As a symbol of the world, then, in all its fundamental aspects, this image is the most artistic, the most exact and complete known to us.

World Soul This concept is related ideologically to that of the Great Mother and to that of the moon as a source of change and transmutation. It has certain negative characteristics, e.g. a tendency to divide and multiply—which is the essential prerequisite for all creative and reproductive processes (31). Only in literature is the

World Soul a single whole, and it is then equivalent to the 'mystic void' of Hindu and Hebrew traditions.

Worm Jung defines the worm as a libidinal figure which kills instead of giving life (31). This comes from its underground associations, its base characteristics, its connexion with death and with the biological stages of dissolution and the primary. Thus, it is death which the worm symbolizes—but death which is relative from the point of view of what is superior or organized; basically, like the snake, it denotes crawling, knotted energy.

Woven Fabric The phrase 'the web of life' is an eloquent expression of the symbolism of woven fabric which is not only concerned with ideas of binding and increase through the blending of two elements (the warp and the woof—the passive and the active), nor is it merely equivalent to creation; rather does it denote the mystic apprehension of the world of phenomena as a kind of veil which hides the true and the profound from sight. As Porphyry observed: 'The ancients called the heavens "a veil" because, in a sense, they are the garments of the gods.' And as Plato said: 'The one and only Demiurge commands the secondary demiurges'— that is, the mythological gods—'to bind the immortal to the mortal in a symbolic fabric'. In addition to the symbolism of weaving, this idea embraces that of the Gemini (signifying the dual composition of all things in existence, one part being immortal and the other mortal). Plutarch observed that weaving was invented by Isis with the assistance of her sister Nephthys (40). The legend of the 'Web of Penelope' is related to this. Guénon sees the warp and woof as equivalent to the horizontal and vertical limbs of the cosmic cross, where the upright represents the various states of being and the horizontal the degree of development reached by these states. He also mentions that the two lines of the loom can be identified with the masculine and the feminine principles, and that this is why, in the *Upanishads*, the Supreme Brahma is designated 'He upon whom the worlds are woven as warp and woof'. At the same time, the alternation of life and death, condensation and dissolution, the predominance of *Yang* or of *Yin*, are, for the Taoists, like the alternating 'waves' of thread in the weave of the fabric (25). Apart from this essential symbolism, a fabric has further symbolic meanings deriving from its colour, form and function (where applicable). Piobb, with particular reference to Scotch tartans, has pointed out that certain types of fabric are characterized by patterns with an esoteric purport (48). Ornamental designs have the same symbolic significance whether they appear in a fabric, or are engraved on a stone or painted in a miniature (see *Graphics*). The veil, as an elemental form of weaving and as clothing, is symbolic of 'wrapping', that is, of matter. The seven veils in Salome's dance, or in the myth of Ishtar, correspond to the seven planetary spheres and their respective influences.

Yang-Yin   A Chinese symbol of the dual distribution of forces, comprising the active or masculine principle (*Yang*) and the passive or feminine principle (*Yin*). It takes the form of a circle bisected by a sigmoid line, and the two parts so formed are invested with a dynamic tendency which would be wanting if the division were by a diameter. The light half represents the *Yang* force and the dark half denotes *Yin*; however, each half includes an arc cut out of the middle of the opposing half, to symbolize that every mode must contain within it the germ of its antithesis. Guénon considers that the Yang-Yin is a helicoidal symbol, that is, that it is a section of the universal whirlwind which brings opposites together and engenders perpetual motion, metamorphosis and continuity in situations characterized by contradiction. The entrance to and exit from this movement lie outside the movement itself, in the same way that birth and death stand apart from the life of the individual in so far as it is conscious and self-determined. The vertical axis through the centre of the Yang-Yin constitutes the 'unvarying mean' or, in other words, the mystic 'Centre' where there is no rotation, no restlessness, no impulse, nor any suffering of any kind. It corresponds to the central zone of the Wheel of Transformations in Hindu symbolism, and the centre or the way out of the labyrinth in Egyptian and western symbolism. It is also expressive of the two counterbalancing tendencies of evolution and involution (25).

Year   More than a symbol, the year is, as it were, the prototype of all cyclic processes (the day, the span of human life, the rise and fall of a culture, the cosmic cycle, etc.). All cycles are composed of an ascending and a descending phase, i.e. evolution and involution; sometimes, cycles are also subdivided into three or, more frequently, four phases (seasons of the year, ages of man). The overall division of the cyclic process, however, need not necessarily be symmetrical. Thus, in a cycle composed of twelve units, such as the year (or the wheel of the Zodiac), the ascending and descending phases can be taken either as 6 plus 6 (symmetrical division) or 8 plus 4 (asymmetrical division). The former is a more geometrical, the latter a more empirical division. The year is usually represented by the figure of an old man in a circle, with two or three outer rings containing such items as: the names of the months, the cycle of work appropriate to each month, the signs of the Zodiac and so on. Often the circle of the year is, in its turn, enclosed in a square the corners of which are occupied by four figures personifying the four seasons. The tapestry of the Creation, in Gerona cathedral, is a famous example. Two interesting points in connexion with the annual cycle are: (i) in Chinese tradition, the cycle is divided into two equal parts, corresponding respectively to darkness/death, and light/life; (ii) there was a primitive belief that every man undergoes a process of regeneration every year, from December to June, symbolizing death and resurrection (51) (Plate XXXII).

Yoke Like the sheaf or bunch, the yoke is a symbol of union and discipline; but by virtue of its association with the ox, it is also symbolic of sacrifice (50).

Yoni Like the mandorla, the Yoni is the gateway, or the zone of interpenetration wherein two circles intersect. Indians, in order to ensure regeneration, make an image of the Yoni in gold, and pass through it (21).

Youth and Old Man These two figures personify the rising and the setting sun. Another similar idea is that which considers each sun as the offspring of its predecessor; this provides us with an explanation of the great number of solar gods born of other sun-gods (35). In addition to this system of 'continuous connexion', or of circular links, the Old Man is always the father (the master, tradition, contemplation, the celestial sovereign, justice), while the Youth is the son (the governed, subversion, intuition, the hero, boldness). The counterbalancing formula of Youth-Old Man loses its equipoise once the Youth is a mature man and the Old Man decrepit, because the latter then becomes infantile and asexual.

Z

Zenith The zenith is a symbol which can be synonymous with that of the central hole in the Chinese heaven known as *Pi*, as well as with that of the peak of the mountain-temple, or the pyramid, or the sacrificial stake, or the pillar of the world (18). It is the point through which mystics believe their thoughts may pass out of space into non-space, out of time into timelessness. Hence, the importance of the formal likeness of this symbol with that of the hole.

Zodiac One of the most widespread of symbols, despite its complexity. In almost every land and age its characteristics are the same—the circular form, the twelve subdivisions with their corresponding signs and their relationship with the seven planets. The Mesopotamian cultures, Egypt, Judea, Persia, India, Tibet, China, America, Islam, Greece and Northern Europe—all were acquainted with zodiacal symbolism. The name of this circular 'form' comes from *zoe* (life) and *diakos* (wheel); and the basic element of this 'wheel of life' is found in the Ouroboros (the snake biting its own tail), symbolizing the *Aion* (duration). The general significance of the Zodiac concerns the process by which 'primordial energy, once fecundated, passes from the potential to the virtual, from unity to multiplicity, from spirit to matter, from the non-formal world to the world of forms', and then returns along the same path (52). This accords with the teaching of oriental ontology, which holds that the life of the universe is split into two opposing yet complementary phases: involution (or materialization) and evolution (or spiritualization). Applying this belief to the Zodiac, the first six signs (from Aries to Virgo) come to represent involution, while the other six (from Libra to Pisces) relate to evolution. This pattern refers not only to the evolution of the cosmos in the broadest sense, but also to specific phases of this process as well as to any given period in the development of the manifest world as such (for example, a period in history, the lifetime of a race or of an individual, the period of the world's existence, the time taken in carrying out a task) (52). As evidence of the great antiquity of this symbol, we would point to the zodiacal signs in the rock-paintings in the Cueva de Arce (at the Laguna de la Janda, Cadiz), the celestial maps in the stone-engravings at Eira d'os Mouros (in Galicia), and the sculpting of the cromlech at Alvão (in Portugal), not to speak of the numerous other examples of the same kind of thing: but there is no conclusive evidence of the existence of a truly systematic understanding of Zodiacal symbolism before the time of king Sargon of Agade (2750 B.C.), who was known to possess a work of astrology containing forecasts of the eclipses of the sun. From the time of Hammurabi (2000 B.C.) man's study of the heavens began to assume a more scientific character. But the Zodiac, and the characteristic signs as we know them today, cannot, in the opinion of Berthelot, be traced back farther than the tablet of Cambyses (6th century B.C.); this, however, does not invalidate the theory that the separate elements that contributed to the symbolic pattern of the Zodiac as a whole were of much greater antiquity than this. For example, the mystic twelvefold vision of the world; and the symbol of the ram associated with the mythic Ram and with the Primitive cult of the sun; and also the Gemini. Marc Saunier has commented, in connexion with the twelve-part division of the Zodiac, that spreading into our solar world from an unknowable unknown, through the twelve luminous doors of the Zodiac, it becomes concentrated into the form of the sun whence it radiates outwards to the seven planetary spheres which refract its unity in the gamut of sounds, rhythms and colours (49). As Jung notes, according to Manichean belief the demiurge builds a cosmic wheel, related to the *rota* and the *opus circulatorium* of alchemy and identical in that it signifies sublimation (31). It is almost unnecessary to point out that this form of motion, rotation on the vertical plane—descending and ascending—echoes the Platonic theories of the soul's 'fall' into material existence and its need to find salvation by returning along the same path. The most important and definitive adaptations of the zodiacal cycle—for other variants arise by analogy—are, first, that which equates the twelve signs with monthly periods, and the complete cycle with the year (commencing with March—with the spring), and, secondly, that corresponding to the great cycle (lasting 25,920 years) of the precession of the equinoxes, whereby, every 2160 years, the equinox withdraws by the space of one sign (thirty degrees). The fact that the figures which make up the zodiacal pattern are mostly animals has prompted Schneider to suggest that the constellations may owe their curious names to an earlier religion of totemistic origin, whose basic features were subsequently applied to the heavens through the process of catasterism (50). Piobb has observed that the Zodiac, besides being a process, may also be understood as a circuit and that its twelve-part division springs from the way in which the quantitative becomes qualitative (in vibrations, sounds or colours) and hence the ecliptic is a zone of energy differing in potential between its entrance (Aries) and its exit (Pisces). He also notes that, if one wishes to grasp the ancient conceptions, one must regard the Zodiac as a totality comprising twelve ideographs which, in sum, epitomize the dodecagon (48). It is clear that every twelve-part scheme alludes to the zodiacal pattern. The signs (q.v. under separate headings) are as follows: Aries, Taurus, Gemini, Cancer, Leo, Virgo, Libra, Scorpio, Sagittarius, Capricorn, Aquarius, Pisces (40). According to Senard, these twelve signs are derived from the four Elements combined with the three modes or *gunas* (levels) known as *sattva*, *rajas* and *tamas* (corresponding, firstly, to a situation—or level—of superiority or of essence; secondly, to an intermediate or transitional situation: and, thirdly, to the level of the inferior and material). But we cannot here go into Senard's theory of the signs of the Zodiac, beyond noting, briefly, the meanings that he attributes to each of them: Aries he interprets as the urge to create and transform: Taurus as undifferentiated magnetism; the Gemini as creative synthesis, or imagination; Cancer as gestation and birth; Leo as individuation, will; Virgo as intelligence; Libra as equilibrium; Scorpio as histolysis; Sagittarius as coordination and synthesis;

Capricorn as ascesis; Aquarius as illumination; and Pisces as mystic fusion (52). Mertens-Stienon founds his study of the Zodiac upon an article by the Hindu T. Subba Rao, published in October 1881 and translated into French for *Le Lotus bleu* in 1937, drawing also upon the work of Blavatsky and Dupuis (the latter favouring an almost exclusively astronomical interpretation of the myths). Mertens Stienon, then, divides the zodiacal signs into three quaternaries, although in our view a better division would be the inverse of this—four ternaries, forming a triunity for each of the seasons of the year (as well as for the cardinal points). He supports the view that the Zodiac may serve to symbolize and analyse the phases of each and every cycle, together with the evolutive stages which it embraces. He distinguishes between the astronomical Zodiac (the constellations) and the intellectual Zodiac (symbols), affirming that it was the constellations that took their names from the symbols. For instance, since, in Egyptian times, so much importance was attached to the symbolic bull and ram, this was why, astronomically speaking, these figures came to mark the vernal equinoxes which, in our era, coincide with Pisces. He shows that the apparent orbit of the sun through the twelve divisions corresponds to twelve degrees or stages in the action of the active principle upon the passive. These stages are denoted in mythology by the avatars of the creator-god—by his metamorphoses and manifestations. The precise symbolism of each sign springs from: (*a*) the number it bears in the series of twelve signs: (*b*) its situation within the series as a whole; (*c*) its situation within each of the four ternaries; (*d*) its symbolic figure; (*e*) the ideas related to this figure; and (*f*) the concomitant planetary symbolism. In the symbolism of the Zodiac one can sense the resolve to create, as in the Tarot pack, an all-embracing archetypal pattern—a kind of figurative model to serve as a comprehensive definition of each and every existential possibility in the macrocosm and the microcosm. As is the case with other symbolic forms, zodiacal symbolism is the product of the *serial* intellection of the universe, arising out of the belief that all things occupy positions and situations in space-time which are limited and typical, and implying, not determinism, but belief in the 'system of destinies', that is to say, the theory that certain antecedents must cause certain consequences and that any given situation must have ramifications that are neither replaceable nor arbitrary. Regarding the application of the Zodiac to the cycle of human existence in the concrete sense, there are certain obvious affinities with symbols pertaining to medicinal rites, as Schneider has shown. It is to Jorge Quintana, and his *El gobierno teocrático de Mohenjo-Daro* (Ampurias, IV), that we owe our knowledge of an octonary zodiac dating from the proto-Indian period of the third millennium before our era. This zodiac is composed of the following signs: *edu* (the ram), *yal* (the harp), *nand* (the crab), *amma* (the mother), *tuk* (the scales), *kani* (the dart), *kuda* (the pitcher) and *min* (the fish). There are obvious parallels between most of these signs and those of the dodecanarian Zodiac. The supreme god of the proto-Indians was equated with the sun, crossing, in his procession through the constellations, the corresponding degrees of the Zodiac, whence he derives his title of 'god of the eight forms'.

Zone   Every zone or area of space holds a symbolic significance deriving from its level on the vertical axis and its situation in relation to the cardinal points. In the broadest sense, zone may, by analogy, be equated with degree or mode. The colours are really only zones of the spectrum, and, by this token, any arrangement of zones is susceptible of interpretation as a serial whole.

BIBLIOGRAPHY OF PRINCIPAL SOURCES

BACHELARD, GASTON. *La Psychanalyse du feu*. Paris, 1938 (1).
— *L'Eau et les Rêves*. Paris, 1942 (2).
— *L'Air et les Songes*. Paris, 1943 (3).
BAYLEY, HAROLD. *The Lost Language of Symbolism*. London, 1912 (repr. 1951) (4).
BEAUMONT, A. *Symbolism in Decorative Chinese Art*. New York, 1949 (5).
BENOIST, LUC. *Art du monde*. Paris, 1941 (6).
BERTHELOT, René. *La pensée de l'Asie et l'astrobiologie*. Paris, 1949 (7).
B. G. P. *Diccionario universal de la mitología*. Barcelona, 1835 (8).
BLAVATSKY, H. P. *The Secret Doctrine*. London, 1888 (9).
CARO BAROJA, Julio. *Algunos mitos españoles*. Madrid, 1941 (10).
CEPOLLARO, A. *Il rituale mitriaco*. Rome, 1954 (11).
COLA, J. *Tatuajes y amuletos marroquíes*. Madrid, 1949 (12).
CHOCHOD, Louis. *Occultisme et magie en Extrême-Orient*. Paris, 1945 (13).
DAVY, M.-M. *Essai sur la Symbolique Romane*. Paris, 1955 (14).
DIEL, Pail. *Le Symbolisme dans la mythologie grecque*. Paris, 1952 (15).
DONTENVILLE, Henri. *La Mythologie française*. Paris, 1948 (16).
ELIADE, Mircea. *Tratado de historia de las religiones*. Madrid, 1954 (17).
— *Images et Symboles*. Paris, 1952 (18).
ENEL. *La langue sacrée*. Paris, 1932 (19).
FERGUSON, George W. *Signs and Symbols in Christian Art*. New York, 1954 (20).
FRAZER, Sir James G. *The Golden Bough*. London, 1911–15 (21).
FROBENIUS, Leo. *Histoire de la civilisation africaine*. Paris, 1952 (22).
FROMM, Erich. *The Forgotten Language*. London, 1952 (23).
GHYKA, Matila. *Philosophie et mystique du nombre*. Paris, 1952 (24)
GUÉNON, René. *Le Symbolisme de la croix*. Paris, 1931 (25).
— *Man and his Becoming according to the Vedānta*. London, 1945 (26).
— *L'Esotérisme de Dante*. Paris, 1949 (27)
— *Le Roi du monde*. Paris, 1950 (28).
— *Aperçu sur l'Initiation*. Paris (29).
JACOBI, Jolan de. *The Psychology of C. G. Jung*. London, 1951 (30).
JUNG, C. G. *Symbols of Transformation* (Collected Works, 5). London, 1956 (31).
— *Psychology and Alchemy* (Collected Works, 12). London, 1953 (32).
— 'Psychology of the Transference'. In *The Practice of Psychotherapy* (Collected Works, 16). London, 1954 (33).
— 'The Relations between the Ego and the Unconscious'. In: *Two Essays on Analytical Psychology* (Collected Works, 7). London, 1953 (34).
KRAPPE, A. H. *La Genèse des mythes*. Paris, 1952 (35).
LEHNER, Ernst. *Symbols, Signs and Signets*. Cleveland, 1950 (36).
LÉVI, Éliphas. *Les Mystères de la Kabbale*. Paris, 1920 (37).
LOEFFLER-DELACHAUX, M. *Le Symbolisme des contes de Fées*. Paris, 1949 (38).
MARQUÈS RIVIÈRE, J. *Amulettes, talismans et pantacles*. Paris, 1950 (39).
MERTENS STIENON, M. *L'Occultisme du zodiaque*. Paris, 1939 (40).
ORITZ, Fernando. *El Huracán*. Mexico, 1947 (41).
PANETH, L. *La Symbolique des nombres dans l'Inconscient*. Paris, 1953 (42).
PAPUS. *Traité méthodique de science occulte*. Paris, 1891 (43).
— *La Science des nombres*. Paris, 1934 (44).
— *Initiation astrologique*. Paris, 1919 (45).
PINEDO, Ramiro de. *El Simbolismo en la escultura medieval española*. Madrid, 1930 (46).

PIOBB, P. V. *Formulaire de l'haute magie*. Paris, 1937 (47).

—— *Clef universelle des sciences secrètes*. Paris, 1950 (48).

SAUNIER, Marc. *La Légende des symboles, philosophiques, religieux et maçonniques*. 2nd edn. Paris, 1911 (49).

SCHNEIDER, Marius. *El origen musical de los animales-símbolos en la mitología y la escultura antiguas*. Barcelona, 1946 (50).

—— *La danza de espadas y la tarantela*. Barcelona, 1948 (51).

SENARD, M. *Le Zodiaque*. Lausanne, 1948 (51).

SEZNEC, Jean. *The Survival of the Pagan Gods*. New York, 1953 (53).

STAR, Ély. *Les Mystères de l'Etre*. Paris, 1902 (54).

—— *Les Mystères du verbe*. Paris, 1908 (55).

TEILLARD, Ania. *Il Simbolismo dei Sogni*. Milan, 1951 (56).

TESTI, Gino. *Dizionario di Alchimia e di Chimica antiquaria*. Rome, 1950 (57).

WILHELM, Richard. *Lao Tse und der Taoismus*. Stuttgart, 1925 (58).

WIRTH, Oswald. *Le Tarot des imagiers du Moyen Age*. Paris, 1927 (59).

ZIMMER, Heinrich. *Myths and Symbols in Indian Art and Civilization*. New York, 1946 (60).

ZOLLINGER, Gustav. *Tau oder Tau-T'an, und das Rätsel der sprachlichen und menschlichen Einheit*. Berne, 1952 (61).

ADDITIONAL BIBLIOGRAPHY

ADAM, Leonhard. *Nordwestamerikanische Indianerkunst.* Berlin, 1923.
ADRIAN, P. G. *Réflexions sur l'univers sonore.* Paris, 1955.
AELIANUS, Claudius. *De Natura Animalium.* Jena, 1832.
AGRIPPA, H. C. *Opera.* Lyon, XVI century.
ALBERT, M. *Le culte de Castor et Pollux en Italie.* Paris, 1883.
ALCAZAR, Luis. *Vestigatio arcani sensus in Apocalypsi.* Antwerp, 1619.
ALCIATI, Andrea, *Emblemata.* Paris, 1580.
ALLBERRY, Charles. *Symbole von Tod und Wiedergeburt im Manichäismus.* Eranos Jahrbuch 1939. Zurich, 1940.
— *Allegorien und Embleme.* Vienna, 1900.
ALLEAU, René. *Aspects de l'alchimie traditionnelle.* Paris, 1952.
— *De la Nature des symboles.* Paris, 1958.
ALLEN, Emory A. *The Prehistoric World or Vanished Races.* Cincinnati, 1885.
ALLEN, J. R. *Early Christian symbolism in Great Britain and Ireland before the XIII century.* London, 1877.
ALLEN, Maude Rex, *Japanese Art Motives.* Chicago, 1917.
ALLENDY, — *Le Symbolisme des nombres.* Paris, 1948.
AMADES, Joan. *Mitología megalítica.* Ampurias III. Barcelona, 1941.
AMMAN, Jost. *Beschreibung aller Stände.* Frankfurt, 1568.
ANDRAE, R. *Ethnographische Parallelen, Neue Folge.* Leipzig, 1889.
ANDRAE, Walter. *Die ionische Säule, Bauform oder Symbol?* Berlin, 1933.
ANTONIADI, E. M. *L'Astronomie des prêtres égyptiens.* Paris, 1936.
ARATUS, Paulus. *Emblemas sacras y profanas, seguidas de un discurso . . .* Rome, 1589.
Archeological Institute of America. *Mythology of all Races.* Boston, 1925–32.
Ars memorandi or *rationarium evangelistarum.* (With verses by Petrus de Rosenheim.) Pforzheim, 1502.
ARTEMIDORUS DALDIANUS. *Onirocriticon libri V.* Leipzig, 1864.
ARTIN, YAKOUB. *Contribution à l'étude du blason en Orient.* London, 1902.
AUBER, C. A. *Histoire et théorie du symbolisme religieux.* Paris, 1884.
— *Histoire du symbolisme religieux avant et depuis le Christianisme.* Paris, 1844.
BACHELARD, Gaston. *Lautréamont.* Paris, 1939.
BACHOFEN, J. J. *Der Mythus von Orient und Occident.* Munich, 1926.
— *Mutterrecht und Urreligion.* Leipzig, 1927.
BALTRUSAITIS, Jurgis. *Art sumérien, art roman.* Paris, 1934.
— *Le Moyen Age fantastique.* Paris, 1955.
BARBERINO, Francesco. *Memorie Imprese e Ritrati.* Bologna, 1672.
BARBIER DE MONTAULT. *Traité d'iconographie chrétienne.* Paris, 1890.
BARRETT. *Lives of the alchemystical philosophers with a catalogue of books in occult chemistry.* London, 1815.
BAUER, A. *Chemie und Alchemie in Österreich bis zum beginnenden XIX. Jahrhundert.* Vienna, 1883.
BEARD, Daniel C. *The American Boy's Book of Signs, Signals and Symbols.* Philadelphia and London, 1918.
BECQ DE FOUQUIÈRES. *Les Jeux des anciens.* Paris, 1873.
BEDA. *Opera.* Cologne, 1612.
BEIGBEDER. *La Symbolique.* Paris, 1957.
BELL, Eric Temple. *La Magie des Nombres.* Paris, 1952.

BERCHEM, Egon von. *Die Wappenbücher des Deutschen Mittel-Alters*. Basel, 1928.

BERGER, E. H. *Mythische Kosmographie der Griechen*. Leipzig, 1904.

BERJEAU, J. Ph. *Early Dutch, German and English Printer's Marks*. London, 1866.

BERNOULLI, R. 'Spiritual Development as Reflected in Alchemy', etc. In *Spiritual Disciplines* (Papers from the Eranos Yearbooks, 4). New York and London, 1960.

BERTHELOT, P. E. M. *Introduction à l'étude de la chimie des anciens et du Moyen-Age*. Paris, 1889.

— *Les Origines de l'Alchemie*. Paris, 1885.

BERTHELOT, P. E. M., and RUELLE, C. E. *Collection des anciens alchimistes grecs*. Paris, 1887–88.

BIDEZ, J., and CUMONT, F. *Les Mages hellénisés*. Paris, 1938.

BIENKOWSKI, P. *Les Celtes dans les arts mineurs gréco-romains*. Cracow, 1928.

BIRINGUCCIO, Vannoccio. *De la Pirotechnia*. Venice, 1540.

BOCCACCIO. *Genealogia deorum gentilium*. Venice, 1472.

BOCCHIO, Achille. *Symbolicarum quaestionum de universo genere*. Bologna, 1555.

BOCHART, S. *Hierozoicon, sive bipertitum opus de Animalibus S. Scripturae*. London, 1663.

BOISSAER, Jean-Jacques. *Emblematum Liber*. Frankfurt, 1593.

BONGUS, P. *De mystica numerorum significatio*. Venice, 1585.

BORGES Y GUERRERO. *Manual de zoologia fantástica*. Mexico, 1957.

BORNEMANN, S. *Die Allegorie in Kunst Wissenschaft und Kirche*. Freibrug im Breisgau, 1899.

BORNITUS, Jacobus. *Emblemata ethico-politica*. Mainz, 1669.

BOWES, James Lord. *Japanese Marks and Seals*. London, 1882.

BOWRA, C. M. *The Heritage of Symbolism*. London, 1943.

BRANT, Sebastian. *Stultifera Navis*. Basle, 1497.

BRÉAL, M. *Semantics*. London, 1900.

BRETON, André. *Cahiers G. L. M. 7*. Paris, 1938.

— *L'Amour fou*. Paris, 1937.

BRIFFAULT, Robert. *The Mothers*. London and New York, 1927.

BRILLANT, M. *Les Mystères d'Eleusis*. Paris, 1920.

BRIQUET, Charles Moïse. *Les Filigranes*. Paris, 1907.

BRUCK ANGERMUNT, Jacobus. *Emblemata politica*. Cologne, 1618.

BRUNE, Johan de. *Emblemata of Zinnewerck*. Amsterdam, 1624.

BRYANT, Jacob. *Analysis of Ancient Mythology*. London, 1807.

BUDGE, E. A. Wallis. *Amulets and Superstitions*. London, 1930.

— *Egyptian Magic*. London, 1899.

BUHLER, Karl. *Ausdruckstheorie*. Jena, 1933.

BULARD, Marcel. *Le Scorpion symbole du peuple juif*. Paris, 1935.

BUREN, E. Douglas van. *Symbols of the Gods in Mesopotamian Art*. Analecta Orientalia. Rome, 1945.

BURNOUF, E. *Le Vase sacré et ce qu'il contient . . .* Paris, 1896.

BURTON, William, and Hobson, R. L. *Handbook of Marks on Pottery and Porcelain*. London, 1909.

CADET DE GASSICOURT and ROURE DE PAULIN. *L'Hermétisme dans l'art héraldique*. Paris, 1907.

CAILLIET, E. *Symbolisme et âmes primitives*. Paris, 1936.

CALLET, Ch. *Le Mystère du langage*. Paris, 1928.

CAMBRIEL, L. P. F. *Cours de philosophie hermétique ou d'alchimie*. Paris, 1843.

CAMERARIUS, Joachinus. *Symbolorum et emblematum centuriae*. Mainz, 1668.

CAMILLI, Camillo. *Imprese illustri di diversi . . .* (with illustrations by Girolamo Porro). Venice, 1586.

CAPUA, Johannes de. *Hortus Sanitatis*. Mainz, 1491.

CARTARI, Vincenzo. *Le Imagine dei Dei degli Antichi.* Venice, 1625.
CARTER, D. *The Symbol of the Beast.* New York, 1957.
CARUS, Paul. *Chinese Philosophy.* Chicago, 1898.
— *The Soul of Man.* London, 1891.
— *The History of the Devil.* London, 1900.
CASANOVA, Ludovicus. *Hieroglyphicorum.* Lyon, 1626.
CASSIRER, Ernst. *Antropología filosófica.* Mexico, 1951.
— *Idee und Gestalt.* Berlin, 1921.
CASTELLANOS DE LOSADA, Basilio Sebastián. *Compendio del sistema alegórico y diccionario manual de la iconología universal.* Madrid, 1850.
CAUSSINO, Nicolao. *Symbolica aegyptiorum sapientia.* Paris, 1647.
CHAFFERS, William. *The Collector's Hand Book of Marks and Monograms on Pottery and Porcelain.* London, 1898.
CHAIGNET, A. E. *Pythagore et la philosophie pythagoricienne.* Paris, 1873.
CHARBONNEAU-LASSAY, L. *Le Bestiaire du Christ.* Brussels, 1940.
— *L'Ésotérisme de quelques symboles géométriques chrétiens.* Paris, 1960.
CHARLES, E. *Roger Bacon. Sa vie, ses ouvrages, ses doctrines.* Paris, 1861.
CHASSANG, A. *Le merveilleux dans l'Antiquité.* Paris, 1862.
CHRISTIAN. *Histoire de la Magie.* Paris, 1863.
CHOMPRE, P. *Dictionnaire abregé de la fable.* Paris, 1727.
CIRLOT, J. E. *El Ojo en la Mitología, su simbolismo.* Barcelona, 1954.
— *Hacia una cienca de los símbolos.* In « Sumario », VIII, 22. Barcelona, 1952.
COBARRUBIAS Y HOROZCO, Sebastián de. *Emblemas morales.* Madrid, 1610 and 1951.
COLONNA, E. *Materiae Signa.* New York, 1888.
COLONNA, Francesco. *Hypnerotomachia Poliphili.* Venice, 1499.
COLLUM, V. C. C. *The Tressée Iron-Age Megalithic Monument.* London, 1935.
CONTENAU, G. *La Magie chez les assyriens et les babyloniens.* Paris, 1947.
COOK, A. B. *Zeus, a Study of Ancient Religion.* London, 1914–40.
COOMARASWAMY, A. *Elements of Buddhist Iconography.* Cambridge, Mass., 1935.
— 'Symbolism of the Dome.' *Indian Hist. Quart.* XIV, 1, 1935.
— 'The Inverted Tree.' *Quart. Journ. Myth. Soc. Bangalore,* XXIX, 2, 1938.
CORBIN, Henry. *Terre céleste et corps de résurrection.* Paris, 1960.
CORDUERO, Moise. *Le Palmier de Déborah.* Mantua, 1623.
— *Le Jardin des Grenades.* Cracow.
COURT DE GEBELIN, A. *Monde primitif.* Paris, 1773–82.
CREUZER, Frédéric. *Les Religions de l'Antiquité considérées principalement dans leurs formes symboliques et mythologiques.* Paris, 1825.
CRUVEILHIER, J. *Paracelse, sa vie et sa doctrine.* Paris, 1842.
CUMONT, Franz. *L'Aigle funéraire des Syriens et l'apothéose des empereurs.* Paris, 1910.
— *Les Mystères de Mithra.* Brussels, 1900.
— *Recherches sur le symbolisme funéraire des Romains.* Paris, 1942.
— *Textes et monuments illustrés rélatifs aux mystères de Mithra,* 1896–99.
CYLIANI. *Hermès dévoilé.* Paris, 1832.
DAMMARTIN. *Traité sur l'origine des caractères alphabétiques.* Paris, 1839.
DANIÉLOU, Jean. *Les Symboles chrétiens primitifs.* Paris, 1961.
DANZEL, Th. W. *Symbole, Daemonen und Heilige Türme.* Hamburg, 1930.
DARMSTAEDTER, E. *Der babylonisch-assyrisch Lasurstein.* In 'Studien zur Geschichte der Chimie'. Berlin, 1937.
DAVID, Madeleine V. *Le Débat sur les écritures et l'hiéroglyphe aux XVII et XVIII siècles.* Paris, 1965.
DEBIDOUR, V.-H. *Le Bestiaire sculpté en France.* Paris, 1961.
De DAT, Giuiliano. *Il secondo cantare dell'India.* Rome, 1494.
DELAAGE. *La Science du vrai.* Paris, 1882.

DELALAIN, P. *Inventaire des Marques Typographiques.* Paris, 1866.
DELATTE, A. *Hergarius.* Liège, 1938.
DELEHAYE, Hippolyte. *Légendes hagiographiques.* Brussels, 1905.
DELLA PORTA, G. Battista. *Fisionomia dell'Uomo.* Padua, 1627.
DEONNA, E. *Quelques réflexions sur le symbolisme.* Rev. Hist. Rel. Paris, 1924.
DIERBACH, J. H. *Flore mythologique* . . . Dijon, 1867.
DIGBY, G. W. *Meaning and symbol.* London, 1955.
DINET, P. *Cinq livres des hiéroglyphiques.* Paris, 1614.
DIONYSIUS, pseudo-. *Divine Names,* etc., tr. C. E. Rolt. London, 1920.
— *The Celestial Hierarchies.* London, 1935.
DOBERER, Kurt Karl. *The Goldmakers.* London, 1948.
DORE, Henri. *Researches into Chinese Superstition.* Shanghai, 1914.
DUCHAUSSOY, Jacques. *Le Bestiaire divin ou le symbolique des animaux.* Paris, 1958.
ELEAZAR, Rabbi Abraham. *Uraltes Chymisches Werck.* Leipzig, 1760.
ELIADE, Mircea. *Méphistophélès et l'Androgyne.* Paris, 1962.
— *Myths, Dreams and Mysteries.* London, 1960.
ELLIS, Havelock. *The World of Dreams.* London, 1924.
EMERSON, Ellen Russel. *Indian Myths.* Boston, 1884.
ENDRES, F. C. *Mystik und Magie der Zahlen.* Zurich, 1951.
ENGELBRECHT, A. *Hephaestion von Theben und sein astrologisches Compendium.* Vienna, 1887.
Eranos-Jahrbuch. Zurich.
EVOLA, G. C. *La Tradizione Ermetica.* Bari, 1931.
FABRE D'OLIVET. *The Hebraic Tongue Restored.* New York, 1921.
— *La Musique expliquée.* Paris, 1928.
FAIR Publishing Company. *A Century of Texas Cattle Brands.* Forth Worth, 1936.
FAULHABER and REMMELIN. *Wortrechnung.* Nuremberg, 1914.
FAULMANN, Karl. *Das Buch der Schrift.* Vienna, 1878.
FAYE, E. de. *Les Apocalypses Juives.* Paris, 1892.
FENN, Waldemar. *Gráfica prehistórica de España y el origen de la cultura europea.* Mahon, 1950.
FERRANDO ROIG. *Simbología cristiana.* Barcelona, 1958.
FERRERO, Guglielmo. *I Simboli in rapporto alla storia e filosofia del diritto.* Turin, 1893.
FIGUIER, G. *L'Alchimie et les Alchimistes.* Paris, 1856.
FINGESTEN, Peter. 'Spirituality, Mysticism and non-objective'. In *The Journal,* XXI-I. New York, 1961.
FISSER. *Le symbole littéraire.* Paris.
FLAMEL, Hortensius. *Le Livre rouge: Résumé du magisme, des sciences occultes et de la philosophie hermétique.* Paris, 1842.
FRAENGER, Wilhelm. *Altdeutsches Bilderbuch.* Leipzig, 1930.
FRANCISCUS DE HOLLANDIA. *De Aetatibus Mundi Imagines,* 1545.
FRANCK, Adolphe. *Darstellung und Deutung der Allegorien.* Hamburg, 1880.
— *La Kabbale.* Paris, 1843.
— *Paracelse et l'alchimie au XVI siècle,* 1857.
FRANKFORT, H. *Cylinder Seals.* London, 1939.
FREEMAN, Rosemary. *English Emblem Books.* London, 1948.
FRIEDENSBURG, Ferdinand. *Symbolik der Mittelaltermünzer.* Berlin, 1913.
FRIEDMANN, Hermann. *Wissenschaft und Symbol.* Munich, 1948.
— *Symbolism in the Dura Synagogue.* New York, 1963.
FREUD, Sigmund. *The Interpretation of Dreams* (Standard Edition of *Works,* vols. 4–5). London, 1953.
FROBENIUS, Leo. *Das Zeitalter des Sonnengottes.* Berlin, 1904.
FUENTE LA PEÑA, Antonio de. *El Ente dilucidado.* Madrid, 1677.

GAILLARD, Louis. *Croix et Swastika en Chine.* Shanghai, 1893.
GATTEFOSSÉ, R. M. *Les Sages écritures.* Lyon, 1945.
— 'Métaphysique préhistorique.' *Bull. Soc. Préhist. Maroc,* 1934.
GEBER. *Works.* Trans. Richard Russell. London, 1928.
GERLACH, Martin, *Allegorien und Embleme.* Vienna, 1900.
— *Allégories et Emblèmes.* Vienna, 1882.
GESSMANN, G. W. *Die Geheimsymbole der Chemie und Medizin des Mittelalters.* Graz, 1899.
GIARDA, Christoforus. *Icones symbolicae.* Milan, 1628.
GIEHLOW, Karl. *Die Hieroglyphenkunde des Humanismus in der Allegorie der Renaissance, besonders der Ehrenpforte Kaisers Maximilian I.* Vienna, 1915.
GIOVIO, Paolo (Paulus Jovius), *Dialogi,* 1562.
GISBERT, Combaz. *L'évolution du stûpa en Asie: les symbolismes du stûpa.* Mélanges chinois et boudhiques. Brussels, 1933.
GISSEY, Odo de. *Les Emblesmes et Devises du Roy, des Princes* . . . Paris, 1657.
GOBLET D'ALVIELLA. *La migration des Symboles.* Paris, 1891.
GOLDSMITH, Elizabeth Edwards. *Ancient Pagan Symbols.* London, 1929.
— *Life Symbols as Related to Sex Symbolism.* London, 1924.
— *Sacred Symbols in Art.* London, 1912.
GOODENOUGH, E. R. *Jewish symbols in the greco-roman period.* New York, 1953–54.
— *Symbolism in the Dura Synagogue.* New York, 1963.
GOULIANOF. *Essai sur les hiéroglyphes d'Horapollon.* Paris, 1827.
GOULD, Charles. *Mythical Monsters.* London, 1886.
GRANDVILLE. *Les Fleurs animées.* Paris, 1874.
GRAVELOT and COCHIN. *Iconologie par Figures.* Paris, *c.* 1789.
GREEN, Henry. *Andrea and his Books of Emblems.* London, 1872.
GREINER, R. H. *Polynesian Decorative Designs.* Honolulu, 1922.
GRILLOT DE GIVRY, Emile Angelo. *Witchcraft, Magic and Alchemy.* Boston, 1931.
GROLLIER, Charles de. *Résumé Alphabétique des Marques de Porcelaine.* Paris, 1927.
GROSSLEY, Robert. *A Great Revelation.* London, 1899.
GRUEL, Léon. *Recherches sur les Origines des Marques Anciennes qui se rencontrent dans l'Art et dans l'Industrie du XVᵉ au XIXᵉ siècle. Part Rapport au Chiffre Quatre.* Paris, 1926.
GUBERNATIS, Angelo de. *La Mythologie des plantes.* Paris, 1878.
GUÉNON, René. *Symboles fondamentaux de la science sacrée.* Paris, 1962.
GÜNTER, H. *Psychologie de la Légende.* Paris, 1954.
GUILLAUME, Paul. *La Psychologie de la Forme.* Paris, 1937.
HAATAN, Abel. *Traité d'Astrologie judiciaire.* Paris, 1895.
HARLESS, A. G. C. A. *Jacob Böhme und die alchymisten.* Berlin, 1870.
HARTLAUB, G. F. *Der Stein der Weisen.* Munich, 1959.
— *Zauber der Spiegels.* Munich, 1951.
HAUTECOEUR, Louis. *Mystique et architecture. Symbolisme du cercle et de la coupole.* Paris, 1954.
HECK, Johan Georg. *Iconographic Encyclopaedia of Science, Literature and Art.* London–New York, 1851.
HEITZ, Paul. *Basler Büchermarken bis zum Anfang des 17. Jahrhunderts.* Strasburg. 1895.
— *Elsässische Buchermarken bis Anfang des 18. Jahrhunderts.* Strasburg, 1892.
HELLPACH, Willy. *Geopsyche* Stuttgart, 1950.
HENSELING, Robert. *Das all und wir.* Berlin, 1936.
HENTZE, Carl. *Mythes et Symboles lunaires.* Antwerp, 1932.
HERAS, P. E. *¿ Quiénes eran los Druidas?* Ampurias. Barcelona, 1949.

HERMES TRISMEGISTOS. *The Divine Pymander*. London, 1923.
— *Oeuvres*. Paris, 1945.
HEWSON, William. *Illustrations of Tracts on the Greek-Egyptian Sun-Dial*. London, 1870.
— *The Hebrew and Greek Scriptures*. London, 1870.
HILD, J. A. *Etude sur les démons dans la littérature et la religion des Grecs*. Paris, 1881.
HINKS, Roger. *Myth and Allegory in Ancient Art*. London, 1939.
HIRTH, Georg, Muther and Richard. *Meisterholzschnitte aus Vier Jahrhunderten*. Munich, 1893.
HOEFER. *Histoire de la Chimie depuis les temps les plus reculés jusqu'à notre époque*. Paris, 1842–43.
HOMEYER, Karl Gustav. *Die Haus- und Hof-Marken*. Berlin, 1870.
HOPPER, F. *Medieval Number Symbolism*. New York, 1938.
HORAPOLLO. *The Hieroglyphics*. New York, 1950.
HORNUNG, Clarence Pearson. *Handbook of Designs and Devices*. New York, 1946.
HOROZCO Y COBARRUBIAS, Juan de. *Emblemas morales*. Segovia, 1589 and 1604.
HOWELL, James. *The Parly of Beasts; or Morphandra Queen of the Inchanted Island*. London, 1660.
HOYOS SÁINZ, Luis de. *Manual de Folklore*. Madrid, 1947.
HROZNY, B. (Fr.) *Symbola ad studia Orientis . . .* Prague, 1949.
HUBAUX, J. and LEROY, M. *Le Mythe du Phénix dans les littératures grecque et latine*. Liège, 1939.
HUBER, M. *Die Wanderlegende von den Siebenschläfern*. Leipzig, 1910.
HUMBERT, J. *Mythologie grecque et romaine*. Paris, 1901.
HUNTER, Dard. *Papermaking Through Eighteen Centuries*. New York, 1930.
IAMBLICHUS. *On the Mysteries of the Egyptians*. London, 1895.
— *Des Mystères*. Paris, 1895.
IBERICO, Mariano. *El sentimiento de la vida cósmica*. Buenos Aires, 1946.
JACKSON, J. W. *Shells as evidence of the migration of early culture*. Manchester, 1917.
JACQUEMAR. *La pierre philosophale et la phlogistique*. Paris, 1876.
JEAN, M., and MEZEL, A. *Maldoror*. Paris, 1947.
JUNG, C. G. See WILHELM, Richard, and JUNG, C. G.
—, and KERENY, I. *Introduction to a Science of Mythology*. London, 1951.
— *Mysterium Coniunctionis*. London, 1963.
— (with Joseph L. Henderson, Marie-Louise von Franz, Aniela Jaffe). *Man and His Symbols*. London, 1963.
JUNIUS, Adrianus. *Emblemata*. Antwerp, 1565.
KALLIR, Alfred. *The Victory of V*. London, 1958.
— *Sign and Design*. London, 1961.
KARLGREN, B. 'Some fecundity symbols in Ancient China.' *Bull. Mus. Far East*, No. 2, Stockholm, 1930.
KARST, J. *Mythologie arméno-caucasienne et hétito-asiatique*. Strasburg, 1948.
KATZ, David. *Gestalt Psychology*. London, 1951.
KENDRICK, T. D. *Anglo-Saxon Art*. London, 1938.
KERVYN DE LETTENHOVE. *Le Toison d'or*. Brussels, 1907.
KHUNRATH, H. *Amphitheatrum Sapientiae aeternae solius verae Cabalae, Mageiae, Alchemiae, Cabalisticum . . .* Hanau, 1609.
KING, Charles William. *The Gnostics and their remains, ancient and mediaeval*. London, 1864.
KINGSLAND, W. *The Esoteric Basis of Christianity*. London, 1893.
KIRCHER, A. *Aedipus aegyptiacus hoc est universalis hieroglyphicae veterum doctrinae instauratio*. Rome, 1652.

KIRCHGÄSSNER, Alfons. *La Puissance des Signes*. Paris, 1962.
KOCH, Rudolf. *The Book of Signs*. London, 1930.
KOPP, H. *Die alchemie in alterer und neuerer Zeit*. Heidelberg, 1886.
KOTANY, Heishichi. *Japanese Family Crests*. Kyoto, 1915.
KÜHN, Herbert. *The Rock Pictures of Europe*. Translated by Alan Houghton Brodrick. London, 1956.
KÜNSTLE, Karl. *Ikonographie der christlichen Kunst*. Freiburg im Breisgau, 1926–28.
KUNZ, Georg Frederick. *The Magic of Jewels and Charms*. London, 1915.
KUNZ, G. F. and STEVENSON, C. H. *The Book of the Pearl*. London, 1908.
KURTH, Willi. *The Complete Woodcuts of Albrecht Dürer*. London, 1927.
KUTSCHMANN, Th. *Geschichte der Deutschen Illustration*. Goslar, 1900.
LAARSS, Richard Hummel. *Das Buch der Amulette und Talismane*. Leipzig, 1923.
LAJARD, F. *Recherches sur le culte du cyprès piramidal* . . . Paris, 1854.
— *Recherches sur le culte public et les mystères de Mithra en Orient et en Occident*. Paris, 1867.
LANG, A. *Myth, Ritual and Religion*. London, 1887.
LANGE, R. *Japanische Wappen*. Berlin, 1903.
L'ANGLOIS, P. *Discours des hiéroglyphes* . . . Paris, 1584.
LANOÈ-VILLÈNE. *Le Livre des Symboles*. Paris, 1921.
LANZONI, Francesco. *Genesi, Svolgimento e Tramonto delle Leggende storiche*. Rome, 1925.
LAUFER, B. *Jade. A study in Chinese archaeology and religion*. Chicago, 1912.
— *The Diamond. A study in Chinese and hellenistic Folk-Lore*. Chicago, 1915.
LAYARD, John. *The Lady of the Hare*. London, 1944.
LEBRUN DE VIRLOY. *Notice sur l'accroissement de la matière métallique*. Paris, 1888.
LEDESMA, Alfonso de. *Epigramas y hieroglyphicos*, 1623.
LEE, Gordon Ambrose. *Some Notes on Japanese Heraldry*. London, 1909.
LEISEGANG, Hans. 'The Mystery of the Serpent.' In *The Mysteries* (Papers from the Eranos Yearbooks, 2). New York and London, 1955.
— *La Gnose*. Paris, 1951.
LE VOILE D'ISIS. *Les Gemmes*. Paris.
LÉVY-BRÜHL, Lucien. *L'expérience mystique et les symboles chez les primitifs*. Paris, 1938.
LIBAVIUS, Andreas. *Alchymia* . . . *Recognita Emendata et Aucta*. Frankfurt, 1606.
LINNAEUS. *Systema Naturae, sive Regna trib Naturae systematice proposita per classes, ordines, genera et species*. Leyden, 1735.
LIPFFERT, Klementine. *Symbol-Fibel*. Kassel, 1955.
LITTLE Gem Brand Book Company. *Little Gem Brand Book*. Kansas City, 1900.
LOEFFLER-DELACHAU. *Le Symbolisme des contes de Fées*. Paris, 1949.
LOISY, A. *Les mythes babiloniens et les premiers chapitres de la Genèse*. Paris, 1901.
LÜDY, Fritz. *Alchemistiche und Chemische Zeichen*. Berlin, 1929.
LULL, Raymond. *De Auditu Kabbalistico, sive ad omnes scientias introductorium*. Strasburg, 1651.
MAACK, Ferd. *Die heilige Mathesis*. Leipzig, 1924.
MAASS, E. *Orpheus*. Munich, 1895.
MACCIO, Paolo. *Emblemata* . . . Bologna, 1628.
MADHIHASSAN, Dr. S. 'Über enige Symbole der Alchemie'. In *Die Pharmazeutische Industrie*, 24, 41–45. Aulendorf i. Württ., 1962.
— 'Ouroboros as the earlier symbol of the Greek Alchemie'. In *Igbal*. Lahore, 1961.
MAHNKE, Dietrich. *Unendliche Sphäre und Allmittelpunkt*. Halle, 1937.
MALLINGER, J. *Les secrets ésotériques dans Plutarque*. Paris, 1946.

MARMOL, F. de. *Dictionnaire des Filigranes*. Namur, 1900.
MARNEFFE, Alphonse de. *Les Combinaisons de la Croix et du Triangle Divin dans les Blasons et les Marques de Marchands*. Charleroi, 1939.
MARTINO, P. *Parnasse et Symbolisme*. Paris, 1954.
MAURY, A. *Croyances et légendes de l'antiquité*. Paris, 1863.
McCLATCHIE, Thomas R. H. *Japanese Heraldry*. Yokohama, 1877.
MEINER, Annemarie. *Das Deutsche Signet*. Leipzig, 1922.
MENARD, L. *Hermès Trismégiste*. Paris, 1867.
MENARD, René. *La mythologie dans l'Art ancien et moderne*. Paris, 1878.
MENDO, Andrés. *Principe . . . en emblemas*. León de Francia, 1662.
MENDOZA, Carlos. *La Leyenda de las plantas*. Barcelona, 1889.
MENESTRIER, François. *La philosophie des images énigmatiques*. Lyon, 1694.
MERTENS STIENON, M. *Space and the Cross*. London, 1935.
— *Studies in Symbolism*. London, 1933.
MICHELET, J. *Origines du droit français cherchés dans les symboles et formules du droit universal*. Paris, 1900.
MONEROT, Jules. *La poésie moderne et le Sacré*. Paris, 1945.
MOREAU, J. *La construction de l'idéalisme platonicien*. Paris, 1939.
MORGAN, L. H. *Ancient Society*. New York, 1877.
MORTILLET, Gabriel de. *Le signe de la croix avant le Christianisme*. Paris, 1866.
MUELLER, Niklas. *Glauben, Wissen und Kunst der Alten Hindus*. Mainz, 1822.
MUNSCH, René H. *L'Ecriture et son dessin*. Paris, 1948.
MUTHER, Richard. *Die Deutsche Bücherillustration der Gothik und Frührenaissance (1460–1530)*. Munich, 1884.
MYLIUS, Joannes Daniel. *Philosophia Reformata*. Frankfurt, 1622.
NAGLER, Georg Caspar. *Die Monogrammisten*. Munich, 1858–79.
NANYO, Kyokai. *Family Crests*. Tokyo, 1940.
NAVILLE, E. *La religion des anciens égyptiens*. Paris, 1907.
NENTER, *Bericht von der alchymie*. Nuremberg, 1727.
NICOLAI, Johannis. *Tractatus de Siglis Veterum*. Lyon, 1703.
NINCK, Martin. *Die Bedeutung des Wassers im Kult und Leben der Alten, Eine symbolgeschichtliche Untersuchung*. Philogus (Leipzig), 1921.
NOOT, Jan Van der. *XII Boeken Olympiados*. Antwerp, 1579.
NOTT, Stanley Charles. *Chinese Culture in the Arts*. New York, 1946.
NÚÑEZ DE CEPEDA, Francisco. *Emblemas sacros*. León, 1682.
NUTT, Alfred. *Studies on the Legend of the Holy Grail*. London, 1888.
OBERMAIER, Hugo. *Fossil Man in Spain*. New York, 1924.
OGDEN, C. K., and RICHARDS, I. A. *The Meaning of Meaning*. London, 1923.
OKADA, Yazuru. *Japanese Family Crests*. Tokyo, 1941.
ONIANS, R. B. *The Origins of European Thought*. London, 1954.
OPPEL, Karl. *Das alte Wunderland der Pyramiden*. Leipzig. 1868.
ORIN, J. M. H. *Le plan divin dévoilé*. Paris, 1890.
ORTIGUES, Edmond. *Le Discours et le symbole*. Paris, 1962.
PALLADINUS. Jacobus, of Teramo. *Belial*. Heilbronn, 1448.
PALLISER, Fanny Bury. *Historic Devices, Badges and War Cries*. London, 1870.
PANOFSKY, Erwin. *Hercules am Scheidewege*. Leipzig, 1930.
— *Meaning in the Visual Arts*. New York, 1955.
PANOFSKY, E. and D. *Pandora's Box*. London, 1956.
PAPUS. *Initiation astrologique*. Paris, 1919.
PARRINDER, Geoffrey. *West African Religions*. London, 1949.
PASSERI, G. B. *Thesaurus Gemmarum Antiquarum*. Florence, 1750.
PATRICK, S. *Parable of the Pilgrim*. London, 1665.
PAVITT, William Thomas and Kate. *The Book of Talismans, Amulets and Zodiacal Gems*. London, 1914.
PELADAN, J. *Les idées et les formes*. Paris, 1901.

PERRY, W. J. *The Children of the Sun.* London, 1923.
PERYT SHOU. *Symbolik und magische Zahlentheorie.* Berlin, 1923.
PETRASANTA, Silvestro. *De symbolis heroicis.* Antwerp, 1635.
PICARD, C. *Les origines du polythéisme hellénique.* Paris, 1931.
PICINELLI, D. Filippo. *Mondo Simbolico ampliato.* Venice, 1670.
POISSON, Albert. *Nicolas Flamel.* Paris, 1893.
— *Roger Bacon, Lettre sur les prodiges de la nature et de l'art.* Paris, 1893.
— *Théories et Symboles des Alchimistes.* Paris, 1891.
PORTAL, F. *Des Couleurs symboliques.* Paris, 1837.
POUCHET, F. A. *Histoire des sciences naturelles au moyen âge,* etc. Paris, 1853.
PRAMPOLINI, Giacomo. *La mitologia nella vita del popolo.* Milan, 1937–38.
QUINTANA VIVES, Jorge. *Aportaciones a la interpretación de la escritura protoindia.* Madrid, 1946.
— *El gobierno teocrático de Mohenjo-Daro,* Ampurias, IV. Barcelona, 1942.
RADIN, Paul. *The Road of Life and Death.* New York.
REGNAUD, P. *Le Rig-Véda et les origines de la mythologie indo-européenne.* Paris, 1892.
REINACH, S. *Cultes, mythes et religions,* Paris, 1908–23.
REINER Imre. *Das Buch der Werkzeichen.* St. Gallen, 1945.
RENOUARD, Ph. *Les marques typographiques Parisiennes des XVᵉ et XVIᵉ siècles.* Paris, 1928.
REPULLÉS, E. *El simbolismo en la arquitectura cristiana.* Madrid, 1898.
RIPA, Cesare. *Iconologia, or Moral Emblems.* London, 1709.
RISCO, Vicente. *Mitología cristiana.* Madrid, 1963.
— 'Fieras de romance'. In *Revista de Dialectología y tradiciones populares.* Tomo XIV. Madrid, 1958.
RIS-PAQUOT, Oscar Edmond. *Dictionnaire encyclopédique des marques et monogrammes.* Paris, 1893.
ROBERTS, W. *Printer's Marks.* London, 1892.
ROBSON, Thomas. *The British Herald.* Sunderland, 1830.
ROSENHEIM, Petrus de. *Ars Memorandi, or Rationarium Evangelistarum.* Pforzheim 1507.
ROUGIER, L. *L'origine astronomique de la croyance pythagoricienne en l'immortalité céleste des âmes.* Cairo, 1933.
ROUSSEAU, René-Lucien. *Les Couleurs.* Paris, 1959.
RUSCELLI, Girolamo. *Le imprese illustri.* Venice, 1572.
RUTH-SOMMER, Hermann. *Alte Musikinstrumente.* Berlin, 1916.
SAAVEDRA FAJARDO, Diego de. *Idea de un príncipe . . . empresas,* 1640.
SABATHIER. *L'Ombre idéale de la sagesse universelle.* Paris, 1679.
SABBE, Maurice. *Le Symbolisme des marques typographiques.* Antwerp, 1932.
SAINTYVES, P. *Les saints successeurs des dieux.* Paris, 1907.
— 'Pierres magiques.' *Corpus de folklore Préh.* II, 1934.
SAMBUCUS, Joannes. *Emblemata cum aliquot nummis antiqui operis.* Antwerp, 1564.
SAN MARTE. *Neue Mitteilungen aus dem Gebiete historisch-antiquarischer Forschungen,* II.
SAULCY, F. Caignart de. *Histoire de l'Art judaïque tirée des textes sacrés et profanes.* Paris, 1858.
SAXL, KLIBANSKY and PANOFSKY. *Saturn and Melancholy.* London, 1964.
SAYCE and MARCH. 'Polynesian Ornament; a Mythography or a symbolism of Origin and Descent.' *Journ. Anthrop. Inst.,* 1893, XII.
SCHELTEMA, Frederik Adama van. *Die Kunst des Abendlandes.* Stuttgart, 1950.
SCHWAB, Gustav. *Gods and Heroes.* London, 1947.
SCHEDEL, Hartmann. *Liber Chronicorum.* Nuremberg, 1493.
SCHEIL, V. *Esagil ou le temple de Mardouk à Babylone.* Paris, 1913.

SCHEFFER, T. von. *Hellenistiche Mysterien und Orakel.* Stuttgart, 1940.
SCHENCK, Georg. *Monstrorum Historia memorabilis.* Frankfurt, 1609.
SCHMIDT, Albert M. *La Littérature Symboliste.* Paris, 1947.
SCHMIEDER, K. C. *Geschichte der Alchemie.* Halle, 1832.
SCHOLEM, G. G. *Major Trends in Jewish Mysticism.* London, 1955.
SCHUILER CAMMANN. *Cosmic Symbolism of the Dragon Robes of the Ch'ing Dynasty.* In Art and Thought.
SCHWALLER DE LUBICZ, R.-A. *Propos sur Ésotérisme et Symbole.* Paris, 1960.
SCOTT, Thomas. *Philomythie or Philomythologie.* London, 1616.
SELIGMANN, Kurt. *Mirror of Magic.* New York, 1948.
SILBERER, Herbert. *Problems of Mysticism and its Symbolism.* New York and London, 1917.
SILVESTRE, L. C. *Marques Typographiques.* Paris, 1867.
SIMPSON, William. *The Buddhist Praying-wheel.* London, 1896.
SIMROCK, K. *Traces of a Hidden Tradition in Mediaeval Mysticism.* London, 1900.
SKEAT, Walter W. 'Snakestones and stone thunderbolts as subject for systematic investigation.' *Folklore,* 1912, XXIII.
SMITH, William Robertson. *Lectures on the religion of the Semites.* London, 1927.
SOLÓRZANO PEREIRA, Ioannes. *Emblemata . . .* Madrid, 1651.
SOTO, Hernando de. *Emblemas moralizados,* 1599.
SOUSA DE MACEDO, Antonio de. *Eva y Ave o Maria triunfante.* Murcia, 1882.
SPENCER, Herbert. *Principles of Sociology,* 1876–96.
STAFFORD, Thomas Albert. *Christian Symbolism in the Evangelical Churches.* New York–Nashville, 1942.
STEKEL, W. *Dichtung und Neurose.* Wiesbaden, 1909.
— *The Interpretation of Dreams.* New York, 1943.
— *Technique of Analytical Psychotherapy.* London, 1939.
STROEHL, Hugo Gerard, *Blumen und Blüten in der Japanischen Heraldik.* Vienna, 1907.
— *Heraldischer Atlas.* Stuttgart, 1899.
— *Imitationsfiguren in der Japanischen Heraldik.* Berlin, 1910.
— *Nihon Moncho, Japanisches Wappenbuch.* Vienna, 1906.
Symbollon. Basle.
TACCHI VENTURI, P. *Storia delle religioni.* Turin, 1934–36.
THOMPSON, Tommy. *The A.B.C. of Our Alphabet.* London–New York, 1942.
THOMSON, Thomas. *History of chemistry.* London, 1930.
THURNWALD, R. 'Das Symbol in Lichte der Völkerkunde.' *Zeitschrift f. Aesthetik u. allgem. Kuntswiss,* XXI.
TIFFEREAU, C. T. *Les métaux sont des corps composés.* Paris, 1855.
TONDELLI, Leone. *Gnostici.* Turin, 1950.
TOPSELL, Edward. *The History of Four-footed Beasts and Serpents; Describing at Large their True and Lively Figure, their Several Names, Conditions, Kinds, Virtues . . .* London, 1658.
TORMO, Elías. *El simbolismo en el arte.* Madrid, 1902.
TRITHEIM, J. *Polygraphie et universelle escriture cabalistique.* Paris, 1561.
TSUDA, Noritake. *Handbook of Japanese Art.* Tokyo, 1935.
TYLOR, Edward. *Anthropology.* London, 1881.
— *Primitive culture; Researches into the Development of Mythology, Philosophy, Religion, Language, Art and Custom.* London, 1871.
TYPOTIUS, Jacobus. *Symbola varia diversorum principum.* Arnheim, 1679.
ULMANN, Paul. *La Croix de Saint-André dans la sculpture romane, bas-reliefs mithratques et doctrines albigeoises.* Paris, 1947.
ULSTADT, Philipp. *Coelum Philosophorum, seu De Secretis Naturae.* Paris, 1544.
URBAN, Wilbur Marshall. *Language and Reality.* London, 1939.
VAGANAY, L. *Le problème eschatologique dans le IVᵉ livre d'Esdras.* Paris, 1906.

VALERIANO, Giampietro. *Hieroglyphica.* Basel, 1556.
VILLAVA, Juan Francisco de. *Empresas espirituales.* Baeza, 1613.
VILLIERS, Elizabeth. *The Mascot Book.* New York and London, 1923.
VINYCOMB, John. *Fictitious and Symbolic Creatures in Art.* London, 1906.
VOLKMANN, Ludwig. *Bilderschriften der Renaissance.* Leipzig, 1923.
WAITE, A. E. *The Holy Grail.* London, 1933.
WEBBER, Frederick Roth. *Church Symbolism.* Cleveland, 1927.
WECHSSLER, Edward. *Die Sage vom Heiligen Graal.* 1898.
WESTERHOVIUS, A. H. *Hieroglyphica oder Denkbilder der alten Völker.* Amsterdam, 1741.
WESTON, Jessie L. *Works.*
WILHELM, Richard, and JUNG, C. G. *The Secret of the Golden Flower.* London, 1932.
— *The I Ching.* London, 1970.
WILKINS, John. *Mathematicall Magick.* London, 1680.
WILLIAMS, Charles Alfred Speed. *Outlines of Chinese Symbolism and Art Motives.* Shanghai, 1932.
WILLIAMS, John. *An Essay on the Hieroglyphics of the Ancient Egyptians.* London, 1836.
WINCKELMANN, J. J. *Versuch eine Allegorie.* Leipzig, 1866.
WIRTH, O. *Le Symbolisme hermétique dans ses rapports avec l'alchimie* . . . Paris, 1931.
WOLFF. *Mythologie der Feen und Elfen von Ursprunge dieses Glaubens bis auf neuesten Zeiten.* Weimar, 1828.
WON KENN. *Origine et évolution de l'écriture hiéroglyphique et de l'écriture chinoise.* Paris, 1926.
YAMAGUSHI, H. S. K. *We Japanese.* Miyanoshi-Hakone, 1937.
ZIEBER, Eugène. *Heraldry in America.* Philadelphia, 1895.
ZIMMER, Heinrich. *Kunstform und Yoga im Indischen Kultbild.* Berlin, 1926.
ZIMMERMANN, Werner. *Geheimsinn der Zahlen.* Munich, 1944.
ZYKAN, J. 'Drache und Perle.' *Articus Asiae* VI, 1–2, 1936.

INDEX

Note. Main entries in the dictionary are not included. Cross-references in bold type are to main entries in the dictionary.